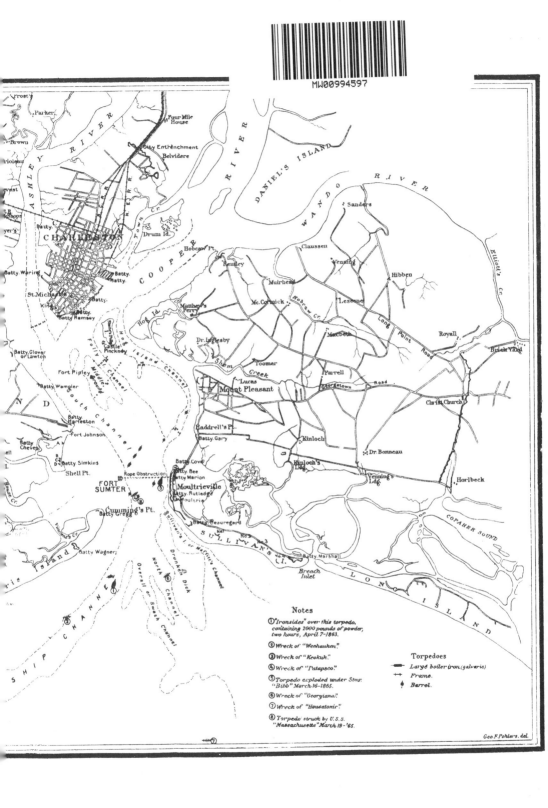

Notes

1. "Ironsides" over this torpedo, containing 2000 pounds of powder, two hours, April 7-1863.
2. Wreck of "Weehauken."
3. Wreck of "Keokuk."
4. Wreck of "Patapsco."
5. Torpedo exploded under Stm: "Bibb" March 16-1865.
6. Wreck of "Georgiana".
7. Wreck of "Housatonic."
8. Torpedo struck by U.S.S. "Massachusetts" March 19-'65.

Torpedoes

— Large boiler iron (galvanic)
↔ Frame.
⚓ Barrel.

Geo.F.Pohlers, del.

Gustavus Vasa Fox of the Union Navy

Gustavus Vasa Fox
of the Union Navy

A Biography

ARI HOOGENBOOM

The Johns Hopkins University Press
Baltimore

© 2008 The Johns Hopkins University Press
All rights reserved. Published 2008
Printed in the United States of America on acid-free paper
2   4   6   8   9   7   5   3   1

The Johns Hopkins University Press
2715 North Charles Street
Baltimore, Maryland 21218-4363
www.press.jhu.edu

Library of Congress Cataloging-in-Publication Data

Hoogenboom, Ari Arthur, 1927–
Gustavus Vasa Fox of the Union Navy : a biography / Ari Hoogenboom.
p.   cm.
Includes bibliographical references and index.
ISBN-13: 978-0-8018-8986-8 (hardcover : alk. paper)
ISBN-10: 0-8018-8986-3 (hardcover : alk. paper)
1. Fox, Gustavus Vasa, 1821–1883. 2. United States. Navy—Officers—Biography.
3. United States—History—Civil War, 1861–1865—Naval operations. I. Title.
E467.1.F79H66 2008
973.7'5092—dc22
[B]   2008000585

A catalog record for this book is available from the British Library.

Frontispiece: "Mr. Fox, with a forehead like the dome of St. Peter's"
(Oliver Wendell Holmes to John Murray Forbes, 1 June 1866, Fox Papers, New-York
Historical Society). Photograph courtesy of Hagley Museum and Library.

Special discounts are available for bulk purchases of this book. For more information,
please contact Special Sales at 410-516-6936 or specialsales@press.jhu.edu.

The Johns Hopkins University Press uses environmentally friendly book materials,
including recycled text paper that is composed of at least 30 percent post-consumer
waste, whenever possible. All of our book papers are acid-free, and our jackets and
covers are printed on paper with recycled content.

For
my seafaring father
Ari Hoogenboom
(1895–1951)
and
my sea-loving son
Ari Arthur Hoogenboom

CONTENTS

In a letter written to Gustavus Vasa Fox on 26 December 1865, Admiral David Dixon Porter remarked, "We are indebted to you more than any other man for our Naval Success." Porter was right. The man most responsible for the U.S. Navy's performance in the Civil War was Assistant Secretary of the Navy Gus Fox. In effect, he was chief of naval operations (a position that did not officially exist until the twentieth century). He consulted with Secretary of the Navy Gideon Welles on matters great and small, and together they formed an efficient team. Fox had been a naval officer for eighteen years and was connected by marriage to the politically powerful Francis Preston Blair family. He understood the demands of politicians (victories in war) and the needs of line officers (ships, guns, and men) and could explain their needs to each other and reconcile their differences. Welles depended on Fox to persuade congressmen to support naval appropriations, and Fox stressed to admirals the connection between successful expeditions, public opinion, and political support for the war.

Welles was a hands-on administrator who approved all decisions, but he deferred to Fox's grasp of naval matters, involving commanders, ships, guns, and strategy. Because Welles was a shrewd judge of character and Fox a shrewd judge of ability, they jointly selected squadron commanders. Fox customarily made lesser appointments, with Welles's approval. Together, they ignored an entrenched seniority system and replaced commanders found wanting.

Fox was primarily responsible for the types of vessels purchased for the blockade (fast, light-draft, wooden steamboats) and for combating Confederate ironclads (heavily armored, big-gunned, turreted monitors, with a low freeboard). The son of an inventor of textile machinery, Fox was an innovator. He was an early advocate of ironclad vessels and, after witnessing the encounter of the *Monitor* and the *Virginia/Merrimack*, led the navy to adopt the monitor design for its ironclads. Realizing that in that battle, armor had triumphed over gunpower, he immediately ordered a reluctant John A. Dahlgren to design a more powerful, fifteen-inch gun, which proved able to destroy Confederate ironclads.

Fox influenced the development of naval strategy and was also the key figure in its implementation. The Blockade Board, for example, which he helped create, recommended establishing bases on the Confederate coastline to sustain blockading vessels. Gaining possession of a suitable harbor required a large expedition, and Fox was aware of the challenge he faced in organizing the armada that secured Port Royal Sound. That expedition got underway largely because he attended to everything from minor details to convincing Lincoln of its necessity. In addition, he insisted that its commander make Port Royal Sound its objective, rather than settling on easier, less satisfactory targets. Its superior anchorage made Port Royal well worth the effort.

Fox was preeminent in determining naval operations. Because the prewar navy was small, he knew most naval officers, whether they remained loyal to the Union or became Confederates. His service in the Coast Survey helped him implement the blockade, and skippering mail passenger steamers acquainted him with state-of-the-art steamboats. In addition, by dealing with the large crews and hundreds of passengers on those steamboats, he quickly developed both administrative and social skills.

During the Civil War Lincoln often sent for Fox. He called on him not only for information on naval matters but also for companionship. Fox was buoyant and optimistic and had a well-deserved reputation as a storyteller. When there was depressing war news, Lincoln found Fox good company. Lincoln called on Fox both at the Navy Department and at his home (where Lincoln sometimes stretched out on a couch). Close contact with the president made Fox a Lincoln man, much like John Hay, Lincoln's private secretary and Fox's boon companion.

In preparation for his unique role in Civil War naval affairs, Fox served a long apprenticeship in the navy and a shorter one in the business world. His great talents probably would not have been utilized by the Lincoln administration but for his fortuitous marriage to Virginia Woodbury, whose sister Minna was married to Lincoln's postmaster general, Montgomery Blair.

■ ■ ■

The Fox Papers of the Naval History Society Collection at the New-York Historical Society is an unparalleled archive for insights into naval operations during the Civil War. Line officers in their unofficial correspondence with Fox often felt free to tell him what they would not say in official correspondence with the Navy Department. The Naval History Society Collection also includes important collections of John Ericsson and Henry A. Wise papers. The diary of Virginia Fox may be found in the Woodbury Family Papers at the Library of Congress. In the Manuscript Division of that library are Fox letters and references to him in the Blair Family Papers, the Gideon Welles Papers, and the papers of naval officers.

A vast quantity of primary source materials has been printed in *Official Records of the Union and Confederate Navies in the War of the Rebellion* (Series I, 27 vols., Series II, 3 vols., plus Index vol.).

The Naval History Society in 1918 and 1919 published in two volumes a generous selection of the *Confidential Correspondence of Gustavus Vasa Fox: Assistant Secretary of the Navy, 1861–1865*, edited by Robert Means Thompson and Richard Wainwright. Admiral John D. Hayes edited, with authoritative footnotes, *Samuel Francis Du Pont: A Selection from His Civil War Letters*, 3 vols. (Ithaca: published for the Eleutherian Mills Historical Library by Cornell University Press, 1969). The *Diary of Gideon Welles: Secretary of the Navy under Lincoln and Johnson*, edited by John T. Morse Jr., first appeared in 1911, and in 1960 Howard K. Beale published an authoritative version of this useful source.

A large number of valuable secondary sources on the naval history of the Civil War are cited in this biography. At the risk of leaving out some that deserve special mention, I wish to single out the following authors and their works that have been most helpful. John Niven, *Gideon Welles: Lincoln's Secretary of the Navy* (New York: Oxford University Press, 1973), appreciates the contribution of Welles to the success of the navy. Rowena Reed's *Combined Operations in the Civil War* (Annapolis: Naval Institute Press, 1978) is an invaluable source on the cooperation and lack of cooperation of the navy and army. Edward William Sloan III, *Benjamin Franklin Isherwood, Naval Engineer: The Years as Engineer in Chief, 1861–1869* (Annapolis: United States Naval Institute Press, 1965), details the contributions of that brilliant engineer and clarifies the differences among competing steam engines. Finally, there are two accurate and succinct chronological works and a dictionary that I have checked with constantly. The *Civil War Naval Chronology, 1861–1865* (Washington, D.C.: Naval History Division, Office of the Chief of Naval Operations, Navy Department, 1961) includes apt quotations, gleaned from the *Official Records of the...Navies* and other collections. The same Naval History Division produced the eight-volume *Dictionary of American Naval Fighting Ships* (1959–81), with additional essays on monitors, Confederate vessels, and related topics. E. B. Long and Barbara Long, *The Civil War Day by Day: An Almanac, 1861–1865* (New York: Doubleday, 1971), enhanced its usefulness with a comprehensive index beyond belief.

■ ■ ■

A John Simon Guggenheim Memorial Foundation Fellowship and grants from the American Philosophical Society facilitated my research on Fox in New York and in Washington. The incomparable Fox Papers of the Naval History Society Collection are at the New-York Historical Society. To its staff and especially to Wilmer R. Leech and Arthur J. Breton I owe a heavy debt of gratitude. I am also grateful to John Knowlton of the Manuscript Division of the Library of Congress, where the Blair and Woodbury family papers are housed, as well as numerous other collections pertaining to the naval history of the Civil War. For help on this as well as other projects, I wish to thank Sherrie Warman, Brooklyn College's interlibrary loan librarian, and Omar Alzindani of that library's reference desk. Thanks are also due to Bill Nelson for drawing new maps of the operational areas. The other maps are reproduced from *Official Records of the Union and Confederate Navies in the War of the Rebellion.*

Scholars have been generous in sharing their source materials and insights with me. Robert V. Bruce gave me his microfilm copy of Virginia Fox's diary; Admiral John D. Hayes discussed with me Fox's relations with Samuel Francis Du Pont; John A. Kouenhoven sent me material on James B. Eads; John Niven shared his views on the Welles-Fox administration of the Navy Department; Edward William Sloan III lent me Fox materials I had overlooked; and C. Norman Guice provided me with Fox letters to and from Charles Henry Davis. I am especially indebted to Craig L. Symonds, who, upon reading the entire manuscript, offered valuable suggestions for its improvement, and to Brian R. MacDonald for expert copy editing. For meticulous care in converting the manuscript into a book I am grateful to Robert J. Brugger and Anne M. Whitmore of the Johns Hopkins University Press.

Friends and relatives have offered encouragement and answered questions. David Herbert Donald has not only answered queries about Lincoln but has inspired me for more than a half century. To Grady McWhiney I owe a special debt for sharing with me his consummate knowledge of the Civil War. Michael Burlingame provided information about Fox's close friend, John Hay, and helped me find elusive items. My daughter Lynn, whose interest in the Civil War goes beyond her favorite subject, William Tecumseh Sherman, applied her editorial skills to the entire manuscript. Finally, my wife Olive, intimately acquainted with the four Woodbury sisters (one of whom married Fox and another, Montgomery Blair), contributed to and edited this work.

I have dedicated this biography of a sailor to my father, a Dutch sailor, and to my son, who, like me, is a teacher. My father, who went to sea when he was twelve, jumped ship in New York in 1920 and, although an illegal immigrant, joined the Coast Guard and became an American citizen. He was a carpenter, never had a vacation, and died in a construction accident. I owe him much, but his most valuable gift to me was teaching me to work. My son, who resembles the grandfather he never knew, saved his allowance when a young boy to purchase a skiff to wander around in. Now, a lover of Shakespeare as well as the ocean, he is the principal of Abraham Lincoln High School in the Coney Island section of Brooklyn.

Gustavus Vasa Fox of the Union Navy

CHAPTER ONE

Midshipman Fox

My son Gustavus Vasa Fox, now sixteen years of age, of an athletic, healthy and robust constitution, has an unconquerable desire for the situation of a midshipman in the navy which has increased with his growth, and strengthened with his strength.

Jesse Fox to Caleb Cushing, 5 December 1837

This . . . youngster is a coon dog—no getting to the windward of him—bold—fearless and powerful.

Henry A. Wise, Journal, 21 June 1839

At 3:00 a.m. on 12 April 1861, Fox arrived at a rendezvous off Charleston, South Carolina. He was in the *Baltic,* with provisions for Fort Sumter. The only vessel awaiting him was the lightly armed *Harriet Lane.* Three tugboats to run supplies to Sumter and three naval vessels to protect them had not arrived. Fox decided to use the *Baltic*'s longboats to row the provisions to Sumter. Three hours later, when the *Pawnee* arrived, its captain, loath to start a civil war, refused to accompany the *Baltic* to the harbor entrance. Undaunted, Fox headed in, escorted by the *Harriet Lane,* and discovered Sumter was under fire. The Civil War had begun. Fox hoped to send in reinforcements that night, but the naval officers insisted on waiting for the expedition's other vessels.

Returning to the rendezvous point, Fox and the *Baltic* "made signals all night" in heavy seas, looking for the missing *Pocahontas* and *Powhatan.* By morning it was too rough to land anything by longboats, and Fox resolved to go in that evening in a captured schooner. He was not allowed that futile gesture. By two o'clock that afternoon, about when the *Pocahontas* arrived, Sumter surrendered. The powerful *Powhatan* never did arrive. Instead of dying in a heroic attempt to reinforce Sumter, Fox evacuated its garrison.

Fox was mortified. After months of planning and weeks of activity to secure an adequate naval force to succor Sumter, nothing went right. Stormy weather, botched orders, and the mysterious detachment of the *Powhatan*, which he deemed essential for his mission's success, brought failure. A friend's hope that Fox might save the Union, as Gustavus Vasa saved Sweden, came to nothing. Fate, carelessness, and machinations beyond his control made irrelevant his experience at sea. And on top of all else, Fox had to remain silent, because full disclosure of what went awry would damage the war effort. Lincoln, however, considered neither the expedition nor Fox a failure. Because he valued Fox's expertise, he created a position for Fox where he could utilize his experience and play a major role in saving the Union.

■ ■ ■

Born in Saugus, Massachusetts, on 13 June 1821, Gustavus Vasa Fox was named for Sweden's King Gustavus, who reigned from 1523 to 1560. He was the founder of the Vasa dynasty, which ruled Sweden into the era of Napoleon. Neither of Gus's parents, Dr. Jesse Fox nor Olivia Flint, was Swedish American. They may have read or seen Henry Brooke's popular play, *Gustavus Vasa: The Deliverer of His Country* (1739). Despite his medical training, Gus's father was more interested in designing textile machinery and manufacturing cotton cloth than in practicing medicine. The year cloth was first manufactured in Lowell, Gus turned two and his parents moved there. With his father still practicing some medicine, Gus later recalled being "dragged round to see dying people," which "made him shrink from such scenes."[1]

Gus received his early education in Lowell, where he grew up with his older sister and brother, Harriet Amanda and George Henry. More than thirty years later, a teacher remembered him as "a bright open-faced, black-haired, black-eyed, chubby boy, full of honesty and full of pluck." Gus, who would never lack an appetite, was especially fond of his mother's mince pies. He also acquired a "fancy" for cats on visits to relatives in the country. As "a bit of a boy," he industriously collected minerals and fossils. Although as an adult he dismissed his "inferior" collection, he took pains to store it with his sister and to add specimens to it from time to time. He later donated about a thousand specimens to the Lawrence High School. In Lowell, young Gus made the connection that shaped his life when he met Colonel Isaac O. Barnes. Barnes and his wife, Hannah Woodbury, virtually adopted him and began to foster his career. "From my earliest recollection," Fox later wrote, "he has stood prominent in my mind and affections and I never knew him to do a wrong or suggest one, or even an act of unkindness."[2]

Gus received more schooling than most children of his time. He attended the recently opened Lowell High School (a classmate was the future politician and general Benjamin F. Butler). There Gus was remembered for excelling in snowball fights, for missing a Fourth of July excursion to Newburyport because of a broken arm, and for participating in a hunt with shovels and hoes for Indian relics near the Chelmsford line. After Lowell High School, Fox attended Phillips Academy at Andover, Massachusetts, for a year and a half, beginning in 1835. Although his brother George pursued a career in business, his parents intended Gus for the ministry, with its "promise of usefulness in this life and assured hope hereafter." When the ministry did not work out, his family settled for law, which he studied for the remainder of 1837 in Barnes's office. Finding, though, that Fox had his heart set on a naval career, his parents decided to "gratify" his "unconquerable desire" to be a midshipman.[3]

Fox had the necessary political connections to secure a naval appointment. Jesse Fox was one of Lowell's "most reputable citizens." An active Whig, he had just been elected a representative to the Massachusetts General Court. He asked Caleb Cushing, the Whig representative of his district, to "intercede with the Hon. Secretary of the Navy in behalf of my son." He also prevailed upon his colleague Dr. Elisha Bartlett, the first mayor of Lowell and one of America's most distinguished physicians, to urge Cushing to secure Fox's appointment. He "has by natural endowment all the qualities to fit him for the pursuit, upon which he is so ardently bent on entering," Bartlett testified. Joined by Daniel Webster, John Quincy Adams, and four other Whigs in the Massachusetts congressional delegation, Cushing recommended Fox as a "young gentleman well-qualified to be commissioned as a Midshipman in the Navy."[4]

Because Democrats were in power, Fox's crucial political connection in securing a naval commission was his friend and law tutor, Isaac Barnes, and his wife Hannah. Levi Woodbury of Portsmouth, New Hampshire, was Hannah's brother. He had been Andrew Jackson's secretary of the navy (1831–34), before becoming secretary of the treasury under both Jackson and Martin Van Buren (1834–41). Shortly after Woodbury took over the Treasury Department, Jackson appointed Barnes naval officer in the customhouse of the port of Boston. Barnes was also involved in the Lafayette Bank of Boston. He was a business ally as well as a customhouse colleague of David Henshaw, who was collector of the port of Boston and the Democratic boss of Massachusetts. He was also head of the Commonwealth Bank of Boston (a so-called pet bank), in which the Jackson administration had deposited federal funds.[5]

Close association with Henshaw enabled Barnes to influence the few Democrats in the Massachusetts congressional delegation. Through his family tie to Woodbury, Barnes also had access to the Van Buren administration. In January

1838 Barnes went to Washington, saw Woodbury and members of the Massachusetts congressional delegation, and coordinated their support for Fox, who on 12 January 1838 was appointed acting midshipman.[6]

Because there was not yet a United States naval academy, naval officers received most of their training on board ship. On 23 April 1838 Secretary of the Navy Mahlon Dickerson ordered Fox to the new twenty-gun U.S. sloop of war *Cyane* in Boston, and on 2 May he reported to Commander John Percival. The *Cyane* sailed on 24 June 1838 for duty in the Mediterranean Sea. It was Fox's good fortune that his maiden voyage was also the maiden voyage of a good ship and that his commanding officer was "Mad Jack" Percival, a legendary figure in the old sailing navy.[7]

Percival had gone to sea at thirteen, commanded vessels at twenty, been impressed into and escaped from the British navy, and fought in the War of 1812. Humorous and irascible, rough in manner and excitable in temper, decisive and brave, Percival was a superb seaman. Knowing the navy could be "one of the worst of schools for any well brought up boy," Percival made it his responsibility to teach and care for young midshipmen under his charge. Two decades before Fox joined the *Cyane*, Percival advised a father to tie a grindstone around the neck of his son and toss him overboard rather than send "him to sea in the Navy where he would be sure to imbibe the very devil in him and go to the devil, both body and soul."[8]

Shipboard life in the old navy varied from tyranny to anarchy, depending on how captains used their arbitrary power. Because many men were needed to work the guns in battle (the *Cyane*'s complement was 200 men), there was a surplus of hands when a man-of-war was simply being sailed. Work for officers and seamen was often more boring than arduous. Frequently undisciplined, seamen fought among themselves nearly as much as they worked. Officers were often ignorant and debauched. Drunkenness was common among them and their men, who were often flogged for that vice. Although strictly disciplined when on duty, midshipmen usually were ignored in their steerage quarters—where quarrels, frequently fomented by bored older officers, were often settled by duels. Manipulated, intimidated, and coerced by superiors, a midshipman "on board an American man of war" led "a dog's life."[9]

Despite his eccentricity, Percival had "good sense and good feeling" and did not neglect his young charges when they were off duty. He was both a captain and a schoolmaster to Fox and other midshipmen, and on two occasions he informed Jesse Fox candidly of his son's progress and failings. Seven months after Fox joined the *Cyane* and five months after sailing, his conduct gratified Percival. Writing from Messina, on the strait between Sicily and Italy, Percival reported that Fox "executed all orders with an alacrity and a judgment beyond his years." He studied assiduously, Percival continued, and his morals were as "yet uncontaminated and I will endeavor to keep them so, in not indulging him too much on shore in this libidinous climate." Lest Jesse Fox think his son "too perfect," Percival admitted he had committed "some very trivial juvenile indiscretions" and was "not so economical." With "very little cause to complain or find fault with him," Percival pledged to "take care that he obtains his warrant in due and proper time."[10]

Cheerful and gregarious, Fox was good company. It was on the *Cyane* that he met his fellow midshipmen, John L. Worden, Henry A. Wise, and Axel Adlersparre, a guest Swedish officer, who later as assistant minister of the Swedish navy would follow Fox's lead and advocate the building of monitors. Fox, Worden, and Wise were friends for life. Their naval careers would intersect in the future, but never more memorably than on 9 March 1862 when all three were on the deck of the *Monitor* immediately after it encountered the *Virginia*.[11]

Travel broadened Fox. He could not imagine "a more formidable place" than Gibraltar and sailed away with a new respect for Britain's "strength and power." Genoa, Fox thought, was "the most beautiful city I have yet seen. There are Palaces here that a Republican can have no conception of." Paintings by old masters—"Raphael, Michael Angelo etc"—that covered the palaces' rooms recalled the frescoed ceilings that adorned the churches. After writing of marble pillars with gold sequins and elaborate fireplace screens, he decided it "useless to describe these fairy places for none but those who see will believe." Fox "had the pleasure of going to the Opera" with Captain Percival, who made sure his charges were introduced to Italy's cultural offerings. Even here, Fox was more aware of art and architecture than of music, describing the opera house but neglecting to mention what opera they had seen. Other sights worthy of mention included the house of the fabled violinist and composer Nicolò Paganini and the street where Columbus—whose first landfall in America Fox later researched—was born and the church where Columbus was christened. Predicting that he would remember the "gorgeous palaces and churches" and would never forget "the *beautiful women*," Fox left Genoa "with regret." Percival could curb but not eradicate the libido in the robust seventeen-year-old boy.

Fox cared less for Naples, where splendor and poverty mingled. With friends, he climbed Vesuvius at two in the morning and "roasted Eggs in the fiery fissures and cracked a bottle of wine on the edge of the unfathomable crater." Upon descending, he visited the "disinterred" cities of Pompeii and

Herculaneum, which Vesuvius had buried. Not surprisingly, Fox was pleased to be a midshipman in the navy but missed his family and especially Isaac Barnes, from whom he wished to receive "a letter . . . more than from anyone else."[12]

Awed at first by his new surroundings on the *Cyane,* Fox carefully controlled his behavior until he had been at sea for almost a year. In late May 1839, however, he "officiously meddled in a matter in which he had no concern or right to interfere," lost his temper, and used offensive language to a fellow officer. For impropriety, for breaching discipline, and for his "highly reprehensible" violation of the rules of the service, Percival suspended Fox from duty. A written apology would lift the suspension, but Fox refused to write it. Instead, with sass to spare, he joined with two other acting midshipmen to ask Percival if "playing Dominoes for amusement *only*" was contrary to the rules of the service or the internal regulations of the *Cyane.*[13]

It was crucial for Fox to apologize. His probationary period was drawing to a close, and he needed Percival's recommendation to become a warranted midshipman and to continue in the navy. Finally, on 21 June 1839, he apologized "to the Service" and to Percival, but not to the officer to whom he had used offensive language. He regretted "that in the warmth of passion" he broke navy regulations by "candidly expressing" his "most sincere opinion of Doctor Buckner T. Magill." Fox added that "ignorance, not obstinacy (as may have been supposed) . . . delayed" his apology.[14]

Percival accepted Fox's apology (which met the form if not the spirit of the rules). He was not taken in by the lame excuse for the delay and roared that Fox was "a damned sea lawyer." Percival wrote Jesse Fox that he had to suspend his son from duty for twenty-seven days "before his contumacious spirit would yield to make proper atonement, which he ultimately did, or I should not have recommended his having a warrant." Fox was bold and fearless, as Wise admiringly noted on the day Percival returned him to duty. Percival apprehended that the time Fox "spent in my friend Barnes' office" had encouraged a spirit of litigation ("little adapted for the service") more than a spirit of subordination. "I hope," Percival continued, "the lesson he had learned will be a sufficient warning to him to not be putting his hand in another's fire." Percival recognized that Fox possessed "talents and abilities," that he could "make a good officer, but he must learn that a subordinate spirit and obedience to the usages of the Service are the first letters of the Alphabet he should . . . practice." Percival's letter, arriving in Lowell around the time Jesse Fox nearly died of typhus fever, produced more than the usual admonitions from family and friends.[15]

A month after he had restored Fox to duty, Percival recommended him for a midshipman's warrant. Fox had improved his mathematics and diligently studied the practical art of seamanship and was "constitutionally well adapted for a Sea officer, being robust, stout and healthy." He was temperate, kept out of debt (Fox had a credit of $6.68 on 30 September 1839), exhibited good habits and moral conduct, and would "when sufficiently disciplined make a good officer." Percival acknowledged that Fox "occasionally evinced a litigious and restless disposition under restraint" (attributed to his "months in a *lawyer's office*"), which Percival had "in a *great degree*, subdued, and brought into obedience with the usages of the service." Fox received the warrant on 5 March 1840.[16]

In September 1839 Percival turned over the *Cyane* to Commander William K. Latimer, and Fox was confident enough of Percival's good opinion to ask for a letter stating his "Character, Talents and Qualifications." Under Latimer, Fox did not totally master his temper and govern his tongue, nor did he lose his capacity to justify his behavior. "I regret very much sir," he wrote Latimer, "that the direct contradiction of my word and positive refusal to obey my order by one of the men should have caused a momentary passion sufficient to have made me disregard the Regulations of the Service and forget the respect due the Quarter Deck."[17]

Despite his lapses, Fox was getting on well, and he reassured his parents and Barnes that he would not "slight" their advice. "I hope," he wrote Barnes, "that you will see Capt. Percival, he can tell you of my moral character, & my attention to studies and duties. He has told me frequently that he can find no fault with either, whether he has changed his mind or not I do not know." Fox sent Barnes a miniature of himself ("an exact likeness") for which he bartered about a dozen "reefers," or short, close fitting, jackets. He speculated that "they would hardly tolerate my long hair at home." His morale was good, and he liked Captain Latimer. He reported that rumors of war with Britain provoked the "universal" wish in the Mediterranean squadron "to cope once more with the would be mistress of the seas." Having returned via the West Indies, the *Cyane* completed its three-year Mediterranean cruise at Norfolk, Virginia, on 16 May 1841. Latimer praised Fox for his deportment and zeal, his assiduity in discharging his duties, and predicted his future success before the board of examiners.[18]

After three and a half years' service, Fox received a three-month leave of absence. The young man of twenty returned to the home he left as a boy not yet seventeen. The high point of that vacation—at least from Fox's perspective five years later—was a visit with Hannah Barnes to the Elms, the Portsmouth,

New Hampshire, home of her brother, Levi Woodbury. Although he probably had known the Woodbury children since he was a child, Fox, on this visit, noticed Virginia Lafayette—the fourth of five children and the third of four daughters—in a special way. She was seventeen, tall, slender, pretty, studious, pious, and "promising" with a "steady, sensible eye" and a diffident manner. She was, however, delicate and prone to illness, seemingly caused more by the failure of her psyche than of her body. Virginia had discovered that she could get more than her share of her parents' attention by pleading illness. Despite or perhaps because of her fragility, the robust Fox found Virginia attractive.[19]

Fox was fortunate in his next assignment. Complying with his request, the Navy Department ordered him on 30 October 1841 to the receiving ship at Boston. Over the next fourteen months, Fox served first on the *Columbus*—a seventy-four-gun ship of the line—and then on the *Ohio*. Although the ninety-gun *Ohio* was powerful and fast and handled like a frigate (a British naval officer in 1840 called it "the perfection of a line-of-battleship"), its huge crew made it expensive to operate. For most of its sixty-three years (1820–83), it was a decommissioned receiving ship at Boston.[20]

The duties on board receiving ships were not difficult. They involved recruiting, housing, and distributing enlisted seamen. With few officers on the huge decommissioned vessel, Fox's quarters were spacious. He also had more opportunity to study for his midshipman exams than if he were at sea. In addition, the nearness of his home in Lowell and the Woodbury home in Portsmouth and his ties with Isaac and Hannah Barnes, who now resided in Boston, made Fox's assignment perfect. "That young Fox came down yesterday for Aunt Barnes," Virginia's oldest sister wrote their mother from the Elms on 21 July 1842, "as Uncle B. was so much engaged he could not come." Fox dined with them on "cherry pie, & preserved *Iceland moss*" and had "plenty to eat." He had the range of the house and its books and did as he pleased, including sitting on a plank under a "glorious old oak" with Virginia. When he carved her initials on that plank, "it was," Virginia recalled, "the *first* evidence of Gus' feelings towards me!" Because Boston was ideal for Fox, he did his best to prove that he was ideal for the Boston receiving ship. Commander George F. Pearson, his superior officer, commended his energetic, intelligent, and gentlemanly behavior and recommended him to the "Board of Examiners as a young officer of much promise."[21]

After more than a year in Boston, Fox requested orders to the recently launched twenty-gun sloop of war *Saratoga*—a slightly longer, improved version of the *Cyane*—being fitted out at the Portsmouth Navy Yard for duty off West Africa. The recent Webster-Ashburton Treaty (1842) not only squelched rumors of war but also required that Britain and the United States maintain joint squadrons on the African coast to suppress the slave trade. The department granted Fox's request, and he left Boston in December 1842 to join the *Saratoga*, with a number of enlistees in his charge. Although Fox received a four-day leave over Christmas 1842 to make "arrangements preparatory to . . . leaving the United States," the *Saratoga* spent the winter at Portsmouth. Finally, on 16 March 1843, commanded by Josiah Tattnall, it weighed anchor on its maiden voyage for New York, to make additional preparations for its African cruise. Able and fearless, Tattnall was a superb officer. Later, as a captain in the Confederate navy, he had, at Port Royal, to flee a superior fleet (organized by his midshipman Fox) and at Norfolk had to scuttle the famous ironclad *Merrimack/Virginia*.[22]

As the light wind out of the northwest shifted to the southeast, the *Saratoga* cleared the harbor. Then the weather thickened, the wind increased, and Tattnall took in his topgallant sails and double-reefed his topsails. Before midnight, a gale of snow, hail, and rain out of the east, with a "tremendous" sea, battered the *Saratoga*, which soon lost any idea of its precise position, but knew it was "embayed" by the shore to the west and south and by the Isles of Shoals to the east. Tattnall carried "an awful press of canvas, to work off shore," but to no avail. Unable to furl the frozen sails, they were "simply hauled up" and helped drive the *Saratoga* before the raging storm. At about nine the next morning, they discovered one of the Isles of Shoals to windward and steered for the harbor under close reefed foresail. But, Fox reported, "every force applied to the ship, tended to set her . . . drifting slowly towards the awful line of breakers to leeward of us" and then "breakers were suddenly discovered ahead." With no escape from "this hell of waters and rocks around us," Tattnall ordered the helm put down, the mizzen mast cut away, two anchors with 300 fathoms of chain let go, and then the main and foremasts cut away. For one moment, the *Saratoga* "bowed her head as if to follow her anchors to the bottom, but, as she rose and fell, we felt ourselves for the 1st time comparatively speaking safe." It took eight minutes to dismast the ship. If Tattnall had delayed five minutes, all 150 hands and the vessel would have been lost. Miraculously, no one was hurt.[23]

Tattnall noted that "at great personal hazard" Fox had been in the thick of the action. He struck the first blow at the main mast and, while cutting the fore rigging, jumped clear of the foremast as it came crashing down. "To you both who have watched me from childhood," Fox wrote the Barneses (who thought of him as their "only boy"), "it will be gratifying, when I tell you (not vainly) that my conduct during the gale has met the approbation of the Cap't

& oldest officers. I can boast of this only to my own relations, it is a sweet reward for any peril."[24]

Towed back to Portsmouth, the *Saratoga* had to be rigged anew. Many of the sails and spars had been recovered, but some spars, along with the masts, had to be replaced. "Our noble ship so lately a wreck" received two masts on 4 April 1843 and began to look itself again. Although Fox visited his friends at Elm Place every time he went on shore, he was troubled about his examination. He was afraid that if he went to Africa with the *Saratoga* he would not get back to Philadelphia in September to attend the naval school. "I shall lose a great deal at my examination," he agonized. In order to be examined, he resolved to ask to return to the *Ohio*, when the *Saratoga* arrived in New York. "If," Fox asked Barnes, "I find any difficulty in getting orders to the Ohio, what Tyler man in Washington is there, that you know, that can help me?" Fox felt "no delicacy about applying to anyone." Although he cared "so little about parties," he knew what political pull could accomplish in the navy. Fox trusted Barnes would land "one of John Tyler's offices" and "if you do not now," Fox predicted, "you will certainly come in for spoils." Fox later told Barnes, "I am a democrat as far as any of your family are concerned."[25]

Sympathizing with Fox's need for schooling, the Navy Department on 26 May ordered him to the razee *Independence*, flagship of the Home Squadron, commanded by Commodore Charles Stewart and stationed in New York. Fox spent a delightful summer in New York harbor on the *Independence*. A hero for capturing the *Cyane* and *Levant* in the War of 1812, Stewart was a mild disciplinarian who interfered little with his squadron officers, and Isaac McKeever, captain of the *Independence*, was renowned for his kindness. The ship was anchored off the Battery (the southern tip of Manhattan), and with musicians in its crew, the officers enjoyed "little dancing parties nearly every week." Dignitaries, including President John Tyler, visited the *Independence*. Occupied with bringing a bevy of women to the ship, Fox was the only officer to miss meeting Tyler. Despite his disappointment, he claimed he would "rather be sitting by a party of pretty faces than shake any man by the hand." Fox thought that "in full dress, with cocked hat on, sword etc.," he "looked like anybody but myself," but one of the women amazed and pleased Fox by presuming, on the basis of resemblance, that he was related to the Woodbury family of Portsmouth. Besides shipboard diversions, Fox's parents visited him, and his sister Harriet Guild, who was married and a recent mother, lived in Brooklyn. Still a sea lawyer, Fox took time from his idyllic summer to query the fourth auditor of the Treasury Department, in charge of naval accounts, if an officer performing the duty of a higher grade was entitled to the pay of that grade. He must, he learned, first be on foreign service or under specific orders from the secretary of the navy.[26]

In late September 1843 Secretary of the Navy David Henshaw (who had been Isaac Barnes's close associate in the Boston Customhouse and in banking ventures) ordered Fox to attend the school at the Naval Asylum in Philadelphia. The orders took almost a month to reach Fox, who did not report until 9 November to the governor of the Naval Asylum, Commander William W. McKean. Early in the Civil War, McKean commanded the East Gulf Blockading Squadron, and his daughter Tish was a close friend of the Woodbury sisters. Because the asylum was full, Fox and other midshipmen roomed at a boardinghouse until space became available.[27]

Determined "to get a good number at the examination," Fox through McKean asked Henshaw to allow him to remain at the boardinghouse. The partitions between the rooms at the asylum did not reach the ceiling, he complained, and the noise of continual "skylarking" reverberated everywhere. Fox also noted that at the asylum the lights were put out at ten o'clock, "the very time a person wishes to pursue his studies with the most vigor." McKean agreed that midshipmen "consider their apartments as a steerage," and Henshaw granted Fox's request. Grateful, he studied diligently and did not take a leave of absence for the Christmas holidays.[28]

Recitations began at 9:00 a.m. and continued until 1:30 p.m. The first four days of the week were devoted to mathematics and the last two to languages. These subjects were basic tools for those who would navigate and serve on foreign stations. With the examination scheduled for 1 June 1844, Fox in January was aware that "it is rapidly approaching." He was so busy and wrote so little that by the end of March he feared his ability to write had departed. "If the space thus created has been filled by *mathematics*," he told Barnes, "you and I will both rejoice."[29]

Fox did not study all the time. On Saturday, 6 January 1844, dining with John L. Worden, his "very strong personal friend" from the *Cyane*, gave Fox's morale a boost. In March, his peers, confident that he was intelligent, mature, and fair, named him to a committee of three to investigate charges of theft and of passing a counterfeit banknote against a fellow midshipman. The committee concluded the accused was guilty and, "for the honor of their corps and their grade," reported its findings to Secretary of the Navy John Y. Mason.[30]

Fox was worried about the hostility of politicians, particularly Democrats, to the navy. Friends of the navy, he thought, were getting "very scarce" in the House of Representatives. He feared Congressman John P. Hale of New Hampshire, a leader of those "thirsting for the downfall of the Navy." (Years later, Hale, still around, thirsted for Fox's downfall.) Fox also felt threatened by William Parmenter of Massachusetts, who, as chairman of the House Naval Committee, was sponsoring legislation that would reduce by attrition the number of officers in each grade. Promotions would be postponed for years, and, Fox complained, the hospitals would be filled with aged midshipmen. It was even rumored that his class would not be examined. Having already spent six years as a midshipman and with no "appetite for more of the same kind of servitude," Fox asked Barnes to influence Parmenter to drop this legislation. Fox had hoped for a Democratic victory in 1844 (to benefit Barnes and therefore himself), but he feared that the navy would "suffer by it."[31]

Congressional hostility to the navy reinforced Fox's cynical attitude toward politics and politicians. "The only reason the Navy has not been entirely annihilated" by Congress, he wrote Barnes, "is that . . . a majority of the members, have relations in the Navy." Indeed, Lieutenant Harry Ingersoll's father, Representative Charles Jared Ingersoll, a Philadelphia Democrat, responded to Hale's attack. "I don't give one of them credit for honesty either in their attack or defense of the Navy," Fox exclaimed.[32]

Despite his fears, Congress did not destroy the navy, nor did Fox fail his examination, which was given in early May, rather than in June. Commodore James Biddle, for the board of examiners, certified, on 3 May 1844, that Fox had passed his examinations in seamanship and mathematics. Within a week, he was relaxing in Boston on the receiving ship *Ohio* and in late May went home to Lowell for ten days. His warrant as a passed midshipman was dated 30 May 1844. A month later, he was ordered to the *Preble* in New York for an African cruise.[33]

Master Fox

It is impossible for me to forget, that poor Midshipman Smith of Salem, who was put under my especial charge by his Mother . . ., is now dead, and that I am now occupying the room of our little master, who was attacked by the fever.

Fox to Isaac O. Barnes, 28 February 1845

I slept on deck with my rifle in hopes to have a shot, and had the pleasure of hearing, for the first time in my life, the whistle of a shot near my head. I suddenly felt a strong desire to preserve my head . . . and walked quietly below and "turned in."

Fox to Virginia L. Woodbury, 13 (24) June 1847

Fox benefited from shipboard training and study at the Asylum. The enthusiastic boy matured into a brash young man, who occasionally had to be reined in. His dreams of glory, however, eluded him. The greatest danger and most harrowing experience in his life occurred not in war but in a malaria epidemic on shipboard. His wartime service in Mexico was of little subsequent use, but work and study on the Coast Survey yielded him valuable knowledge.

■ ■ ■

The African cruise of the *Preble*, a sixteen-gun sloop of war, under Commander Thomas W. Freelon, was short and disastrous. Bucking head winds during most of September 1844, the *Preble* took thirty-three days to reach Funchal, Madeira, a voyage that took the *Saratoga* thirteen days. "No island," Fox told Hannah Barnes, "is hailed with more joy after such a passage, than this," with its "delicious fruit and rich wines and delightful rides over a country which blooms with all the production of every zone."

Looking for the African Squadron, the *Preble* arrived on a Sunday at Santa Cruz, Tenerife, the largest of the Canary Islands. Ordered ashore, Fox and a fellow officer landed "amid a crowd" of lepers who displayed "horribly distorted" limbs and "loathsome" infections, while demanding alms. The officers observed soldiers going to mass "with their arms and martial music" and learned that the African Squadron and its commodore, Matthew C. Perry, were at Porto Praia, São Tiago, the largest of the Cape Verde Islands. The *Preble* remained at Tenerife long enough for Fox and his buddy Henry A. Wise to climb its fabled 12,198-foot peak (Pico de Teide), visible from 100 miles at sea.[1]

By late October the *Preble* had found Perry and was about to depart for five months of "dark and horrible cruising," 3,000 miles down the African coast in search of slave ships. Fox assured Hannah Barnes that the "squadron thus far has enjoyed excellent health," thanks to Perry's sanitary regulations that caused "considerable mirth and some growling." Ships were smoked with smudges, dried with coal stoves, and well ventilated; men had to wear a flannel undershirt night and day, bathe every week, and not be on the African shore later than eight o'clock.[2]

The *Preble* did not take that "dark and horrible" cruise down the coast. Because of an insurrection in Portuguese Guinea (Guinea-Bissau), Perry ordered it to Bissau. Although Washington had not responded to his request for guidance, Perry had earlier protected the African Americans settled in Liberia by the American Colonization Society. Now, under the pretext of protecting American commerce, he ordered the *Preble* to prop up Portuguese colonial power. American brigs and schooners (invariably from Salem, Massachusetts) traded on the Guinea Coast, but Perry probably felt obliged to Portugal for letting the U.S. African Squadron be based in the Cape Verde Islands. On 3 November the *Preble* arrived at Bissau, located forty-five miles from the coast on the Geba River estuary. At the request of the beleaguered governor, it anchored "very close" to the shore to aid the town if it was attacked. Too far from the sea to benefit from its breezes, the anchorage was "completely landlocked." The eye, Fox noted, "rests on nothing but those low level lands, partly submerged, and covered with rank vegetation and animal matter, that in its decay and corruption, give out that fearful 'malaria.'"[3]

The men on the *Preble* did not take the revolution seriously. Sixty "sick looking Portuguese negroes" and three European officers garrisoned the "dilapidated" fort, whose dozen pieces of artillery were "in the last stages of decomposition." The Portuguese had native allies, but they were primarily interested in the "grog and grub" distributed at the fort. The governor claimed 5,000 natives were trying to capture the fort, but seeing skirmishes convinced Fox that 500 was a closer estimate of rebel strength. An enterprising Salem brig was selling obsolete arms that Fox guessed General Henry A. C. Dearborn had condemned for use by the Massachusetts militia. During a rebel attack on the fort, the *Preble* opened fire and "desperately wounded" a rebel, which discouraged attacks on the ship's side of the fort.[4]

For sixteen days, Fox recalled, "we lay, confident, secure, and happy." Life on the *Preble* was so normal that the midshipmen were infuriated when Freelon, to promote the circulation of air, would not permit them to secure some privacy by putting up a latticed bulkhead across the crowded steerage apartment, shared by ten officers. When not fretting that they were "subject in our most private moments to the gaze of every man in the ship," they went hunting. Lured by plentiful game, Fox and friends incautiously waded in "mud and water" after sunset.[5]

On 19 November, the day after Fox and his cohorts complained of their lack of privacy, a case of "African fever" (malaria) appeared on the *Preble*. By 23 November five men were afflicted, including Midshipman Jesse M. Smith of Salem, whose mother had put him under Fox's "especial charge." Alarmed, Freelon up-anchored and sailed to Porto Praia. When the *Preble* arrived there, six days later, it had forty-seven men on board with fever, including Freelon who became delirious. Perry ordered the *Preble* to Porto Grande (Mindello) on nearby São Vicente, which was healthy and the best harbor in the Cape Verde Islands. On the way there, both Fox and Master William A. Henry "had a pain across the back, one of the first symptoms" of African fever. Having been on that "after sunset" hunting expedition, both of them, Fox wrote, "'turned in' anxious for the morrow to know our fate; I awoke in perfect health, my first step was to the Master's room, I found them bathing his forehead to allay the burning heat, his pulse was up to a hundred and twenty and his face wore an expression of deep anxiety."[6]

The *Preble* arrived at Porto Grande on 3 December with 67 on the sick list, which number increased to 93 cases in a crew of 144. Buildings were rented and erected on shore to house the sick, and the ship was cleansed, ventilated, and purified with fire. A cemetery was established "in a little valley near the town" for the sixteen who died. Midshipman Smith, who had been delirious most of the time since he was stricken, died the day the *Preble* arrived at Porto Grande, while Henry, who was disheartened and expected to die, "never lost his senses till a few hours before his death," ten days after he took sick. "The depression of spirits that follows an attack of this fever," Fox noted, was compounded by absence from home. He thought he could "defy the fever" with his mother or sister to care for him, but without them he prayed for deliverance.[7]

Fox and a fellow officer were the only members of the ill-fated hunting party to escape the disease. By Christmas only two or three men remained seriously ill, but besides the sixteen who died, nineteen were so "broken up" they were sent home. With the remaining convalescents still debilitated, Perry ordered the *Preble* to Madeira. From there, Fox reported on 28 February 1845 that "the hurry, hustle, activity and fun of a man of war has been resumed. The old fiddle, cast aside by the men at Bissau, is touched with new life and the men at this moment are 'shuffling down' in the gangway, forgetting . . . their sixteen messmates who sleep under the sod at Porto Grande." But Fox could forget neither Midshipman Smith nor the image of Smith's mother, "who will be crazy at his loss." He was constantly reminded of William Henry, whom he, as acting master, had replaced as the *Preble*'s navigating officer and whose room he now occupied. His brush with death made Fox long for letters from Virginia Woodbury, to whom he was writing regularly.[8]

With a crew too unhealthy for duty on the African coast, the *Preble* remained at either Madeira or the Cape Verde Islands, waiting for orders to return home. Freelon, who had recovered, was sufficiently impressed by Fox to make him an acting lieutenant (which on foreign service meant more pay). Fox was "comfortable, happy and in perfect health." He was "kind and lenient to the men" with one exception. He demanded that a seaman named Tripp prove he was innocent of an alleged offense. When dissatisfied with Tripp's defense, he peremptorily called all hands to witness his punishment, which presumably would be a flogging with the cat o'nine tails.[9]

Commander Freelon intervened, spoke to the officers and crew, ordered that Tripp not be punished, and mortified Fox.

When he protested, Freelon responded that he did not intend his remarks "to reflect upon your conduct. . . . But you must be aware of principle of Law and equity that requires that every accused person shall have the benefit of any doubt that may rest upon the minds of his judges. This doubt existed in my mind . . . and it . . . existed also in your own mind, as you required him to *prove his innocence* of the offense alleged against him; a thing that is next to an impossibility." Freelon further told Fox, a spirited young man of twenty-four, that he had to comply with the general orders of the ship.[10]

After several months, the *Preble* was ordered home, and on 25 September 1845 it arrived in New York. On leave for three months, Fox visited his sister and her family in Brooklyn before going home to Lowell. Political affairs had turned to his advantage. Isaac Barnes and his friend, the historian George Bancroft, had found favor in the James K. Polk administration. Barnes had been named the U.S. marshal at Boston, and Bancroft the new secretary of the navy. Fox's leave expired on 27 December 1845. He hoped that Bancroft would delay his orders long enough for him to be sent to the Coast Survey when it commenced its work in the spring.[11]

While waiting orders, Fox speculated that there would be no war with Mexico. He was appalled by the possibility that the Texas navy (four rotten vessels, whose officers were failed U.S. Navy midshipmen) might be incorporated into the U.S. Navy. Not only would he be outranked by incompetents, but money needed to build ten war steamers would be wasted reconditioning four potential "coffins." Besides visiting New York, Fox in March saw the Woodburys in Portsmouth. There, he attended a temperance tea party at the Jefferson House, where there were, he exclaimed, "refreshments of coffee, tea & cakes & everything that is bad."[12]

As Fox hoped, on 9 April 1846 Samuel Phillips Lee of the U.S. Coast Survey requested his services, having heard that he was available and a good officer, and Bancroft ordered him to Baltimore. Perhaps Virginia Woodbury's sister Minna, who was engaged to Lee's brother-in-law Montgomery Blair, influenced Lee to choose Fox. Influence alone, however, did not secure his appointment to the Coast Survey. Fox had mastered mathematics and navigation at the naval school.[13]

Fox reported to Lee for duty on 4 May 1846. Even though the United States declared war on Mexico a few days later, he spent the summer charting Chesapeake Bay on board the Coast Survey schooner *Nautilus*. "From daylight till dark we are at work," he wrote Hannah Barnes, "frequently going without dinner till the day's work was finished." Once dinner arrived, a shipmate recalled, Fox ate large quantities of rice pudding. After dinner, at around nine o'clock, he went on deck, smoked a cigar "lying down on the hard planks," and dropped off to sleep. "Notwithstanding dews, wind and my hard pillow," he claimed to "sleep sweetly till morning." He was "stronger, happier and brighter" than during the past idle winter, when he slept half his time away in "a state of stupidity." A husky youth who had become a somewhat overweight young man, Fox hoped but could not report "with certainty, that this active life has *thinned* me." In early September, he moved ashore to Annapolis, Maryland, where he worked on charts, "too large a scale to be constructed" on board the *Nautilus*. He was pleasantly situated with a quiet family on the principal street. When cold weather came at the end of November, Lee and his men sailed the *Nautilus* into winter quarters at the Washington Navy Yard.[14]

With the Mexican War going on, Fox and his survey colleagues wanted to participate in the expedition to take Vera Cruz. Lee succeeded in getting himself and several of his officers, including Fox, transferred to the Coast Survey

brig *Washington,* undergoing repairs at the Philadelphia Navy Yard. Lee suggested to the navy secretary John Y. Mason that the *Washington* join the squadron in the Gulf of Mexico for "active naval duty" and use its hydrographical
equipment to survey Mexican ports. Mason accepted Lee's suggestion and
made Fox acting master of the *Washington.* Fox got along with Lee, who in the
Civil War distinguished himself at New Orleans and as commander of the
North Atlantic Blockading Squadron. But Lee tended to be irascible, and Fox
did not become his close friend.[15]

Before leaving for Philadelphia, Fox spent three "very pleasant" weeks at
"Browns," the boardinghouse where Levi Woodbury, who had become a
Supreme Court justice, and his family stayed in Washington. On New Year's
Day, he accompanied Judge Woodbury to President James K. Polk's White
House reception and to the receptions of Vice President George M. Dallas,
Secretary of the Navy John Y. Mason, and Dolley Madison, who at seventy-
eight was still the queen of Washington society. Fox, however, was more interested in Woodbury's daughter Virginia than in the politicians. He spent a
memorable Christmas with her and was not deterred to find that she felt
healthy as rarely as he felt ill. "Miss Virginia," he noted, "gets a little sick for
a day or two but is soon about again, though she only rides out."[16]

Lee sent Fox and his other Coast Survey officers to Philadelphia in early
January to expedite repairs on the *Washington.* Lee was busy in Washington
winding up his "surveying business," settling accounts, and getting instructions for his forthcoming cruise to Mexican waters. Estimating that the *Washington* would take five or six weeks to repair, Fox feared the army would gain
the glory of capturing Veracruz's great fortress, San Juan de Ulloa. His chances
for glory seemed slim. In June the *Washington* was scheduled to leave the war
zone to survey the "more perilous" Gulf Stream.[17]

The *Washington* was repaired on schedule, but recruiting a crew was difficult, because the merchant marine paid better than the navy. "Common seamen" out of Philadelphia and New York were paid $22 a month, which was
$3 or $4 more than petty officers and $10 more than seamen in the navy. The
Navy Department refused to authorize Lee to offer a $20 bounty for recruits
($15 for each seaman, and $5 a head for the landlords of sailors' rooming
houses, who, as labor contractors, delivered men to the *Washington*). To get a
crew, Lee paid the bounty, though he called it "a recruiting expense," when
Secretary Mason complained about his action.[18]

Frustrated by the delays, Fox almost joined a vessel departing in February
for Veracruz. Then, a faulty chronometer enabled him to visit the Washington
Naval Observatory. With Congress adjourned, the city seemed "dull and stu-

pid," without even "a drunken man to be seen in the streets." Fox saw Virginia and probably accompanied her on an hour's drive, which apart from reading and writing was her only activity.[19]

Without its full complement, but with three guns and "barrels of apparatus for scientific purposes," the *Washington* sailed for Veracruz on 7 April 1847. Fox presumed correctly that Veracruz had already fallen, but he hoped that they would find "somebody that will shoot at us." The voyage began with an "omen from the heavens" that Fox, lying flat on the deck, gazed at for two hours. "After a beautiful display of the Aurora Borealis, an arch of bright light detached itself, and rising, divided the heavens, as perfect as the belt of Saturn."[20]

On 1 May 1847, after a "rough and stormy" passage, the *Washington* arrived at Veracruz, where an American flag flew over Fort San Juan de Ulloa and an "immense fleet" filled the harbor. Having missed dragging heavy naval guns four miles (40 mules and 300 men moved them only ten or twelve yards in an hour) and the "terrible excitement" of firing them, Fox was "crazy to have a chance . . . to fight." He reflected that the thousand or so soldiers dying of disease would be remembered only by their families, while the few men who died in battle would be given magnificent funerals. The *Washington* dropped fifteen miles down the coast to a better anchorage at Anton Lizardo and on 4 May, having been ordered by Commodore Matthew C. Perry, under whom Fox had served on the coast of Africa, to help blockade the Laguna de Terminos, sailed east toward Yucatan.[21]

For ten days, the *Washington* blockaded the eastern passage (the Barra de Puerto Real) into the Laguna de Terminos. Then, Perry decided to open it up under American control and to reoccupy the town of Laguna (Cuidad Carmen) at the Laguna's western end. With inlets at either end of the long Isla del Carmen, the Laguna was in 1847 a part of Yucatan. Whether Yucatan was the independent La Republica Chica (the Tiny Republic) or a part of Mexico was impossible to determine. It had seceded a couple of times, but it also had a strong unionist Santa Anna party that proclaimed its reincorporation into Mexico. Yucatan was a source of war supplies for Mexico from Cuba, Europe, and even the United States. Transshipped into smaller boats at Campeche, supplies proceeded down the coast into the Laguna and from it to the Rio Grijalva (Tabasco River), and then upriver past Villahermosa (Tabasco) to Cárdenas, a hundred miles upstream. From there, supplies went overland to Mexico City.[22]

"The only point on the Mexican coast," Fox exclaimed, "now held by the military is Tabasco." It was defended, he estimated, by 2,000 "regulars and rancheros," though the actual figure was nearer 900. Although Perry had bombarded Villahermosa in October 1846, Mexican reinforcements and supplies continued to pass through it. When Perry decided to attack it again despite the rainy and sickly season, Fox had his heart set on being a part of the expedition. Perhaps, he prophesied, "this is the last opportunity I shall ever have" of getting into a battle. "Don't say anything to Pa or Ma," he warned Barnes, "about my hopes of going on this expedition."[23]

Fox and the *Washington* almost missed the expedition. As Perry's squadron of fifteen vessels approached the mouth of the Rio Grijalva, the *Washington* was headed toward Veracruz in the opposite direction. Upon learning the expedition was underway, it reversed course to join Perry. On Sunday, 13 June, Fox worked feverishly to lighten the *Washington* so it could cross the bar at the river's mouth and to prepare for the trip seventy-two miles upstream to Villahermosa. Although a "crashing" thunderstorm doused the squadron that evening, Monday dawned beautifully, and Perry's four small steam gunboats towed three bomb brigs, a schooner, and the *Washington* (which touched bottom several times) over the bar. The gunboats also towed forty pulling boats, crammed with 1,050 men from the squadron's larger vessels, and seven surfboats, each loaded with a brass field gun. At seven o'clock on the evening of 14 June 1847, the expedition started upstream with Perry's flagship the *Scorpion* (commanded by Josiah Tattnall) leading the way, as it towed the *Washington*. Fox intended to write his "dearest Ginny" as they progressed upriver, but could not, he explained, because of the crowd, noise, confusion, and excitement of going into "an engagement from which there was a possibility of never coming out alive." Near daybreak, an overhanging branch knocked two men into the river from "a boat towing astern." After the men were recovered, the *Scorpion* and the *Washington* anchored until daylight, when the other steamers and their tows caught up.[24]

Wasting no time, the expedition continued to push up the deep, serpentine river. It was about 200 yards wide with "perfumed flowers" crowding its low banks. Meeting slight resistance, the flotilla at sundown encountered some obstructions in the river, eight miles below Villahermosa. The Mexicans fired several shots as the squadron anchored, but were silenced by a few discharges from its large guns. Worried by the obstructions, Perry decided to land at daylight. That evening the Mexicans returned, fired more shots, and for the only time in his life Fox heard one whistle by his head.[25]

Rising at dawn, on 16 June, the 1,100-man landing force and ten artillery pieces were in boats ready for the attack by seven o'clock. When a probe of the obstructions drew fire, Perry, "with his broad pennant flying, pulled into our midst," Fox reported, "and rising in his boat gave the word to land. Such a yell arose from our sailors, as never before awoke the silence of these woods, and with a rush like a coming tempest," they reached the shore. "The bank was twenty feet high, and very steep, but men and artillery ascended" and met no resistance.[26]

By eight o'clock, they were marching on a narrow winding path toward Villahermosa. Despite the thick vegetation, the Mexicans did not harass the mile-long column of rapidly tiring sailors. "Cannon, ammunition, three days' provisions, all the arms and apparatus for the sick were carried and dragged through the mud, over stumps, and under a burning sun, without a breath of fresh air," for a distance of more than six miles. Fox discarded most of his clothes. Overcome by heat and exertion, some officers and men had to be carried. Their "gigantic exertions" proved unnecessary. Lieutenant David Dixon Porter cleared the obstructions by exploding submerged barrels of powder and, with four steamers, took Villahermosa. (Fox admired Porter for his feat, and, in the late 1850s, when he was stationed at Portsmouth, they became friends.) "When we emerged from the chaparral," Fox reported, "the Fort lay before us, the stars and stripes above it, and beyond, the Town, bright under the rays of the setting sun." Giving "three tremendous cheers," the sailors managed to enter "the town in fine order and at a rapid pace," despite a sudden downpour.[27]

The Tabasco expedition resulted in few immediate casualties. No Americans were killed and only a half dozen were wounded, Fox estimated, while perhaps ten or fifteen Mexicans were killed. The following month, however, yellow fever and malaria broke out in the squadron. With no battle to realize his dreams of glory and to relieve frustrations created by the awful march, Fox was contemptuous of the Mexicans' "miserable cowardice." He took a trombone for loot, but soon lost it. Bravado kept him from seeing that the Mexicans had wisely retreated before a superior amphibious force that would not stay. Perry remained for five days before moving downriver, leaving a company of marines and a few small vessels, which yellow fever and guerrilla harassment soon forced out of Villahermosa.[28]

By July, Perry returned the *Washington* to its Coast Survey duties. Making a fine run, it landed dispatches at Mobile, Alabama, and then stopped at Pensacola, Florida, for ten days to prepare for its Gulf Stream work. There, Fox received letters from Virginia, Barnes, and home. During his last three days at Pensacola, he was "in town and on the move, from light till very late," rounding up men who failed to return to the vessel from their shore leave. Departing from Pensacola in late July, he was sorry not to stop at Havana for some "really good cigars," as the *Washington*, "without a breath of fresh wind," floated by at four miles an hour on the Gulf Stream current. By 30 July it was between Florida and the Bahama Banks and making its routine observations.[29]

Even though he ignored Perry's advice to avoid night dews and the hot sun and to wear thick clothing, Fox continued to enjoy "perfect health." When sleeping, he told Barnes, "I wear nothing but a ribbon around my neck, never have a covering at night of more than a sheet, and make it an invariable rule to get in a draft of wind," provided by the ventilating "wind sail." He also took frequent showers. His main complaint on the *Washington* was the lack of fresh provisions. "Only think," he exclaimed, "of eating for fourth of July dinner nothing but salt meat, the only thing approaching freshness being apple sauce made from old dried apples." Fox blamed his loss of five pounds in three months on "our confounded living" in Mexico. Life in the Gulf Stream, where the *Washington* remained until it returned to Philadelphia in September, was not much better.[30]

On the other hand, Coast Survey shore duty, with good food and good companionship, was enjoyable. In September Fox ran up to New York to hire for the Coast Survey three of the best chronometers obtainable, brought them back to the *Washington*, and rated them with great care.[31]

Fox's next assignment was the Coast Survey Office in Washington, where he anticipated a fall and winter with "no lack of fun." Virginia and her family would be in town. He and four other officers rented a house with an "elegant parlor," which was cheaper than a hotel and preferable to a boardinghouse. New Year's Day 1848, Fox reported, was warm, misty, and muddy and "a day especially set apart and devoted to drinking egg nog and apple toddy. To obtain these drinks," one could go "into any open home, shake hands with anybody, bow to everybody and *fall to.*" While making the rounds, Fox chanced on Levi Woodbury, whom he accompanied for part of the afternoon.[32]

Participation in the Tabasco expedition appeared to give Fox a touch of arrogance. Although he did not deign to attend, he derisively described the New Year's Day crush at the White House, which had awed him the previous year. "Nothing is doing at the Capitol," he wrote Hannah Barnes. "The House is too noisy to be interesting and the Senate too crowded for comfort and the Supreme Court by far too stupid." But the older woman knew that those high-spirited, disparaging remarks—even calling her brother Levi and his colleagues stupid—were designed to amuse her and were from a young man being hailed at the capital as a conquering hero. The adulation was temporary, as was the exultation it engendered in Fox.[33]

CHAPTER THREE

Lieutenant Fox

China

The Chinese . . . are a huge engine which we cannot help admir-
ing but how anxiously we desire to see the steam "let on" and
the mass move. Once started and the work becomes easy from
their own aptness . . . one third of the inhabitants of this earth
take their appropriate position amongst their brethren of the
West.   *Fox to Barnes, 22 January 1850*

The winter of "fun" proved shorter than Fox expected. On 13 January 1848
Secretary of the Navy Mason detached him from the Coast Survey and ordered
him to the twenty-gun sloop of war *Plymouth*, which was about to depart for
East Asia. Designed by Samuel Pook and launched at the Boston Navy Yard in
1844, the *Plymouth* was an "exceptional ship." It was stiff and "dry in rough
weather, . . . very fast in both light and heavy winds, and also very handy." Fox
anticipated he would be broadened by service in the Far East. He looked forward to collecting mineral and animal specimens for his growing cabinet of
curiosities. He also wanted to become acquainted with the Chinese people.
That hope was frustrated, but Fox met knowledgeable "old China hands," who
helped him grasp the potential of an industrious, ingenious people. The
friendships he formed halfway around the globe with members of mercantile
families later proved useful to Fox in learning steam navigation and in finding
suitable blockading vessels.[1]

■ ■ ■

Fox joined the *Plymouth* at the Brooklyn Navy Yard as acting master in late
January and, after a freezing trip, arrived at Norfolk on 18 February 1848.
With no stove on board, it was cold enough for Fox to wish that its 12,000
pounds of powder would explode and provide instant heat. Although torn from
the glamour of Washington, Fox was delighted with the *Plymouth*, its officers,

and its destination to join the East India Squadron. The *Plymouth*'s commander, Thomas R. Gedney, who requested Fox be made his navigating officer, was "notorious for his kindness of disposition and good temper" and kept "liquors to match" his fondness of "good living." Nor did Fox have to stand watch, as he did when master on the *Preble* and *Washington*. He could confine himself to his duties of navigation and observation, leaving time for reading and study. Besides learning French, an old teacher advised him to purchase books on geology, mineralogy, botany, and Chinese history. Fox also asked Barnes to send books.[2]

Fox spent a few days in Washington at the end of February checking the accuracy of the *Plymouth*'s chronometer and compass cards. The death and funeral of John Quincy Adams slowed work in all government offices, making Fox's errand take longer and giving him more time with Virginia. "You have a great deal of trouble getting chronometers," teased Virginia's sister Frances. Because Virginia was "more delicate than usual" and he was leaving on a 60,000-mile cruise that would take years, their parting on 27 February left Virginia emotionally upset and Fox anxious about her health and the future of their love. Months would elapse before they would hear from each other, even if letters were sent by steamship, at the prohibitive cost of $1.80 per letter. While not engaged, Fox and Virginia apparently were contemplating matrimony in the distant future. There were sound reasons to wait. Fox had no fortune, his salary was low, and promotions to better-paying grades were by seniority and very slow. Virginia did not relish being married to a naval officer who from time to time would be absent on three-year cruises. Nevertheless, they dreamed that her father would be elected president, bringing Fox choice shore assignments and making their marriage possible.[3]

On 9 March 1848 the *Plymouth* set sail for Hong Kong via the Cape of Good Hope, with Rio de Janeiro its first stop. On board was Dr. John Wesley Davis, the former Speaker of the House of Representatives and the new commissioner to China. Bad weather plagued the ship, and near the equator "light winds and deluges of rain" became prevalent. Fox informed his "dear Pet"— the family nickname that reflected Virginia's pampered status—that he got up at sunrise and read and studied until breakfast. To determine the position and course of the ship, he made observations and calculations until dinner at two o'clock and for a half hour afterward. Next, he smoked his daily cigar, while playing whist with Gedney, Dr. Davis, and Lieutenant George W. Doty. Without supper, coffee, tea, or liquors, Fox went to bed at eleven o'clock. This ascetic course was probably at Virginia's behest. (Hannah Barnes had a drinking problem, making Fox and Virginia especially aware of the corrosive effects of liquor.) On Sundays, no whist was played and an officer read the Episcopal prayers and morning service. The prayer book Virginia had "placed so feelingly" in his hands helped Fox "attend with thoughts in harmony with the occasion."[4]

When a man fell overboard, the routine was broken. Because the ship was traveling fast and only a frightened, tongue-tied midshipman saw the man fall, precious moments were lost before the cry "Man overboard" was heard. He was already a half-mile astern when the ship hove to and a boat was lowered. Although the sailors tossed floating objects overboard, the man, who was tiring rapidly with waves breaking over his head, could not get to them. While the rest of the 220-man crew watched and hoped, sailors, straining at the oars of a small boat, reached the drowning man and lifted him "from death into life."[5]

The *Plymouth* took fifty-four days to sail to Rio de Janeiro. The contrast between the spectacularly beautiful harbor and the "narrow streets, horrible vehicles, howling slaves, and . . . vile stench" of Rio de Janeiro overwhelmed Fox. His estimate that two-thirds of the population was "imperfectly formed" revealed more about him than about Brazilians. At a party given by Consul Gorham Parks for the officers of the *Plymouth* and the Brazil Squadron, Miss Jones, a large, "well rounded" blonde American in a low-cut dress, was "the belle." Fox hurriedly assured his slender, delicate Pet that she was "far too gross" for him to "fancy."[6]

While Fox approved the higher necklines on the dresses of the "Portuguese ladies," their darker complexions troubled him. "I think if time accustomed the eyes to endure them it would not banish from the mind, the fact of African blood having mingled with theirs." His racially inspired hypercriticism transformed their modesty into a "solemn, chilling, reserved" manner. Reviling miscegenation and probably remembering the *Preble*'s disaster at Bissau, Portuguese Guinea, Fox declared the Portuguese and their descendants "the vilest race of people on the earth." When more rational, he acknowledged that they had built "quite a decent city" at Rio, although "slavery and squalid wretchedness" obscured its virtues. Fox disliked slavery but, like many northerners, he abhorred the African victims more than he despised its perpetrators.[7]

The *Plymouth* remained at Rio for more than three weeks. Upon its arrival, Fox heard the "astounding news" of revolutions in Paris and elsewhere in Europe and of renewed antiforeign hostilities at Canton, near their destination. With Virginia's encouragement, he was studying French and hoping to go to France for two years on a leave of absence. With his Woodbury connection, Fox felt he could get a leave if the Democrats won in 1848. He wondered whether the French monarchy would "melt" into a sister republic "without an awful explosion." Although delayed by a court-martial—in which Fox, the sea lawyer, acted as counsel—the *Plymouth* departed Rio on 28 May, before the mail steamer arrived.[8]

The *Plymouth* made excellent time. "Far down in the south Atlantic," at sunrise 13 June, Fox beheld Tristan da Cunha, "A snow capped mountain standing in majestic loneliness, amidst a waste of waters." Sighting a "huge whale enjoying himself in the foaming waves" became an everyday occurrence, and the *Plymouth* "found a great variety of aquatic birds." Apparently ignorant of Samuel Taylor Coleridge's *Ancient Mariner* and his legendary curse, Fox "shot an albatross which measured ten feet across the wings," preserved its head for his museum, and used a quill from one of its wings to write of his deed. Impressed by how aquatic birds were adapted to their environment and were phenomenal navigators, Fox speculated "whether heaven designed them as wonders, or *going to sea* so much makes them so." Seeing men warped by the sea, Fox was led to that evolutionary speculation more by observation than through scientific knowledge. The *Plymouth* passed 300 miles south of the Cape of Good Hope on 21 June, avoided the "gigantic seas" for which that cape was notorious, and rapidly proceeded across the Indian Ocean, sighting only two Dutch ships on the whole voyage.[9]

Out of sight of land since Tristan, the *Plymouth* anchored at Meio Bay, Java, on the Straits of Sunda, on 21 July. In fifty-four days, it had covered nearly 9,000 miles. Fox was proud of his accurate navigating. At Meio Bay, the *Plymouth* took on water, and Fox bathed in a beautiful stream and hunted unsuccessfully in the thick undergrowth. He also dove for shells and coral in the bay for seven hours. He stopped, after seizing a shell fish, which plunged long darts into his fingers, instantly coloring them blue. The darts were brittle and painful to extract, and it was over a week before he regained the use of his middle finger. After three days at Meio Bay, the *Plymouth* ran up the Sunda Strait to the "neat" village of Anyer Lor for fresh provisions. There, the men, "with the recklessness of sailors," spent their money on "about a hundred [Java] sparrows, thirty monkeys, twelve small deer, a great many turtle doves, and real turtles, and many other birds and animals." On the next lap of the voyage, the *Plymouth*'s rigging was "filled with delightful songsters," and the monkeys amused the crew by riding about the deck on the backs of unhappy pigs. Experiencing delightful weather in the China Sea, the *Plymouth* arrived at the Portuguese town of Macao on 15 August 1848 and five days later anchored in the Chukiang or Pearl River, twelve miles below Canton.[10]

Initially, nothing went right for Fox in China. The *Plymouth* made the

Pearl River estuary its base, anchoring usually at Macao, on the left, when entering the estuary, and occasionally at Hong Kong, on the right. Although the Portuguese had been at Macao since 1557, Fox preferred the recently established (1841), flourishing British town of Victoria on Hong Kong Island. When he lost his appetite and a side of his face and both hands were swollen, local residents told him it was from excessive handling of Chinese lacquered ware. Fox was disappointed to find only a letter from his sister, even though mail via steamships took only two and a half months. Worse, he heard that the Democrats had nominated Lewis Cass for the presidency, rather than his patron Levi Woodbury. Because the "South will not go for him" as it would have for Woodbury, Fox felt certain his party would lose. With dreams of interesting assignments fading, Fox told Virginia that he would "stay at sea now till your Pa comes in," presumably after winning the nomination and election in 1852.[11]

Fox was still unwell on the evening of 31 August, when a typhoon struck the *Plymouth*, "dozens of merchant vessels, a great many Chinese junks & smaller crafts," at Cum-sin-mum. It was one of the many harbors formed by the hundreds of islands in the mouth of the Pearl River. While a few ships, like the *Plymouth*, rode out the typhoon at anchor, junks and small craft were sunk, dismasted, or driven ashore. Two villages—one with 5,000 inhabitants— were destroyed, while Canton, Hong Kong, and Macao suffered enormously. Near the *Plymouth*, a large ship sank, and, though its masts were still above water, its captain, his wife, their five children, and most of the crew perished. Many of the vessels at Cum-sin-mum were loaded with opium, and because the Chinese on shore were "pilots, fishermen or pirates" as the occasion demanded, they seized chests of opium driven ashore from wrecks. To protect private property—albeit tons of a narcotic—Gedney sent Fox and fourteen men to defend from 4,000 Chinese a washed-up English brig loaded with opium worth $400,000. Working feverishly with his men for twelve days, including two Sundays, to save the cargo and float the brig, Fox seemed unconcerned by the devilish nature of the cargo he broke the Sabbath to save.[12]

Life soon improved for Fox. He went "on duty" at Hong Kong for what amounted to a month-and-a-half vacation. Living with Sandwith Drinker of Philadelphia, whose family was in the United States, Fox rose at seven, breakfasted at eight, strolled on the veranda to view the harbor shipping, and read until four, when he dined with his host. After eating, they went horseback riding from five until seven, then rested over soda water and cigars before going out for an evening visit with one of several American families in Victoria. Hong Kong was a "mass of granite," with "no trees, no flowers, nothing to soften the glare of the white buildings & grey rocks." After 9 October, when

Commodore David Geisinger appointed him acting lieutenant, Fox was less critical. By 25 October he was in his "snug little room" on the *Plymouth* at Macao with his fat, contented, crooked-tailed cat Thomas (given him by the captain of a Siamese frigate). Fox preferred Thomas's "gentle & subdued" affection to the "rough & course" devotion of a dog.[13]

When the *Plymouth* went to Hong Kong to take on fresh water, its delighted officers entertained six American ladies. The *Plymouth* was in "beautiful order," entirely black outside and everything white inside except the clean, bright, contrasting guns. Impressed that they could not soil their handkerchiefs by rubbing the guns and the deck, the ladies declared Fox's room, which they loved, to be that of an unmarried man. After three days, the *Plymouth* returned to Macao, where shallow water forced it to anchor five miles from a town with few social attractions.[14]

For a week, beginning 19 November 1848, Fox visited the "vast Hive" of Canton. Actually, he saw only the 800 yards along the river, with a depth of 200 yards, allowed to European and American traders. Like all "foreign devils," he would have been insulted and probably attacked if he had visited Canton proper. Having come 15,000 miles to see China, Fox complained, "All is closed against us." He could not "obtain an accurate idea of the people," who were cut off from "all improvements" from abroad. Still, he was charmed by the "wonderful and useful" objects the Chinese produced "without the aid of machinery" and purchased a sandalwood box for Virginia.[15]

What he did see of Canton, Fox found crowded and unattractive. Its five-to-seven-foot-wide streets and its two-story, tile-roofed houses of unburned bricks were home to a million people and an additional 400,000 lived on 84,000 boats in the 100-yard-wide Pearl River. Some junks were "magnificent" in size and gilding, and all had an eye painted on the bow and on the stern a huge, contorted, fierce dragon. Although Fox visited a Buddhist temple, "filled with idols," he could learn little of Buddhism. Westerners, occupied with "making money," told him that the devotions of Buddhist priests resembled a Roman Catholic mass and claimed that the Chinese were indifferent to religion. But while returning downriver, Fox caught sight of two awe-inspiring pagodas and declared them "the great guardians of this strange and wonderful people."[16]

In December 1848 the *Plymouth* brought envoy Dr. John Wesley Davis to Manila to visit the Spanish governor of the Philippine Islands. Staying with people from Lynn, Massachusetts, Fox purchased scarves, cuffs, and handkerchiefs of pina cloth (invisibly knotted pineapple-leaf fibers) for his sister and Virginia and visited the large beautiful lake of Laguna de Bay. Later, he was entertained, with Davis, by a village and its impressive padre, with food, drink,

music, and dancing. Fox delighted everyone by waltzing with one of the graceful, "handsome little Filipino girls." Impressed by the accomplishments of the
Roman Catholic Church, he perceived that religion, not arms, kept the Philip-
pines loyal to the Spanish crown. "The conquerors have passed away," he
noted, "the converted remain to continue their allegiance." Despite the heat,
Fox waltzed again and again, when the consul at Manila threw a party to introduce the *Plymouth*'s officers to a dozen Spanish ladies and a few gentlemen.
Enjoying the happy, good-humored, and unreserved Spanish women, he was
taken aback when a matron lit a cigar (single women abstained). Upon reflection, he decided it was no worse than elderly American women taking snuff.[17]

Back in Macao, Fox was bored as 1849 began. Occasional parties—even one
attended by an old friend from Madeira, Captain Amaral of the Portuguese
navy, now governor of Macao—could not dispel his mood nor could exotic
Chinese food cheer him. He declared that cuisine "a horrible collection of
most villainous compounds." With the rise in Chinese xenophobia, foreigners
were blamed for the smallpox epidemic, then raging in Canton. Agitators
demanded that foreigners be expelled and offered rewards for certain English
heads. Fox feared that foreigners could not trade safely in China until Europeans inflicted on it the "horrors of war." Bored by the "monotony" of his existence and frustrated that, after nearly a year in China, he remained "as profoundly ignorant" of the Chinese as were those on "the other side of the
globe," Fox concluded that the little known about China "hardly repays the
toil and trouble of . . . the research." With his growing hostility to China and
the Chinese, Fox longed for home.[18]

With warmer weather, life was less boring. To beat the heat, Fox shaved his
crown, leaving a fringe of hair "a la Friar" and spent the dog days of summer
gazing at the Dog Star (Sirius). He and Virginia had "adopted" that bright
star, and he knew she was also gazing at it. Hearing in June that Boston Harbor had almost frozen over, Fox lamented the *Plymouth* was on "a waste of
boiling water." He kept cool and conjured up images of home by purchasing
some New England ice at five cents a pound. (A 400-ton cargo had melted
down to 200 tons by the time it arrived at Hong Kong.)[19]

News, although delayed, helped while away time. When, in June 1849, word
of the California gold rush "swept off a great many foreigners from China"
and left those who remained "fluttering with the excitement," Fox merely
said, "the devil with the mines of California." He was surprised by news of
the strength of the antislavery and protariff people in Congress. He hoped the
controversy over slavery in the Mexican cession would be "settled quietly,"
feeling it would be "ridiculous" for "a great people" to "fall to pieces in giving

berth to those negroes." With growing love and gratitude for her prayers, Fox continued to write long letters to Virginia and to purchase gifts for her, as well as for friends and relatives. These gifts included six silk dresses, costing a total of $37.80, for his sister Harriet Guild in Brooklyn.[20]

The social life at Macao improved in late spring, when Samuel Wetmore Jr., a New York merchant whose company had a Canton branch, arrived. Fox found his well-educated bride, Sarah Boerum Wetmore—the daughter of a U.S. Navy captain—enchanting and "very fond of conversation" in which "truth and sincerity and frankness shine forth." For a whole month, Fox and the *Plymouth*'s first lieutenant Thomas Jefferson Page arrived at her home nearly every afternoon and stayed until eleven (even though she banished cigar smokers to the far end of her veranda). Always at home with the very young, Fox enjoyed a children's costume party at the home of Paul S. Forbes, the American consul at Canton, and socialized with his cousin, Robert B. Forbes. Fox regretted that unlike Portuguese families in Macao, who did not let business rivalry prevent associating with their countrymen, the Wetmores and the Forbeses carried their bitter business rivalry into their social life. Fox profited from associating with both families. The Wetmore connection later helped him learn steamboat navigation, and the Forbes connection proved useful in acquiring ships for the Navy Department in the Civil War.[21]

Fox enjoyed horseback riding. Reflecting on a ride with Emilie Rawles, a gritty sixteen-year-old, who though thrown twice (once on her face) would not quit, made Fox aware that he did not fancy "animal courage" in women.

> For my part [he wrote Virginia], I had rather see a girl timid as a fawn, and yet if my feelings were analyzed it might be found that it was for no other reason than that your sex should be obliged to lean towards ours for protection from danger. The excess of almost any feeling in woman, is a *blessing*, and we love it, rather than that even distribution which ensures so calm an existence. You need not attempt to argue this point with me, Miss Pet. I know your ideas and I am determined to stand by mine, and will not be convinced. As long as your *practice* is a *little* different from your frigid theory I won't *growl*.

In theory, Virginia approved of Emilie's grit. In practice, no one could lean longer and harder than Virginia, and Fox loved her for being a burden.[22]

The idyllic social life at Macao came to an abrupt end. On 22 August 1849 Fox's dear friend Governor Amaral was hacked to death while horseback riding. His assassins escaped with his head, for which posters in Canton offered a $50,000 bounty. An efficient, vigorous administrator, Amaral, by breathing new life into Macao, was "particularly obnoxious" to those Chinese most hostile to foreigners. The *Plymouth*, which had moved upriver to Whampoa for the typhoon season, immediately returned to Macao. While anchoring there, a sailor, the second to do so in two months, fell from the main yard and died instantly when he hit the white pine deck. With Macao resembling a chaotic armed camp, the Wetmores soon left for England, and the delightful evenings on the veranda were over. In addition, a huge Chinese pirate fleet of fifty-eight junks commanded by Shap-ng-tsai threatened shipping in the Hong Kong–Macao area. Although the British navy and a typhoon destroyed his fleet, the Chinese government bought off Shap-ng-tsai by appointing him a mandarin at Canton.[23]

After he had helped capture two junks loaded with pirated goods, Fox suspected that "American and English people have been regular traders with these pirates—in other words, receivers of stolen goods—and that we have taken a couple of their crafts." This experience gave Fox a deeper understanding of what was going on:

> Very little law exists here. Notwithstanding treaties and Consular Courts, both English and Americans are engaging in an immense contraband trade with the Chinese. There is not more than one "house" that ever dreams of paying duties, bribing and smuggling is systematized to perfection. The U.S. Congress established courts here for the trial of "offenses against law," & it is much ridiculed; who are the Judges, except the Commissioners [Paul S. and Robert B. Forbes], the very ones most deeply engaged in this traffic. Dr. Davis dare not represent the true state of things, and the English Gov't persists, as it drains China every year of $20,000,000 of specie. This is ruining the Country politically, and I have no doubt, the immense quantity of opium is doing the same morally. Our Gov't would move in the matter if it knew the true condition of things.[24]

During the fall and winter of 1849 and 1850, Fox added to his "museum" and swore off cigars, while eagerly awaiting the arrival of Joseph Balestier, the recent U.S. consul at Singapore, who was coming to negotiate commercial treaties in Southeast Asia. The *Plymouth*, with Fox as navigating officer, was scheduled to take Balestier from place to place on what promised to be a "magnificent cruise among new wild and strange people." Fox expected "to pick up much useful information."[25]

Fox spent ten days at Hong Kong, in late January and early February, procuring charts to navigate the relatively unknown waters of Southeast Asia. He stayed with the Drinkers, breakfasted with the Rawles, and went horseback riding. Fox also joined Robert Forbes on his first trip in his steamboat *Spark*. It boasted a whistle—a "new feature, unknown to foreign boats." Three English-made sea steamers, with cabins and engine below deck, already plied the Pearl River, but this American-style, broad-beamed river steamboat, drawing little water, with machinery and state rooms on its deck, was a "totally different craft" and more practical for river transportation. Built and dismantled in America and assembled "without difficulty" in the Far East, the *Spark* confirmed the faith of Fox and his messmates "that under any circumstances our country will become—'The smartest nation, In all Creation.'"[26]

As he prepared to leave for Southeast Asia, Fox tempered his earlier dismissal of the Chinese with the paternalistic observation that they were "capable of great advances under proper tuition." Limited personal observations of the Chinese and contact with Sir John Bowring, the British consul at Canton, and Dr. Peter Parker, a medical missionary who doubled as secretary of the American legation there, helped Fox perceive "more favorable traits" of the Chinese "than most foreigners allow."

Although Fox still claimed the Chinese had "no inventive genius," he admired their "many ingenious deviations from our manner of conducting things." He called them "a huge engine." Starting that engine, Fox decided, was the task of "the Saxon race. . . . John Bull has tried them with his horns [Opium War of 1840], and now let Brother Jonathan try them with 'soft sawder.'" If flattery could convince the Chinese to drop their prejudices, welcome Americans into the interior, and adopt Western ways, "the workshops of all Europe and America could not supply the Chinese with what a few years unrestricted intercourse would lead them to require." Fox had caught a vision of Young America: "What a destiny for the United States, to be the lever which shall move Asia to its regeneration; it may be, with San Francisco as a fulcrum."[27]

CHAPTER FOUR

Lieutenant Fox

Diplomacy and Home

It is certain Uncle Sam will not look with unconcern if any European power reaches out its hand towards these [Hawaiian] islands.   *Fox to Virginia L. Woodbury, 22 November 1850*

San Francisco . . . occupies the same position as [to] Polynesia & Asia which N. York does to the West Indies and Europe, & when the line of states . . . shall connect these two cities, our country may . . . distance all competitors.

Fox to Virginia L. Woodbury, 31 January 1851

In an era of poor communications, American naval officers were involved in diplomacy that sought to expand the commerce and influence of the United States. While in East Asia and completing his circumnavigation of the globe on his way home, Fox caught a vision of a greater United States stretching from coast to coast. It would tap the wealth of Asia and Europe, enabling it, in time, to outstrip all rivals. The acquisition of California, the simultaneous discovery of gold there, and its subsequent rapid development seemed providential to Fox, and the spirit of "manifest destiny" enhanced his nationalistic fervor for the Union.

■ ■ ■

On 22 February 1850 both the *Plymouth* and the *St. Marys* sailed from Macao. The *St. Marys* left "for Manila & home," while the *Plymouth*, with Philip F. Voorhees, commander of the East India Squadron, on board, "kept S.W. for Cochin China" (Vietnam). On 25 February it arrived at Tourane (Danang) Bay, the nearest (forty miles) safe anchorage to the capital city of Hue. After the yellow hills beyond Macao, Fox loved the "blue mountains" and the "greenery of the vegetation." He picked a bouquet of tropical flowers, collected a few choice rocks, admired a canoe made on "the basket principle" of wattled bamboo, and was inspired by a Buddhist temple, with its 120-foot dome "rent by fissures," admitting sunlight. He found the people "perfectly civil" but filthy, with black teeth and red lips and mouths from chewing betel nut. He noted that the men wore "very graceful black crepe turbans," folded like Dolley Madison's turbans. Having earlier had commercial relations with the French, Cochin China, also called Annam, had, by 1850, expelled European merchants and missionaries.[1]

Joseph Balestier, who tried to mask his ignorance with bluster, proved to be an inept diplomat. His hopes to open Vietnam for American trade were based on a blunder by Fox's old captain, "Mad Jack" Percival. When he visited Danang Bay in the frigate *Constitution,* five years earlier, Percival was convinced that a French missionary was confined under sentence of death. He landed at the head of an armed party, took hostages, captured three men-of-war, and demanded the release of the Frenchman, who could not be found. After two weeks, he returned the vessels and hostages and departed.[2]

Balestier, who had been consul at Singapore, convinced the Zachary Taylor administration that apologizing for Percival's conduct would open negotiations for a treaty. The president's letter of apology (echoing communications to Native Americans) threatened that if a treaty was not forthcoming he would "send his fire ships to see why his majesty of Cochin China has so bad a heart." A translation muting the "fire ships" was forwarded to the Annamese emperor, who refused to see Balestier. Local officials insisted that neither an apology nor a treaty was necessary. No one was hurt or killed by Percival's actions, and they did not wish to buy or sell anything. Even when Balestier insisted that his rajah would retaliate with ships and soldiers because his letter had been spit upon, the Vietnamese held firm. On 15 March, after refusing a Vietnamese "present of provisions," the *Plymouth* got underway, and though Balestier wished to move northwest up the coast opposite Hue for yet another attempt, adverse winds closed this early chapter in American relations with Vietnam. Fox warned Barnes to be discreet in using his description of "this precious humbugging diplomatic expedition . . .; if the administration find me telling you what an ass they have made of themselves they will mark me."[3]

Ten days later, the *Plymouth* anchored ten miles off Paknam, the port city of Bangkok, Siam (Thailand). The voyage had been enchanting. With every sail answering to favorable breezes, the *Plymouth* moved so effortlessly it seemed "to sleep over the sea," passing "numerous beautiful islands," including the "Woodbury group" named by Edmund Roberts, an American diplomatic agent related by marriage to Levi Woodbury.[4]

The Gulf of Siam abounded with aquatic snakes, and Fox collected a poisonous one and an innocuous one for his "museum." The United States and Siam had signed a treaty of friendship and commerce in 1833 (negotiated by Roberts). Balestier's mission was to modify the high-tonnage duties, which deterred American vessels from visiting Bangkok. With the thermometer at 98 degrees and cholera raging in Bangkok and Paknam, Commodore Voorhees allowed only Balestier and his translator to go ashore. Among the visitors welcomed aboard was Prah Nai Wai, the commander in chief of the Siamese navy. He was a friendly thirty-year-old relative of the king, proud of his ability to calculate latitude and longitude and of his well-constructed, eighty-foot boat, designed to be rowed or sailed. "Willing to brave the cholera" to see Bangkok, Fox felt cheated by Voorhees's refusal to let them go ashore.[5]

To the delight of all, the day after Balestier went ashore, the *Plymouth* got underway and visited villages and islands in the Bight of Bangkok, where the crew could buy curios, hunt, and swim. Fox took observations, charted these islands for the Bureau of Navigation in Washington, and named one with "beautiful white beaches" and "magnificent woods" Ko Pet for Virginia. (Ko, or more properly Koh, is the Thai word for island.) While they were at Koh Pai, Balestier "unexpectedly joined" the *Plymouth*, which then left the Bight of Bangkok.[6]

Balestier had once again bungled his negotiations. Fox soon read a letter from Admiral Prah Nai Wai to Voorhees giving the details of "the second failure of our ascetic, testy envoy." When he was not allowed to hand President Taylor's letter to the king, Balestier "left the house in anger and broke off all friendly intercourse," leaving Bangkok on 22 April 1850. In his letter, Prah Nai Wai made it clear that Balestier's "excitability" was so apparent the ministers feared he might, if allowed before the king, "produce a quarrel or disturbance" and endanger existing friendly relations with the United States. Should the Americans wish to negotiate, Prah Nai Wai requested, they should send a "prudent & well disposed person not inclined to anger." Balestier denied that he was angry and excited. "This charge is absurd," he exclaimed to Voorhees, "I behaved as I did at Touron [Tourane], you saw me there." "Yes," replied Voorhees, "and I must say I thought you were highly excited and showed a great deal of temper."[7]

With Balestier back on board, the *Plymouth* headed for Subi (also known as South Natuna or Flat) Island off the northwest coast of Borneo. The ship called first at the Island of Pulo Obi, off Cape Cambodia, to replenish its water supply. There, Fox added another specimen to his collection, but handling the four-and-a-half-foot green poisonous snake caused his face to swell. When

they reached the Natuna Islands, sailors climbed sixty or seventy feet up the
trunks of coconut palms and, with their traditional cry of "Stood from under,"
dropped bunches of coconuts, narrowly missing their messmates below. After
"living on 'salt junk' and worm eaten bread and . . . rusty water, the milk from
a cocoa nut" was "re-freshing . . . beyond language to express."[8]

On 18 May the *Plymouth* anchored at Subi Island, whose 300 inhabitants
had "tenderly cared for" the survivors of the American ship *Mary Ellen*. On
the following day, Balestier, Voorhees, Fox, and some other officers visited the
Daltoo, enjoyed refreshments of sweetmeats and coconuts, and presented him
with a sword and a gold medal from President Taylor. To the Pungalai, second
in rank in whose house the shipwrecked Americans actually stayed, they gave
a carbine and ten gold buttons. Fox was captivated by the "extremely handsome" Malay women, who, when they shook hands "first touched their bosom
and then laid their delicate fingers within ours, their eyes cast down as if we
were the first of the opposite sex they had beheld." Wearing two pieces of
strategically folded cotton cloth, leaving their arms and shoulders bare, these
women, with "their modest behavior and downcast look," gave Fox and his
companions, he noted, "the only bright vision we have seen this cruise."[9]

On the morrow, when the Natunans visited the *Plymouth*, Balestier almost
ruined the good impression he had made. He scowled at the Pungalai for being
late and turned on his heel and walked aft, leaving Voorhees to make amends.
Although Balestier returned, Fox thought his action expressed his view (to
which Fox objected) "that the only way to treat these people was to make them
fear us." When the guests departed with gifts, the *Plymouth* weighed anchor
and stood away for Kuching, Sarawak, on the northwest corner of Borneo.[10]

The *Plymouth* arrived off Kuching on 26 May 1850. Because Sir James
Brooke, the almost legendary rajah of Sarawak, who was a British subject, was
in Bangkok negotiating for Great Britain, the *Plymouth* did not stop. It sailed
360 "delightful" miles northeast to Labuan Island (which the British had
recently acquired) in Brunei Bay, arriving on 6 June. The sultan of Borneo,
whom Fox considered "crushed by the power of Great Britain," resided at
Brunei, fifteen miles up the Brunei (Limbang) River from the bay. Fox was
intrigued by air plants hanging from huge trees, admired camphor trees, and
found a upas tree. He obtained some of its poisonous milk and sent one of its
leaves to Virginia. For his museum, he purchased "a number of the peculiar
weapons of the Malay tribes" and became thoroughly exhausted searching for
beds of coal.[11]

With the aid of British officials, who translated and interpreted, Balestier
negotiated an advantageous treaty for the United States. With nine articles

taken "verbatim from the English" treaty, Fox concluded, "it has been formed by the permission of the English with a poor man they are holding by the throat."[12]

Despite success at Brunei, Fox thought the voyage "devoid of interest & information" and was happy on 27 June to get underway for Macao. Blaming most of his disappointment on Balestier, he lamented, "We might be standing for Macao with a box full of treaties. . . . Even the barbarians will not remember our flag to the elevation of the American character. I love my country too well to see these shadows thrown over her."[13]

As the *Plymouth*, "under a cloud of sail," ran before the monsoon toward Macao at the rate of 200 miles a day, it resembled a floating menagerie. Commodore Voorhee's "pride was an orangutan from Borneo," whose round face partook "wonderfully of the characteristics of humanity." There were "some thirty monkeys owned by the sailors," who dressed them in different styles, "having earrings in their ears, & some have even been taught to chew tobacco." There was also a gibbon swinging from point to point "with the most surprising certainty." "Superior to all," Fox believed, were his "*eleven cats.*" Most of these were Malay cats, whose short tails gave them "a cunning appearance" and "determined" Fox to introduce the breed into Massachusetts.[14]

Arriving in Macao the evening of 8 July 1850, Fox was happy to return to what seemed "almost a home." Five months of accumulated mail brought some marvelous news. He would be going home via San Francisco and Cape Horn in the brig *Dolphin*. Voorhees appointed Fox its acting first lieutenant, "a position," Fox explained, "assigned to Lieut's of eight years standing & as I am not yet promoted, duty to myself requires that I should accept the place though it keeps me away several more months." His desire to circumnavigate the globe and to visit countries he described with exaggeration as "almost the only ones I have hitherto omitted" would be gratified.[15]

Receiving his orders on 13 July 1850, Fox left the "magnificent" *Plymouth* "with regret," reporting on board the *Dolphin* the next day. Having suffered many deaths from sickness, the *Dolphin* had become "entirely officered from the Plymouth." Its commander was Fox's friend Thomas Jefferson Page, who came out in the *Plymouth* as second lieutenant and with whom he had called on Sarah Wetmore. "We are confined in space," Fox noted, "but otherwise delightfully situated for we all mess together & know each other thoroughly." Having doubts about their surviving Cape Horn, Fox dispersed his "family of pets," leaving his favorite, Minna—named after Virginia's oldest sister—with nine-year-old Kate Drinker (the future painter Catherine Drinker Janvier). Fox spent part of his last evening in Hong Kong with his dear friends the

Rawles, whose unfailing and wholehearted hospitality, he feared, would be for him "forever lost." He went on to a "grand dinner" and did not get back to the *Dolphin* until one o'clock. On 22 July, the *Dolphin* set off for home.[16]

The *Dolphin*, called by Fox a crazy little dancing brig, arrived off Manila Bay on 27 July in a gale "that would have done credit to the Cape of Good Hope." With a long line of white breakers under its lee (the side of the ship sheltered from the wind), it dashed in rather than spend "a night of anxiety off a 'lee shore.'" Even in Manila Bay, the gale continued with such force that it was two days before the *Dolphin* communicated with the shore. Fox was impatient to renew old friendships and eat "delicious" mangoes. Although he enjoyed the scenery, he called the people "a yellow degenerate race, beneath both the Spanish & Indian in appearance." On 7 August 1850 the *Dolphin* weighed anchor for San Francisco and whatever islands the winds might blow it near.[17]

After "33 days and 15 hours" of headwinds and light breezes, the *Dolphin* covered the 1,800 miles to the Bonin Islands (Gasawara Jima). In his journal letter, Fox teased Virginia (who gloried in her delicate health) that their location would not interest "invalid young ladies who travel only" from a sofa in Washington to those in Portsmouth and who peruse the works of Carlyle and Lamartine. Anchoring at Port Lloyd, Fox was surprised to discover the whaler *Aeronaut* of Mystic, Connecticut. In 1848, off the coast of Brazil, it was the first vessel the *Plymouth* spoke to after leaving the United States and was now on a new voyage. The Bonin Islands, which had recently been inhabited, provided sweet potatoes and other fresh provisions, primarily for whalers. The *Dolphin* was too late for the island's specialty—300-pound turtles, available from February to August; it did, however, purchase seven barrels of potatoes for fifteen dollars. Fox acquired five pumpkins from a Hawaiian woman settler, who took "a strong prejudice" in his favor (which he attributed to his lately cultivated moustache). She lured him into her hut with the promise of pumpkins and offered him her body as well. If Fox's version, written to Virginia, is to be believed, the spell was broken when he saw she was an "ugly old woman and the romance vanished & so did I with my five pumpkins!"[18]

On 17 September 1850 the *Dolphin* sailed from the Bonin Islands, moving out of the tropics. Fox enjoyed the cool breezes that made the days "invigorating" and required "a double blanket" at night. Albatrosses appeared, but the "little Brig" was too unstable to shoot them from the deck, and Fox recalled "what Pet said about the poetry." Virginia obviously had rectified Fox's ignorance of *The Rime of the Ancient Mariner*. The *Dolphin* crossed the international date line, repeating 6 October, and anchored in Honolulu harbor on 22 October.[19]

"Our visit to Honolulu," Fox wrote, "was short but full of interest." On arriving, he and his mates were surprised to learn of Zachary Taylor's death and of changes in the cabinet. Elisha Hunt Allen, the new consul there, proved to be "the same little gentleman with gold specs" Fox had met at Elm Place, who would spend the next thirty years promoting closer Hawaiian-American relations. Fox attended parties given by Allen as well as by Dr. Gerrit Parmele Judd—the medical missionary who was currently the finance minister of Hawaii. Fox was impressed by the heir to the throne, who, with his brother, was "under the surveillance of Dr. Judd." Fox regarded Honolulu as "a miserable spot . . . with neither trees, walks or pavements. . . . The influx from California," he observed, "has destroyed the native character of the place and one meets more Americans than natives." In a generation, he predicted, "these islands must fall into the hands of some power for support, or perhaps, the tide of emigration from the U.S. via California, will repeople them & annexation will follow!"[20]

The *Dolphin* left Honolulu on 6 November 1850. It winged along toward San Francisco at a rate of 200 miles a day, but the decks were covered with water, and the rolling and pitching caused "books, swords, canes, curios & crockery" to rattle and crash about the officer's living quarters. Eating became almost ridiculous. "One moment we lean over the table as if in thankfulness for our food," Fox commented, "the next we bend so far back as if drinking a bumper."[21]

Fox read Walter Scott novels and thought about his missionary hosts and their impact on Hawaii. Although he recognized their civilizing influence and the hostility they endured by interposing themselves "between the rapacity of the traders & merchants and the ignorance of the natives," Fox, an anti-Calvinist Episcopalian, lamented that these "agents of Heaven were Presbyterians, bigoted, unforgiving & stern, enemies to all social enjoyment as well as to the healthful, innocent exercises of the natives." A bon vivant if not a hedonist New Englander, he did not care for "New England austerity & abstemiousness." He loathed its "bigotry and uncharitableness" that dictated: "This man will not go to Heaven if he smokes cigars, plays cards, or drinks a glass of wine, he must be immersed, or he must be elected." Rejecting "preachers of brimstone," whose "worship is fear & solemn awe" rather than love, Fox thought people were attracted to religion "by charity & gentleness & mercy."[22]

Fox's fundamentally religious nature received a further stimulus on the evening of 22 November 1850. "The night was dark & wild," he wrote, "a fresh breeze & heavy sea, a cold, clammy fog hung over the water, contracting our vision and preventing necessary observations." He and his fellow officers were quietly discussing one of Scott's novels when they were "startled" by the fearful cry, "breakers ahead, close aboard!" Everyone rushed on deck fearing "shipwreck & death," but the *Dolphin* hauled off and avoided the breakers of the "iron-bound coast" fifty miles north of San Francisco. Fox ascribed their escape to God, whose mercy answered prayers. Three days later, the *Dolphin* entered the Golden Gate. Fox was in the United States, but the distance he had to travel around Cape Horn exceeded that from China to New York around the Cape of Good Hope. "I am farther from you," he told Virginia, "than when I left Hong Kong four months ago."[23]

Before proceeding to San Francisco, which was in the throes of the gold rush, the *Dolphin* anchored off Sausalito. "This," Fox explained, "is the anchorage for men of war formerly, on account of its shelter & excellent water, now in consequence of its central, commanding situation, yet, sufficiently removed from the different cities to prevent the men from deserting, without unusual precautions & exertions." The *Dolphin* lost only one deserter, presumably to the California gold mines. Fresh provisions were scarce, because of the gold rush, and "required a fortune to purchase."[24]

On 29 November, the *Dolphin*, "ran across the bay" and anchored off San Francisco, amid "a forest of masts far exceeding in density the appearance of N. York at the busiest season." Over the next two weeks, Fox met old navy friends (particularly from the Coast Survey) and Washington acquaintances, who regaled him with tales of chicanery and violence. "I saw enough," Fox wrote Virginia, "to convince me that all our preconceived ideas of the rapidity with which civilization & commerce may arise, are here set at naught." The contrast with the listless inactive Mexican village San Francisco had been in 1845 was enormous. Fox was both awed and appalled. "Now it seems like one vast fair, a holiday, a New England Militia Muster; everybody one meets is hurrying forward as if to a fire & excitement, the most intense, sets on every feature. The streets are crowded, men walk in the middle of the streets, their hats pulled down, moustache uncombed, trousers rolled up & their whole bearing denoting an agony of thought and purpose."[25]

Apart from its natural setting and its feverish restlessness, San Francisco's most noticeable characteristics were gambling and drinking:

The central part of the City is devoted to these amusements. The lower floor of nearly every building has a gambling room & drinking bar; a vast hall, adorned with paintings and containing some 20 tables with different games. At each one of these sits the operator and his partner with piles of silver and gold, coined & raw from the mines. A band of music sends its strains to far into the distance, and many of its tables are occupied by French & Spanish girls whose beautiful smiles lure to the games. Day and night there is scarcely a cessation, the men with full pockets stream in with joyful anticipations depicted upon their countenances, whilst the fleeced depart with all the bad passions of their hearts flashing from their blood shot faces. . . . Vast numbers are drinking all the time. Fights are common, and I frequently heard the exclamation when a row commenced—"Don't shoot!" At two different rooms I [was] shown tables where since my arrival at San F. deliberate murder had been committed. This is the open villainy and degradation visible to the public, in broad day.[26]

Living conditions were cramped and expensive. Many slept in their offices, because a room with a canvas ceiling in a boardinghouse cost thirty dollars a week and hotels were "small, carelessly kept and exorbitant." Fox saw no "residence of any size in the place, certainly not one that would be called comfortable in the east." Thinking their residence temporary, people put up with overpriced inconveniences. Perhaps the high point of Fox's visit was a "small Washington" dinner party hosted by James and Mary Blair. Fox thought their "little cottage" among the best homes in that city. A former naval officer, Blair was a younger brother of Montgomery Blair and consequently the brother-in-law of Virginia's sister Minna. Because Mary Blair had just come from Washington, Fox was eager for news of the Woodbury sisters. Mary told him "much of Mrs. Minna, Mrs. Frank & the beautiful Nell (Virginia's youngest sister), & last of Miss Virginia," or as she called her, "Ginnie." Fox also called on Jesse Benton Frémont and reported that she and Colonel John C. Frémont lived directly opposite the Blairs "in a little affair scarcely larger than an omnibus. Dining room, reception room & sleeping room all in one."[27]

Despite its vices and prices, Fox valued San Francisco for patriotic and personal reasons. He exaggerated that it was "the only harbor of capacity from Cape Horn to Behring's Straits." He predicted that when "civilization & internal works shall connect" San Francisco and New York, "our country" can be called "The Middle Kingdom," a "title which the Chinese have arrogated to themselves." To give "our nation the means of preternatural growth," Providence, he thought, delayed the discovery of gold until it acquired California.[28]

California also offered great opportunities to naval officers, whether they resigned or remained in the navy. James Blair, who engaged in shipping, was worth $150,000. Steamers connected San Francisco to the East Coast with the interruption of a short overland trip across the Isthmus of Panama. If he could secure such a command, his salary, plus a "percentage on the gold dust" carried, would total more than $7,000 a year and enable him to acquire "a small fortune. . . . Plenty of young men in the Navy," Fox mused, "compete successfully with the rough old men of the merchants service, most of whom have served their apprenticeship as common sailors." Knowing how to get desired orders, Fox asked Barnes to use "his own and everyone's influence to obtain me one of these steamers," and asked Virginia to see if her father could bring the influence of the Supreme Court to his aid. Nursing these aspirations, Fox on 18 December started the 17,000-mile voyage home.[29]

The voyage to Valparaiso, Chile, was long and monotonous. Officers and men ate potatoes, rice, beans, ham, salt pork, and hard tack, while anticipating strawberries and cream at Valparaiso. On 22 January 1851 the *Dolphin* met the Nantucket whaler *Mohawk*, 2,500 miles west of Valparaiso (southeast trade winds had forced the *Dolphin* to run to the southwest). The *Mohawk*'s captain came on board bringing beautifully addressed letters for home written by his "pretty" and, Fox assumed, "refined & educated" wife, who was with her husband on the *Mohawk*, and a gift of several bunches of bananas, which was the first fresh fruit on board the *Dolphin* since Manila. Touched that the captain's wife, who had an infant to care for, would spend years on the *Mohawk*, the *Dolphin*'s officers "sent her a large bundle of papers from various parts of the world." The *Mohawk* had touched at Juan Fernandez (Robinson Crusoe's uninhabited island) in December and had marooned one of its men there for misconduct. According to the captain, they had found strawberries, quinces, peaches, and apples growing there. Because it seemed cruel to bypass the abandoned sailor "whatever may have been his offenses," the *Dolphin* planned to pick him up and get some fruit from that fabled island.[30]

Unfortunately, unfavorable winds and calms plagued the *Dolphin* as it headed east toward Valparaiso. Even the bananas, given by the captain of the *Mohawk*, dried up without ripening. Fox attempted to harpoon a twelve-foot shark but failed because of "his tough hide, the dullness of the harpoon & the weakness" of the cast. Two days later, 15 February 1851, during a heavy rain and a rough sea, the ship's cooper, while "reefing topsails . . . fell from the fore top sail yard, a distance of 60 ft., and striking a heavy iron rod outside the vessel, fell into the sea. Life buoy, spars, and many ropes were instantly thrown to him & fell within his grasp, but stunned by the shock of his fall he only made one or two ineffectual struggles, threw his arms wildly into the air and disappeared." A more dreadful death could not be conceived, with "the vessel almost within his reach," Fox noted. "Sailors believe death comes from the visit of the shark, & this, certainly will confirm their superstition."[51]

After seeing no land for sixty days, the *Dolphin* sighted Más Afuera, a "lofty, solitary, volcanic rock." The following day, Juan Fernandez was sighted, but adverse winds kept the *Dolphin* thirty miles away from that "huge pile of lofty mountains." Finally, on 21 February, the *Dolphin* reached the coast of Chile and anchored at Valparaiso on 23 February.[52]

For over a month, the *Dolphin* remained in Valparaiso, preparing to round Cape Horn. Responsible for refitting the vessel, Fox, as first lieutenant, was extremely busy, so he stayed with the vessel while other officers visited Santiago. With the U.S. frigate *Raritan* in port, Fox socialized with its officers, and he saw some of the many Americans living in Valparaiso. One evening, when he was virtually alone on the *Dolphin*, the first lieutenant of the *Raritan* and his wife paid him an unexpected visit. Fox broke out a bottle of champagne he had saved to drink at Cape Horn and gave the lieutenant's wife a "sword made of sharks teeth." When they departed, he "burned a blue light that lighted up every ship near" them, to her delighted cries of "bueno." Fox did not think Valparaiso (Vale of Paradise) lived up to its name. "No grass, no green trees meet the eye, only dingy houses & parched, yellow hills that seem moving dust when the wind freshens." He dismissed Chileans as lazy and indicted them for their barbarous treatment of animals. "You can scarcely conceive," he wrote Virginia, "the cruelty of the common people to their beasts."[53]

Fox's impressions of Chile were negative until he ventured on horseback into the interior. The taste of Chilean grapes and wine was irresistible, the horsemanship of Chilean women, riding sidesaddle, was astounding, and the beauty of Chilean valleys was stunning. Clambering "with difficulty" up a hill in the center of the city of Quillota, Fox beheld a plain ten-miles wide and thirty-miles long. It was "one luxuriant mass of vegetation, divided by a silver stream in refreshing contrast to the tropical green," and in the distance were the snow capped Cordilleras, including Aconcagua, the mightiest peak (22,835 feet) in the Western Hemisphere. Looking down upon the City, Fox thought, "it appeared to have been laid out in the midst of a garden, each square enclosing a perfect mass of foliage entirely hid from the streets." That night, Fox "almost forgot & forgave" the bedbugs in his hotel room and dreamed that he "was again looking down upon the valley of Quillota. It was," Fox concluded, "the most delightful trip I have ever made."[54]

The *Dolphin* left Valparaiso on 28 March 1851, while the *Raritan*'s band played and its officers and crew gave it a farewell cheer. The wind was so still that oarsmen in the *Raritan*'s boats had to tow the *Dolphin* out to sea. Regretting leaving "an agreeable port," Fox had the disquieting thought that the *Dolphin* was heading for Cape Horn, but was cheered to be going home. No sooner had the *Dolphin* cleared the lighthouse than the breeze freshened, deluging its decks with water, causing "hogs, chickens & ducks" and hundreds of articles to float about. Adverse wind caused the *Dolphin* again to pass Juan Fernandez and Más Afuera, but, then, the wind shifted and the *Dolphin* sped rapidly south.[35]

On Good Friday, 18 April, at midnight, the north wind was so powerful the *Dolphin* took in sail and in a short time was hove to, or stopped. On Monday Fox wrote Virginia:

Saturday the wind grew stronger & the waves larger, & at one P.M. the wind inclined to the N.W. and it was determined to take advantage of it & run S.E. though a sailor will tell you that "scudding" is dangerous. The little Brig went off beautifully. The winds seemed to scream with delight as they dragged us on & the great waves gathered behind us as if jealous of our speed. We displayed but a bit of sail, but as the sun declined, it seemed as if even that would be reft [taken] from us by the increasing storm. How the web & woof held I know not for they opened until the outline of ribs & spars could be traced through them, & the great cordage which retained their corners, grew small with their tension, so that each fibre became erect as if charged with electricity.

As the day passed away the waves seemed released from the earth so long their resting place. My God, never shall I forget their vast size, their majestic advance &, through Him, their harmlessness! Nothing approaching them in size had I ever seen, therefore, I gazed with the interest & awe of a novice. I probably saw the largest for I watched long fascinated. . . . The whole waters within sight to the N.W. seemed to have accumulated into one vast mountainous ridge, which rose as it advanced until the heavens were almost shut from view, before us a descending plain seemed to lead into the dark abyss of the ocean, behind the roaring sea caused a tremor in the vessel long before it reached us, the motion was as if the very wood & iron felt fear. When it approached the vessel & curled over towards us, I knew a millionth part of its mass would sweep us into eternity. I shut my eyes and trusted alone in Him who thus far had carefully & safely guided us.

Nor was the trust in vain. All Saturday night the sea rolled towards us, I could *feel* each awful advance, yet the [Easter] morning dawned & we were still speeding safely before the gale. Yesterday [Easter Sunday] it continued unabated, spars secured outside by heavy iron bolts, where they have remained secure three years, were wrenched away & scattered upon the waters. Sea after sea broke over us, the fires could not be lit & we ate bread & water. Snow, hail & rain came with the blasts & finally, we had had no observation for six days. Today we [are] around the Cape, the ocean is smooth & occasionally the sun shines out & a breath of air only moves over the track of the storm. I describe only enough to make you share my feelings & would talk longer but for the cold. It is snowing and I am writing with a pair of buckskin gloves on that just allow my fingers to move.

Rounding Cape Horn on Easter Sunday, the *Dolphin* went above 57 degrees south latitude, or the equivalent of Labrador in October.[36]

The voyage to Rio de Janeiro was routine. Fox amused himself by collecting two varieties of sea birds for his cabinet. With his scientific impulses triumphing over superstition, he tried but failed to secure "the immense white albatross." The weather grew warmer, with May first dawning beautifully, making his longings for home intense. He hoped to hear at Rio de Janeiro that he would get his steamer. If that wish was not granted, Page suggested he apply for the Naval Observatory in Washington, which would be pleasant in the winter. When the *Dolphin* arrived at Rio on the evening of 7 May 1851, Fox received two letters from Virginia but no news of his coveted assignment. After a stay of four days, the *Dolphin* left Rio and, on 24 June 1851, arrived in New York, where its officers and men could boast they had circumnavigated the globe. Fox would not see Page again, but late in the Civil War he thought long and hard about his command, the powerful French-built Confederate ironclad *Stonewall*.[37]

CHAPTER FIVE

Captain Fox / Agent Fox

Capt. G. V. Fox, U.S. Navy, late master of the Panama steamer "George Law," and now the newly appointed agent of the Bay State Mills in Lawrence, in this State, was, yesterday morning, married at Portsmouth, N.H., by the Rev. Dr. Burroughs, to Miss Virginia L. Woodbury, third daughter of the late Judge Woodbury.

"Marriage in High Life," 30 October 1855, Fox Scrapbook

Fox had resolved to seek command of a mail steamer for two reasons. He had best learn all he could about steamships, because steam, not sail, was the navy's future. Also, command of a mail steamer would be lucrative, and he was relatively poor. With the death of his politically powerful patron, Levi Woodbury, the probability of choice assignments vanished. His prospects in the navy changed to long voyages and slow promotions, accompanied by a prolonged courtship of Virginia, who would not marry someone away for three years at a clip. Weighing his love for the navy against his love for Virginia, Fox renounced the navy, as well as Virginia's fortune, to marry her.

■ ■ ■

Upon completion of the *Dolphin*'s cruise at New York, Fox received the customary three-month leave. It was interrupted by service on a court-martial, by angling for the command of a mail steamer, and by the death of his most influential patron. Fox returned to Lowell around 15 July 1851 and probably visited Virginia at Portsmouth shortly thereafter, but her joy over his return gave way, on 4 September, to mourning the sudden death of her father Levi Woodbury. His death was a personal blow to Virginia, who was still the much pampered "Pettie," and a professional blow to Fox, who had counted on Woodbury to further his career. The hopes had been substantial. Thomas Hart Benton and the Blairs had been pushing Woodbury for the 1852 Democratic presidential nomination, and Fox owed much of his success to his Woodbury connection. Not only were the ambitious dreams of Virginia and Fox destroyed by her father's death, but their relationship (sustained by correspondence for three and a half years) cooled. Fox was promoted on 26 September 1851 to master (his warrant was dated from 29 August 1851), after serving as acting master for more than six years.[1]

Fox was partially successful in his quest for a mail steamer. Democratic congressmen Robert Rantoul Jr. (of Beverly, Massachusetts) and Charles H. Peaslee (of Concord, New Hampshire), as well as commodores David Geisinger and Joseph Smith, wrote William S. Wetmore of the Collins Steamship line in New York supporting Fox for the command of a Collins Line steamship. Wetmore was the cousin of Samuel Wetmore Jr., Fox's friend at Macao. At the time, congressmen and commodores influenced the personnel decisions of American mail steamship lines. In 1847 Congress encouraged their development by providing liberal subsidies for carrying mail between New York and Liverpool (Collins Line); between New York, New Orleans, Havana, Kingston, and Aspinwall (Colon) on the Isthmus of Panama (Law Line); and between Astoria, Oregon, San Francisco, and Panama City (Aspinwall Line). Built in New York, under the eye of a special Navy Department superintendent, these mail ships were supposed to be readily converted "into war steamers of the first class."[2]

None of them, however, could be used by the navy. Commodore Matthew C. Perry supervised the program, but the Navy Department neglected to clarify his vague orders. The Collins liners were sumptuous but unsafe, fast but impossible to convert into first-class war steamers. They were without traverse bulkheads to seal off a section of the vessel to isolate a leak or avert a disaster. They even lacked steam whistles. In a fog, they relied on a seaman in the bow blowing "a fisherman's tin foghorn." The Collins Line appointed Fox chief officer (second in command) of the *Baltic* in November 1851, and the Navy Department gave him a leave of absence to acquire "a practical knowledge of steam navigation."[3]

Fox remained on the *Baltic* for nearly two years, learning to navigate one of the largest and fastest steamers afloat. In August 1852, while he was first officer, the *Baltic* made a record passage from Liverpool to New York (nine days and thirteen hours) that stood for twelve years. His commanding officer, Captain Joseph J. Comstock, commended Fox's "industry and faithful discharge of his duties." When Comstock was ill, Fox assumed command of the *Baltic* and satisfied both Comstock and Collins Line officials.[4]

In late February and early March 1852, Fox had charge of the *Baltic* on an excursion from New York to Washington and back. The "unbounded liberality" of this trip was designed to increase the federal government's support of the Collins Line. The *Baltic* was jammed with visitors, some of whom got "gloriously drunk." At times more than 2,000 were on board—including President Millard Fillmore, most cabinet members, many senators and congressmen, General Winfield Scott, members of the diplomatic corps, and "a goodly number of beautiful and elegantly dressed ladies." Abigail Fillmore, the president's wife, and five congressmen accompanied the *Baltic* back to New York, with the latter praising the *Baltic* and urging additional federal support for the Collins Line. For Fox, the contrast between his recent service on the crowded, wildly pitching *Dolphin* and entertaining a vast throng of dignitaries on board the huge (280 feet long, 2,700 tons, with two 35-foot paddle wheels), opulent *Baltic* was startling. Its grand saloon exuded an "air of elegant comfort" amid "oriental magnificence." It had stained-glass windows, costly wainscoting, rich gilding, luxurious sofas, marble-topped tables, and "handsome spittoons" (masquerading as flower vases). While learning steam navigation, Fox met and dealt with America's economic and political elite.[5]

A few months after the Washington excursion, on 9 July 1852, the Navy Department promoted Fox to lieutenant. As befitting his new rank, he began casting about for a command of his own. Although Comstock and Collins Line officials gave him very favorable letters of recommendation, Fox remained chief officer of the *Baltic* on the New York to Liverpool run until April 1853. Just as Fox expected to be appointed captain of a large steamer "within a very few days," his latest six-month leave of absence from naval service expired. Six weeks later, Secretary of the Navy James C. Dobbin ordered him to the USS *Princeton* at Norfolk, Virginia. Fox played for time until late June, when Dobbin ordered him *forthwith* to the *Princeton*. Although George Law of the United States Mail Steamship Company had nominated Fox to command the *Ohio*, final approval came after the *Princeton* sailed. A resentful Fox reflected that things would have been different had Levi Woodbury, New Hampshire's original favorite son for 1852, been president, rather than Woodbury's old law student Franklin Pierce.[6]

The second screw steamer to bear the name *Princeton* had recently been constructed in Boston. It utilized the engines designed by John Ericsson and some of the timber from the earlier *Princeton*, the first screw steamship in the U.S. Navy. From July to September 1853, the new *Princeton* served as the flagship of Commodore William Branford Shubrick's Eastern Squadron, which Pierce had ordered to protect American fishing rights off the coasts of Nova Scotia, Newfoundland, and Labrador. The Convention of 1818 gave Americans

the right to fish within the three-mile limit off specified coasts of Newfoundland and Labrador and to dry their fish in the unsettled areas of those coasts.
In the early 1850s, British provincial authorities, backed by London, interpreted that convention to circumscribe the privileges of American fishermen
by drawing lines from headlands to close bays of considerable expanse abound-
ing with mackerel and herring. Americans were even stopped from navigating
the Gut of Canso (between Cape Breton Island and the mainland of Nova
Scotia) and could not purchase supplies in British colonial ports.[7]

The *Princeton* stopped at Halifax, Nova Scotia, and in late August was at
Charlottetown on Prince Edward Island. Fox blamed Nova Scotia politicians,
the descendants of Tories, and not the common people for "this fish row." A
thoroughgoing expansionist, he thought the American government should
have reacted earlier and more strongly to the fishing crisis. He found Prince
Edward Island "a garden of Eden" and claimed that within sixty miles of
Halifax, Nova Scotia, there were more harbors where a ship of the line could
get in and out against wind and tide than in "the whole world put together."
In the United States, on both the Atlantic and Pacific, only Newport, Rhode
Island, could compare. "For Heaven's sake," Fox importuned, "let us get this
country. Then we shall have a North a worthy rival of the great West. God
never meant this rich portion of domain to remain long in such unworthy, lazy
hands."[8]

"We are not permitted to make a row," Fox lamented, even while admitting
there was no pretense for one. The British had seized only two fishing boats
(one of which they had released), and the English officers "have treated us
remarkably well." Despite his reluctance to go on this cruise, Fox admitted he
was glad to "visit lands whose wealth I had no idea of." He would visit the
Magdalen Islands, coal at Sydney on Cape Breton Island, and stop at St. John's,
Newfoundland, before returning to Portsmouth, New Hampshire, by mid-
September 1853. There he finally got his orders to the mail steamer *Ohio* at
New York.[9]

Belonging to the U.S. Mail Steamship Company—known as the George
Law line—the *Ohio* was less sumptuous than the *Baltic* but equally useless for
the navy. It left New York on the fifth day of each month. It refueled at Kingston, Jamaica, proceeded to Aspinwall (Colon), Panama, where it discharged
mail, freight, and passengers bound for California and received mail, treasure,
and passengers from the Pacific Mail steamer that had left San Francisco on
the first of the month. The *Ohio* then returned to New York, arriving on about
the last day of each month.[10]

As captain, Fox was responsible for everything on board. Initially, he had to insist that the stewards clean the vessel at Aspinwall, because they had been leaving quarters filthy until they received tips from incoming passengers. Among both passengers and crew members, thievery and drunkenness were persistent problems. On 7 October, two days after putting to sea with his new command, the valise of a steerage passenger was rifled and a portion of its contents were found under a sleeping Panama Railroad laborer, whom Fox clapped into double irons in a lifeboat. On that same day, he confined a delirious man in single irons for safekeeping. Two days later, Fox had to confine his third officer William Lawson in double irons for drunkenness and disobeying orders. He released Lawson the next day, after ordering him to seaman's duties. On a subsequent voyage, while leaving New York on 5 January 1854, Fox discovered his first officer "drunk and unfit for duty," discharged him, and sent him back by the pilot boat. In quick succession, Fox placed in irons a drunk who interfered with coaling the ship, a thieving steerage passenger, and waiters who sold the ship's stores to passengers.[11]

On 29 January, Fox gave up the command of the *Ohio* but remained with the George Law line. When the captain of the *Philadelphia* was sick in mid-February, Fox commanded that steamer on its regular run between New York and New Orleans via Havana and gained what proved to be the invaluable experience of navigating the lower reaches of the Mississippi River. Upon returning to New York, he took command of the *George Law*. It was large enough to ship a crew of 100 and to carry 849 passengers, efficient and fast enough to sail nonstop to Aspinwall and back in nineteen days, and impressive enough to be named for its owner.[12]

While running a tight ship, Fox cut an imposing figure. His "studious care for the interests of the company" and his gallant behavior endeared him to his superiors and his passengers. Virginia Woodbury's brother-in-law Montgomery Blair—in San Francisco to settle his brother Jim's estate—met a young woman named Kiger, who, having sailed on Fox's ship, was his "enthusiastic admirer."[13]

While he was captain of the *George Law*, Fox's relationship with Virginia Woodbury had reached a crisis. Montgomery Blair was "distressed" by her health and observed: "I think Gin is rather sick at heart than in body however & she must cure herself of that. If Fox will come up to the mark—why well and good, but if he continues to play off she ought to quit thinking about him. She is one of the finest women I know & ought not to waste her thoughts on people that do not appreciate her." On hearing more about Virginia's indisposition, Blair exclaimed, "What on earth does she fool herself so far about that affair," but Virginia and Fox were more attached to each other than Blair suspected. The oak leaves she embroidered on a pair of slippers for Fox constantly reminded him of the special tree and bench where he carved her initials. For years he wore those slippers, until Montgomery's brother Frank carried them off. "I note," Montgomery later wrote to his wife Minna, "what you say of Gin's pleasure at my mention of Fox. Well! She's a crazy person isn't she!" Blair resolved to "try & hit Fox's ship" upon his return, for Virginia's sake, but doubted if he could "get up an intimacy with him. . . . He has I think other views now."[14]

Blair apparently did not "hit" the *George Law* and had no opportunity to alter Fox's irresolution. One problem was that Virginia had demanded as a condition of marriage that Fox resign from the navy. She could not bear the thought of his absence three weeks each month, while on his run to Panama, and possibly for over three years, if he was returned to active duty and ordered to a foreign station. While her father lived, she had assumed that if she and Fox married he would receive good shore assignments. On Christmas Day 1849, she wrote "a letter from Mrs. Fox—13 years hence—" to her "Ma" in which she imagined that in 1862 "Pa" would be president and she and "Gus" would have seven children and be happily domiciled in the commandant's quarters (with a roof of gold) in the San Francisco Navy Yard. But in 1854 Levi Woodbury was dead and Fox was at sea.[15]

Fox had a dilemma. Virginia was bright, well read, and attractive, but she was sickly, and her diminished political connections were of no use to him unless he remained in the navy. Even if she married, Virginia was determined to retain control of the $21,000 she had in municipal, railroad, and bank bonds. The navy, which had been Fox's life since 1838, had too many officers, and a strict seniority system slowed promotions. As captain of the *George Law*, Fox brimmed with self-confidence and believed he could also be successful as a captain of industry. Indeed, with a hundred crewmen and hundreds of passengers, Fox was more a manager than a navigator, and with that in mind he explored job options outside the navy.[16]

Upon landing a job in a textile mill, Fox gave up the sea to marry Virginia. His new position came not through the Woodbury connection but from naval acquaintances. He left the *George Law* on 3 July 1855 and two days later received a one-year furlough from the Navy Department "to test" his new position. Fox proceeded to Lawrence, Massachusetts, to succeed Captain Oliver Hazard Perry as the "agent"—in effect plant manager—of the Bay State Mills, which Amos and Abbott Lawrence had organized in 1846 and had been operating since 1848. Samuel Lawrence provided Fox with a home, which, although unfurnished, satisfied Virginia. Fox later mused that if it were not for the home, "*perhaps* something very *pleasant* in this life would never have happened." By mid-October, Fox had his "new and elegant mansion" (as it was described by a Boston newspaper) furnished sufficiently for Virginia to occupy. On 20 October, at the Elms, her family home in Portsmouth, they signed a wedding contract, specifying that after marriage Virginia's property and all that she might inherit subsequently would remain in her hands for "her own separate use." On Monday morning, 29 October 1855, Gustavus Vasa Fox and Virginia Lafayette Woodbury were married. Accompanied by friends, the couple took a train to Boston, where they enjoyed a "splendid wedding dinner," given them by Virginia's uncle and aunt, William and Julia Clapp of Portland. Following the dinner, the Foxes took a train to their partially furnished house in Lawrence.[17]

Fox's marriage brought him more than Virginia. It brought him companionship in her close-knit family. He would become its most beloved member, Montgomery Blair's dearest friend, and the children's cherished Uncle Gus. In Lawrence, Fox and Virginia quickly became social leaders. With his assets totaling $5,600, they spent $3,757.85 on their home. This amount included $1,678 for furniture, $489 for silver, $468 for carpets, $341 for "pictures, portraits, & engravings," $324 for a piano, $290 for crockery, and $168 for "kitchen furniture and fixens." With three domestic servants, the Foxes entertained generously, during their first two years together, and ran their annual expenses up to $2,500. "Did ever anybody see such a nice specimen of house-keeping as Virginia exhibits," exclaimed her younger sister Nell. "She ought to have a gold medal awarded by the Essex County Society for the improvement of the condition of men & women. I really don't know what more they could do to make everybody happy around them." Fox and Virginia joined the Grace Episcopal Church, where they rented a pew for thirty dollars annually and presented the organist and his wife a sterling pitcher and tea set. Convinced that the Foxes were "really making something out of Lawrence," Virginia's mother appeared surprised and relieved as she boasted of Fox's "refined taste . . . for everything beautiful in art & nature" and of "his devotion as a husband."[18]

A year after Fox resigned from the navy, the Panic of 1857 produced a sharp, though short, economic depression that proved disastrous for him. Samuel Lawrence, the treasurer of the Bay State Mills, plunged it into bankruptcy by improperly using its funds in a futile attempt to save his own company, Lawrence & Stone. The Bay State Mills was reorganized in 1858 and renamed the Washington Mills. An investigating committee reported to the Bay State shareholders that with the plant's machinery and accounts in good order, Fox had performed his duties "with fidelity, punctuality, and diligence." He had economized "in small things and large," voluntarily cut his own salary in half, and, regarding him as both "efficient and successful," his employers kept him on as their agent. In addition, the panic also hurt Isaac Barnes to whom Fox lent approximately $2,000. Less income put a crimp in the life-style of the Foxes, as they cut their expenditures back to $2,000 in 1858 and $1,700 in 1859. Fox learned that navigating a company through the world of business with its sudden tempests could be as risky as rounding Cape Horn.[19]

Economic adversity did not affect the status of the Foxes in Lawrence. In October 1858 the local Democrats unanimously nominated Fox—"an old school Democrat" who "has never been active in politics"—for representative in the Massachusetts General Court, as the legislature was called, but he lost the ensuing election. He proved his mettle as a man of action in fighting two fires. When the "Bangor Block" building caught fire early one morning, he connected a fire hose with the Washington Mills hydrant before the fire department engines were in service, and its "voluminous streams of water" were mainly responsible for containing and extinguishing the blaze. He again proved a hero when the Pemberton Mills collapsed on the afternoon of 10 January 1860. Its "outrageously defective" cast iron pillars and inadequate floor timbers gave way, plunging 650 workers into a hellish pit of burning rubble. From the neighboring Washington Mills, Fox again used its hoses to fight the harrowing fire and "labored heroically, regardless of his own life." Still, more than 100 men, women, and children perished.[20]

The coroner's inquest blamed the tragedy on the Eagle Iron Foundry of West Boston and on the architect and superintendent of the mill's construction, but a letter to the *New York Herald*, with a Lawrence dateline, charged that "tyrants" and "task-masters" drove textile mill workers like slaves. Virginia Fox responded with a letter to the *Lawrence Sentinel*, which she deceptively signed "Wife of a Worker." Not mentioning that her husband's work was managing the Washington Mills, she attacked the *Herald* letter as a bogus work of fiction, possibly written by an "inefficient, or faithless workman." The operatives of Lawrence, she countered, were not "white slaves" but "well educated and respectable American men and women," earning "liberal wages."[21]

Despite the real or imagined virtues of Lawrence, Fox and most of his absentee employers were unhappy with each other. "I esteem our Boston managers as gentlemen," Fox told Montgomery Blair, "but have a thorough contempt for them as operators in this business." Although twice dissuaded by his friends among the directors from resigning, Fox reported that as of 21 June 1860, "I have at length cut adrift from our sinking concern and have swum safely ashore." He was relieved to be out of a firm he felt "sure will be wrecked by

Boston mismanagement." The final break came after the directors ignored his advice to bid forty-three and one-half cents per yard to supply flannel for the U.S. Navy; they insisted it could be made for thirty-eight cents and won the contract at that price. The next lowest bid at forty-four cents vindicated Fox. Because Virginia took his resignation "very pleasantly," Fox perceived that she found living in Lawrence "more a duty than a pleasure." He resolved that "the crown of Sicily shall not prevent me devoting this summer to my little sick wife, who will see Niagara and whatever else she expresses an interest for."[22]

Fox immediately "broke up house keeping at Lawrence." The company agreed to pay him the $1,600 back pay it owed him and to compensate him for "land and improvements about the house." Virginia was already in Washington, where she was spending a month with her sister Minna (Montgomery Blair's wife) before visiting her sister Frank (Frances) and her husband Archibald Lowery at Tubby Hook, on the northern tip of Manhattan Island. To keep Fox in town, his friends wished to run him for mayor, but he continued to wrap up his affairs. He resigned from the vestry, gave up their pew and sold its cushions, returned unused groceries, and paid bills.[23]

After visiting his family in Lowell, Fox rendezvoused with Virginia at Tubby Hook. To reach her, he walked thirteen miles in four hours, after spending the night of the Fourth of July in lower Manhattan. Five days later, they left to tour Niagara Falls and Canada. After viewing the falls from various points on 14 July, Virginia had a "*very* high fever," a sore throat, a pain in the chest, an upset stomach, accompanied by loose bowels, throwing up, coughing, and loss of voice. "Heartbroken" over exposing her to the spray from the falls, Fox planned to return to Tubby Hook. When Virginia felt "much better" the next day, they took a boat to Montreal. By 17 July, "thanks to Croton oil"—a drastic cathartic that purged and blistered its victims—she had recovered. Apart from the Victoria Bridge across the St. Lawrence—the "greatest bridge in the world"—the Foxes were disappointed with Montreal and quickly decamped for Quebec City, where, with "good servants" and a "very nice corner room," they stayed until 24 July.[24]

An ensuing boat trip down the St. Lawrence and up the scenic Saguenay River was the high point of the Foxes' vacation. Among the passengers, Fox enjoyed the company of the renowned travel writer Bayard Taylor and especially that of Anna, Charlotte, and John Bloodgood of Mobile, Alabama, the children of a "rich & dead" cotton broker. After going ashore at Rivière du Loup, Fox was in "high spirits." He had both discovered a waterfall Taylor had missed and raced and beaten the Bloodgoods, although to win that race, he had almost overturned his calash. "There's that American walking," Virginia overheard an Englishman exclaim, "he's been everywhere, has a very sick wife on board, he don't look like being sick of life soon, such a quantity of cigars as he smokes!" While Virginia took laudanum (opium) for her pain, Fox accepted her indisposition and was his irrepressible, enthusiastic self on the fjord-like Saguenay River, arguing with Taylor about the origin and height of the cliffs lining its shore, paddling about Ha Ha Bay in a rented birch bark canoe, and bringing Virginia offerings—"flowers & leaves, blueberries, raspberries, dogwood," from the hillsides.[25]

The Foxes returned to Tubby Hook, via Quebec City, Montreal, Lakes Champlain and George, and the Hudson River Valley. Occasionally, Virginia was pleased. She liked the black waiters, hot dishes, and new furniture in their Montreal hotel and found Lake George "picturesque in extreme." But often she complained. The 200 guests at Fort William Henry Hotel were "not fashionable," and at Saratoga, New York, the waters were acrid and disagreeable, the food wretched, and the children who should have been in bed ruined all style at a dance she and Fox attended. "Nothing could induce" her to remain, and they got up at five o'clock to return by rail to Frank's home.[26]

In late August, Fox and Virginia moved their temporary headquarters from Tubby Hook to the Elms, her family home in Portsmouth. Anxious to get back to work, Fox explored with William A. Aspinwall the possibility of commanding either the *Atlantic* or the *Baltic* (neither was available) and considered entering the mining profession. He had collected minerals since childhood, and one of the few investments he made, with his modest funds, was in a Michigan mining company. That company, however, thanks to the chicanery of its agent, failed to pay its taxes and was sold to a friend of the agent, who became part owner. Fox decided to investigate the lowdown actions of the agent and to explore the possibility of managing a copper mine on the south shore of Lake Superior.[27]

Armed with letters of introduction, Fox left the Elms in mid-September for the Midwest by way of Canada. He was charmed by the lakes and mountains of New Hampshire and Vermont and preferred Toronto's wide streets and the "light buff stone" of its public buildings to the narrow streets and "dark, black limestone" structures in Montreal and Quebec City. On a side trip northwest from Toronto to Collingwood, he remonstrated with an Anglican clergyman, who was furious that the Prince of Wales, who was touring Canada and the United States, had refused to meet with Orangemen. Fox insisted that the Orangemen—an anti-Catholic political organization—deserved to be ignored. Having supervised Irish employees at Lawrence and run for office as a Democrat, Fox had too much experience with Roman Catholics to sympathize with nativist bigotry.[28]

Fox traveled by rail from Toronto to Detroit and Chicago. He was delighted with the perfect ventilation in his berth in the Michigan Central sleeping car and with the prairie sunrise, which was like "an ocean changed to grass." Impressed by the homes and stores in Chicago, Fox was bothered by its "miserable outskirts," flatness, and lack of tides to carry off refuse. He visited Virginia's friend Adele Cutts Douglas, whose husband Stephen A. Douglas was the northern Democratic nominee for president. For half an hour, they chatted about Chicago and Washington, politics and her husband. As befitting a great niece of Dolley Madison, Adele was "very handsome" and in "superb" style, but her conversational powers, Fox assured Virginia, were not equal to those of his own "little wife."[29]

Returning to Detroit, Fox caught the side-wheel steamer *Cleveland* for Copper Harbor on Michigan's Keweenaw Peninsula. The trip up Lake Huron to the Sault Sainte Marie Canal was delightful. Linking lakes Huron and Superior, the canal locks, completed five years earlier, fascinated him, but the Native Americans, eking out a "base existence" on the shores of the Saint Marys River, were not, he assured Virginia, "the Indians of our imagination." Fox found a "beautiful cabinet specimen" of copper at the Keweenaw Peninsula, but discovered mining operations had been suspended at Copper Harbor. When he confronted the crooked agent, he "professed a willingness" to enable investors to regain possession of their property. His word proved worthless. Having found no opportunities in copper mining, Fox was again thinking of returning to "steamboating" when he reached Portsmouth on 28 October, as the 1860 presidential campaign drew to a close.[30]

CHAPTER SIX

Fort Sumter

I cannot shrink from a solemn duty, which, if successful is preg-
nant with great results for our beloved country.
Fox to Virginia Fox, 8 April 1861

The presidential election of 1860 solved Fox's unemployment problem. The victory of the Republican nominee, Abraham Lincoln, led South Carolina, Georgia, Florida, Alabama, Mississippi, Louisiana, and Texas to secede from the Union and to create in early 1861 the Confederate States of America. When Fox was in the navy, politics had interested him only as a means of furthering his career. He was a Democrat primarily because of his connection with Levi Woodbury. Fox did not like slavery, but the question of whether to allow it to extend into the western territories did not appear to interest him. Because he had no permanent address, he was unable to vote in 1860. Had he been able to vote, he probably would have voted for Stephen A. Douglas, although Virginia's brother-in-law Montgomery Blair campaigned for Lincoln. Secession, however, was anathema to Fox, who revered the Union. He was a patriotic nationalist who believed it was the manifest destiny of the United States to expand, not to contract. Disunion would shatter his dream of America outstripping all other nations, and he was determined to help hold the Union together.

■ ■ ■

The news that South Carolina would call a convention to consider secession reached Portsmouth on 17 November 1860, the day Fox had saved a boy who had broken through thin ice on a pond. With secession sentiment growing in the Deep South (South Carolina seceded on 20 December), it was obvious that the Union was in danger. In December the Foxes returned to Tubby Hook to spend Christmas with Virginia's sister Frank. Just after Christmas, Major Robert Anderson, who commanded the Union troops at Charleston, moved his

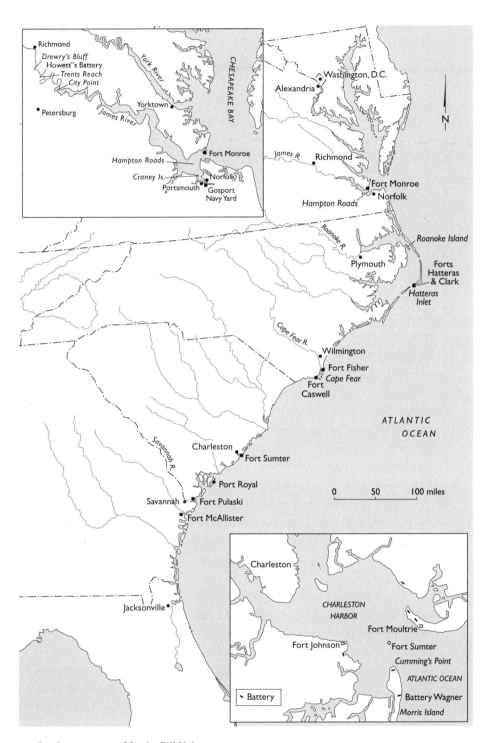

Southeastern coast. Map by Bill Nelson.

command from Fort Moultrie to the less vulnerable Fort Sumter, on an island in Charleston's harbor. In addition, President James Buchanan stiffened his attitude toward secession. On 5 January 1861 he dispatched from New York a merchant vessel, the *Star of the West*, to reinforce Anderson with 200 men, arms, and ammunition. A few days later, Fox met his former boss Marshall O. Roberts, president of the United States Mail Steamship Company and owner of the *Star of the West*. He would have given Fox command of the *Star*, he insisted, had he known Fox was in New York. The next day, 9 January, the unarmed *Star of the West*, while flying the U.S. flag, attempted to reinforce Anderson and was fired upon by South Carolina batteries. Anderson was about to return their fire when the ship turned back. Sumter's guns remained silent.[1]

The Buchanan administration ignored the insult, and six additional lower southern states seceded from the Union. Had Fox, with his impassioned love of the Union and his impetuous love of action, been in command of the *Star of the West*, instead of the cautious John McGowan, it is likely that he would have held his course for Sumter and that Anderson would have engaged the South Carolina batteries. Emboldened by the success of their audacity, South Carolinians increased and strengthened their batteries, making Anderson's position more tenuous and a successful relief expedition more difficult.[2]

When Fox heard that the *Star of the West*—the ship he should have commanded—had turned back, he began to wrestle with the problem of how Sumter could be reinforced. He and Virginia moved into the St. Germaine Hotel in New York City. She wished to consult Dr. Oliver Wolcott Gibbs on the state of her health, while Fox wished to consult his acquaintance George William Blunt, who, as editor of *Blunt's Coast Pilot*, was knowledgeable about Charleston harbor. Gibbs recommended that Virginia have surgery by James Marion Sims, the leading gynecologist of the day, and Fox tried out his thoughts about the relief of Sumter on Blunt. The *Star of the West* incident, Fox fumed, disgraced the country and dishonored the flag. Sumter could be relieved, and he wanted to do it. Referring to John A. Dahlgren's *Shells and Shell Guns* (1856), Fox told Blunt that in 1855, during the Crimean War, British and French gunboats at night ran by Russian batteries 1,000 yards distant at Kinburn at the mouth of the Dnieper River. "He could do the same," Fox insisted, "with three steamers at Charleston, as the distance he could keep from Fort Moultrie was greater than that of Kinburn."[3]

In late January, Fox worked on his relief plan. Blunt, who was helping him, wrote Lieutenant General Winfield Scott outlining Fox's ideas and extolling his qualifications "to the highest degree." Fox also wrote of his plan to Montgomery Blair in Washington, who "laid it before" Scott on 30 January. Having just heard from Blunt, in whose judgment of sailors he had great confidence, Scott invited Fox to Washington, but his letter "laid a week" in the post office. A subsequent telegram via Blunt reached Fox on 4 February. "A jovial old man," Blunt shook the telegram in Fox's face "with delight beaming from every feature." While Virginia's "heart died within" her, they rushed out to wire Scott that Fox would catch the first train in the morning. Arriving back at the hotel, Blunt, looking like a "proud father," told Virginia that Gustavus Vasa "saved his country from her enemies & *this* Gustavus Vasa will save his." Virginia managed a smile, but that evening her eyes filled with tears while she watched Fox calmly play chess with an acquaintance. Her own approaching surgery heightened her anxiety. After a restless night, she woke Fox at five o'clock. To soothe her, he insisted that reinforcing Sumter was a "*peace* measure" that would discourage an attack and "*perhaps* prevent entirely a civil war."[4]

In Washington on 6 February, Fox had breakfast with Scott, who treated him "very kindly." He remembered the Woodburys "with great affection" and dispelled Fox's apprehension that he would not accept a plan someone else originated. Scott told Fox that "there were worse things than bloodshed & he didn't mind shedding a little if it would preserve the Union, it was a good country & worth preserving." Fox conferred several times with Lieutenant Norman J. Hall, of the Fort Sumter garrison, who was in Washington and could, on his return, brief Anderson. On 7 February Fox explained the project to Secretary of War Joseph Holt and the next day presented it to Scott in writing.[5]

Fox assumed that obstructions prevented deep-draft, heavily armed war vessels from entering the harbor. He planned to employ a "large, comfortable sea steamer" to carry troops and stores to the bar off Charleston and then to utilize two powerful light-draft New York tugboats to run them into the fort. Accompanying these vessels would be the efficient revenue cutter *Harriet Lane* and the, unfortunately, inefficient USS *Pawnee*. If the landing was opposed, Fox would move the *Pawnee* and the *Harriet Lane* up to the bar and, supported by Anderson's guns, destroy or drive away hostile vessels. The only remaining obstacles, Fox concluded, "are the forts on Cummings point, and Fort Moultrie, and whatever adjacent batteries they may have, distant on either hand from mid channel about ¾ of a mile. Two hours before high water, at night, with half the force on board of each tug, within relieving distance of each other, [I] should run into Fort Sumpter." He had faith in his plan and its chances for success. "The Union looks better," Fox wrote Virginia on 7 February. "My plan will be adopted if it becomes certain that reinforcements must be sent."[6]

On 8 February the Confederate Constitution was adopted, and the next day Jefferson Davis was appointed provisional president of the Confederacy. With these events, Buchanan feared reinforcements would provoke South Carolinians to attack Sumter, and he did not wish to start a civil war. "I would not trust them," Fox wrote Virginia, "but old Buck may know better." Although the cabinet discussed Fox's plan, nothing came of it. Neither did anything come of a similar relief expedition of four revenue steamers organized by Scott, Holt, and Secretary of the Navy Isaac Toucey, nor from a proposal by John Murray Forbes of Boston. Despite the urging of Scott, Buchanan would not reinforce Sumter unless he was requested to do so by Anderson, and he knew that Anderson, reluctant to bring on war, would make no request. Upon giving Fox the news, Scott "seemed much disappointed and astonished." With less than a month remaining of his term, Buchanan decided to leave the deepening Sumter crisis for Lincoln to resolve. While the Buchanan administration debated and waited, Fox returned to New York to be with Virginia as she underwent surgery with Dr. Sims and convalesced slowly at the newly established Woman's Hospital at 83 Madison Avenue.[7]

Fox's plan fared better with the incoming Lincoln administration. The new postmaster general, Montgomery Blair, backed his kinsman's idea. Once again, Fox traveled to Washington, leaving the still hospitalized Virginia alone. On 13 March, accompanied by Blair, Fox discussed with Lincoln his plan and a possible visit to Fort Sumter. Two days later, Fox attended a cabinet meeting, where he answered objections to his scheme by Scott, now in opposition because of increased batteries at the mouth of Charleston Harbor, and by General Joseph G. Totten, chief of engineers. Most of Lincoln's cabinet favored evacuation, but the president remained uncommitted. "Uncle Abe Lincoln," Fox reported to Virginia on 19 March, "has taken a high esteem for me and wishes me to take dispatches to Major Anderson at Fort Sumpter with regard to its final evacuation and to obtain a clear statement of his condition which his letters, probably guarded, do not fully exhibit. I have really great curiosity to see the famous Fort." Fox obviously wanted to check on the viability of his plan of relief, but his cheerful reference to "evacuation" suggests that, in the face of cabinet and military opposition, even he could be reconciled to abandoning Sumter. Within the two-week-old Lincoln administration, hostility to secession, balanced by fear of civil war, produced halting, uncertain, and inconsistent views, which Fox, despite his strong nationalism, reflected.[8]

At 8:30 p.m. on 21 March, Fox arrived at Fort Sumter, remained an hour and a quarter, and left Charleston that evening for Washington. To get to the besieged fort, he acquiesced when Governor Francis W. Pickens inferred that his purpose was peaceful and insisted that Fox be accompanied by Confederate Commander Henry J. Hartstene, an old navy intimate, who also had been captain of a mail steamer. Fox brought Anderson three letters. One from Pickens referred to the "peculiar circumstances" of Fox's visit, which he permitted because "I confide in you as a gentleman of Honor." A second letter informed Anderson that he had been nominated lieutenant colonel and colonel by brevets, and a third from Secretary of War Simon Cameron to Winfield Scott requested "accurate information" about Anderson's command. Fox received a list of the fort's scanty provisions and learned that it could hold out on half rations until 15 April, conversed with officers, and then accompanied Anderson to the ramparts. There they "saw the distant batteries by moonlight," heard but could not see a rowboat, and talked. But as Anderson's surgeon, Samuel W. Crawford, noted in his diary, "The conversation that took place we do not know."[9]

Unfortunately, neither Fox nor Anderson was clear about their conversation. Kenneth Williams observes, "The sailor confused the soldier, and the soldier confused the sailor." Aware that Fox had planned a relief expedition (Lieutenant Hall had returned to the fort with that information), but anxious to be evacuated, Anderson argued that the loss of life accompanying a landing would outweigh any advantages that it might gain. Besides, even if Sumter was held, it was surrounded by hostile batteries that would have to be carried before the fort could be of military value to the federal government. Somewhat taken aback by Anderson's lack of enthusiasm for his plan (Fox wondered if he harbored "Southern sympathies"), aware that evacuation was a possibility, and inhibited by Pickens's belief that his mission was one of peace, Fox, Anderson thought, "merely hinted" about relief, and Fox said he "made no arrangements with Major Anderson for reinforcing or supplying the fort." But Fox did more than hint. He knew Anderson had been briefed on his plan, and he pointed to the spot he thought most feasible for a landing.[10]

Anderson certainly considered a relief expedition because the next day he reported: "I have examined the point alluded to by Mr. Fox last night. A vessel lying there will be under the fire of thirteen guns from Fort Moultrie, and Captain [John G.] Foster says that the pan-coupe, or immediately on its right— [is] the best place to land. . . . The Department can decide what the chances will be of a safe debarkation and unloading at that point." Without specific orders, Anderson continued to assume that he would be evacuated and did not put his men on short rations. Four days after Fox's visit, Lincoln's confidant, Ward Hill Lamon, assured Anderson that his force would be withdrawn.[11]

Fox returned to Washington on 24 March. There he bucked a swarm of office seekers to get his travel expenses and to see "Abe often, also Mrs. L." Mary Lincoln, Fox reported to Virginia, "is Lady Like, converses easily, dresses well and has the Kentucky pronunciation like old Mrs. Blair," Montgomery's mother. With Lincoln, Fox talked about Sumter. They assumed that Anderson was on short rations and would hold out until 15 April. Remembering the rowboat he could not see from Sumter's ramparts, Fox was convinced that small boats with muffled oars could approach Sumter virtually undetected. But evacuation, as Lamon had assured Anderson, was in the air, and on 26 March Fox wrote Virginia: "Sumpter is to be given up."[12]

Lincoln, however, decided not to give up Sumter. On 27 March Stephen A. Hurlbut, an old Charleston-born friend from Illinois, had at Lincoln's behest recently visited South Carolina. Hurlbut told him that Union sentiment there was dead and that evacuating Sumter would lead to a demand that Fort Pickens off Pensacola, Florida, also be abandoned. This prediction was confirmed in a disturbing way by Winfield Scott's advice that both Sumter and Pickens be given up to "soothe" the remaining slave states contemplating secession. Hurlbut's firsthand observations contradicted the wishful thinking, inspired by Secretary of State William H. Seward, that a voluntary federal withdrawal from Sumter, or anywhere else, would promote a counterrevolution against secession and the reconciliation of the North and South. Hurlbut warned that an attempt to reinforce Sumter would certainly lead to war and that even an expedition to provision that fort would be resisted. If Hurlbut was right, evacuation would destroy the Union peacefully and even a feeble attempt to save the Union by maintaining a federal presence in the seceded states would result in war.[13]

Pledged to preserve the Union, Lincoln was prepared to risk war. On 27 March, after receiving Hurlbut's report, he asked Fox for the details of his plan. At nine o'clock on the morning of 28 March, Fox sent to the White House a memorandum, which was soon lost, but Lincoln had already "agreed upon, and directed" its contents. That evening, following his first state dinner, Lincoln asked his cabinet to remain, apparently informed it of Scott's suggestion that Pickens be abandoned, and asked it to meet at noon the next day to decide Sumter's and the nation's fate. At that formal meeting, Secretary of the Treasury Salmon P. Chase and Secretary of the Navy Gideon Welles joined Montgomery Blair to favor reinforcing Sumter. Buttressed by this support, Lincoln wrote both Welles and Secretary of War Simon Cameron on 29 March:

"I desire that an expedition, to move by sea, be got ready to sail as early as the 6th. of April next, the whole according to memorandum attached." He asked them to cooperate in getting off Fox's expedition. Specifically, the Navy Department was to ready for one-month's service at sea the *Pocahontas* at Norfolk, the *Pawnee* at Washington, and the *Harriet Lane* at New York. The War Department was asked to provide 200 men and twelve months' supplies for 100 men "in portable shape, ready for instant shipping." Lincoln's decision, however, was not final. He instructed the War Department to "conditionally engage" a large steamer and three tugboats, and he verbally ordered Fox to New York to make tentative preparations for the expedition.[14]

Organizing the relief expedition proved frustrating. The steamer, tugs, and desiccated provisions (which were imperishable and compact) had to be secured quietly lest federal efforts to secure an important loan be imperiled by a war scare. Fox wanted to charter the *Baltic*, on which he had served. It was owned by his friend, shipping magnate William H. Aspinwall, who along with Charles H. Marshall (a commission merchant and head of the Black Ball packet line) had enthusiastically supported his Sumter plan. But now, on Saturday, 30 March, they were "astonished at the idea of Govt attempting it declaring that the time has past and that the people are reconciled to leaving this position and making the stand on Pickens. . . . We argued . . . til midnight," Fox reported to Blair. "They propose making no move til Tuesday on account of the loan," he continued, "promising that they can get me ready in time after that. I really think they doubt my word in the matter. . . . You have no idea of the fears existing with these gentlemen and I am not sure that they will decline all participation. So fall away, in the hour of peril, hands and hearts that should stand by our Govt. I am real heart sick, not discouraged, at the delays, obstacles and brief time allowed for a vital measure that should have had months' careful preparations."[15]

Having recently returned from Washington, where he had been exposed to Seward's views, Marshall declined to participate, making supplies more difficult to obtain. Although Aspinwall remained "very averse to the movement," he let Fox have the *Baltic*. By Tuesday noon, the loan bids were safely in, and Fox then secured desiccated provisions. They were stored in two-and-one-half-bushel sacks for fast unloading from either tugs or the *Baltic*'s ten longboats. Convinced that the main threat to his plan would come from Confederate naval forces, Fox ordered the heaviest howitzers for the tugs. To destroy any vessels attempting to intercept his boats, he counted on an "efficient naval force" (especially 300 experienced sailors, whom Welles had promised him, in

the recently returned, powerful *Powhatan*). Delays and objections, both political and military, left Fox dejected. "I feel like abandoning my country, moving
off somewhere. I am sick down to my heel."[16]

On Monday, 1 April, Fox was encouraged when Lincoln invited him to
Washington to shape the necessary orders. The next morning, before rushing
to the president's side, Fox had to pick up Virginia at the hospital, where, after
six weeks, she was being discharged. On the way to the depot, he told her that
he was going directly to Washington. With "a most hasty kiss," he placed her
on a departing train for Tubby Hook and assured her that her brother-in-law
Archibald Lowery was on board. Unknown to Fox, Lowery had missed the
train. In Washington, where Seward was trying to prevent the relief of Sumter, Fox experienced further frustrations. "My expedition is ordered to be got
ready, but I doubt if we shall get off," Fox complained. "Delay, indecision,
obstacles. War will commence at Pensacola," he predicted. "There the Govt is
making a stand," and if southerners "fire upon reinforcements, already ordered to land, Fort Pickens and the ships will open upon the whole party."[17]

Lincoln, nevertheless, decided on Thursday, 4 April, to relieve Sumter. After
a long conference with a Virginia Unionist, he realized that not even the voluntary evacuation of Sumter would ensure that Virginia would remain in the
Union. He also heard from Anderson that day that he had not placed his garrison on short rations and could not hold out until 15 April. If Lincoln allowed
Anderson to be starved out, the administration would be, as Seward and other
critics charged, without a policy. Through Cameron, Lincoln ordered Fox to
"take charge of the transports . . . in New York" and "succor Fort Sumter" and
urged Anderson to "hold out, if possible, till the arrival of the expedition."[18]

With detailed orders from Winfield Scott, Fox sped to New York on 5 April
to whip his expedition into shape. The next day, when news arrived that Lincoln's 11 March order to reinforce Fort Pickens (with troops on board the
Brooklyn) had not been carried out, the last possibility that Lincoln might
abandon the Fox expedition, and with it Sumter, disappeared. The Union had
not been dramatically upheld at Fort Pickens, efforts to shift the focal point of
the secession crisis from stormy Charleston to calm Pensacola had failed, and
Lincoln had reached the point of no return. In a move calculated to avoid any
responsibility for starting a civil war and any recognition of the Confederacy,
Lincoln on 6 April ordered Robert S. Chew, a State Department clerk, to notify
Governor Pickens that "an attempt will be made to supply Fort-Sumpter with
provisions only; and that, if such attempt be not resisted, no effort to throw in
men, arms, or ammunition, will be made, without further notice." On 8 April

Chew handed Pickens an unaddressed, unsigned copy of the notice and told him that he "was not authorized to receive any communication from him in reply."[19]

Despite Lincoln's decision to "succor" Sumter, Seward's earlier determination to reinforce Fort Pickens undermined Fox's expedition. On 29 March he got Lincoln to approve the organization of a secret Pickens expedition by Captain Montgomery C. Meigs, a talented army engineer, who in turn enlisted the audacious naval officer Lieutenant David Dixon Porter. Orders to send to Pickens the powerful *Powhatan,* under Porter's command, were signed on 1 April by Lincoln, at the behest of Seward, who believed he was the administration's strong man. He did not inform Secretary of the Navy Gideon Welles or Secretary of War Simon Cameron of his interference in their departments.[20]

But on that same day Welles, cooperating with Fox and with Lincoln's approval, ordered Commandant Andrew H. Foote of the Brooklyn Navy Yard to fit out, "at the earliest possible moment," the *Powhatan.* Fox deemed its 300 sailors, howitzers, and "fighting launches" essential for the success of his plan. Twenty minutes later, the implementation of the Seward-Meigs-Porter plan began, when Foote received an almost identical telegram from Lincoln with word that the *Powhatan* would sail on a secret mission and that further orders borne by a "confidential messenger" would follow. The messenger proved to be Porter with orders from Lincoln giving him command of the *Powhatan* and instructing Foote that "under no circumstances" was he to "communicate to the Navy Department the fact that" the *Powhatan* was "fitting out." Because Welles had already ordered the *Powhatan* fitted out, Foote was puzzled by such an unusual order delivered by a man he did not trust. Porter had been hobnobbing with southern naval officers in Washington. For a few days, Foote obeyed the new order, while Fox and Welles were unaware that the *Powhatan* had been detached from the Sumter expedition.[21]

Foote was a boyhood schoolmate of Welles's, and he tried to let Welles know that something was going on. On 4 April he wrote that in obedience to "government" orders not directly from the Navy Department he was cooperating with Meigs in fitting out an expedition, and the next day he telegraphed that he hoped the *Powhatan* would sail that evening. At that point, Welles realized that something was seriously amiss. Vague references to government orders bypassing the Navy Department were troubling, but the planned departure of the *Powhatan* that evening was alarming. He had only that day ordered Samuel Mercer, *his* captain of the *Powhatan,* to command the naval force of the *Powhatan, Pawnee, Pocahontas,* and *Harriet Lane* in support of Fox's expedition. Welles telegraphed Foote to hold the *Powhatan* until further orders, and Porter and Meigs telegraphed Seward for clarification.[22]

Seward went to Welles, who became infuriated upon learning of Seward's meddling. By midnight, they were before the president, who forced Seward to order Porter to restore the *Powhatan* to Mercer and Fox's Sumter expedition. With a stroke of malevolent genius, Seward signed his own name (instead of Lincoln's) to the slow telegram he sent. By the time it arrived the next day at 3:00 p.m., Porter had sailed in the *Powhatan*, and, even worse for Fox, Mercer did not relay his orders to the next senior officer of the Sumter expedition. A messenger with Seward's telegram to Porter overtook the *Powhatan* before the Narrows, but Porter, with Lincoln's name on his original order, rejected the clarification he had requested from Seward and claimed it was "too late to change his plans." He stubbornly remained on course for Pensacola, where it turned out the *Powhatan* was not needed. Incredible as it seems, Fox, who had arrived back in New York on the evening of 5 April, did not know of Seward's machinations nor would he hear, until 13 April, that the *Powhatan* had been detached from his expedition.[23]

Fox divided his three days in New York between his wife and his expedition. By day, he energetically carried out his authorization by the War Department to purchase provisions and to charter tugs and his old ship the *Baltic*. In the evenings, he tried to cheer Virginia with "amusing anecdotes" of Lincoln's cabinet and with the delightful word that Lincoln planned to appoint him assistant secretary of the navy at $3,500 a year, if Congress would create the office. Fearful her "feelings would overpower" her, Virginia wept so much she "could scarcely speak to G[us] alone." In contrast, Fox was bursting with happiness. His expedition was about to sail. Besides provisions, the *Baltic* took on 200 raw recruits and sixteen boats to deliver them at Sumter. At 7:00 p.m. on 8 April, Fox boarded the *Baltic* as it passed through the Narrows, and the expedition was underway.[24]

Missing the evening tide, the *Baltic* was forced to anchor inside Sandy Hook. There, Fox pondered his last frustrating weeks and his next perilous days. "You can form no idea," he wrote Montgomery Blair, "of the trouble and heart sick obstacles which have met us from the limited time allowed. To Wm. H. Aspinwall and Russell Sturgis, I am deeply indebted for assistance." To Virginia, Fox justified his course:

> I feel deeply dearest wife the pain I cause you, but nevertheless I cannot shrink
> from a solemn duty, which, if successful is pregnant with great results for our

beloved country. I am afraid we are too late, from no fault of mine, but I pray earnestly that I may be permitted to do something for a country dear to me above all others. There is no personal peril to those whom God selects to act a prominent part. I feel none, *not the least.* I confide completely in His great arm and the faithful prayers of a dear wife. . . . Now do not brood. . . . What a picture of happiness God has framed for us "together" in the past. *It will continue* if we confide in Him. I feel my mother's sublime faith, that we have but to perform our *duty*, leaving the mysterious results to be worked out in his appointed time.

Having invoked duty, country, God, and mother, Fox said "farewell." Always self-confident, he assured Virginia he would be back shortly.[25]

Despite Fox's careful planning, almost everything went wrong. "Constant steady bad weather and heavy sea" plagued the expedition. The *Baltic* got underway the morning of 9 April, reached the rendezvous off Charleston at 3:00 a.m. on 12 April, and found only the *Harriet Lane.* The diverted *Powhatan* would never arrive, the *Pocahontas* was seriously delayed, and gales prevented the *Yankee* and the *Uncle Ben*, the tugs en route, from arriving. The third tug, the *Freeborn*, never left New York. Fox would have to use the *Baltic*'s longboats to run supplies to Sumter. By 6:00 a.m., the *Pawnee* arrived, but when Fox asked it to accompany the *Baltic* to the harbor entrance, while he landed provisions, its commander Stephen C. Rowan refused. His orders were to report to Mercer of the *Powhatan*, and he was "very averse to doing anything to commence a war."[26]

Undaunted by Rowan's refusal, Fox headed in with the *Harriet Lane* (under Captain John Faunce) as an escort and discovered Sumter was under fire (it had been since 4:30 a.m.) and that "Major Anderson was replying gallantly." War having commenced, Rowan was eager to cooperate. The heavy seas moderated a little, and Fox wanted to "attempt a couple of boats" that night, 12 April. Short of hands, having only one armed launch, and hoping for reinforcements, the naval officers overruled him, promising him they would defy the batteries and escort him in the next morning. While the *Pawnee* and the *Harriet Lane* remained in close, Fox and the *Baltic* returned to the rendezvous point and "made signals all night," looking without success for the *Powhatan* and the *Pocahontas.*[27]

By the morning of 13 April, weather conditions had worsened. The waves were so high that the *Baltic* had to anchor four miles outside of the *Pawnee* and *Harriet Lane*, and it was too rough for the longboats to land reinforcements. At 8:00 a.m., Fox and the senior army officer, Lieutenant Edward Hudson, clambered into a boat and pulled away for the *Pawnee*. As they drew near, Fox was horrified by "black volumes of smoke issuing from Sumpter. The barbarians, to their everlasting disgrace," he anguished, "redoubled their fire, and through the flames and smoke the noble band of true men continued their response." Down to their last resort, Rowan offered Fox a captured ice schooner to carry provisions and men to Sumter. "I accepted it," Fox reported, "and the night of the 13th I should certainly have gone in, and as certainly been knocked to pcs. My tug boats I knew could not have reached Charleston in the weather we had experienced since leaving N. York, and the Powhatan, I now learned, by a note from Capt. Mercer to Capt. Rowan . . . was 'detached from duty off Charleston.'" After months of planning and weeks of activity to secure an adequate naval force to relieve Sumter, Fox was reduced to committing suicide in an unarmed sailing vessel.[28]

The suicide did not come off. Sumter surrendered at about 2:00 p.m., 13 April (when the *Pocahontas* arrived), and instead of dying in a valiant attempt to succor the beleaguered garrison, Fox transported Anderson and his men back to New York. On the way, Fox assuaged some of Anderson's anger and frustration. He thought Fox should have told him more during his 21 March visit to Sumter and was bitter about the government's neglect of him and his command. Fox explained that Lincoln, while committed to uphold federal authority, had made certain that if war came, the South would fire the first shot and that it would be aimed at provisions, not reinforcements. Fully aware of Lincoln's intent, Fox had prepared a note to be delivered to Governor Pickens with the first boatload of provisions. It emphasized: "If your batteries open fire it will be upon an unarmed boat, and unarmed men performing an act of duty and humanity." Fox (who was at sea and had no idea how the North had reacted to the attack on Sumter) assured Anderson "how anxious the Prest was that they (S.C.) should stand before the civilized world as having fired upon bread. . . . I also explained," Fox reported to Blair, "the reasons for holding the fort, far superior to any military ones, and told the Major that I thought the Govt would feel particularly gratified at the result."[29]

Lincoln was neither a Machiavellian genius who manipulated the Confederates into starting the Civil War nor a bumbling neophyte pushed by events beyond his control. Both consistent and flexible, he was determined to uphold the Union. To preserve it, he explored various means short of war. He toyed with the idea of giving up Sumter while reinforcing Pickens, near less volatile Pensacola. But as the possibility of a peaceful restoration of the Union grew dim, Lincoln made certain that federal forces would not fire the first shot and that, if the South attacked the Fox expedition, it would shoot at a humane mission bringing bread to a hungry garrison. Lincoln had remained consistent to his plea to secessionists in his inaugural address: "In *your* hands, my dissatisfied fellow countrymen, and not in *mine,* is the momentous issue of civil war."

Because Anderson was fatigued and overwrought, Fox composed for him his stirring one-sentence report which began: "Having defended Fort Sumter for thirty-four hours, until the quarters were entirely burned, the main gates destroyed by fire, the gorge walls seriously injured, the magazine surrounded by flames, and its door closed from the effects of heat, four barrels and three cartridges of powder only being available, and no provisions remaining but pork, I accepted terms of evacuation offered by General Beauregard."[30]

The siege of Fort Sumter profoundly affected Fox and, through him, the Union navy. Fox believed that the bombardment demonstrated that Scott's aide George Washington Cullum (an engineer with firsthand knowledge of Sumter) was wrong in thinking that its thick walls had rendered it impregnable and that while under fire it could not be reinforced. "Had the Powhatan arrived the 12th," Fox insisted, "we should have had the men and provisions into Fort Sumpter, as I had everything ready, boats, muffled oars, small packages of provisions, in fact everything but the 300 sailors promised to me by the [Navy] dept. A tug would have accomplished it, but with more risk alongside of the Fort. Capt. Foster the Eng[ineer] of Fort Sumpter says we would have got in and so does Hartstein [Hartstene] of their navy."[31]

After thirty-four hours of bombardment by thirty-three guns and seventeen mortars, "impregnable" Sumter was a burning shambles. Successfully provisioning the fort, Fox believed, would have delayed surrender only a few days. "These facts," Fox thought, "will make a stir, for not one was ever presented in all the discussion we had." His Sumter experience taught him that the shot and shells of modern ordnance could destroy a fort. That experience confirmed his conviction that naval forces could run by forts and, with their mobile-gun platforms, reduce them. His Sumter experience also left him obsessed with capturing Charleston to avenge his personal humiliation.[32]

Fox's anger and frustration over the detachment of the *Powhatan* were monumental. He soon discovered that it was Seward who, as Fox put it, "interfered with the other depts as the last hope of preventing the reinforcing of Sumpter. And it did prevent it, and I had the mortification of witnessing the surrender of the Fort with no part of my proposed plan arrived, in fact deprived by treachery of all power of accomplishing it, and losing reputation with the general public for the failure because I cannot state the facts at this crisis ... without injury to the Govt." The thought of "that timid traitor W. H. Seward

... who paralyzes every movement from abject fear" made Fox apoplectic. "His bitterest enemy," Virginia Fox cried, "could not have played him a baser trick." Fox felt all the more humiliated because the Confederates and the news dispatches had assumed that vessels hovering off the bar outside Charleston's harbor were part of a 9,000-man expedition, leading people to wonder how it could have failed. In reality, Fox had only 200 raw recruits in a chartered steamer supported by two undermanned naval vessels.[33]

It mattered less what other people thought when Lincoln wrote:

I sincerely regret that the failure of the late attempt to provision Fort Sumpter should be the source of any annoyance to you. The practicability of your plan was not, in fact, brought to a test. By reason of a gale, well known in advance to be possible, and not improbable, the tugs, an essential part of the plan, never reached the ground; while, by an accident, for which you were in no wise responsible, and possibly I to some extent was, you were deprived of a war vessel, with her men, which you deemed of great importance to the enterprize.

I most cheerfully and truly declare that the failure of the undertaking has not lowered you a particle, while the qualities you developed in the effort have greatly heightened you in my estimation. For a daring and dangerous enterprize, of a similar character you would to-day be the man, of all my acquaintances, whom I would select.

You and I both anticipated that the cause of the country would be advanced by making the attempt to provision Fort Sumpter, even if it should fail; and it is no small consolation now to feel that our anticipation is justified by the result.[34]

CHAPTER SEVEN

Ships for the Blockade

> I understand that there is some opposition to the appointment
> of Capt. G. V. Fox to the clerkship we talked of. My wish, and
> advice is, that you do not allow any ordinary obstacle prevent his
> appointment. He is a live man, whose services we cannot well
> dispense with. *Lincoln to Welles, 8 May 1861*

Responding to the attack on Sumter, Lincoln called up 75,000 militia on 15
April 1861 to suppress "combinations" obstructing the laws of the United
States. Four days later, he proclaimed a blockade of the insurrectionary states.
An effective blockade would prevent the Confederacy from importing arms
and other manufactured goods and paying for them with cotton exports. To
make the blockade a reality, from Chesapeake Bay to the Rio Grande, required
bases on that enormous coastline and the addition of hundreds of armed, fast
steamships to the forty-two steam and sailing ships in the Union navy. Establishing and tightening the blockade were the navy's primary tasks, and breaking the blockade was a major Confederate objective. To help Secretary of the
Navy Gideon Welles make the blockade a reality, Lincoln insisted that Fox be
in the Navy Department.[1]

■ ■ ■

On 18 April Fox rejoined an "unnerved" Virginia at Tubby Hook. Although
mortified by abuse in the press, Fox remained calm, said little, and insisted
neither Virginia nor her family tell anyone of "the treachery," lest it be known
how badly the Lincoln administration had bungled the Fort Sumter expedition. Unable to bear the stinging criticism directed at her husband for its failure, Virginia hoped Fox would "give up *public life.*" But a few days later, when
he asked her whether he should take command of a "new *Pacific Steamer*" at
$4,000 or $5,000 a year or take the assistant secretary of the navy post Lincoln
had promised him at $3,500, she said she "would rather live on $500 a year
. . . than have him go to sea."[2]

Fox attended to family matters, while awaiting his summons to Washing ton. He persuaded his nephew Charlie Guild to postpone enlisting until he could check out things for him in the navy. He saw Virginia's physician Dr. Sims, who said she "could come anytime for her treatment." Although Virginia told Fox she would not go to Sims without him and that she "should go mad" if he went to Washington (which was poorly defended and somewhat isolated for a week following the 19 April Baltimore riots), he left Tubby Hook on 25 April to see Lincoln. On his way, Fox stopped in New York City, saw Aspinwall, who, with $5,000 from William B. Astor, had just hired the side-wheel tugboat *Yankee* (one of the tugs from Fox's expedition), had it armed with two thirty-two-pound guns, and wanted Fox to take it to Annapolis. Because it was on the way to Washington, Fox agreed. He was appointed an acting lieutenant by Samuel L. Breese, commandant of the New York Navy Yard, who ordered him to Fort Monroe and Annapolis to convoy ships with provisions and troops for Washington. Fox hoped to destroy the two privateers reported to be cruising in Chesapeake Bay. He returned to Tubby Hook that evening, practiced with a pistol, and on 26 April left New York with the *Yankee*.[3]

After an uneventful trip, the *Yankee* reached Annapolis on 29 April, the same day the Maryland House of Delegates rejected secession. Massachusetts troops, Fox proudly reported, commanded by his "old schoolmate" Benjamin F. Butler, had communications open to the capital. That evening, by a special train provided by Butler, Fox arrived at the Washington home of Montgomery and Minna Blair. "We were all charmed to see Fox," Nell told her mother, "& Blair literally hugged him," but she was exasperated to have heard from her mother that Virginia was "depressed" over Fox's treatment. The "governing power here," Nell responded, "appreciate Fox's services & award him all credit," and, annoyed with Virginia, quoted Macbeth, "I can 'not minister to a mind diseased.'" Blair confirmed Fox's suspicion that Seward was the culprit who had diverted the *Powhatan*. Fox was assuaged, however, after seeing Lincoln and receiving his handsome letter.[4]

Lincoln had intended Fox to be assistant secretary of the navy, but because that post had not yet been created, he suggested that Fox take a command at sea. Believing that "the naval war will be only one of blockade," Blair convinced Lincoln that Fox's expertise and energy were needed in the Navy Department. Welles balked at appointing Fox as chief clerk (the highest subordinate position in the department). He had already promised William Faxon, his trusted associate from the *Hartford Press*, that he would be his chief clerk, starting on 8 May. That very day Fox handed Welles a note from Lincoln stat-

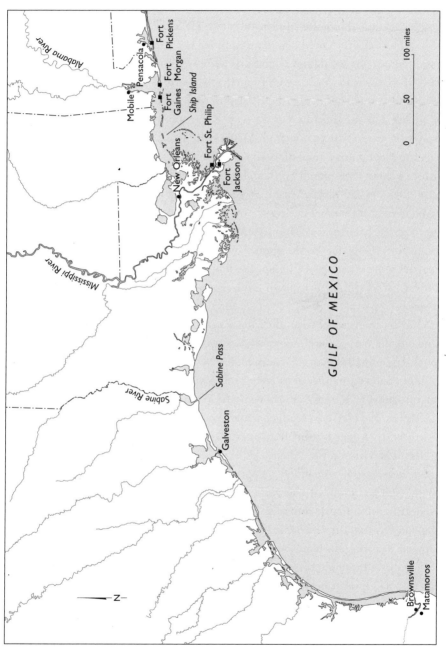

New Orleans and the Gulf Coast. Map by Bill Nelson.

ing he wanted Fox appointed to the Navy Department, because he was a "live man," whose services they needed. After spending the rest of the day with Fox, Welles realized that Lincoln was right and appointed him chief clerk at $2,200 a year. Both Fox and Faxon were mollified by assurances that in July Congress would create, and Fox would fill, the office of assistant secretary of the navy. Impressed by the magnitude of the task before him, Fox went to work the next morning, abandoning plans to accompany Nell to New York.[5]

Fox was superbly equipped for his Navy Department tasks. He had years of naval experience, had served in the Coast Survey, and had skippered sophisticated steam vessels. He was connected to the powerful Blair family, and Lincoln quickly grew fond of him. Lincoln respected him professionally, consulted with him frequently, and relied on his judgment. Political connections and friendships with line officers enabled Fox to mediate between politicians and sailors. He could explain political imperatives to naval officers and naval strengths—and limitations—to politicians. In addition, personal characteristics qualified him for his position. Powerfully built, he had boundless energy and enthusiasm for the Union, for the navy, and for the ships, guns, and men in whom he had placed his faith. Like Lincoln, Fox was a superb raconteur, and, like Lincoln, he knew when to tell a story. Fox was self-confident and unafraid to make decisions, but he did not rely solely on his own experience. In maturing his Fort Sumter plans, for example, he worked with George W. Blunt, whose knowledge of Charleston's harbor was unparalleled. Usually, Fox's enthusiasms were for the plans and designs of those in whose genius he placed his faith. On the whole, his enthusiasms served the Union well and his diligence, abetted by Welles's judgment and strength, infused new life into the Navy Department.

Before the war, naval officers contemptuously dismissed the Navy Department as "the most rickety and stupid of all" government offices. Its staff of seventy-four sticklers for "forms and red tape" worked a six-hour day, from 9:00 a.m. to 3:00 p.m. Faced with a Herculean task, Welles on 20 May 1861 extended the hours to 4:00 p.m., barred unofficial visitors and unexcused absences, and forced "behindhand" clerks to work after hours, until their daily tasks were completed. Nevertheless, Fox observed "that a private concern would be ruined by conducting business as it is carried on here." Twenty additional clerks soon augmented the staff. In contrast to the clerks, Fox worked until ten o'clock most evenings. Charles Henry Davis, superintendent of the Naval Almanac, who on occasion helped Fox with his enormous correspondence, noted, "He has a gigantic capacity for work . . . and makes all difficulties yield before him."[6]

Fox provided Welles with professional knowledge of nautical matters. In the absence of a chief of naval operations, Fox filled that role, first as chief clerk and after 1 August 1861 as assistant secretary of the navy. Faxon, who became chief clerk after Fox's promotion, handled routine administrative matters, while Fox planned and coordinated naval movements. As Fox later observed to Welles, "When Faxon and I were together there were really two Ass't Sec'ys. a civil and a naval one."[7]

Fox's role as a coordinator was crucial. The Navy Department had been organized in 1842 into five bureaus, whose heads—usually naval officers—were appointed by the president and confirmed by the Senate and were undisturbed by the spoils system. Presidential appointment and secure tenure gave bureau heads independence, even though they served under the secretary of the navy. When Fox took office, the chief of Navy Yards and Docks since 1846 was the venerable Captain Joseph Smith, under whom Fox served as a young midshipman in the receiving ship *Columbus*. John Lenthall, a professional naval architect, had headed Construction, Equipment, and Repair since 1853; and, since 1854, Horatio Bridge had been in charge of Provisions and Clothing. Dr. William Whelan headed Medicine and Surgery; and Andrew A. Harwood had just taken over the Bureau of Ordinance and Hydrography, whose chief and principal clerks had resigned to join the Confederacy. In addition to these regular bureau heads, Welles created a Bureau of Detail to advise him on personnel and appointed Captain Hiram Paulding to head that post. According to Charles Henry Davis, Fox found the new bureau "rather an incumbrance than a convenience" and preferred "to answer most of the applications himself."[8]

Prior to Fox's arrival, Welles had responded energetically to the crisis. He had ordered home all but three of the thirty vessels on foreign stations and, while hoping to save the Norfolk Navy Yard, following Virginia's secession, ordered its destruction if necessary. Although the yard was not threatened, naval officers, exercising what John Niven calls "bad judgment and faulty execution," burned nine vessels on 20 April. These included the *Plymouth* and *Dolphin*, on which Fox had served, and the powerful steam frigate *Merrimack*, which two days earlier had been reported ready for sea. Worse, these nervous naval officers destroyed only part of the navy yard and none of its ordnance. Its more than 1,000 heavy guns would supply Confederate batteries, and its dry dock and other facilities were sufficiently intact for the Confederates to refloat the *Merrimack* on 30 May. To replace vessels lost at Norfolk and add to the Home Squadron (which at full strength numbered only twelve ships), Welles on 21 April ordered each commandant at the Philadelphia, New York, and Boston navy yards to procure for blockade duty "five staunch steamers" capable

of carrying a nine-inch pivot gun. On 22 April Welles authorized the organization of a "flying flotilla" of small vessels for service in Chesapeake Bay and its
tributaries. Fearing the secession of Maryland, he approved embarking the
corps of midshipmen at Annapolis on the *Constitution* on 24 April and removing the Naval Academy to Newport, Rhode Island, where it remained until the
war's end.[9]

When Fox joined the department, naval operations and the acquisition of
new vessels became his chief responsibilities. A week earlier, Winfield Scott,
loath to invade the South in the summer on dry land with ninety-day volunteers, suggested his long-range Anaconda Plan to sever and crush the Confederacy with a naval blockade and joint army-navy operations down the
Mississippi. Conceiving this, essentially naval, grand strategy was easier than
executing it. Gunboats had to be built for river operations, and good ships and
proper bases were needed for the blockade. With the owner of every rotten
ship eager to sell it to the government for an exorbitant price, vigilance was
needed to acquire blockaders that were light-draft, fast, and seaworthy. Joint
expeditions had to be planned to control the Mississippi and to secure good
harbors as bases for blockaders. These harbors had to be close to blockaded
ports but not vulnerable to Confederate attack.[10]

To plan a viable blockade, Fox consulted with the head of the Coast Survey,
Alexander Dallas Bache. He suggested, and Fox agreed, that a Blockade Board
should be constituted to "condense all the vast information in the [Army] Engineers Department, Coast Survey, and Navy, for the use of the blockading
squadron," but Welles did not constitute such a board until 20 June. Before the
Blockade Board got underway, Welles and Fox sought advice from experts at
hand. On 29 May Welles required that the Navy Department bureau chiefs
have a board meeting every Monday morning at ten to advise on specific questions and to make general suggestions. Not waiting until Monday, the bureau
chiefs met on Friday and recommended that twenty-five gunboats be built
immediately, that fifty whaleboats be purchased to enable boarding parties
from blockaders to inspect stopped vessels, and that construction be commenced on the remaining three of the seven steam-screw sloops of war authorized by Congress.[11]

The bureau chiefs had confirmed what Welles and Fox had already decided.
On 24 May Fox spoke of plans to build fifty new gunboats. By a stroke of luck,
the navy's engineer in chief, Benjamin Franklin Isherwood, had recently designed engines for two Russian gunboats. The Navy Department adopted his
detailed drawings of the vessels and their machinery. On 28 May Fox wrote
Virginia, who was at her family's home in Portsmouth, that her sister Nell

could "announce officially" that two of the sloops of war would be built at the navy yard there and that she should come up with two "euphonious Indian names for them." Indian place-names were another of Fox's enthusiasms, and it became the "settled policy of the Department to name its vessels from this inimitable vocabulary." The Navy Department turned down "Laconia" as "foreign" but adopted Virginia's suggestion of "Kearsarge." By early June, U.S. navy yards were constructing all seven sloops of war, and in July the Navy Department contracted with private shipyards for the construction of twenty-three small light-draft "ninety day gunboats." The building of these well-planned vessels gave Fox little trouble. Lenthall's Bureau of Construction, of which Isherwood was a part, and navy yard personnel knew what they were about and, when gunboats were built privately, experienced naval officers supervised their construction. Fox, for example, could rely on Commodore Francis H. Gregory in New York, who showed "great zeal," adding to the efficiency and hastening the completion of the ninety-day gunboats. When the first of these were launched in New York and in Brooklyn a month ahead of schedule, Captain Samuel Francis Du Pont of the Blockade Board declared "that nothing has yet been built in the English or French navy to compare with them."[12]

Although Fox had plunged into his enormous task of coordinating naval operations, his restless nature and energy occasionally tempted him to stray from his Navy Department desk. Before the dawn of 24 May, he accompanied the *Pawnee*, commanded by Rowan, as it left the Washington Navy Yard for Alexandria, Virginia. Besides sailors, this amphibious expedition included New York Zouaves (famous for their gaudy uniforms and intricate drill) under the dashing Colonel Elmer E. Ellsworth. Fox's presence "was exceedingly acceptable" and, as John A. Dahlgren, commandant of the Navy Yard, observed, "had an excellent effect in impressing all concerned with a sense of the importance which the Department felt in the operation." Meeting scant resistance, the Union forces occupied the town. After impulsively hauling down the Confederate flag from a local hotel, Ellsworth was killed by its proprietor, who, in turn, was killed by one of the Zouaves. Both the North and the South had their first martyrs. Fox accompanied the body of Ellsworth, who was Lincoln's personal friend, back to Washington, where it lay in state in the White House.[13]

When Virginia learned that Fox had accompanied Ellsworth to and from Alexandria, her anxiety increased. As Fox worked at the department each evening, concern for his wife's health was on his mind. It is plausible that he coped with her infirmities by working hard, that he compensated for his sexual frustration and assuaged his guilt for not being at her side by energetic attention to duty. It is also possible that without Virginia's real or imagined sicknesses, his devotion to the navy would have been at a more normal and less effective level. Apparently, he never questioned the reality of his wife's afflictions and her distress. After Dr. Sims examined Virginia in New York on 16 May and pronounced her well, despite her "nausea & sickness," Fox thought him no help. "I shall not let you go near the Dr.," he declared. To soothe Virginia, he predicted, "You will be *happy* and look on the sunshine and not on the clouds" and promised her, "you shall have your own way in everything *always*." Even though for long periods Virginia did not leave her couch, she brought strengths to the marriage. She was intelligent, well read, and a wonderful conversationalist. In these virtues Fox found support, and he needed her. "How I wish you were here," he wrote in late spring, but Virginia, avoiding the heat of Washington, spent the summer in Portsmouth.[14]

Much of Fox's feverish activity in May and June was connected with instituting the blockade. Charles H. Marshall, who had refused in April to help Fox provision his Fort Sumter expedition, complained to him in May that only the Chesapeake was efficiently blockaded. Another New Yorker, Fox's friend Alfred Crea, protested "the extraordinary and disheartening delays of the Navy Department," which "undoubtedly" would result in mass meetings denouncing the competence of Welles and Fox. Crea relayed the rumor that the *Wabash* had delayed its departure for a week "to replace an incompetent Gunner! The next excuse may be the want of tooth picks!" Responding in haste, Fox challenged him, "Come on and take my place for a week and you will feel better."[15]

Despite the anxiety of Marshall and Crea, the Navy Department had not been idle. As of 30 April, the *Cumberland* was blockading Norfolk, Virginia, and the mouth of the James River; on 10 May, the *Niagara* began blockading Charleston, South Carolina; sixteen days later, the *Brooklyn* blockaded New Orleans and the *Powhatan* (still under Porter's command) blockaded Mobile, Alabama. Two days later, the *Union* initiated the blockade of Savannah, Georgia. These vessels, however, did not necessarily remain stationed off these ports. Three days after the *Powhatan* blockaded Mobile, it captured a schooner near the Southwest Pass of the Mississippi River. The *Niagara* moved from Charleston to the Gulf, where it captured a schooner off Mobile. The *Union* took prizes off North Carolina and Charleston, as well as off Savannah. The Navy Department moved its few vessels about to achieve a semblance of a blockade, but Marshall and Crea were essentially right. Apart from Hampton Roads, the blockade was not yet effective.[16]

Confederate commerce destroyers and privateers, as well as merchant vessels, eluded the blockade. Initially, Fox had to protect commerce from privateers. Immediately following the attack on Fort Sumter and before any privateers existed—a host of shipowners, merchants, bankers, and insurance company executives pressed the Lincoln administration to arm and protect California mail steamers (which carried $40 million in gold to New York annually) from anticipated attacks by privateers. Welles pledged that the navy would do all in its power to protect commerce and ordered the capture of any privateer. The Confederacy authorized privateering, on 6 May 1861, and also decided to raid Union commerce with Confederate government vessels, either fitted out at home or acquired abroad.[17]

Apparently, only twenty Confederate privateers put to sea (mostly in 1861), and their success was limited even before the blockade was effective. The most disruptive cruise was that of the brig *Jefferson Davis*, formerly a slaver, which slipped out of Charleston on 28 June 1861. Under the command of Louis M. Coxetter, it began the last classic privateering cruise in history. It took nine sailing vessels, terrorized the coast as far north as Nantucket, Massachusetts, and forced Fox to order the *Iroquois* and four other vessels to find and destroy it. They failed, but the *Davis* was a losing proposition even before it was wrecked, on 18 August 1861, while entering St. Augustine, Florida. Only two of its prizes made it to port and brought a return. It released three prizes with prisoners and burned one prize, and another was burned when it ran aground running the blockade. When still another prize, the *Enchantress*, was recaptured by blockaders, a New York court nearly hanged its prize crew as pirates. The pirate issue first arose following the capture, off Charleston on 3 June 1861, of the privateer *Savannah*. Given the certainty of reprisals, the Lincoln administration decided on 3 February 1862 to regard the crew of privateers as prisoners of war.[18]

The *Davis*'s most memorable, and temporary, prize was the schooner *S. J. Waring*. Its black cook, William Tilghman, fearful that his capture by the *Davis* would result in enslavement, took an axe and killed three members of the prize crew, retook the vessel off Charleston, and brought it into New York six days later. With such a showing, Coxetter could not interest investors in further privateering ventures. By late 1861 privateers had ceased to be a problem for Fox. The increasing efficiency of the blockade made it virtually impossible for privateers to send prizes to friendly ports. Confederate investors turned to far more lucrative blockade-running steamers. Always fast, usually small, and mostly of British registry, these vessels carried war matériel and other items from Bermuda and the Bahamas to southern ports in exchange for cotton.[19]

The Confederate government was more interested in disrupting Union commerce than in prize money. Its navy secretary Stephen R. Mallory, on 14 June 1861, ordered Commander Raphael Semmes, who at New Orleans had readied the CSS *Sumter* (a converted merchantman) to "do the enemy's commerce the greatest injury in the shortest time." After eluding the blockade on 30 June, the *Sumter* arrived at Cienfuegos, Cuba, on 6 July. With it were seven prizes, which Semmes hoped to leave there until they were adjudicated by a Confederate admiralty court. Consistent with the rule (first proclaimed by Britain on 1 June and later adopted by other neutral nations) excluding prizes from their ports, the captain general of Cuba restored the vessels to their owners.[20]

Although Semmes managed to send a couple of prizes back to New Orleans, he could not spare men for prize crews and feared the prizes would not get through the Union blockade. His only option was to destroy his captures, excepting Union vessels with neutral cargoes, which he ransomed. Midshipman Alfred Thayer Mahan suggested to Fox that a sailing vessel with a masked pivot gun and a crew of a hundred could lure the *Sumter* close enough to board or sink and volunteered "to lead the enterprise." Semmes arrived at Gibraltar in January 1862, where, in April, he abandoned the *Sumter* with its leaking boilers and rotting hull. It was patched up, renamed the *Gibraltar*, and under British colors ran the blockade into Wilmington, North Carolina, at least once in 1863.[21]

The vessels that Confederate commerce destroyers and privateers took had virtually no effect on the Union war effort. The alarm they provoked in Union shipping circles was their contribution to the Confederate cause. That alarm forced Fox to divert ships from the blockade. The *Vincennes, Iroquois, Pembroke, Marion, Dale,* and two revenue cutters tried to find the *Jeff Davis* off the New England coast. On board the *Sumter,* Semmes was delighted to learn from 21 November 1861 newspapers, taken before he burned the ship *Vigilant* of Bath, Maine, that the *Powhatan,* the *Niagara,* the *Iroquois,* the *Keystone State,* and the *San Jacinto* were all searching for him. After he arrived at Gibraltar, the *Kearsarge, Tuscarora,* and *Ino* were off that harbor, awaiting the *Sumter*'s departure prior to its abandonment. The *Nashville,* another Confederate cruiser, escaped from Charleston on 26 October 1861, sailed to England, and then, on 28 February 1862, slipped into Beaufort, North Carolina. Even though it burned only a clipper ship and a schooner, the *Nashville* forced

Fox and Welles to divert from the blockade the *Connecticut, James Adger,* and *Curlew.*[22]

The South's most successful commerce destroyers would be built in England, while Union naval vessels were constructed at home. In planning gunboats and sloops of war, Fox was an advocate of beauty as well as power. On 21 February 1862 he gave Benjamin F. Delano, naval constructor at the New York Navy Yard, detailed advice about beautifying the "new fast sloop" he was designing. "I am led to this," Fox explained, "because in every part of the world our merchant ships are the admiration of all sailors, and I cannot understand why we are not able to approach them with our men of war." He thought the Mohican class of steam sloops appeared to have "hollow" sides, and he disliked "her cut water [bow]." Above all, he thought the new side-wheel double-ender gunboat *Miami* "a disgrace . . . in every part of her. She is a great clumsy, ugly, eight knot boat, and . . . looks like a bowl at each end." Fox made suggestions for the new fast sloops. He wanted them to have a "perpendicular stem, very light oval stern of a *regular* curve, sides rounding, not only from the rail to the water, but from the fore to the mizzen chain. . . . I advocate these matters," Fox emphasized, "because I am proud of our Navy and feel a deep interest, and I know how much people go for looks. Luck even gets attached to a beautiful craft, but never to an ugly one." A few months later, Fox asked shipbuilder William Henry Webb to design a 175-foot gunboat and pled, "Give her a clipper look which no man-of-war has."[23]

Looks were important, but Fox stressed "speed is the great desideratum," and steam engines (which so often broke down) were the greatest challenge. He complained that the *Niagara* "goes 10 knots only. The Pawnee was to have gone 16 and goes 8. The Pensacola's engines by [Edward N.] Dickerson cost $328,000 and barely got the ship to New Orleans at the rate of 6 knots but cannot bring her back." To achieve the best hulls and machinery, Fox ordered the navy's constructors to share their expertise and urged private builders to do the same. To Paul S. Forbes, his friend from his Hong Kong days, who planned to build a 300-foot steamer that would make 15 knots, Fox furnished all the information he could. He would do the same "to any respectable outsider asking only reciprocation for the public good," he added. "I have done this because I want you to beat us if you can. . . . I will rejoice and be thankful and give praise to the man who builds the best and fastest ships, and the most successful engines . . . whether he be an insider or outsider." Fox asked Naval Constructor Delano to share his expertise and instruct Forbes about "the solid manner in which our navy ships are built," adding, "I do not wish to see our Constructors beaten, so I would suggest that you get up a vessel of about the same tonnage . . . provided you will agree to beat him in speed." These large fast vessels were slow in construction and too late for the Civil War, but in postwar tests the navy won the race against "outsiders."[24]

Because converted merchant marine vessels were the backbone of the blockade, the department had to be wary lest it be fleeced by unscrupulous shipowners. On 19 April 1861 the navy chartered the *Keystone State* for five weeks, while naval vessels were returning from foreign stations. It was an eight-year-old wooden side-wheel steamer owned by the Ocean Steam Navigation Company of Philadelphia. When it proved to be an effective blockader, Fox wanted to buy it. He estimated that it cost its owners $150,000, and he was willing to pay $125,000 for it, but he called their exorbitant price a "swindle" and "out of the question." Welles on 28 May ordered the *Keystone State* returned to the Ocean Steam Navigation Company, stating that the government would neither purchase nor lease any boat from it in the future. That threat brought the company around. On 10 June, the navy purchased the *Keystone State* for $125,000 and had it fitted out and at sea by 21 July. Its successful career as a cruiser and blockader confirmed Fox's judgment of its worth.[25]

Fox depended on advice from navy yard commandants, especially those at New York, Boston, and Philadelphia. He often had to choose from among conflicting opinions, and he made one of his soundest decisions in his first weeks in office. "There is great pressure," he wrote Du Pont, "to fit out twenty Sloops of war from sailing vessels but I resist and say steam—Am I right?"[26]

An effective blockade required successful diplomacy as much as sound ships. Realizing that British intervention had to be avoided and that Seward would play a crucial role in staving it off, Fox quickly forgot his fury with Seward for interfering with the Sumter expedition. He dined with the charming and "very polite" secretary of state on Friday, 7 June, and reported on Sunday that Seward "sent for me and read his dispatches to me just written to England— also those received." Because these crucial dispatches involved Britain's reaction to the blockade, Seward correctly informed the Navy Department of their contents but informed Fox rather than Welles, probably because Fox was directly involved in implementing the blockade and possibly because he was more forgiving than Welles. The Sewards and Foxes soon enjoyed a dinner as a result of the blockade. Seward invited them to "dine off the tortoise," which had been captured on a blockade runner and sent by Fox to Seward as a gift.[27]

By mid-June, a conciliatory move by Britain and the rapid deployment of blockading vessels encouraged Fox. With the *Keystone State* in mind, he wrote, "We are getting out clear of the grasp of these sharks who have swindled us in ships when our necessities gave us no option. There are 21 vessels in and on the way to the Gulf, 19 on the Atlantic, 10 in the Chesapeake and Potomac and 3 in the W. Indies—and more going, so I think our own ships will do the work now—especially as John Bull is backing down." Britain had followed up its neutrality proclamation of 13 May 1861—which recognized the blockade but regarded the South as a belligerent able to commission privateers and commerce destroyers—with the 1 June proclamation. It closed British ports to the prizes of both the North and the South. Adopted by other nations, this proclamation discouraged Confederate privateers, because it forced their prizes (virtually all of which were slow-sailing vessels) to run the Union blockade of southern ports. After the *Sumter* lost its prizes in Cuba, the Confederate navy resorted to burning the vessels it took on the high seas.[28]

Fox thought the department was getting clear of shipowner "sharks" in mid-June, because it was using George D. Morgan in New York and John Murray Forbes in Boston as purchasing agents. Forbes, who had amassed a fortune in shipping and multiplied it in railroading, was a patriotic and shrewd businessman, who knew merchant vessels and gave his thoughtful advice and valuable services free.[29]

Fox and Welles's main purchasing agent, George D. Morgan, was not as selfless as Forbes. His relations with Welles and the Republican Party provoked questions. Married to the sister of Welles's wife, Morgan was a business partner of Governor Edwin D. Morgan of New York, his cousin who also chaired the Republican National Committee, and their wholesale grocery, banking, and brokerage company handled Welles's investments. "Can you not give me something," Morgan begged Welles on 26 April, a week after Lincoln proclaimed the blockade. "My business is gone & I should like to be employed here by you." Playing upon Welles's prejudices, Morgan insinuated that Moses Hicks Grinnell and Simeon Draper, two lieutenants of Thurlow Weed (who, as Seward's ally, was despised by Welles), profited exorbitantly from sales of ships to the navy, because they controlled Samuel L. Breese, commandant of the New York Navy Yard. Abetted by William H. Aspinwall, Morgan also attacked Samuel M. Pook, the navy's purchasing agent in New York, who was a distinguished naval architect and senior naval constructor at New York. Morgan produced convincing data that, while Pook expertly evaluated the blockading capacity of vessels, he knew nothing of their monetary value.[30]

Shipowners were not the only "sharks" in New York harbor. Commander H. S. Stellwagon, who urged the navy to acquire the screw steamers *Kensington*, *Cambridge*, and *Mercedita* (all roughly 900 to 1,000 tons), warned Fox of an influence-peddling scheme. An agent assured the owner of the *Mercedita*

that the government would buy his vessel if he would split 10 percent of the sales price among four prominent New Yorkers. The *Mercedita*'s owner refused to "swindle the U.S.," but he would not reveal the names of the four notables, the agent, or the government department the agent purportedly represented. By June, Welles's eagerness to stop the navy from being fleeced outbalanced his fear of hostile criticism, and he made Morgan the navy's New York purchasing agent. What Forbes did for nothing in Boston, Morgan did for a handsome 2.5 percent commission in New York, where the volume of purchases were at least ten times that of Boston.[31]

Morgan plunged into his task. Fox's 1861 correspondence beginning in June overflows with Morgan's communications, as well as occasional letters from Forbes, with whom Morgan cooperated. "I have two letters from Mr. Forbes," Morgan reported from New York on 20 June, "in regard to vessels & am to meet him to morrow morning at 9 o'clock at his office in Boston where we shall have a list of the best ships for sale.—I have also been busy here and there are a great number of ships which I can buy on reasonable terms." Despite the navy's demands, a buyer's market for ships prevailed. Northerners owned 98 percent of the American merchant marine, whose tonnage was second only to that of Britain. Many of these vessels were idle, partly because war had destroyed the cotton export trade, partly because their owners feared the depredations of Confederate privateers.[32]

Although Morgan had wide discretion, he checked frequently with Fox. He needed guidance when owners offered unusual vessels, ranging from ferryboats (to be converted into gunboats for rivers and sounds) to the spectacular 4,114-ton Collins liners *Adriatic* at $600,000 and the 2,800-ton *Baltic* and *Atlantic* for $300,000 each. The liners were tempting, but Fox resisted. They cost too much money, drew too much water, and were too old. At Fox's behest, Morgan purchased several tugboats, which when armed with small "guns and howitzers" were useful. "Oh! those blessed ubiquitous tugs," Du Pont later rhapsodized to Fox, "they were your thought, and . . . no estimate can be placed on their value." Fox also preferred steamers at 1,200 tons, but Morgan, insisting "such could not be found," purchased the new 1,725-ton sidewheel steamer *Connecticut* for $200,000 (his most expensive purchase) and the 1,517-ton side-wheeler *Rhode Island* (built in 1860 and rebuilt the next year after it caught fire) for about $185,000. They proved to be effective blockaders and powerful tow boats of underpowered or disabled vessels. Fox remonstrated strenuously when Morgan agreed to purchase the thirteen-year-old New London whaler *Charles Phelps*. Morgan persuaded the department to "accept her," because "she is far superior" to previous purchases and "is cheap" (it was utilized as a coal supply ship at Hampton Roads), but he promised in the future to "let old ships and old steamers alone."[33]

Morgan and Forbes both suggested ways to save time and money. When they met in Boston on 21 June, Morgan called the government penny-wise and pound-foolish for refusing to pay cash for vessels. Earlier Forbes had suggested to Fox that ships be purchased with 6 percent treasury notes, saving the government the discount on the notes. Morgan claimed that shipowners wanted cash and sold the treasury notes they received at a larger discount than bankers, depressing the market value of the treasury notes. The government would be better off, he argued, paying cash borrowed in the open market by regular bids. With the government taking its time to pay, the sellers of the *Connecticut* and *Rhode Island* were annoyed in late July that the value of treasury notes had fallen 2½ to 3 percent since the month-earlier date of sale.[34]

Forbes and Morgan emphatically stated that rigorous inspection by a navy constructor prior to accepting a vessel inflated its cost. Forbes told Fox that he had three to five ships available but warned that the chance of rejection by a public inspector (and the "taint" that would result) would increase their cost by 5 to 10 percent. Morgan chimed in that "few owners will allow the Naval Constructor to bore and examine" their ships for rot, although they would allow a discreet merchant or ship carpenter inspector to bore. Fox agreed to use a mercantile inspector, who proved sufficiently "cautious & prudent" to reject the *Spirit of the Times*, which had been highly thought of by Morgan and Forbes.[35]

The two businessmen sought to avoid inordinate delays at the overworked and inefficient Boston and New York navy yards. They preferred having the local navy agent (a private merchant) coal the vessels they purchased. But upon discovering that the Boston navy agent was "formerly an *alderman* always a mere politician," Forbes did his best to keep vessels out of "*his* clutches for supplies." Because Fox wanted the bottoms of naval vessels coppered and U.S. navy yards were too busy, he authorized Morgan to have the work done at a good private yard.[36]

Morgan and Forbes occasionally were enthusiastic about bargains that were ill-suited for blockading or searching the high seas for privateers. Beautiful sailing ships and large deep-draft steamers were cheap, while the 800-ton, single-deck, fast steamers Fox wanted were scarce and proportionately more expensive. Morgan wanted to buy the 2,000-ton *Ericsson*, but Fox resisted the temptation of a good cheap vessel, whose size limited its usefulness. After finding only one propeller-driven steamer suitable out of ten inspected, Morgan and Pook advocated purchasing twenty barks. These three-masted sailing vessels were "cheaper and nearly as fast as most of the propellers" and could cruise for long periods of time at little expense, but Fox was not interested.[37]

A frugal businessman and a deepwater sailor at heart, Forbes balked at paying a 25 percent advance on the "real value" of "*wide* shoal vessels" that could operate in shallow waters, when magnificent deep-draft ships could be purchased for the same price. Although Fox wanted steamers that, in David Dixon Porter's phrase, could run "on the grass in the dew," he did let Forbes acquire the beautiful, fast, 895-ton, clipper ship *Ino*. In July 1861 the typical Confederate privateer was a schooner or a brig, and Fox used the *Ino* and other armed clippers to protect "our homeward bound vessels from all parts of the world." But when the Confederacy replaced sailing privateers with steam commerce destroyers, the *Ino* become obsolete as a cruiser. Its hard-driving skipper, Josiah Perkins Creesy, who had commanded the legendary clipper ship *Flying Cloud*, proved disobedient and was dismissed within a year.[38]

In general, Morgan and Forbes were vigilant and intelligent buyers who supplied the navy with useful vessels that fell within Fox's parameters. Relying on Morgan and Forbes exclusively saved the government money. Sellers could not play competing agents off against each other, and influence-peddling schemes were frustrated. In Boston, for example, the asking price of vessels temporarily went up 20 to 25 percent when the firm of Glidden & Williams insinuated to owners that for a commission "*their influence* would get the vessels accepted." Fox immediately assured Forbes that east of New York no vessels would be purchased except "through your board. . . . We mean to have you act unfettered" and in secret. By the end of 1861, Morgan had bought eighty-nine vessels for $3.5 million (about $900,000 less than asking prices) and earned $70,000 in commissions. Morgan's lucrative arrangement, while advantageous to the government, left Welles open to insinuations of corruption by Senator John P. Hale of New Hampshire and, in the New York press, by the *Times, Herald,* and *Tribune.* Fox defended Welles and enlisted Blair's support, lest there be a move to oust Welles from the cabinet.[39]

Throughout the war, the blockade was Fox's highest priority, and he worked tirelessly to purchase and build an adequate navy. His demands ruffled feathers and exasperated commanders. On 30 June 1862, after his wife overreacted to his complaints about Fox, Du Pont replied:

> He is impulsive and sensitively alive to the success of his Department—and with our people what else is there that can sustain a man, a political appointee in an office, but *success?* He has been all and all to us this war, nor could he have been this but that Mr. Welles or a man just like him had held the first place—

and all the past administrations of the Navy put together can in no manner compare with this last year in energy, development, and power. I am often fretted by him but in details, very provoking it is true, but these sink when I reflect that we have two hundred ships of war with rifle cannon now on the ocean—when in March '61 we had not one within reach to save the Norfolk Navy Yard.[40]

CHAPTER EIGHT

Implementing the Blockade

The President [has] been told up and down by Mr. Fox, *who is the Secretary* . . . that the blockading squadron cannot keep at sea in the winter without depots for coal.

Du Pont to Sophie Du Pont, 26 July 1861

The Navy Department . . . has a vitality and energy never seen there before.   *Du Pont to Sophie Du Pont, 30 August 1861*

Not only did Fox want the navy to acquire suitable vessels at reasonable prices; he wanted these boats used advantageously. Deploying and supplying blockading vessels required bases. Acquiring those bases necessitated planning, and Fox realized that experts had best do the planning. Implementing plans and organizing expeditions to seize bases successfully, however, depended upon administrative energy, of which Fox had an abundant supply.

■ ■ ■

Although Alexander Dallas Bache of the Coast Survey and Fox suggested in May that a Blockade Strategy Board be constituted, Welles did not think it necessary and preferred to rely on his bureau chiefs and Fox. By 20 June Welles had changed his mind. Not only had Fox reminded him of Bache's proposal, but Francis Preston Blair had told him that "very active" Confederate agents were purchasing English screw steamers to break the blockade. Blair's information had come from John Charles Frémont, who was in England. On 27 June 1861 this carefully chosen board of military and civil-service personnel, consisting of Bache, Major John G. Barnard of the Corps of Engineers, and Captain Samuel Francis Du Pont, its chair, convened in Washington, with Commander Charles Henry Davis as its secretary. Du Pont had blockaded in the Mexican War and was the navy's leading strategist; Davis was an expert oceanographer; Barnard had been the superintending engineer of fortifications at the mouth of the Mississippi and at Mobile, Alabama; and Bache, since 1843, had supervised the study of American coastal waters.[1]

Welles asked the board to select two Atlantic coast ports—one in South Carolina and the other in Georgia or Florida—to serve as coaling stations for blockaders. Du Pont thought the board could complete its work in a week, but Bache, whom Du Pont suspected was trying to enhance the utility and prestige of the Coast Survey, wanted to condense in a "manual" all available information for the blockading squadron.[2] Fox agreed with Bache.

Battling heat and flies, the Blockade Board studied the coast from the Chesapeake Bay to the mouth of the Mississippi. It exceeded Welles's original orders and produced six "memoirs" and four supplementary reports that carefully considered what coastal operations would be necessary to sustain the blockade. Its "Report of Fernandina, Florida, 5 July 1861" suggested that the blockade would be well served by Fernandina's capture; the "Report on Bulls Bay, St. Helena Sound, Port Royal Bay, 13 July 1861" argued that any of those points could serve as a base for the blockade, but feared that Port Royal Sound, although it would make the most desirable base, was too formidable to attack; and the third memoir, "Coast of North Carolina, Its Sounds and Inlets, 16 July 1861," adopted Fox's "idea of war" by recommending that North Carolina's inlets be obstructed by sinking "old vessels laden with ballast." This "stone fleet" obstruction was suggested to Fox by shipping magnate William H. Aspinwall. In these three important reports, the board focused on the blockade but did not conceive that its bases might be used for combined army and navy campaigns against Charleston, Savannah, and the coastal railroad.[3]

Despite its name, the Blockade Strategy Board did not originate strategy. It worked out details and means of implementing the blockade and provided invaluable data for future operations. For example, its fifth memoir, "New Orleans and Its Approaches, Mississippi Sound, 9 Aug. 1861," provided information a fleet could use in attempting its capture, but it shied away from that bold move and recommended that the Mississippi be obstructed. Strategies were left to Fox and Welles.[4]

Members of the Blockade Strategy Board had an ideal vantage point to observe the federal government, especially the Navy Department. Du Pont, who had feared that government machinery could not "expand immediately into the expenditure of some five or six hundred millions and the raising and organizing a half million of men," was surprised when the government did it with "great energy . . . and much less stickling with forms and red tape" than he had expected. He was even more surprised when "the Navy Department, hitherto the most rickety and stupid of all of them," exhibited new energy. Du

Pont ascribed the new vitality to Fox, who overcame reluctance on the part of Lincoln and the cabinet to implement the work of the Blockade Board.[5]

Du Pont and his close friend Charles Henry Davis soon discovered that there was a downside to Fox's energy and enthusiasms. "One of his characteristics is that he prefers planning and projects to execution," Du Pont complained, "so you are always afraid that he is going to propose some change." Davis noted the same trait. "These uncertainties, caprices, or feeble workings (whatever they may be called)—these sudden changes in Fox's mind sometimes cause me serious anxiety. They disturb confidence and lessen security." On the other hand, Davis recognized that Fox "is very, *very* clever, very prompt in the business of the department, and very even-minded." He thought, "it will all come right," despite Fox's tendency to "revel in some brand-new speculation."[6]

In addition to expert advice from the Blockade Board, Fox by July was receiving suggestions from line officers. His unofficial correspondence, which grew enormously, gave the men who were trying to carry out Navy Department strategy an opportunity to suggest how policies could best be effected. These officers had faith in Fox (he was, after all, one of them), and they were more candid and direct in private letters to him than in official reports to Welles. Fox's confidential correspondence with his old colleagues proved a fruitful source of ideas for the Navy Department and provided feedback on how its ships and guns, its tactics and strategies were succeeding or failing. Crucial information was funneled to him, and the knowledge he gained strengthened and confirmed his preeminence in determining naval operations.

Lieutenant David Dixon Porter, who was blockading the Southwest Pass of the Mississippi River with the *Powhatan*, for example, regaled Fox with sound observations and unsound prejudices. Amusing, outspoken, egotistical, prone to malign, and known as "Lying Dave," Porter called Chief Naval Constructor John Lenthall "an incubus" and suggested he was disloyal; claimed Chief Engineer Benjamin F. Isherwood "can't make an engine"; and attacked senior officers, who were getting commands, as "rum sucking," brainless "old foggies." He believed that his seventy-year-old commander, Flag Officer William Mervine of the Gulf Blockading Squadron, was a myth, because he never heard from him, and declared that "this blockade is the greatest farce on earth." With the *Powhatan*'s deep draft limiting its effectiveness, Porter urged Fox to "hurry up your small steamers" and also to support Commander John A. Dahlgren's development of rifled guns, whose range and accuracy far exceeded "old fashioned" smoothbore ordnance. Porter observed that "no ship has any business at sea now without a battery of rifled guns." Porter also gave Fox the bad news that the *Sumter*, commanded by Raphael Semmes, had on 30 June escaped to sea, eluding the *Brooklyn* (which was too far out from the Mississippi's Pass à l'Outre). Typically, Porter lamented that, if he had been listened to, this and other calamities would have been avoided. To Porter's repeated complaint that his promotion to commander was five years overdue, Fox responded, "Take a fort."[7]

While the Blockade Board was meeting, Congress assembled in a special session on the Fourth of July. For personal as well as professional reasons, Fox worked for the election of Montgomery Blair's brother, Francis Preston Blair Jr. of Missouri, as Speaker of the House. If Blair won, he would appoint a House Naval Committee friendly to the Welles-Fox administration of the department and would kill bills attempting to make hastily recruited officers a permanent part of the navy. Fox was also unhappy with the bill drawn up by his friend John Murray Forbes and Richard Henry Dana Jr. (author of *Two Years before the Mast* and an authority on admiralty law). Their bill would create a volunteer navy, paralleling the volunteer army, which was a distinct organization from the regular army. When Blair was not elected Speaker, he decided to join the army and in July 1862 resigned from Congress. In his new position, he became one of the most outstanding political generals to serve in the war. Even without Blair as Speaker of the House, the Navy Department did well. Neither the Forbes-Dana bill nor any bill to integrate volunteer officers on the navy list passed Congress. On 24 July Congress authorized the temporary increase of the navy (approving what the Lincoln administration had been doing since April). Under this law, the navy throughout the war appointed "acting officers," and the seniority of career naval officers was not jeopardized.[8]

On that same July day, the bill creating the office of assistant secretary of the navy passed Congress. That evening Lincoln assured Fox he would be nominated to this position, which had been created for him. The salary—equal to the sea pay of a captain, or about $4,325—gratified Fox, especially because assistant secretaries in other departments earned $3,000. "You see the importance of my having remained here as Ch. Clk.," Fox gloated to Virginia, recalling that his decision to accept it had left her "terribly dejected." Plagued by ill health, she missed her "dear, dear Gus" intensely "at *all* times but especially *Sundays*," longed to be back in "our dear Lawrence *home*, where we were so happy *in each other*," and worried that Fox might be seduced by the temptations of a wartime capital. "I hope —— will be ordered off," she told Fox. "I don't believe him to be a very *desirable* companion for any one—*is he* dear Gus?" Quoting 1 Cor. 15:33, "Evil communications corrupt good manners," Virginia added, "but my dear H[usband]'s are I hope & believe incorruptible!"[9]

On Sunday, 21 July, the Union army suffered a sharp defeat at Bull Run in Virginia. Although Fox postponed a long-planned visit to navy yards culminating at Portsmouth, he assured Virginia on Monday that "all is pretty quiet. . . . We commence again and rely upon our cause and our God." By Tuesday, Fox was more apprehensive. The army appeared demoralized, and Washington appeared vulnerable to an attack, which he feared might come that evening. Word reached Fox that, with artillerists in short supply, General Joseph K. F. Mansfield wanted some naval officers to help defend the Virginia forts guarding the approaches to Washington. With his usual enthusiasm, Fox asked available officers to go, but relied on the discretion of Du Pont, at whose place they rendezvoused. Du Pont (and others) did not want "to go and interfere with the [army] officers in the forts at a mere suggestion of the chief clerk." As Du Pont confided to his wife, "I felt that if my services were wanted I was entitled to some official request . . . from General Mansfield or General Scott, through the Secretary of the Navy." Although it was 11:00 p.m., Du Pont, not wishing to obey yet unwilling to disobey what might be construed as an order, decided to remain at the ready and immediately go to the forts if three guns—the signal if Washington were attacked—sounded.[10]

There was no attack, but if there had been the naval officers could not have gotten to Virginia in time. This concern over protocol in an emergency and the rank-conscious thinking of Du Pont and fellow officers illustrate how necessary Fox's appointment as assistant secretary of the navy was. Without the title, Fox was a forty-year-old civilian, who, when in service, had been junior to every major naval commander in the Civil War.

On Wednesday, 24 July, Fox reported to Virginia that, while there was still danger, "Jeff Davis has not yet captured us." By the next day, he assured her that the southern army, or part of it, fled "in as great a panic as our people." Identifying with the helplessness of the afflicted and hearing unfounded rumors of Confederates "murdering . . . our wounded on the field & *in the hospital*," Virginia added her concerns for them, to those for herself. On learning that Dr. Sims had sailed to Europe, she hoped "his health will be benefitted & that he will learn something in his *specialty* for the good of us poor suffering women. Thank God, dear Gus, that you are a man!"[11]

With the invasion scare over, Fox returned to planning naval operations. He insisted on, and Lincoln and the cabinet agreed to, a joint army-navy expedition to take Fernandina or Bulls Bay (Du Pont quipped that he hoped the latter would not be another Bull Run). General-in-Chief Winfield Scott approved and named General Thomas West Sherman to command the military side, while Fox, with Welles's approval, determined that Du Pont should proceed to New York to organize and lead the expedition. By pouncing "upon two ports little suspected and watched," Du Pont thought the August expedition would "strike terror and do away with the recent reverse" at Bull Run, but speed was essential before "hurricanes may come and make it a second Armada."[12]

Fox was impatient for the expedition to sail. But planning sessions with military leaders for this combined operation with 12,000 troops revealed the impossibility of an August departure. On the first of that month, the day Lincoln appointed Fox assistant secretary of the navy, Du Pont reported that after meeting with "General Scott & Co. . . . it was agreed that the 10th of October instead of 7th September was a better day—but the *fast* people, Fox & Co., are flaring up at what they call delay." Scott was afraid the men would get sick in September, and Du Pont agreed that "*Mosquitoes* are worse than Minié balls."[13]

As the responsibilities of his forthcoming expedition weighed upon him, Du Pont became more deliberate. The audacious Blockade Board planner began to evolve into the cautious admiral, and, as he reflected, he was not eager to lead the expedition. He was not consumed with ambition, and until Bull Run he had been content to serve on the Blockade Board, which on 26 July got out its fourth memoir, covering the South Carolina and Florida coasts, and on 9 August released its memoir on New Orleans and the mouth of the Mississippi. Formerly a conspicuous opponent of seniority, Du Pont was annoyed when Fox and Welles changed regulations to enable John A. Dahlgren, who was not even a captain, to command the Washington Navy Yard. He claimed this effort by Fox and Welles to appoint by merit ignored "all military propriety and justice. I had to serve twenty-two years at sea before I could get a navy yard; now a commander who [has] not yet commanded a sloop of war is eligible."[14]

If Fox feared, as Du Pont suspected, that he was not the ideal leader for the expedition, he nevertheless stuck with Du Pont. After he prepared "a *rough* draft" of what his "instructions should be," Fox sketched them out for Du Pont's consideration. Du Pont found Fox's draft "in the highest sense complimentary." It gave him full authority to prepare and organize in cooperation with the army an expedition to invade and occupy the seacoasts of rebel states, ordered him to New York "as early as practicable," and urged him to "lose no time in getting afloat."[15]

For almost three months (since 9 May), Fox had worked days, nights, and

Sundays at the Navy Department. Ships were acquired and expeditions planned, and Congress, which would adjourn on 6 August, not only had passed legislation on 24 July to expand the navy but on 3 August authorized an iron-clad program. With much accomplished, Fox on the next day, an extremely hot Sunday, entrusted Du Pont's orders to Charles Henry Davis, after failing in his attempt to hand deliver them to Du Pont. He then departed to spend a few days with Virginia in Portsmouth. The trip mixed business with pleasure. As planned, he probably visited the Philadelphia, New York, Boston, and Ports-mouth navy yards. In New York, he secretly conferred with George D. Morgan about potential blockaders (knowledge of his interest would raise the prices), inspected and approved the purchase of two excellent side-wheel steamers— the 1,675-ton *DeSoto* and the 1,558-ton *Bienville*—and probably also looked at the five ferryboats the department soon ordered. Fox also visited some of the five private shipyards and two ironworks busy on contracts awarded them by the New York naval constructor, Samuel Pook.[16]

Fox was back in Washington by Monday, 12 August. Offensive expeditions to strengthen the blockade occupied Fox in the late summer and fall of 1861. "Don't you think," he anxiously asked Du Pont on 17 August, "we better con-nect you officially with the hurrying off of the bought vessels etc., at New York?" While Du Pont was organizing a major expedition to secure a base for the blockade, Fox and Welles in early August decided to attack the weak Con-federate forts on the Hatteras Inlet to Pamlico Sound in North Carolina. Fox's old friend Major General Benjamin F. Butler conceived this joint army-navy operation to retrieve prestige he had lost following his poorly coordinated attack and repulse on 10 June at Big Bethel, Virginia. After the army's subse-quent debacle at Bull Run, the Navy Department was anxious to lift sagging northern spirits with a victory. Also, if not taken, these forts would prevent the sinking of stone-laden schooners in Hatteras Inlet, as Fox suggested and the Blockade Board recommended.[17]

Although Fox remarked that Butler wanted "too much of the fleet," the expedition was small. Its objective was limited to occupying Fort Hatteras and Fort Clark until the inlet was sealed. Fox and Welles did not envision an at-tempt to secure Pamlico Sound. Butler had only 860 infantry and an artillery company to take the forts, and Flag Officer Silas H. Stringham, commander of the Atlantic Blockading Squadron and naval head of the expedition, had on 16 August only one vessel near Hatteras. Of Stringham's steamers, the *Union* was in Baltimore for repairs; the *Penguin*, with a boiler unfit for service at sea, was up the Potomac at Aquia Creek, looking for invaders; and Stringham feared the powerful *Wabash* drew too much water. Sympathetic to Stringham's plight,

Fox asked Du Pont to hurry off the *Susquehanna* in Philadelphia and the *Flag* in New York.[18]

Despite Stringham's reluctance, the expedition left Hampton Roads on 26 August. It arrived off Hatteras the following day, and on the next day began bombarding the forts and landing troops. The heavy surf destroyed the landing boats after they had landed 315 wet, disorganized men and before they could land provisions. But the bombardment by the steam frigates *Minnesota* and *Wabash*, the sailing frigate *Cumberland* (towed by the *Wabash*), and the steam sloop *Susquehanna*, steaming in a circle, proved successful. After two and a half hours, the Confederates abandoned Fort Clark, but Fort Hatteras remained in their hands at 6:00 p.m., when a stiff breeze prevented further firing. With calmer seas the next day, the intense bombardment resumed and continued until 1:30 p.m., when Flag Officer Samuel Barron surrendered Fort Hatteras "unconditionally."[19]

"Our Hatteras expedition," Fox crowed, "was of national importance besides useful for our naval credit." Although the forts were weak and poorly defended, northerners rejoiced in this first substantial victory. The ease with which the navy took the forts led Fox to question the conventional wisdom that a combined army and navy attack on such installations was necessary and to exaggerate the capacity of the navy to reduce forts. Success at Hatteras set a pattern of relying too heavily on naval power when attacking forts. This pattern was followed until the summer of 1863.[20]

Easy victory raised expectations. Fox dropped his initial plan to abandon the Hatteras forts after blocking the inlet with stone-laden schooners. Although urging that the Hatteras and Ocracoke inlets be used as bases for further operations, both Stringham and Butler, to Fox's disgust, raced home to tell of their heroic deeds. When Butler awakened Fox with the good news, Fox asked him why he had come back. Fox's congratulatory telegram and Welles's order to Stringham—to press his advantage and secure the "inland sounds and passages"—found him and the *Minnesota* in New York. Fox and Welles feared that "all has not been done that should be" at Hatteras. Welles urged that the *Minnesota* should be at "her Post," that "the hulks should be sunk, and the other important points secured."[21]

Lincoln did not share the enthusiasm for utilizing the North Carolina sounds for ultimate attacks on Norfolk, Virginia, and Beaufort, North Carolina. Nor was the army, with its concern for defending Washington, interested in providing troops for a back-door approach to Norfolk. Fox also soon realized that offensive operations in the sounds would take ships from the blockade. He knew that an effective blockade—crucial in staving off British intervention on

behalf of the Confederacy—was more important than Beaufort or even Norfolk. And, in September 1861, he knew and the British knew that the blockade
was an ineffective "paper blockade" and that its legality could be challenged.
The British steam sloop *Rinaldo* anchored for forty hours off Beaufort "without sighting any United States cruisers" enforcing the blockade. To the South's
dismay, Britain chose to regard the blockade as legal. It preferred not to risk
war, and, as the world's preeminent naval power, it had blockaded in the past
and assumed it would have reason to blockade in the future. If so, recognizing
the legality of a loose blockade would be a useful precedent.[22]

But with no guarantee that the British would continue to regard the blockade as legal, the Navy Department had to make it more effective. To guide and
to goad Stringham to greater activity, Fox forwarded him copies of reports
from consular agents about potential blockade runners. (Throughout the war,
Fox utilized these reports from Canada, the Bahamas, Bermuda, England, and
elsewhere to keep track of blockade runners and commerce destroyers.) On
9 September he asked Stringham what he needed to hold and obstruct the
North Carolina inlets. Stringham angered Fox by remaining with eleven ships
at Hampton Roads, awaiting more vessels for operations in shallow inlets,
while three southern ports were uncovered. When Fox on 14 September chided
him for not sending vessels "immediately southward," Stringham took it as
the reprimand it was. Smarting that the department regarded his energy listless and his ideas grandiose, Stringham on 16 September resigned command
of the Atlantic Blockading Squadron, before Welles and Fox could remove
him.[23]

Fox and Welles utilized the border between North and South Carolina to
divide blockading squadrons. On 18 September Welles appointed Du Pont
commander of the South Atlantic Blockading Squadron and his friend Captain
Louis M. Goldsborough commander of the North Atlantic Blockading Squadron. Having returned to Boston in August from a two-year cruise in the *Congress*, Goldsborough wanted a short leave before returning to sea. He sent his
forceful wife Elizabeth to secure a leave for him from Fox. She wrote Goldsborough that Fox said he could have his leave, but that his services were needed
and that, although Fox knew him to be loyal, southern navy and army officers
were being eyed suspiciously.[24]

Indeed, Welles and Fox had to be cautious. Naval officers usually, but not
always, followed the lead of their home state. Those from the cotton states,
like Fox's former captain Josiah Tattnall, almost invariably joined the Confederacy, as did for the most part those from the seceded states in the upper South,
like Fox's close friend Thomas Jefferson Page. Officers, like Du Pont, from

border slave states that did not secede remained loyal to the Union. Franklin Buchanan was an interesting exception. He mistakenly assumed Maryland would secede and resigned on 22 April 1861. When Maryland failed to leave the Union, Buchanan tried to rescind his resignation but Welles dismissed him, and he joined the Confederate navy. A few officers from seceded states were more loyal to the Union than to their home state. Perhaps long tours of duty abroad representing the nation—not a particular state—made them more nationalistic. The most famous and the greatest Civil War naval officer, David Glasgow Farragut, was born in Tennessee, spent his childhood in New Orleans and on a Mississippi plantation, settled in Norfolk, and abandoned it for New York the day after Virginia seceded. Perhaps the most striking example of a nationalistic officer was Percival Drayton. A member of an aristocratic South Carolina family, Drayton despised slavery (but not African Americans, who, he believed, would become productive citizens), ardently supported the Union, efficiently attacked South Carolina fortifications commanded by his older brother, and was denounced as "infamous" by that state's legislature. How these officers made up their minds can only be conjectured, but Goldsborough's thoughts can be followed on a paper trail.[25]

Had Fox been privy to Goldsborough's reaction when he heard of secession, while off Montevideo, Uruguay, Fox would not have been so certain of his loyalty. On 28 January 1861 Goldsborough opposed secession, but declared, "Come what may, I never can unsheathe my sword in anger against the South." Should there be a peaceful separation and "the army and navy all broken up," he instructed his wife, "get for me the highest berth you can in the Southern Navy or if there is to be no Southern Navy, the best berth a Southern Confederacy will afford me." On hearing these sentiments in late March, his wife warned him to "*keep cool!*" be quiet, and stick to your post of duty. "*I am at the helm,*" she assured him. But before he received his wife's admonition, or heard of the attack on Sumter, the "audacious" course of South Carolina and President Buchanan's "cowardly" failure convinced him that he was a Union man. "I, for one," he wrote his wife, "cannot understand the idea that a man in our country owes a higher allegiance to his state than to country. . . . From her it is, and not from any state that I hold my commission and to her it is that I mean to cling come weal or woe!" Goldsborough and his ship were ready to fight "in a righteous cause," but the thought of civil war made his "heart bleed."[26]

Anxious that Goldsborough—a Marylander—not compromise his usefulness, Fox telegraphed their mutual friend John Murray Forbes to urge Goldsborough not to ask to be relieved. Goldsborough took the advice and got the important and lucrative command of the North Atlantic Blockading Squadron. Vessels captured while running the blockade were condemned and sold with one-half of the proceeds going to the federal government, 45 percent to the officers and crew of the capturing vessel, and 5 percent to the commander of the blockading squadron. For almost two years as a blockade squadron commander, Du Pont's share of prize money was at least $65,000 and possibly as much as $75,000.[27]

With the appointment of Goldsborough, over thirteen of his seniors, and of Du Pont, over eighteen of his, Fox and Welles struck a blow against seniority. It was an essential blow that substituted merit and vigor in place of mediocrity and the debilitating effects of superannuation. On 31 August they replaced the tenth captain on the list, William Mervine, as commander of the Gulf Blockading Squadron with the thirty-eighth captain, William W. McKean. Four captains, all senior to Goldsborough, had to be removed from his squadron. "Things," gloated Du Pont, "have taken an active turn, and this day is an epoch in naval history—seniority and rotation have seen their last day. Selection with as much regard to seniority as the good of the service will admit is now the order of the day." Fox realized that senior officers resented what was to a large extent his action. A few months later, he dismissed the high praise of Captain Uriah Phillips Levy (who in his seventieth year wanted to be in charge of the Boston Navy Yard) by observing, "All those old fellows would poison me if they could."[28]

Goldsborough and Du Pont realized that their primary responsibility was to maintain the blockade. Toward that end, the Navy Department urged on Goldsborough the difficult task of obstructing the North Carolina inlets. With ambitious schemes to control the North Carolina sounds temporarily abandoned, a modest attempt in late September failed to take Roanoke Island. Confederate gunboats controlling Pamlico Sound made it impossible to obstruct the Oregon and Loggerhead inlets. Although the Hatteras forts remained in Union hands, the pounding surf on 2 October prevented Commander Henry S. Stellwagon from properly positioning the stone schooners in the inlet, and he gave up in disgust and asked for a new command. Committed to blocking inlets, the department persisted, and finally, on 14 November, Lieutenant William N. Jeffers of the tug *Underwriter* (recently purchased by Morgan in New York) obstructed Ocracoke Inlet with three schooners. But, as Jeffers predicted, "another channel will be found." With eighteen other stone schooners sunk either en route to Hatteras or at anchor at Hampton Roads and one returned to its owners, blocking North Carolina inlets failed ignominiously. Fox, however, did not give up on his "idea of war." The department assembled a stone fleet of obsolete whalers for use at Charleston and Savannah.[29]

The Hatteras operation was never more than a sideshow, compared to the expedition Du Pont was preparing in New York. In August, September, and October, Morgan, Naval Constructor Samuel M. Pook, the navy yard under Commandant Samuel L. Breese, and private shipyards worked feverishly to purchase and ready ships. Morgan wrote Fox almost daily with suggestions and queries. His basic problem was that few vessels could meet the navy's meticulous peacetime standards, and meeting those standards in converting ships for war purposes caused inordinate delays. For example, rust-resistant copper-fastened and copper-bottomed vessels, powered by low-pressure boilers in the hold, rather than on deck, were difficult to acquire. In addition, vessels sent to the navy yard for conversion never seemed to emerge. If there were to be a Du Pont expedition and an effective blockade, Morgan begged Fox to relax the navy's standards. He wanted him to "scatter" the work among private shipyards and to appoint Pook's son as an assistant constructor to help his harassed father, who Morgan feared would break down. When Fox approved the purchase of iron-fastened boats, Morgan rejoiced, "we shall soon be through."[30]

Fox also heard from Du Pont, who wrote about converting merchantmen to men-of-war, repairing the *Wabash*, adding vessels to his fleet, writing orders for his officers, coaling his ships, installing Parrott rifled guns, storing powder, and loading army transports. In early September, Du Pont feared that not one purchased vessel in five would be ready in time. Later that month, he complained that "when the vessels are once at the Navy Yard, until it is understood they are to be part of my command, *we* are paralyzed." Even when it was known the ships were for Du Pont, the navy yard proceeded "very slowly." Nevertheless, thanks largely to Pook, a veritable armada was ready by mid-October. Worn out from his labors and fearful that Fox might disapprove his alterations and their cost, Pook was gratified by his congratulations "upon the auxiliary navy you have had so much to do towards creating."[31]

During September and October, Fox's primary concern was Du Pont's expedition. Fox had problems both in New York and in Washington. Readying ships in New York required him to make a multitude of decisions, as revealed in his correspondence with Du Pont and Morgan. More important, Fox and Welles had to prevent the Du Pont expedition from being sidetracked. Convinced that Washington was vulnerable to a Confederate attack, civil authorities, as well as General George B. McClellan, were reluctant to commit troops for an expedition down the Atlantic coast. In mid-September "another panic" about Washington's safety threatened troops for the Du Pont expedition.

Welles pushed on, bringing "matters with great spirit before the cabinet," and Lincoln told Secretary of War Simon Cameron that the joint expedition "must be ready to move . . . very early in October."[32]

At a confused conference on 1 October 1861, where Fox played a leading role, Lincoln made the final decision. While looking for General Thomas West Sherman, the military commander of the expedition, Du Pont encountered Fox. He took him to "Seward's where the President was, to have a final discussion on the expedition—just as if," Du Pont remarked, "it had not been settled six times that it was to go." He was a bit disconcerted when Lincoln failed to recognize him and had to be reminded by Fox that he was the naval commander of the expedition. Seward, Du Pont recounted, "pokes a cigar at Fox who, sitting on the same sofa with Lincoln, puffs smoke into the president's eyes. Meantime there is a desperate hunt going on all over town" for Cameron, McClellan, and Sherman, while Seward intoned "There's nobody nowhere tonight!"

At last Cameron and Sherman drifted in, and the meeting got underway. Fox sought information about an 8,000-man expedition under General Ambrose E. Burnside (who had asked him for a naval aide-de-camp). Neither Lincoln, Cameron, nor Seward was aware of it. Cameron hinted that Seward planned it, because he "regulated all the business of all the departments," and Lincoln said he would go back to Illinois if he had forgotten something that important. Assistant Secretary of War Thomas A. Scott then arrived and confirmed that there was indeed a Burnside expedition, to secure the Potomac River and Chesapeake Bay. It also became obvious that the War Department had confused it with the Du Pont–Sherman expedition. When Burnside ordered a Rhode Island regiment to Washington, the War Department, thinking it was part of Sherman's command, insisted it go to New York. "So it went, cross-purposes for a week," Du Pont sighed, "which would doubtless have ended in some great snarl, but for the fortunate circumstance of Fox being roused to a suspicion that something was going on to override *his* favorite expedition."

At 11 p.m., with Du Pont feeling very sleepy, McClellan walked in "with a lighted cigar." At this point, burdened by the knowledge that "it would cost so much money," Lincoln feared they would have to give up the expedition. Du Pont "said nothing but thought of all our work this summer—and of all the fixed determinations of the Cabinet." Fox somehow prevailed, and the conference determined to send off the expedition. McClellan agreed to part with 14,000 men in lieu of new, untrained regiments. Significantly Fox, not

Welles, represented the Navy Department at this conference. The question to be decided was one of naval operations, and it was Fox's ideas that carried the day.[55]

As the dynamic force behind the Du Pont expedition, Fox was determined to make it a success. He gave Du Pont most of the ships and officers he desired. True, Fox annoyed Du Pont by sending the powerful screw steamer *Iroquois*, which Du Pont wanted for his expedition, to search for the Confederate cruiser *Sumter*, but, being responsible for all naval operations, Fox could not ignore merchant pressures.[54]

Fox also determined the expedition's objective. He insisted that it be Port Royal, the best harbor between Charleston and Savannah. The Blockade Board had recommended that Bulls Bay, South Carolina, or Fernandina, Florida, be taken in preference to the more formidable Port Royal, and Du Pont's orders signed by Welles on 12 October 1861 allowed him to select his target. When Fox journeyed to New York at the behest of Du Pont prior to his departure on 15 October, Fox argued that he attack Port Royal. Du Pont wrestled with this problem on the way to Hampton Roads. Although reluctant to attack Port Royal, which he feared was defended by 200 guns, Du Pont had to admit that his squadron had "swelled into an armada" of more than fifty vessels. Because "Port Royal alone admits the large ships," he reasoned, it would be a superior base for the blockade. Du Pont consulted with his fleet captain, Charles Henry Davis, whom Fox already had convinced, but Du Pont also wanted "God's direction to come to a right judgment."[55]

Fox persisted and prevailed. After Du Pont arrived at Hampton Roads, Fox visited on 22 and 23 October and persuaded Du Pont to attack "the *big* place." Du Pont, in turn, secured the approval of General Thomas West Sherman. Fox helped Du Pont arrange "many details" and was impressed by the naval officers' enthusiasm, by the cooperation between Goldsborough and Du Pont, and by the fleet of troop transports and naval vessels. "Two ferry boats and a tug," Fox optimistically wrote Welles on 22 October,

> arrived yesterday in the midst of the gale and performed admirably giving the Como[dore, Du Pont,] renewed hope in regard to reaching their destination. The whole roads are filled with vessels as far as the eye can reach all filled with troops or bristling with guns. The gale is fortunate. It gives time for the final arrangements of signals, towing etc. besides the average promise of good weather which follows every gale. There is a great deal of enthusiasm here; the high tone and vigor of these two Flag Officers has awakened a fire in the hearts

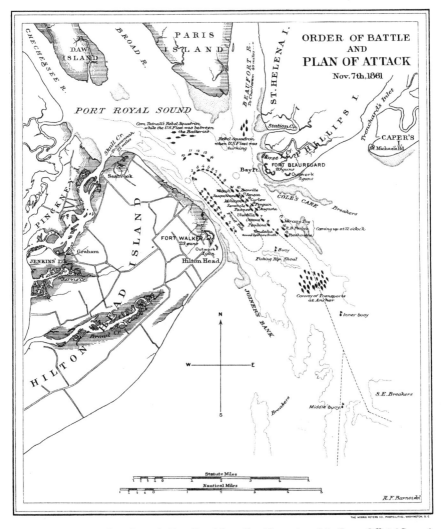

Order of battle and plan of attack (Port Royal Sound), 7 November 1861. From *Official Records of the Union and Confederate Navies*, 12:262.

of all. Gen'l Sherman is now near me and even his pale blue eyes light up at the magnitude of the expectations of those around him.

The fleet would sail, Fox said, as "soon as the weather gets smooth and the wind shifts off shore."[36]

Fifty vessels departed a week later, when the foul weather apparently abated. As he got underway, Du Pont told Fox, "The ships of my squadron are in as high condition as I can expect—and I am thankful to the Department for its endeavors to make it as efficient as possible, & to your practical, intelligent & personal supervision & zeal I shall ever recur whatever the results in store for us may be."[37]

A subsequent gale heightened the anxiety of Fox, Welles, and Lincoln as they waited in Washington for news from Port Royal. Even though foul weather scattered the fleet and Sherman's landing craft and ammunition were lost in the storm, the Port Royal expedition was spectacularly successful. Deprived of the army's support, the navy alone attacked Fort Walker and Fort Beauregard, each with 13 guns, guarding the entrance to Port Royal Sound. On 7 November, Du Pont, with fifteen vessels mounting 157 guns, chased up the Beaufort River a small Confederate squadron, under Josiah Tattnall (who years earlier had been Fox's captain), and in three hours compelled Fort Walker to surrender. Later that afternoon, the Confederates abandoned Fort Beauregard, giving the Union fleet control of Port Royal Sound.[38]

Although Du Pont had fought his ships well, it appeared to Fox and Welles that, had he been more energetic, his gunboats could have captured Fort Walker's fleeing garrison. But the department was in no mood to cavil over Du Pont's caution. The navy had gained, for the blockade and for future offensive movements, a strategic base within eighty miles of Charleston, the spiritual capital of secession. The victory also demonstrated the vulnerability of the Confederacy's coast to amphibious operations and struck fear in the hearts of southerners. The naval victory over incomplete and inadequately armed forts reinforced Fox's belief that naval power alone could reduce forts.[39]

Fox's mind-set was confirmed by the praise and reports he received from the expedition's commanders. Du Pont found his success "more complete and more brilliant than I ever could have believed." Claiming there was nothing on the Potomac like "scientifically constructed" Fort Walker, Du Pont exaggerated the Confederate defenders' bravery, maintaining that their two long-range rifled guns "never missed" and put an "awful hole" through the main mast of his flagship, the *Wabash*. "When they once broke," he continued, "the stampede was intense and not a gun was spiked. In truth I never conceived of such a fire as that of this ship on her second turn." Fox could "take the credit," Du Pont insisted, for the victory, and Charles Henry Davis, the captain of the *Wabash*, commended Fox for his "labors, cares, and responsibilities, in assisting, fostering, and promoting this expedition." Davis also praised Fox for courageously setting aside the claims of seniority in naming Goldsborough and Du Pont to their commands and "heartily" congratulated him on the result of his "decided and responsible course of action."[40]

CHAPTER NINE

The Monitor
and the Peninsula

The ringing of plates on plates
Still ringeth round the world.
War yet shall be, but warriors
Are now but operators.
  Herman Melville, "A Utilitarian View of the Monitor's Fight"

Oh for a General of Genius.   *Fox to Virginia Fox, 2 July 1862*

Fox was optimistic in January 1862. Three major Confederate cities were endangered. Acquiring Port Royal augured well, not merely for the blockade but
also for coastal operations, including the capture of Charleston, the heart of
rebeldom. Plans for a big expedition to take New Orleans were afoot. In Virginia, the Army of the Potomac waxed in strength daily and would in time,
with the cooperation of the navy, move on Richmond, via the peninsula between the York and James rivers. Northern shipyards were launching conventional wooden gunboats and working on unconventional ironclads. Fox hoped
these ironclads would prove more than a match for the ironclad that Confederates were improvising at Norfolk on the hull of the raised *Merrimack*. Before
the Peninsula campaign could get underway, the most novel battle in naval
history, between the *Monitor* and the *Virginia/Merrimack*, resulted in a stalemate. Containing the *Virginia* made the massive joint operation possible. To
Fox's dismay, victory, which seemed so close, proved elusive. The Peninsula
campaign failed, and Richmond remained the capital of the Confederacy.

■ ■ ■

The effect of Du Pont's victory at Port Royal cannot be exaggerated. With Port
Royal Sound as a base, the blockade was infinitely strengthened. Fox complied
with Du Pont's request that a floating machine shop be fitted out at Port Royal

to repair the steamers' frequent mechanical breakdowns. From his Port Royal base, Du Pont cut water communication between Charleston and Savannah (9 November). With the occupation of Tybee Island (24 November) and control of Wassaw Sound (early December), he boasted on 5 December that Savannah was "more effectively closed than a bottle with wire over the cork."[1]

In addition, seven stone-laden whalers were sunk at Savannah on 17 December, and, three days later, Charles Henry Davis skeptically, but skillfully, sank sixteen stone-filled whalers in a checkerboard pattern in Charleston's main ship channel. During the night of 25 to 26 January, thirteen additional stone whalers were sunk in Sullivan's Island channel, leaving open only the shallow and more easily guarded Swash and North channels. But the results were only temporary, as Charles O. Boutelle of the Coast Survey predicted. In May 1862 he found that new and deeper channels had bypassed the wrecks. Although both Du Pont and Davis, as members of the Blockade Board, had agreed to the idea of obstructing inlets, and Bache presented the board evidence in its support, Du Pont complained the stone fleet "was a hobby of Fox's which nothing could put out of his head," and Davis called it a "maggot" that "had got into Fox's brain." Despite its fleeting success, Herman Melville's judgment, "A failure, and complete / Was your Old Stone Fleet," was closer to the truth than Fox's hopes.[2]

On 8 November 1861, the day after Du Pont was victorious at Port Royal, Captain Charles Wilkes of the USS *San Jacinto* unwittingly endangered the blockade. With his unerring knack for causing trouble, Wilkes forcibly removed Confederate commissioners James M. Mason and John Slidell from the British mail steamer *Trent*, en route between two neutral ports and delivered the prisoners to Fort Warren in Boston Harbor where they were confined. Wilkes carried out this violation of British neutrality with no authorization, and northern public opinion was ecstatic. Welles reflected that mood, when he told Wilkes he had the "emphatic approval of this Department." Lincoln was pleased, and Fox predicted "Wilkes will be sustained by the Administration and the Country." Already unhappy with the Union blockade stifling imports of cotton for their textile mills, the British were outraged, demanded an apology, and prepared for war.[3]

Cooler heads prevailed. Approaching his deathbed, Prince Albert softened the tone of British demands. Upon hearing of Wilkes's act, Montgomery Blair (in whose house Virginia and Gus were staying) called it "a bad move" that would "produce trouble." He was the only cabinet member to counsel Lincoln to give up Mason and Slidell. Although some naval officers, like David Dixon Porter, were "crazy for a fight" with England, Fox and officers like Louis

Goldsborough were not. If war came, Fox planned on "fighting England by coaling our steamers in France & *attacking* her coasts," but he informed Lincoln of the limitations of the American navy.[4]

Lincoln regularly consulted Fox on naval matters and, informal westerner that he was, often dropped in at Blair House to see him. "He distorts his features terribly," Virginia observed on 12 November, "& throws himself around promiscuously." Before she and her sister Minna brought in tea, "Gus said he had been full length on the sofa!" Although Lincoln seemed in no hurry to resolve the crisis, Fox convinced him that, because the superior British navy could accomplish a major southern objective and destroy the Union blockade in a month, Mason and Slidell would have to be released. On Christmas Day, Gus and Virginia Fox, the Blairs, and other guests enjoyed a "*plain*" but "agreeable" dinner at the White House. Later, the president met with his cabinet and Senator Charles Sumner, a strong advocate of peace with Britain, to discuss the *Trent* crisis. All came around to the view that the prisoners should be given up, and on New Year's Day, at the "small, quiet" port of Provincetown, Massachusetts (selected by Fox to avoid "any popular excitement"), Mason and Slidell boarded the HMS *Rinaldo.* Complying with British demands on this matter averted war and seemed to improve the Union's relations with Britain.[5]

An even more serious threat to the blockade than Wilkes's rash act was taking shape at the Norfolk Navy Yard. Having raised the scuttled and burned *Merrimack* on 30 May 1861, the Confederates converted it into an ironclad ram. Their secretary of the navy, Stephen R. Mallory hoped ironclads would be able to lift the blockade. Although Fox and Welles were aware of Confederate plans and knew that a Union ironclad program was necessary, they initially concentrated on fast, light-draft wooden steamers to catch blockade runners. Yet Virginia noted on 5 November 1861 that Fox "has desired iron ships made ever since he came here." These vessels interested neither John Lenthall, the head of the Construction Bureau, nor Chief Engineer Benjamin F. Isherwood, who called them a "humbug." In truth, the pioneering British and French armored vessels (*Warrior* and *Gloire*) drew too much water and would run aground and be useless at the entrance to virtually all southern harbors. An early proposal by John Laird & Sons of Birkenhead, England, to build ironclads for the Union was for frigates whose draft of twenty-four or twenty-five feet of water would limit their usefulness. Besides, Welles was determined to rely on American shipyards for vessels. Although the proposal was rejected, Fox did not rule out help from the Lairds.[6]

Among Fox's correspondents, John Murray Forbes was most interested in ironclads. In June he was enthusiastic about two iron steamships under construction in South Boston and made calculations about encasing them in armor. When their owners, who had before the war sold ships to South Carolina "at high prices," talked of profiting $50,000 each from the steamers, Forbes angrily yet delicately exclaimed to Fox, "I would see them dxxd . . . first." Lenthall believed that an iron merchant ship could not be converted into an efficient armored warship, but the avaricious ironmongers convinced Forbes that adding armor plate to wooden frames and pitch-pine planks would be more buoyant than an all-iron vessel and draw less water. Forbes suggested that the navy experiment to determine the minimum thickness of iron plates required to withstand bombardment from a distance of a third to a half mile. He noted that if vessels were designed with 45-degree sides to deflect blows, thinner armor plate would be required, and vessels would draw less water. By 26 July he reported to Fox that he had collected for the department "quite a lot of Pamphlets from England" on ironclad vessels, including data comparing hammered with rolled iron plates as well as "*hammered* slabs of steel."[7]

On 19 July Senator James W. Grimes of Iowa introduced ironclad legislation, suggested by Welles. It authorized Welles to appoint a board of three officers to evaluate plans for "iron or steel-clad steamships or steam batteries" and appropriated $1.5 million for their construction, but did not include the request by Welles and Fox for $50,000 "to try experiments with iron-plating." Cornelius S. Bushnell, an entrepreneur and old associate of Welles's, lobbied the bill through Congress. When Lincoln signed it on 4 August, the Confederates had for two weeks been implementing plans to shield the salvaged *Merrimack* with four inches of armor plate. On 8 August Welles appointed two of his bureau chiefs, Joseph Smith and Hiram Paulding, and the ubiquitous secretary of the Blockade Board, Charles Henry Davis, to the Ironclad Board.[8]

While knowledgeable about vessels, the members of the new Ironclad Board knew little about ironclads. Nor did American naval architects and shipbuilders have experience in designing or constructing them. But Joseph Smith, the board's leading spirit, had a good mechanical mind. After the board advertised for designs, Fox on 13 August (despite Welles's hostility to awarding contracts to foreign firms) contacted the Lairds' New York agent, John T. Howard. "I hope you have written out about the floating battery. I wish they would tender for two." Because of the shortage of wood in England, English shipyards had been constructing iron ships, and the Lairds were on the cutting edge of ironclad technology. Fox's fears seemed confirmed, when, in early September, the Ironclad Board, having considered seventeen designs out of many submissions, rejected all but two and cautioned that top-heavy armament would make even those unstable. The two selected were a gunboat (*Galena*), designed by Naval Constructor Samuel M. Pook's son Samuel Hartt Pook for Bushnell, and a frigate (*New Ironsides*), submitted by Merrick & Sons of Philadelphia. Bushnell immediately traveled to New York to consult anew with John Ericsson, a brilliant engineer who had significantly improved the screw propeller. Having already suggested changes in Pook's design to better accommodate a steam engine, Ericsson assured Bushnell that the Pook-Bushnell gunboat would be stable and would sustain shot from a six-inch gun.[9]

Ericsson then showed Bushnell his own model and plans (developed years earlier) for "a floating battery absolutely impregnable to the heaviest shot and shell." Emperor Napoleon III of France had rejected it in 1854. Although Ericsson had written Lincoln about it on 29 August 1861 and five days later sent its plans to the Ironclad Board, it was not seriously considered. Ericsson's failures had been heavily publicized. The twelve-inch gun "Peacemaker," which was bored under his direction, had exploded on board the *Princeton* in 1844 (Virginia Fox was among the survivors who were there), and during the next decade his "caloric," or hot-air, engine, had failed. Bushnell discovered that Ericsson had designed an ingenious "ironclad shot-proof steam battery of iron and wood combined," whose hull was "wholly of iron and the upper vessel of wood." It had a low freeboard (top deck close to the waterline) and mounted two large guns in a heavily armored revolving turret. Theodore Ruggles Timby had patented a "revolving fort" in 1843, and the idea of British naval captain Cowper Phipps Coles for "revolving towers" had been published in *Blackwood's Magazine* of December 1860. But Ericsson was the first to conceive of a turret on a vessel. His enthusiasm for his floating battery convinced Bushnell. He showed the model and plans to Welles, who was impressed and asked the Ironclad Board to examine Ericsson's model.[10]

On 13 September Bushnell presented Ericsson's unconventional design to the Ironclad Board in the presence of Lincoln and Fox. Fox was predictably enthusiastic, Lincoln thought there might be something in it, and Smith and Paulding were skeptical (although Smith was open-minded). Davis, who had been absent at the first meeting and was briefed at the second, was hostile. With the board expressing fears of "another Ericsson failure," Bushnell rushed to New York and overnight fetched Ericsson. Fortunately, Welles asked Smith, who had decided the Ericsson design was worth the gamble, to treat the testy inventor "tenderly." A diplomatic query from him about the craft's stability triggered Ericsson's eloquence, which impressed even Davis.

After consultation, members of the Ironclad Board asked Ericsson to meet with them that afternoon in Welles's office. At the end of an even more impressive performance, Ericsson promised to deliver his ironclad, which he named the *Monitor*, in ninety days, for $275,000. Without hesitation, Welles told him to commence work immediately, that a contract would follow. Lacking complete faith in Ericsson's *Monitor*, the Ironclad Board insisted in the contract of 4 October that it be tested under enemy fire before being accepted by the navy, but the board did give Ericsson 100 days to deliver the vessel. The board also approved (but without the enemy-fire requirement) the gunboat *Galena* and frigate *New Ironsides*, its selections from the earlier submissions. While Ericsson's first task was to build the *Monitor*, Fox, fearing a war with Britain, spoke to him about designing a more powerful seagoing "vessel of extraordinary speed and . . . invulnerable, so far as the tower was concerned, as a fit match for the 'Warrior.'"[11]

While enthusiastic about the untried *Monitor*, Fox explored other ways of neutralizing the *Merrimack* and meeting possible threats from abroad. On 1 November 1861, a week after the keel of the *Monitor* had been laid, Fox (without consulting Welles) asked Howard, the Lairds' agent: "Do you believe we could buy an entire Iron Frigate in England, all ready for sea?" Nothing came of that query, but John Lenthall, head of the Bureau of Construction and Repair, and Chief Engineer Benjamin F. Isherwood, goaded by Fox, abandoned their earlier hostility to ironclads. Together, they planned a double-turreted ironclad using the Coles system of "revolving towers." Fox was fearful that a sufficient quantity of four-and-one-half-inch iron plates, for the sides and towers, would not be available in the United States. He wrote Howard, "I am strongly in favor of getting the plates in England. . . . I should like to have your address there, in case we should send abroad, and will ask you to talk with Laird & Son, as *time* is the great object." By late November, Lenthall and Isherwood had matured their plans for a 216-foot vessel, but, as Fox feared, thick iron plates in quantity for it and vessels of its class would have to be obtained from abroad. A mission to line up these plates (of which Welles was aware) failed because a $10 million appropriation to build twenty ironclad gunboats was delayed in the Senate until 7 February 1862. John P. Hale of New Hampshire, the head of the Naval Affairs Committee, was responsible for the delay. Without four-and-one-half-inch iron plates, Union ironclads were primarily armored with one-inch plates laminated together to obtain the desired thickness. Apart from Hale's opposition, Fox thought that Du Pont's success at Port Royal with wooden vessels stalled the appropriation.[12]

By the end of 1861, the Navy Department had three ironclads under construction: the broadside frigate *New Ironsides*, Bushnell's gunboat *Galena*, and Ericsson's turreted *Monitor*. Before the conventional *New Ironsides* and the

Galena were completed and before the unconventional *Monitor* was tested, the department had committed itself to turreted vessels. A week after Lincoln on 13 February signed the appropriation for twenty gunboats, the Navy Department advertised for proposals for three types of ironclads: for river service, for harbor defense, and for coast defense. It insisted that the latter two types be turreted, but it hesitated between turrets modeled on Ericsson's *Monitor* or the Coles system of towers, advocated by Lenthall and Isherwood. The department did not reach a final decision until the *Monitor* was tried by battle.[13]

The *Monitor* was launched on 30 January 1862 at Greenpoint, Brooklyn, on the East River in New York Harbor. Although it took four rather than three months to build, the *Monitor*'s rapid construction illustrated Ericsson's inventive brilliance and his organizational genius (as well as that of his three partners). It also testified to the North's almost limitless facilities and skilled workers. From Ericsson's drawings and specifications, the plates, turret, steam engine, and other parts of the *Monitor* were fabricated, primarily in New York State, and assembled in Greenpoint. Fox telegraphed his congratulations upon its launching and urged Ericsson to "Hurry her for sea, as the *Merrimack* is nearly ready at Norfolk." At the New York Navy Yard (where, Ericsson complained, "the nice system of doing work . . . is not calculated to forward matters"), the *Monitor* was armed with two eleven-inch Dahlgren guns, taken from the gunboat *Dacotah*. Defects in the *Monitor*'s engines and steering mechanism, revealed in trials, were quickly remedied. On the morning of 6 March 1862, towed by the tugboat *Seth Low* and accompanied by two gunboats, it left the New York Navy Yard for Hampton Roads.[14]

While Ericsson rushed the *Monitor* to completion, Fox was planning naval expeditions. He wanted to capture Roanoke Island, North Carolina, to facilitate an attack on Norfolk, Virginia, via its back door. He also wanted to sever the Confederacy by taking New Orleans and other points along the Mississippi and its tributaries. On 8 February a joint army-navy expedition, under General Ambrose E. Burnside and Flag Officer Goldsborough, captured Roanoke Island. Two days later, a flotilla, under Commander Stephen C. Rowan, destroyed Confederate gunboats at Elizabeth City, North Carolina, secured Albemarle Sound, and cut Norfolk's main supply line. Goldsborough remained off Roanoke Island planning a joint army-navy attack on Norfolk, where the *Merrimack* was being clad in iron. "That dock-yard at Norfolk is an infernally sore thing to us," he exclaimed, "& have it we must!!"[15]

With plans to attack Richmond from the east, utilizing his base at Fortress Monroe on Hampton Roads, McClellan felt he could not spare men for the back-door approach to Norfolk. By February, Fox focused on Hampton Roads,

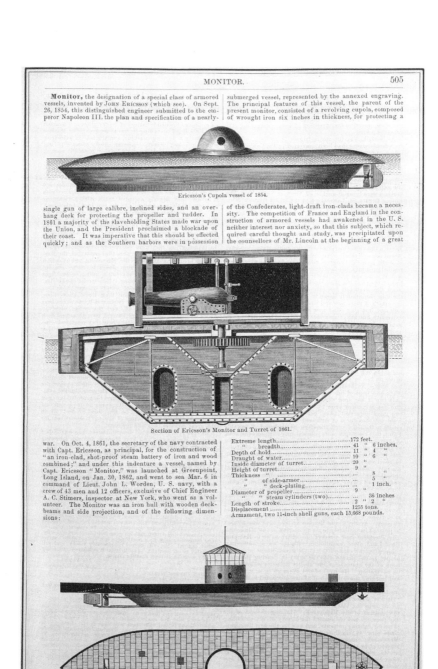

Monitor, the designation of a special class of armored vessels, invented by JOHN ERICSSON (which see). On Sept. 26, 1854, this distinguished engineer submitted to the emperor Napoleon III. the plan and specification of a nearly-submerged vessel, represented by the annexed engraving. The principal features of this vessel, the parent of the present monitor, consisted of a revolving cupola, composed of wrought iron six inches in thickness, for protecting a

Ericsson's Cupola vessel of 1854.

single gun of large calibre, inclined sides, and an overhang deck for protecting the propeller and rudder. In 1861 a majority of the slaveholding States made war upon the Union, and the President proclaimed a blockade of their coast. It was imperative that this should be effected quickly; and as the Southern harbors were in possession of the Confederates, light-draft iron-clads became a necessity. The competition of France and England in the construction of armored vessels had awakened in the U. S. neither interest nor anxiety, so that this subject, which required careful thought and study, was precipitated upon the counsellors of Mr. Lincoln at the beginning of a great

Section of Ericsson's Monitor and Turret of 1861.

war. On Oct. 4, 1861, the secretary of the navy contracted with Capt. Ericsson, as principal, for the construction of "an iron-clad, shot-proof steam battery of iron and wood combined;" and under this indenture a vessel, named by Capt. Ericsson "Monitor," was launched at Greenpoint, Long Island, on Jan. 30, 1862, and went to sea Mar. 6 in command of Lieut. John L. Worden, U. S. navy, with a crew of 43 men and 12 officers, exclusive of Chief Engineer A. C. Stimers, inspector at New York, who went as a volunteer. The Monitor was an iron hull with wooden deckbeams and side projection, and of the following dimensions:

Extreme length	172 feet.	
" breadth	41 "	6 inches.
Depth of hold	11 "	4 "
Draught of water	10 "	6 "
Inside diameter of turret	20 "	
Height of turret	9 "	
Thickness "		8 "
" of side-armor		5 "
" deck-plating		1 inch.
Diameter of propeller	9 "	
" " steam cylinders (two)		36 inches
Length of stroke	2 "	2 "
Displacement	1255 tons.	
Armament, two 11-inch shell guns, each 15,668 pounds.		

Ericsson's Monitor of 1861.

Drawings of the Monitor. From *Johnson's (Revised) Universal Cyclopaedia,* 8 vols. (New York: A. J. Johnson & Co., 1889–90), 5:505.

Norfolk's front door. At his suggestion, he and John G. Barnard, chief engineer of the Army of the Potomac, discussed a "joint Naval and land attack" on Norfolk by either the Elizabeth or Nansemond rivers. Not as yet completed, the *Merrimack* was commissioned on 17 February as the *Virginia.* It threatened to control Hampton Roads and the James River and to hamper McClellan's proposed operations on the peninsula between the James and the York rivers. Sensing that McClellan's objective should be the Confederate army at Bull Run, Lincoln, already troubled by McClellan's inaction, was uneasy about the shortcut to Richmond. Fox was in almost daily consultation with McClellan and with Lincoln, who often dropped in on the Foxes' new quarters. Although Lincoln did not seem to mind, their rooms "looked mighty little like *a home* to" Virginia and were quite noisy, with some raucous young bloods from the British legation above them.[16]

The demands on Fox's time were enormous. On 5 March, Virginia noted, dinner had to wait, because McClellan "sent for Gus." Two days later, the "President sent for Gus," she wrote, and dinner was "put off again." After tea that day, the Foxes went to McClellan's, "as Gus wanted to see him on business." Upon their return, Fox went to see Welles, but, while Fox was gone, Lincoln and his secretary John G. Nicolay called. Nicolay went off to fetch Fox, while Lincoln, in the half-hour he spent with Virginia, could not contain his exasperation with McClellan. "I'll tell you how things are, state a proposition to you. Suppose a man whose profession it is to understand military matters is asked how long it will take him & what he requires to accomplish certain things, and *when* he has had all he asked & the time comes, he does *nothing.*" Lincoln elaborated, "There has been an immense quantity of money spent on our army here on the Potomac & there is nothing done—the country & Congress & everyone is anxious & excited about it."[17]

Seward came in before Fox returned, and, when he told Lincoln and Virginia that he hoped to see Fanny Kemble, the actress, who lived in their building, the conversation took a lighter turn. They talked about Kemble's failed marriage to a Georgia plantation owner, Pierce Butler. He "married a *great* woman to elevate himself," Seward said, which resulted in "*a devil* of a time generally." The chitchat amused Lincoln, but he wanted to talk with Fox about clearing hostile batteries from the right bank of the Potomac. Fox had been "growling all winter at the blockade of the Potomac," but McClellan, with his move to the Peninsula in mind, did not wish to assault the batteries.[18]

The next afternoon, Lincoln asked Fox to go to Fortress Monroe at Hampton Roads. He wanted him to decide what ships could be spared at Hampton Roads to cooperate with the army in keeping the Potomac open to navigation.

Anticipating no immediate crisis, Fox, on that Saturday evening of 8 March, left for Fortress Monroe with his friend Lieutenant Henry A. Wise, Virginia's sister Nell, and two young women from the Welles household.[19]

As Fox went down the Potomac, he had no idea that the *Monitor*, commanded by his friend John L. Worden, had narrowly escaped disaster on Friday, while en route to Hampton Roads. Fox later recalled that "Worden had no confidence" in the *Monitor*, and its voyage down the coast was not inspiring. Rough seas off the capes of the Delaware coast had broken over the *Monitor*'s deck and into its four-foot-high blower pipe, causing the blower belts to slip, overheat, and break. With no ventilation, the engine room filled with gas, and members of its gang passed out and had to be carried to the top of the turret to be revived by fresh air. The tug pulled the *Monitor* inshore to calmer waters, where the belts were repaired, and it proceeded through less ruffled seas. After midnight, the *Monitor* again encountered a heavy sea, entangled its steering ropes, and for half an hour, before they were cleared, yawed from side to side unmanageably, severely straining the hawser by which it was towed. The remainder of the trip was uneventful, with the *Monitor* arriving at Hampton Roads at nine o'clock on Saturday evening, 8 March.[20]

The *Monitor*, however, was too late to prevent the havoc wreaked that day by the *Virginia* (completed only three days earlier), commanded by Franklin Buchanan. It rammed the razee frigate *Cumberland*, burned the frigate *Congress*, and damaged the steam frigate *Minnesota* (which had run aground). Union guns wounded Buchanan and damaged some of the *Virginia*'s plates and its smokestack (making it slower), and part of its ram went down with the *Cumberland*. But it had won an awesome and instructive victory. "Ever since my connection with the Department," Fox observed ten days later, "I have used every proper opportunity to awaken an interest in iron-clad vessels and very many associated with me, and most especially the Secretary, have felt an awakening, but the public slept. Most fortunately we have met with a disaster—This is the Almighty's teaching always—success never gives a lesson." News of the disastrous lesson nearly panicked the cabinet, especially Secretary of War Edwin M. Stanton, who had replaced Cameron in January. With faith in the *Monitor*, Welles tried to reassure his jittery colleagues, but they, under Stanton's influence, planned to obstruct the Potomac with stone ships. Welles thought that idea was absurd, because it would accomplish a Confederate objective. The cabinet was worried, but, Welles told Virginia, "the President and all" were "delighted" that Fox had gone to Hampton Roads.[21]

Fox knew nothing of the devastation caused by the *Virginia* until he arrived at Hampton Roads, early Sunday morning, 9 March 1862. Abandoning Nell and the Welles ladies, he immediately took command because Goldsborough was at Roanoke Island. Ignoring protocol and ruffling feathers, he suggested to the senior naval officer, Captain John Marston, that the Roads be cleared of sailing vessels and that steamers be ready "to move off in a moment." He took a steam tugboat out to the *Minnesota* (still hard aground), inspected its damage, and observed its new protector, the *Monitor,* which was lying nearby. It had arrived, Fox later told Ericsson, "at the moment the novelist would have produced her." Fox returned to the tugboat and watched with Wise as the *Virginia* (now commanded by Catesby ap Roger Jones) steered for the *Minnesota,* but at 8:45 it encountered the *Monitor.*[22]

An indecisive three-and-a-half-hour battle followed between two novel and untested vessels. The adversaries fired slowly and deliberately. From its two eleven-inch Dahlgren smoothbore guns, the *Monitor* fired forty-one solid cast iron shots, each weighing 168 pounds. It was hit twenty-two times without significant damage by the forty-six shots aimed at it by the *Virginia,* which also fired at and further damaged the *Minnesota.* To Worden's relief, the *Monitor*'s turret (his major concern) continued to function smoothly, after sustaining heavy shots, while its fire "freely" stripped off the *Virginia*'s iron. Isaac Newton, engineer of the *Monitor,* thought that if the elevation of its guns had been depressed by one degree the *Virginia* would have surrendered in an hour. When the *Virginia* tried to ram the more maneuverable and skillfully handled *Monitor,* it could strike only a glancing blow. But a shell, exploding close to the lookout hole of the *Monitor*'s pilothouse, damaged it slightly and temporarily blinded Worden.

The *Monitor* hauled off (enabling the *Virginia* to claim victory), while Samuel Dana Greene took command. He discovered that the damage to the pilothouse was not sufficient to stop fighting, headed toward the *Virginia,* and fired five additional shots. But Jones, with his vessel drawing twenty-two feet and an ebbing tide, was steering for Norfolk, where the *Virginia* went into dry dock for repairs, having suffered significant damage in two engagements. The *Monitor* did not pursue. The position of its pilothouse prevented firing directly over its bow, and the *Virginia* was faster; consequently, with no pilot, Greene did not want to risk striking obstructions, running aground, or possible capture. He also told Fox that he feared the *Monitor*'s pilothouse was "very much injured," endangering its steering apparatus. The *Monitor* returned to lay by the *Minnesota* until it floated.[23]

Fox was overjoyed, relieved, and impressed. He and Wise immediately boarded the *Monitor* and found Worden, its only casualty, "lying begrimed with powder, bloody, and almost sightless." "Have I beat her off?" he asked.

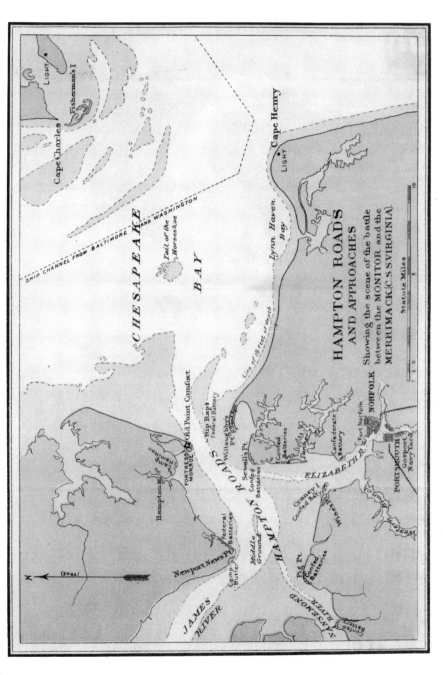

Hampton Roads. From *Official Records of the Union and Confederate Navies*, 7:3.

"Jack!" Wise exclaimed, "You have saved your country." Fox "gave him the sympathies of a shipmate and friend and congratulations upon his fortitude and success." He then asked Greene to assemble the officers and crew on deck, where he thanked them in the name of the Navy Department for their "great services." At 6:45 p.m. that Sunday, with telegraphic communications between Fortress Monroe and Washington restored, Fox wired Welles that the ironclads had fought and the *Virginia* had retired; that the *Minnesota*, although "somewhat injured," would soon be afloat; and, despite Greene's concern, "the *Monitor* is uninjured and ready at any moment to repel another attack." He then telegraphed Ericsson, "Your noble boat has performed with perfect success."[24]

Despite his jubilation, Fox was not carried away. The battle, he told McClellan (whose plans on the Peninsula required that the *Virginia* be neutralized), showed "a slight superiority in favor of the 'Monitor.'" Knowing that the *Virginia* "is an ugly customer," Fox realized it was too optimistic "to believe we are yet clear of her. Our hopes are upon the 'Monitor.'" The day after the battle, Lincoln saw Worden, learned that the *Monitor* could be "boarded and captured very easily" by jamming its turret and drowning its machinery with water down its stack, and agreed with him that it "should not go sky-larking up to Norfolk." On 11 March, Fox, through Montgomery Blair, assured Lincoln "that the Monitor shall take no risk excepting with the Merrimack."[25]

Because Marston, the senior officer present, was "not efficient," Fox remained at Hampton Roads until Wednesday, when Goldsborough returned from Roanoke Island. Apart from ordering unwieldy sailing frigates out of Hampton Roads and calling in maneuverable gunboats, Fox took care of mundane items, like securing a proper mooring buoy for the *Monitor.* Even though the *Virginia* remained a formidable threat, he thought the results of the battle had been decisive. The *Monitor* saved the *Minnesota*, neutralized the *Virginia*, and enabled McClellan to make Fortress Monroe his base of operations for his Peninsula campaign.[26]

Witnessing the *Monitor*'s success in the trial of battle convinced Fox that the navy should model its ironclad program on Ericsson's creation. As Fox and Wise came ashore at Fortress Monroe, after the battle, with Fox wishing that the *Monitor* had had enough offensive punch to sink the *Virginia*, their eyes fell upon "the Union gun," an experimental fifteen-inch columbiad (for coastal defense), designed by the army's ordnance expert Thomas Jackson Rodman. Presumably after sounding out Wise (an authority on ordnance), Fox decided to ask John A. Dahlgren, in whose ability to solve ordnance problems he had great faith, to develop a fifteen-inch naval gun. The army ordnance people at Fortress Monroe, agreed with him that "nothing can stop the *Mer-*

rimack here except the *Monitor* and the big guns" (the fifteen-inch columbiad and a twelve-inch Rodman rifle).[27]

Two days after the historic battle, Fox wired Dahlgren, "We must have more of these boats with 15-inch guns." He also asked if heavier wrought-iron shot could be used in the *Monitor*'s eleven-inch guns. In his excitement, Fox wrote Senator James W. Grimes of the Naval Committee, "The lesson of Sunday is for 20-inch guns." Dahlgren advised against using heavier wrought-iron shot, fearing that if his eleven-inch gun burst in its turret, the *Monitor* would be totally disabled. But despite misgivings, he promised to design "as large guns as you want with solid shot." Fox's enthusiasm for the *Monitor* and its dramatic performance against a Goliath of a vessel made it easier for him to persuade the administration, Congress, and the people of its worth. Even with the fifteen-inch gun, many naval officers, including Du Pont, thought the uncomfortable, unseaworthy, revolutionary vessel was invulnerable but still lacked offensive power.[28]

A "*tired out!*" Fox arrived back in Washington on Thursday, 13 March. He got little rest. Communications from McClellan, hand-delivered by General Irwin McDowell, asked him if the *Monitor* could "keep the *Merrimack* in check, so that I can make Fort Monroe a base of operations?" Fox told McDowell he thought the *Virginia* would be confined to Hampton Roads above Fort Monroe and telegraphed McClellan that "the *Monitor* is more than a match for the *Merrimack*, but," he added, "she might be disabled in the next encounter. I can not advise so great dependence upon her."[29]

At breakfast the next morning, Lincoln sent for Fox and asked him to go that evening to New York to consult Ericsson and to charter fast steamers to ram and sink the *Virginia*. A few days earlier, Ericsson had annoyed Fox a bit by declining his invitation to inspect the *Monitor* with Chief Engineer Alban C. Stimers, who had been on board during its maiden voyage and momentous fight and whom Fox later praised as "the inspiring spirit of that engagement." Ericsson told Fox he was aware, even before the *Monitor* had been half-completed, that on future monitors the pilothouse should be relocated and its ventilation improved. At present, he was rushing, in response to the Navy Department's February advertisement, to complete his design for "the Swift impregnable turret carrier" and had decided to "stick to my drawing table." He and his associates were competing against the Coles-inspired turrets on the proposed Lenthall-Isherwood ironclad. He resented "the most unexpected march which Mr. Isherwood stole upon me in relation to my cylindrical impregnable, steam revolving turret."[30]

On Saturday morning, 15 March, Fox talked ironclads with Ericsson. They discussed improvements the department deemed necessary on the six additional enlarged monitors the government wanted Ericsson and his associates to build. Having observed what James Phinney Baxter calls the "triumph of armor over guns at Hampton Roads," Fox insisted that the new monitors carry fifteen-inch guns. Anticipating some of the Navy Department's demands, Ericsson planned in the new monitors to place the pilothouse on top of the turret, which would improve communications, increase visibility, and allow a new monitor to fire over its bow without blowing away its wheelhouse. They also discussed the "swift turret carrier" on Ericsson's drawing board. When Fox had first suggested it in September 1861, he had hoped it would be "a fit match" for the British *Warrior*. He had in mind a conventional high-sided ironclad, but Ericsson was designing a super monitor with a *"flush deck only 18 inches out of the water."* Spellbinder that he was, Ericsson convinced Fox, an enthusiastic innovator, that it would be seaworthy.[31]

While Fox's grandiose dreams challenged Ericsson, they disturbed Dahlgren. On 17 March the Navy Department ordered Dahlgren to design fifteen- and twenty-inch guns. He regarded that order, to design guns without experimentation, impulsive and fraught with difficulties and dangers. Already concerned about heavy charges in his eleven-inch guns, he wondered if iron could be cast strong enough to prevent huge fifteen-inch guns from bursting. Even though Fox was not an ordnance expert, Dahlgren knew he had consulted with knowledgeable artillery and ordnance men in both the navy and the army. Still, Dahlgren regarded Fox as ignorant and arrogant. Worse, Dahlgren and Rodman (whose columbiad inspired Fox) were bitter rivals. Each accused the other of plagiarizing his designs.[32]

Obeying orders, Dahlgren on 4 April sent Ericsson plans for the fifteen-inch gun. A few days later, he had drawings ready for the Fort Pitt Foundry, where fifty guns were on order and where the Rodman gun had been cast. Dahlgren thought it best to use the Rodman method of "hollow" casting, rather than his own, because the only fifteen-inch gun—the Union gun—had been cast in that manner. Although the navy's fifteen-inch gun bore his name, he regarded it as more a Rodman than a Dahlgren, but Rodman had nothing to do with the navy gun. Given the reluctance of both Dahlgren and Rodman to be associated with the gun, Ericsson wanted to call it "the *Fox Gun*."[33]

"When Rodman's fifteen-inch gun was introduced," Charles Henry Davis recalled a year later, "Dahlgren pronounced against it, and . . . demanded to be openly acquitted of, any responsibility concerning it. Fox decided against his dictum, and, himself, on his own authority and charge, took the matter out of the hands of the Bureau of Ordnance," which Dahlgren dominated. At the time, Dahlgren suppressed his anger over Fox's interference, but four years later complained that Fox exercised "an insufferable tyranny over the Navy—and has entirely deranged it in fastening his notions upon everything—Retiring officers, and assigning duty without regard to anything but his own will—absorbing every function of the Depart—filling the Bureaus with his own creatures, and spending money in every fancy that entered his pate. . . . Nothing could exceed the insolent tyranny of Fox." During the war, though, Dahlgren did not reveal his feelings to Fox, who fostered his career. Indeed, their wartime correspondence is marked by cordiality.[34]

Tyrant or not, Fox could order Dahlgren, but Ericsson had to be cajoled. After a few days of reflection, Fox wrote Ericsson on 18 March, reiterating his support for a super–*Monitor* style "fast boat" and suggesting improvements for the six new monitors. After reviewing his conversations with those on board the *Monitor* during its passage to Hampton Roads and his eyewitness impressions of its "contest with the 'Merrimac,'" Fox concurred "fully in the plans which you showed me in New York Saturday." He also promised that in three or four days Dahlgren would forward to him the outside dimensions of the fifteen-inch gun for the new monitors. In addition, Fox offered, in a "kind spirit" to the testy inventor, ten "suggestions of detail," including fifteen-inches of armor on the turret, "the 'ram' now so popular," an equipoise rudder forward to be used in action only, twelve-feet high ventilator and smoke pipes, and comfortable accommodations for officers and crew, including a raised "gallery" on deck for exercise. "We ought," Fox concluded, "to have a dozen 'Monitors' at least, instead of six. How many can be made in the country, including your fast boat?" Complimenting Fox's "perfect" mastery of the subject, Ericsson responded favorably to his suggestions and warned that Dahlgren "not add a single inch of length for the 15 inch gun," because the diameter of the turret could not be increased. He also assured Fox that "the building of a dozen Monitors is a mere trifle with the enormous engineering capabilities of the United States at this moment."[35]

Fox envisioned "fast boats that will cross [the Atlantic] to the *enemy's country*," with twenty-inch guns mounted in two turrets protected by twenty-five inches of iron plate. He anticipated that after the battle at Hampton Roads, "the most enormous Calibre of ordnance must immediately come into use," and he wanted to be prepared. "You startle me," Ericsson responded to requests for fifteen-inch and twenty-five-inch thicknesses on turrets, but he appreciated Fox's "boldness" that proved "we are now going to have a navy ahead of all other nations." The capacity of rolling mills and considerations of buoyancy led Ericsson to decide on eleven-inch armor on the turrets of the new monitors, arranged so additional four-inch plates could be bolted on.[36]

But Fox's demand for two turrets on the "fast vessel" depressed Ericsson and "utterly dispelled" his hope for the United States to be "at the head of the Naval Powers." The 300-foot, fast vessel Ericsson planned could sustain only one turret with two twenty-inch guns and the armor Fox wanted. Despite Fox's arguments, Ericsson remained adamantly opposed to two turrets, arguing that the weight of an additional turret could be used to provide more armor. Fox reasoned that a minor turret mishap on a single-turret vessel would render it helpless. He told Ericsson to go ahead with his plans for the swift single-turret carrier "and at the same time let us . . . make a larger vessel with two turrets." Happy with the go-ahead for his seagoing monitor, Ericsson graciously said that "anything which my head or hands can effect, is entirely at the command of your department." As long as there was a possibility of European intervention, Fox was in a hurry for "the big ship." Sensing the deterring effect of the navy's "revolving fort upon a raft," Fox complied with requests by foreign powers for drawings of the *Monitor*.[37]

Fox and Ericsson agreed completely on how to improve the monitor design for coastal service. Accordingly, ten new coastal monitors—known as the Passaic class—were contracted for $400,000 each in the early spring of 1862. All but one were launched in the late summer and fall of 1862 and commissioned by early 1863. Ericsson, who built six of them, had not underestimated the North's industrial capacity. At 1,875 tons displacement (twice that of the original *Monitor*, but drawing the same ten and a half feet of water) and armed with a fifteen-inch as well as an eleven-inch Dahlgren smoothbore, they featured changes Fox and Ericsson had discussed in their correspondence. Ericsson and Chief Engineer Alban C. Stimers called on Fox on 2 April 1862. That evening the three of them discussed monitors with Lincoln at the White House.[38]

To facilitate monitor construction, the Navy Department ordered Stimers to New York as inspector of ironclads. He was to assist Rear Admiral Francis H. Gregory, whose office oversaw the construction of naval vessels by private contractors on the Atlantic coast. Having supervised the building of the original *Monitor* and served in it at Hampton Roads, Stimers was an enormous help to Ericsson and became the leading spirit in what became known as "the Monitor Bureau." Stimers, Ericsson reported to Fox in April 1862, "knows all about the wants of a vessel of war, I therefore cheerfully defer to his judgment" about "the arrangements for officers, crew, stores, ammunition &c. of the Impregnables . . . and feel greatly obliged to him for his efficient assistance."[39]

Fox was in constant communication with Ericsson to hurry, to suggest, and to criticize. On 5 June, for example, Fox, having seen preliminary drawings of Ericsson's "seagoing turret ship," feared it did not meet "the requirements of an Ocean Steamer." In addition, he feared, correctly it turned out, that the Passaic class of monitors would not have the speed of nine knots and lamented: "We seem to . . . lag astern John Bull in the matter of speed." Construction proceeded rapidly, even though Ericsson complained to Fox on 6 July, "Our men observed the great festive day of the nation with so much spirit last Friday that they were unfit for work yesterday. This being Sunday we lose three valuable days in succession."[40]

By the summer of 1862, Fox and Ericsson had reconciled their differences sufficiently for the Navy Department to contract for two seagoing monitors, costing a total of $2.3 million. The *Dictator,* a single-turreted vessel armed with two fifteen-inch guns, would be more than twice as large as the new coastal monitors, while the even larger *Puritan* was to be double-turreted. The *Dictator* was commissioned in November 1864 and joined the North Atlantic Blockading Squadron. Although designed to achieve fifteen knots, its service speed was only nine knots and its twenty-foot draft limited its usefulness, but its skipper John Rodgers declared it "steers beautifully" and "is a great triumph." Ericsson had agreed to arm the *Puritan* with twenty-inch guns, but casting such experimental guns delayed its completion, and with the end of the war construction ceased. By early 1865, Ericsson had won his argument with Fox and built the *Puritan* with a single turret, because Fox wanted thirty inches of freeboard for a voyage to Europe, which he hoped "would win a moral victory that might save blood and treasure." These deep-draft, seagoing monitors were designed to combat the British and French navies, should those nations intervene in the Civil War. As the threat receded, their need diminished. The Union navy had greater need for shallow-draft armored vessels to operate in southern rivers and harbors. Nevertheless, by the war's end, the *Dictator* was ready for the Confederate *Stonewall.*[41]

While Fox and Ericsson were planning bigger and better monitors, the original *Monitor* made McClellan's Peninsula campaign possible. "I have such a lively faith in the gallant little Monitor," McClellan wrote Fox, "so I have determined on the Fort Monroe movement." Because a vast army had to be moved down the Potomac to Fortress Monroe, and its flanks on the York and James rivers had to be protected, control of those rivers and of Hampton Roads was imperative. To bottle up the *Virginia* at Norfolk, Stanton offered the Navy Department the stone fleet he had assembled to block the Potomac (derisively called "Stanton's navy" by Lincoln). McClellan also liked the idea. Although he had enthusiastically blocked channels at Charleston, Fox opposed using Stanton's hulks at Norfolk, when meeting with Stanton and Lincoln. He may have anticipated its capture or simply had faith in the *Monitor*.[42]

Stanton did not think the *Monitor* should be relied on and Charles Ellet Jr., a gifted civil engineer, agreed. He was in Washington promoting, without success, his pet project of high-speed rams to sink Confederate gunboats. Fox's spirited opposition to utilizing Stanton's stone fleet hurt Stanton's feelings and exacerbated his hostility toward Welles and especially Fox. Lincoln, Stanton complained, "leans to the judgment of Mr. Fox, who he seems to think is in possession of the entire amount of knowledge in the naval world." Although admitting his ignorance of "the naval world," Stanton, a few days after Fox bruised his ego, commissioned Ellet a colonel and ordered him to create a ram fleet to operate "on the Western waters."[43]

McClellan began moving his army from Alexandria to Fortress Monroe on 17 March. His chief engineer, General John G. Barnard, pored over charts with Fox on 18 March and talked "siege guns, Norfolk, Yorktown, &c." with him on 22 March. McClellan wanted the navy to bombard Yorktown's defenses, but Fox, worrying "about a second Visit from the Merrimack," reminded Lincoln that Goldsborough's "first duty was to take care of the Merrimac." Not wanting the army people to "say that the Navy could not help," Fox told Goldsborough that if he could spare ships to "knock down the town for them, they consider it as saving several months in the campaign." If naval support was limited or nonexistent, McClellan obviously anticipated a long siege, rather than the quick assault Lincoln had in mind.[44]

On 6 April, the day after that siege began, Fox left Washington to gain "more accurate information of the squadron & affairs" at Hampton Roads. There were reports that the *Virginia* (*Merrimack*) "was coaling & expected out," so Virginia Fox supposed that "Gus expected to see the battle." The *Virginia* came only as far as Craney Island on 7 April, probably because of bad weather. It was so wet and boggy that it took Fox three hours on horseback to ride three miles to McClellan's tent before Yorktown, where he consulted, dried off, and spent the night. He promised to support McClellan with mortars and "with ships as far as their capacity permitted" and apparently agreed to ask Lincoln to send more troops to Yorktown. Fox saw Lincoln on 11 April, and, Virginia noted in her diary, "Gus obtained an order for Gen[eral] Franklin's division to go to McC[lellan]."[45]

The *Virginia*, however, limited the "capacity" of the navy to support McClellan, whose move up the peninsula to Richmond had bogged down at Yorktown. On 11 April the *Virginia* rounded Sewell's Point, entered Hampton Roads, and enabled its escorts to capture three Union provision transports. Both it and the *Monitor* cautiously avoided a return engagement. Even if the *Virginia* did not attack the *Monitor*, it was valuable to the Confederacy. "A man here," Virginia Fox noted on 18 April, "to see Gus about destroying the Merrimac; asked what they would give him if he accomplished it—$500,000! He seemed surprised. Gus says it is equal to 100,000 men to the rebels—protects Norfolk and the James River, and keeps our fleet . . . from going to Yorktown." Although the *Washington Star* estimated that 1,500 schemes to destroy the *Virginia* had been proposed to the Navy Department, virtually none was taken seriously. Without much faith, Fox relayed to Goldsborough the notion of the French Prince de Joinville (François Ferdinand d'Orléans), who was on McClellan's staff, that the *Virginia*'s propeller could be fouled with a hawser. Fox did charter two "sound" vessels (the *Illinois* and the *Arago*, at $1,300 a day each) for "an extra hazardous employment," to ram the *Virginia*. The crews of both vessels refused to attack the *Virginia*, while those of the *Vanderbilt* and the *Ericsson* were willing, but never had the opportunity. These boats were also rented to run down the *Virginia* (apparently, at $3,000 a day).[46]

"The Navy," Fox complained to Goldsborough, "is suffering severely from the condition of things at Hampton Roads. The great public not understanding why *we* cannot take Yorktown. The feeling here," which Fox and Lincoln apparently shared, "is that McClellan has put himself into a very tight place, and that a rush past the batteries at Yorktown only can relieve him, or very greatly assist him." With the *Galena* (like the *Monitor* one of the three original ironclads ordered by the Navy Department) due any day, Fox urged that Goldsborough take it and some other "brave fellows" above Yorktown. "The golden opportunity is now present to save the Army, and immortalize the Navy," he argued. Fox did "not feel very great anxiety" about such a move, since "a passage at night, under full steam, across the line of fire, has been demonstrated by this war to be easy of accomplishment." In April 1862 it was not yet clear that running by forts was meaningless without adequate troops to seal them from succor. When the *Galena* arrived, Goldsborough dismissed it— before a trial by battle—as "a most miserable contrivance" and did not attempt to run by Yorktown. The *Galena* was an experimental ironclad, and its two- to two-and-one-half-inch armor was not reassuring.[47]

Carefully monitoring the month-long siege of Yorktown, Fox spent the night of 3 May in McClellan's tent. While his host bragged he would bag

18,000 Confederates on the morrow, the Confederates were already evacuating that town. Because Fox liked to have a trophy of each battle, he returned home with "muskets, long spikes of wood with steel points and cartridge boxes and bags, &c., &c.; plunder from the field of Yorktown." He distributed some of these spoils among members of the naval committees of Congress. At York-town, some of the cartridge bags were "made from the Bay State Shawl," manufactured at Lawrence under Fox's supervision.[48]

Still, Fox was more interested in Confederate artillery emplacements than in his versatile Bay State shawl. Having seen all the defenses of Yorktown ("but 50 guns and none pointing up river"), he was "satisfied that if [John S.] Missroon had pushed by with a couple of gun boats, the Navy would have had the credit of driving the army of the rebels out, besides immortality to him-self." While Fox thought the water batteries "insignificant," Goldsborough thought the fifty guns formidable.[49]

Although Fox got on well with Goldsborough, they differed in their person-alities and responsibilities. Goldsborough was cautious, while Fox was auda-cious. A career naval officer, Goldsborough did not understand that in a democ-racy public opinion was important to the navy. "The great public in our country unfortunately," he wrote Fox, "is very apt to misjudge Naval & mili-tary matters, because it is seldom correctly informed about them, & because of the disposition of every fool in the land to write & talk about things of which he scarcely knows the meaning." A political appointee with expertise in naval operations, Fox had to prod naval officers and reconcile their requirements and judgments with political realities. In constant contact with Lincoln, Welles, Blair, and various congressmen, Fox realized that dramatic victories would help morale, get appropriations passed, and provide vessels for his command-ers, while conspicuous failures would do the opposite. He emphasized that the escape of the Confederate commerce raider *Nashville* on 17 March from Beau-fort, North Carolina, was "a terrible blow to our naval prestige," rather than a direct negative effect on the Union war effort.[50]

Thirsting for naval victories, Fox advised Goldsborough to send his gun-boats up the James and York rivers. Because the *Virginia* drew so much water, "they would be soon out of her reach." He was "radiant" when he heard that Lincoln, at Fortress Monroe to hurry military operations, had ordered Golds-borough to send on 8 May the *Monitor, Galena,* and three other vessels to shell Confederate batteries on Sewell's Point. Lincoln's hope was to induce the *Vir-ginia* out far enough for Fox's costly rams to sink it. It came out briefly, but not far enough to ram.[51]

Fox was right about the *Virginia*'s deep draft. Three days later, following

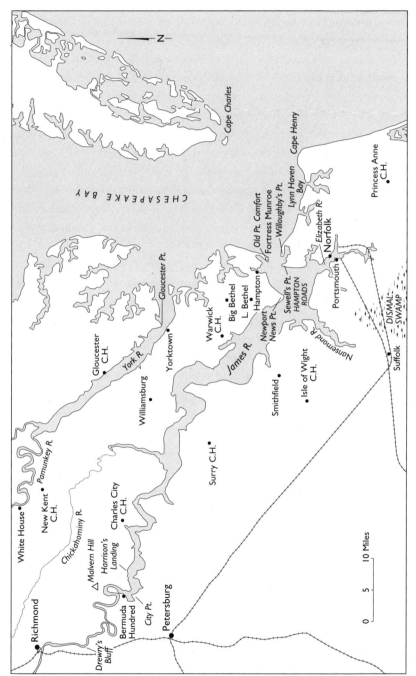

Southeastern Virginia. Map by Bill Nelson, derived from *Official Records of the Union and Confederate Navies*, 8:3.

the Confederate evacuation of Norfolk, Flag Officer Josiah Tattnall scuttled
the *Virginia* because it could not ascend the James. Goldsborough immediately
ordered the James River Flotilla, including the *Monitor* and the *Galena*, up
that river, where on 15 May at Drewry's Bluff, eight miles below Richmond, it
was repulsed by the guns of Fort Darling. The draft of the *Monitor* restricted
its movements, the flotilla's guns could not be elevated effectively, and the
inadequate armor of the *Galena* was pierced by Confederate gunners, some of
whom under Catesby Jones had just arrived from the *Virginia*. John Rodgers,
who commanded the flotilla, wrote to his wife "that the Galena dont compare
in efficiency or comfort to the Monitor."[52]

"The destruction of the *Virginia*," Confederate Captain Franklin Buchanan
wrote Jones, "saved Richmond, for if you all had not been at the Bluff Richmond would have been shelled, and perhaps taken." With dreams of new lau-
rels for the navy, Fox had hoped that Goldsborough's available gunboats would
"dash" by Fort Darling and take Richmond, and Buchanan thought it a distinct possibility. The repulse by Fort Darling at Drewry's Bluff disappointed
both Fox and Lincoln. Word that McClellan was not discouraged exasperated
Lincoln, who wanted him to be aggressive and more than merely not discouraged. Trying to rein in Fox's ideas of unilateral naval capabilities (which
Buchanan shared), Goldsborough realistically told him, "without the Army
the Navy can make no real headway to-wards Richmond." In cooperation with
McClellan, "we shall have Richmond," he predicted.[53]

While cooperating with McClellan, Goldsborough echoed McClellan's cautious nature. Richmond, which Fox thought on 3 June was "about to fall," was
not to be had. Fox longed to send Goldsborough off to Wilmington, North
Carolina, to "knock down" Fort Caswell, but he had to remain "watching over
the Army of the Potomac," protecting its provision transports. Gunboats ascended the York and Pamunkey rivers and patrolled the James up to Drewry's
Bluff. By 16 June Goldsborough sounded less sanguine about taking Richmond.
He reported to Fox that Confederate obstructions in the James River at
Drewry's Bluff made it "wholly impassable" for gunboats. Only a joint attack
could take Fort Darling, but McClellan felt he was not strong enough to provide troops to flank that fort. Taking McClellan's doubling of the enemy seriously, Goldsborough believed in mid-June "beyond a doubt" that Richmond
defenders "now amount to 200,000 men." Growing more impatient by the
day, Lincoln insisted on 17 June that Fox go to Hampton Roads and report back
to him. Virginia Fox said that on the way there Fox consulted all night with
Lieutenant Robert H. Wyman, commander of the Potomac Flotilla, and all
night at City Point with Commander John Rodgers, of the James River Flo-

tilla. She made no mention of a meeting with Goldsborough. Fox and Welles were becoming impatient with his caution.[54]

Beginning at the end of June, the Seven Days Campaign pushed McClellan back, cut him off from his main base at White House on the Pamunkey River, and postponed the capture of Richmond. On Saturday evening, 28 June, Lincoln was depressed, as he waited for news at the War Department. He asked Fox to join him "immediately." With McClellan retreating toward the James River, while the navy protected his transports as they moved from White House to his projected new base at Harrison's Landing, Fox also was downcast. The most positive news he could focus on was that McClellan had "lost no guns ammunition or provisions, only men!"[55]

A superb storyteller, Fox stayed until ten o'clock and "kept the President in good spirits telling anecdotes." A few days later, on 2 July, after reporting that "Uncle Abram is cool and sure but Stanton looks sick," Fox cried, "Oh for a general of genius." With the blockade in mind, he wrote Virginia, who was in Portsmouth, that the retreat "is most fatal to us as I fear it will bring down France and perhaps England upon us." Fox hoped that the huge seagoing monitors he and Ericsson were planning would meet that threat.[56]

After McClellan fell back to Harrison's Landing, Fox and Welles tried to infuse some spirit into the Peninsula campaign. On 6 July, they appointed Charles Wilkes (who earlier had seized Mason and Slidell from the *Trent*) commander of the James River Squadron, having him report directly to the department, rather than through Goldsborough. Incensed by this slight, Goldsborough asked on 15 July to be relieved as commander of the North Atlantic Blockading Squadron. Welles and Fox were "not sorry to have him quit," because he seemed "used up." From his strong position at Harrison's Landing, abetted by formidable naval support, McClellan still threatened Richmond via the James River, but he demanded more reinforcements before taking the offensive.[57]

Anxious for that offensive, Fox "took the liberty" to go to the War Department. He suggested that troops from South and North Carolina, from the West, and "every drilled soldier" at Washington be sent to McClellan. To defend the capital, he would call up 100,000 militia. Except that Ambrose E. Burnside in North Carolina was ordered to join the Army of the Potomac, Fox's drastic advice was ignored. Probably retaliating for Fox's rejection of his advice to block Norfolk, Stanton did not spare Fox's feelings. "Having a little sense of mortification therefrom," Fox wrote General Barnard on 23 July, "I have not been into the War Dept since." Fox was so frustrated that he snapped at Virginia for whining about her loneliness, "Don't you think somebody else's heart aches to be alone besides your own." He was "discouraged to see the waste of such great efforts" and complained that "a combination of errors great in the aggregate have given the day against us." The administration's reluctant support of McClellan, combined with the caution of McClellan and Goldsborough, were certainly among the errors Fox had in mind.[58]

"There seems much apathy," he observed in late July, as Henry W. Halleck, the army's leading theoretician of war, took command of the armies of the United States (McClellan remained in command of the Army of the Potomac). "The impotent conclusion of a magnificent commencement is too disgusting to contemplate with any degree of satisfaction or patience." Yet Fox perceived a ray of hope. "Halleck has more brains for the cabinet [as an adviser to it] than for the field and I think will do well here. He is our only hope."[59]

That hope withered quickly. With McClellan adamant about reinforcements, Halleck ordered the Army of the Potomac back to Washington. Wilkes and the Navy Department were dismayed; they had envisioned a joint army-navy operation up the James, culminating in Richmond's surrender to the navy. Instead, as Fox reported to Senator James W. Grimes on 5 August, "The Army of the Potomac rests quietly under the great guns of the Navy." Over the next few weeks, the James River Flotilla covered the army's withdrawal from the Peninsula. "Thus the great combined movement," Rowena Reed notes, "begun with such promise of a rapid and decisive victory, came to an inglorious end."[60]

CHAPTER TEN

The Mississippi

We are refused swords, Pistols, rifles and muskets with cartridges, by both Army and Navy. I am trying to get clothing,
also, refused by both. . . . Our men have not been paid. . . . Thus
we go here, and you wonder why I have the blues.

Foote to Fox, 27–28 September 1861

The passing of the forts, Jackson and St. Philip, was one of the
most awful sights and events I ever saw or expect to experience.

Farragut to Fox, 25 April 1862

The war in the West was different than in southern coastal regions, where the
navy maintained the blockade, or in Virginia, where huge armies confronted
each other north and east of Richmond. In the West, the Mississippi and its
tributaries were the transportation arteries of a vast region, facilitating rapid
movements by joint army and navy forces. On the upper Mississippi, a river
navy had to be created under chaotic conditions. On the lower Mississippi, an
armada had to be assembled to take New Orleans. Severing the Confederacy
by a giant pincer movement, down and up the Mississippi, provided opportunities for impulsive, daring actions and stunning accomplishments. It also produced the navy's and the army's greatest Civil War heroes.

■ ■ ■

Ironically, it was the War Department that built the first Civil War ironclad
vessels. On 7 August 1861, more than a month before Ericsson presented plans
for the *Monitor* to the Ironclad Board, the War Department contracted with
James B. Eads of St. Louis, Missouri, for seven light-draft ironclad river gunboats. From the start, though, the Navy Department was involved with these
vessels. In April, a few days before Fox entered the Navy Department, Eads
proposed that it arm a center-wheel, catamaran snag boat (a vessel that re-

moved river obstructions) and base it at Cairo, Illinois, to interdict Confederate river commerce. Because operations on western rivers were then the army's responsibility, Welles referred Eads to the War Department. He also asked John Lenthall, chief of the Bureau of Construction, to design a river gunboat and ordered Commander John Rodgers and Constructor Samuel M. Pook to help the army create a flotilla on the upper Mississippi River. On 1 June Lenthall gave the army his plans for a 436-ton stern-wheeler drawing five feet, disclaiming, "It does not seem to be practicable to make" an efficient armed steam vessel for the Mississippi. He suggested that western steamboat builders be consulted and that Pook make necessary modifications. With General-in-Chief Winfield Scott's approval, the War Department went ahead, and Eads won the contract for what became known as the Cairo class of river gunboats.[1]

Although Eads built these river gunboats, they were essentially Pook's creation. At 512 tons, they carried thirteen guns and were protected by sloping two-and-a-half-inch iron sides. Much of their topsides were unprotected, and their pilothouses were deathtraps, with little armor. Strenuous efforts were made to complete these vessels by 10 October 1861, but it was January before they were ready. Two additional ironclads were ordered by General John C. Frémont (then commander of the Western Department, in which the Mississippi River Gunboat Flotilla was lodged). Frémont had Eads convert a ferry boat into the five-gun *Essex* and a snag boat into the formidable sixteen-gun *Benton*. The *Essex* was ready by November 1861, and the *Benton* was commissioned on 24 February 1862. With faith that water-borne, thirteen-inch mortars could compel forts to surrender, Fox persuaded Frémont to order thirty-eight mortar boats—actually log rafts—for the Western Flotilla.[2]

While Eads was building and converting gunboats, Rodgers improvised. He purchased three wooden river steamers at Cincinnati, converted them into gunboats, without armor, and on 12 August arrived with them at Cairo to patrol the Mississippi. When Frémont complained, "I don't like Commander Rodgers," and asked that he be replaced by "some younger" and presumably more pliant officer, Fox transferred Rodgers, at the end of August, despite his prodigious labors. For his replacement, Fox selected Captain Andrew H. Foote, an older officer, who had commanded the New York Navy Yard at Brooklyn. He had experience in building and equipping vessels and would be indispensable in readying the Eads boats for service.[3]

Foote immediately swung into action. In St. Louis on 5 September, he reported to Frémont, who was "discouraged" and talked so "sadly about the state of things along the river" that Foote feared he had an impossible task.

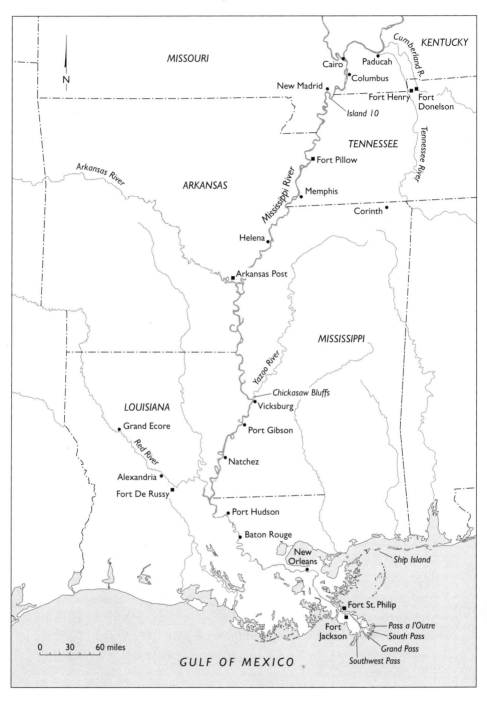

Mississippi River, from Cairo to Fort Jackson. Map by Bill Nelson.

Moving on to Cairo, Foote arrived at midnight and discovered that Rodgers with two of his gunboats had just left for Paducah, Kentucky, with Brigadier General Ulysses S. Grant. Foote commandeered a steamboat, caught up with the expedition, and participated in Grant's seizure of Paducah, which controlled the mouth of the Tennessee River. It was the start of a productive partnership and the harbinger of successful army-navy operations on western waters. Somewhat encouraged, Foote returned to St. Louis and conferred with Frémont, who, he told Fox, "(no doubt from your letter overestimating me) received me very cordially and seemed desirous to obtain my views fully."[4]

Participating in the movement against Paducah was far simpler than readying new vessels for action. "I have the blues," Foote complained to Fox on 27 September. Trying to organize a fleet or flotilla was a difficult task under the best of circumstances, but Foote's task was doubly complicated. He was "away from a Navy Yard . . . in this wilderness of Naval wants," outfitting an army flotilla, which was commanded by naval officers. "We are still without a Quarter Master, the connecting link between us and the Army," he complained, and consequently "we cannot from either Army or Navy get any powder." After looking in vain "to regular sources of supply," Foote turned his eyes towards irregular sources. For example, he asked the energetic Indiana governor, Oliver P. Morton, for the powder he needed. Making matters worse, John C. Frémont was a difficult superior. He "suddenly requires a good many things without consulting me in my Department," Foote complained, and furthermore, "papers going to Genl. Frémont's Quarters can seldom be found again and we are suffering from it now."[5]

The response from Fox cheered Foote. He was sending him 300 drilled men, including many New England fishermen. Although by 2 November "Guns, powder, shell, small arms, as well as all or most material stores" had arrived and were quickly sent downriver to Cairo, Foote still had problems. The Mississippi at St. Louis was too low to float a fully equipped gunboat, which Foote knew would draw more than six feet of water and be of limited use at Cairo. His lack of rank, he told Fox, hampered his usefulness. The army regarded his captaincy equal to a lieutenant colonelcy. Recently, a colonel, against Foote's and Frémont's wishes, had ordered a gunboat to accompany his regiment, and at Cairo Ulysses S. Grant would have deprived the flotilla of storage space, already assigned to it, were it not for Frémont's specific order.[6]

Lack of money was Foote's biggest headache. Eads's boats were being "kept back by want of money" and so, too, were the thirty-eight mortar boats, whose construction Frémont asked Foote to expedite. "This moment," Foote added as a postscript, "the Contractor of the Mortar Boats, comes into my office and says he cannot get a cent of money and will stop work and leave town to avoid his workmen mobbing him. I relate the incident to show the position in which you have placed me, and the obloquy likely to rest upon my hitherto considered honest name."[7]

Despite the headaches, Foote persevered, as did Fox. In response to the cries for help, Fox "made several calls upon the War Department, about the money," and was assured that "it was remedied." Also, on 19 November, by addressing Foote as "My dear Flag-Officer," Fox informed him that his lack of rank had been remedied. "I am grateful to you," Foote responded, "for my Flag." He also wrote that he had been cheered by news of Du Pont's victory at Port Royal and praised Fox for his part in "planning and aiding" that expedition. When, a few days later, the first two Eads gunboats were launched at St Louis, Foote discovered that they drew five and a half feet and could barely get down river to Cairo for their completion.[8]

Despite his new rank and Frémont's ouster on 2 November 1861, Foote continued to be frustrated by his military superiors. Major General Henry W. Halleck, the commander of the newly created Department of the Missouri, was more ignorant than Frémont of "the wants of men of war, or even Western Gun Boats," and questioned Foote's "judgment about Navy matters." Worse, Halleck stopped the construction of the mortar boats and delayed the gunboats' action by not providing the men to handle them. Reflecting the army's attitude, Grant suggested that the thirty to forty drunkards he had in the guardhouse be transferred to the gunboats. Feeling desperate, Foote turned to Fox. "I present the whole matter to you knowing that your resources will apply the corrective, as you have, superadded to good sound judgment, great experience in naval matters and wants."[9]

Fox "begged and beseeched" the War Department to take care of Foote's needs and discovered that the army hardly had any mortars ready for Foote to install in the log rafts. An ardent advocate of mortar boats, Fox felt certain that their arcing "bombshells" would be effective against elevated "earth forts," like Donelson on the Cumberland River. He complained of the delay to Lincoln, who became "very much exercised in the matter," especially after he learned that only two mortar beds were ready for Foote at Pittsburgh. Lincoln told Stanton to issue a "peremptory order" to the ordnance officer at Pittsburgh to ship mortars "to Cairo instantly" and telegraphed Foote on 23 January that he wanted the "rafts with their 13 inch mortars" ready "at the earliest possible moment." Demanding a daily telegram on their progress, he told Fox's sidekick Henry A. Wise of the navy's Ordnance Bureau, "I wont leave off until it fairly rains Bombs."[10]

Unable to spare more men from the navy (500 had been sent), Fox told Foote he had advised Halleck "to obey orders about furnishing you with men." Anticipating some of these problems, Fox had desired "to transfer the whole thing to the Navy." But Foote realized that a change of that sort would cause complications and further delays. "Now we are so entwined with" the army, he wrote on 31 January, "and our supplies and building & other accommodations coming from them, a change would be embarrassing." Foote hoped by "straining every nerve to get men" that by "next week . . . we shall make a move with seven of the Gun Boats & a land force. I have to send men from different Gun Boats," he complained, "to make up crews for four of the iron clad boats."[11]

With the four ironclads and three wooden gunboats (but without mortar boats), Foote left Cairo on 2 February 1862 for a joint expedition with Grant. With the Tennessee River full enough to float ironclads, the time was right for an expedition against Fort Henry. On 4 February Grant began disembarking his 15,000 men five miles below the fort, and two days later, at 11:00 a.m., both troops and gunboats advanced on the fort. Dense forest and bad roads, made worse by two days of heavy rain, delayed Grant's men, while Foote's gunboats engaged Fort Henry, which was defended by fewer than 100 artillerymen. Most of its garrison had been moved eleven miles overland to the more substantial Fort Donelson on the Cumberland River. After three hours' bombardment by the flotilla, Fort Henry surrendered to Foote. Of his vessels, only the *Essex* suffered significant damage. Its boiler was hit, scalding twenty-eight men, some fatally. Over the next three days, the three wooden gunboats ascended the Tennessee River as far as Florence, Alabama. They captured the partially completed Confederate ironclad *Eastport* at Cerro Gordo, Tennessee, while the Union ironclad *Carondelet* destroyed the Memphis and Ohio Railroad bridge above Fort Henry. Foote's victory gave "intense satisfaction" to Lincoln, Congress, and the Navy Department. Fox rejoiced that Foote's "sublime patience" and hard labor was "crowned with victory," and, as his own reward, he savored "another fort knocked over by the Navy."[12]

Grant immediately moved to besiege Fort Donelson (defended by approximately 21,000 men). Recognizing that Foote and his gunboats were "a valuable part of our available force," he awaited their ascent of the Cumberland before launching an assault. After repairing some of the battle damage at Cairo, Foote, at the urgent request of Halleck and Grant, left on 11 February for Donelson. Still short of men, he told Fox he took all he could, leaving skeleton crews in the rest of his squadron. He regretted he did not have ten extra days, for by then eight mortar boats and three additional ironclad gunboats would be ready. On 14 February Grant hoped that the flotilla would repeat its Fort Henry success. With the army relatively quiescent, Foote's four ironclads and two wooden gunboats attacked Donelson. Rather than exploit his long range guns, Foote closed in on the fort. Because Donelson was on high ground, its gunners poured a withering, plunging fire on the gunboats, whose topsides were relatively unprotected. The steering on two of the ironclads was disabled, and Foote, who was in the exposed pilothouse of his flagship, was injured in the foot. As they drifted downstream, the rest of the squadron withdrew.[13]

A long siege seemed inevitable. The following day, Foote told Grant he had to repair the two gunboats in Cairo, promising to return in ten days with more gunboats and mortar rafts to reduce the fort. While they conferred, the Confederate garrison attempted to break out. Sensing that the moment for a coordinated counterstroke had come, Grant, supported by shells lobbed into the fort from the long range guns of two relatively uninjured gunboats, attacked, driving the Confederates back. The next day, they "unconditionally" surrendered.[14]

The effect of the capture of Fort Donelson can hardly be exaggerated. Militarily it saved Kentucky for the Union, threatened the Confederacy's hold on Tennessee, and helped to gain control of the Mississippi River. The unconditional surrender of its garrison devastated southern morale and gave the North the boost it badly needed. That dramatic surrender also drew attention to the generalship of Ulysses Grant. His confident, rapid movements, his ability to understand the enemy and to keep it off balance, and his capacity to sense the moment for a decisive counterstroke became apparent.[15]

With the fall of those forts, Union forces occupied on 4 March the strong fortifications at Columbus, Kentucky. Foote's dispatch with the welcome news arrived the evening of 4 March, during a party at Welles's home. While rejoicing, Fox "felt a pang" that the mortar boats had not been able to bombard the "Gibraltar of the West." He wanted his faith in building them confirmed, and he wanted the navy to take Confederate forts by raining "13 inch shells upon them," which would deflate the army engineers who built fortifications. They, Fox exaggerated to Foote, "are all alike, conceited, puffed up, imbued with a contempt of the Navy, and have all their lives been trying to prove impossible what you have demonstrated possible, viz:—to attack forts successfully with vessels." He was proud of Foote's "work attained without the efficient cooperation from anyone. . . . I *think* we shall work out a reward for you," he wrote on 8 March. "We shall try." On that day, however, the *Virginia* wreaked havoc at Hampton Roads, and Fox's attention turned to coastal, seagoing, and river monitors.[16]

Fox realized that the Union was fortunate in having an engineering and organizational genius in St. Louis, who was comparable and perhaps superior to Ericsson. James B. Eads (who had built river gunboats for Foote's Western Flotilla) responded to the Navy Department's February advertisement for turreted, river ironclads, with plans for single- and double-turreted river monitors. In the fourth week of May 1862, Eads contracted with the Navy Department to build two stern-wheel, single-turreted monitors and four larger quadruple-screw, double-turreted monitors. Both models had a "turtleback" deck, but the forward turret on the larger vessels was designed by Eads, while the other turrets were after Ericsson's model. The guns in the Eads turret were on a huge steam-powered platform, which was lowered into the hold, where the guns were loaded and then raised, run out, aimed, fired, and returned to the hold for reloading. Eads had proposed to use his turrets exclusively on these vessels, but Fox insisted that each have an Ericsson turret, because it had withstood the test of battle. Eads cheerfully complied and checked with Ericsson about minor modifications. Excited to be a part of the cutting edge of naval technology, Eads wrote Ericsson, "I think with you that America is about to make all the World wonder. I am thankful for being born in this era." His stern-wheelers drew only four and a half feet and attained a speed of seven and a half miles per hour, while the double-turreted vessels drew six feet and had a service speed of nine knots. With seasonal changes in the depth of rivers, six feet was the maximum practical draft for naval vessels operating on the Mississippi and its tributaries.[17]

Unlike Ericsson, who had sophisticated shipyards available on New York's East River, Eads had to build the Union Iron Works at Carondelet, Missouri, seven miles below St. Louis. The plant could roll three-inch-thick iron plates, which were superior to three one-inch laminated plates that were used on Ericsson's monitors. The Union Iron Works consisted of a large machine shop and four ship houses, under which the boats were built. By the fall of 1862, the Eads shipyard, boasting an illuminating gas–generating plant, was in full swing, employing between 500 and 600 men, who worked day and night. The lighter stern-wheelers were launched in January and February 1863, with the *Neosho* commissioned on 13 May and the *Osage* on 10 July 1863. Eads's two-turreted, Milwaukee-class monitors followed. Richard H. Webber calls them "perhaps the most sophisticated successful monitors of the Civil War." The *Winnebago* and the *Chickasaw* were commissioned in April and May 1864, and the *Kickapoo* and the *Milwaukee* in July and August 1864. As the *Winnebago* neared completion, Fox was "very much struck" by the Eads turret and contemplated its use on oceangoing monitors.[18]

The monitors Fox began promoting in March 1862 were not available on the Mississippi for more than a year. Foote had to make do with ironclads that had proved vulnerable in the close-up attack on Fort Donelson. On crutches and pained by his wounded foot, which refused to heal, Foote prepared for an assault on Island No. 10, downriver from Columbus. Situated on a sharp bend in the Mississippi, it was upstream and south of New Madrid, Missouri. It was heavily defended by many of the Confederates who had evacuated Columbus. Moving overland, Brigadier General John Pope captured New Madrid on 14 March and occupied the West Bank of the river. To keep those defending Island No. 10 from escaping down the east bank of the Mississippi, he needed the flotilla's support. On that same day, Foote, with seven gunboats and ten mortar rafts, left Cairo for Island No. 10. To compel its surrender, he began on 16 March a three-week, long-range bombardment. Although he claimed the "mortar shells have done fine execution," they did little damage.[19]

Despite Fox's dreams of a fleet subduing a fort, a combined army-navy operation, as envisioned by Pope, was necessary to take Island No. 10. Initially, Foote refused to risk gunboats when Pope needed him to seal off the garrison's escape. Two and a half weeks later, Commander Henry Walke of the *Carondelet*, having persuaded Foote to let him run by Island No. 10, accomplished it in a thunderstorm on the night of 4 April. In another thunderstorm, two nights later, the *Pittsburg* followed. On 7 April these gunboats silenced Confederate batteries on the east bank, Pope landed his troops, and Confederates began fleeing Island No. 10. That evening, its batteries surrendered to Foote, and, on the next day, the garrison's main body, unable to escape, surrendered to Pope. Pope's carefully coordinated army and navy operation proved a brilliant success. The campaign convinced Assistant Secretary of War Thomas A. Scott (who was present) that the commander of the Gunboat Flotilla should be directly under Halleck's orders. He reported to Secretary of War Stanton that Pope believed he could have taken Island No. 10 three weeks earlier, if Foote had been obliged to obey his orders. Pope's published report, criticizing Foote, infuriated Fox and other navy men.[20]

Driving down the Mississippi, Foote on 14 April commenced the bombardment of Fort Pillow, Tennessee (approximately forty miles north of Memphis), using Fox's mortar rafts. With Foote's wound unhealed and his health deteriorating, Fox (following Foote's suggestion) named Charles Henry Davis as his successor. On 9 May Davis relieved but did not replace Foote. Having been slated to head a bureau, Davis blamed Fox for his "disagreeable," tentative position and regretted that he relied on him as "my real friend." The following day, the eight-vessel Confederate River Defense Fleet attacked the

Union mortar rafts and gunboats bombarding Fort Pillow at Plum Point Bend, rammed and sank two gunboats in shallow water, and chased the remaining Union vessels into shoal water, where the deeper-draft Confederate vessels could not follow. When Fox got the news, he exclaimed, "Davis is overmatched & things are not well managed." He agreed with him that he belonged elsewhere and ordered Farragut up the Mississippi from New Orleans. The briefly victorious Confederate fleet returned under the guns of Fort Pillow, Union gunboats were quickly refloated and repaired, and the naval bombardment of Fort Pillow continued until the Confederates evacuated it on 3–4 June. It had become untenable, not because of mortar shells, but because the Union had isolated it by capturing Corinth, Mississippi, and cutting the Memphis and Chattanooga Railroad.[21]

Despite the misgivings of Fox, Davis remained in command. With a sixty-eight-gun fleet of five gunboats accompanied by the ram fleet, created by Colonel Charles Ellet Jr., he sailed to within two miles of Memphis on 5 June. Ellet had in two months fitted seven steamboats with rams for the War Department and was as much a rival as an aid to Davis, with whom he barely communicated. Stanton had vaguely instructed Ellet to move upon the enemy with the "concurrence" of Davis but had not placed him under Davis's command. Totally inexperienced and supremely self-confident in military and naval matters, Ellet wished to spearhead attacks, while Davis preferred keeping the rams at the rear and on the wings of his squadron. Early the next day, on 6 June, the twenty-eight gun, eight-vessel Confederate River Defense Fleet emerged from the Arkansas shore to save Memphis. With two of his rams, Ellet rushed ahead, followed by Davis and his gunboats. In the melee that followed, Ellet was mortally wounded, while three Confederate vessels were destroyed, four were captured, and one escaped down river. By 11:00 a.m., the mayor of Memphis surrendered his city, first to Ellet's son Charlie and then to Davis, as the rival Union forces continued their separate ways.[22]

Fox and Welles were elated, but Davis thought the department's official letter was not sufficiently friendly. "If it had been Foote, who is the Magnus Apollo of the Department," he complained to his wife, "the kind word would have been said." He yearned to be in Washington at the head of the new Bureau of Navigation. "About the bureau," he told his wife, "it is uncertain. Mr. Fox's preferences, and friendships, are like the loves of a flirting young lady, capricious, ephemeral, superficial. I was once to have a squadron, then a bureau, and here I am playing second fiddle to Foote." Fox was not as capricious as Davis felt, nor as unfriendly as he feared, but he was, as Davis thought, a man of quick, impulsive decisions. Above all, he responded to victories. After

17 June Davis no longer played second fiddle. He replaced Foote as flag officer, and a month later he became commodore. To Fox's delight, Congress provided for additional naval officers and created the ranks of rear admiral, commodore, and lieutenant commander. Congress also gratified one of Fox's ardent desires. It transferred (as of 1 October 1862) Davis's Gunboat Flotilla to the Navy Department. A month later, on 7 November, over Stanton's objections, Lincoln transferred Ellet's Ram Fleet to the Navy Department.[23]

The victory at Memphis opened the Mississippi River for the Western Flotilla all the way to Vicksburg, Mississippi. It was 250 miles (as the crow flies to the south, but not as the river bends). On 1 July 1862 Davis and the Western Flotilla joined Flag Officer David G. Farragut's fleet above Vicksburg. Having last met at Port Royal Sound in February, the two flag officers had traveled in opposite directions and had managed in five months to circle the Confederacy.

■ ■ ■

A native of Tennessee, Farragut had married a southerner and lived in Norfolk, Virginia. The day after Virginia seceded from the Union, 18 April 1861, he left for New York. Despite his forthright stand for the Union, the Navy Department, leery about southern officers, was slow to use him. But his work on naval ordnance and in establishing the Mare Island Navy Yard in California marked him as an officer of energy and ability, whose peers rated him bold and impetuous. Proceeding slowly, the Navy Department appointed him on 30 September to the Board for Better Organization of the Navy. It met at the New York Navy Yard to retire inefficient officers. When Fox and Welles needed an officer of caliber and nerve to lead an offensive against New Orleans and up the Mississippi River, they tapped Farragut.[24]

From the start of the war, New Orleans was a Union objective. In Winfield Scott's Anaconda Plan, its capture would culminate a combined drive of the army and gunboats down the Mississippi River. By the fall of 1861, Fox and Welles were discussing a naval assault on New Orleans, moving upriver from the Gulf of Mexico. Plans to take New Orleans began to gel after Du Pont's 7 November 1861 success at Port Royal Sound emboldened Commander David Dixon Porter on 12 November to present his plan for taking New Orleans to the Navy Department. Two days' bombardment of Fort Jackson and Fort St. Philip by thirteen-inch mortars, mounted on schooners, would enable wooden warships to run by and capture the city, he argued. Then a small army accompanying the squadron could garrison the reduced forts and occupy New Orleans.[25]

The plan appealed to Fox and Welles. Fox was certain wooden naval vessels

could run by hostile forts and that thirteen-inch mortars, which he had persuaded Frémont to order for the Western Flotilla, could reduce forts. Lincoln
agreed to the plan, and on the evening of 14 November he joined Fox, Porter,
and Welles at McClellan's house to secure 10,000 troops for the "big expedition." Fox suggested using the troops being raised in New England for service
in the Gulf by his Lowell friend, Major General Benjamin F. Butler. Butler
shared the interest of New England manufacturers in liberating southern cotton for their mills. As early as 2 November, he had orders to sail to Ship Island
in Mississippi Sound on 20 November. Lincoln, McClellan, and Governor John
A. Andrew of Massachusetts were delighted to ship Butler, who was controver-
sial, flamboyant, and quarrelsome, to a war theater so remote that it took
weeks for dispatches from it to reach Washington.[26]

Fox and Welles carefully picked the naval leaders of the New Orleans expedition. Within a few days, Porter was ordered to prepare and command a fleet
of twenty-two mortar schooners to bombard the forts below New Orleans. Because that task took him to New York, Fox and Welles had him ask Farragut
(who was Porter's foster brother) if he was willing to fight the South. After
Porter reported favorably, they brought Farragut to Washington and found
him enthusiastic and confident that he could take New Orleans with two-
thirds the vessels Fox proposed. Unlike Fox and Porter, Farragut had little faith
in mortars, which Porter had predicted would reduce the forts in forty-eight
hours. But Farragut believed, as did Fox, that wooden steam sloops of war
could run by the forts. Meeting Farragut, whose optimism outran his own, Fox
began to wonder if he was "too enthusiastic," but Fox and Welles knew the
"big expedition" needed a bold and impetuous leader. Remaining in Washington to plan the expedition and shape his orders, Farragut was in fine fettle.
Virginia Fox found him a "very pleasant and gay" dinner guest. "He's crazy
for an advance," she observed, "thinks the South playing brag on all points,"
and eager to be off. On 9 January 1862 he was appointed commander of the
West Gulf Blockading Squadron, and on the 20th he received his orders.[27]

Farragut was to enforce the blockade from Mobile Bay to the Rio Grande.
His most important task, the department told him, was to reduce the forts
defending New Orleans, taking "possession of it under the guns of your squadron . . . until troops can be sent to you." Welles signed the orders, but Fox, as de
facto chief of naval operations and with ideas of the navy unilaterally destroying forts and capturing cities, shaped the instructions. Farragut told Fox that,
if he got the vessels promised, he would "not complain of the want of force,"
but he disturbed Fox by adding, "there may be more places for *light draft vessels* than we can supply immediately." As Farragut prepared to depart for the

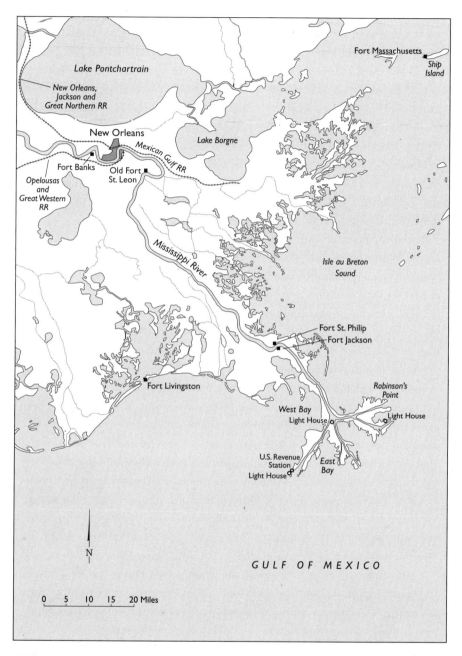

Delta of Mississippi and approaches to New Orleans. Map by Bill Nelson, derived from *Official Records of the Union and Confederate Navies*, 18:131.

Gulf, his "greatest anxiety" was "for the sick & wounded." Anticipating heavy casualties, he asked for a large number of tourniquets and a hundred iron beds for a hospital ship. He was also anxious that Fox send him good mechanics, because Du Pont informed him that steamers were "constantly getting out of order." Farragut left Philadelphia with his "miserably slow" flagship *Hartford* on 28 January, stopped at Hampton Roads until 2 February, and on 20 February arrived at Ship Island, off the coast of Mississippi, to rendezvous with Butler's troops, who would arrive in army transports.[28]

The day after Farragut left Hampton Roads, Iowa senator James W. Grimes of the Naval Committee wrote Fox excitedly that taking New Orleans was politically imperative, as well as militarily useful. "This Government will crumble to pieces," he stated, "unless something is speedily done. The trouble will be in the north west, where a sentiment is growing up that is perfectly indescribable & that will soon become uncontrollable. The attack upon & capture of New Orleans will relieve us of this difficulty. . . . The country looks to the Navy. You are our only solution, move Heaven and Earth & do it *at once.*"[29]

As Farragut sailed for the Gulf, Fox began to worry that they had picked the wrong man. Thinking Farragut wanted the light-draft steamers for the assault on New Orleans, rather than for blockading, Fox found his dispatches "discouraging." Uneasy and anxious for firsthand information, Fox on 24 February turned to Porter, who tended to twist everything to his own advantage. Fox asked him for an appraisal of Farragut's performance, because "*it is not too late to rectify our mistake.*"[30]

"It is too late," Porter responded over a month later from the South West Pass of the Mississippi. "I see no reason why he should not be competent to do all that is expected of him." Then Porter confided, "I never thought Farragut a Nelson, or a Collingwood; I only consider him the best of his rank . . .; but men of his age in a seafaring life are not fit for the command of important enterprises." Porter said that Farragut was physically strong and mentally alert, and was likable, zealous, and brave, but added that he "has no administrative qualities, wants stability, and loses too much time in talking." Farragut, indeed, was more a fighter than an administrator. Porter's remarks, revealing more of his ambition than of Farragut's capacity, were, as he said, too late to harm Farragut. And Farragut's subsequent dispatches assured the department that he wanted small steamers, drawing less than five feet of water, for the blockade, not for taking New Orleans.[31]

On the slow voyage to Ship Island, Farragut mulled over his plans. Unless the Navy Department objected, he hoped, while waiting for Porter's mortar

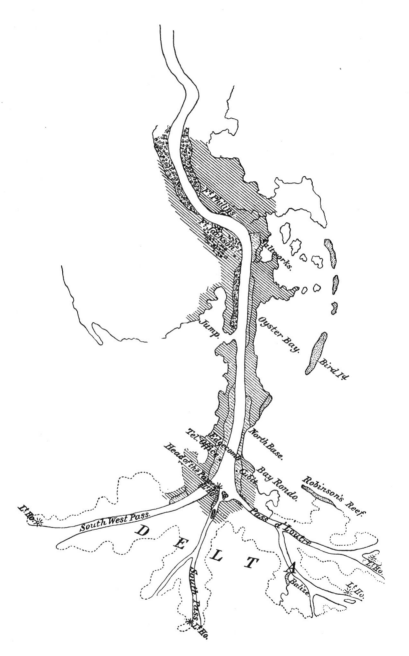

Sketch of the Mississippi River above the Head of the Passes [1857]. From *Official Records of the Union and Confederate Navies*, 16:636.

schooners, to "pitch into Fort Livingston . . . to give my men practice." It controlled Barataria Bay, through which Fort Jackson and Fort St. Philip on the Mississippi could be reinforced and supplied from the west. Welles and Fox did object. "If we fail," Fox wrote, "let it be at the main point, where, if you succeed all other victories are cast in the shade."[32]

Even before hearing from Fox, Farragut concentrated on the "main point." Two days after arriving at Ship Island, he dispatched the *Brooklyn* to the Head of Passes to maintain the blockade, and, after having had Coast Survey personnel ascertain that the Southwest Pass of the Mississippi possessed the deepest channel, began moving his heavy vessels over its bar. The *Hartford* got over on 13 March, before Farragut ran into trouble. "The Mississippi & Pensacola are lightened as much as . . . possible," he reported to Fox on 21 March, "they both draw 18 feet, the Mississippi forward and the Pensacola aft—we hope to tip them to 17 feet and tug them over." Dragging these vessels through the mud was laborious and dangerous. Their inadequate power was abetted by small steamers, tugging on hawsers under the direction of Porter (who had arrived by mid-March) and by sailors straining at capstans winding up lines, attached to kedges (anchors) dropped ahead. Two sailors were killed, when a hawser parted, while they worked to get the *Pensacola* through the mud. After two weeks (7 April), a stiff southerly wind raised the water sufficiently to get it and the *Mississippi* across the bar. It was not possible to get the steam frigate *Colorado* into the river. It was Farragut's most powerful ship, but it drew twenty-two feet.[33]

Losing both time and the element of surprise, Farragut was frustrated. He was also annoyed at having to borrow coal from Butler's army to get his ships across the bar, and he urged Fox to send him an adequate supply. Aware of the propensity of his vessels to run aground in the Mississippi, he asked Fox for "six kedges of from one to two thousand pounds, ten Hawsers from Eight to Eleven inches." For his mortar fleet, Porter requested "6 eight-oared boats; 10—7 in. hawsers; 8—sixteen hundred pound anchors, with chains." Squadron commanders depended on Fox. He had John Lenthall check on coal sent to Ship Island and saw that Farragut's and Porter's needs were met. Pleased with his powerful fleet, Farragut thanked Fox "for your exertions to send me this force."[34]

Even with his fleet of seventeen vessels, mounting 154 guns and twenty-one mortar schooners, Farragut had a difficult task. Fort Jackson and Fort St. Philip mounted 100 guns, a chain supported by hulks was stretched across the river below the forts, fire rafts were ready to drift down upon the Union fleet, and the uncompleted but potentially dangerous ironclad *Louisiana*, the armored ram *Manassas*, as well as thirteen small gunboats were above the forts. General Barnard, at Fox's request, provided Farragut and Porter with detailed information about the forts and estimated that a huge fleet of 300 to 400 guns, six ironclads, and an army of 10,000 were needed to take them. On 18 April Porter's mortars began to bombard Fort Jackson, and on the night of the 20th the gunboats *Itasca* and *Pinola*, under heavy bombardment from the forts, cut the chain. After five days, 5,000 mortar shells inflicted some damage and a few casualties, but repairs were made quickly and almost all of Fort Jackson's guns remained in working order.[35]

With Porter running low on shells and fuses, Farragut, in the early hours of 24 April, steamed through the opening in the chain and, under heavy fire and dense smoke, ran by the forts. The Confederate flotilla attacked, with the *Manassas* pushing a fire raft into Farragut's flagship *Hartford*, which "in a moment . . . was one blaze all along the port side." Although Farragut briefly thought "it was all up with us," his officers and crew managed to extinguish the fire, while the *Mississippi* demolished the *Manassas* with two broadsides. Losing only one gunboat in "a kind of guerrilla" melee, Farragut's fleet destroyed all but two of the Confederate gunboats. The "passing of the forts," Farragut wrote Fox the next day, "was one of the most awful sights and events I ever saw or expect to experience." In writing Montgomery Blair, Butler praised Fox for predicting "the exact way in which the Forts could be passed," before adding, "By the by tell him his mortar fleet is a *humbug*."[36]

Farragut demanded the surrender of New Orleans on 25 April 1862, the same day he wrote Fox. Although the mayor delayed for four days, he had no choice but to comply. The Confederate army had decided New Orleans was indefensible, and the river was so high that Farragut's guns could fire over the levee into its streets. He had not reduced the forts that guarded New Orleans, but he had carried out his instructions from Welles and Fox to "appear off that city and take possession of it under the guns of your squadron . . . keeping possession until troops can be sent to you." Butler's army did not arrive until 1 May, and Farragut's 250 marines could not prevent the Confederates from evacuating 3,000 troops, machinery for making iron plates for gunboats, railroad rolling stock, and war matériel.[37]

Butler's troops were delayed by the necessity of capturing the forts Farragut had run past. Following Porter's advice, Butler landed on 27 April behind Fort St. Philip and was instrumental in forcing the surrender to Porter of both it and Fort Jackson on 28 April. Striving to polish a tarnished military reputation, he was annoyed that Porter neglected to give credit to the crucial presence of the troops and insisted that the forts surrender "to the mortar flotilla."

Farragut also frustrated Butler's quest for glory by dashing past the forts and compelling the surrender of New Orleans. "This I deem wholly an unmilitary proceeding on his part to run off and leave forts behind him unredeemed," Butler complained to his wife, "but such is the race for the glory of capturing New Orleans." Had Farragut awaited the surrender of the forts and reached New Orleans simultaneously with Butler's army of occupation, could the Confederates have been prevented from pulling everything of military value out of New Orleans? Perhaps, but the Confederates realized that once Farragut got between New Orleans and the forts, both were doomed, and they had best remove all they could from New Orleans.[38]

"How happy I am," Fox wrote Farragut on 12 May, "at having relied entirely upon the Navy to capture N. Orleans." Exulting in "the magnificent achievement," Fox bragged to Porter, "England has no such record, and the Navy (as I intended it should) has effected it all." Fox's doubts about Farragut's capacity were dissipated by his "unparalleled achievements. . . . I am sure I have never read anything equal to it," Fox told Farragut. "Having studied up the localities and defenses in conceiving this attack, I can fully appreciate the magnificent execution which has rendered your name immortal." With the additional news of the fall of Norfolk on 10 May and the scuttling of the CSS *Virginia* on 11 May, Fox rejoiced that "the rebellion seems caving in all around." He anticipated "very little difficulty in taking the whole coast."[39]

"The only anxiety we feel," Fox reminded Farragut on 12 May, "is to know if you have followed your instructions and pushed a strong force up the river, to meet the Western Flotilla. . . . The opening of the Mississippi is of more importance than Mobile, and if your ships reach Memphis in the next few days Beauregard's army is cut off from escape." With Halleck advancing on General P. G. T. Beauregard at Corinth, Mississippi, Fox envisioned a role for the navy in his capture. Fox had reason to be anxious. In his report of 29 April to Welles announcing the fall of the forts and New Orleans, Farragut added, "As soon as I see General Butler safely in possession of this place I will sail for Mobile with the Fleet." Having destroyed four forts above New Orleans, Farragut optimistically believed there were no further impediments between his fleet and Memphis and reasoned erroneously that he had obeyed his 20 January order "to push a strong force up the river to take all their defenses in the rear."[40]

Fox's anxiety was heightened by the arrival at Hampton Roads on 8 May of Captain Theodorus Bailey, Farragut's second-in-command at New Orleans. He brought dispatches and captured rebel flags, which he, along with Fox, presented to Congress the following day. While dining at Willard's, Bailey responded "None," when Fox asked how many ships Farragut had sent up the Mississippi. "Impossible," Fox exploded, "the instructions were positive." He was further unnerved by Bailey's opinion that Farragut "had *forgotten* them. I have hardly slept since," Fox wrote Farragut on 17 May. Later reports that some of Farragut's vessels had gotten as far as Vicksburg contradicted Bailey and cheered Fox. But he was depressed when the New York press reported on 16 May that the fleet had returned to New Orleans. These reports "distressed the President so much" that Fox immediately dispatched the *Dacotah* to notify Farragut to carry out his 20 January instructions "to go up and clear the river with the utmost expedition."[41]

From Washington, Fox, Welles, and Lincoln had an overall perspective of the war, but they had poor communications with many line officers. Although information could be exchanged with Goldsborough of the North Atlantic Blockading Squadron and with Davis of the Western Flotilla with relative ease, delays increased with Du Pont of the South Atlantic Blockading Squadron and William W. McKean of the East Gulf Blockading Squadron, and were at their worst with Farragut. For example, Fox learned on 27 April from Richmond papers, "New Orleans Taken by the Fleet," and was the first to give Lincoln the good news, but more than ten days elapsed before word arrived from Farragut via Bailey. At that point, Fox feared that Farragut was making a "terrible mistake" by going after Mobile and losing "a golden opportunity" to cut off Beauregard's escape.[42]

Neither Fox's fears nor his hopes materialized. Farragut went neither to Mobile nor up the river, and Halleck's advance on Corinth was so slow that Beauregard evacuated it, slipped through his fingers, and escaped south. On 7 May, too early to have heard from Fox, Farragut reported to him that the *Oneida*, with seven or eight gunboats, should have been at Vicksburg, Mississippi; that the *Brooklyn* was at Baton Rouge two days earlier; and that he would go upriver that day in the *Hartford*. Refreshing his memory after Bailey left by rereading his orders, Farragut probably realized that there were more "impediments" between him and Memphis than the four forts he reduced. He also knew that his squadron was in no condition to attack Mobile. "I did not wish our enemies to know the fact," Farragut confided in Fox, "but I have scarcely a vessel fit to go out of the River for active service, they are so battered, by getting foul of each other as well as the shot—but in the River they will get along." Farragut estimated that the "large ships except the Mississippi will do very well, with our own repairs," but that "nearly every Gun Boat must go into a Dock yard for repairs." He wanted more vessels, especially a monitor to attack the Confederate ironclad ram *Arkansas,* which was nearing completion. "It would be most gratefully received, as worth all the gunboats in the river."[43]

As usual, Farragut was confident and optimistic. He anticipated little trouble in taking possession of the river and effecting a junction with the Western Flotilla, before turning his attention to Mobile. "I shall push down there," he reported to Fox, as though it were a matter of days or weeks, "as soon as I get back from up the River." Vicksburg, however, proved to be a formidable "impediment." On 18 May, eleven days later than Farragut's estimate, it refused to surrender to Union gunboats, led by the *Oneida,* commanded by Samuel Phillips Lee. Farragut had, indeed, as the New York papers reported, returned to New Orleans with his large vessels, but his gunboats remained before Vicksburg, while he ordered Porter and his mortar schooners up the river to bombard that citadel and arranged with Butler for troops to commence in mid-June "a succession of attacks on the various bluffs" between Baton Rouge and Vicksburg. Farragut and Porter warned Fox that clearing the Mississippi was complicated by the "dilapidated condition" of the gunboats, by mosquitoes (unlike the army, the navy was without "bars"—mosquito netting), and by the "fever, dysentery, and diarrhoea" that afflicted officers and men. Fox suggested that incapacitated seamen be replaced by those on storeships "and supply their places with enlisted contrabands, as they are termed." Benjamin F. Butler, when in command at Fortress Monroe, Virginia, in July 1861, gave that name to escaped slaves. A clever lawyer, he refused to return them to their owners because they were "contraband of war."[44]

By 25 June, 3,200 Federal troops and Farragut's squadron were opposite Vicksburg. On the next day, Porter's mortars began to bombard Vicksburg's defenses. To Porter's disgust, Brigadier General Thomas Williams prudently, if not heroically, declined to coordinate an assault with the mortar attack. He began the more deadly task of digging a canal across Swampy Toe (a peninsula formed by a loop in the river opposite Vicksburg) to enable vessels to bypass Confederate guns, but gave it up a month later. As always, Porter exaggerated the effect of his mortars, but even if Williams had carried the forts, he could not have held them. The Confederates were reinforcing Vicksburg with 15,000 men. Because Williams, supported by the navy, could not take Vicksburg, Farragut's fleet ran by Vicksburg on the morning of 28 June and on 1 July joined Flag Officer Davis and his Western Flotilla north of Vicksburg. Farragut demonstrated again that wooden ships could run by forts with minimal damage, but his dash had no practical effect except to lift northern morale. Running by Fort Jackson and Fort St. Philip cut them off, and, when threatened by a besieging army, they surrendered; but running by Vicksburg, with its rail connection to the East, did not isolate it. It remained in rebel hands. Abandoning wishful thinking, Fox and Welles by mid-July asked Secretary of War Edwin M. Stanton for an army to cooperate with Farragut at Vicksburg.[45]

A big army seemed even more necessary after 15 July. The Confederate ironclad *Arkansas* emerged that day from the Yazoo River and engaged the fleets of Farragut and Davis. Fox concluded that Davis "was caught napping," but he later heard through Foote that Farragut failed to tell Davis that he had learned from a deserter that the *Arkansas* would "certainly" come out that day. Though damaged, it anchored under Vicksburg's guns and survived an attempt to destroy it on 22 July by the Ellet ram *Queen of the West*. Having run past Vicksburg during the battle on 15 July, Farragut's fleet headed downstream on 25 July. Falling water imperiled its deep-draft vessels.[46]

Fortunately for Farragut, the Confederates seized the offensive. Supported by the *Arkansas*, they moved downstream in an attempt to retake Baton Rouge, but the attack fizzled when, on 6 August, engine failure forced the *Arkansas*'s crew to scuttle it. "Farragut," Fox commented, "cannot conceal his joy at getting rid of the Arkansas and I do not wonder at it. An accident has given her to our arms, not courage or judgment or prudence or foresight."[47]

Fox wrote those comments on August 20 in Portsmouth, where he had escaped from his grueling Washington routine. But he did not escape business entirely. Although he was going fishing that afternoon, the day before he had inspected the construction of ironclads in Boston with Admiral Gregory and Engineer Stimers and had reported to Welles on their progress. He also noted that enlistments were up. Although most of them were landsmen, they were of "a superior class," and luckily "steamers do not require so many seamen."[48]

While in Portsmouth, Fox continued Navy Department work. He checked on the wooden screw sloop of war *Ossipee*. He was told it would not be ready until December, because "the contractors on the engines are losing money and therefore work as few hands as possible." He apparently was able to hurry them, because it was commissioned on 6 November 1862. He also visited the "very fine" local library and "picked up quite a number of soft Indian names" for Union vessels. Fox loved Indian names for ships, but officers and crews often despised them. "The weather," Fox told Welles, "has been most delightful, dry cool east winds, and clear October sunshine. I feel entirely different bodily and mentally than when I left Washington."[49]

When Fox arrived back in "dear, hot, dusty, muddy, cold, dry, damp, healthy, feverish Washington" on 27 August 1862, he thought of what had been accomplished and what remained to be done. The Union navy controlled the Mississippi, except for Vicksburg and Port Hudson. It had performed creditably at

Hampton Roads during the evacuation of the Army of the Potomac from the Peninsula and, with the launching of the *Passaic* at Greenpoint on New York's East River, had acquired the first of a new improved class of monitors. But, in the Azores, Captain Raphael Semmes had hoisted the Confederate flag on the commerce destroyer *Alabama*. And in the Carolinas, Wilmington and Charleston, where the rebellion began, remained in Confederate hands and open to blockade runners.[50]

CHAPTER ELEVEN

More Ironclads

The greatest experiment of the age, the result of which will overturn all preconceived ideas of attack and defence and place the Navy on a permanent footing of preeminence, [is] . . . the new Monitors.

Fox to Ensign Charles P. Clark, 17 November 1862

By the summer of 1862, the navy had been phenomenally successful. Fox had helped make possible the impressive string of victories at Hatteras, Port Royal, New Orleans, Fort Henry and Fort Donelson, and Memphis. In addition, the navy's actions in the abortive Peninsula campaign were critical: the navy made it feasible by neutralizing the *Virginia,* facilitated it by controlling the York and Pamunkey rivers, and saved it at Harrison's Landing. With gunboats on the James River, the navy gave the campaign an avenue and a chance of success. The failure below Richmond, at Drewry's Bluff, on 15 May, however, signaled the end of quick and easy naval victories. A tougher future was confirmed, when on 28 June Farragut ran by Vicksburg with no tangible result. Only tedious, formidable, combined army-navy operations could take either Richmond or Vicksburg. McClellan, however, did not feel strong enough to push up the James River, and only 3,000 soldiers under Brigadier General Thomas Williams supported Farragut at Vicksburg. Lack of support from the War Department had cooled Fox's ardor for combined operations, heightened his chauvinism for the navy, and increased his faith in heavily armed ironclads.

■ ■ ■

Fox told Du Pont in June that "my duties are two fold; first, to beat our southern friends; second, to beat the Army." After the War Department and then Halleck rejected Fox's plea for a joint operation up the James River to Richmond, he visited that department more for news at its telegraph office than for planning cooperative ventures. On 5 August he wrote Senator James W. Grimes: "I don't know how army matters are going, I am a little disgusted. They must give us 10,000 men under *our* command [and] we will keep the Mississippi open. Six weeks at Vicksburg and no soldiers, Williams good for nothing, and now the conquest abandoned." A month later, he complained to Grimes, "There is but one General who has done justice to gun boats and the Navy, and success and good fortune never deserted him—viz: Burnside" in North Carolina. The transfer from the War to the Navy Department of the Western Gunboat Flotilla on 1 October 1862 and the Ellet rams on 7 November was a victory for Fox. The Navy Department's complete control of the renamed Mississippi Squadron promoted efficiency, but it also tended to separate rather than coordinate the army and the navy. With McClellan's amphibious plans abandoned, combined operations were shelved, and the War and Navy departments followed their own agendas.[1]

Fox's disillusion with generals coincided with his growing confidence in the navy's new ironclads. Not only were new monitors nearing completion (the *Passaic*, the first of its class, was launched on 30 August 1862), but also the formidable broadside *New Ironsides*, armed with fourteen eleven-inch smooth-bores and two 150-pound Parrott rifles, was commissioned on 21 August 1862. After the Confederate victory, at the Second Bull Run, over John Pope's Army of Virginia on 29–30 August, Fox lamented, "The soldiers are in most excellent condition and spirits but we have no chief to lead them."[2]

With nineteen gunboats on the Potomac, Fox knew Washington was in no immediate danger. There were, of course, rumors about its fall "and the public buildings being blown up." He heard of these at 11 p.m. on 2 September, "when in burst [William Thomas] Carroll Clk. of the Supreme Court who had just arrived from Phila.," as Fox and Blair "were smoking our segars." Fox assured Virginia, "We can take care of ourselves here disgraceful as is the bickerings and inefficiency of those who control the war matters. We are going to be hard pushed . . . but we are not going to be captured or blown up." Aware of the carnage of battle, he sent his nephew Charlie Guild (who wished to give up his Navy Department clerkship to enlist in the army) to nurse the wounded "to show him the terrible reverse of a soldiers life." A devout Episcopalian, who was convinced that God would lead the righteous Union to victory, Fox sighed, "His ways are past finding out." For a moment, he wondered, "Perhaps as a judgment upon the South their independence will be given them by the Almighty. It will be their greatest punishment."[3]

Although confident the gunboats could prevent a frontal assault on Washington, Fox realized Lee's invasion of Maryland, following his victory over

Pope, endangered the capital. He had confidence in McClellan (who had been restored to command) "for organization and defence," but not when "we resume the offence." On 6 September he told Virginia, "if we are beaten badly I cannot see but what we shall have to take to the gun boats and leave Washington to its fate." On the other hand, he realized, "If we beat them their position is most perilous." On the evening of 7 September, McClellan "stopped with his staff at our house to see me and has gone off full of hope and confident of suc cess. I am not at all sure." Fox assumed McClellan would encounter "the best Gen'l. of modern times," Thomas J. ("Stonewall") Jackson near Frederick, Maryland. "The chances are all on McClellan's side but they have always been and yet we did not win." If his worst fears materialized, the gunboats were ready to evacuate the government, and Fox arranged with George Washington Riggs, the banker, to store his "baggage . . . in case of a retreat as he passes for a Secesh."[4]

Fox admitted on 6 September, "We are having a dark spell just now." His gloom had been deepened by the death from rheumatic fever, on 4 September, of his nine-year-old niece Maria Blair, whom he loved like the daughter he never had. Past military failures and feared failure in the current campaign discouraged Fox from cooperating with the army, just as his enthusiasm for ironclads encouraged his penchant for unilateral naval action. Nor was he alone. "Seward was here," Fox told Virginia on 6 September, "to get us to attack Charleston," which was "his remedy for all evils." While Fox knew that taking Charleston was no panacea, he also knew the political and diplomatic value of its capture. Seward's plea had its effect. That same day, Fox wrote to a member of Du Pont's squadron predicting "our next blow will be Charleston, purely naval and the day is fast approaching." To Senator Grimes, he wrote, "I trust we shall give you Charleston before Congress meets" in December. Fox's faith in the navy may have been extreme, but his faith was not unique in the fall of 1862. "If it be the design of Divine Providence to save the country," Senator Henry B. Anthony of Rhode Island exclaimed, "it must be done by a miracle or by the navy."[5]

Although Fox's fears for Washington did not materialize, his lack of faith in generals continued. McClellan stopped Lee at Antietam on 17 September, but, as Fox apprehended, he did not seize the offensive but allowed Lee and his men to return unmolested "as an *army*" back to Virginia. In addition, the "shameful surrender of Harper's Ferry" to Jackson, prior to Antietam, Fox lamented, "has deprived us of the substantial fruits of the victory." McClellan's failure to follow up his victory at Antietam exasperated Lincoln. "To tell the truth," he remarked, "I am tired boring with an auger that won't take hold." Lincoln replaced McClellan on 5 November with Fox's favorite general, Ambrose E. Burnside, who proved a failure on 13 December at Fredericksburg. With the War Department preoccupied with overland campaigns and loath to provide troops for joint seacoast ventures, Fox followed his predilection for "purely naval" expeditions to take the major blockade running ports of Wilmington, Mobile, and Charleston. He was emboldened by the number of ironclads nearing completion, the navy's string of successes, and a thirst for more naval glory. Renowned as the seat of the rebellion, Charleston was an attractive target, and, on a personal level, Fox hated it for frustrating his Sumter relief expedition.[6]

While preparing ironclads for a sweep down the coast to knock off Wilmington, Charleston, and Mobile, Fox worked to improve the men, the officers, and the administration of the navy. In these efforts, he was helped by Senator Grimes. On 28 May 1862 Fox begged Grimes to "add a proviso" to the naval appropriations bill "abolishing the spirit ration and forbidding any distilled liquors" except for medicinal purposes on naval vessels. "All insubordination, all misery, every deviltry on board ships can be traced to *rum*. Give the sailor double the value, or more, and he will be content." In June, Fox predicted to Marcus Spring, who shared his humanitarian goals, that getting "rum out of our ships" will begin "the second great era; the first was [after we] threw the 'cats' overboard" and stopped flogging seamen. Abhorring "brutal tyrants," Fox realized that "Christian officers" of "fine instincts" like Du Pont and Foote fought well "from a higher impulse than fleshy courage." Grimes and Congress responded to his plea with legislation on 14 July. The centuries-old practice of lining up daily for two dips of grog ended on 1 September 1862. Nor could sutlers on board naval vessels continue to sell exorbitantly priced liquor by the bottle. Many sailors did not appreciate the reform. Lieutenant Stephen B. Luce told Fox in January 1864 that among experienced petty officers one of "the crowning sorrows appeared to be the stopping of their grog."[7]

Naval officers, among whom alcoholism was a problem, benefited from the prohibition of spirits, as did seamen. Had a regulation against distilled liquors been put into effect earlier, it might have saved the career of Commander Overton Carr. He had been an efficient officer with the Wilkes Exploring Expedition of 1838–42 but, while captain of the *Quaker City* in 1861, was "frequently inebriated" at sea and "constantly" while in port. Carr and another officer of the same rank with the same problem were court-martialed and furloughed, rather than dismissed, by Welles and Fox, who hoped they would stop drinking and return to sea, where they were needed. A worse loss occurred eight days before the ban went into effect. The "noble" sloop of war *Adiron-*

dack ran aground in the Bahamas. Fox was "afraid to whisper *why* she was lost," but Du Pont shared his fear with his wife. Its captain, Guert Gansevoort, had been drunk.[8]

Unfortunately, officers could smuggle liquor on board more easily than common seamen. Alcoholism, though reduced after the new regulation, continued to cause difficulties. "I can't stand a man that drinks," Sylvanus W. Godon of the *Susquehanna* wrote Fox, just before departing for Rio de Janeiro in April 1865, "and here in one day I report" three officers. Drink made them not only inefficient but also "destructive" examples for the midshipmen on board.[9]

In July 1862 Congress, with Grimes working closely with Fox, improved the morale of officers by creating the rank of rear admiral and increasing the number of positions in the lower ranks. "I congratulate you," Du Pont wrote Fox, "upon the most important legislation you have got through for the Navy—the greatest in a half century." The legislation set the number of rear admirals at 9, commodores at 18, captains at 36, commanders at 72, and the remaining junior officers at 144 in each rank. Farragut was the first to be promoted to the rank of rear admiral. He was soon joined by Du Pont and Goldsborough. Striking another blow against seniority, Fox and Welles relied on the selections of an advisory board, created on 16 July, but Fox noted, "They only skipped the notoriously inefficient."[10]

Welles, Fox, and Grimes also improved the Navy Department by increasing its bureaus from five to eight. After the 5 July 1862 act, sponsored by Grimes, the department's bureaus were Yards and Docks, Equipment and Recruiting, Navigation, Ordnance, Construction and Repairs, Steam Engineering, Provisions and Clothing, and Medicine and Surgery. The Bureau of Detail was eliminated. Fox had taken over its difficult function of selecting (detailing) officers for commands, assignments, and promotions, focusing on himself both the frustrations of the disappointed and the disgust of the critical. Du Pont, for example, complained that "a drunkard, an utterly worthless demi-lunatic, and an inborn skulk" were "nominated for promotion on the *retired list*." He noted that in "the reorganization of the Navy Department a bureau was left out, the most important of all, the Bureau of Detail—and hence such extraordinary procedures."[11]

But the men in Du Pont's examples were not nominated by Fox but by an advisory board of naval officers. Although a bureau would have diffused complaints, it probably would not have been an improvement over Fox, who knew the officers, and Welles, with his sound judgment. In time, Du Pont's friend Charles Henry Davis, who took over the Bureau of Navigation, helped Fox in detailing officers. The modest increase in Navy Department personnel (considering the volume of business generated by the war) required the addition of a third story to its building. "We have," Fox told Du Pont, "erected a fine flag staff thereon and shall not raise the American flag upon it until Charleston falls. If you will send us Sumpter's flag it shall go up under the American flag."[12]

Future naval and marine officers were on Fox's mind. He appealed, apparently without success, to the unfriendly chair of the Senate Committee on Naval Affairs, John P. Hale, to "elevate" the Marine Corps by taking its officers from the graduating class at West Point, which would give the navy "thoroughly trained soldiers." If that idea should not be acceptable, Fox suggested that Marine Corps officers be required to interchange with army officers of the same rank for three years at a time. Such an arrangement would improve the Marine Corps and would be valuable for army officers involved in joint operations.[13]

Before Fox entered the Navy Department, the *Constitution* had moved the Naval Academy (established in 1845) and its midshipmen from Annapolis, Maryland, to Newport, Rhode Island, where Fox wanted to keep them. Prodded by him, the Coast Survey evaluated Coasters Harbor Island off Newport and found it "provokingly feasible" as a permanent site for the Naval Academy. "Why can't you present that island and poor house to the Govt," he urged Rhode Island Senator Henry B. Anthony, "and get the school into it before we hire buildings for another year. You people are not alive to the ease with which the school could be fixed upon that spot, which is eminently fitted for it."[14]

Curriculum changes at the academy were imperative. "The navy," Fox observed to the academy's superintendent, George S. Blake, in May 1862, "is undergoing a great revolution"; its victories had provided an opportunity "to place the school on a firm basis to meet all the requirements of the times. All improvements and changes," Fox realistically noted, "are better done in war than peace." Specifically, Fox urged that the academy establish a steam-engineering professorship, because on the *Monitor*—the vessel of the future— there were "four line officers, and four engineers." Fox wanted future engineers to know navigation and ordnance and future deck officers to learn steam engineering. He also wished to couple the study of ordnance with iron-armor plating. Although Blake realized that Fox's suggestions would "require considerable changes in the Academic Course," he worked to institute them. Fearing he had gone overboard about teaching new technology, Fox reaffirmed that "seamanship is of the utmost importance, in my opinion, notwithstanding steam, and ironclads." In addition, both Fox and Blake wanted midshipmen to have good Christian teachers to instill morals and, unless their parents filed a written objection, wanted mandatory attendance at Sunday religious services. By December 1864 Blake had instituted a course on the theory of the steam engine, was consulting with Isherwood, and had plans for a workshop for practical instruction.[15]

Because secession had decreased enrollment, Fox was delighted when Attorney General Edward Bates decided Lincoln should ignore the district system for Naval Academy appointments. With this change, the president could fill 70 vacancies and bring the student body up to the 464 allowed by law. Appointees had to be between the ages of fourteen and seventeen (for those already in the navy, the maximum age was stretched to eighteen). If he could, Fox would have doubled the student body in 1862 to meet the navy's needs. Political pull and social standing secured appointments, but the board of admissions fairly and rigorously applied standards. When a young Woodbury kinsman of Fox's, accompanied by Uncle Barnes, failed the academy's entrance test, Fox insisted, "the good of the service is the first consideration and that I know has been the single purpose of the board. I have great satisfaction in believing that no consideration would lead them to swerve from their trust, and therefore I am happy." In 1864 he got sons of his sister and brother appointed to the academy, but "little Fox" was sent home for a year to mature, while Gus Guild (Charlie's younger brother) was "more steady, though but little inclined to study." Although Fox could get boys into the academy, he could not and would not keep them there if they were found wanting.[16]

Having himself been an inexperienced boy "launched from home" without a guide, Fox put in place a guide for those who followed. At his behest, Welles wrote an orientation letter for entering midshipmen that Frederick Engle of the Naval Asylum praised for its capacity "to reach young hearts." Fox also requested that Edward Everett, orator and statesman, write a letter "that has some *ring* about it; some inspiration—something that will awaken their ambition and their pride—something that they may seek in their hours of relaxation for a renewal of their hopes and an elevation of their character."[17]

Although committed to reform, Fox, during the second half of 1862, devoted his energy mostly to the building of improved versions of the *Monitor.* By the summer of 1862, the coastal monitor program was well under way. Contracts had been awarded, at private yards on the East Coast, for ten vessels in the Passaic class. They were larger, better ventilated, more powerful, and had more armor than the *Monitor.* Each was armed with one fifteen-inch smoothbore, developed at Fox's insistence, and an eleven-inch one. The pilothouse on these vessels was on top of the turret and did not impede the firing of its guns. In May 1862 the Navy Department had also contracted with George W. Quintard for the *Onondaga*. It was a double-turreted monitor that Fox was anxious to develop, because a damaged turret would make a one-turreted vessel helpless.[18]

Fox also had prodded John Lenthall, head of the Bureau of Construction and Repairs, and Engineer in Chief Benjamin Franklin Isherwood to design the Miantonomoh class of double-turreted monitors. They had planned to use Cowper Phipps Coles's towers or turrets (throwing Ericsson into a tizzy), but following the success of the Ericsson turret at Hampton Roads, Fox insisted they use it, rather than the Coles tower. Although four of these vessels were built slowly and well at government navy yards, only one saw action. It was the *Monadnock*, commissioned in October 1864, which proved to be the most seaworthy Civil War monitor.[19]

Before any monitor of the Passaic class could be battle tested, the department in September and October 1862 contracted for nine improved monitors of the Canonicus class. They were a bit longer, narrower, and heavier than Passaic-class vessels; drew eleven and a half rather than ten and a half feet of water; were more heavily armed, with two fifteen-inch guns; and had a five-inch iron glacis, protecting the vulnerable base of the turret. Five of these vessels, built on the East Coast, were commissioned by 1864, but contracts for four of them were let to incompetent firms on the Ohio River (three at Cincinnati and one at Pittsburgh) and were not completed in time for war service.[20]

To supervise the construction of vessels and machinery in private shipyards on the Atlantic Coast, the Navy Department set up a "General Inspectors Office, Ironclad Steamers." It was based in New York under Francis H. Gregory. With orders for the Passaic and Canonicus classes of monitors, this office became known as the "Monitor Bureau." It dealt directly with Fox and Welles, bypassing Lenthall and Isherwood, who concentrated on vessels constructed and repaired in the government's navy yards. Gregory was a hardworking septuagenarian, but the leading spirit in the Monitor Bureau was Chief Engineer Alban C. Stimers. He supervised the construction of the *Monitor* and was on board for its battle with the *Virginia*. Unquestionably, he knew more about monitors than any other naval officer. He worked incredibly hard, but he was inordinately ambitious (coveting Isherwood's job), somewhat paranoid, and self-confident beyond his capabilities. With Stimers's ambition, Ericsson's testiness, and Lenthall's and Isherwood's coolness toward monitors, bad blood developed between the Washington bureaus and the Monitor Bureau. To get the utmost from these four capable men, three of whom were men of genius, Fox mixed tact, flattery, challenges, and orders. Because Lenthall and Isherwood knew what they were about, Fox dispensed most of his psychology on Ericsson and Stimers, who in 1862 were running the experimental and virtually untested monitor program.[21]

The Inspectors Office tried to ensure that minimal standards were met by the private shipyards constructing most of the navy's ironclads. Rushed to completion, they met the navy's immediate needs, but Fox realized they were poorly built. "We found ourselves in the condition of utter helplessness, with regard to the construction of iron vessels and plates," he explained, and had to use the material at hand, which often proved to be inferior. The same rigid test used by the English and French navies "would reject all of our plates," he stated. He realized that "all the vessels we are now constructing so rapidly, will rot, and disappear, with nearly the same haste with which they have been constructed." To build durable iron ships, the government would have to erect ironworks to produce superior plates and construct vessels at navy yards. To meet its urgent need for ironclads during the Civil War, the Navy Department could not rely on its navy yards (which were geared to building wooden vessels), but had to depend on the rapid, albeit shoddy, work of private establishments.[22]

Fox's correspondence with Ericsson was voluminous. Much of it concerned the planning of the *Dictator* and *Puritan* and the big guns Fox wanted them armed with. Ericsson warned Fox that constructing those large vessels would require four times more labor and take twice as long as building four smaller craft. "Would it not be better to have the latter than the former?" he queried. Ericsson was confident that a Passaic-class monitor with a fifteen-inch gun throwing a 450-pound shot could sink the *Warrior, Black Prince,* and any other five-inch ironclad vessel in the British navy. Apparently, he did not think the oceangoing *Dictator* and *Puritan* essential for the defense of the United States. Fox disagreed. He worried that vastly reduced cotton exports combined with the continued success of Robert E. Lee's Army of Northern Virginia might tempt Britain to break the blockade. Fox wanted monitors that could fight on the high seas, either deterring the British government or, if it did intervene, defeating the British navy.[23]

Throughout much of 1862, Ericsson and Stimers worked well together. Ericsson found Stimers useful in planning the quarters and storerooms of the new monitors and deferred to his judgment. Unfortunately, Stimers spread himself too thin, thinking he could do everything. In April 1862 Ericsson was annoyed to discover that Stimers was drawing plans for a modified monitor. He would have been appalled if he had realized that Fox had encouraged him.

The Stimers version was "head, body and tail the same and yet a different animal," Ericsson told Fox, "so utterly defective" with "not a redeeming feature in the whole production." Ericsson also thought "it was a great breach of professional courtesy in Mr. Stimers to put forth plans under my invention." Still, Ericsson did not wish to hurt Stimers, whom he called "my excellent friend." He asked Fox to order "him to devote his whole time to the superintendence of the 6 vessels we are now building and desiring him to leave the planning of the intended vessel for the present." Although offended that Ericsson had to have his own way, Stimers was willing to humor him and not lose his "great genius, skill and experience." Believing he could produce "superior vessels," Stimers later told Fox, "it would be easy for us to improve upon those which should subsequently be built." The notion that he could improve on Ericsson's designs would prove disastrous.[24]

By early August, Fox longed for a light-draft monitor, carrying more than the three-inch side armor Eads planned for his monitors. "I wish somebody of brains," he wrote Ericsson, "would give us a six foot draft boat of great velocity and high pressure for the western waters, impregnable like your boats." But to achieve invulnerability on a monitor, the weight of two-inch deck, five-inch sides, and eight-inch turret armor would draw ten feet. Fox realized that "10 feet gives us the main part of the Mississippi most of the year," but "6 would be better, and I trust you will turn over in your brain a six foot invulnerable 10 knot boat . . . for all kind of shore & river work." Ericsson responded with "a general plan of a Swift and powerful Monitor Ram for the Mississippi, of 10 feet draught," but no six-footer, which Fox soon deemed indispensable. Fox even hoped briefly for "an impregnable 4 foot boat."[25]

Ericsson's fertile brain was diverted for a short time from ironclad vessels to "Monitors on shore." It was an idea for highly mobile field artillery, a horse-drawn version of a modern tank. Montgomery Blair, a West Point graduate, liked it, and Fox "mentioned it to the Army Ordnance and the Asst. Secy. of War," but told Ericsson, "It is pretty hard work to get anything started here, and I doubt if anything can be done, unless it is proved." Fox and Blair thought Ericsson should "make a set and prove how easily it can be accomplished." On 27 September, however, Fox warned Ericsson, "Your brain is mortgaged to us to a certain extent." He urged him,

> Think of the ironclads, the six footers, the Puritan and the Dictator! . . . I feel
> that we are incomplete without the six footers: the enemy will draw himself
> into his shell after the ten footers have hammered him, and we can't get him
> out. I beg of you to look at this—20 feet for foreign nations; 10 feet for coast

defense and harbor work; 6 feet for rivers. The series seems incomplete without them. I rely upon you, and there are several shops ready to go into them.[26]

By early October Ericsson sent Fox "calculations and plans for the 'six footer.'" These plans, however, were not complete, and Ericsson told Stimers that he "must make out all the drawings for them." Already overworked, Stimers gave little direction to the draftsmen working on them. Ericsson also warned Fox, "There are many important points connected with the proposed plan which require explanation," but explanations were not made to Fox or Stimers. Although Fox was anxious for the six-footers, Ericsson's genius and Stimers's energy were diverted from their development by Fox's plans for capturing Charleston. Indeed, Fox failed to acknowledge the receipt of Ericsson's plans for the six-footer, as his restless mind pondered overcoming the obstructions between Fort Sumter and Fort Moultrie at the entrance of Charleston's harbor. To solve that problem, Fox turned to Ericsson and Stimers, and plans for the six-footer were shelved.[27]

Ericsson predictably had a solution for overcoming the obstructions. Fox assumed that these defenses were piles, abetted by "floating rafts, torpedoes and ropes anchored to foul the propellers" and believed that torpedoes would have to blast open the channel. Responding to Fox's pleas, Ericsson, by December, had readied four rafts, equipped with torpedoes and designed to be pushed by monitors blasting their way through Charleston's obstructions.[28]

Ericsson and Stimers were also busy making adjustments to the *Passaic* and monitors of its class. The *Passaic* was launched on 30 August 1862 and commissioned on 25 November 1862, with Captain Percival Drayton in command. On hand to inspect it and advise Ericsson were captains John Rodgers and John Worden, who were to take command of other Passaic-class monitors. Attempting to soothe the irascible Ericsson, Fox wrote, "Sailors you know are conservative and impatient, slow to change old ideas and restless under efforts necessary to reach perfection, but when the hour of trial comes they will not disappoint the just expectations of the country, nor the production of your skill and genius." The presence of the captains turned out to be essential. When launched, the *Passaic* had no compass, no arrangement for being towed, and an unsatisfactory anchoring system. These shortcomings were readily fixed. Smoke, resulting from firing guns inside its turret, was its most serious problem. It took Ericsson weeks to design a "muzzle box" that successfully contained the smoke.[29]

Apart from design flaws to be anticipated in the first model of a class, the workmanship on the speedily built *Passaic* was appallingly bad. In a trial run, the steering apparatus broke two or three times. Its commander, Percival Drayton, was "anxious to get away," and with repairs completed, he left New York on 27 November for Hampton Roads. Off Cape Charles, Virginia, he "had a regular burst-up of the boiler, owing . . . to very bad work and fastenings not half the proper size." He had to stop at the Washington Navy Yard for repairs. In addition, the "compressing arrangement" on its fifteen-inch gun (the muzzle ring) entirely gave out, obliging Ericsson to send a repair crew to Washington to alter and repair it. Drayton believed the *Passaic* would prove useful, but that it would have been more useful if it had been built more faithfully to specifications and fitted out with more intelligence: "She is only another illustration of the ill consequences which result from the Navy Department giving itself completely up to the popular man of the moment, who always, it seems, starts with the idea that all human knowledge is in his head and that genius supplies the place of all experience. Ericsson I believe to be honest, but . . . a little unfortunate in his friends."[30]

One of those friends was the "negligent and overbearing" T. F. Rowland of the Continental Iron Works. There, the *Passaic*'s hull was constructed with a sheer of more than twenty inches, when Ericsson's plan called for twelve inches. That "extraordinary blunder" made the vessel low amidships, high out of the water in the bow, and difficult to trim. Drayton blamed Ericsson, and Ericsson blamed Rowland. But Ericsson also blamed Drayton for not stowing his coal properly, leaving his bow too high.[31]

Fox was disappointed, discouraged, and annoyed. His vision of a fleet of monitors taking Wilmington, Charleston, and then Mobile was, at least for the present, an illusion. "We have at length got the Passaic here but in a melancholy condition," he reprimanded Admiral Francis Gregory of the New York Inspectors Office. "From the imperfect construction of the stays of her boiler and their inadequate size and number, we have lost the use of this vessel in the contemplated operations." Experts estimated it would take six weeks, day and night, to repair it. "Doubling this, which is the only safe rule," the *Passaic* would be in Washington until March 1863. "If the other boilers," Fox warned Gregory about the remaining Passaic-class vessels, "which are understood to be after similar plans, are no better stayed, we shall have the same trouble and disaster." Realizing that Stimers was primarily responsible for the faulty stays, Fox added, "Isherwood thinks an Engineer ought to have known of this trouble in inspecting the boilers during construction." Fox urged Gregory to hurry the *Montauk* to take the place of the *Passaic*. "It is very hard to lose this vessel and [I] think it could have been avoided by skillful attention."[32]

The *Passaic*'s shortcomings strained further the relations between Isherwood, Ericsson, and Stimers. Fox wanted harmony, but above all he wanted the best vessels possible. To improve the *Passaic*, "we have ordered Mr. Isherwood to examine and report upon the working of the boilers, engine, turret & c., & c., for the purpose of placing before you," Fox wrote Ericsson, "all the information possible, and I know you will understand and appreciate our motives." Fox reiterated his faith in "this most admirable and unsurpassed product of genius of the highest order." He stressed that the department and Isherwood were not engaging in faultfinding, but were trying to identify "minor details," which Fox was confident Ericsson would perfect. Fox also reminded Ericsson that "being myself responsible that some twenty [monitors] are now underway," his own reputation was at stake. "It is briefly whether I shall be considered an Ass or a very sensible man." Ericsson appreciated Fox's "very kind" letter, but added, "I hope you will not think me egotistical if I say that Mr. Isherwood's experiments will be of no use to me excepting indeed that they may reveal some defective workmanship." With his ego (which certainly was enlarged) intact and ideas unchanged, Ericsson kept working.[33]

As the chief inspector of ironclads, Stimers should have caught errors in the construction of the *Passaic*. "The responsibility," Fox warned him, "rests entirely upon you to guard against the defects" of the *Passaic* "in the vessels yet to come out." Stimers, who controlled neither his hot temper nor his inflated ego, was difficult to handle. In response to Fox's detailed criticisms, he was obsequious to Fox, critical of Ericsson, and contemptuous of Isherwood. He congratulated Fox on his "correct judgment," suggested that Ericsson bamboozled nonprofessionals in setting valves on steam engines, and castigated Isherwood for an "absurd" idea on the cause of foaming.[34]

The testiness of both Ericsson and Stimers was exacerbated by the "malpractices" of the chief engineer of the *Montauk*. Unless checked at once, he would "ruin the boilers of that vessel." He blew off the boilers under thirty-five pounds of pressure and allowed cold seawater to return. He also shifted steam from one boiler at full pressure into the other boiler filled with cold water. These acts, causing unequal temperatures between the top and bottom of the boilers, would "strain the joints and crack the plates." For this "foul play," Ericsson, having talked it over with Stimers, blamed "the malign influence" of Isherwood, whom they believed was "bitterly and openly hostile" to the monitor fleet.[35]

Fox defended Isherwood, cautioned Stimers, and pled for harmony. "I doubt the propriety of Mr. Stimers putting on to Isherwood's shoulders any 'malign influence' against the Monitor fleet." One of his clerks detailed the engineers "months in advance to enable" Stimers to eliminate those who were incompetent. Careful supervision was essential because there was a shortage of engineers sufficiently competent to maintain and, in case of accident, to repair the complicated machinery on board a monitor. Cooperation, Fox told Ericsson, was equally essential: "Mr. Stimers and Mr. Isherwood belong to a military family and it is impossible for the former, to talk as openly about the latter, as the Officers tell me Stimers does, without laying himself liable to be called upon to prove all he says. . . . I have no friends in all this business except those who most earnestly and zealously work to defeat the public enemy, and all those who are banded together to work to the same end, should endeavor to do it with harmony." Flawed though Stimers was, Fox needed him. "Please hurry Stimers," he pleaded, "with the drawing of the six footers, so we can advertize. I suggest for the battery, one two hundred pound rifle and one 11 inch smooth bore." With Ericsson too busy perfecting monitors and designing rafts to deal with Charleston obstructions, Fox and Ericsson turned over to Stimers the fleshing out of Ericsson's preliminary plans for the light-draft monitor.[36]

Fox had been uncharacteristically pessimistic about the *Passaic*. It was actually repaired by Christmas 1862 and had become a novel attraction in the capital. Lincoln and the cabinet inspected it on 6 December, and on 15 December Virginia Fox recorded:

> All went to Yard to see Passaic—1½ ft only out of the water. I thought it a part
> of the wharf—& kept saying—Where is the vessel? The tower immense & 15 in
> gun in it—(at last Gus' dream is realized). So dark below they burn lamps in
> the day—otherwise looks comfortable. Jesse W[oodbury] Paymaster—he is
> happy *but* complains of dampness there. It is not a ship—only a huge machine
> for carrying & working *two* immense guns (cannon) in safety. All is subordinate
> to that.

As the new year of 1863 drew near, Fox was again optimistic about a sweep down the coast by monitors. With the *Passaic* off to Hampton Roads and seven other monitors of its class either commissioned or about to be commissioned, Fox looked forward to the fall of Charleston.[37]

CHAPTER TWELVE

Charleston

The Fall of Charleston is the fall of Satan's Kingdom.

Fox to Du Pont, 3 June 1862

Ardent defenders of the Union tended to exaggerate Charleston's importance. No one exaggerated its importance more than Fox. Charlestonians were the first to secede, the first to fire on the Stars and Stripes, and the frustrators of Fox's scheme to relieve Fort Sumter. Charleston had become a symbol of rebellion for northerners and of independence for southerners. On both sides, its psychological value enhanced its military significance. Still, Charleston's role in the South's war effort was more than symbolic. Until mid-1863, it was the blockade runners' favorite port, regularly receiving war matériel and exporting cotton, which was "the coin of the realm." Fox was aware of the economic importance of Charleston. In his mind it was also synonymous with the rebellion, and he wished to "go squarely at it by the Channel, so as to make it *purely navy.*"[1]

■ ■ ■

Du Pont tried to rein in Fox's expectations. Although he told his wife that "Charleston should be taken by a large army, squeezed at the same time by a fleet," he was not that direct with Fox. He did tell him on 25 May 1862 that he had "pushed the Gunboats into *Stono*" River, giving the army a base on James Island. At the opposite end of James Island stood Fort Johnson, which was, Du Pont thought, poorly defended from the rear and the "Key" to Charleston Harbor. From it, Fort Sumter could be bombarded. Insisting that he and his men would do all in their power to take Charleston, he warned Fox not to underrate the navy's task. While he dismissed Charleston's landward defense as "nothing," its seaward defense, after a year's work, was formidable. Fort Sumter and Fort Moultrie, abetted by batteries, could effectively concentrate their fire on the main channel into Charleston's harbor. "Then you know," Du

Pont warned Fox, "we go into a bag, no running past, for after we get up they can all play upon us." Du Pont, however, exaggerated the power of the batteries surrounding "Rebellion Roads," the "cul-de-sac" he feared would trap him in the harbor, if he succeeded in getting into it.[2]

A month after the Union foothold on James Island was acquired, General David Hunter, after a setback, evacuated it. Army and navy officers were aghast, because James Island was essential for a combined operation against Charleston. Believing that Charleston could be taken only through "James Island . . . where our army can have a firm base of operations in complete communication with its own transports, and our fleet," Captain Percival Drayton was infuriated. "That James Island evacuation was most disgraceful," Fox exploded. "Had they only held their position it would have prevented re-enforcements leaving for Richmond." But news that the army had pulled out strengthened his belief that the navy had to take Charleston. "You will have to do it," he told Du Pont, "as you have done everything else, alone."[3]

In late August 1862, the failure of Pope, "a lying braggart without brains," at Second Bull Run increased Fox's desire for Charleston, and the new ironclads seemed to place it within the navy's grasp. By then, Fox, realizing that Charleston was "where all the munitions go for the use of the rebels," had military as well as political reasons for wanting to take Charleston. The *New Ironsides*, with its formidable broadside batteries and four-and-a-half-inch plate, Fox reported to Du Pont, "seems a success. . . . We must have Charleston with her and two monitors, and I think we can get them to you next month. The Pres't is most anxious and you know the people are." Although Du Pont was "sure of ultimate success," he warned Fox, "Do not go it half cocked about Charleston—it is a bigger job than Port Royal," which "You & I planned . . .—let us consult together again—Loss of life is nothing, but *failure* now at Charleston is ten times the failure elsewhere."[4]

"Du Pont is here," Fox reported to Virginia on 2 October, "*looking* like an Admiral as he has always behaved like one. We shall settle the doom of Charleston at this time." Their "long and earnest conversations on the capture of Charleston," Du Pont thought, resulted in "Fox modulating his sanguine hopes and impulsive certainty into a calm investigation of all the difficulties." But when Du Pont discovered that government officials—especially Seward—also had "a marked appetite" for Charleston's capture within six weeks, he warned Fox "not to allow the Cabinet ministers or unhealthy public opinion to push him prematurely into an operation." With public opinion, as reflected in the fall elections, going against the administration, all its politicians demanded victories. Constantly worried that an ineffective blockade would provide a pretext for European intervention, Seward was even more anxious for Charleston. He told Du Pont that "the occupation of the whole coast and every port is much more important abroad than the capture of Richmond." Ironically, the growing effectiveness of the blockade—depriving English textile manufacturers of southern cotton—was a reason why Britain might intervene.[5]

On 18 October Du Pont again suggested to Fox that the attack on Charleston "might be a joint movement of Army and Navy." Unfortunately, Du Pont did not forcefully state his views. "It is not in my nature to press things," he told his friend Congressman Henry Winter Davis. Fox conceded that the army could have a force on James Island to take possession, after the navy captured the city. But Du Pont noted, "Fox's Navy feelings are so strong and his prejudices or dislike of Army selfishness so great . . . that he listens unwillingly to combined movements." Indeed, Fox had learned that neither Halleck nor Stanton was interested in supplying troops for joint ventures with the navy, and, when they were provided, as Du Pont discovered at Port Royal, they were poorly trained, badly led, and in small numbers. Attempting to "induce an enlarged view of a joint expedition," Du Pont told Fox that "*certainty* of success" was more important than "undivided glory." Although Fox agreed, "Oh, yes, indeed, the success must be paramount," Du Pont failed to exploit the opening. He did not insist that success could be achieved only by landing a large enough army on James Island to take Fort Johnson, which he knew was the key to Charleston Harbor. He simply marveled that Fox was a "Curious man, but very smart and smarter every day."[6]

With Du Pont too diffident to insist on a combined operation, Fox remained confident that ironclads could take Charleston, and Wilmington, North Carolina, as well. When not riled up about Charleston, Fox acknowledged the growing importance of Wilmington, which was more difficult to blockade than Charleston. He assumed that ironclads would take it, as they swept down the coast toward Charleston. As early as August 1862, Daniel L. Braine of the *Monticello* was taking soundings of the mouth of the Cape Fear River, on which Wilmington was located. By mid-December, the approaching readiness of ironclads, the recent disastrous defeat of the Army of the Potomac at Fredericksburg, and Lincoln's desire "*to strike a blow*" led to a flurry of activity in the Navy Department. Captain Drayton, of the monitor *Passaic*, observed that Fox, with his restless mind and nervous energy, focused chaotically on Wilmington. "Though the popular clamor centers upon Charleston," Fox, on 15 December, wrote Samuel Phillips Lee, the commander of the North Atlantic Blockading Squadron, "I consider Wilmington a more important point in a military and political point of view."[7]

Fox recognized that the shallowness of Cape Fear River bars made access to Wilmington difficult but not impossible. He hoped Lee could utilize the four ironclads that would soon head south. When Lee came to Washington for planning, Drayton claimed it was difficult to get Fox "over the charts." When they did study them, he insisted, "There is plenty of water." Fox based his belief on Braine's recent assurance that at high tide there was twelve feet of water at the entrances to the Cape Fear River and that the Confederate cruiser *Nashville* (which drew thirteen feet) had gotten into Wilmington, although it ran aground and had to be lightened. The *Passaic,* with seven-days' coal, drew eleven feet, while the *New Ironsides* drew almost sixteen feet. Fox had some basis for this reasoning. Having served with Lee in the Coast Survey, he realized that channels shifted and that deeper narrow ones did not always appear on its charts. For example, the 1858 Coast Survey chart revealed a maximum depth of seven feet on the Stono River bar, and yet Charles O. Boutelle of the Coast Survey found a channel sufficient for gunboats—including Drayton's *Pawnee* with its ten-foot draft. Through his friend Blunt, Fox secured four pilots in New York familiar with the Cape Fear River and sent them to Lee.[8]

Realizing that Lincoln was "most anxious as to time," Fox ordered ironclads to Beaufort, North Carolina, in preparation for an attack on Wilmington. With its repairs completed, the *Passaic* (towed by the *State of Georgia*) and the original *Monitor* (towed by the *Rhode Island*) left Hampton Roads for Beaufort on 29 December 1862 and encountered a storm off Hatteras that sank the *Monitor* and almost sank the *Passaic.* Although the *Passaic,* with less of a deck overhang and a rounder hull, was more seaworthy than the *Monitor,* it was shipping water that its pumps could not expel, and, to avoid foundering, Drayton ordered all shot thrown overboard. That costly storm led Fox and Welles to reconsider the attack on Wilmington. In addition, a 27 December reconnaissance of the New Inlet Bar, Cape Fear River, found barely enough water to carry the monitors over it. Lee believed there was more water at the Western Bar, but local pilots at Beaufort claimed "there was nothing like water enough" for the *Passaic.* In despair over the loss of the *Monitor,* Fox decided with Welles to concentrate on Charleston and not to risk the navy's few monitors in shoal water.[9]

On 6 January Welles ordered the *New Ironsides* and the monitors *Passaic, Montauk, Patapsco,* and *Weehawken* to Du Pont "to enter the harbor of Charleston and demand the surrender of all its defenses." A 10,000-man army under General Hunter was also on its way to Port Royal, but Welles emphasized that the capture of Charleston "rests solely upon the success of the naval force." After the fall of Charleston, Fox and Welles wanted Du Pont to send the *New Ironsides, Patapsco,* and *Weehawken* to Pensacola "to strike a blow at once at Mobile." Later, when more monitors were available, they were prepared to risk them in the shoal waters of the Cape Fear River.[10]

The monitors, Fox believed, were "the greatest experiment of the age," but he was troubled by their lack of seaworthiness. He realized that there would be problems towing them to Charleston and Mobile. Once they were at those points, though, he was confident they would destroy harbor defenses. The monitors, Fox reasoned, were impregnable platforms for huge guns that, despite flaws and delays, could be constructed quickly and cheaply. By December 1862, he claimed, "there is no workshop in the country capable of making steam machinery or iron plates and hulls that is not in full blast with Naval orders" and predicted that in a year sixty ironclads would be in commission.[11]

The worst "hurricane" (probably a northeaster) in "several years" struck the East Coast on 20 January 1863, heaping a "terrible load of anxiety" on Fox. When it began, John Rodgers in the Passaic-class *Weehawken* was heading for Hampton Roads. "During the heaviest of the gale," Rodgers wrote Fox, "I stood upon the turret and admired the behavior of the vessel. She rose and fell to the waves and I concluded then that the Monitor form had great seagoing qualities." Fox was relieved and overjoyed. "With that reckless daring so characteristic of him," Fox told Du Pont, Rodgers "cast off his tow and pushed out to sea and rode it out beautifully. . . . The loss of the Monitor brought up the 'I told you so' people, Rodgers courage has extinguished them." To Rodgers, Fox exclaimed, "Your brave act has been of more use to us than a victory." Fox assured Du Pont, "Every succeeding vessel we build stronger and better and with improvements that will render them perfectly safe at sea." Indeed, after the anticipated fall of Charleston, he wanted Du Pont to send both the *Passaic* and the *Montauk,* not to the Gulf, but North for "greater strengthening." Brimming with confidence in the five ironclads and in Du Pont, Fox assured him of his "intense interest as you go forward to retake the City where this wicked rebellion first tore down the Stars and Stripes."[12]

Despite high hopes, January 1863 proved a bad month for the navy. A daring surprise attack by Confederate army gunboats at Galveston, Texas, on the first day of the month prompted Union blockaders to flee to New Orleans. On its last day, the Confederate ironclad rams *Chicora* and *Palmetto State,* under the cover of fog, emerged from Charleston Harbor, rammed the *Mercedita,* damaged the *Keystone State,* and shelled two other ships, but the blockade of Charleston was not broken. "The Charleston matter," as Fox called it, "gave us very little concern . . . and I fancy the knowledge you have acquired" about the rams "is worth more to us, than our loss is gain to the enemy." Hoping to spur Du Pont, Fox predicted that he would soon wipe out the navy's "disgraceful" behavior at Galveston.[13]

Du Pont was not sure he could wipe out the Galveston disgrace, and the army, with which he preferred to cooperate, was of no help. On 2 February generals Hunter and John G. Foster (who had been at Sumter with Anderson) conferred with Du Pont at Port Royal. Neither had "any plan [n]or been sent with any," Du Pont commented to his wife. With a strong Confederate presence on James Island, he did not see "what much they can do to help us to take the city, but will be of vast importance afterwards, if it pleases God that we should succeed."[14]

Foster did have a plan of attack. With 17,000 well-provisioned Confederate soldiers on James Island, he rejected that back door to Charleston. It was now well defended and too wide at its upper end "to be covered by guns from the ironclads." Meeting with Lincoln, Stanton, Halleck, and Fox on 15 February, Foster suggested that the "ironclads . . . protect him upon Morris Island whilst he erected batteries to reduce Sumter." That idea, Fox told Du Pont, "was so insignificant and so characteristic of the Army, that I could not help expressing myself to that effect." He protested that "it would be utterly an Army movement and the Iron Clads might go to Mobile, that they were built expressly to go by Forts and take Charleston; if, as is reported, *the obstacles* in the harbor had nearly, if not entirely, disappeared, he wished them to go in in a straight line and utterly disregard the shots from the Forts, not even return them," and steam into "Rebellion Roads."

With the navy's earlier success at New Orleans clearly in mind, Fox "asked General Halleck what would be the result of the ironclads reaching a position off the city. He replied the entire evacuation of James Island." Later, when George W. Cullum, Halleck's chief of staff, joined them in Halleck's office, Fox repeated the question, and Cullum agreed with Halleck that "it would be all up with them if we could pass the forts." To Fox's query, "Why attack the forts?" Foster grudgingly admitted, "If we could get to the city it would be no use." Opposed to a siege, Lincoln "*earnestly*" wanted Fox to reconnoiter Charleston's defenses with Foster and to see Du Pont.[15]

Fox wanted to go, but Welles convinced Lincoln that Fox should remain in Washington. "Told him," Welles recorded in his diary, "it was a time when the active force of the Department was most wanted, it being near the close of the session of Congress, when every variety of call was made, and delays to answer are inadmissible; and some important bills were to be acted upon and engineered through." Welles also argued that Du Pont's pride might be touched by such an errand. But it was Fox's capacity to convince congressmen of the navy's needs that made him indispensable to Welles.[16]

Fox could best convince congressmen with victories. Aware that the country was growing "very impatient," he reminded Du Pont that "finances, politics, foreign relations, all seem to ask for Charleston." Fox urged Du Pont to utilize Ericsson's rafts to clear rope obstructions and "torpedoes" (mines) and pass Sumter without pausing to batter it, possess Charleston Harbor, isolate the forts guarding its entrance, and place Charleston under the guns of the ironclads. Du Pont, however, shrank from that task. Welles deplored "the signs of misgiving and doubt which have recently come over him—his shirking policy, getting in with the army, making approaches, etc. It is not what we have talked of, not what we expected of him—is not like the firm and impetuous Farragut."[17]

Ericsson feared that Fox expected too much from the monitors. He believed that, with fifteen-inch guns, they would prevail against any ship, and he was reasonably confident they could run by fortifications. But he anticipated that Du Pont would attack, rather than run by Sumter, and warned Fox "you have not guns enough" to subdue a powerful fortress. "I hope I may be wrong," Ericsson concluded, "but at the same time pray that you will not commence the attack until you have all your turrets present." Ericsson's caution made Fox concede that the monitors might not be impregnable. "Du Pont will very soon be at work against the enemy with the ironclads," Fox wrote Farragut, "and if anything is left of them they will go directly to you" to take Mobile.[18]

Misgivings about reducing Sumter and fear that the monitors were vulnerable led Fox to again urge Du Pont to run by Sumter. "I hope you will hold to the idea of carrying in your flag supreme and superb, defiant and disdainful, silent amid the 200 guns, until you arrive at the center of this wicked rebellion and there demand the surrender of the forts, or swift destruction. *The President and Mr. Welles are very much struck with this programme.* . . . The sublimity of such a silent attack is beyond words to describe, and I beg of you not to let the Army spoil it."[19]

Lincoln endorsed the program because of Fox's enthusiasm. "I should be very anxious about this job," Lincoln remarked several times to Fox, "if you did not feel so sure of your people being successful." Not totally carried away, Fox conceded to Du Pont, "if the obstructions prevent this, it will be time enough to assist the Army in laying siege. I believe you will do what is *best* in the most superb manner and you will be successful." Anticipating that success, Fox on 2 April 1863 asked Du Pont to "send all the Iron Clads, that survive the attack upon Charleston immediately to New Orleans reserving for your squadron only two." Fox explained that operations against Mobile and Wilmington were being postponed because Lincoln insisted that the ironclads be sent to open the Mississippi between Port Hudson, Louisiana, and Vicksburg. He especially wanted to possess that stretch of the Mississippi where supplies coming down the Red River could be interdicted.[20]

Fox's compliments, expectations, and exhortations inspired Du Pont to ridicule, rather than to action. Although Du Pont demanded more monitors (which Fox strained to get him), he lacked confidence in them. He conceded that they were impregnable but argued that the slow fire of their two guns gave them little offensive punch. Monitors lent themselves to Fox's strategy of getting by forts and cutting them off from their succor, but Du Pont refused to seriously considered running silently by Sumter. "We'll do it if it can be done," he told Fox, but "to *get there*," he thought, "we shall have to batter and pound beyond any precedent in history." Although Du Pont thought, "the probabilities are *all* against us," he failed to tell Fox. To get into Charleston Harbor, he believed, his fleet of thirty-two guns would have to "silence two or three hundred" guns, avoid obstructions, and not run aground, lest a monitor be captured. A monitor based in Charleston Harbor, Du Pont feared, could destroy the blockaders.[21]

Du Pont's cautious temperament was poles apart from the impetuous nature of Farragut or Fox. Du Pont anticipated defeat, unless "it pleases God to give us a victory at Charleston." Fox forced him into his splendid victory at Port Royal, and Fox tried to force him into an even greater victory at Charleston. "I never proposed taking Charleston," Du Pont wrote his friend James Stokes Biddle on 25 March 1863. When earlier in 1862 Hunter evacuated James Island, which Du Pont knew was the best approach to Charleston, he took it calmly, while Percival Drayton, other naval officers, and Fox were apoplectic. About to lead a naval assault on Charleston, though, Du Pont looked back on that abandonment as "the golden opportunity gone." Du Pont believed firmly in joint army-navy operations, but by March 1863 the army units available to him were paralyzed by a quarrel between Hunter and Foster. "In reference to Charleston," Du Pont concluded, "I cannot see where and how the troops are going to help us—the day has gone by for them, I fear, until we do the work."[22]

Du Pont had no stomach for an exclusive naval attack on Charleston's defenses or for a Farragut-style run through the obstructions past the forts. Feeling as he did, he should have told Fox and Welles that he knew their proposed attack would fail and, if they continued to insist on unilateral naval action, resigned his command. He clung to his command, though, in part because John A. Dahlgren, whom he despised, had for months been angling to replace him. Du Pont's hints, however, were enough to worry Fox and Welles. "Fox," Lizzie Blair Lee reported to Samuel Phillips Lee on 6 April, "has grown thinner in two weeks & I never saw him look as anxious as now."[23]

Du Pont attacked on 7 April 1863 and "failed," he told his wife, "as I felt sure we would." In two hours, seven monitors, the *New Ironsides,* and the lightly armored *Keokuk* fired a total of 136 shots (125 at Fort Sumter) as compared to over 2,000 fired by Sumter alone. Five monitors were damaged, and the *Keokuk* (an ironclad, but not a monitor) was so seriously hit that it sank the next day. Convinced that his fleet inflicted little damage on Sumter, Du Pont withdrew, deciding not to risk his monitors by renewing the attack the next day. From his flagship *New Ironsides,* he could not see that the Dahlgren-Rodman fifteen-inch guns on the monitors had inflicted considerable damage. It was significant enough, in fact, to threaten to bring down Sumter's northeast face. Although Du Pont believed his repulse proved that the monitors, with their fifteen-inch guns, and the *New Ironsides* were failures, the monitors had more offensive punch than he realized or his champions later conceded.[24]

Fox first heard on 10 April of the repulse "from Rebel sources" and was convinced that Du Pont was "feeling the ground; it was not the true attack." Confident that Du Pont would utilize the experience gained, Fox predicted, "The real attack would be made in the morning, so as to have all day for the work." Two days later, he was appalled to learn that "the Rebel account [was] too true." Mirroring her husband's mood swings, Virginia became "awfully blue over war matters."[25]

Fox himself was too resilient, too self-confident, to remain devastated. He planned to visit Du Pont and Charleston to reconnoiter its defenses, inspect the monitors, and discuss future moves. Unfortunately, once again, Welles would not let him go and ordered him to New York to consult with Ericsson about monitor problems revealed by the attack. Both Fox and Du Pont would have benefited from a face-to-face meeting. Presumably, Du Pont would have been more forthright than he had been the previous October, and Fox, following the repulse, would have been more attentive to Du Pont's concerns. Fox would have been enlightened, and Du Pont less apt to feel abandoned by the department and blamed by it for the defeat. But they neither met nor corresponded after the repulse. Rather than admit he was too optimistic about the capacity of the monitors, Fox reflected that Du Pont neither tried to steam past the forts nor adhered to his own battle plan.[26]

Loading a fifteen-inch gun inside a monitor during the attack on Fort Sumter, 7 April 1863. From *Frank Leslie's Illustrated History of the Civil War*, p. 450. Courtesy Hagley Museum and Library, Wilmington, Delaware.

If there had ever been a chance of success, Du Pont made it highly unlikely. He planned not to achieve victory but to minimize his losses. He delayed the attack until the ebb tide, rather than the incoming one, so damaged vessels would drift out to sea rather than into the harbor. He abandoned his original idea of bombarding the northwestern face of Sumter because of "heavy fire" from Fort Sumter and Fort Moultrie "and the nature of the obstructions" of which, because he had failed to reconnoiter, he knew little. He had little faith that Ericsson's torpedo raft, attached to the bow of the lead monitor, could blast a path through the obstructions, which at the time of his attack consisted of a rope between Sumter and Moultrie with a network of turpentine barrel floats, but no torpedoes. In theory, the torpedo raft could easily have cut the rope, but pushing it with an underpowered monitor in a strong tidal current

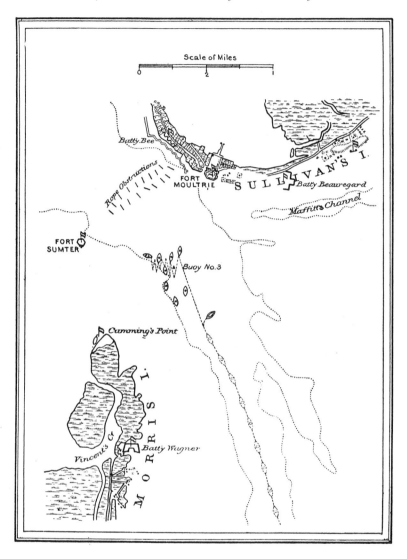

Plan of the approach and attack on Fort Sumter, 7 April 1863. From *Official Records of the Union and Confederate Navies*, 14:90.

was difficult if not impossible. When John Rodgers in the lead monitor, *Wee-hawken*, tried to use the Ericsson raft, he did so without its torpedo (justly fearing that it was too dangerous). The raft became tangled with his anchor chain and had to be cut loose.

Rodgers made no attempt to break through the rows of buoys (which he presumed were attached to torpedoes), and the attacking ironclads remained—like sitting ducks—in the vicinity of red buoy number three, which had served as the target, during practice, for seventy-six Confederate guns. The failure to advance rendered Du Pont's most powerful vessel, the *New Ironsides*, useless, as it yawed in the "narrow channel and rapid current," collided with two monitors, and failed to fire on Sumter. Perhaps a commander like Farragut would have "damned" the nonexistent torpedoes, cut through the network of buoys, gained possession of Charleston Harbor, and compelled the abandonment of the forts and the surrender of Charleston, as Fox hoped and Halleck conceded could happen. But, without the cooperation of a well-trained, competently led army (Hunter's force was neither), running by the forts might have proved as meaningless as running by Vicksburg.[27]

Although they were disappointed both by the outcome of the attack and by the "tone and sentiment" of Du Pont's reports, Fox and Welles refrained from casting blame. Chief Engineer Alban C. Stimers, however, was hostile. He claimed that before the assault, Du Pont had ignored his advice on how to use the Ericsson torpedo rafts (which Stimers had tested) and had already decided not to use them to blow up obstructions. In addition, Stimers's inspection of the monitors the day after the engagement revealed only minor damage, which in Stimers's opinion left them with "sufficient enduring powers to enable them to pass all the forts and batteries" if the torpedo rafts were used to clear the obstructions. Ericsson, citing engineers' reports, agreed that the monitors sustained "very trifling damage" and added, "It has often given me pain to think our fighting *machines* are entrusted to officers who know nothing of mechanics and *therefore* have no confidence in their vessels."[28]

Despite Ericsson's pain, Fox soon concluded that he had probably erred in his belief that the monitors could penetrate the obstructions and take Charleston unilaterally. The unanimous opinion of the monitor captains—especially John Rodgers and John L. Worden—who all agreed with Du Pont that their vessels even when armed with the fifteen-inch gun lacked the offensive punch to overcome "stone walls," was for Fox disappointing but decisive. He became convinced that Charleston would have to be taken by a combined army-navy operation, led by neither the incompetent Hunter nor the overly cautious Du Pont.[29]

Defeat at Charleston poisoned relations between Du Pont and Fox, primarily because of Stimers's opinion, which Fox had in fact discounted. But Du Pont officially suggested that Fox approved, prior to its publication in the *Baltimore American*, the critical article, "A Disgraceful Result," by C. C. Fulton, echoing the views of Stimers with whom he had witnessed the assault. Although Fox had a close relationship with Fulton and at times planted articles in the *American*, he had not seen the article and certainly would not have approved it. Fox said he had "given Admiral Du Pont my confidence and esteem to the fullest extent, and the extraordinary insinuations in his dispatch . . . are as unjust to me as they are unworthy of him." Nevertheless, a year later, Fox still had sufficient "confidence and esteem" to offer Du Pont, through Charles Henry Davis, the command of the Pacific Squadron, but because it neither was classified as war service nor was similar to the squadron he had commanded—six vessels compared to sixty or seventy—Du Pont rejected the overture.[30]

On 4 June 1863 the aggressive (but ailing) Andrew Hull Foote was ordered to replace Du Pont as commander of the South Atlantic Blockading Squadron, and on 12 June Brigadier General Quincy Adams Gillmore (who a year earlier with rifled guns had compelled the surrender of Fort Pulaski on the Savannah River) replaced Hunter as commander of the Department of the South. When Farragut asked "what was the trouble with Du Pont," Fox replied "that he was recalled because he despaired of success." "Foote," Fox cheerfully wrote, "is going down to take a turn at the Rebels. . . . The attack will probably be in conjunction with the Army upon Morris Island."[31]

Fox soon had his faith in the monitors restored. On 17 June 1863 the powerful *Atlanta*, a Confederate ironclad ram, moved into Wassaw Sound, Georgia, to attack the *Weehawken* and the *Nahant*. In the ensuing battle, John Rodgers, captain of the *Weehawken*, demonstrated that he had underestimated the offensive punch of his eleven- and fifteen-inch guns. The *Atlanta* ran aground, was freed, proved unmaneuverable, and ran aground again, altogether firing six harmless shots at the *Weehawken*. In fifteen minutes, the *Weehawken*'s big guns hit the *Atlanta* five times. The fifteen-inch gun was devastating and compelled the *Atlanta*'s surrender, undermining the criticisms voiced by Du Pont and Dahlgren and vindicating Fox. Often critical of Fox, Charles Henry Davis noted, "The recent attack on Fort Sumter was a disappointment to Fox, on account of guns and monitors both. But this fight of Rodgers's, one of the most remarkable in naval history, . . . completely justified Fox's bold determination in behalf of guns and vessels." Fox, Welles, Lincoln, and Congress were ecstatic, and Rodgers was promoted to commodore and ordered north to command the *Dictator*.[32]

When Foote, before he could relieve Du Pont, died of Bright's disease later that month, Fox and Welles had to make a further change. The death "of our great Admiral" was a "terrible calamity," Fox mourned. Foote was replaced by their second choice, John A. Dahlgren, who relieved Du Pont on 6 July. In record time, Fox hurried Dahlgren off to cooperate with the army at Morris Island, whose north end faced Fort Sumter. As Fox realized, Gillmore, like

Foster, planned to utilize the monitors for landing on Morris Island, capturing Fort Wagner, and shelling and destroying Sumter. The monitors presumably could then penetrate the obstructions, move into the harbor, and demand Charleston's surrender. Although Fox earlier had ridiculed Foster's plan, he now backed it and went over Halleck's and Stanton's heads to secure from Lincoln more troops for Gillmore. When in August Lincoln asked, "Why, with more force than Du Pont had, they did not go up at once and take Charleston?" Fox replied, "Charleston cannot be taken by a purely naval attack."[33]

Dahlgren and Gillmore proved no more successful than Du Pont and Hunter. Four days after Dahlgren's arrival, troops were landed on Morris Island covered by the bombardment of four monitors, but Fort Wagner held out. An assault on 18 July, spearheaded by the Fifty-fourth Massachusetts Colored Infantry, failed with the frightful loss of more than 1,500 killed, wounded, or missing Union soldiers. While Fox was now committed to joint, cooperative operations with the army, General-in-Chief Halleck and the War Department had become "very much opposed to doing anything at Charleston." During the siege of Fort Wagner, Dahlgren reported that Gillmore's 6,000 men were inadequate, but when Fox, at Welles's behest, asked for more troops, Halleck "rebuffed" him, saying, if they "would take care of the Navy he would take care of the Army." Dahlgren observed, "Stanton and Halleck are opposed to any move on Charleston; Fox and Gillmore are strong for it. Fox carries it, but the slow progress gives Stanton the advantage." After Fox requested more troops and Welles saw Lincoln, Stanton promised to send Gillmore 5,000 more men. When, like all naval commanders, Dahlgren was also short of men, Fox suggested that he "get Contrabands for Seamen and Coal heavers."[34]

From 17 to 23 August Gillmore and Dahlgren intensified their attack on Wagner and bombarded Sumter. While these two ordnance experts reduced it to rubble, their relationship deteriorated. Even if the War and Navy departments cooperated in Washington, a successful combined operation required a hearty cooperative spirit on the part of line naval officers and army field commanders. Dahlgren's six monitors and the *New Ironsides* were under severe fire and sustained damage and casualties. For example, Fleet Captain George W. Rodgers and Gordon Woodbury (a Virginia Fox relation) were decapitated when a shot from Wagner shook loose part of the lining of the *Catskill*'s turret.[35]

Ericsson, Fox told Dahlgren, was "overwhelmed at the sad accident" and asked for "sketches" that would enable him to make design changes to avoid "similar accidents in the vessels coming forward." Fox added, "It would be of the greatest advantage to the Department if you would request the iron clad captains to make constant reports, minute in all particulars, with your endorsements thereupon to enable us to strengthen and guard from the accidents of such fearful cannonading." No doubt at Fox's behest, Welles had already officially asked Dahlgren for a weekly report with sketches of the damage inflicted on the ironclads.[36]

In early September, the slow progress at Charleston inspired newspaper articles, by Miles O'Reilly, that were critical of the monitors, hostile to Dahlgren, and friendly to Du Pont. Written in fact by Charles G. Halpine of Hunter's staff, these articles would have "annoyed" Fox even more had he realized that Halpine utilized private letters, from Gillmore's command, supplied to him by Halleck. "The N.Y. Herald articles," Fox wrote Virginia, "are the results of the contest about Monitors, the removal of Du Pont &c. &c. I stake my reputation on the result, that with these vessels we will win back all the fortified places of the U.S. and defend our shores against foreign aggression. I take no interest whatever in the *discussion* knowing that *success* at Charleston will settle all controversy." By October, Welles and Fox realized that Gillmore was behind the attacks on Dahlgren and the monitors. Dahlgren realized it a bit later.[37]

There was, however, only limited success at Charleston. Further bombardment forced the Confederates to abandon Fort Wagner on 6 September, but the next day, when Dahlgren demanded the surrender of Sumter, Beauregard told him "to take it if he could." Without Gillmore's cooperation, Dahlgren tried to take Sumter, but an assault at 1:00 a.m. on 9 September by 500 sailors and marines failed miserably. While the mutual hatred of Dahlgren and Gillmore hampered further action, the Navy Department became more realistic about capturing Charleston. After Du Pont's repulse, Fox and Welles thought its capture probable, with the navy a "cooperating force," aiding the army. In time, however, they believed that, while the "moral effect of taking Charleston was not to be questioned," the military advantage would be negligible, because "the port was closed."[38]

Neither Fox nor Welles blamed Dahlgren for the failure to take Charleston. "Fox says," Wise assured him, "you have done 'nobly' and even if nothing else be effected, the mere fact that you have closed the Port of Charleston is of immense importance and value." Fox continued to encourage Dahlgren, counseled patience, and begged him to ignore "the newspapers." But, realizing the importance of public opinion, Fox himself could not ignore the hostile press. Along with Ericsson, he planted press releases in friendly newspapers and commended editors for favorable remarks. Harsh realities, however, forced him and Welles to redefine "success" with respect to Charleston.[39]

The tactical changes at Charleston and articles attacking the monitors disturbed Ericsson. Having designed the torpedo rafts to clear the way for monitors to dash into Charleston Harbor and reduce its city to "ashes," he disapproved the systematic bombardment of Sumter. "It is truly unfortunate," he wrote Fox on 13 September 1863, elaborating on a point he had made the preceding February, "that your original plan of breaking up the obstructions and running past the forts has not been carried out. It is now evident that unless you order the Rafts to be employed at once the prestige of the Monitor system will receive a fatal blow. . . . To silence, destroy, take and hold mud forts is not work that Monitors are suited for."[40]

Although Fox agreed that attacking land forts was not the duty of any ship, including the monitors, he disagreed "entirely" that they were losing their prestige. The "marvelous" monitors, Fox assured Ericsson, were "becoming immortalized by their endurance." Repeated disappointments at Charleston had made him cautious about running by the forts. While he had complete confidence in Dahlgren's persistence, he conceded, "If the obstructions cannot be removed or passed, we must be content with holding the mouth of the harbor and with long range rifles on Cummings Point rendering the city untenable." The Yankees and the Rebels deceived each other. The monitors were not, as Fox and Welles would have the world believe, invulnerable, nor were the Rebel torpedoes (mines) and obstructions at Charleston as extensive as the Confederates wanted Union forces to believe. The Rebel deception, however, was more effective. It dissuaded both Du Pont and Dahlgren from entering Rebellion Roads.[41]

Torpedoes especially spooked Dahlgren, after the Confederate *David* used a spar torpedo to damage the *New Ironsides* on 5 October 1863. He sent Fox drawings of the *David* and urged that it be produced in quantity and turned on the enemy. The Navy Department developed a torpedo boat, the *Stromboli*, renamed *Spuyten Duyvil*, which saw service on the James River. By late 1863 Ericsson improved his antiobstruction torpedo raft with a 600-pound charge of powder. But, like its predecessor, it had to be lashed to a monitor's bow. Dahlgren's tests showed it would be effective against "piles, chains, network, and torpedoes" on a smooth sea (which seldom occurred off of Charleston). It was judged "too cumbersome and complicated" to attack enemy ironclads.[42]

Dahlgren did like the "time torpedoes" developed by Benjamin Maillefert and ordered 100 of them on 16 February 1864 to clear the channel into Charleston Harbor. The next day, however, the Confederate submarine *H. L. Hunley* began a new chapter in naval warfare, using a spar torpedo. It sank the wooden steam sloop of war *Housatonic*, before accidently sinking itself. After that,

Dahlgren's wooden vessels kept their steam up and went out to sea each night. Even though he ordered torpedoes, he did not use them to penetrate the obstructions, which by 1865 were augmented with torpedoes.[43]

Dahlgren continued to attack Sumter. On 26 October 1863, abetted by land batteries, he launched a two-week bombardment, leaving it in ruins. Sheltered by its rubble, the Confederate infantry held on. By then, Beauregard had removed its guns to strengthen the inner ring of Charleston's defenses, making Rebellion Roads the cul-de-sac Du Pont earlier had feared. Although the Navy Department finally gave up on taking Sumter, Dahlgren, by utilizing monitors inside the bar at the entrance of the harbor, effectively blockaded Charleston.[44]

Fox appreciated the work of Dahlgren and his monitors in virtually closing the port, but his hatred of Charleston lingered. "As a naval feature," he wrote Dahlgren in January 1864, "the work at Charleston is done but, politically and morally, we ought to enter far enough to burn the city by naval fire and accomplish the destruction of their naval forces as well as get a more secure anchorage." For this destruction, monitors were necessary, and on that score he was discouraged. "I have been to New York looking at the iron-clads. I doubt if you get the Onondaga, Tecumseh, Canonicus and Manhattan before the first of March. It is melancholy, but patience to those who win is a quality admired by the world."[45]

Although Dahlgren was not able to burn Charleston, Fox valued his efforts and would not replace him. In May 1864 Fox mentioned to Porter that "Dahlgren wants to come home. Poor fellow, hard work, forty-two courageous and persistent attacks, poor health, and the papers discussing and cussing him. The [admiral's] square-flag is not the pleasant place Washington Navy Yard was. I don't think we can let him home just now." At the end of the war, Dahlgren proudly wrote Fox, "The inside blockade by the Monitors has never been beaten." Despite the navy's efforts, Charleston did not surrender until 18 February 1865, when William Tecumseh Sherman's army forced its evacuation.[46]

CHAPTER THIRTEEN

The Light-Draft Debacle

The want of a light draft ironclad has been so imperative that
the Department was justified in taking great risks to obtain one.

Fox, 15 December 1864

Regarding the monitor as the naval vessel of the future, Fox committed the
navy to its use in the present. By late 1862 Ericsson was planning two seagoing
monitors to meet the threat of foreign intervention, and ten coastal monitors,
drawing ten feet of water, were already nearing completion. With their shallow draft, substantial armor, big guns, and low cost, the coastal monitors were
preeminently suited for operations in southern waters. To penetrate further
into the Confederacy, Fox yearned for an invulnerable river monitor, drawing
only six feet of water. In October 1862 Ericsson responded with preliminary
plans for a light-draft monitor but was too busy to elaborate on them. With
Fox's approval, Ericsson asked Chief Engineer Alban C. Stimers to make
detailed drawings, based on Ericsson's plans. The results of that request were
disastrous.

■ ■ ■

Fox relied on Stimers, despite Stimers's volatility. Apparently able, obviously
energetic, and with great faith in monitors, Stimers was very useful. His telling Fox, "You are the Navy Department," no doubt enhanced Fox's good opinion of him. Ericsson also valued Stimers, but as a draftsman, filling in the
details of his plans, not as a naval architect or inventor. Fancying himself in
those roles, Stimers felt he could improve on Ericsson's work. Fox was aware
that in April 1862 Ericsson was appalled by Stimers's drawings of a modified
monitor, but they both realized that, except for Ericsson, no one else knew
more about monitors than Stimers. It seemed to make sense to ask Stimers to
flesh out Ericsson's plans for the new class of light-draft monitors. Busy getting monitors and rafts off to Charleston, Stimers assigned the task to a com-

petent, but "unsteady," draftsman. Ericsson assumed Stimers would not alter the dimensions of these six-footers, and Fox assumed Stimers would consult Ericsson before making changes.[1]

By the end of December, though, Stimers had altered the dimensions of the light drafts. Claiming they would "draw ten inches too much water," he added to their length and beam, necessitating a new set of drawings. In mid-January, while questioning Stimers about the planned attack on Charleston, Fox urged him, "Hurry all you can the plans for the six footers." Stimers did consult with Ericsson about their armament, but not about the fundamental changes he had made on the original plans.[2]

When Ericsson saw Stimers's plans on the morning of 24 February 1863, he told Fox he was "repudiating all responsibility in regard to the light draughts." He believed his plans submitted in October were good enough for contractors to bid on and that, had the Navy Department proceeded, it would have "a light draft fleet very nearly ready for action." He was "disappointed to learn . . . that other plans were wanted and more particularly" that Isherwood and Stimers "had decided on changing propellers, boilers, &c." He complained that his objects of "impregnability, dispatch & dispensing with iron" in his "simple open plate Iron Tank Encased in Timber . . . have all been lost." The timber, for example, was so reduced in thickness "that the sides are not shot proof." Ericsson hardly knew what the department should do. If it could get bids on the basis of his original proposal, "it would be well," but he feared that was improbable. He warned Fox that contracts must have "ample provisions as to changes that you may deem proper to make. . . . Some internal changes may readily be made and the thing come out well enough." Nevertheless, Ericsson reiterated, "Only do not hold me responsible."[3]

Fox and Welles were in a quandary. Because the light drafts had already been delayed, they resolved to go ahead. Even if Ericsson's criticisms were correct, he did hold out the possibility that the shortcomings of Stimers's light drafts could be remedied while the vessels were being constructed. Because Stimers's plans were more fully developed than Ericsson's early sketches, both Lenthall and Isherwood considered them preferable, though neither evaluated them critically. Both were also sufficiently hostile to Stimers to give him enough rope to hang himself.[4]

Although Stimers's plans were not complete, the Navy Department began to contract for their construction in March 1863. "The Department as I understand it," Fox wrote him on 16 March, prior to Stimers's departure with rafts for South Carolina, "only furnish the general plan, contractors making their own working drawings." Most of them, however, did not make their own detailed drawings but waited for drawings to be sent from Stimers's office. Sub-ordinates worked on plans for the six-footers in Stimers's absence, and by 19 April Stimers assured Fox, "I shall soon have the principal detail plans of the Light Drafts in the hands of the workmen." By the end of the month, with the plans still not ready, he estimated that "nearly all" of them would be ready by 1 June. Even though the drawings were by his subordinates, Stimers insisted, "all important matters . . . received my earnest attention."[5]

When the failed 7 April attack on Charleston exposed several shortcomings on the Passaic-class monitors, the six-footers were once again neglected. Fox wanted to use the battle scars to instruct and improve the monitors in service as well as the new Canonicus class that was under construction. Ericsson, how-ever, was not anxious to be instructed by the complaints of the "gallant" mon-itor commanders.[6]

Fox once again had to interpret and mediate—this time, between men of sail, unhappy that they were being forced into fire-breathing monsters, and the brilliant, egotistical, headstrong, irascible inventor of those fire-breathing monsters. Having pushed the sailors, Fox now cajoled the engineer. On Mon-day, 20 April, he conferred with Ericsson, and on 24 April he wrote from Wash-ington, reiterating improvements deemed necessary by monitor captains. They wanted a stronger pilothouse on top of the turret, more protection for the turret's base, jam-proof turret gears, and a fully operable turret when steam pressure fell. In addition, they called for a less vulnerable deck, another an-chor, and "a proper system of ventilation." Fox stressed that without better ventilation no one could remain aboard, that medical officers had protested the foul air, and that "smoke from the lamps has already affected several of the crew." Anxious for solutions to these problems, he wrote in a similar vein to Stimers.[7]

Ericsson and Stimers addressed these and other problems that Fox pointed out. Fox was neither an engineer nor a naval architect, but he had skippered steamships, was the son of an inventor of textile machinery, and grasped mechanics. He read plans critically and worked to anticipate problems. He was concerned, for example, that tangled rope obstructions, like those at Charles-ton, could easily foul the propeller and render a monitor helpless. He also thought wider peepholes, to scan the horizon, were necessary. Stimers's pro-posal that "steel saw plate . . . sharp as a knife" be attached to each propeller blade to prevent fouling was not adopted, and a propeller basket tried on the *Passaic* reduced its speed too much to be useful. While both Stimers and Erics-son presented Fox with plans for enlarged peepholes, Fox thought Ericsson's plans were "infinitely superior." Although Stimers was useful, Fox relied on

Ericsson to review and revise Stimers's work. "Your brain," Fox told Ericsson, "has answered every call that my anxiety has made upon it either by argument or some ingenious mechanism that meets every difficulty." Fulsome flattery kept Ericsson working day and night for the Union navy. Fox was an enthusiast with great faith in his men and machines, and he constantly cheered and urged on his commanders and the makers of the tools of naval warfare.[8]

Fox was constantly on the lookout for technological developments that would improve the monitors and their guns. In March 1863, upon reading about Bessemer steel in an English periodical, he asked Abram S. Hewitt, the prominent New Jersey iron manufacturer, his opinion of Bessemer steel. "Will it make large guns? Will it answer for large plates as well as wrought iron? Can it be cast in immense masses? For example the Pilot Houses of our turret vessels are eight feet in diameter, seven high, eight inches thick, and weigh about twenty-eight tons." If Hewitt thought they could be cast, Fox was willing to order two dozen pilothouses from England, because he assumed "the Bessemer process has not been tried" in the United States. Hewitt dashed the "sanguine hopes" Fox entertained for Bessemer steel, and he concluded that the "articles must have been exaggerated." Fox turned to Hewitt, because he had just been in England studying gunmetal, which he manufactured at cost for the Union war effort. Fox also wanted to know if it was feasible "to cast Pilot Houses out of Dahlgren's gunmetal." He asked, "How can the Government get a fifteen inch smooth bore cannon that will be perfectly safe with 100 pounds of common cannon powder. Dahlgren says it can't be done. If it cannot, the defence, for the first time in history is stronger than the attack."[9]

Hewitt was not interested in casting pilothouses, but he knew about guns. He pulled no punches. "*Today* the means of attack are superior to the means of defense. . . . *Today* England & France could take every one of our seaports" because, Hewitt elaborated, "we have no guns which can penetrate their Iron Clads," with their four-and-a-half-inch to five-and-a-half-inch solid plates. Our ironclads with their layers of one-inch plates riveted together "cannot resist the shots from the improved ordnance now in general use in Europe. . . . This improved ordnance is produced by the use of wrought iron and steel in lieu of cast iron for heavy guns." Hewitt declared that "the conflict between the Merrimack & the Monitor proved that our guns were good for nothing" and disparaged the fifteen- and twenty-inch guns made of cast iron, which Fox favored. To make heavy guns out of wrought iron and steel required twenty-five- to thirty-ton steam hammers, and there were none in the United States. Because these steam hammers were useful only for making heavy ordnance and would have no peacetime application, the government would have to supply them. Mixing flattery with truth, Hewitt complained that no one in the administration or Congress was interested in these developments except Fox. By 1864 Ericsson, encouraged by Fox, was designing a thirteen-inch wrought-iron gun, strengthened with thin hoops, for the *Dictator*; but it was not adopted.[10]

Hewitt continued to send Fox alarming information about the latest European metallurgical developments for heavy ordnance. Fox remarked to his friend Peter H. Watson, an assistant secretary of war, that Hewitt "was somewhat of an enthusiast" about "better guns." He was high on the Whitworth system of "hexagonal rifling," which "is now everywhere admitted in Europe to be the best yet devised." If the Rebels were to get ten-inch Whitworth "guns which will stand charges of 50 pounds of powder you may bid goodbye to the monitors," Hewitt told Fox, "if they ever get within 800 yards and are fairly hit." To keep them out of Rebel hands, Hewitt urged the government to "buy every Whitworth 10″ & 7″ gun that can be made this year." With the blessing of Watson, Hewitt planned another trip abroad "to buy tools for making guns here" and to acquire Whitworth guns as well as the steel guns made by the Krupp Works of Essen, Germany. Hewitt exaggerated the value of rifled ordnance, which tended to burst, and underestimated the power and practicality of Dahlgren's smoothbores. Apparently, the navy got neither Whitworth nor Krupp guns.[11]

Nowhere was ordnance tested against armor more severely than at Charleston. And Fox and Welles realized that no one would be more competent than Dahlgren to report on the offensive and defensive capabilities of the monitors. Dahlgren's critical, yet appreciative, report of 28 January 1864 included useful comparisons with the *New Ironsides*. From 10 July to 7 September 1863, the "battering received" by monitors was "without precedent; the *Montauk* had been struck 214 times; the *Weehawken* 187 times, and almost entirely by X-inch [ten-inch] shot. What vessels have ever been subjected to such a test?" As could be expected, Dahlgren was not keen about the fifteen-inch Dahlgren-Rodman gun. Because rapidity of fire was more valuable than size of projectile against earthworks at Charleston, he preferred the more rapid fire of two eleven-inch guns in a turret. In contrast, the *New Ironsides*, with its battery of fourteen eleven-inch smoothbores and two 150-pound Parrott rifles threw more weight against Morris Island defenses than all the monitors. The Passaic-class monitors drew eleven and a half feet of water (ten to eleven feet was ideal on the southern coast); their speed was about seven knots; their peculiar steerage, when mastered, was not difficult to control (they pivoted with more celerity in less space than any other class of vessel); and each had a complement of eighty men. The *Ironsides* drew about fifteen and a half to sixteen feet, had a speed of six to seven knots, was difficult to keep in position against the tide, and had a crew of 440 men. Its draft restricted it to midchannel, the absence of armor on its bow and stern made it "very vulnerable to a raking fire," and the direction of its broadside was "limited laterally."

Dahlgren believed the defects of both the casemated frigate *Ironsides* and the monitors were "easily remediable." He observed that the Navy "Department could not have been more judicious in preferring a number of monitors to operate from a heavy frigate as a base." Had Welles and Fox built exceedingly powerful vessels, like the French *Gloire* (which drew twenty-eight feet) or the British *Warrior* (drawing twenty-six feet), they would have been "perfectly impotent" in the shallow waters of the southern coast. "There is very little navigable water on this coast which is not accessible to the monitors," Dahlgren observed. Indeed, with "four little monitors" supported by the *Ironsides,* Dahlgren had virtually closed Charleston, by moving monitors up into that port's channels. Despite muted criticism of the fifteen-inch gun, Fox could not have hoped for a more positive evaluation of the monitors.[12]

While Charleston had become difficult for blockade runners, they were still getting in and out of Mobile and Wilmington with relative ease, and Fox wanted to possess these ports. In early 1864 Farragut was planning to gain control of Mobile Bay, while S. P. Lee longed to assault Wilmington. They needed monitors, but the Casco class of twenty light-draft monitors, planned by Stimers, which were to be ready by early 1864, were delayed both by design changes and by the political necessity of building them at yards of "very limited facilities," located from Portland, Maine, to St. Louis. Fox was infuriated by delays of the light drafts as well as of the Canonicus-class monitors. Upon receiving the "iron-clad bureau bill," along with a letter from the Atlantic Works (a light-draft contractor), he exploded at Stimers.

> It foreshadows delays, those horrible bills for additions and improvements and everlasting alterations, all of which have cursed our cause and our Department. . . . The light drafts that were wanted for the coming campaign will not be done until the whole contest is concluded, though six of them would have given us the vitals of the South. What is the reason?—additions, alterations and improvements. The first monitor did more than all the others put together, because she was on time. . . . If I were asked to name the wish of my heart at this moment, it would be for twelve of the first monitors and twelve light drafts, upon which not a single alteration, addition or improvement had been added. The most melancholy picture of engineering skill are those turrets of the Agamenticus class—contract price of $140,000—alterations, additions and improve-

ments of $130,000. I hear that in some of them three or four smokestacks were made, each thrown away for some trifling objection. So I am told that several whole pilot-houses have been laid aside for similar reasons, and other like extravagant changes, all of which may appear clear to the professional mind, but to us it comes like the sudden destruction of bright hopes.

Fox's anger over waste and delays was heightened by awareness that influential congressmen, hostile to him and to monitors, would pounce upon any extravagance or failure in their construction.[13]

Telling Fox, "it is the most severe rebuke I ever received," Stimers defended himself and shifted the blame to Ericsson. He denied discarding smokestacks or pilothouses for trivial reasons, but conceded that the cost of improvements had been higher than expected. He blamed at least six weeks of the *Canonicus*'s delay upon the "utter failure" of Ericsson's "gun carriage friction gear," designed to adsorb recoil and "to double the rapidity of fire." Ericsson maintained that the mechanism (with alterations) was fine and that the gearing on the *Canonicus* failed because Stimers did not follow his working drawings and conducted a "hasty and improper" trial of the new gun carriage. Their once cordial and productive relationship had been strained by differences over the six-footers and, in February 1864, was exacerbated by their faulting each other for the delay of the Canonicus-class monitors. Ericsson complained to Fox that Stimers "has too much to look after . . . and therefore must leave to inexperienced hands that which can scarcely be effected by the most experienced. I have several times . . . told him in the most emphatic manner that no man living could satisfactorily perform the task of superintending the Iron Clads put under his care much less plan" the light drafts. That task "demands the whole time and mind of the most skilful."[14]

Much of Fox's ire that was directed at Stimers was aroused by Stimers's failure to reject contractors' shoddy work. In March 1864 Welles specially charged Fox to investigate frauds and noted that Fox was "greedy" to get hold of swindling contractors. By April Fox discovered that "negligence in inspection has become an evil that must be crushed" and found a new reason to chastise Stimers. On 15 April 1864, before the new *Chenango* got out of New York harbor, its boiler blew up, scalding to death thirty-three men. Fox suspected that its boiler was "not stayed according to specifications," but engineer James W. King said inferior iron that inspectors should have condemned was at fault. Fox also reminded Stimers that the *Octorara* "went to sea without Kingston Valves"; the *Juniata* "never was good for anything"; the *Wyalusing* had to come back to rectify "the most simple omissions"; and the "iron of the boiler of the *Osceola,* of which the Department has a piece, is not fit for a wheel-barrow. . . . By what authority," Fox demanded, "does any person consent to, and accept for the government inferior work?" Fox reminded Chief Engineer Stimers, "Not an inspecting engineer has been reported for passing bad work, yet not a vessel has gone out that has not been grossly neglected." Having reamed out Stimers, Fox queried, "Is there no way to get some of these light-drafts afloat in a month?"[15]

Within two weeks, Stimers got a light draft afloat, but just barely. Although Fox had high hopes for these vessels, they were failures. When the *Chimo,* the first to be completed, was launched at Boston on 5 May 1864, it was only three inches out of the water, without its turret or stores. If those had been in place, it would have sunk. On 16 May Stimers wrote Fox that amidships it was twenty-one inches above the water and in two weeks would be on the way to New York. On 31 May Stimers was optimistic enough about the five light drafts launched or about to be launched that he suggested commanders for them. Deluding himself about his serious design problem, Stimers told Fox, "If they were six inches more out of the water and were armed with the ten inch solid shot gun using say 40 lbs of powder they would be decidedly the best vessels we have for this war." They proved to be useless; Stimers had mis-calculated on a monumental scale.[16]

Because of reassurances from Stimers, Fox initially did not realize the extent of the light-draft disaster and thought modifications would rectify the problem. "You notice," he wrote Ericsson on 3 June, a month after the *Chimo* was launched, "our friend Stimers falls short somewhat in his calculations on the light drafts. It can be remedied if judgment is used in dispensing with the weights." Having asked Admiral Gregory to investigate the problem with engineers and to submit their findings to Ericsson, Fox added to Ericsson, "I will thank you to assist the Admiral." He emphasized that a "failure to even one of these light drafts" will tarnish the reputation of all monitors.[17]

But Ericsson, hostile to Stimers for changing his original plans for the six-footers, would not discuss the light drafts with Gregory in Stimers's presence. Feeling desperate, Stimers, on 8 June, told Fox that Ericsson wanted the light drafts to fail to destroy him (because he considered Stimers "a formidable rival") and to bring Fox "to grief" (because he considered him an "utter" in-competent). Within a week, Welles and Fox replaced Stimers, as general inspector of the ironclads, with William W. W. Wood. On 16 June Ericsson met with Gregory and Wood and decided to convert the *Chimo, Casco,* and *Naubuc* into torpedo boats, by removing their turrets, deck plating, and vacuum en-gines. Ericsson also "strongly advised" that the remaining hulls be deepened twenty-two inches (eliminating their light-draft feature); be strengthened, lest "they break in two in a seaway"; and be completed with a casemate for two eleven-inch guns, instead of a heavy turret. Gregory hoped, "If it can be done," these steps "will make something" of "the little Stimerites." Fox confessed to Ericsson that, with "so many elements of trouble being before us, it must be left entirely to your superior skill to work out the problem with celerity and economy." In June and again in August, Fox visited the *Chimo* in Boston, found it "very backward," and looked at three or four light-draft hulls in New York.[18]

Fox clung to the hope that Ericsson could avoid "great alterations" in one light draft, the *Tunxis*. He wanted "to get her into the Sounds of North Carolina where there never is any sea." Ericsson warned Fox that "no mechanical expedient avails," beyond deepening and strengthening the hull. Its trials revealed to Gregory's satisfaction that it had "a fatal weakness in the bottom." Stimers, nevertheless, supervised minor modifications of the *Tunxis* at the Philadelphia Navy Yard, but Ericsson and Gregory were proved right. Upon departing on 21 September 1864, the *Tunxis* took on water so fast it nearly swamped before getting back to the navy yard. Agreeing with Ericsson, Cornelius K. Stribling, the commandant of the yard, told Fox there was no way the light drafts could be improved. If they were stripped of their protective overhang and their sides were raised, they would draw more water and be even slower. Yet William W. W. Wood, who succeeded Stimers and apparently shared his blindness, assured Fox in November that the altered light drafts at New York "are progressing rapidly towards completion and will make very serviceable vessels." Only eight of the Casco-class vessels were finished when the war ended, and none of them saw action.[19]

Fox's faith in Stimers had backfired. Usually Fox's impulsive zealous enthusiasms worked out, but he should have heeded Ericsson's warning. He could have avoided Stimers's disaster and had his six-footers, if he had contracted in May 1862 for twenty-four, instead of just four, of James B. Eads's double-turreted, Milwaukee-class river monitors. In early 1863, not realizing how successful the Eads river monitors would be, Fox regarded Ericsson's designs, even as interpreted by Stimers, as the surest way to secure serviceable light-draft monitors. By late 1863 Eads's monitors had progressed enough to be judged successful, and Farragut wanted them "to operate in the shallow waters of Texas." The successful trial of Eads's novel turret in late February 1864 confirmed their value. Farragut got the *Chickasaw* and the *Winnebago* in the spring of 1864 and used them with great effect at Mobile Bay.[20]

Although responsibility for the light-draft-monitor debacle was shared, those who were or should have been involved minimized their role. As head of the department, Welles approved their construction, but he relied on Fox for such decisions. It was Fox's misplaced enthusiasm that led the department to forge ahead. Fox should have realized that Stimers was stretched too thin and made certain that he checked his plans with Ericsson or that Lenthall and Isherwood double-checked Stimers's plans. Unfortunately, Ericsson, while repudiating responsibility for Stimers plans, continued to encourage Fox by conceding that with changes they might turn out well. Most seriously, the personal feelings of several of the principals apparently outweighed their patriotism. Stimers's inflated ego disdained advice, and Ericsson, Lenthall, and Isherwood left him to sink or swim. Superintendent Admiral Gregory, as well as Fox, failed to insist that the bickering Stimers and Ericsson consult with each other. Unfortunately, when both Stimers and his boats sank, it was the navy that suffered.[21]

Although Ericsson suspected it, not even he realized just how badly Stimers had erred until the *Chimo* was launched. Before Congress's Joint Committee on the Conduct of the War, which subsequently investigated the light-draft debacle, Ericsson protected Gregory by not telling the whole truth. He admitted to Fox on 13 January 1865:

> Admiral Gregory's presence, the other day, prevented my entering as fully as I intended into the subject of the testimony. The threatened question: "did you state your objections to Stimers' plan to the Admiral Superintending" was a subject I could not admit to in the Admiral's presence, as I had almost implored of him to make a demand on me that would give *official form to my objections*, long before you put the work in hand.

If, indeed, Ericsson early realized Stimers's plans were flawed beyond those he mentioned in his letter of repudiation and failed to communicate those objections officially or unofficially to Gregory or Fox (with whom he was in regular contact), his responsibility (despite his letter of repudiation) for the light-draft debacle is substantial. When pressed by the committee, Fox stated that Stimers drew the plans and supervised the construction of the *Chimo*. The committee agreed that the light-draft monitors were Stimers's responsibility.[22]

CHAPTER FOURTEEN

Vicksburg

Porter . . . goes west to immortalize himself.

Fox to Virginia Fox, 1 October 1862

Fox had frustrations on the Mississippi River as well as at Charleston. Even though the formidable Confederate ironclad ram *Arkansas,* victimized by its engine's failure, had to self-destruct on 6 August 1862, the river from Vicksburg, Mississippi, to Port Hudson, Louisiana, remained in the hands of the enemy. Admiral Farragut's fleet and Commodore Charles Henry Davis's Gunboat Flotilla could run by fortifications but could not cut them off, and bombarding with David Dixon Porter's mortar boats had little effect. The western Confederate states of Arkansas, Louisiana, and Texas were able to float supplies down the Red River and across the Mississippi to eastern Confederate states. The strongholds of Port Hudson and Vicksburg would have to be taken by the army with what support the navy could offer. Because the army would not be ready to take the offensive for months, Davis retired upriver and prepared for the transfer of his flotilla from the War Department to the Navy Department. Farragut and his fleet moved downstream to defend New Orleans from resurgent Confederate forces.

■ ■ ■

During what Davis called "this period of comparative repose," Fox decided to replace him, as of 1 October 1862, with the aggressive intriguer David Dixon Porter. Fox knew Porter's defects, but he also knew Porter was a fighter. Earlier in July, after the *Arkansas* escaped, Porter wrote Fox that "Davis . . . deserves to lose his command." Fox had wanted Davis to "give them one more drubbing" (to ensure his promotion to rear admiral) before coming to the Navy Department as head of the Bureau of Navigation, a position he coveted. When in September, Davis complained of fever, chills, and diarrhea, Fox moved him immediately to the bureau. Forgetting his ill health and his request to come home for a few weeks, Davis complained to his wife that his transfer from the Western Flotilla "is one of those sudden ideas and impulses of Fox of which I have often spoken to you and constituting a peculiarity and distinctive feature of the operation of his mind." Fox was impulsive and moved quickly, but in this case his timing was best both for the service and for Davis, whom Fox regarded highly on personal and professional levels. Davis got his promotion and his bureau, which enabled him to help Fox on personnel matters, while Porter, who was an excellent organizer, beefed up the Mississippi Squadron for the campaign against Vicksburg.[1]

When Davis went upstream, Farragut dropped down the Mississippi and with some of his vessels moved into the gulf. For him, the period of repose provided an opportunity to attack Mobile. Despite the loss of his best officers (whom Fox had called to the "imperative" duty of commanding monitors), the rampant sickness in his command, and the "dilapidated condition" of his fleet, he wished to attack. "My whole time," he told Fox, "is taken up repairing vessels." He asked for additional gunboats and vessels "of a draft that I can run any where," good men (rather than boys), and "a smart Pay Master, for looking after the supplies."[2]

Fox had difficulty supplying Farragut's needs and dampening his ardor for Mobile. "We don't think you have force enough, and we do not expect you to run risks crippled as you are. . . . It is a dark time for us just now," Fox wrote on 9 September 1862, as Lee was invading Maryland, "and the country asks for another naval victory, but my opinion is that *wood* has taken risk enough and that iron will be the next affair." Because the iron monitors (then under construction) would first strike Charleston, Farragut would have a long wait. The wooden gunboats he wanted were protecting Washington, and seven fast steamers, composing Wilkes's Flying Squadron (soon to be joined by five more ships), were in pursuit of the Confederate commerce raiders *Florida* and *Alabama*. With "broken down vessels" filling the navy yards, Fox complained that "it takes as long to repair as to build a ship." Unable to send additional vessels, Fox was willing to give Farragut "mechanics, machinery or anything else you require" to make repairs at Pensacola. With respect to Mobile, Fox wanted Farragut to "act on your own judgment." He added, "We only expect a blockade now and the preservation of New Orleans."[3]

Farragut was annoyed that Fox and Welles did not want him to attack Mobile, but, if vessels had been lost in such an attack, the blockade would be endangered. Because it took weeks for mail to reach him and over a month to send a message and get a response, Fox and Welles had to rely on Farragut's judgment. To improve communications with him at New Orleans and points between, Fox urged Congress to appropriate money for a cable, exclaiming to Senator James W. Grimes, "What is the cost of it compared to its power!"[4]

Farragut, exercising his judgment, chose to stress Fox's yearning for a naval victory rather than his unwillingness to risk wood. "I agree with you," he wrote Fox on 11 October, "that this is the time for a diversion, by an attack on Mobile." Exuding confidence, he told Fox, "I feel no fears for New Orleans & never have." Having heard that Lincoln "did not like my coming out of the River," Farragut pointed out that, once the *Arkansas* was destroyed, the three ships and three gunboats he left at New Orleans were more than sufficient protection. The Confederates, he noted, "have nothing, but our fears to operate upon! They have tried all sorts of lies, to frighten us—& I am sorry to say they succeed very often." Farragut realized that Mobile would be difficult, but he relished the task. "At Mobile it is different," he explained to Fox, "they have 3 or 4 Iron clads in construction & no doubt they would be very formidable in shoal water, where our ships can not operate—but let them come outside of the shallows, & I flatter myself I will show you how far wood can stand against iron—particularly any thing built in shallow water."[5]

On 23 December 1862 Farragut still itched to attack Mobile, but he needed 1,500 to 2,000 soldiers to "threaten" Fort Gaines at the entrance to Mobile Bay. Despite Fox's warning of Confederate ironclad rams, Farragut's "best information" was that one ironclad, completed at Selma up the Alabama River, needed eight feet of water to get downstream to Mobile and another ironclad was not finished. "Mobile," he confidently told Fox, "can be taken at any moment, & by Wooden Ships. . . . Had I my own way, it would be to attack Mobile first & then have my whole available force free for the River & Texas & the Rio Grande."

Farragut did not have his way. Although he had not on 23 December received any specific orders, he did see those of General Nathaniel Prentiss Banks (who had replaced Benjamin F. Butler). From Bank's orders, he learned that Lincoln regarded "the opening of the Mississippi River as the first and most important of our military and naval operations." Immediately obeying what he called "my implied orders . . . to assist the Army to attack Port Hudson & Vicksburg," Farragut declared, "I am all ready . . . with the 4 ships—& several G. Boats." Farragut and Butler had cooperated well. When Farragut ran out of funds to pay laborers (who were repairing his vessels) and mortar boat crews (who were "clamorous to be discharged as fast as their times expire"), Butler lent him $25,000. Butler also had fitted out "a small fleet of steamers in the Atchafalya," which he intended for Farragut's use in shallow waters. "I will put them," Farragut declared, "in the Red River & clear it out so soon as I get above Port Hudson—which I hope will be in a week or two, the moment the Army is ready we will be there." Although Farragut assumed that orders to support Banks were on their way, he characteristically assured Fox, "I trust that I will never want instructions to aid in the great work where there is an opening."[6]

But Banks was not ready to move for a couple of months, and before Farragut could go up the Mississippi, his squadron was disgraced at Galveston. The navy took that port in October 1862, and the army occupied it on 24 December. On 1 January 1863 the Confederates (under Major General John B. Magruder), using two "cottonclads" (improvised gunboats that had cotton bales for armor and were loaded with army sharpshooters) and two smaller tenders, attacked the Union squadron of six vessels (under Commander William B. Renshaw). Meanwhile, other units assaulted the Federal garrison. The Confederates boarded and captured the *Harriet Lane*, but not the *Westfield*, which Renshaw blew up (inadvertently killing himself) after it ran aground. The remaining Union vessels under Lieutenant Commander Richard L. Law abandoned the blockade and fled. This "disreputable and pusillanimous conduct" made Fox apoplectic. Not only was the navy surprised, but the conduct of Renshaw and Law was "too cowardly to place on paper." The raising of the blockade, Fox feared, would lead to foreign intervention. He hoped that retaking Galveston quickly would prevent that disaster. Trying to salvage something from the Galveston affair, Fox used it in a futile effort to motivate Du Pont at Charleston.[7]

Even before hearing from Fox, Farragut ordered Commodore Henry H. Bell with "a large squadron," including the *Brooklyn*, to retake Galveston and restore the blockade. Without a pilot and fearful of running aground, Bell, on 10 January, ineffectively "bombarded" Galveston "from the *ocean*," Fox contemptuously noted. To Farragut, he complained, "I can only tell you how much embarrassment is caused by Law's panic and the neglect of Bell to retake the place." To compound Farragut's and Fox's headaches, Raphael Semmes's *Alabama* appeared off Galveston the day after its bombardment and sank one of Bell's vessels. On 16 January the Confederate commerce destroyer *Oreto*, better known as the *Florida*, escaped from Mobile. "This squadron," Farragut exclaimed, "is eating its dirt now . . . Galveston skedaddled, the *Hatteras* sunk by the *Alabama*, and now the *Oreto* out." If the government had let him take Mobile, Farragut lamented, the *Florida* would not have escaped. Galveston and the abandoned blockade, not the *Alabama* and *Florida*, were Fox's main worry in February 1863. Although Galveston was not retaken until 2 June 1865, Britain and France did not intervene.[8]

While Farragut itched to take Mobile, Porter was busy converting the army's Western Flotilla into the navy's Mississippi Squadron. With Fox urging him to show "an economical administration over our West Point friends," Porter spoke not merely of keeping expenditures down but of making his squadron self-supporting. "I hope to pay expenses," he assured Fox on 30 October, "by seizing contraband cotton. I have two steamers down the river for cotton, niggers and horses." On 10 November he anticipated that a sweep of the river below Helena, Arkansas, would yield 8,000 cotton bales. For operations on Mississippi tributaries, he asked Fox to get Welles to authorize purchasing ten light-draft stern-wheelers at $30,000 each, and, with his faith in mortar boats unshaken, he asked for an additional fifteen to reduce forts. Apart from the mortar boats, Welles was "inclined to grant everything" Porter asked for. He and Fox wanted "success beyond a doubt." Fox urged Porter to be ready to move down stream to Vicksburg, so the navy could not be accused of delaying the army. Thinking of the incalculable military and political importance of isolating the Confederate West by controlling the entire Mississippi, Fox emphasized, "The opening of that river as early as possible is the imperative act to be considered above even the capture of Charleston."[9]

Like his predecessor Davis, Porter was "extremely anxious to get possession of Ellet's Rams." Never a part of the Western Flotilla and commanded by army personnel, the Ram Fleet remained under War Department control. Porter told its commander, Alfred Ellet, that he would "not permit any naval organization on this River besides the Mississippi Squadron" and would not allow Ellet to move his vessels. At a long cabinet meeting on 7 November 1862, Fox and Welles fought Porter's battle and "beat" Stanton, who lost his temper. Lincoln approved Porter's proposal that the Mississippi Marine Brigade and Ram Fleet be created. "The cool man always wins," Fox crowed, but his victory was not complete. The Marine Brigade and Ram Fleet remained an army organization under the command of Brigadier General Alfred Ellet, but Lincoln placed him under Porter's orders. Fox had "little confidence" in that arrangement and anticipated friction between Ellet and Porter. Conscious that he had offended the War Department, Fox advised Porter "to be incontrovertibly right in case of a difference with the Army" and to "give us success, nothing else wins."[10]

In proposing the Mississippi Marine Brigade, Porter had caught a glimpse of the Marine Corps of the future. The concept of a Marine Brigade was originated by Ellet and Lieutenant S. Ledyard Phelps of the navy in August 1862, while on a joint expedition up the Yazoo River, and adopted by Porter. "My idea," he explained to Fox, "was to have a Brigade that I could throw on shore at any place," but in particular "to make a combined attack on Vicksburg. I don't trust the Army; it is very evident that Grant is going to try and take Vicksburg without us, but he can't do it. As he heaves in sight inland our guns will commence on the water side, and if the Ellet Brigade is organized, we will have our troops in town before he does and the flag flying on the mud works." From November 1862 to March 1863, Ellet was off recruiting men for the Marine Brigade, as Grant probed in the direction of Vicksburg. Porter told Fox that guerrillas would force Grant to turn back from his overland move into Mississippi via Holly Springs, because "these soldiers cannot get along out of sight of a Gun Boat." Porter was half right; Grant would pull back, but it was the Confederate army, not guerrillas, that harassed his supply line.[11]

Recruits were in short supply. While Ellet was raising his brigade, Porter begged Fox in early December to fill his half-manned squadron with able-bodied seamen. Fox assured Porter that he would do his best. On the East Coast, however, there were eight blockaders, five ironclads, and four tugs ready for crews, creating "an unusual pressure and seems to forbid sending you any men or even 'boys.'" The manpower shortage forced the navy to turn to the obvious solution. "Du Pont and Farragut want men," Fox continued, "but we have written them that they must take negroes."[12]

Military necessity and close contact with Lincoln pushed Fox to recruit African Americans and to favor emancipation. In late 1862 Fox, an ebullient raconteur and an optimist with a grasp of the overall military and naval picture, was a comforting presence for Lincoln. The stalled Army of the Potomac discouraged Lincoln, who, in early November 1862, replaced McClellan with General Ambrose E. Burnside. After Burnside's disastrous defeat at Fredericksburg, Virginia, on 13 December, Lincoln sent for Fox even more frequently. Adding to Lincoln's woes was a cabinet crisis, during which Seward and his antagonist Chase resigned. Lincoln accepted neither resignation, and the crisis passed, but the wounds did not heal.[13]

While Fox cheered Lincoln, Lincoln influenced Fox. On 28 December Fox and Montgomery Blair had "a long political talk," which Virginia found "interesting, but too personal to *preserve*" in her journal. Blair deplored the "Abolitionists," who had precipitated the cabinet crisis and predicted that the Emancipation Proclamation, freeing slaves only in territory controlled by the Confederacy on 1 January 1863, would be "ineffectual" and "divide the Northern people—a Popes bull against the Comet." Apparently, neither Fox nor Virginia was convinced by Blair, because she commented, "Nous verrons! [We shall see!]" Fox obviously favored emancipation a month later, when Virginia, whose views tended to mirror his, advocated it as she argued with her friend,

Adele Cutts Douglas, Stephen A. Douglas's widow, who upheld her late husband's views. "I told her circumstances had changed; he would have been a Republican now and in favor of anything to aid in putting down these rebels!" Before the war, Fox tolerated slavery to preserve the Union, but the South seceded to preserve slavery. It became clear to Fox that, if the Union was to be saved, slavery had to be destroyed and that former slaves had to help man the navy's ships.[14]

Indeed, Porter was already replacing "lazy deck hands on transports" with "contrabands," liberated, along with cotton and horses, on his downriver sweeps. He found these African Americans a valuable addition to his squadron. While on the Arkansas River on 16 January 1863—after the Emancipation Proclamation—Porter wrote Fox:

> The Squadron is chock full of niggers, including women and children. I take all
> that come. . . . I let them all know they are free. . . . What injustice to these poor
> people, to say that they are only fit for slaves. They are better than the white
> people here, who I look upon as brutes, and half savages. I have shipped about
> four hundred able bodied contrabands and owing to the shortness of my crews,
> have to work them at my guns. This does not include the men on board the
> transports, powder vessels and store vessels, and at Cairo, I suppose we have five
> hundred and I intend to make it a thousand or more if necessary. We must meet
> the devil with fire.[15]

Some officers in Porter's squadron were not enthusiastic about enlisting African Americans, but they had to bow to necessity. With only thirty-five men on board, Commander Selim E. Woodworth, of the *General Sterling Price,* felt "compelled to have recourse to contrabands" for the 100 additional men he needed. Blacks outnumbered whites in the crew of Woodworth's previous command, as they did on all vessels of the Mississippi Squadron. To instruct these inexperienced men in the ways of the navy, Woodworth pleaded with Fox to send experienced warrant and petty officers to Porter's squadron.[16]

Thanks to the hastily recruited African Americans, Porter was ready to support the army. Happily for Fox and the Union cause, Porter and General William T. Sherman worked well together. Porter accompanied Sherman's army of 30,000, whom Grant ordered down the Mississippi and up the Yazoo River for an assault on Vicksburg. He witnessed Sherman's frustrating defeat on 29 December 1862, at the easily defended bluffs near Chickasaw Bayou. Porter told Fox that Sherman's men "fought like devils" and would have succeeded but for terrible weather. Determined to have a success somewhere, Sherman and Porter planned to go back up the Mississippi to the Arkansas River to attack Fort Hindman at the village of Arkansas Post, fifty miles up that stream. "It was all arranged," Porter told Fox, "before McClernand came," and, outranking Sherman, took command of the expedition. John A. McClernand was an incompetent without plans, leaving Porter "to guess at every thing and anticipate events." At Arkansas Post on 11 January 1863, it was the murderous fire of Porter's thirteen gunboats, following the failure of McClernand's assault, that compelled Fort Hindman's 5,000-man garrison to surrender to Porter.[17]

News of Porter's victory at Arkansas Post overjoyed Fox. Its timing was fortuitous, he explained, because "the disgraceful affair at Galveston has shaken the public confidence in our prestige." Goading on Porter, an acting rear admiral, Fox promised him, "If you open the Father of waters you will at once be made an Admiral." While anxious to control the Mississippi, Fox reminded Porter that, among his widespread responsibilities, it was "of vital importance" to keep open General William S. Rosecrans's communications up the Cumberland River in Tennessee. With five of Rosecrans's transports recently captured by Confederate raids, Lincoln was worried, and the War Department was clamoring for more naval protection.[18]

Knowing that Porter was both a fighter and a lying braggart, Fox warned him to exercise self-control. Fox had heard from Brigadier General Frank Blair, who was serving under Sherman, that some in the army were "very jealous of the Navy." Noting that "the flaming army correspondence misleads nobody," Fox advised Porter, "keep cool, be very modest under great success as a contrast to the soldiers. Let them all see that the public service is your guide." Fox soon would know a great deal about Porter's activities, because Fox's nephew Charlie Guild, whom Porter liked, had in January 1863 become Porter's secretary. In his long letters, Charley conveyed his admiration for Porter to Fox.[19]

Victory at Arkansas Post was sweet, but it was not Vicksburg. True, 5,000 of the enemy had been removed from the Federal army's rear, but Arkansas Post was attacked only because of failure at Chickasaw Bayou. Doubting that the army could take Vicksburg, Fox thought it pointless for Porter to bombard it. By 19 January Fox and Welles had concluded that the wisest course was to dig a canal—not across Swampy Toe, but upriver a few miles at Duckport—that would divert the Mississippi and render Vicksburg useless. "My impression," Fox wrote Porter, "is that it would be cheaper and better to set the whole army to work upon the new spot and turn the river clear of the hills and let Vicksburg go. . . . The moment the canal is opened away you go to Port Hudson, Banks [who as yet had not moved] will never take that so it must come from you and Grant to really open the river." Fox continued in a vein that showed how he and Lincoln influenced each other in their almost daily contact. "I dislike to see you all set down for a long siege at Vicksburg. The Country cannot stand it at home or abroad. The President is of my opinion that you better cut through farther back and do it at once."[20]

Grant experimented from January to March, but his Vicksburg problem remained unsolved. He not only had men digging the Swampy Toe Canal and the suggested Duckport canal, but he also explored the possibility of bypassing Vicksburg to the west via a cut further upriver to Lake Providence and the Tensas River to the Red River. On the east shore of the Mississippi, attempts were made to approach Vicksburg through a back door, the Yazoo Pass opposite Helena, Arkansas, and, when that failed, Steele's Bayou. The Duckport canal did not divert the river and was too shallow, while the Swampy Toe Canal was of little use, because an enemy battery commanded its entire length. Porter was enthusiastic about the Lake Providence, Yazoo Pass, and Steele's Bayou possibilities, but Grant had his doubts. Joint probes revealed these shallow, narrow, twisting routes through tree-lined bayous, creeks, forks, and rivers were easily obstructed and defended by the enemy.[21]

These probes did not improve Grant's reputation in Washington. Lincoln, Fox told Farragut on 2 April, was

> rather disgusted with the flanking expeditions and predicted their failure from the first and he always observed that cutting the rebels in two by our force in the river was of the greater importance. Grant who I judge by his proceedings has not the brains for great work, has kept our Navy tailing through swamps to protect his soldiers when a force between Vicksburg and Port Hudson, the same length of time, would have been of greater injury to the enemy.

Porter, however, had faith in both Grant and Sherman, who, he had told Fox in early March, "are on board almost every day. Dine and tea with me often; we agree in everything, and they are disposed to do everything for us they can, they are both able men, and I hope sincerely for the sake of the Union that nothing may occur to make a change here." Porter's strong support of Grant probably muted Fox's complaints about him, which, given Fox's proximity to Lincoln, was very important.[22]

Despite some vessels "tailing through swamps," Porter had what Fox called "the true idea" of blockading the Red River, but it proved hazardous. In early February the ram *Queen of the West,* under Colonel Charles R. Ellet, ran by Vicksburg, destroyed three Confederate supply vessels, and steamed up the Red River. After seizing another prize, the *Queen* ran aground, on 14 Febru-

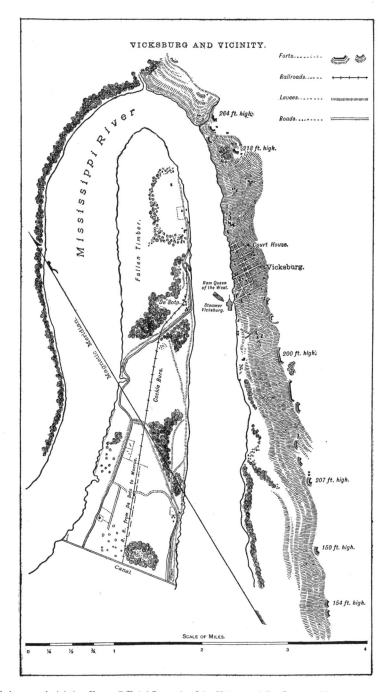

Vicksburg and vicinity. From *Official Records of the Union and Confederate Navies,* 24:221.

ary, and was captured. The ironclad *Indianola*, which Porter sent to help the *Queen* blockade the Red River, ran by Vicksburg on 13 February. On 24 February the Confederate *Queen* and three other vessels captured it. When word of the *Indianola*'s loss reached Washington on 3 March, Lincoln twice sent for Fox to explain the disaster. Mistakenly imagining "the telegraph is finished to New Orleans," Porter asked the department to inform Farragut about the *Indianola*, because its capture threatened "serious disasters to our vessels off Baton Rouge." To Fox's consternation, within ten days the Confederates had acquired two formidable Union vessels and ruined Porter's blockade of the Red River.[23]

Farragut got the news by 2 March. Hoping to recapture the *Queen* and the *Indianola*, he made a costly run past Port Hudson, on 14 March. General Nathaniel P. Banks did not simultaneously assault its batteries as planned and failed to divert Confederate gunners. The USS *Mississippi* was destroyed, the *Richmond* and *Monongahela* were damaged, and only the *Hartford* and *Albatross* got through to the mouth of the Red River. Farragut's move did shield Banks's transports from the *Queen* and her consorts and interrupted the flow of rebel supplies via the Red River. Lincoln and Fox applauded his audacity, which helped starve Vicksburg. In retrospect, Farragut regretted his action, knowing his depleted force was "unable to prevent the crossing of cattle and hogs at and above Natchez."[24]

Unbeknownst to Farragut, the *Indianola* had been destroyed by a ruse, more than two weeks earlier on 26 February. Porter had converted a coal barge into an imitation monitor, with paddle wheel boxes to look like a turret, logs to look like guns, and pork barrels to look like a smokestack, and sent it down river. Amid an enormous barrage, it drifted by Vicksburg's batteries, alarmed the *Queen of the West*, which fled downstream, and scared Confederates into blowing up the *Indianola*. News of its destruction reached Fox long before he learned from Rebel papers that "the noble old frigate *Mississippi*" was lost. He lamented, "could we have telegraphed" Farragut that the *Indianola* was destroyed, the *Mississippi* would still be afloat. Fox used this illustration to urge Senator Henry Wilson to push through Congress an appropriation for a cable to New Orleans, which was far less costly than replacing the *Mississippi*.[25]

Despite a moment of cheer at Porter's successful ruse, Fox in early April was aware of the bottom line. Three vessels had been lost between Vicksburg and Port Hudson, and the powerful *Queen* still remained in enemy hands. Because he was largely responsible for naval operations, he smarted from newspaper attacks on Welles. The Horace Greeley accusation in the *New York Tribune*, "that the 86 years that the Navy has been in existence has not recorded so many disasters as have taken place within the last year," especially rankled Fox. Yet, he realized, "The people . . . will have nothing but success," and he acknowledged, "they are right."[26]

Fox demanded an end to the failures, which he ascribed to incompetence and even to treachery on the part of Union officers. Earlier, he and Welles called for the court-martial of officers involved in the Galveston disaster. The loss of the *Queen of the West* prompted Fox to remark, "Having protested in cabinet meeting against this ram fleet under soldiers and as at present organized, I was prepared for trouble though not on such a large scale." He expected incompetence from soldiers afloat, but not from naval officers. He questioned the capacity of Lieutenant Commander Watson Smith, who had the misfortune to command the two gunboats on the impossible Yazoo Pass expedition. That expedition bogged down before the almost submerged Fort Pemberton, where the Tallahatchie and Yallabusha rivers form the Yazoo River. Fox suspected that George Brown, the commander of the *Indianola*, "acted treacherously. . . . We have lost our best vessels," Fox lamented, "without much of a fight" and most humiliatingly they were "captured by . . . horse marines."[27]

On the other hand, Fox and Welles were understanding when aggressive hard-fighting commanders met defeat. They praised Farragut, who ran past Port Hudson. Fox wrote "to the heroic commander of the *Mississippi*," Melancton Smith. "The noble old ship is gone, but the Navy and the country have gained an example. . . . I beg of you to remember me most kindly to Alden, McKinstry, Macomb, and the other captains who behaved so well. We feel no regret here at the attempt, for the unflinching qualities displayed make us forget Galveston." With Du Pont's attack on Charleston momentarily expected, Fox hoped for the same fighting qualities and predicted that "if we are successful, they will lose heart all round, otherwise look out."[28]

Although Du Pont's 7 April attack on Charleston failed, Porter on 16 April was optimistic. But he warned Fox, "Vicksburg is harder to take than Charleston." He was willing to put "our crazy old turtles [Eads ironclads]" anywhere there was "the least chance of gaining an inch." He also assured Fox that, although George Brown "acted like a fool," because he had not "managed his vessels as I told him," he was loyal, and, although Watson Smith was ill, failure at Fort Pemberton was the army's fault. Porter, however, made no excuses for Alfred and Charles Ellet of the Marine Brigade and Ram Fleet, both of whom he despised. Dismissing them as brave but brainless and insubordinate, he "got rid of" the combined Marine Brigade and Ram Fleet in April and May by sending it up the Tennessee River to protect the communications of the Army of the Cumberland, under General William S. Rosecrans.[29]

Meanwhile, Grant had enlisted Porter's aid to carry out a daring plan to take Vicksburg, which was situated on the east bank of the Mississippi River. Because probes from the north had failed, he wished to march his army down the west bank of the Mississippi to a point south of Vicksburg. There he needed transports and barges to ferry his men to the more advantageous terrain of the river's east bank. On 16 April Porter ran by Vicksburg with seven gunboats and three army transports, towing barges. The gunboats were only slightly injured, but one transport was destroyed and another damaged. Still the vessels that got through would be able to move Grant's men across the river. While cooperating with Grant, Porter told Fox he was "quite depressed with this adventure, which as you know never met with my approval." Porter's misgivings were accentuated because McClernand (for whom he had contempt) instead of Sherman (whom he admired) commanded the advance troops. McClernand was not ready for a quick move across the Mississippi to capture Grand Gulf (forty-five miles south of Vicksburg), which the Confederates were steadily strengthening. By 25 April Porter was convinced that Grand Gulf could not be taken by storm and suggested running by and landing troops below it. Grant, however, preferred an amphibious assault, following a naval bombardment. For five and a half hours on 29 April, Porter's vessels fired at the Grand Gulf batteries with little success. At that point, Grant decided neither to attack nor to risk running by the Confederate batteries with transports loaded with soldiers. Instead, he unloaded his troops and marched them further down the West Bank.[30]

Porter was disappointed. His squadron was chewed up and seventy-six men were killed and wounded for "nothing at all." Yet, he assured Fox that he liked Grant "very much" and did not try "to influence" him. He recognized that Grant had "the entire responsibility of the move" and was "taking the safe course." After sunset, Porter attacked again, while the empty transports, and then the squadron, ran by Grand Gulf to a point six miles downstream, where they ferried 10,000 men across the river to Bruinsburg. On 30 April Grant had his army on the east bank of the Mississippi and ready to move on Vicksburg.[31]

On 3 May the Confederates evacuated Grand Gulf, which had Grant at its rear and Porter at its front. While Grant marched relentlessly northeast toward Jackson, Mississippi, Porter headed downstream, rendezvousing with Farragut that evening at the mouth of the Red River. The next day, Porter pushed up the Red River, with eight vessels, and on 7 May accepted the surrender of Alexandria, Louisiana. He turned it over to Banks, who, he told Fox, was "gallivanting about the country 'avoiding a direct attack'" on Port Hudson. Prevented by low water from proceeding further, Porter left several vessels to blockade the Red River. By 14 May he was again below Vicksburg with a few vessels, ready to help Grant, when Grant arrived at Vicksburg's back door.[32]

While Grant was crossing the Mississippi on 30 April, Fox was preoccupied with the recent crossing of the Rappahannock River by General Joseph F. Hooker's Army of the Potomac. By that date, Hooker occupied a position at Chancellorsville, above Lee at Fredericksburg, threatening to cut him off from Richmond. Hooker's campaign had begun auspiciously, but, schooled by previous disappointments, Lincoln closely monitored developments. The battle of Chancellorsville, which began on 1 May, ended on 4 May with a Union defeat. As he often did when distressed by military reverses, Lincoln called for Fox. On Sunday, 3 May, Fox and Lincoln left the War Department telegraph office at 11:00 p.m., hoping Union forces under John Sedgwick at Fredericksburg and Hooker's main force had Lee in a vise. Fox confided to Virginia his fear that "Lee may escape them." Rather than press forward, Hooker fell back and on 4–6 May recrossed the Rappahannock. Outnumbered by more than two to one, Lee had won a stunning victory. On 5 May, in answer to Lincoln's query, Hooker confirmed that the "Rebels re-occupied the heights of Fredericksburg" and added, "it is not of the slightest consequence." Although a storm that night cut telegraph communication, by morning Lincoln had Richmond newspapers detailing Hooker's retreat up to the Rappahannock and the rupture of Confederate communications by Union cavalry to within five miles of Richmond. Envisioning an offensive capitalizing on the cavalry's work, Lincoln sent Fox to Hooker with the newspaper intelligence and his personal message, "Stick to them, I'm with you."[33]

Fox found the army back across the Rappahannock "at their old quarters at Falmouth." He was dismayed to discover "Hooker cool, clear and satisfied ... when he lost his first line of defense and could not fight!" Virginia Fox, who knew Hooker intimately, because he had wooed her older sister Frances, wondered when was he "ever otherwise" than "cool, clear and satisfied." Fox reported that all were "in good spirits," but after the storm the "ground was abominable just now to maneuver." Lincoln, however, "was just *disgusted!*" when he learned of Hooker's whereabouts. Taking Halleck with him, he left for Falmouth an hour after Fox. With Hooker letting him hold on to his hope for an offensive, Lincoln felt better. On 16 May he repeated to Fox the amusing talk of pickets across the Rappahannock: "The rebs call out, 'Yanks, going to take Richmond?'; Yank replied, 'What makes you dress so poorly?'; Reb answers, 'We don't put on our best clothes to kill hogs.!!'" Contrary to Lincoln's hopes, the next offensive in the East would be Lee's and it would be partly designed to divert Union troops from Grant's move on Vicksburg.[34]

Abetted by Porter, Grant was giving Lincoln and Fox a great deal to cheer about. On 14 May, he captured Jackson. He then turned west, marched along the railroad to Vicksburg, and defeated Pemberton at Champion's Hill (16 May) and Big Black River Bridge (17 May). By 18 May he had Pemberton bottled up in Vicksburg. Pemberton could hold out, but there was no way he could escape. As it filtered back to Washington five days later, news of this "glorious success" gave Fox the intense pleasure of breaking out "a bottle of champagne to drink General Grant's health." Although it was only two weeks after the Chancellorsville defeat, Virginia Fox exclaimed, "Thank God, this looks like the beginning of the end." The following day, the Foxes rejoiced further over the news, "Vicksburg ours!"[35]

The Vicksburg report was premature. Grant failed in his initial assault on 19 May. Two days later, he tried again with naval support. Porter lobbed mortar shells "on the works and town all night," and in the morning he coordinated intense shelling with the army's assault, but the attack failed. Unwilling to throw away more lives in assaults, Grant besieged Vicksburg. "With the navy holding the river," he recalled, "the investment of Vicksburg was complete." Porter helped the siege by landing a battery of heavy naval guns manned by naval personnel. He also ordered a flotilla up the Yazoo River, which forced the Confederates to destroy a "fine" navy yard and three steamboats, including an unfinished 310-foot "monster" that would have caused the Union "much trouble."[36]

While Grant began to besiege Vicksburg, Banks, having gallivanted up the Red River, moved on Port Hudson. Farragut aided him with only the *Hartford* and *Albatross* and some smaller vessels, noting, "My vessels are pretty well used up, but they must work as long as they can." By 26 May Banks had Port Hudson besieged, and Farragut was harassing its defenders with mortar shells day and night. Assaults by Banks on 27 May and 14 June failed, but his siege continued. Farragut supported it with fire from his ships and mortar schooners and by landing four nine-inch guns and four twenty-four pounders for a breaching battery, manned by the officers and crew of the *Richmond*.[37]

Lee's invasion of the North in June did not relieve the pressure on Vicksburg or Port Hudson, as Lee had hoped. To deter Lee, Fox suggested to Lincoln that General John A. Dix (whose troops at Yorktown, Virginia, were not tracking Lee) move up the James River to "raid" Richmond, but nothing came of that idea. The Army of the Potomac, under Hooker's replacement, General

George G. Meade, defeated Lee at Gettysburg, Pennsylvania, on 1–3 July 1863, and on 4 July Lee's army began an unmolested retreat south. That same day on the Mississippi, Vicksburg surrendered, and on 9 July Port Hudson surrendered as well. Wholehearted cooperation between the army and navy had made these operations a success. Grant, whom Fox came to realize had more than enough "brains for great work," was generous in his praise of the navy's contribution at Vicksburg. "Without its assistance," Grant wrote, "the campaign could not have been successfully made with twice the number of men engaged. It could not have been made at all, in the way it was, with any number of men without such assistance." The navy's control of the Mississippi and its capacity to ferry troops across it were crucial to Grant's brilliant campaign. In addition, during the siege, mortar schooners fired 7,000 shells, gunboats 4,500, and naval guns on shore an additional 4,500.[38]

On a personal level, June was a miserable month for Fox. While Grant and Banks were tightening their grip on Vicksburg and Port Hudson and Lee was operating northwest of Washington, Virginia Fox suffered from bronchitis, nausea, and diarrhea. Lest he disturb her rest, Fox slept on the floor for days and tried to arrange for her departure to New York or Portsmouth. Montgomery Blair suggested she leave town on a stretcher with his family. His sister Lizzie Blair Lee thought she should be moved to her family's home at Silver Spring, and Henri Mercier, the French minister, invited her to accompany him to New York aboard the French man-of-war that was standing by to evacuate him because of Lee's invasion. Refusing these offers, Virginia, on 2 July, had Fox take her to her sister Frances Lowery's home at Tubby Hook at the northern end of Manhattan Island. Relieved that Virginia was in good hands, Fox returned to Washington on 5 July and rejoiced over Lee's defeat at Gettysburg, Grant's victory at Vicksburg, and the imminent surrender of Port Hudson.[39]

Fox anticipated a counterstroke by Meade that would destroy Lee. "Much to the disgust of everybody," there was no counterattack. "Lee's army has escaped," Fox lamented to Farragut, "though we were three to one and his army reduced one half and thrown upon a swollen stream yet he was permitted to cross though it required twenty four hours to do it. The destruction of that army would have ended the military power of the South." Initially thinking Lee had "left forty thousand of his army of invasion behind," Fox told Porter, "The rebellion is going overboard fast."[40]

Although disappointed by Lee's escape, Fox was proud of the navy's role—especially that of Farragut and Porter—in the "final opening of the Mississippi." Although some "*young* officers" thought Farragut rash, his aggressive style delighted Fox. "You smashed in the door in an unsurpassed movement" at New Orleans, he told him, "and the success above became a certainty. . . . Your last move past Port Hudson has hastened the downfall of the Rebs. The President with his usual sagacity predicted it the moment you were by." Fox also praised Porter, who was now a rear admiral. The promotion, "which I promised to obtain for you when the Mississippi was opened," was "nobly gained." Contrasting him with Du Pont, Fox told Porter, "Our Iron Clads at Charleston were only dented, yours have been perforated through & through in every engagement yet we get no dispatches from you that they are failures, and that nothing can be done. . . . If the Mississippi had been opened when we determined upon continuing work upon Charleston we should have sent for you as one that knows no failure and that loves fighting."[41]

Fox realized, though, that love of fighting was not enough. He had learned from defeat at Charleston and victory on the Mississippi that unilateral action by the navy failed, while well-coordinated, combined operations succeeded. He abandoned the notion that the navy alone could take Charleston, did his best to secure troops for the joint efforts of Gillmore and Dahlgren to carry Fort Wagner, and predicted in July that they "will certainly take Charleston." In this cooperative mood, the Navy Department had no immediate orders for Farragut or Porter, because "the movements of the Army" were unknown. "I wish," Fox wrote Farragut, "they would give you the troops you have so often asked for and with Porter and his Iron Clads an attack be made upon Mobile." To Porter, Fox emphasized cooperation with the army "in the future as . . . in the past." Fox realized that Porter had to deploy many vessels in "picket duty" on the Mississippi and its tributaries, but hoped that he and "that noble old chief Farragut" could "hitch teams" and capture Mobile. While fearing his river ironclads would break in two "in the least seaway," Porter was willing to serve under Farragut, but he warned Fox (who no longer needed the warning) that "the only way to be successful is a perfect combination of Army and Navy—it is useless for either branch of the service to attempt any thing on a grand scale, without the aid of the other."[42]

Fox's hope of striking at Mobile "whilst all rebeldom is in an infernal panic" was not realized. Like Fox, Grant was eager to move on Mobile, but Halleck preferred a campaign in trans-Mississippi Louisiana. With the Mobile campaign postponed, Farragut received a leave north, where, Fox assured him, "you will find a nation ready to acknowledge how well you have performed every duty imposed by this unfortunate rebellion." Porter felt he could not take the leave Fox sent him "while there is any thing left to do" on the rivers. Fox wanted him to fit out, as "tinclads," ten to twelve vessels to cooperate with Banks and make certain that communications be kept open to William S. Rosecrans's army at Chattanooga, after his defeat at Chicamauga, on 19–20 September 1863.[43]

Ironically, the muddy Mississippi and its tributaries, rather than the briny Atlantic, produced the two great admirals of the Civil War. It was on that river that Farragut and Porter were resourceful, aggressive, and victorious. Fox was proud of them and felt that they had vindicated his judgment.[44]

CHAPTER FIFTEEN

Washington

> Here, take this card to Captain Fox; *he* is the Navy Department.
>
> *Abraham Lincoln, ascribed*

> Fox . . . at times . . . is officious. Most men like to be, or appear to
> be men of authority, he as well as others. I have observed, that
> when he knows my views and desires he likes to communicate
> them to the parties interested, as his own. . . . These are little
> weaknesses . . . and I permit [them] to give me no annoyance.
>
> *Welles, 13 August 1863*

The South was not seized by the "infernal panic" Fox hoped to capitalize
on. Although Lincoln declared the "Father of Waters again goes unvexed to
the sea," the two halves of the split Confederacy were far from conquered.
Some of the Mississippi's tributaries were still vexed, because southern armies
largely controlled the Red River to its west and threatened the Tennessee to its
east. The western half of the Confederacy, however, was more of a diplomatic
headache than a military threat. Difficulties in maintaining the blockade at
Galveston, Texas, worried Fox, Welles, and Seward, with their persistent fear
that Britain or France would use naval lapses as a pretext for intervening on
the side of the South. The threat of intervention waned with the success of
Union arms, but the occupation of Mexico City on 6 June 1863 by Napoleon
III's France aroused a fear that it would attempt to restore Texas to a French-
created Mexican empire. To offset threats of intervention and aggression,
there was a desire in Washington to conquer the trans-Mississippi Confederacy, which enabled Porter and Sherman, with Halleck's blessing, to concoct the
disastrous Red River campaign. It did not originate with Fox and Welles, who,
despite differences, functioned admirably as a team in Washington. While
struggling to build and to adequately man the navy's ships, they coped with
hostile congressmen, patronage-hungry politicians, and corrupt contractors.[1]

■ ■ ■

If anything, after defeat at Gettysburg and Vicksburg, the Confederacy became even more doggedly determined. At Charleston, an assault on Fort Wagner failed on 11 July, and a second attack, following a massive naval bombardment, failed on 18 July. That attack was immortalized by the bravery and sacrifice of Robert Gould Shaw's Fifty-fourth Massachusetts Colored Infantry. In between those attacks, draft riots—especially in New York City from 13 to 15 July—aroused "infernal panic" in the North, hope in the South, and personal anxiety for Fox.[2]

Although he had heard about the working-class violence in lower Manhattan, Fox had assumed until 18 July that his wife, Virginia, and her sister Frances and her family at Tubby Hook, in northern Manhattan, were out of harm's way. He was horrified to learn that they had been frightened by the dozen Irish laborers who were blasting rocks and building roads on their place. "They are jealous of the negroes getting their work and lowering prices [wages] by coming North," Virginia reported. "The *draft* is the great cause of discontent; they are mad that those who can pay three hundred dollars for a substitute can get off!" Because Virginia and the Lowerys were isolated in a rich enclave on the Hudson River and there were reports of violence at nearby Fort Washington, Spuyten Duyvil, and Harlem, they feared for their lives and made plans to flee to New Jersey. The workmen proved no threat, however, and, by 22 July, life returned to normal.[3]

A week later, on 29 July, with the nightmare of the New York draft riots over, Fox got to New York to witness the launching in Greenpoint, Brooklyn, of the *Onondaga*, the navy's first double-turreted monitor. He then crossed the East River to Manhattan, caught a train, arrived at Tubby Hook by noon, and surprised a chagrined Virginia who "was meditating a splendid toilette for him!" Happy to find her whole—even if dressed informally—Fox told her she "must never travel without" the six-barrel pistol he brought her.[4]

The next morning at ten o'clock, he returned to the debilitating heat of Washington. A few days later, on Sunday, 2 August, he spent "a pleasant cool day" cruising the Potomac on board the *Baltimore* with Welles and his family and other Navy Department people. Also with them was Lincoln's secretary John Hay, who regretted that the lunch was "fearfully disproportioned" to their "enormous appetites." That salubrious, if spartan, excursion inspired a second trip, as far as the capes of the Chesapeake, on 6 August (the day of thanksgiving for the victories at Gettysburg and Vicksburg), which for Fox had a different outcome. The violent thunderstorm they encountered seemed to cause a "cold in the bowels" that would plague him for a couple of weeks.

Nevertheless, he continued to work and, on the following Sunday, was strong enough to ride out to the Blairs at Silver Spring. Still "sick from a bilious cholick" on Tuesday, he decided to go North for a week.[5]

Shared excursions were only one indication that Fox and Welles worked well together. Intensely proud men with very different personalities, they complemented each other, making a harmonious and effective duet. Welles was austere, shrewd, deliberate, cautious, and suspicious. Fox was ebullient, impulsive, enthusiastic, optimistic, and full of faith in, and hope for, his men and vessels. If they failed, though, he could be devoid of charity. Both Welles and Fox were able and energetic, loyal to Lincoln, and devoted to the Union. Trained to obey his superiors, Fox carried out Welles's orders. Welles deferred to Fox's grasp of technical naval matters and was ever aware that his closest ally in the cabinet, Montgomery Blair, was married to Fox's sister-in-law.[6]

If Welles had been a lesser man, jealousy might have poisoned their relationship. Welles was often caricatured as a superannuated incompetent, who was ignorant of naval affairs and a burden to Lincoln. By many, Fox was regarded as the actual head of the Navy Department. Because he functioned as chief of naval operations, line officers, like Du Pont, referred to him as *the Secretary* and considered Welles an old man with neither force nor intelligence. In 1863, after hostility toward Fox replaced friendship, Du Pont believed even more strongly that Fox "governed" the Navy Department, and Du Pont's friend, Congressman Henry Winter Davis, who was Blair's archenemy, regarded Welles as an "old fool," whom Fox kept in ignorance.[7]

The most serious threat to the Welles-Fox partnership occurred in the summer of 1863. On 27 March 1863 the British shipbuilder John Laird, defensive for having built the *Alabama* and fearing that he might not be able to deliver the rams he was completing for the Confederacy, claimed on the floor of the House of Commons that Welles and Fox, through an unnamed agent (John T. Howard, whose letters he quoted and who actually was his friend and agent), had asked him to build ships for the Union navy. On 11 April Laird threatened to expose Howard and publish his letters if the federal government denied "the statement I have made." A copy of that threat was forwarded to Fox, who passed it on to Welles without acknowledging the full extent of his correspondence with Howard. Claiming he allowed none but Americans to build ships for the navy, Welles wrote Senator Charles Sumner on 19 May, indignantly denying Laird's insinuation that the Navy Department had tempted him to violate British neutrality. Sumner, who was chair of the Foreign Relations Committee and had well-placed English friends, was striving to prevent the Lairds' rams from reaching the Confederacy. Publication of the Welles letter to Sumner by the *New York Times* on 6 August prompted Howard to inform Welles that he had a letter from Fox, conflicting with Welles's denial.[8]

Actually, the Lairds, through Howard, had initiated contact with the Navy Department. The department rejected Howard's proposal of 10 May 1861 that the Lairds build deep-draft ironclad frigates for the Union. Later, on 13 August 1861, when Fox became worried about securing ironclads to counteract the *Virginia*, he told Howard that he hoped the Lairds would bid on "the floating battery." On 1 November 1861, a week after the keel of the *Monitor* had been laid, Fox asked Howard, "Do you believe we could buy an entire Iron Frigate in England, all ready for sea?" Furthermore, in 1861, fearful that a sufficient quantity of four-and-one-half-inch iron plates for ironclads would not be available in the United States, Fox asked Howard if they could be supplied by Laird & Son. Welles had never been foolishly consistent. Not only was he willing to buy the four-and-one-half-inch plates abroad, but, later, to deprive the enemy of vessels capable of lifting the blockade, he was willing to purchase the rams the Lairds had built for the Confederacy. To keep abreast of British technology, the Navy Department, late in the war, ordered through Freeman Harlow Morse, the U.S. consul at London, "Twin Screw Engines" from the Canal Iron Works, located at London Docks.[9]

But Howard's claim that Fox, through him, had approached the Lairds caused Welles to reassess his assistant. Welles's trusted friend, Chief Clerk William Faxon, who was critical of Fox, thought him "forward, and too ready with his letters substituted for those of the Secretary or chiefs of bureaus." He suspected that "Fox took upon himself to correspond with Howard and perhaps" Laird, after Welles "turned them off." Although Fox's unofficial correspondence was voluminous, Welles signed virtually all important official correspondence, including orders written by Fox. Conceding there might be something in Faxon's surmise, Welles, nevertheless, was certain that Fox would not "go contrary to my decision." He thought Fox wished to be regarded as a man of authority, and may have been "anxious to give himself notoriety. ... Orders which I frequently send to chiefs of bureaus and others through him, he often reduces to writing signing his own name to the order. ... Admiral [Joseph] Smith, Lenthall, and Dahlgren have been vexed by them." Even so, Welles claimed not to be annoyed. Although Faxon thought Fox may have "committed himself and the Department," Welles, conceding that Fox "doubtless wrote Howard," concluded, "There can, I think, have been no committal, for Fox is shrewd, and has known my policy and course from the beginning."[10]

While Welles was ruminating in his diary about Fox's shortcomings, Fox was, with Virginia, en route from New York to Portsmouth. On 15 August, the day after their arrival, he wrote Welles to control the damage the Laird-Howard revelations might do to their relationship. He stressed the exploratory nature of his requests through Howard to the Lairds and claimed they were a ploy to goad Lenthall and Isherwood to design an ironclad, because "Isherwood thought iron clads a humbug and Lenthall shrank from touching the subject." Fox also strolled on the beach that day, and, although Virginia begged him not to jump in the cold Atlantic, he was "too ocean crazy to desist," even though he had been unwell for a month. On 18 August, having journeyed to Portsmouth, Howard interrupted Fox's few days of swimming and fishing to discuss their correspondence. According to Virginia, Howard agreed with Fox that Laird "did wrong to publish his private letters & he wrote & told him so & that he made the proposal for the L—— & not the Department to the L." Howard, Fox reported to Welles, "has three letters from me which contain expressions similar to what I wrote you last week. . . . To explain my notes, written in the dark days following the first Bull Run, it is necessary to know that he presented himself . . . as an agent of Laird." Despite his protestations, Fox wisely and unofficially had sought bids through Howard from the Lairds. In 1861, with the Confederacy rushing the *Virginia* to completion and the Union ironclad program a huge question mark, Fox would have been remiss if he had not explored the quick acquisition of ironclads. In any event, his damage control in August 1863 appeared successful.[11]

News in September of failures at Sumter and the Gulf and high-handed behavior off the coast of Japan required more of Fox than damage control. The day before Dahlgren's sailors and marines were repulsed at Sumter, another poorly planned, ill-coordinated attack in the Gulf totally failed. On 8 September a joint army-navy expedition at Sabine Pass on the Texas-Louisiana border, apparently originating with Banks, lost two of its four gunboats. The first inkling the Navy Department had of it came from Commodore Henry Haywood Bell's dispatches, detailing his cooperation in response to Banks's request. When Farragut, who was in Washington, read Bell's dispatches, he predicted the movement would end in a disaster. He realized that the expedition, while nominally "joint," would not combine an army assault with a naval bombardment, leaving the gunboats to reduce the forts. Also in September, Fox was "sorry" to learn that two months earlier the *Wyoming*, avenging an insult to the American flag, destroyed three Japanese vessels in the Strait of Shimonoseki. Because Japan had ordered "War Steamers" from private American shipyards and the Navy Department had shared details for their construction, Fox was especially chagrinned by the *Wyoming*'s action. After that regrettable incident and the failures at Charleston and Sabine Pass, the navy was quiescent in the fall and winter of 1863 and 1864, as it gathered strength for assaults on Mobile and Wilmington.[12]

More manpower was essential for increased strength. But the War Department's administration of the draft, in the fall and winter of 1863 to 1864, weakened the navy and angered Fox and Welles. Despite African American enlistments, the shortage of seamen became even more acute in the late spring and summer, as the three-year hitch ended for the large number of men who had signed up when the war started. The wealthy could avoid the draft, but skilled workers could not, even if their contributions as civilians were considered essential for the war effort. Sixty men—many of them experts—were drafted from ordnance works, where they were far more valuable than in the army. In addition, maritime towns discouraged naval enlistments, because those enlistments were not credited toward draft quotas. To make matters worse, these towns offered large bounties to at least 5,000 seamen who joined the army. In February 1864 Captain James Alden of the *Brooklyn* wanted to confer with Fox about "our ineffectual attempts to obtain men," after spending weeks in Boston and New York to ship a crew. Two months later, Samuel Phillips Lee of the North Atlantic Blockading Squadron complained that the crew of his flagship, the *Minnesota*, "are about all gone" and that the rest of his blockaders were "suffering for men."[13]

Congress passed a law making it possible to transfer sailors from the army to the navy. Fox claimed 10,000 of them were willing to live on bread and water if they could get "out of this sojering." Stanton, however, refused to give these men to the navy. With the shortage worsening, Welles requested in late March 1864 the transfer of 12,000 seamen from the army, and asked Fox to negotiate with Halleck, whose attitude "disgusted" Fox. "There has been a sorry display of the prejudices of some of the military authorities," Welles noted. "Halleck appears to dislike the Navy more than he loves his country." Alerted by their complaints, Lincoln sent for Fox and Welles and asked Welles to write a gently phrased order for the transfer, which he signed and sent to Stanton.[14]

The shortage of sailors was so acute that officers, among them Reigart B. Lowry and Stephen B. Luce, offered Fox similar long-range solutions. Lowry suggested an apprentice system that would recruit boys and train them on a vessel, like his command, the sailing frigate *Sabine*. Fox and Welles liked the idea. In August 1864 Lowry and his frigate were ordered to Norfolk, where by December he was in charge of instructing and disciplining 200 boys. Before commanding the monitor *Nantucket* in late 1863, Luce had served on the fac-

ulty of the Naval Academy (1860–63) and, in the summer of 1863, had taken
the academy-training frigate *Macedonian* to Europe. That experience made
him an advocate of shipboard training before commissioning Naval Academy
graduates. In January 1864 his major concern was not the Naval Academy, but
the impending loss of "the best class of Petty officers," the boatswains and
the gunners. To solve that problem, he too advocated a training ship for boys.
With a "drill ship . . . we may soon raise a *new class of men*," and petty officers
could be recruited from among those boys who demonstrated the greatest
aptitude.[15]

In the fall of 1863 Fox worked by day and dined pleasantly by night, while
Virginia remained in Portsmouth. Continuing to enjoy Fox's company, Lincoln
"came over" one evening with a "musket on his shoulder" and invited Fox
"to shoot with him" and Assistant Secretary of War Peter H. Watson. In the
"shooting match" (probably the "musket" was a Spencer repeating rifle), Lincoln was second to Watson, and Fox proved the poorest shot. On 19 November
Fox was at Gettysburg when Lincoln gave his immortal address. With Henry
A. Wise, Fox frequently dined with Lincoln's secretary John Hay, and at times
they were joined by the bon vivant painter Emanuel Leutze. Wise was head of
the Bureau of Ordnance, a celebrated author under the pseudonym of Harry
Gringo, and the son-in-law of Massachusetts statesman and orator Edward
Everett. On at least one occasion, after dinner Fox, Wise, and Hay went on to
the Canterbury Music Hall—a "very low" theater "where the principal attraction is the 'development' of the female performers, and where *double entendre*
always brings down the house." They would usually end their evenings with
stewed oysters at Harvey's Oyster Saloon. On 10 September they were joined
for dinner by Joe Hooker and Daniel Butterfield, his chief of staff, at Wormley's. They drank moderately and talked immoderately about adventures in
bygone wars and years and the retribution England deserved for its current
behavior.[16]

Fox declared:

> When the time comes, a publication will be made of insults and wrongs on
> every sea—of ports closed to us and opened to the enemy—of flags dipped to
> them and insultingly immovable to us—of courtesies ostentatiously shown
> them and brutally denied us—that will make the blood of every American boil
> in his brain-pan. We shall have men enough when this thing is over.

His companions suggested taking Canada, but Fox, with blockade running in
his brainpan, had other ideas. "We will make no fight on Canada, that will fall
of itself. But we will cast our eyes at Bermuda at Nassau at the Islands that

infest our coast, nurseries of treason & piracy against us, by whose aid England has been at war with us & we at peace with her. We have found it is not good for these possessions to lie so near for our discomfort." With the end of the war, "we will turn to these Islands and we will say 'Get out.'"

Having disposed of a portion of the British Empire, Fox spun yarns to the delight of Hay. "Fox," Hay recorded, "was more than unusually funny tonight," as he told of the "delightful . . . usages of society on the coast of Africa," where

> when you dine with a native prince, the etiquette is to appear naked. . . . He says one of his brother officers once made a present to a native King of a cocked hat a green velvet waistcoat and a skillet. On dining with him the next day, the grateful host appeared in the cocked hat with the flaps drawn down like elephants ears over his chops, the green velvet waistcoat pulled to bursting over his stomach . . . the second button left open to display his umbilical development, his testicles stored in the skillet and his male organ fastened to its handle, . . . the skillet being moored around his loins by cowhide thongs.

Understandably, Lincoln, with his earthy sense of humor, enjoyed Fox's company.[17]

Much as Fox delighted in his dinners with Wise and Hay, he missed Virginia. "I hope you will grow stronger," he wrote on 16 September. "It is my only earnest prayer in our relation for your confinement to the house is a great deprivation to both of us. If we could only walk to the [Lafayette] square 'together' or even over to Min's often, without risk to yourself I should indeed be grateful and happy." Fox would ask for "nothing in this world if we could go tramping off together for one mile. That dreadful Dr. [Sims] made a promise that we should walk . . . that distance and no injury to you." His failure to keep that promise was for Fox a disappointment.[18]

In hopes of walking without pain and no longer being "nervous & anxious," Virginia resolved on a further gynecological procedure. She returned on 9 November 1863 to New York's Woman's Hospital and placed herself under the care of Dr. Sims's former assistant, by then surgeon in chief Dr. Thomas Addis Emmet. Angry that Sims had not restored Virginia's health, Fox forbade her going to the hospital. After telling him "it was *too late*," she complained in her diary, "I thought he would be delighted. How I have suffered—for want of encouragement." On 10 November she underwent a twenty-minute procedure without ether (although the doctor recommended it), leaving her "exhausted!" as she was wheeled off to bed and given whiskey. Emmet assured Virginia that nine-tenths of women had her "troubles." She was "thankful" that she was in his care and assured him that she "had several homes & was as well known as an invalid as a London street beggar & if [he] could enable me to walk it would add greatly to his reputation."[19]

Fox became reconciled to the procedure and hopeful of good results. Because Emmet was an avid collector of autographs and prints, he asked Virginia for a Lincoln autograph and those of prominent Rebels in her possession. Grateful for Virginia's treatment and for her pleasant room, Fox sent Emmet photographs and charts and arranged to have the brother of his wife, Catherine Emmet, who was an ailing prisoner of war, sent home to Alabama. Although, beginning on 5 December, Virginia sallied forth to shop for Christmas, she remained at Woman's Hospital over a month, returning to Tubby Hook on Christmas Eve. "Gus thinks I look well & is glad I have tried Dr E," Virginia recorded, when Fox arrived on Christmas Day. While he came to New York to spend Christmas with Virginia, he also came for the launching on 26 December of the huge single-turreted monitor *Dictator*, which he and Ericsson had hoped Virginia would christen. Not only did a severe cold keep her from appearing, but Fox, Arch, and Woodbury Lowery were too late for the launching. With Virginia unable to accompany him, Fox left for Washington, at 10:30 a.m. on 28 December.[20]

Virginia's health did not improve. She assumed on 31 December that "*severe* blistering" had saved her "from another attack of bronchitis," and Fox, cheered by that news, exclaimed, "'severe' blisterings are good." Although better for a few days in mid-January, she soon had little appetite and felt "dispirited, weak, disappointed that after suffering so much to be well" she "should be sicker & more separated from Gus than before." To add to her woes, a clogged smoke pipe at Tubby Hook nearly asphyxiated the entire household on 19 January, leaving everyone dizzy with severe headaches and violent nausea. On 24 January Fox and Virginia left for Washington. They had hired a private railroad car, with a bed. What should have been an easy trip was delayed twelve hours, when their engine derailed. In Washington, Virginia was delighted to find that Gus had moved her piano into their rooms, and, as in the past, their dinners were provided by the celebrated caterer James Wormley.[21]

In the exciting wartime capital, Virginia's morale improved. She had spurts of energy, followed by excessive fatigue. On her parlor sofa, she suffered from a variety of ills that left her dizzy, bilious, nauseous, feverish, coughing, aching, dysenteric, or with combinations of these symptoms. Illness did not dampen the affection Gus and Virginia had for each other. On a cold day in January, "too raw to go out," Virginia made a dessert and recorded that "Gus rose after tasting it & kissed me saying 'A success Pettie.' Bless my pudding tasting boy!" Despite frequent bouts of illness, she made calls, visited her sister Minna Blair almost daily, went out for drives, heard "Mrs. Lincoln's Marine Band," attended the opera with Gus (who had no ear for music), and, when wives were invited, joined Gus for dinner. On 16 March, despite her "sick headache," she "dressed in noire" and with Gus went to a three-hour, eleven-course dinner with six kinds of wine at the Italian minister Joseph Bertinatti's home. Gus "was in high spirits," and Virginia told Bertinatti: "I never expected to go to Italy & he had brought Italy to me." They were so pleased that they stopped off "to *describe* it" to Minna.[22]

While Fox enjoyed the Washington social scene in early 1864, he continued to work diligently at the Navy Department. Although his services were usually appreciated both in and out of government, in February Congressman Henry Winter Davis, Blair's enemy and Du Pont's friend, attacked Fox's and Ericsson's monitors. In what Welles called a vindictive and malignant speech, Davis disparaged Fox's nautical ability by calling him a "cotton-spinner." In addition, Fox's chief nemesis, Senator John P. Hale of New Hampshire, who was chair of the Naval Committee, in mid-February 1864, unbeknownst to the rest of Congress, slyly and maliciously slipped into the Naval Appropriation bill an $825 reduction of Fox's salary, lowering it to $3,500. "Gus," an outraged Virginia reported, "refuses to let his friends try & restore it—is not working for money—but for his Country he says."[23]

While his own salary was cut, Fox was trying to ferret out corruption among naval contractors in Boston, New York, and Philadelphia. In this effort, he was aided by Henry S. Olcott, an investigator borrowed from the War Department, and William E. Chandler, who would in two decades be secretary of the navy. Professing "to be a gentleman by education and socially," Olcott thought of himself as a special commissioner and threatened to quit if he was referred to as a "detective." They investigated contractors who bribed clerks to receipt for goods not received and those who overcharged for goods delivered. Initially, Olcott asked whether Fox and Welles expected him "to make any case to suit personal prejudice or political purpose." In his reply, Fox "pointedly disclaimed anything but a broad, honest, patriotic inquiry into the public business, with a view to reformation of abuses." Apart from frauds, he objected to demands by politicians that navy yard personnel be fired if they were not ardent Lincoln men.[24]

Fox found little support in the press. In New York, Horace Greeley's *Tribune* was friendly to Hale and to Chase, who disliked the Blairs (and Fox by extension); James Gordon Bennett's *Herald* opposed the Lincoln administration; Henry J. Raymond of the *Times* was anxious to politicize the navy yards; and William Cullen Bryant's *Post* was published by Isaac Henderson, the New York navy agent whom Fox and Welles had arrested and tried as a corruptionist. Henderson counterattacked through Bryant, who wrote Lincoln alleging the existence of widespread distrust of Fox's "capacity and integrity." His wastefulness and corruption enabled profiteers to obstruct the war effort and to "seek to overthrow the Union party," and his management of the navy had destroyed "our commerce at sea." Bryant's accusations were false. Fox was scrupulously honest. He returned a beautiful set of furs sent to Virginia by a monitor contractor, saying they were tempting, but "it is not right for me to accept." Fox concluded that the navy should buy its own supplies and dispense with navy agents. By December 1864 Welles and Fox were appointing naval officers as navy agents.[25]

Ironically, Fox's zeal was inspired in part by Hale, who hoped to embarrass Fox and Welles. Hale had L. C. Baker, a provost marshal and a detective, investigate those suspected of defrauding the navy, especially in New York. It was, for Hale, a defensive move because in late 1863 he had been exposed for accepting a $3,000 bribe thinly disguised as a retainer from a convicted corruptionist. On 1 February 1864, with "a sprawling mass of suspicions," Baker called on Welles, who soon concluded that Baker was "wholly unreliable" and confirmed Olcott's observation that "there is something contemptible in the name of detective." Realizing that fraudulent contractors had taken advantage of the government, Welles put Fox in "special charge of the matter." Virginia reported that Gus was "so excited over the rascality of the Contractors" that he wanted them arrested. Happily for Fox, Congress in the spring of 1864, at the behest of the War Department, permitted military and naval contractors to be tried by court-martial. As a result, Charles W. Scofield of Philadelphia and the Smith Brothers of Boston were tried and convicted during 1864 and 1865. Senator James W. Grimes of the Naval Committee told Fox that convicting Franklin W. and Benjamin F. Smith and "the immaculate" Henderson would be the equivalent of two victories, "for it will be the end of stealing in the Navy." Tried in a civil court, Henderson escaped conviction on a technicality. Rascals like the Smiths, Henderson, and Scofield had prominent friends— Charles Sumner, Henry J. Raymond, and Thurlow Weed, for example—who appreciated their lavish contributions to the Republican Party.[26]

Political influence pervaded the navy yards. Demands made on these employees during Lincoln's reelection campaign irritated Welles and Fox. The chief concern of Henry J. Raymond of the *New York Times*, who in 1864 became chairman of the Union (Republican) National Committee, was raising campaign funds. He levied "contributions" from contractors and navy yard employees and even wanted to fire skilled workers who would not pay their "assessment." John W. Forney, secretary of the Senate and proprietor of the *Philadelphia Press,* abetted by a Philadelphia alderman, demanded that Fox replace a "rank Copperhead" at the navy yard with a reliable Lincoln man, because "it will have a great effect upon the coming election in the First district." The commandant of the navy yard, Cornelius K. Stribling, told Fox that "master workmen are afraid to ask to have men discharged for fear it may be the cause of Members of Congress using their influence to have them dismissed, because some good supporter of the Member has been dismissed for his unfaithfulness or incapacity."[27]

Besides being badgered for assessments and obliged to get out the vote, navy yard workers, like servicemen, were not paid on time. On 26 February 1864 George W. Blunt, Fox's warm friend in New York, warned, "Unless you pay the workmen in the Navy Yard more punctually you will have trouble." Their pay was a month overdue, and they were "being robbed" by extortionate money lenders, called "shavers. It is," Blunt wrote, "cruel." The men were paid on 29 February, but only for January, still leaving them a month behind. "If you knew how they were shaved you would feel as I do," he told Fox; "besides we want all their votes next fall." Blunt also noted that lack of punctuality explained why the Navy Department relied so often on disreputable suppliers. Reputable establishments paid their bills promptly, but the U.S. Treasury paid bills "in not less than 60 days," and "to make good that loss of interest the house must have two prices, one to the trade the other to the government. No respectable house can do this as the cry would be that the U. S. was cheated and no explanation would set it right before the public so that as you say you fall into bad hands." Indeed, John Murray Forbes argued with justification that failure to pay its bills on time cost the government more money than cheating and bribe taking.[28]

Henry J. Raymond lobbied hard for Charles W. Scofield's release, obviously hoping for a share of his booty for the Republican Party. With Lincoln silently acquiescing, Raymond lectured Welles on the necessity of politicizing navy yard personnel. At the New York Navy Yard in Brooklyn, Union Party officials estimated in early August that half of its 7,000 employees opposed Lincoln's reelection and that 6,000 of them could be fired without impairing the yard's efficiency. They demanded that its commandant, Admiral Hiram Paulding, not interfere with political assessments, that he be removed, and that the present assistant constructor be fired. Raymond claimed that Welles gave him "assurances of a disposition to remedy all these evils," but Welles said nothing of this to Fox. When apprised in October by Hay of Raymond's demands, and of Lincoln's plea to satisfy them, Fox was outraged. The department was ready to turn out anyone hostile to the administration, but Fox doubted if there were any. He saw Lincoln who, by then feeling optimistic about the election, said he would not interfere and would "turn the whole matter over" to Welles. Despite the efforts of Fox and Welles, the navy yards were heavily involved in politics, and vessels were delayed. Ericsson reminded Fox on 9 November 1864 that "the Dictator would have been in commission ere this but for the election."[29]

Fox was not totally above politics himself. In the last moments of the 1864 presidential campaign, he responded to the plea of Captain William H. Wiegel, the assistant provost marshal in Baltimore, to furlough from the Potomac Flotilla fireman James Logan, who with his brawn ("muscular force") was "worth to us on election day 150 votes" and more in the fifteenth and seventeenth wards. In addition to furloughing Logan, Fox sent Wiegel a check. A few days after the election, Wiegel frankly told Fox of "the influence your cheque for $75 possessed over the sordid minds of many voters. I kept an open house all day, and as a consequence, in my precinct (the 3rd.) of the 15th. Ward, where there are only two hundred voters Mr. Lincoln's majority was over 275, and the 1st. and 4th. precincts about the same proportion. I think we have done *nobly*, yet if I had $1,000 I could have given 15,000 majority instead of 12,000 only; but I will not complain." Booze, brawls, and bribes had much to do with the impressive turnouts achieved in this and other nineteenth-century elections.[30]

After the election, party leaders pressed Lincoln to pardon Scofield. On 16 December 1864 Welles informed Scofield's lawyer that he adamantly opposed any remission for "a very bad man," whose association with yard employees was demoralizing and pernicious. Undeterred, the lawyer went to Lincoln, who then sent for Fox to apprise him of the facts in the case. Welles noted, "Not infrequently when parties fail with me, they go to the President, and of course state their ill success, but, claiming to have a case press him to act and he, knowing from them my decision, sends for Fox to get the facts. It is not a very satisfactory way, but the President's peculiarity." Lincoln had great faith in Fox's judgment and so did Welles. Although, where fraudulent contractors were involved, Welles "would not be oppressive," Fox, he noted, "is violent against these men, who, he believes, are hypocrites and rascals." Fox gave Lincoln the facts on 16 December, and on the following day Lincoln called at the Navy Department and heard additional information gathered by William E. Chandler, who investigated frauds at the Philadelphia Navy Yard. Scofield, for example, had seduced with cash payments the clerk of the storekeeper at the Philadelphia Navy Yard "to receipt for 70,000 pounds when there were but 50,000." He was not released.[31]

Despite the waste of corruptionists, Welles and Fox accomplished a great deal. In his December 1863 annual report, Welles noted that the navy had 588 ships, armed with 4,443 guns, and manned by 34,000 seamen. They were blockading more than 3,500 miles of shoreline and patrolling more than 3,600 miles on the Mississippi and its tributaries and an additional 2,000 miles of coastal rivers, inlets, and sounds. "The North," Fox proudly wrote Freeman H. Morse, the American consul at London, "seems to respond to every call upon it, men, money, ships, Engines, munitions, all come forth with the alacrity of Alladin's Lamp. . . . Mr. Welles has a right to be proud of his work. The boldness with which he adopted radical changes of Vessels and armaments has been rewarded by success, and history will do him justice." Although Welles boasted that more than 1,000 blockade runners had been captured, Fox was not satisfied. On the same day that Welles dated his report, 7 December 1863, Fox sent Admiral S. P. Lee a list of blockade runners (most running into Wilmington), urging more diligence on the part of the North Atlantic Blockading Squadron.[32]

Because maintaining the blockade was of paramount importance, Fox worked to keep the blockading squadron commanders on their toes. Throughout the war, the Navy Department forwarded to them extracts from consular dispatches to the State Department relating to suspicious vessels they should look for. It also relayed to them news reports of successful blockade runners. Although some blockade runners were privately or publicly owned Confederate vessels, most were of British registry. Virtually all of them picked up their cargoes—a portion of which by Confederate law had to be war matériel— in either the Bahamas or Bermuda. In early 1864 Dahlgren, Farragut, and Lee responded to Fox's demands for greater effectiveness. Dahlgren assured him that, although there were no new assaults on Sumter, four monitors were blockading Charleston effectively. Farragut wrote on 13 February, "those publications about vessels running into Mobile are false." He claimed it had been six weeks since the last one evaded his blockade. A week later, Lee reminded Fox that the two widely separated entrances to Wilmington doubled his problem. Because the blockade had been strengthened there the previous fall, twenty-three blockade runners had been destroyed or captured, and he suspected that the runners were not being replaced as fast as they were lost. In the spring of 1864, Farragut was planning to gain control of Mobile Bay, while Lee continued to hope for sufficient military support for an assault on Wilmington.[33]

Throughout the war, the blockade steadily became more effective. The classic estimate is that one in ten blockade runners was lost in 1861, one in eight in 1862, one in four in 1863, one in three in 1864, and one in two in 1865. Stretching 3,550 miles, it was the most ambitious blockade in history, and, at the onset of the war, neither southerners nor Europeans thought it could succeed. Thanks to the efforts of Fox and Welles, the "stringent Union naval blockade" was an unexpected success in unexpected ways. David G. Surdam's careful study shows that it "suppressed, if not totally prevented," coastwise shipping between Confederate ports, which increased the strain on the "rickety" southern railway system. The blockade, furthermore, prevented the improvement and expansion of southern railroads, which at best had difficulty in supplying southern armies. While a considerable amount of war matériel did penetrate the blockade, it nevertheless "affected the Confederacy's ability to import essential war materiel, especially small arms." Surdam concludes that the two most important achievements of the Union blockade were the disruption of intraregional trade (which did not occur to Fox) and "denying the Confederacy badly needed revenue from exporting raw cotton and other staple products" (which was a primary aim for Fox).[34]

In the summer of 1864, some of Fox's merchant marine friends wanted to fit out privateers to intercept blockade runners, especially at Wilmington. Robert Bennett Forbes of Boston and Joseph J. Comstock of New York pushed to do so, but Robert's brother John Murray Forbes warned Fox to be cautious. It seemed "very dangerous to our friendly relations with England." Fox, nevertheless, told Comstock on 28 July that the navy could give him "some old 32s [cannon] and the balls—nothing else." Fox thought that a boat going sixteen knots "would during the summer months make a fortune. . . . Our fast boats have been so long on the blockade that their speed has run down." But two days later, after Fox discovered the State Department would not authorize privateers, he told John Murray Forbes that any privately owned vessel sent out after blockade runners would have to become part of the navy. Because half of a naval vessel's prize money went into the navy's pension fund, "the matter will not pay, but I am most anxious to have it tried." Fox hoped private competition would shake up the blockading squadron off Wilmington. Although Fox was ready to order Forbes's vessel to cruise fifty miles outside of Wilmington, one-half the prize money was discouraging. Neither Forbes nor Comstock sent out vessels.[35]

Prize money helped inspire the ill-fated Red River campaign, which de-
layed Farragut's assault on Mobile. It was the brainchild of General-in-Chief
Halleck, who ordered it in January 1864. Both General Nathaniel Prentice
Banks, that campaign's commander, and Grant, who until 12 March 1864 was
subordinate to Halleck, realized that Mobile was a more important objective
and agreed reluctantly to a Red River campaign. William T. Sherman and
Porter, however, were anxious to go up the Red River. On 21 December 1863,
Sherman proposed to Porter that after a "movement up the Yazoo River . . . ,
. if you will, I will . . . go up the Red River as high as Shreveport and make that
rich country pay in gold or cotton for all the depredations on our [Mississippi]
river commerce." Porter immediately (27 December) queried the commander
of the *Choctaw*, off the mouth of the Red River, about its defenses and depth.
The raid's military value was questionable, its rationale, with its mix of diplomatic, political, and economic objectives, was dubious, but its promise of plunder was seductive. The Union presence in the Confederate trans-Mississippi
West would discourage what they suspected were French ambitions for Texas.
Liberating vast stores of cotton would keep textile mills in New England hum-
ming, politicians in office, and pour revenue into the U.S. Treasury and prize
money into the pockets of the men in Porter's squadron.[36]

Neither Fox nor Welles advocated a Red River campaign, though they did
want the navy to cooperate with the army in joint expeditions. "Sherman and
myself," Porter wrote Fox on 13 January 1864, "have been trying to concoct
something by way of keeping our hands in" and wished to "visit Shreveport"
before the spring campaign for Atlanta commenced. On 30 January, Sherman
suggested to Porter that "March 1 should be fixed as the date for us to enter
Red River," and by 13 February Porter had decided to take every ironclad vessel in his fleet up the river.[37]

On 12 March Porter's "large fleet of ironclads" began its ascent of the Red
River in support of a 30,000-man army commanded by Banks. Because he was
outranked by Banks, whom he considered an incompetent political general,
Sherman decided not to accompany 11,000 of his troops, who were a part of
the expedition. Porter arrived at Alexandria before Banks and had his men
scouring the countryside for cotton (whether owned by Unionists or Rebels).
By 24 March he reported to Welles that he had 2,021 bales as a prize of war,
and the next day he told Fox that he expected to "capture ten thousand bales
before I leave the River." Charlie Guild (who was Porter's secretary) assured
his Uncle Gus that the cotton had been seized by General Kirby Smith "for
war purposes" and belonged to the Confederate government. Porter did not
tell Welles that his men stenciled the bales "C.S.A." to "legitimize" their sei-

There was an old man up Red River
Found it hard his expenses to River,
So he went for some Cotton
That Jack had just Got in
And Therefore refused to deliver —

Captured Red River Cotton, caricatured by D. D. Porter. Jack Tar is thumbing his nose at Major General Nathaniel Prentiss Banks and cotton speculators carrying scales and a carpetbag of greenbacks. Courtesy Collection of The New-York Historical Society, New York.

zure before marking them "U.S.N." In contrast, prize law did not apply to the army, which seized cotton for the U.S. Treasury, making soldiers jealous and angry.[38]

Ignoring the advice of experienced pilots, Porter gambled on rising water over the next month and took his largest ironclad, the *Eastport*, over the rocks and falls above Alexandria. He told Fox that they would have to pull the boats through the narrow rapid channel "by tying one boat to the trees and work them through with *her* steam Capstan." He added jocularly, "If we are kept up the River 'till next fall dont be surprised." It took two and a half days of hard work to get the *Eastport* over the rocks, but Porter had little trouble getting ten other gunboats and thirty transports over. On 3 April he moved up river toward Shreveport. Taking some of his lighter vessels, he got as far as Loggy Bayou on 10 April. There, he learned that Banks was in retreat, having been defeated two days before at Sabine Crossroads. The next day, Porter faced disaster, as he backed downstream until he could turn his boats around. Seriously threatened by rapidly falling water, he was harassed by snipers and field artillery. He lost two transports and had to blow up the stranded *Eastport* before reaching the impassable falls at Alexandria on 27 April. In Washington, Fox learned from Richmond papers the agonizing news that "Porter will have to destroy his fleet if the Army retreats."[39]

Fox heard more bad news that April. Off Newport News, Virginia, on 9 April, the Confederate boat *Squib* rammed a torpedo into the steam frigate *Minnesota*. The torpedo's fifty-pound charge of powder caused a "tremendous explosion," inflicting minimal damage, but raising maximum apprehensions of future attacks. In contrast, the descent of North Carolina's Roanoke River on 19 April by the formidable ironclad ram CSS *Albemarle* was a present danger. It rammed and sank the Union gunboat *Southfield*, forced the gunboat *Miami* to flee, and enabled the Confederates to capture Plymouth, North Carolina, and to gain control of the Roanoke Valley. Anxious to confront the *Albemarle* with the powerful monitor *Tecumseh*, which drew too much water to get into the sound, Fox asked Ericsson to have "camels" made to lift it over a bar with eight feet of water. But the 700 tons required to lift the *Tecumseh* three feet out of the water would be "so costly tedious and difficult to construct" that Ericsson advised against it. Fox was vexed further when he learned that, on 30 April, the *Harriet Lane* (which was in Confederate hands) and two smaller vessels escaped through the Galveston blockade.[40]

Worst of all, Fox and Welles learned that the Richmond newspapers were accurate. Porter's fleet was, in late April, trapped above the rapids at Alexandria. His predicament, Porter characteristically reported, was "without any fault of mine." There was only three feet, four inches of water "on the falls," with seven feet needed to get his ten gunboats over, and, as he said, "no amount of lightening will accomplish the object." To Fox, he lamented, "Our expedition which promised so much, and which I hoped would have been commanded by Sherman, has been disastrous from the time Banks took command, . . . and will continue to be so until that high functionary is consigned to that oblivion he so justly merits."[41]

Ironically, an army engineer, with whom Banks cooperated wholeheartedly, saved the "backbone of the Mississippi Squadron." Lieutenant Colonel Joseph Bailey of Wisconsin was familiar with the temporary dams loggers used to float logs down shallow streams. He proposed damming the Red River to float the gunboats over the rapids. Porter was skeptical. "If damning would get the fleet off, he would have been afloat long before," he punned. But Bailey's plan was the only hope for saving his gunboats.[42]

Banks supplied 3,000 soldiers, primarily from Maine and New York regiments, who worked around the clock. They included Maine woodsmen, who felled the trees, and African Americans, who worked in water up to their necks. Porter (who was ill) and his men were "strangely apathetic" at first. They neglected to lighten their gunboats by removing guns, armor, and stores. An irate officer on Banks's staff discovered cotton in the hold of every gunboat. On 9 May four of Porter's lighter-draft vessels got over the falls when part of the dam gave way, briefly forming a chute. Bailey and his men immediately began building new "wing dams on the upper falls." At this point, Porter's sailors began working feverishly at lightening their vessels. By 13 May they were over the falls and had clear sailing to the Mississippi. Porter's report of 16 May accurately credited the saving of his fleet to Bailey, Banks, and the men of the Maine and New York regiments. But with respect to Banks, Porter wrote privately to Fox, "I think my *weakness* is generally giving people more credit than they deserve." He added, "I had some trouble to hold Banks to his work," insinuating that Banks was about to pull out before the dams were completed. Regretting his involvement in "that ridiculous and disgraceful affair," Porter vowed "I shall be sure of my man before I cooperate with any Soldier."[43]

Porter was fortunate that his superiors were understanding and preoccupied. He, not Banks, had made the decision to risk the fleet above the falls. By the time Sherman could have fought his way up to Shreveport, the Red River would have fallen so low that Bailey could not have worked his miracle. Luckily for Porter, the Red River was remote from Washington, where in early May all eyes were focused on Grant's advance in the Wilderness of Virginia. Lincoln had appointed Grant in command of all Union armies, and he was with the Army of the Potomac. Full of anxiety, Lincoln on 6 May dropped in on Fox at the Navy Department. "I have nothing to do," Lincoln said, "and have been over to Stanton's, and have now come here. The fact is, I cannot keep still, I am so anxious to hear something about the army." After asking Fox if he had any news, Lincoln commented, "Grant has got on the wall and kicked away the ladder—like Cortez in Mexico, he has burnt his ships."[44]

In contrast to Porter's lack of charity for Banks, Fox told Porter, "I am sorry for Banks—it has utterly extinguished him." Rather than criticize Porter, Fox and Welles assured him they were confident in his "judgment . . . on the Red River." They did not admonish him for putting his vessels at risk and rejoiced that they were saved. "We are much relieved," Fox wrote Porter on 25 May 1864, "at receiving your telegram yesterday that the ironclads were out of the river, through the instrumentality of Colonel Bailey's conception. . . . Bad as things looked," Fox, ever the optimist, added, "I had a confident presentiment that even the elements would be mastered in saving that fleet." Although the

Navy Department thanked Bailey handsomely, Fox could not refrain from noting that "the cases shall be multiplied where the Army has leaned upon our boats for salvation and returned no thanks." With his faith in Porter unshaken, Fox assured him of a leave and hinted at the command of a blockading squadron. "After you get your feathers smoothed and oiled, I don't see why you should not come East, if you so desire it."[45]

Fox also warned Porter about his acquisition of cotton up the Red River. The Treasury Department was coming under fire for trading with the enemy (which Welles consistently opposed). Secretary of the Treasury Salmon P. Chase "in conversation with Mr. Welles," Fox told Porter, "endeavored to throw blame upon you in regard to dealings in cotton. We understand this to be a move . . . to defend himself at our and your expense." Telling Porter to be prepared, Fox suggested that "facts in this matter of trade had better be noted, and perhaps a history of it reported to the Department with your own dealings, such a paper as can be yielded to any Congressional committee that should call for it."[46]

Porter had already gotten wind of congressional interest in alleged "cotton speculations and frauds on the part of officers in the West," including himself. On 11 May, while Bailey was building wing dams, Porter self-righteously lied to Welles that he "would not walk ten steps out of the way of my duty for all the cotton in the South" and "not one instance occurred since we entered this river where officer or man failed to respect private rights . . . or took so much as an egg" without paying for it. In truth, Porter was not heavily involved with cotton speculators, although William Halliday, who was on his flagship, realized a fortune from the Red River campaign. Rather than trade for cotton, Porter simply seized all the cotton he could, claimed it belonged to the Confederate government, and shipped 6,000 bales to Cairo, Illinois, as prize of war. In November 1864, at a dinner party including Fox and Hay, "Porter talked in very indecent terms of abuse of Banks, saying that the fleet got ahead of the army & stole the cotton which the army intended to steal . . . & said he would stand the criticism as long as he had his pockets full of prize money." Later, when he testified about the Red River campaign before the Joint Committee on the Conduct of the War, Porter flatly declared that "Cotton killed that expedition," that speculators controlled it, that the navy seized no prize cotton, and that Banks was responsible for the expedition's failure. In the end, the efforts of Porter and his men—even bailing some cotton—came to nothing. In the spring of 1865, the Supreme Court decided that prize law did not apply to inland seizures, and profits from their sale went to the U.S. Treasury.[47]

If Porter had declared that cotton inspired a risky campaign that made little military sense, he would have been closer to the truth. The army and his fleet escaped a total disaster, but they were diverted, in the spring of 1864, from the more urgent objective of Mobile.

CHAPTER SIXTEEN

Commerce Raiders
and Ironclad Rams

The contest between the "Kearsarge" and the "Alabama" has had the effect of a *coup d'etat* both in France and England. . . . I was mightily amused at the astonishment shown in reference to the XI in. guns.   *Frederick M. Edge to Fox, 21 July 1864*

Fortune is an uncertain wench, but she generally sticks to those who fight it out with her, she loves perseverance & courage, & they will accomplish much even against her *will*.

Farragut to Porter, 7 May 1864

Early in 1864, elusive Confederate cruisers were still preying on Union commerce, and the Confederacy was building two formidable ironclads (the *Albemarle* in North Carolina and the *Tennessee* in Alabama) to harass blockaders. Fox relied on monitors designed by Ericsson and Eads to destroy the Confederate ironclads, but to find Confederate commerce destroyers on the world's oceans necessitated fast, seaworthy, wooden, state-of-the-art steamships. In truth, these vessels were also used on the lower Mississippi and formed the outer ring of ships at blockaded ports. They were the necessary complements to the revolutionary ironclad creations.

■ ■ ■

From the beginning of the war, no problem vexed Fox more than Confederate commerce destroyers. Even though they did the Union cause little direct harm, they inflicted significant indirect damage. Commercial interests mounted enormous pressure on the Navy Department to divert vessels from the blockade or coastal expeditions to search for Confederate raiders. Finding them was a frustrating task. The raiders were elusive, and, although most of them were ultimately caught or laid up, even after the war ended, the crippled American merchant marine would never regain its preeminent position.[1]

The most successful southern commerce raiders were British-built vessels. On 1 July 1862 Fox and Welles were certain that the fast steamer *Oreto,* at Nassau in the Bahamas, was destined for the Confederacy. It left Nassau on 7 August and, avoiding Union warships, took on its battery at nearby Green Cay. Rechristened the *Florida,* it sailed on 17 August, but yellow fever, afflicting both captain and crew, forced it to Cuba. It later was shelled by blockaders as it entered Mobile Bay on 4 September. The *Florida* was damaged, but Fox, unhappy that it had escaped from Nassau and Cuba, was even more disappointed that it was not destroyed at Mobile Bay. He urged the blockaders to be more vigilant. Quarantined because of yellow fever and badly in need of repairs, the *Florida* did not get underway until 16 January 1863, when, to Fox's chagrin, it once again ran the Mobile blockade.[2]

Like the *Florida,* the *Alabama* was built at Liverpool, England (where it was referred to as the *290*), and on 29 July 1862 it sailed from that port as the *Enrica.* At a rendezvous in the Azores, it received its armament. With Raphael Semmes in command of a crew "of 110 of the most reckless sailors from the groggeries and brothels of Liverpool," it put to sea on 24 August as the *Alabama.* By 7 December 1862 it had captured twenty-six vessels (burning several whalers and grain-filled vessels) while sailing from the Azores to the east coast of North America and the Caribbean. The depredations of the *Alabama* created heavy pressure on the Navy Department for its destruction. Because he did not have ships to search for the *Alabama,* Fox especially felt the heat. Not wishing to impair the blockade, he and Welles had to rely on overseas squadrons. As Welles explained to Charles Wilkes, the commander of the West India Squadron, "we must make the most of the force we have." He emphasized that "the first great and imperative duty of your command is the capture and destruction of the *Alabama* . . . , and similar cruisers of a semi-piratical character that are depredating our . . . commerce." Wilkes's squadron, however, caught only blockade runners, like the British *Peterhof,* on 25 February 1863, off St. Thomas, which led to a long international dispute over the legality of its seizure.[3]

Fox plotted the whereabouts of Confederate cruisers. Bits and pieces of information came to the Navy Department from the crews of burned vessels, from observations of neutral, and therefore unharmed, vessels, and from consular agents in foreign ports. Almost always weeks old, the information was at times erroneous. On 19 October 1862 Fox learned from the captain of the *Bril-*

liant that sixteen days earlier the *Alabama* was about 1,000 miles east of New York and would rendezvous off Cape Breton Island or Nova Scotia with a supply vessel, carrying guns and coal. Accordingly, the department ordered the *San Jacinto* away from the Wilmington blockade to Cape Breton Island to intercept the *Alabama*. On that day, the *Alabama* was 500 miles closer to New York and planned to rendezvous with its supply vessel at Martinique in the West Indies. The skipper of the *Brilliant* had also heard that the *Alabama* could rendezvous and pick up letters at five other points, including Martinique. Five days later, with no further news, Fox decided to send the *Dacotah* (with yellow fever on board) to the cold climate of Cape Breton and the *San Jacinto* (with a healthy crew) to the West Indies, including Martinique. On 3 November (when his information from the *Brilliant* was a month old), Fox heard that on 29 October the *Alabama* was heading northwest about 250 miles east of New York.[4]

By early November, Union warships were looking for the *Alabama* from Nova Scotia to the West Indies, from the Azores to Bermuda. In addition, the governor of New York and the Boston Board of Trade begged the Navy Department for an ironclad to protect their ports. On 19 November the powerful *San Jacinto* discovered the *Alabama* at Martinique, but Semmes escaped that rainy night and took on coal from 21 to 24 November at the Venezuelan island of Blanquilla. With the evasive *Alabama* again on its destructive way, a frustrated Fox continued to track and anticipate its moves.[5]

The success of Confederate cruisers in 1863 and early 1864 vexed Fox further. Following the victory of the Confederate cotton clads at Galveston on New Year's Day 1863, the *Alabama* appeared off Galveston on 11 January and sank the U.S. gunboat *Hatteras,* and five days later the *Florida* escaped from Mobile. Farragut was chagrinned at the lapses of his West Gulf Squadron, and Fox and Welles were equally distressed.[6]

In late January, the *Florida* and *Alabama* burned northern vessels in the Caribbean. A third raider, the *Georgia,* put to sea in April, found the *Alabama* at Bahia, Brazil, and supplied it with 528 pounds of powder on 15 May. After they crossed the South Atlantic separately to the Cape of Good Hope, the *Georgia* returned to the North Atlantic, arrived at Cherbourg, France, on 28 October 1863, and remained there for months, while the *Alabama* spread "panic" in the East Indies. Paul S. Forbes, who was building the *Idaho* for the Union navy, saw the *Alabama* at Singapore and reported to Fox that "her boilers are nearly worn out." Returning across the Indian Ocean, the *Alabama* made repairs at Colombo, Ceylon, coaled at Cape Town, South Africa, and arrived at Cherbourg on 11 June 1864. In the previous five months, Semmes had destroyed only three northern vessels.[7]

While the *Alabama* visited East Asia, the *Florida* remained in the Atlantic. In May 1863 it ranged as far south as Pernambuco (Recife), Brazil, headed north to within 50 miles of New York, crossed the Atlantic, and was laid up in Brest, France, from September 1863 until February 1864. It then crossed the Atlantic and scuttled the U.S. mail steamer *Electric Spark* on 9 July, 100 miles off Cape Hatteras. Hoping the USS *Shenandoah* would catch the *Florida* off the Delaware capes, Fox on 12 July also had the *Juniata* and the *Ticonderoga* searching for it on its presumed course "up the coast." They failed to find it, but, as the *Florida* crisscrossed the Atlantic over the next three months, it burned only one additional vessel, before anchoring at Bahia, Brazil on 4 October 1864.[8]

Fox had little reason to cheer in the first half of 1864. The depredations of Rebel cruisers on the high seas, the threat of the *Albemarle* on the North Carolina sounds, and the disastrous position of Porter on the Red River were only some of his problems. Others were swindling contractors cheating the navy, run-ins with General Henry Halleck over the transfer of seamen from the army to the navy, and the hostile move in Congress that cut his salary. Conditions were so bad that he found Porter's escape from disaster more exhilarating than sobering.

Fox's luck and that of the Union navy improved in June 1864. Three days after the *Alabama* arrived at Cherbourg, the U.S. steam sloop of war *Kearsarge*, under John A. Winslow, positioned itself at the entrance of the harbor awaiting the *Alabama*'s departure. Although the *Alabama* needed repairs, Semmes decided to fight the *Kearsarge*, because the *Alabama* appeared nearly its equal in armament. On 19 June 1864, after an hour's battle, Dahlgren's eleven-inch smoothbores proved superior to British guns. With the *Alabama* sinking, Semmes struck its colors and asked Winslow for assistance. To the annoyance of Winslow, Fox, and Welles, Semmes and part of his crew were picked up by the English yacht *Deerhound*, spirited to England, and not turned over to Winslow. Still Fox and Welles were jubilant over the victory. Welles commended Winslow for rescuing drowning men, but told him he "committed a grave error" in paroling his prisoners, who had made "piratical war on unarmed merchantmen."[9]

The *Kearsarge*'s victory over the British-built and armed *Alabama* surprised naval observers on both sides of the Channel, and the fortuitous location of the victory gave it particular impact in Europe. The enormous interest the duel aroused is reflected in Edouard Manet's paintings *The Battle of the "Kearsarge" and the "Alabama"* and *The "Kearsarge" at Boulogne.* Frederick Milnes Edge, a London journalist, reported to Fox that Laird was taunted in the House of Commons about the sinking of his vessel. French naval officers, who inspected the *Kearsarge* at Cherbourg, were impressed by the Dahlgren smoothbores that destroyed the *Alabama.* They apparently realized that, although their ironclads mounted many guns (from thirty-two to fifty-two), they were of small caliber, and the officers feared that their vessels would be vulnerable to the heavy Dahlgrens.[10]

The French reaction confirmed Fox's view that Dahlgren's nine- and eleven-inch smoothbores were the "best shell guns in existence." Edge predicted that "if you will permit us to see a XV in. here, I am confident it will let you have things your own way hereafter." Fox agreed that openness and publicity of the armaments and armor of the monitors would have a deterring effect on European intervention, so, upon request, he gave drawings of monitors to the ministers of Russia, Prussia, and Denmark. Richard Cobden, the English economist and statesman, who was warmly sympathetic to the North, told Edge "that he is in hopes of hearing of the arrival of the 'Dictator' [Ericsson's seagoing monitor] very shortly. I trust he is right in his anticipations, for he agrees with me that a good sample of your sea-going Ironclads will benefit the cause of the Union hugely in Europe." Ericsson agreed. "The appearance of the Dictator in the British Channel," he wrote Fox, "will create a sensation never before recorded in the naval history of England."[11]

A few months later, the *Florida*'s career ended. Napoleon Collins, commander of the USS *Wachusett*, saw it arrive in Bahia on 4 October and followed it in the following morning. He challenged the *Florida* for an engagement in international waters off Bahia, but its commander Charles Manigault Morris, aware of the fate of the *Alabama* when it met a similar vessel, declined the invitation. At 3:00 a.m. on 7 October 1864, Collins, grossly violating international law and Brazilian sovereignty, steamed past the Brazilian gunboat separating the adversaries and rammed and captured the *Florida.* With Morris and most of his crew ashore, Collins towed off his prize, under fire from the Brazilian fort. On 11 November, he brought the *Florida* into Hampton Roads. During the night of 7 to 8 November, Fox was awakened by a telegram reading "Florida taken" and a second, more detailed telegram. Coming on the eve of the presidential election, the news was especially welcome.[12]

Officially, the United States government disavowed Collins's rash act, and a court-martial found him guilty and sentenced him to dismissal from the navy. Members of the *Florida*'s mostly British crew who were on board when the ship was captured were released from prison in February 1865 with twenty dollars each for passage back to England. If it had not been run into at Hampton Roads by an army transport on 19 November, the *Florida* would have been returned to Brazil. It sprung a leak and, with less than heroic measures taken to save it, sank nine days later in nine fathoms of water. Unofficially, northerners applauded Collins's act, and Fox and Welles were pleased by its result. A court of inquiry found no negligence connected with the fortuitous sinking of the *Florida*. Collins was returned to active duty, after Welles disapproved his sentence, on 17 September 1866.[13]

Between the sinking of the *Alabama* and the capture of the *Florida*, the Navy Department was troubled by the escape of another Confederate commerce destroyer. On a short, devastating, August cruise, from Wilmington, North Carolina, to Halifax, Nova Scotia, and back, the *Tallahassee* destroyed twenty-six vessels, causing an uproar in shipping and insurance circles and a flurry of activity in the Navy Department. On 12 August, the day after the *Tallahassee* scuttled, burned, or bonded seven vessels off Sandy Hook, a telegram from Bradley S. Osbon of the *New York Herald*, addressed to Fox, described the *Tallahassee* (white, two smokestacks, schooner rig), its armament (three guns), crew (mostly soldiers), commander (John Taylor Wood), and its course (southeast).[14]

On vacation in Portsmouth, New Hampshire, Fox did not participate in the fruitless and frustrating effort to track down the *Tallahassee*. Orders from Welles to the New York Navy Yard were not carried out. The *San Jacinto*, which he thought would intercept the *Tallahassee* at Halifax, had not even sailed from New York. Angry, Welles censured Rear Admiral Hiram Paulding, commandant of the New York Navy Yard, for "this delay, in such an emergency" and for not keeping the department informed about the *San Jacinto* or about the instructions he gave to the four vessels he sent after the *Tallahassee*. Without copies of Paulding's orders, the department had no idea whether one of the vessels had "gone to Halifax, or what disposition has been made of them." Actually, one of the vessels arrived at Halifax ten hours after the *Tallahassee* left, on 20 August, with barely enough coal to return to Wilmington, on 25 August. Chagrinned that poor communications prevented the destruction of the *Tallahassee*, Welles instructed navy yard commandants in Boston, New York, and Philadelphia to inform the department by telegraph of the movements of vessels searching for "piratical cruisers." Had Fox, whose sixth sense tended to discover snafus, been in Washington instead of fishing with his nephews in New Hampshire, he might have checked with Paulding to see if the *San Jacinto* had in fact sailed.[15]

Two months later, on 28 October, the *Chicamauga* and the next day the *Tallahassee*, renamed *Olustee*, escaped from Wilmington. Their cruises were brief (approximately a week for the *Olustee* and three weeks for the *Chicamauga*). Each destroyed about a half dozen sailing vessels near New York. Together, they caused the usual distress in shipping circles and fruitless efforts to run them down by Fox and Union cruisers.[16]

The last of the Confederate commerce destroyers was the British-built *Shenandoah*. Originally the *Sea King*, it was, after its maiden voyage to Bombay, India, purchased by Confederate agents, armed at Madeira, and began its cruise on 19 October 1864, commanded by James I. Waddell. He was ordered to "the far-distant Pacific" to destroy "the great American whaling fleet, a source of abundant wealth to our enemies and a nursery for their seamen." Alarmed, New York merchants called unsuccessfully upon Fox to purchase the *Baltic* and *Atlantic* to track down the *Sea King*. Waddell arrived in Melbourne, Australia, on 25 January 1865, having destroyed seven vessels and bonded two. He remained in port for repairs until 18 February. Cruising into the North Pacific and beyond it, through the Bering Strait into the Arctic Ocean, Waddell destroyed twenty-five whalers, before learning on 2 August 1865 that the war was over. Heading back to England, he surrendered the *Shenandoah* to British authorities on 6 November.[17]

Although Waddell regarded his voyage as a "triumph," Fox and Welles had even more contempt for him than for commanders of the other Confederate commerce destroyers. The *Shenandoah*'s "piracy was of the most odious and despicable character," Welles exclaimed. "It was not the plunder of richly laden barks belonging to 'merchant princes,' . . . but the wanton destruction of the property of individuals seeking a humble subsistence in one of the most laborious and perilous of callings, and who could make no show of resistance to the overwhelming force of the pirate." While the *Shenandoah* "inflicted so much individual distress upon persons so little able to bear it, and so little deserving of it," Waddell's cruise had no effect, direct or indirect, on either the Union or the Confederate war effort.[18]

The further a commerce destroyer cruised from the northeastern coast of the United States, the less its overall effect on the blockade. Carrying the Confederate flag, as the *Alabama* did to the East Indies, the *Shenandoah* to the Arctic, and the *Florida* into the South Atlantic to Brazil, did not approach the disruptive effects of the short cruises of the *Jeff Davis*, *Tallahassee*, and *Chicamauga*. Nor did those long cruises cause as much havoc as when the *Alabama* and *Florida* intercepted vessels entering and leaving New York, Boston, and

Philadelphia. Even so Fox and Welles did not let these panics seriously jeopardize the blockade.

■ ■ ■

Although an irritant, the Confederate cruisers did nothing to delay closing the major blockade-running ports of Mobile and Wilmington. Since almost the day after he took New Orleans, Farragut had wanted to attack Mobile. While the strength of the Union navy increased, so did Mobile's defenses. Forts Morgan, Gaines, and Powell guarded the entrance to Mobile Bay, and, in the spring of 1864, the ironclad ram CSS *Tennessee* at Mobile was receiving guns from the Naval Gun Foundry and Ordnance Works at Selma, Alabama. Although the commander of Fort Morgan, Richard L. Page, thought both Morgan and Gaines "very weak," Admiral Franklin Buchanan of the *Tennessee* thought them "very strong" and was impressed by the power of his vessel. "I wish you could see the *Tennessee*," he wrote Catesby Jones, who had commanded the *Virginia* in its epic fight with the *Monitor,* "she is a man-of-war."[19]

More aggressive than impetuous, Farragut needed at least one ironclad, in addition to his wooden ships, to gain control of Mobile Bay and seal off Mobile. Returning to the command of the West Gulf Squadron in January 1864 after a five-month leave, he "made a reconnaissance of Forts Morgan and Gaines," counted the guns on their bastions, and observed the obstructions between them, which forced vessels to pass under the guns of Morgan. He was "satisfied" that, with one ironclad and the cooperation of an army of 5,000, he could run the batteries, destroy the flotilla in the bay, and reduce the forts. Aware that the four double-turreted monitors, drawing only six feet (designed by James B. Eads), were nearing completion at St. Louis, Farragut boasted to Welles, "If I could get these I would attack them at once." In April, he told Fox he feared he would not get ironclads from the North, "but I was in hopes of getting one or two of Eads . . . to fight the Tennessee in the shallow waters"[20]

While Farragut anxiously awaited monitors, Buchanan was getting the *Tennessee* over Dog River Bar into Mobile Bay and into fighting shape. On 14 June, Farragut informed Fox, while lying outside Mobile Bay "watching Buchanan," that he had fresh intelligence from four German or Danish carpenters, who "had been at work upon all the rams." They reported that the *Tennessee*'s sister ship *Nashville* was being plated at Mobile and approaching completion and that Buchanan, at night when the sea is "very smooth . . . will come with his whole force" and attack Farragut's fleet. Again Farragut pleaded with Fox, "If we had one ironclad we could go in at any moment," but without an ironclad going in would be useless. Farragut's deep-draft wooden vessels "could not get at their ironclads after we got in, and they could choose their distance on the flats to cut us up." Thirteen days later, Fox responded that ironclads were on their way. He cautioned Farragut that Porter had some reservations about using the Eads river monitors at Mobile and warned, "If you conclude to attempt anything, I hope you will look out that the torpedoes are removed. They have this system of *warfare* very well arranged now."[21]

Farragut got not one but four monitors. Welles ordered two Eads monitors—the *Winnebago* and the *Chickasaw*—as well as two Ericsson monitors—the *Manhattan* and the *Tecumseh*—to join Farragut's fleet. With the last of the designated ironclads, the *Tecumseh*, arriving on the evening of 4 August 1864, Farragut characteristically attacked early the next morning. His wooden vessels fared better than the *Tecumseh*, which after firing the first shot at Fort Morgan struck a torpedo (mine), and sank with nearly all on board. The loss of its gifted commander, Tunis Augustus M. Craven, was as great a loss for Fox as was the ship. Fearing more torpedoes, the *Brooklyn*, at the head of the line of wooden vessels, stopped, while it and Farragut's flagship the *Hartford* were under fire from Fort Morgan. Lashed by his fleet captain Percival Drayton to the rigging and seeing that the advance of the whole fleet was arrested, Farragut reputedly and memorably shouted, "Damn the torpedoes! Full speed ahead!"[22]

The *Hartford* "dashed ahead," and the fleet followed. After Farragut's gunboats captured, injured, or dispersed the three gunboat consorts of the *Tennessee*, "one of the fiercest naval combats on record" began. With its maneuverability inversely proportioned to its impregnability, the *Tennessee* bore down on the *Hartford* but could ram neither it nor the other vessels. Although their guns worked slowly, Farragut's monitors steadily fired on the *Tennessee*, while his wooden vessels attacked it with their guns and with their bows "at full speed." A huge fifteen-inch shot from the monitor *Manhattan* broke through the iron plating of the *Tennessee*, and the four *Chickasaw* eleven-inch guns pounded its stern. It was rammed twice by other vessels and was struck a glancing blow by the *Hartford*, followed by a broadside of nine-inch guns at twelve feet. After an hour and a quarter, Buchanan surrendered. His steering gear had been shot away by the *Manhattan*, his smokestack had been blown away by the *Hartford*, several of his port shutters had been jammed, and the *Manhattan* was about to fire its fifteen-inch gun at close range. With Farragut in control of Mobile Bay, blockade runners could no longer reach Mobile. With pardonable pride, Farragut told Fox, "we did our work 'up brown.'" Fort Powell surrendered to the *Chickasaw* that afternoon. Two days later, the *Chickasaw* compelled Fort Gaines to surrender, and on 23 August, Fort Morgan surrendered. It had been sealed off by the army and bombarded by Farragut's fleet.[23]

In Washington, Fox and Welles anxiously awaited news from Mobile. On 6 August at 9:00 p.m., Fox telegraphed his old schoolmate, General Benjamin F. Butler, commander of the Army of the James, to "get a Richmond paper to see how Farragut is getting on at Mobile." At 7:00 p.m. on 8 August, Butler's telegram, citing the *Richmond Sentinel,* brought news of Farragut's splendid victory. The triumph was for Fox a vindication of his judgment on tactics, vessels, and guns.[24]

In running by Mobile's forts, Farragut did what Fox had wanted Du Pont to do at Charleston. Welles commended Farragut for having "illustrated the efficiency and irresistible power of a naval force . . . to set at defiance the best constructed and most heavily armed fortifications." The battle of Mobile Bay also confirmed Fox's wisdom in building monitors with their shallow draft, heavy guns, but no rams, which were, he later reminded Welles, "a device, as you know, I always opposed." The four monitors Farragut had going into Mobile Bay were slow, and none of them steered very well. Although the *Tecumseh* sank immediately and the *Winnebago*, with malfunctioning turrets, could fire only intermittently, the *Manhattan* and the *Chickasaw* were invaluable during the battle with the *Tennessee* and later in subduing the forts. James W. A. Nicholson, the commander of the *Manhattan*, was ecstatic about his vessel. At best, its speed was only six knots, and with four inches of seaweed on its bottom it was able to do only four knots, which made it even slower than the *Tennessee*. Despite its lack of speed, Nicholson boasted to Fox that the *Manhattan*, was "impregnable to any ordnance that the Rebels possess" and "that no vessel can be built to stand those XV″ solid shot with fifty—or sixty—pounds of powder."[25]

The battle of Mobile Bay demonstrated the uselessness of rams and ramming. If handled properly, any steam-powered wooden vessel could avoid ironclad rams. The four wooden vessels that rammed the *Tennessee* damaged their bows more then they harmed it. While trying to ram the *Tennessee*, the *Hartford* was rammed in error by the *Lackawanna*. It was the ordnance of the *Tennessee*, not its ram, that hurt Farragut's fleet, and it was the broadsides of his wooden vessels and the big guns of his monitors that forced the *Tennessee's* surrender. After Mobile Bay, Farragut recognized that monitors were "becoming the most important guardians of our shallow waters." Unlike light-draft wooden vessels, their machinery was protected by iron as they passed "under the heaviest batteries and frequently at short distances." Fox could not have hoped for a better vindication of his faith in monitors.[26]

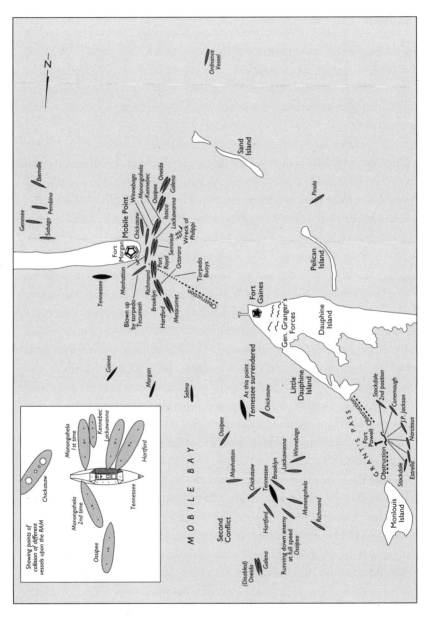

Battle of Mobile Bay, 5 August 1864. Map by Bill Nelson, derived from *Official Records of the Union and Confederate Navies,* 21:600.

The good news from Mobile Bay came just before Fox left Washington for his two-week August vacation in Portsmouth, New Hampshire. He needed the rest. He usually worked at the Navy Department seven days and several evenings a week, and it had been a momentous summer. In June, Fox had mixed business and pleasure when Lincoln took him on a visit to Grant. Fox was brought along for his company and because he was responsible for arranging naval support for Grant's campaign against Lee's Army of Northern Virginia. On 20 June, with Grant besieging Petersburg, Lincoln and Fox (constituting a party of two, Fox proudly told Virginia) left Washington by steamer. They met with Grant the next day at City Point on the James River, then mounted horses and inspected Union lines at Petersburg, where "the troops cheered the Prest, especially the colored ones, with much fervor." On 22 June Fox and Lincoln went up the James River with Butler and S. P. Lee "to Howletts House where the enemy have a battery," and just below that point inspected the twin-turreted monitor *Onondaga*. Again mounting horses, they "rode across Butler's lines," dined with him at Point of Rocks on the Appomattox, and returned by boat to City Point. There they "had an hours visit from Genl Grant." He assured them that "he will surely win," even "though he will have some rebuffs." Fox added, "I think he will." Although Admiral Lee was not pleased, Fox agreed to Grant's desire to increase the obstructions in the James River at Trent's Reach, to prevent Confederate ironclads from threatening City Point. The new obstructions would release two monitors (including the *Tecumseh*) for service elsewhere. With everything "very satisfactory," Lincoln "came back in fine spirits."[27]

While toiling in the debilitating Washington heat, Fox found amusement and affection in his playful cat, who lived in his office. "I take over her breakfast," he reported to Virginia, "and then she raises a row amongst my papers until about 11 when she turns in for a sleep in the sun in the window." With Virginia and Henry A. Wise out of town, his major diversions were dinners with John Hay and occasional trips down the Potomac. He spent the Fourth of July on Chesapeake Bay with the Blair and Welles families.[28]

A week later, to divert Grant who was besieging Petersburg, the key to Richmond, Confederate general Jubal Early with 15,000 men penetrated to the environs of Washington. There, on 11 July, he threatened the capital and burned the house of Montgomery Blair at Silver Spring, Maryland. "Though Min always disliked the house & living there," Virginia Fox observed, "it is natural that its loss should give it a thousand attractions to her it never had before." Concerned that Early might mount "a serious attack" that night and jeopardize Lincoln's safety, Fox "remained at the telegraph office all night."[29]

The following day, Lincoln, Welles, Fox, several senators, and assorted ladies and gentlemen went out to Fort Stevens and viewed the skirmishing, which occurred between the fort and the Silver Spring gate. On this occasion, future Supreme Court Justice Oliver Wendell Holmes Jr. shouted at Lincoln, "Get down, you fool," and General Horatio G. Wright told Fox to put down young Min Blair, whom he was hoisting in the air to better her view. Having accepted the War Department estimate that Early had only 3,000 to 4,000 men, Fox and Welles belittled the threat to Washington. Early withdrew the next day.[30]

Nevertheless, Welles and Fox called on Admiral Lee to "send to Washington three or four of your gunboats." They also informed him that Silver Spring (his father-in-law's house, where his wife and young son summered) "is in the enemy's possession, but not burned yet." Allowing his private concerns to magnify his fears for the capital, Lee left Hampton Roads for Washington on 13 July in his flagship the *Malvern,* much to the distress of Welles and Fox. "The Department," Welles scolded, "disapproves your leaving your station without orders in an emergency like the present. Return to Hampton Roads without anchoring your vessel." Feeling that Fox had always disliked him, Lee blamed Fox for his censure, as did his wife Lizzie and father-in-law Francis Preston Blair Sr., both of whom became noticeably cool to him. Lizzie Lee struggled "to be civil," and old Blair came close to asking Fox to leave the room. In her correspondence with her husband, she began referring to Fox as "Fatty."[31]

Fox knew that Early's raid would not divert Grant. He was certain that, whatever the Confederates do, "Grant will not loosen his hold and the fall of Richd is sure" and victory certain. Virginia's brother Charles Levi Woodbury, a peace Democrat, worried that a Union victory would not assure a stable country. He dreaded a postwar America with millions of free blacks. "I do not share Charles forebodings," Fox wrote Virginia. "Trouble we shall have. A contest for human rights where wrong has so long reigned, entails misery calamity and sacrifices, but God is working it out. I have no anxiety about it." For Fox, as for many other northerners, the war to save the Union had become a war for human rights.[32]

On Saturday evening, 30 July, Fox accompanied the Lincoln family down the Potomac to Fortress Monroe to escape Washington's heat and to see Grant. With them were James C. and Mercy Ann Conkling, other Illinois friends, and Assistant Secretary of War Charles A. Dana. Fox found Grant, who was calling on Sarah (Mrs. Benjamin F.) Butler and "her stylish daughter" Blanche, and brought him on board. The enlarged party visited "Norfolk to please Genl Grant who had never seen the City," and went out to sea "to get a sniff of the ocean air." Before Grant left, he described the failure of the assault the day before, following the mine explosion under Confederate lines at Petersburg, but neither he nor Lincoln "seemed cut down" by the defeat. Despite appalling casualties suffered by the Army of the Potomac over the past two and a half months, they were confident Petersburg and Richmond would fall. In a lighter vein, Fox reported to Virginia, who was fond of Mary Lincoln, that "with her old Springfield friend" she "was for the time being divested of her cares of State and I was surprised to find a good deal of fun in her. Each night we all sat up until after 1 o'clock."[33]

Hard work and the debilitating effects of a Washington summer took its toll on Fox's usual blooming health. The exercise of walking seven miles a day, between his room in Georgetown Heights and the Navy Department, did not seem to help, nor did riding the two horses Admiral Porter sent him. One was a "blooded mare," who had reputedly belonged to Jefferson Davis, and the other a "bay," who, Porter predicted, would cure Fox's "dyspepsia." On the way to Portsmouth for his two week August vacation, Fox complained that he was "nearly sun struck" in New York and Boston. When he arrived in Portsmouth, Virginia observed, "he looks bilious, had diarrhea all summer & dyspepsia—drinks Congress water three times a day, takes oranges for dinner & shares all *with me*!" Fox took the famed mineral water from the Congress Spring in Saratoga, New York, at the behest of Montgomery Blair, who had faith that hydropathy would cure all ills.[34]

Fox's ill health and news of the success at Mobile Bay coincided with an offer of the agency of Washington textile mill in Lawrence. He would be paid $5,000, plus 1 percent on dividends (about $3,300), because its agent was moving to the Thayer Mill. "We both feel rather inclined to accept," Virginia noted in her diary, "as Gus's health is so bad in W[ashington] & the Navy is now organized." Fox was confident that the last major blockade-running port of Wilmington would shortly be shut down, and "Navy operations over by 1*st* Jan[uary]." On 23 to 24 August, he visited Lawrence to explore the position and also saw his mother in Lowell. "I do not see how the devil the Navy Department can get along without you," Grimes wrote Fox, "and yet I do not blame you for accepting ten thousand dollars and Mass. . . . to staying in Washington at $3500 a year."[35]

Despite Fox's interest, no concrete offer followed. The burning of the Thayer Mill in September placed the agency negotiations with Fox on hold, but his friend Joseph S. Fay tried to tempt him with the position of assistant treasurer with the view of becoming treasurer. That position would give him enough free time to live in Boston, which Virginia preferred to Lawrence. Just when Fay was trying to bring him home to Massachusetts, another friend, A. R. Mac-

Donough, offered him "on certain conditions presidency of a new oil Co. in Penna." at $10,000 a year. Fox emphatically responded "*No!*" The fledgling oil industry was too speculative, too volatile, and western Pennsylvania too remote. More important, by 29 August, Fox had decided "the Prest and Mr Welles ought not to be abandoned at this crisis."[36]

Even though Fox could foresee the navy's eventual triumph and had begun to consider his postwar career, he still had plenty of work at the Navy Department. Before he heard the good news from Mobile Bay in August, he had heard troublesome news from North Carolina. The day after Farragut's triumph, the *Tallahassee* escaped from Wilmington to start its short devastating cruise, and the Confederate ironclad ram *Albemarle* left Plymouth, steamed to the mouth of the Roanoke River, and threatened blockading vessels before returning. Union blockaders were on edge, but unbeknownst to them Confederate military authorities were reluctant to risk the *Albemarle* in further combat. Its presence at Plymouth gave them control of the rich Roanoke River Valley.[37]

As commander of the North Atlantic Blockading Squadron, Lee was eager to destroy the *Albemarle,* as were Welles and Fox. After it sank the wooden *Southfield* in April, Lee thought the *Albemarle* had best be attacked with torpedoes, but a "gallant" attempt to blow it up failed on 25 May. Lee then suggested another way to blow up the *Albemarle.* Lieutenant William B. Cushing would attack it with a torpedo attached, either to an "india-rubber boat" or "a light-draft, rifle-proof, swift steam barge." Lee ordered the India-rubber boat, as well as "four tugs to be fitted with torpedoes." Utilizing Lee's ideas, Cushing proposed on 9 July 1864 that the *Albemarle* be attacked by "three low pressure tugs, one or more fitted with torpedoes, and all armed with light howitzers."[38]

By the end of July, the Navy Department had procured an India-rubber boat, which was "packed in a box" and stowed on board the *Brandywine,* waiting to be requisitioned by Cushing. Either Fox was unaware of the stowed package or he and Welles wanted Cushing to have exactly the rubber boat and tug he wanted. After he consulted with them, Cushing was ordered to New York to purchase "a suitable tug and India-rubber boat." As Welles later noted, the department having "selected you for this important and perilous undertaking . . . left the details with you to perfect." By 9 September Cushing had selected his "picket boats," and Fox agreed that he could send them by canal to Chesapeake Bay, where he could meet them. "The torpedo is all that detains them now," Cushing added, "and that will soon be completed."[39]

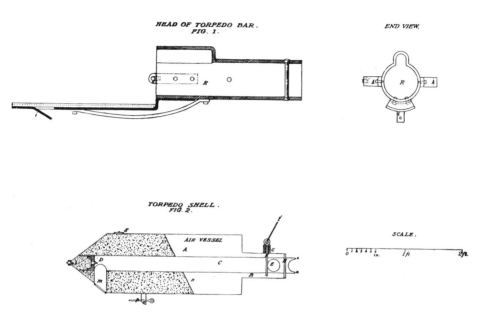

Drawing of Cushing's torpedo. From *Official Records of the Union and Confederate Navies,* 10:623.

On the night of 27 to 28 October 1864, Cushing carried out one of the most daring exploits in the history of the U.S. Navy. With steam picket launch *No. 1,* he ascended the Roanoke River, mounted the pen of logs protecting the *Albemarle,* lowered the torpedo boom, and with a "vigorous pull" exploded the torpedo under the ram's port bow, sending it to the bottom. When his launch was destroyed by the *Albemarle*'s gunfire, Cushing and his men jumped overboard. Two drowned, Cushing and another escaped, and the remaining eleven were taken prisoner. Cushing swam downstream, hid in a swamp, learned from a Negro the good news that he had sunk the ram, captured a skiff, and reached a Union vessel at the mouth of the Roanoke. Immediately on hearing that the *Albemarle* had been sunk, Commander William H. Macomb with his wooden gunboats retook Plymouth, "after a gallant and extremely well-conducted fight," and the vessels that had been watching the *Albemarle* were free to blockade elsewhere. Cushing and Macomb were lauded by Lincoln, Congress, and the Navy Department.[40]

Because Cushing had perfected the details of his exploit, Welles told him, "to you and your brave comrades . . . belongs the exclusive credit which attaches to this daring achievement." Noting his heroism and "innate love of

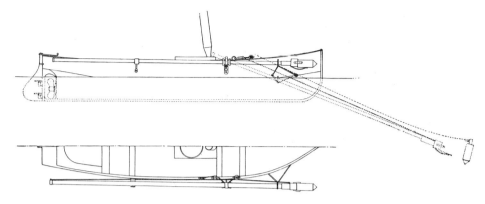

Drawing of Cushing's torpedo launch. From *Official Records of the Union and Confederate Navies*, 10:623.

perilous adventure," Welles gave some fatherly advice along with fulsome praise to the twenty-one-year-old, newly married Cushing. "I trust you may be preserved through further trials, and it is for yourself to determine whether, after entering upon so auspicious a career, you shall by careful study and self-discipline be prepared for a wider sphere of usefulness on the call of your country." Welles had reason to caution Cushing. Two months earlier, he had censured him for his highhanded violation of international law in detaining the British brig *Hound*.[41]

Welles's letter of commendation to Cushing illustrates the Fox-Welles mode of picking and dealing with naval officers. They wanted daring commanders who combined risk taking with careful preparation and sound judgment. They were willing to overlook Cushing's cavalier behavior toward the captain of the *Hound*, because of his heroic behavior on four previous occasions. They had recently replaced his superior, Samuel Phillips Lee, with David Dixon Porter, despite Porter's near disaster on the Red River. Porter was selected because he had energy, ability, and would fight. But friendship with Fox, who championed Porter throughout the war, also enabled him to emerge from it as a naval hero, second only to Farragut. When asked why Lee was removed, Captain Daniel Ammen replied, "because Fox likes Porter the best—that is the whole of it." But Porter was selected not merely because of his closeness with Fox but because that closeness intersected with his capacity to win battles. Success was the bottom line for Fox, who had earlier admired Du Pont.[42]

Having selected their commanders, Fox and Welles would, as they did with Cushing, leave the details to them. They set goals in keeping with the overall strategy of dividing and strangling the Confederacy; procured vessels, which they expected to be used to the fullest extent of their capacity; gave commanders a free hand in achieving those goals; and, having allowed them considerable discretion, demanded success. Their approach worked well except for the assault on Charleston. And, even there, if a Farragut rather than a Du Pont had been in command, the outcome might have been different.

CHAPTER SEVENTEEN

End of the War

You and I know that the motive power of that Department
(with all due respect to the Old Man of the Sea) has been Fox.
That he knows more about it, has more force & industry and
is better fitted in every way to be the head of the Department
than any other man in or out of the Navy.

Charles Baldwin Sedgewick to Henry A. Wise,
22 November 1864

In the fall of 1864, Fox felt it was imperative that Wilmington be shut down
and that Lincoln be reelected. After Farragut's success at Mobile, the South's
only viable contact with the outside world was through Wilmington. The
rebellion is sustained, Fox observed, "not by what entereth into their ports but
by what proceedeth out," and he predicted that Rebel credit would collapse
when cotton exports ceased. Fox and Welles had long wanted to prevent blockade running into Wilmington, but, because of shoal water, a purely naval
attack on Fort Fisher was not possible. In May 1863, shortly after Du Pont's
repulse at Charleston, Fox and S. P. Lee were unable to secure a "small force"
from Halleck for a combined operation to take Fort Caswell, guarding the
Beach Channel of the Cape Fear River. On 2 January 1864 Welles asked Stanton for help in taking Caswell. Its possession would "enable the naval vessels
to lie inside" the mouth of the Cape Fear River, "as is the case at Charleston,
thus closing the port [Wilmington] effectually." Halleck opposed the idea, and
nothing happened. Fox finally made progress when he connected success at
Fort Fisher with success at the polls.[1]

■ ■ ■

In the summer of 1864, Wilmington was still being ignored by the War
Department, and Lincoln's reelection was in jeopardy. Grant in May and June
had suffered enormous casualties, while moving south and east, in an effort to

turn Robert E. Lee's right flank. After six weeks of fighting, there was no breakthrough, and Grant began a long siege of Petersburg, the backdoor to Richmond. With the election in doubt, Fox was able to enlist Lincoln to counter War Department disinterest in a Wilmington operation. On 29 August 1864, the morning Fox returned to Washington from his vacation, after "a red hot saturation for 30 minutes then a cool shower for ten," he checked in at the Navy Department, where all was quiet. He then called on Lincoln "to propose a move to help his election which he took to very earnestly." A few days later, Fox and General Quincy Adams Gillmore discussed with Grant plans for a 1 October joint attack on Wilmington by Farragut (with whom Fox and Welles planned to replace S. P. Lee) and Gillmore. To maintain an element of surprise, Grant wished to keep secret that the joint attack's true objective was Wilmington. On 19 September he had already complained to Fox that the South was aware of "a formidable expedition . . . against Wilmington," and his scouts reported that "*Preparations are even being made which will lead to the evacuation of Richmond* if it becomes necessary to save Wilmington."[2]

Already pushed back to 15 October, the attack was again postponed. It was delayed because Halleck had little use for the navy and joint operations, Grant had little use for Gillmore, and neither wanted to provide the 10,000 troops needed for the joint expedition. In addition, Benjamin F. Butler, in whose department Wilmington lay, thought Gillmore incompetent. Furthermore, with his health "giving way," Farragut did not want to lead the expedition. Consequently, S. P. Lee was replaced as commander of the North Atlantic Blockading Squadron by David Dixon Porter, who was as aggressive as Farragut and better organized. After "a bout" with Stanton on 5 October, Fox felt that the War Department had "commenced operations on the Navy Dept.," and on 28 October 1864 Welles complained to Lincoln that to increase the North Atlantic Blockading Squadron to 150 ships, "every squadron has been depleted," but perhaps to no avail, because "the autumn weather so favorable for such an expedition is fast passing away."[3]

"I go up in the morning," Porter wrote Fox on 15 October from Hampton Roads, "to try and stir Grant up. I am afraid he is not sufficiently interested in this business." Curiously, in view of his earlier high opinion of Grant, Porter told Fox, "Your old School-mate Butler has *charge* of him and he wants to get Richmond (which cannot be done) without outside aid. Take the forts [guarding Wilmington], and Richmond will fall." After visiting Grant, who was not "sanguine about anything," Porter declared, the army "can't move *an inch* & won't move an inch until Wilmington is taken." He thought it "a pity that [James B.] McPherson was killed, & Sherman could not bring his brains here."

Typically, Porter disparaged everyone—even Grant—who did not fall in with his plans.[4]

Even though the Wilmington expedition was stalled, Fox was heartened as the political campaign to reelect Lincoln gathered momentum. Although there were dismaying Union losses, followed by a stalemate in Virginia, successes elsewhere began to lift sagging northern spirits. In early July, news arrived that the *Kearsarge* had destroyed the *Alabama;* in early August, Farragut was victorious at Mobile Bay; and in early September, William T. Sherman took Atlanta. By October, General Philip Sheridan had gained control of the Shenandoah Valley, and later that month Cushing sank the *Albemarle.* By November, northern public opinion was optimistic; people sensed that victory was close.[5]

Fox's loyalty to Lincoln was complete. He understood that Lincoln's "intimation" to Montgomery Blair in September, that he resign from the cabinet, was calculated to conciliate "the Chase and Fremont faction . . . in the eve of the election." Blair, of course, acquiesced. "It seems," Fox wrote Virginia, "rather a summary process and does not appear to me to be frank and true, but politics is not made up of the truest mettle. Blair," Fox added, "pecuniarily is better off—though power is what they want." He took heart from the assurance of his dinner companion John Hay, who was Lincoln's secretary, that "after election it would be all right" for Blair.[6]

On the evening of election day, 8 November, Fox and Welles joined Lincoln and Hay in the War Department telegraph office to await the returns. Not wishing to encounter Stanton, Fox had been reluctant to go, but Stanton, who had recently been ill, remained at home. It was a delightful occasion, because it soon became obvious that "the election had gone pretty much one way." Fox was elated because Congressman Alexander H. Rice, a friend of the Navy Department, was reelected and because, as he exclaimed, "There are two fellows that have been specially malignant to us, and retribution has come upon them both, Hale and Winter Davis." Lincoln, although he had ample reason, did not rejoice at their defeats and gently chided Fox. "You have more of that feeling of personal resentment than I. Perhaps I may have too little of it, but I never thought it paid." Toward midnight, they had a "nice oyster & coffee supper," with Fox amusing the convivial group by "abusing the coffee for being too hot." Fox left between one and two, "convinced the Nation had endorsed & elected Uncle Abe! Great rejoicing over election," Virginia reported, "Serenade & salute at White House." A cough kept her from going with Fox and the Blairs after two to hear the speeches and join the celebration.[7]

Chief Justice Roger Brooke Taney had died on 12 October, giving Lincoln an opportunity to make things "all right" for Montgomery Blair by naming him chief justice. To help Blair's candidacy, Fox asked Benjamin F. Butler to write Lincoln in Blair's behalf. He reminded Butler of their long acquaintance and particularly of "one great occasion, when the scales balanced between McClellan's hostility and my influence in your favor, I won." The Blairs and Fox were disappointed when on 6 December Lincoln named Salmon P. Chase. "Lincoln," Fox told Virginia, "had intended giving Blair the Chief Justice place, but was forced to give it to Chase. L. said he would sooner have eaten flat irons than do it."[8]

Lincoln was reelected, but the Wilmington expedition remained stalled. Grant claimed he could not spare a man, "that it was as much as he could do to hold his lines." Porter grumbled to Fox on election day that Grant "had unnecessarily extended them without the least advantage to himself." But Porter told Fox:

> I got an idea from Butler the other day which I want to improve on. I want two hundred . . . tons of powder in one flat bottomed schooner (Wise will think I intend to ask for Niagara Falls soon). The cost will be one million seven hundred thousand dollars. . . . I propose running the schooner with the powder on to the beach near Fort Fisher & set fire to her, giving the tug which puts her there time to get four miles off. Every living thing within three miles will be killed—not a place containing a gun will be tenable—casemates will go down on the heads of those inside, guns will be capsized, houses will fall, and our own ships at ten miles distance will feel the shock. . . . Butler, (with whom by the way I have struck a great intimacy, & who seems to take kindly to me) says he has the powder in Fort Monroe, & will give it & the schooner.

Carried away, Porter predicted that "Charleston can be taken in a week in that way, & every fort demolished." His success in blowing up obstructions in the Tabasco River probably contributed to his enthusiasm.[9]

With Grant reluctant to commit troops for a conventional assault, Fox adopted the powder ship idea. On Saturday, following the election, he left Washington to consult with Grant and Porter. At Hampton Roads, he inspected the *Florida*, which Collins had just brought in, and found it "dirty." He also found a cat, which he named Jeff Davis and brought home "in a bag." He planned to keep Jeff Davis at the Navy Department in place of Kitty (whom he gave to Mary R. Simpson, when he left for Portsmouth), but Jeff "got away" during his first night in Washington. Meeting with Grant, Porter and Fox discussed plans for devastating Fort Fisher at the Swash Channel of the Cape Fear River, below Wilmington, with a mega-explosion of a vessel loaded with gunpowder. Together they convinced Grant that an enormous explosion would destroy Fisher or at least stun the garrison, permit the fleet to pass, and enable a modest number of troops to capture the fort.[10]

Fox was influenced, no doubt, by the August explosion at City Point, which destroyed a boat, wharf, and buildings. If eight tons of gunpowder could produce such havoc, could not the explosion of 200 or 300 tons severely damage the earthworks of Fort Fisher? Fox was willing to entertain novel ideas, ranging from the stone fleet to monitors with bigger and bigger guns. He was now willing to try "this grand torpedo." By the time of Fox and Porter's November meeting with Grant, Gillmore was out of the picture, and any troops Grant would allocate for an assault on Fisher would be under Godfrey Weitzel, with Butler as the overall commander. As the originator of the powder ship idea, Butler was enthusiastic about its potential.[11]

Fox forged ahead with plans for exploding 300 tons of powder on a vessel running aground in eight feet of water, 450 yards from Fisher. On 16 November he telegraphed Porter, "See if you have any shaky steamer that will carry 300 tons. It will save time. Otherwise I will get a blockade runner. We will go on with this. General Butler left this evening and will cooperate." Four days later, Porter ordered the *Louisiana* to Beaufort, North Carolina, to be stripped of everything but "boilers and machinery" and asked Fox to send the powder to Beaufort. The army and the navy were each to supply 150 tons, but before exploding that quantity of powder in a novel experiment, Fox sought the opinions of experts.[12]

Their advice should have stopped the experiment. The most perceptive and prophetic opinion was by Chief Army Engineer Richard Delafield, who predicted that the powder ship could not get closer than 950 yards, that the guns of Fisher would probably destroy it, and that, if exploded, it would produce "no useful result" on the fort. Major J. G. Benton, commandant of the Washington Arsenal, thought that 200 tons at 100 yards would be effective, but that there would be "great difficulty" in getting that close. At dinner with Wise on 19 November and at dinner the following evening at the Washington Navy Yard with ordnance officers Thomas Poynton Ives and William N. Jeffers and a dozen others, Fox discussed the objections and reservations of Delafield and Benton to the powder ship idea. After observing that the lateral effect of explosions "is very limited," Jeffers stated on 23 November that no serious damage would be produced beyond 500 yards by exploding 300 tons of powder.[13]

Undeterred, Fox convened a meeting of army and navy ordnance bureau officers that evening at the home of Henry A. Wise. With Fox optimistically explaining that "if the explosion will deprive the people in the forts of all power to resist for a period of two or three hours," the fleet could pass into the Cape Fear River and the forts—as at Mobile Bay—would be reduced or occupied. Hope, imagination, and enthusiasm prevailed over the known effects of previous accidental explosions and in the absence of any controlled experiments. The group conjectured that a blast even as far away as 800 yards would uncover Fisher's bombproofs and physically injure and demoralize its garrison. If the powder ship was exploded as it ran aground, the earthworks would be injured. Its guns would be unserviceable long enough for the fleet to pass and for the works to be carried by an immediate assault. Given the overwhelming desire to shut down Wilmington compared with the outlay of 300 tons of powder and a "shaky steamer," the meeting "unanimously decided" to explode a powder ship as soon, and as close to Fisher, as possible.[14]

But Grant was reluctant to commit troops to capture Fort Fisher. "I cannot believe," Fox wrote Lincoln, "that we ought to abandon the attack on Cape Fear defenses after the vast preparations of the navy and the solemn promises of the army." If a substantial force were not forthcoming for a mere fortnight or so, Fox warned Lincoln, "our fleet once dispersed . . . can never be brought together in such force as the present."[15]

Thanksgiving Day was 24 November, and Fox took time out for dinner. He had "sent to Phila[delphia] for the largest turkey to be found," and he and Virginia had as guests his friends John Hay and Henry A. Wise, "the hero" William B. Cushing, and General Nathaniel P. Banks, to whom Fox was indebted for saving Porter's fleet on the Red River. After Thanksgiving, Fox met Butler on Porter's flagship at Hampton Roads, on Sunday, 27 November, "to finally arrange matters." While there, he inspected the recently commissioned, large, double-turreted *Monadnock*, which with its four fifteen-inch Dahlgren guns was the most formidable and reputably the best-built monitor to see service in the Civil War. Given Fox's intimate association with the monitor program, his visit was not perfunctory. He relayed his criticisms to Chief Engineer William W. W. Wood. The turrets could function better, the boilers should be moved aft to improve its trim, and its awkwardly stored boats prevented its guns from being fired in all directions.[16]

After returning to Washington, Fox was uncertain about Grant's plans. On Friday, 2 December, Grant told Porter he could spare only 5,000 men (instead of the 12,000 he had recently spoken of) and that he depended on the powder ship *Louisiana* for success. Because it was not ready, Porter urged Fox to order the Norfolk Navy Yard "to work on her night and day." By 4 December the *Louisiana* was ready for its cargo of powder. Butler and the army had its 150 tons on hand, and Fox assured Porter that "Wise promises everything quickly."[17]

Wise and his Ordnance Bureau did not come through. Although the navy had 150 tons of good powder on hand, Wise decided to use "second-class" powder, stored at the Portsmouth and New York Navy Yards. The vessel his bureau chartered to procure it was misdirected to Provincetown, Massachusetts, and took two weeks to get to Norfolk, arriving too late to be of use. Butler and Grant wanted the expedition to start without the powder ship. "The greater part" of Fisher's garrison had been sent to Georgia to oppose Sherman (who occupied Savannah on 22 December), and Butler was positioned off Fisher to land his troops, under the command of Godfrey Weitzel, on 15 December in beautiful weather. Porter delayed. Because Fisher's guns were formidable and Butler's troops were neither numerous nor impressive, he thought the powder ship necessary. With "only a vague idea of what they are going to do," Porter feared that Butler and Weitzel were "depending on the explosion to do *all* the work."[18]

The powder ship proved a fizzle boat. Although Porter assumed the *Louisiana* would hold 300 tons of powder and not draw over eight feet of water, it was overloaded with 215 tons. Stormy weather prevented its explosion on 18 December and forced Butler's transports to seek shelter at Beaufort, North Carolina. On 22 December Porter wrote Fox again disparaging Butler, despite being on good terms with him. He expressed great faith in the powder ship, which he affectionately called the *Pet*, and declared it was "as buoyant as a cork." It was the "timidity of some of the Commanders in getting the ships close to each other" that he feared. On further reflection, he added, "I think we will take it if nothing happens to our powder vessel, for she will destroy all their magazines without doubt, and with that idea in my head I wish you good night."[19]

On the next night of 23 to 24 December, the *Pet* was finally exploded, but miscalculations by Porter minimized its effect. Rather than run the ship aground, Porter had it anchored "a little way out," but it dragged its anchor to about 1,100 yards from the fort. Worse, Porter had no faith in the electric wires, clocks, and slow matches carefully calculated by Jeffers and Major Thomas Jackson Rodman (developer of the Rodman gun) to secure a simultaneous explosion of all the powder. So Porter ordered the *Louisiana* set on fire. Porter's blaze ruined the work of Jeffers and Rodman and set off a series of harmless explosions that barely disturbed Fort Fisher.[20]

On 24 December and on Christmas morning, without Butler's army on hand, Porter bombarded Fisher. He expended approximately 21,000 projectiles, but did little harm, failing to concentrate on a specific objective. When the fort ceased firing to conserve ammunition, Porter assumed he had silenced it and that the army could move in. After Butler and Weitzel got about 2,500 men ashore on the afternoon of Christmas Day, they discovered that the fort was unharmed. It was also well defended, and with Confederate reinforcements from Richmond threatening to trap their small force, they withdrew.[21]

The expedition against Fort Fisher was a failure. When Lincoln asked what happened, Grant responded that loose talk about it coupled with the squandering of three days of fine weather enabled the alerted Confederates to heavily reinforce what had been a weak garrison. In truth, the navy, and, to a lesser extent, Grant were responsible for what Grant called the "gross and culpable failure." The navy had made the powder ship its own, but its Ordnance Bureau delayed the ship's departure, and Porter rendered it harmless and failed to coordinate both its explosion and his subsequent bombardment with the inadequate army Grant provided.[22]

Porter once again nimbly shifted blame. Having made Banks the goat of the Red River campaign, he now made Butler the goat of the first attempt to capture Fort Fisher. "The coveted prize," he told Fox, "slipped through our fingers owing to cowardice in the army." Porter's official reports to Welles from 26 to 29 December became more and more shrill, as he condemned Butler for not strolling into Fisher and taking possession. He even claimed that three soldiers had entered the fort, killed some Rebels, and came away with a horse and a mule. "Well, sir," he insisted, "it could have been taken on Christmas with 500 men, without losing a soldier; there were not 20 men in the forts, and those were poor, miserable, panic-stricken people, cowering there with fear, while one or two desperate men . . . managed to fire one gun, that seldom hit anyone." Realizing that Porter's word was not to be trusted, Fox asked for "positive testimony as to any soldier entering Fort Fisher." While condemning Butler for not taking the fort with 2,500 men, Porter in a sense absolved him by stating, if General Winfield Scott "Hancock, with 10,000 men, was sent down here, we could walk right into the fort."[23]

Failure at Fisher galled Fox, but Butler was a convenient scapegoat, even though he was Fox's school friend. On 29 December Lieutenant Samuel W. Preston (who was on the powder ship) brought the Navy Department Porter's milder initial report. While visiting the Foxes with Porter's wife George Ann, Preston was "very severe on Butler," whom he thought "could have taken the Fort." Within a few days, naval circles were rife with bad puns at Butler's expense. Ruth Loring, the wife of Chief Engineer Charles H. Loring, presented Virginia Fox with "two slices of Boston cake" (cream pie), observing that "their bakers were better than their Butlers." Not to be outdone, Virginia responded that Butler's "fort is not to take forts even when fortified by 'Uncle Sam's best Porter.'"[24]

On 3 January Fox assured Porter that neither "the valor or skill of the navy, [n]or your own reputation has suffered" and that "neither Stanton nor Grant sustain" Butler. Fox, however, told Porter that around 18 December, before the gale came, "you lost two days of fine weather when the army was with you" and advised him to get a plausible excuse for his delay on the record. Grant's trusted aide, Lieutenant Colonel Cyrus B. Comstock, was with Butler and reported that three precious days of good weather were lost before the navy appeared and before Fisher was reinforced. Nevertheless, Fox was glad that he had brought Porter East. "How mistaken [S. P.] Lee was when he wrote that those big frigates would be of no use in such an attack! I knew from the experience at Hatteras that he was wrong."[25]

Aware that the powder ship had been a debacle, Fox conveniently forgot it. "You will perceive," he wrote Quincy Adams Gillmore, "that the Wilmington expedition has failed and become a ridiculous page in history certainly not from want of proper preparation on the part of the Navy Department, or just appreciation of the difficulties of the enterprise." Fox wished that Grant had adopted Gillmore's early plans and that the big bang had never been attempted. Fox boasted, "The naval part of the expedition was the most complete and upon the largest scale that ever was put into operation by our country, and it did precisely what I promised you could be done by ships, when we talked over the matter upon our visit to Grant. Had the military cooperation been given as you proposed we should now be in possession of Federal Point." Echoing Porter, Fox described the scene at Fort Fisher on Federal Point. "Imagine the fire of the fleet—not a sailor killed by the enemy, who were driven from their guns! Imagine the violence of the army skirmish in front of the works— twelve men wounded, ten by the shells of the fleet, owing to the daring of the skirmishing line, and this is called war!"[26]

Not wanting to give up on Wilmington, Fox and Welles moved to secure a more formidable military force from Grant and enlisted Lincoln in their cause. Welles telegraphed Grant in cipher, "at the suggestion of the President," that he provide sufficient troops to ensure the fall of Fort Fisher. The navy would cooperate in the same manner it did in capturing Fort Wagner off Charleston. If Grant could not supply an adequate army, then Porter's very large fleet will have to be dispersed. Fox telegraphed Grant on 29 December, emphasizing the need for a formidable, combined operation. "Porter will continue his fire" to harass efforts to strengthen Fisher, but its unilateral capture by his huge fleet was impossible. "It is," Fox concluded, "hopeless alone."[27]

Having a month earlier cooperated reluctantly and ineffectively, Grant responded with alacrity and care. By the next day, 30 December, he decided to send the same 4,000 troops reinforced by a brigade of 1,000, all under the command of Alfred H. Terry, an able volunteer officer. Terry had participated in the bombardment, siege, and capture of both Fort Pulaski, off Savannah, and Fort Wagner, off Charleston, and was serving in Butler's Army of the James. One reason for Grant's change in attitude was that Lincoln had made it clear he wanted to end blockade running into Wilmington. The other reason was that the military situation had changed. Sherman had completed his march across Georgia and occupied Savannah on 21 December. Initially, as Dahlgren reported to Fox from near Savannah on Christmas Day, "the plan was to embark Sherman" and transport his army north. Sherman did not like that idea. He was convinced his army could march anywhere and would be healthier on the move than on transports. Because the naval force was not sufficient to transport Sherman, Grant allowed him to carry out his original plan, which was a march through the Carolinas to Richmond, where he would link up with Grant.[28]

Possession of Wilmington was imperative as a supply depot for Sherman. Should Terry need reinforcements, Grant ordered to Baltimore a division from Philip Sheridan's Army of the Shenandoah. If that division proved inadequate, the Twenty-third Corps was told on 9 January to move from Nashville to Baltimore. Grant's instructions to Terry emphasized the need for cooperation and coordination with Porter's fleet. Grant wanted Terry to "consult with Admiral Porter freely," to secure "unity of action," and to promote understanding and prevent future recriminations if the renewed expedition failed. He shrewdly noted, "It would be well to have the whole programme laid in writing." While aware that Porter was adept at shifting blame, Grant added, "I have served with Admiral Porter, and know that you can rely on his judgment and his nerve to undertake what he proposes." Grant suggested that Terry "defer to him as much as is consistent with your own responsibilities."[29]

Porter was not pleased and gave Fox a full measure of his discontent. He hoped for victory, "though the man Grant is going to send here, a volunteer general, is one of Butler's men, who will likely whitewash Butler by doing just as he did. Dont be surprised if I send him home with a flea in his ear, . . . if he comes here with any of his 'ifs and buts,' and stops to consider as to taking the forts. It is the easiest work I ever undertook." Still fearing that "Butler is too cunning for Grant, and will make him do what he pleases," Porter longed for

Sherman, who if present would "make Butler's fur fly." Porter had faith in neither Grant nor black soldiers. He believed only in "my own good officers and men. I can do anything with them, and you need not be surprised to hear that the web footers have gone into the forts. I will try it anyhow, and show the soldiers how to do it." Working himself into a frenzy, Porter itched for another fight. "It is strange, but true, that the desire to kill and destroy grows on a man, the oftener he hears shot whistle." With his huge fleet, Porter bragged, "I could whip the largest fleet John Bull could send out."[30]

Realizing that the attack on Fisher would be renewed with a greater chance of success made Fox feel better. He was able to take kidding from Secretary of State William H. Seward, who "was in splendid spirits" at his New Year's reception, on Monday, 2 January 1865. When Virginia, escorted by Fox and Wise, entered, "He greeted Gus before the room full 'Ah here is the man that did not take Wilmington.'"[31]

Fox could not let on why Seward's jibe did not bother him. Both Grant and the Navy Department were trying to keep the new attack a secret, while Porter spread the report that the troops were to cooperate with Sherman for an attack on Charleston. Communications relating to the attack on Fisher were either in cipher or by messenger. Terry sailed under sealed orders, learning his destination when at sea. Grant suspected that Fox or Gillmore had loosely talked the preceding summer about plans to capture Fisher. Fox defensively wrote Grant on 4 January 1865 that he "trusted to time to enable you to discover all the leaks in the vicinity of your headquarters." To stop further leaks, he told Grant, "I got the President to put" Bradley Sillick Osbon into the Old Capitol Prison. His syndicate sent Porter's "whole plan" to fifteen to twenty newspapers on 27 October on the questionable assumption that the information would not be used until after Fisher was attacked. On 19 December the *Boston Daily Advertiser* and the *Philadelphia Press* published the plans, and on 22 December, two days prior to the attack on Fisher, Porter's "whole plan, copied from our papers, was published in Richmond." Noting Osbon's fate, some members of the press behaved responsibly. Alexander Fulton, publisher of the *Baltimore American*, told Fox he had "information that another expedition was fitting out," and Lawrence A. Gobright, of the Associated Press, informed Fox "that he had such news from Hampton Roads, but had suppressed it." Having just spoken with Lincoln about leaks, Fox warned Fulton "that if any more movements relative to operations in the future are published, summary proceedings in vindication of right and justice shall instantly issue."[32]

While Fox worked to stop leaks to the press, he also cultivated editors to secure articles friendly to the navy and wrote "press releases" for them. Virginia Fox noted on 6 February 1865 that Gus wrote "various articles on Navy matters in the papers—he writes considerably." Among his correspondents were the Fultons of the *Baltimore American*, Horace White of the *Chicago Tribune*, John Russell Young of the *Philadelphia Press*, and William H. Russell of the *London Army and Navy Gazette*. While admirals and generals were often hostile to the press, Fox realized that it shaped the public opinion, which determined how much congressional support the navy would get.[33]

Anxious for victory, Fox was delighted with Grant's wholehearted cooperation and worked to facilitate the combined operation. When Grant needed small boats for landing troops on an ocean beach, Fox strove to get them. Because they were scarce, he telegraphed all navy yards for them and suggested to Grant that the quartermaster at New York "go into the market and purchase all he can find." Indeed the capture of Fisher was imperative for Fox. "The country," he wrote Grant, "will not forgive us another failure at Wilmington, and I have so informed Porter." Victory was, of course, always the paramount consideration, but a second failure at Fisher would confirm the wisdom of Butler and Weitzel and shift blame for the first failure from them to Porter and the navy. Fox knew that a contrast between Porter's bombastic claims and evidence of an ineffectual bombardment would be devastating. Fisher's fall, however, would enhance the navy's reputation and hasten the end of the Confederacy. Realizing victory depended on the army as much as on the navy, Fox telegraphed Grant on 5 January, "Can you not possibly go down the coast for a few days? I think we have fine sea steamer at Norfolk, and I will accompany you. It seems to be worth a few hours of the directing mind."[34]

While doing his best to make the second attempt on Fort Fisher successful, Fox was also writing Grant about a delicate mission. Francis Preston Blair, with Lincoln's blessing, hoped to speak with Jefferson Davis and bring about a quick end to the war. Fox was supposed to accompany both Blair and his son Montgomery to see Grant at Fortress Monroe on 30 December. Fox, however, did not go. He was anxiously awaiting dispatches from Porter about the first attack on Fort Fisher. When Grant heard Fox was not coming, he headed back to his headquarters at City Point. "Poor Blairs," Virginia Fox commented, "will have to follow him there." Francis Preston Blair had written Davis on 30 December that, while his proposed visit to Richmond was unofficial, he wanted "to explain the views I entertain in reference to the state of the affairs of our Country." Buoyed by the Union failure at Fisher, Davis did not respond, and the Blairs returned to Washington. Montgomery reported to the Foxes that "the Rebs there are very cross—not whipped enough yet."[35]

Soon thereafter, however, Jefferson Davis decided to talk with Francis Preston Blair. On 12 January 1865 Blair visited Richmond and carried a letter back from Davis to Lincoln. Davis wished to open negotiations between "two countries," but Lincoln's response stressed his willingness to secure "peace to the people of our one common country." Before traveling to Boston for the funeral of his lifelong friend and benefactor, Virginia's Uncle Barnes, Fox made the preliminary arrangements for Blair's return to Richmond with Lincoln's response. When Fox, who was gone from 8 to 12 January, got back to Washington, Blair was in Richmond. Varina Davis, Virginia Fox reported, "threw her arms around Mr. Blair & kissed him & wept. The same on parting. He is as mum as the Sphinx about the object of his visit." Apparently, Blair hoped Davis would be enticed to renounce secession for a joint effort to rid Mexico of Louis Napoleon's troops, but Davis was not ready to acknowledge that the North and South were "one common country." In a letter to her dear friend Minna Blair, Varina Davis wrote, "We will both pray for our own peace, and God will have his own."[36]

The second attack on Fort Fisher was more formidable and better coordinated than the first attempt. Porter's armada of fifty-nine vessels carrying 627 guns (the most powerful fleet the world had seen) bombarded Fisher from 13 to 15 January with at least 19,682 projectiles weighing 1,652,638 pounds. Having learned from its first attack on Fisher, the Navy Department provided ample coal and ammunition to sustain Porter's steady bombardment. Warned by Fox that he must succeed and not wanting to be exposed as a braggadocio, Porter handled his fleet brilliantly. He planned for every contingency, communicated and cooperated effectively with General Terry, skillfully deployed his vessels, and handled his guns flawlessly. He replaced his fleet's rifled Parrott guns (which had tended to burst in the first attack) with nine-inch smoothbores. After concentrating fire before the assault on the land face, during the assault he fired with accuracy and great effect on concentrations of the 1,900-man Confederate garrison.[37]

Having boasted that sailors would "show the soldiers how to do it," Porter participated in the assault. Terry landed his troops above Fisher, between it and Wilmington. Because he had to protect his rear, he had only 3,300 men for an assault. For the attack on the fort, Porter volunteered a brigade of 1,600 sailors and 400 marines from his fleet. The naval brigade struck first on the ocean side of the fort. Encountering a murderous fire from the defendants (who emerged from their bombproofs), the naval brigade was repulsed with heavy casualties, including the death of extremely able Lieutenant Samuel W. Preston. Porter blamed the attack's failure on "the infernal marines who were running away when the sailors were mounting the parapets."[38]

The disastrous naval assault distracted the Confederates. Attacking on the river side of Fisher, the army gained a foothold within the fort, but was soon pinned down and in danger of being repulsed or captured. At that point, Porter ordered the *New Ironsides* and the gunboats to fire on the Confederate defenders. The accuracy of this naval bombardment turned the tide of the battle. Porter won a great victory. Welles was overjoyed and Fox, who was primarily responsible for assembling and supplying the fleet, was gratified. "I congratulate you," Admiral Gregory wrote Fox, "upon this great event, and consider much of the honor, reflects upon yourself."[39]

The fall of Fort Fisher isolated the Confederacy completely. Blockade runners no longer had an available port of entry. Fearing a Confederate counter-offensive, Porter complained of Grant's "indifference." He called Terry "the most inefficient man in the country," lamented that he had less than 6,000 men and that "a number of them are negroes," and begged Fox to have Lincoln prod Grant into sending 13,000 men to the Cape Fear River. Porter was mistaken about Grant's indifference to Wilmington. Grant was confronting a serious problem on the James River that threatened his City Point base.[40]

Eight days after the loss of Fort Fisher, the Confederate James River Squadron took the opportunity to move down river on 23 to 24 January. Union naval forces on the James, protecting Grant's base at City Point, had been depleted to beef up Porter's fleet. If the formidable Confederate squadron (three heavy ironclads—the *Richmond*, the *Virginia No. 2*, and the *Fredericksburg*—plus eight other vessels) could gain control briefly of the James, it could destroy Grant's stores at City Point and hamper his siege of Petersburg. To Grant's dismay, William A. Parker, commander of the Union's James River Squadron, which consisted of the double-turreted *Onondaga* and ten gunboats, did not confront the Confederates at Trent's Reach. He moved down stream, still above City Point, where his vessels had more room to maneuver. Believing that the Union's obstructions at Trent's Reach were in "bad" condition, Parker feared that his force could not prevent the Confederate squadron from coming down at high water. Grant worried that if the Confederate vessels got past the obstructions, he would get "little assistance . . . from the navy under Captain Parker," who "seems helpless." In Welles's name, Grant ordered the gunboats back upstream and telegraphed Fox, and then Welles, for help.[41]

Fox and Welles responded immediately, as did Lincoln, who had gotten wind of Grant's concern. "The president just sent for me," Fox telegraphed Grant, "and suggested that Admiral Farragut should go down to James River, and leaves for Annapolis in an hour." Fox assured Lincoln that the "fight would be over before he could get there & it would amount to nothing." Fox

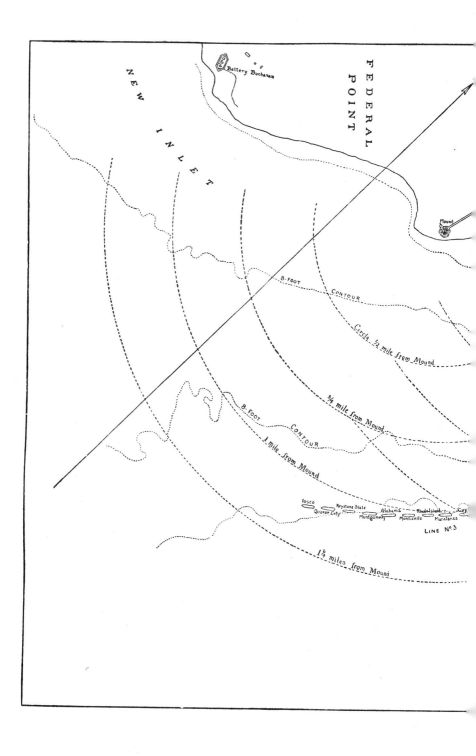

F E D E R A L
P O I N T

N E W   I N L E T

Battery Buchanan

Mound

8-FOOT CONTOUR

Circle ½ mile from Mound

¾ mile from Mound

8-FOOT CONTOUR

1 mile from Mound

Iosco
Quaker City
Keystone State
Montgomery
Alabama
Monticello
Rhode Island
Maratanxa
Guy

LINE Nº 3

1¼ miles from Mound

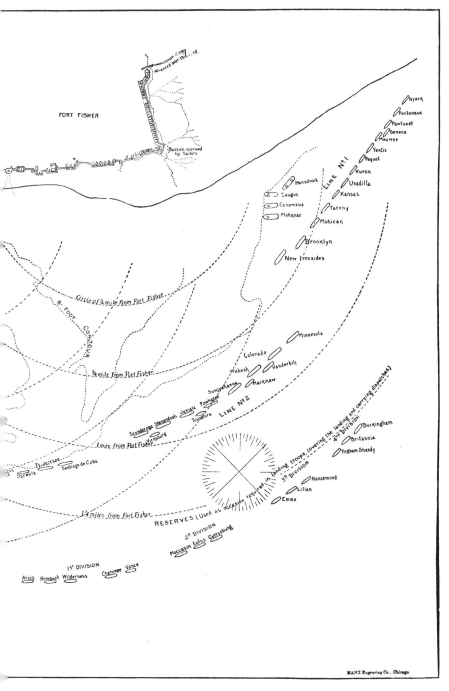

FORT FISHER

I advanced over this line

Bastion stormed by Sailors

Circle of ½ mile from Fort Fisher

8. FOOT CONTOUR

½ mile from Fort Fisher

1 mile from Fort Fisher

1½ miles from Fort Fisher

LINE No. 1

Nyack
Pontoosuc
Pawtuxet
Seneca
Maumee
Yantic
Pequot
Huron
Unadilla
Kansas
Tacony
Mohican
Brooklyn
New Ironsides

Monadnock
Saugus
Canonicus
Mahopac

Minnesota
Colorado
Wabash
Vanderbilt
Mackinaw
Susquehanna
Powhatan
Juniata
Tuscarora
Ticonderoga Shenandoah
Vicksburg
LINE No. 2

4TH DIVISION
required in landing troops, covering the landing and carrying dispatches
Buckingham
Britannia
Tristram Shandy

3D DIVISION
Nansemond
Lilian
Emma

RESERVES (Used as occasion

2D DIVISION
Moccasin Eolus Gettysburg

1ST DIVISION
Aries Howquah Wilderness Cherokee Vance

Santiago de Cuba
T. Jackson
Osceola

MANZ Engraving Co., Chicago

Plan of second attack on Fort Fisher, 13–15 January 1865. From *Official Records of the Union and Confederate Navies*, 11:425.

had already, with Welles's approval, decided to remove Parker and replace him with William Radford, the captain of the *New Ironsides*. Fox assured Grant that the *Ironsides* with its draft of sixteen feet could reach City Point and protect Grant's base. Because the *Ironsides* could go up the James River only a little further, to Bermuda Hundred, Radford asked Fox for an additional monitor to support the *Onondaga, Saugus*, and the captured ironclad *Atlanta* further upstream. He thought the monitors with their fifteen-inch guns were the "best obstructions" and observed, "We could not hold this River, nor could Grant's Army stay here without them."[42]

The anticipated Confederate attack on City Point failed to materialize. As Parker suggested, the obstructions at Trent's Reach were not effective. The *Fredericksburg* got through at about 1:00 a.m. on 24 January, but the other two heavy Confederate ironclads ran aground before reaching the obstructions, as did a gunboat and a torpedo boat, and were stranded by the ebb tide. To protect them, the *Fredericksburg* returned through the obstructions. With daylight, fire from Union army batteries blew up the gunboat, compelled the abandonment of the torpedo boat, and turned back the rest of the Confederate squadron. The *Onondaga*, which with its powerful fifteen-inch guns could have destroyed the Confederate ironclads, was not on hand at dawn. It arrived at about 10:30 a.m., just as the flood tide was beginning to float the grounded ironclads. Before they moved upstream, the *Onondaga*'s fire severely damaged the *Virginia*, but did not hurt the *Richmond*. The damage to the *Virginia* and obstructions at Trent's Reach dissuaded the Confederates from a subsequent attack. "The rebel fleet ran up the river last night," Grant telegraphed Fox on 25 January, "thus showing present danger to be at an end." Delayed all night on his special train to Annapolis, Farragut reported, on 26 January, that Radford had "ample force" and that "all appears to be right."[43]

By the end of January 1865, Jefferson Davis wanted to negotiate an end to the war, but he had run out of bargaining chips. Sherman was moving into South Carolina; Fort Fisher fell on 15 January; and the dash downriver on 23 to 24 January by the powerful Confederate James River Squadron failed, when its most formidable ironclads ran aground. Although Francis Preston Blair had told Davis that Lincoln insisted on "one common country," Davis appointed peace commissioners, who met with Lincoln and Seward at Hampton Roads on 3 February. Neither the Confederate commissioners, who still wanted to negotiate between "two countries," nor Lincoln, who insisted on "one common country," budged.[44]

No longer worried about City Point, Grant wanted Fox to accompany him to the Cape Fear River. They would confer with Porter about establishing a supply route up the river for Sherman's army. "I should particularly like you to go with me," Grant urged Fox, who had been uncertain he could get away. On 27 January they left on the *Rhode Island* for North Carolina. Grant ordered John M. Schofield's Twenty-third Army Corps to the area. Those troops and the navy's capacity to move men, equipment, and supplies upriver and to bombard fortifications led to the capture of Wilmington, North Carolina, on 22 February and Fayetteville, North Carolina, on 11 March. Fayetteville was the head of navigation and the site of the last Confederate arsenal outside Richmond. Porter complained to Fox that the navy did not get its share of credit and that those points would have been captured earlier "had Grant sent Terry men and kept Schofield away." The movement up the Cape Fear River posed yet another threat to Lee's Army of Northern Virginia.[45]

While accompanying Grant to North Carolina, Fox regretted that he could not spend more time with General John Gross Barnard. He was the nation's leading expert on fortifications, and he was with Fox and Grant on the *Rhode Island*. Before the war, Barnard had supervised the defenses of major ports, including New York, Mobile, and San Francisco. During the war, he served on the Blockade Board and designed the elaborate defenses of Washington. "As Chief Engineer of the Army of the Potomac," Fox later noted, "he was the medium through which we consulted with the military department and organized joint operations. More than any other officer of the army with whom I was brought into contact, he understood and appreciated naval cooperation." After the fall of Fort Fisher, Barnard studied its strengths and weaknesses.[46]

Although European powers did not intervene to save the Confederacy, the threat was real. Fox never ruled out the possibility of a foreign war. The French had been in Mexico since 1862, British-built and British-manned commerce destroyers had decimated American shipping, and Americans were itching to annex Canada. Fox was well aware of British and French naval power and the vulnerability of American seaports. "Where is our defence," he asked Barnard, "against naval operations flung upon our coast by a maritime power ready at all times for combat?" Fox had faith in monitors and their fifteen-inch guns, but his faith was neither blind nor complete. He also realized that "our northern ports have deeper water than the southern, and admit the attacks of a more formidable naval force." In addition, Farragut had demonstrated on several occasions that forts could not prevent the passage of vessels across their line of fire.

Probably thinking of Charleston, Fox believed that harbor obstructions offered the best defense. As he mentioned to Barnard, "The rebels have exhibited wonderful talents and energy in the defenses of their harbors." Because obstructions involved military engineering as well as naval science, Fox, in February 1865, placed his idea on paper. He suggested that timbers with torpedoes affixed be attached to small iron boats (the size of large bell buoys) moored "in the Channel in a quincunx form" (four at the points of a rectangle and a fifth in the middle). As many rectangles as necessary could be created. As the occasion demanded, the boats could be moved from their moorings to clear the channel or could be chained together "to form one immense raft." With the war coming to a successful conclusion, he sensed that the mood of the people was one of "indifference and confidence—the fatal results of victory." Fox was right. His admittedly crude idea of a huge torpedo studded raft never floated.[47]

The aborted Confederate attack on the James River was the last serious problem Fox and the Navy Department faced. Once again, it illustrated Fox's pivotal role. Both Lincoln and Grant turned to him when they wanted a quick response, and Grant asked Fox to help plan the move up the Cape Fear River to supply Sherman. Primarily concerned with ships and those who manned them, Fox always acted with the knowledge and approval of Welles. Working together, Welles and Fox made few errors in achieving victory over an enemy that initially controlled thousands of miles of coast and rivers. Admiral Francis Gregory, who supervised the construction of vessels outside navy yards, had ample opportunity to observe that their collaboration was fruitful. He congratulated Welles on the success of the navy and told Fox he trusted "that the future, will insure to you, the *full reward*, for having pulled *your oar*, faithfully and manfully in the great struggle."[48]

After the victory was won, Porter wrote Fox:

> I am not in the habit of complimenting people but dont mind telling you what you already know. We are indebted to you more than any other man for our Naval Success, for tho Mr. Welles is as good as gold, and is in my opinion as able a head (politically and financially) as the Navy ever had, yet he could not be expected to have that professional knowledge which would enable him to act independently of the old officers, who I regret to say were found to be all adrift when their opinions were asked.

Contemplating Fox's departure from the department, Porter added: "You will leave the recollection of a good honest administration which you may always be proud of, and will have your loss regretted by your friends, it is no matter what the contractors or Navy agents say about you."[49]

Although he had been tempted to leave, Fox remained at his post until the end of the war. "I had to let my offer at the Mills go by on account of my duties here," he told Grimes, "and the place was filled. I should not have been happy to have left my duties here for any temptation though I felt like yielding to passion when Congress deliberately reduced my pay." Fox, however, would have been delighted to have been named minister to Switzerland, and he was disgusted when his bribe-taking antagonist, John P. Hale, was named minister to Spain. Fox did feel he deserved a reward. Not given to boasting, Fox, on writing to his friend Grimes, yielded briefly to that temptation.

> The naval blows del[ivere]d upon the Southern coast have not been matters of chance but were arranged deliberately. . . . I doubt whether the author of them, who has less pay than a Col. in Washington could get the mission to Berne. Had he been into a few cotton peculations it might have been given him. However I had rather have the good opinion of Mrs. Grimes than a vote of thanks from a Senate that could tolerate such rascals as Hale."

That rascal had lowered Fox's salary to $3,500, by pegging the pay of all assistant secretaries at that figure, which for the others was a raise. Cutting his pay was bad enough, but Hale, prior to leaving the Senate, also ridiculed Fox's 1861 attempt to provision Sumter and secured a resolution on 5 February 1865 seeking information on that relief expedition.[50]

At a time when Fox and Welles had good reason to feel triumphant, Congressman Henry Winter Davis of Maryland tried to undermine their control of naval affairs. In early February 1865 he moved an amendment to the Naval Appropriations bill, setting up a board of admiralty to administer naval affairs. Welles, and possibly Fox, could see some merit in the idea, which in 1915 emerged as the Office of the Chief of Naval operations, but its sponsor made it an attack on Fox, Welles, and Lincoln's conduct of the war. It was obvious to all that Davis's aim was to weaken Fox, who was de facto chief of naval operations, rather than to build departmental efficiency. Attacking Fox doubly gratified Davis. Montgomery Blair was his rival in Maryland politics, and Davis was a close friend of Admiral Samuel F. Du Pont, who blamed Fox for the failure of his attack on Sumter. Friends of the administration, led by Alexander H. Rice, the chair of the House Naval Committee, defeated the attempt. "Thus," Virginia Fox rejoiced, "Gus & the Dept. triumph over their enemies." Although the Davis amendment was defeated in the House, Davis's ally Benjamin F. Wade introduced it in the Senate, where it suffered the same fate.[51]

Over the previous four years, Fox had trod on many toes and made some mistakes. It is possible that a board of admirals would have avoided those errors. But it is probable that such a board would have respected seniority, been

steeped in tradition, and would not have nurtured innovations, like the monitors. Many senior naval officers chafed under Fox's authority and would have
preferred dealing with a board of admiralty. Welles observed that "Farragut,
like many of the officers is dissatisfied with Mr. Fox" and wanted an admiralty
board. When he served in the navy, Fox had been junior to every officer who
would ultimately command a squadron in the Civil War. As Welles's trusted
adviser on naval matters, he, in effect, had been jumped to the top of the naval
list. Among the disappointed, he was known as "Mr. Fox the maker and
unmaker of Admirals." On the other hand, he had many warm friendships
among his peers from his years in the service, and he retained their high
regard. Men like Porter and Thornton A. Jenkins applauded the shaking up of
the seniority system by Fox and Welles, as did young officers, like Lieutenant
Commander James E. Jouett. "We young officers look to you for positions to
make a name," he told Fox, "you are to be our friend & advocate."[52]

Welles, who could be critical of his assistant, thought there was some truth
in Farragut's remark that Fox "assumes too much and presumes too much."
Welles observed that Fox wanted naval officers to think him "all powerful"
and was "rough" in his "manner and language." Fox's subordinate, Chief
Clerk William Faxon, complained, "I am constantly annoyed by him." In turn,
Welles thought that Fox signed his own name on important orders to give the
"impression that he was at least a coadjutor with the Secretary, in naval operations." It also bothered Welles that Fox shunned "a fair and honest responsibility for his own errors," especially in the light-draft-monitor program. What
Welles and Farragut regarded as assumption and presumption in Fox, Charles
Baldwin Sedgewick saw as positive characteristics. As chair of the House Naval
Affairs Committee until March 1863 and from 1863 to 1865 codifier of naval
laws for the Navy Department, Sedgewick observed that Fox, with his knowledge, "force & industry" was the "motive power of that Department."[53]

Welles, having cataloged what he and others perceived as Fox's shortcomings, dismissed some as minor and excused others as "human nature."
Indeed, Welles should not have complained about Fox signing his own name
to orders because it rarely happened. There are few Fox-signed orders in the
published *Official Records of the Navy*. Furthermore, Fox was more than an
aide to Welles in planning naval operations. He actually wrote or originated a
vast number of important as well as routine orders that Welles signed. For
example, in August 1865, after consulting with John Rodgers of the *Dictator*,
Enoch G. Parrott of the *Monadnock*, Admiral Gregory, and John Ericsson, Fox,
who was in Portsmouth, thought the *Monadnock* should go to the Pacific. "I
suppose," he wrote Welles, "an order better be given . . . to have her entirely

ready for a voyage to the Pacific say by the 20th of Sept. I shall see Rodgers today or tomorrow and will write you in regard to the further necessary orders for himself and Parrot."[54]

Usually, Welles rose above pettiness. Fox, he observed, "is familiar with the service and has his heart in its success." He called him "very serviceable and, to me, considerate, deferring and acquiescing in my decision when fixed, readily and more cheerfully than most others." Welles shrewdly recognized that Fox's "position is a hard one to fill. The second person in any organization, especially if he is true and faithful to his principal incurs the censure and ill-will of the multitude." Would a board of admiralty be an improvement over Fox? On reflection, Welles thought not. There would "be jealousies in the service of such a board, as there are of the Assistant Secretary."[55]

Charleston, which for many symbolized the rebellion, was a point where Fox for a time let emotion cloud his judgment. He was not alone in wanting revenge on that city, but as leader of the expedition whose attempt to provision Fort Sumter touched off the Civil War, he wanted, more than anyone else, for the navy to capture and humiliate Charleston. Sumter proved an expensive and galling symbol for Fox and the Union navy. Charleston, "that den of infamy," was finally evacuated by the Confederates on 17 to 18 February 1865, and Sumter fell not because of the navy but because of Sherman's advance into South Carolina. Fox, who had realized since 1863 that joint operations were necessary to subdue the Confederacy, rejoiced in the army's success and admired generals Grant and Sherman. He was even able to refer playfully to the taking of Charleston by Sherman. "I admire exceedingly," Sherman wrote Fox, "the pleasant wit and style of your allusion to Charleston, and assure you the older I grow the more pleasure I experience at the cordial good feeling that exists between the old Navy & Army."[56]

In the end, Fox was gratified. Charleston was humbled, and he was on hand to witness its humiliation. A flag-raising ceremony at Sumter was planned for 14 April 1865, four years exactly after Fox had evacuated Major Robert Anderson and his command. Fox coordinated attendance at that celebration with a well-earned vacation in the guise of an "inspection trip." On 28 March he and Virginia, accompanied among others by her sister Ellen Woodbury, Gideon Welles's son Edgar, Lincoln's private secretary John G. Nicolay, Charles C. Fulton of the *Baltimore American* (a reward for his support of the Navy Department), and John Murray Forbes and his daughter Alice, boarded the fast side-wheel steamer *Santiago de Cuba*. Forbes had ample reason to be included on the trip. He was a China trade veteran, a railroad builder, an unofficial agent for the Navy Department, and an abolitionist, who helped finance an experimental free-labor plantation at Port Royal, South Carolina. After a rough passage, the *Santiago* on 31 March entered Charleston Harbor, where flag-bedecked naval vessels manned their yards and saluted Fox. His party visited the harbor's fortifications and, on 1 April, toured Charleston in "broken down carriages." They saw "many handsome houses," found John C. Calhoun's unostentatious grave, and took Admiral Dahlgren's tug up the "very pretty" Cooper and Ashley rivers, where "wrecks of torpedo boats" and block-ade runners "abounded."[57]

The *Santiago*, with Fox and his guests, left for Cuba that evening and entered the harbor of Havana on 4 April. They admired the Morro Castle, saw "hundreds of ships, a forest of masts, flags of all nations," and surprisingly the *Harriet Lane*, which the Navy Department believed had been destroyed. Part of Fox's expedition to Sumter in 1861, the ship was captured by the Confederates at Galveston, converted into a blockade runner, and interned by Spanish authorities at Havana.[58]

The *Santiago*'s captain advised the junketeers to stay on board, using the words "dirty, fleas, dark" to describe rooms ashore. Determined "to imbibe all of foreign life" she could, Virginia would not "hear of it." Their room at the Hotel Ingleterra opened on the piazza, with its statue of Queen Isabella, and had magnificent views of the sea, the city, its surrounding hills, and glorious palm trees. The view made up for the room's inadequacies. It had "one pitcher & basin, no slop bucket," a common water closet reached through an open court, and an iron bedstead. Virginia claimed it was so shaky that vibrations from passing carriages "made me giddy & Gus got up & laid on the floor on my blanket shawl." While enjoying the sights of Havana, they noticed "plenty of Southerners looking at us from the corners of their eyes." They took a handsome volante (a two-wheeled carriage with its body ahead of the axle and the driver astride the horse) into the country to view a gorgeous garden. "Gus," Virginia reported, "had been crazy to ride in one with driver in full costume & he did to his entire satisfaction." They also visited the cathedral, where viewing the bust of Columbus (behind which his ashes purportedly reposed) may have inspired Fox's later interest in discovering his first landfall in the New World.[59]

On Friday afternoon, 7 April, Fox, Virginia, and Ellen went sixty miles east by rail to the port of Matanzas. The next morning, they visited a sugar plantation, in the valley of the Gumiere, belonging to the cousin of Congressman Thomas A. Jenckes of Rhode Island. There, they observed "negroes, some native Congoes," cutting sugarcane. They were supervised by "an overseer, *black* with *sword* by his side & *whip* in hand," on a twelve-foot-high platform.

The slaves, some of whom obviously were victims of the outlawed slave trade, brought cut cane, flowers, and coconuts to them, for which they "gave them money." Later that afternoon, they visited an orange plantation that daily sent 4,000 oranges to market.[60]

The close encounter with slavery on the sugar and orange plantations, after four years of slavery-induced conflict at home, moved the Foxes.

> We visited the quarters, a court, in the middle an open shed, with three huge iron kettles was the kitchen for all. The little hut no windows open into the court, four posts, covered with thatched top. Two ft. from ground were fastened a few boards in it. This was the *bed*, no cloths, & just room to move round. The bed, dark, dirty, desolate. Oh, Cuba, these are human beings, with nerves, & souls, look at the South & learn the lessons written in her lost blood! Three hours a day during the sugar season is all they allow the negroes for rest, sleep, eating. They live from five to seven years under this exhaustive system & glad must they be when death puts an end to hunger, whip & toil! They looked fat from eating the cane, but the faces of many reminded me of a bull dog. One especially half clothed, who had been *feeding* Gus, begged him to take more with the most abject "for Massa," "for Massa," all the English he knew.[61]

On Sunday, 9 April, with no Protestant church available in Matanzas, they found an agreeable substitute in the recently discovered Cave of Bellamer. "The sight," Virginia exclaimed, "was glorious, & I silently praised God for this new view of his works. Their beauty will haunt me for this life at least!" Her impulse to glorify God would have been even stronger had she realized that on that Palm Sunday Robert E. Lee surrendered the Army of Northern Virginia to Ulysses S. Grant.[62]

Fox's party boarded the *Santiago* that Sunday afternoon and departed for Port Royal, South Carolina, where they arrived on Tuesday. They took a boat to Savannah on Wednesday, were unimpressed by that city, but the trip back to Port Royal was enjoyable with Fox "full of anecdotes & good spirits." They were impressed on Thursday by what they saw and heard at the large wooden church in the "freed negro village" of Mitchellville. "For the *first* time [William] Lloyd Garrison & George Thompson spoke freely in S.C." They were joined by other antislavery advocates, including Theodore Tilton, of the *Independent*, and Congressman William D. Kelley, all of whom gave good speeches. Virginia confessed, "My feelings were touched & I actually sobbed so I feared I'd have to leave, but controlled myself. 30 years since Garrison had a halter round his neck & was dragged through the streets of Boston for expressing abolition sentiments, & in Baltimore was put in prison to save his life." Although Virginia thought the black minister dwelt too much "on the *un*importance of *color*," she "sat three hours *interested*, but Ellen's democratic [racist] spirit was chaffed." Virginia grimly added, "she had to stand it."[63]

Fox was as moved as Virginia. A few weeks later, he chided Tilton for inadequate coverage in the *Independent* of that marvelous meeting. Tilton responded that a full report of the Mitchellville meeting "would *mar* your memory" of "that height of moral sublimity and rapt religious fervor which you and I had the happiness to witness on that golden day." Fox and Virginia, to a greater extent than their relations, empathized with blacks and were heartened by their progress.[64]

The *Santiago de Cuba* left Port Royal Thursday morning and arrived at Charleston on Friday, 14 April. Fox, Virginia, and their guests, who braved the "small boat pitching frightfully . . . through the rough sea," soon "stood in Ft. Sumpter! *Conquered* a heap of ruins! From the top a slope of broken matter to the very bottom." Accompanied by Dahlgren and Nicolay, they were escorted to the platform, but the flag-raising ceremony was delayed for an hour. Robert Anderson, Henry Ward Beecher, and other celebrants were "outside in the Arago, very seasick & not able to get over the bar." Great cheers greeted their arrival, and the ceremony got under way. Anderson was "much agitated . . . cried when making his speech" and when he raised the torn flag he had struck, men "embraced & many were in tears." A 100-gun salute from Fort Sumter "& all the batteries & Ships in the harbor" followed, prompting Virginia to remark, "It was the bombardment once again!" Beecher, who was stouter, shorter, and less intellectual than Virginia imagined, then gave a "*too long*, discourse." That night, while Charleston Harbor was aglow with lanterns and rockets and enlivened by music and dancing, Abraham Lincoln was assassinated in Washington.[65]

CHAPTER EIGHTEEN

From War to Peace

I look back upon our association with perfect satisfaction and
history will do you full justice for the judgment, firmness and
integrity of your administration. It is my glory to have formed
a part of it.   *Fox to Welles, 30 May 1866*

On Monday morning, 17 April 1865, the pilot boat at the mouth of Chesapeake Bay had dreadful news. "They had a story," Gus told Virginia, "that the
President was assassinated, & an attempt on Seward." Fox, Nicolay, and everyone else, while fearing it might be true, refused to believe it. At Point Lookout,
Maryland, "the *fatal news was confirmed. . . .* What a pall it throws over us,"
especially since, Virginia noted, it happened on "the very night of the Sumpter
celebration." As the *Santiago de Cuba* passed Mount Vernon, Virginia focused
on the singular contributions of Washington and Lincoln and prophesied that
among past and future presidents "None will ever be more honored than
they!" The Foxes found the capital in deep mourning. "All houses small &
great hung with black—a deathly silence prevails" all the way to Montgomery and Minna Blair's home, opposite the White House. Virginia told Minna
of their "trip but the sparkle of the champagne" was gone, while Minna could
scarcely describe the night of 14 April. "None knew who would be murdered
or what revenge might be taken. It seemed like the beginning of the reign of
terror," but it was not. Lincoln, the commander in chief, was among the war's
last casualties. With peace, Welles and Fox had to transform the huge navy
they had assembled into modest squadrons, deployed around the globe. About
to celebrate his forty-fourth birthday, Fox had to consider his transition from
the Navy Department to a new position in or out of government.[1]

■ ■ ■

On Wednesday, Fox attended Lincoln's funeral at the White House, while Virginia, from the front of the Treasury Building, viewed the "very sad & impos-

ing" procession. For an hour and a half, carriages three abreast and mourners on foot passed by with "blacks at the end led by [James] Wormley and two others on horseback." Sharing their grief, Virginia exclaimed, "How my heart ached! What a friend *Gus* has lost!" She was right. Lincoln's death affected Fox's postwar career. Fox's ambition for a diplomatic plum (like the ones his friends John Hay and John Nicolay received) would not be realized.[2]

The war was virtually over, but two Confederate vessels were still at large. The *Shenandoah* was heading for the Bering Sea. It would destroy many whalers before its commander realized the war was over and made it back to England. The powerful Confederate ram *Stonewall* left Lisbon, Portugal, on 27 March and was rumored to be heading for Texas, where Confederate General E. Kirby Smith refused to surrender until 2 June 1865. Fox could do little about the *Shenandoah* beyond wishing that the *Wachusett*, bound for the East Indies, would encounter it off the Cape of Good Hope. He could prepare for the *Stonewall*, however, which was commanded by his old friend and shipmate Thomas Jefferson Page. Fox discussed with Farragut "ironing the cutwaters" of vessels to make them more effective rams. But Farragut, whose vessels rammed the *Tennessee* at Mobile Bay, did not think adding iron to the bows of wooden ships would help them stand the shock. Nevertheless, he said he would ram the *Stonewall*, "iron or not." He characteristically suggested to Fox, "Two of our steamers the class of the Lackawanna or Monongahela, ought to capture the Stonewall either by Boarding or running her down—or both."[3]

Preferring to fight iron with iron, Fox made certain that Ericsson's *Dictator* would be ready for the *Stonewall*. Ericsson was certain the *Dictator* could overtake it, and Fox was confident that the *Dictator*, commanded by the intrepid John Rodgers, would, with its fifteen-inch guns, cave in the sides of the *Stonewall*. The trial by combat never happened. Page took his vessel to Havana and, on 19 May, turned it over to Spanish authorities.[4]

A month after Lincoln's death, Grant's and Sherman's armies celebrated the end of meaningful resistance with parades. It was an army affair, but Fox felt the seating arrangements in the reviewing stands insulted the navy. Welles had requested eighty tickets for admirals, commodores, heads of bureaus, and their families. He received only thirty second-class, yellow tickets, and two first-class, blue tickets, for himself and Fox. Fox told General Christopher Columbus Augur, who was in charge of arrangements, that he was going to "scan" the 1,500 persons with the preferred blue tickets, for the number-one stand, to see if they were more deserving than navy people. "I am very sorry," he added, "that the last great act of this war should be a pageant that by some strange blunder is likely to create bad feeling amongst those of a brother service who have shared with the soldiers the trials of the war but are forgotten in an event so memorable as the review." Augur infuriated Fox by rejecting his note as "not acceptable." Virginia begged Fox, apparently successfully, not to respond.[5]

With peace, the Union had to be reconstructed and the army and navy reconstituted. Fox had little to do with reconstructing the Union, but a great deal to do with recreating a peacetime navy. In politics, he had become more of a Lincoln man than a Blair man. That shift was apparent by late 1862, when he argued with Montgomery Blair in favor of the Emancipation Proclamation, and, along with Virginia, he remained friendlier to black aspirations than other members of the Blair and Woodbury clans. It can only be conjectured whether these views stemmed from their New England background, reinforced by their close association with John Murray Forbes; their Christianity (stressing the great commandments to love God and their neighbors); or their appreciation of the crucial contribution black sailors made to the Union navy. After African Americans were allowed in 1865 to ride on Washington street cars, Virginia was mortified when "two nice looking black men" were insulted by a white woman and, by eye contact, communicated her feeling to one of the men, who responded with a laugh.[6]

Fox had one official opportunity to express his views on Reconstruction and specifically on the political rights of African Americans. In late May, acting as navy secretary when Welles was out of town, he attended cabinet meetings and became acquainted with President Andrew Johnson. "He does not say much," Fox reported, to his friend Senator Grimes, "listens, calls for opinions and does not seem inclined to question Heads of Depts in their specialties." While representing the Navy Department in the cabinet, Fox "had to oppose the Prests Proclamation for bringing N.C. back because it does not give the black man a vote. I suppose my opinion is of no earthly moment to anyone but myself," he told Grimes, "but I was happy to give it because I believe it is right." Several months later, after services at St. John's Episcopal Church on Lafayette Square, Fox and a family friend, Tish McKean, had opposing views of the day's sermon. She thought it too radical and would "hurt the feelings of the returned rebels," but he thought the preacher "must be a Copperhead from his moderation."[7]

Although Fox's views did not affect Reconstruction policy, as Welles's trusted adviser he could influence naval matters. He continued to deploy vessels and to write orders, which Welles read and signed. Personnel decisions were arrived at jointly, an indication that the Welles-Fox partnership still functioned smoothly. Fox continued to oversee the construction of bigger and better ironclads. He corresponded frequently with Ericsson about his *Dictator* and *Puritan* and consulted with John Lenthall, head of the Bureau of Construction, about building new vessels and repairing old ones. His interest was far from perfunctory; his discussions with Lenthall involved technical details, and his opinion carried weight. The constructors at the Philadelphia Navy Yard, who were fitting out the monitor *Monadnock* for the Pacific, recommended to Lenthall "a hole in the pilot house of a foot square with a heavy shutter fitted. I presume," he wrote Fox, who was at Portsmouth, "for the purpose of seeing clearly at sea. You may have objections to so large a hole in the pilot house and it will stand until you get back, or I can hear from you if you think it really necessary to have so large an opening."[8]

With the cessation of hostilities, Fox helped dismantle the navy. Blockading squadrons were pared down, and "blockading" was dropped from their names. On 2 June 1865, the day Kirby Smith surrendered, Fox ordered Admiral S. P. Lee to reduce the Mississippi Squadron to fifteen vessels and to economize by keeping their fires banked. On 14 August the squadron was eliminated. The twenty-three remaining vessels of the North Atlantic Squadron, on 1 July 1865, made it one-sixth its size when Porter commanded it on 1 January 1865. The Navy Department began to auction off its blockaders (which had seen hard use) before they deteriorated further. John Murray Forbes (who negotiated the purchase of many blockaders) told Fox that the sales were not adequately publicized, but he conceded to Fox in July that "your ships sold a great deal better than your limited advertising *deserved*." Many of the vessels hastily built for operations in the South's shoal waters, deteriorating into "naval trash," were unsalable and unsailable. Prewar squadrons were reactivated to protect American commercial interests by showing the flag abroad. Goldsborough took command of the European Squadron on 18 July; Henry H. Bell was appointed commander of the East India Squadron on 31 July; and Sylvanus W. Godon took command of the Brazil Squadron on 12 August.[9]

The African Squadron was abandoned. "I think," Fox wrote Welles on 26 August, "it would be infinitely preferable to give up the African Squadron and have the same force in the West Indies under a special Commander. Such a transfer of ships would increase our influence in the seas adjacent to our coasts and which are really our waters." By December the Navy Department formed a West Indian Squadron. Slave ships could be apprehended as effectively off the Cuban coast as off Africa, and a West Indian Squadron reflected the imperialist ambitions of Seward, Welles, and Fox. The West Indies was an area, Welles explained, "where we have so large a trade, and where, owing to the proximity of the islands to our shores, it is essential that we cultivate friendly relations." Seward and Fox had more than friendship in mind. For strategic reasons, they wanted to acquire the Virgin Islands from Denmark, as well as Alaska from Russia. Fox's close friendship with Waldemar Raasloff, the Danish minister in Washington, facilitated negotiations for the purchase of the Danish West Indies. Although Fox lobbied Charles Sumner (chair of the Foreign Relations Committee) and, in December 1868, President-elect Ulysses S. Grant for its passage, the Senate ignored the resulting 1867 treaty, letting it die. Fifty years would elapse before the United States would acquire those islands.[10]

With peace, Fox thought about his future. He realized his Navy Department position, created for him in order to meet wartime demands, would be terminated, and he was unhappy that Congress had cut his salary. Planning to take a high-paying managerial position, he explored possibilities in textile, iron, steamship, and mining enterprises, while working to improve the navy. In the winter of 1865 to 1866, he rejected several industrial offers and priced himself out of the market for others. In December 1865, he was offered the agency of the Middlesex Mills at Lowell at $7,500, but Virginia did not want to live in Lowell, and Fox wished to explore other opportunities. In that same month, the banker Jay Cooke and associates offered him the presidency of a Pennsylvania coal company at $10,000 a year. Upon learning "that the selling of coal was to be added to the duties of Pres't," Fox demanded "twenty-five thousand dollars of stock at twenty-five, in my name" and the option to purchase an additional $25,000 of preferred stock at 3 percent, when the market value was at 8 percent. The Cooke associates did not meet these demands, and Virginia's hope to live in Philadelphia on a handsome salary evaporated.[11]

Virginia's dreams quickly revived. In January 1866 the shipping magnate William H. Aspinwall planned to establish a new shipping line, headquartered in New York and led by Fox at $10,000 a year ($20,000 if the line did well). Fox accepted the presidency, and Farragut proposed that the Foxes live near him in New York. By the end of February, Aspinwall's plans fell through. "Thus ends our $20,000 a year," Virginia lamented. In March and April, Aspinwall urged Fox to head the Tredegar Iron Works in Richmond, Virginia, at $10,000. Fox said $100,000 "would not tempt him to live among those secesh," but General Joseph R. Anderson of the ironworks urged him to visit Richmond and suggested he could live in Washington. Accompanied by Aspinwall, Fox visited Richmond, found it a "beautiful city like Portland," and was tempted but still refused to work among his former enemies. Knowing they could not live "*poor as mice,*" Virginia was forced to consider living in Lowell.[12]

Clearly, Fox was not anxious to leave the Navy Department. "I do not feel like retiring to other business," he told Grimes in June 1865, "if there is a prospect of accomplishing the following matters, for the Navy." Since early 1862, he had advocated a navy yard for ironclads at League Island, up the Delaware River at Philadelphia. Because ironclads rusted badly in salt water, he wanted a facility located on fresh water in a city and state noted for machine shops and iron production. Ericsson among others pointed out that, to retard rusting iron and rotting wood, it would be best to store monitors out of the water and that League Island was admirably suited for a marine railway system. Fox also wanted "Line officers of the future to be made steam engine drivers." With steam-powered vessels used in battle, commanding officers needed to be ac quainted with the machinery upon which victory depended.

He was especially concerned with improving the quality of officers and enlisted men in the navy. He wanted "a radical change in the enlistment of sailors," who had traditionally been recruited from the grog shop. He advocated their training and education "by a thoroughly improved apprenticeship system which will give us in the future steady good men." He also disliked the practice of allowing members of Congress to recruit future officers through control of appointments to the United States Naval Academy. He wanted "Half the Cadets at the Naval School to be appointed from enlisted apprentice boys." Having eliminated the daily ration of grog, Fox wanted to improve the monotonous diet of men at sea. He called for "a new galley." Because, in his opinion, the Marine Corps had not distinguished itself in the war, he wanted the "Marines to go to the army where they belong." Marine officers had been accused of southern sympathies, and Porter complained of their cowardly behavior in the costly naval assault on Fort Fisher. Fox's fondest wish was that the nation would find the way to "keep a large navy and make [it] useful in peace."[13]

Grimes feared Fox was asking too much, and Fox, well versed in the ways of Congress, realized there were limits to what he could accomplish. Still, apart from keeping a large navy and ridding it of the Marine Corps, Fox either achieved his goals or nudged the navy toward their realization. He got the navy yard at League Island, despite strong New England support for New London, Connecticut. In its curriculum, the Naval Academy increased its stress on steam engineering.[14]

The academy remained important to Fox. He received excellent advice from the distinguished astronomer John H. C. Coffin, who taught mathematics and navigation there. Academy instructors should be experienced, be competent beyond their subject, and be tenured, Coffin emphasized. They should not be subject to the "highly injurious" practice of rotation every three or four years.[15]

Coffin's alarm over the effects of rotation concerned Fox. He was not pleased when Porter, whom he and Welles had selected to head the academy, "ordered all his young men to Annapolis who have been with him in the two squadrons." Among them was Fox's nephew Charlie Guild, but, realizing that he would be accused of favoritism if his nephew got a choice shore assignment, Fox insisted that Charlie go to sea. During the war, Porter had told Fox, "I would ask nothing better after this war is over than to have command of the Naval Academy, and get the right set of officers into the Navy." He wanted "fearless dashing men," rather than "Miss Nancy's." In May 1865, just before Porter took over the academy, Porter and Fox saw a great deal of each other. They went horseback riding, and one evening Fox remained at Porter's house until eleven o'clock. Although Porter stressed derring-do, while Fox emphasized competence, they both wanted able and aggressive officers. To achieve his ends, Porter wanted fresh blood more than experienced teachers. Fox and Porter agreed that the academy belonged at Newport, Rhode Island, but, despite their efforts, it returned to Annapolis, Maryland.[16]

Fox made headway in getting a superior set of sailors in the navy. The prewar navy was often the last refuge of broken-down men, who were no longer vigorous enough for the merchant marine. To attract and train capable, strong young men, R. B. Lowry, with Fox's encouragement, had launched, beginning in August 1864, an apprentice-seaman program on board the sailing frigate *Sabine.* By 1 July 1865 Lowry was using a recruiting circular to attract boys of good character, between thirteen and eighteen years of age, who were "physically sound, well developed," and could read, write, and do long division. Needing parental consent, they would serve until they were twenty-one, when they could become seamen on board a man-of-war, be preferred for appointments as warrant and petty officers, or be honorably discharged. While in training aboard the *Sabine,* apprentices were to be instructed by ship officers and schoolmasters. Along with Farragut, Percival Drayton inspected the *Sabine* in late May and found the apprentices performing in a "most satisfactory" manner.[17]

Naval officers continued to suggest to Fox ways to improve the service. Navy yards provoked constant complaints and inspired suggestions. Paul Shirley put to sea in the *Suwanee,* which had been fitted out at the Philadelphia Navy Yard, and discovered "*cart loads*" of rubbish (including wood chips and blocks, coal, rivets, and even hammers) in its hold, impeding the operation of its pumps. Shirley urged that "stringent orders" require that holds be clean before stowing provisions and stores. Orders had been given to clean the *Suwanee*'s hold, but unskilled navy yard workers were more adept at bringing out the vote of a ward than removing debris from a hold. Fox's old Coast Survey friend, Benjamin Franklin Sands, commandant of the Boston Navy Yard, relayed to Fox his son's observations of the efficient mustering of workmen at the French navy yard at Cherbourg, compared with the time lost "in our process." Fox and Welles were aware that political appointments of navy agents and in navy yards cost the navy time, money, and quality. Their efforts to prosecute wrongdoers and achieve reforms were frustrated by intense pressure on Lincoln and Johnson to keep the navy yards in political hands and even to pardon convicted thieves and swindlers who generously contributed to political campaigns.[18]

From Dr. W. S. N. Ruschenberger, Fox received advice on how to improve the quality of medicine and surgery practiced on shipboard. To attract better doctors, Ruschenberger wished to peg the pay of doctors to that of high-ranking line officers. Ruschenberger suggested his own appointment as head of the Bureau of Medicine and Surgery, while disparaging the reputation of Fox's friend Phineas Horwitz, who would get that post. Naval doctors were reasonably good at setting bones, sawing off shattered limbs, and binding up wounds, but for many other medical problems sailors would have been better off if doctors had been banned from vessels. The Foxes relied on navy doctors, and their experience indicates the state of the medical profession. When in July 1865 Horwitz was out of town, "his assistant," Fox wrote Virginia, "wanted to blister me because I had my old pain with my diarrhea, but I declined." Instead, Fox went on an overnight trip on the Potomac with President Johnson and Welles, which proved to be far more salutary and comfortable than getting blistered would have been. Medical practices in the navy merely kept pace with those in the nation as a whole.[19]

Fox was more concerned about steam engines than medicine. He wanted naval officers to be familiar with the principles of steam engineering, but engines varied, and their champions quarreled bitterly. During the war, the navy was willing to experiment, using engines of various designs to power its vessels. Fox and Welles endeavored to keep inventive minds focused on the war effort. For its class of six fast supercruisers, decided on in 1863 and intended to serve as a threat to Britain rather than to the Confederacy, three were to be built at navy yards with engines designed by Engineer in Chief Isherwood, and the others at private yards with engines by Ericsson (the *Madawaska*), Merrick and Sons of Philadelphia (the *Chattanooga*), and Edward Nicoll Dickerson (the *Idaho*).[20]

Ericsson and Isherwood disparaged each others' engines and the theories of steam engineering upon which they were based. Their hostility, however, did not compare with Dickerson's hatred for Isherwood. A spellbinding lawyer, an unscrupulous polemicist, and an amateur steam engineer, Dickerson convinced the New York press and Paul S. Forbes (who was Fox's friend and a cousin of John Murray Forbes) that the steam-expansion theory he embraced, and on which he based his engines, was sound. Dickerson's problem was not his theory (English engineers and Ericsson thought it had merit), but his failure as a designer of practical machinery. Because of their high opinion of Forbes and to quiet Dickerson, Fox and Welles accepted Forbes's offer of February 1863 to build the *Idaho* with Dickerson's engines. At about the same time, they agreed to put Dickerson's machinery in the double-ender gunboat *Algonquin* and, for comparative purposes, put Isherwood's engine into its sister ship, the *Winooski.* They were taking a chance. In the previous year, Dickerson's machinery in the *Pensacola* had failed Farragut on the Lower Mississippi.[21]

Fox was friendly with Ericsson, Isherwood, and Forbes, and, above all, he and Welles wanted the best combination of speed, size, and dependability in steam engines. They were willing to give Dickerson another chance to show that his theory was serviceable, but by the end of 1863 two surveys had condemned the *Pensacola*'s machinery. In addition to slandering Isherwood's character, Dickerson accused Fox of circulating a pamphlet disparaging his engines and called him a character assassin in the *New York Times.*[22]

Trial runs should have settled the controversy, but the disputants were as adept at inventing excuses as designing engines. When the competing gunboats and the supercruisers were completed after the war, their trials attracted enormous attention because of Isherwood's position, Ericsson's reputation, and Dickerson's vituperation. After delays by Dickerson, the double-ender gunboats were tested side by side, from September 1865 to February 1866, with the result that Isherwood's machinery in the *Winooski* produced more speed, weighed less, and was more compact than Dickerson's engine in the *Algonquin.* Fox was intensely interested in these tests and was posted on Dickerson's evasive tactics by Isherwood and Admiral Gregory. The *Algonquin* was never commissioned. Dickerson had a ready supply of excuses for the *Algonquin,* but the supercruiser *Idaho,* in its trial of May 1866, made only a little over eight knots, with his machinery, rather than the fifteen knots it was supposed to achieve. The navy rejected it, but Paul Forbes persuaded Congress to force its acceptance. Ironically, the navy had the last laugh. It removed Dickerson's machinery and converted the *Idaho* into one of the fastest fully rigged sailing ships afloat.[23]

The reaction of Ericsson to the double-ender trial was curious. Writing to Fox, he argued that the trial proved Isherwood's ideas "falacious" and "utterly erroneous." He believed if Dickerson had "been a good constructing Engineer he would have secured a great triumph for the expanding principle," but concluded it was impossible to make Dickerson's engine "*practically* useful." But Ericsson then stated "no vessel afloat has a better or more Economical engine" than Isherwood's in the *Winooski*. As Isherwood observed to Fox, if Ericsson thought his engine the best afloat, how could the theory upon which it was built be erroneous?[24]

By 1867 Ericsson's ideas and engines were severely tested. His engines in the *Madawaska* were fine-tuned in the fall of 1866. During the 144-hour trial of the engines in January 1867, the *Madawaska* ran into rough seas and at times attained fifteen knots or better. It could not sustain that speed, however, because it rolled excessively and shipped water. Its average speed of under thirteen knots disappointed Ericsson, but the Navy Department accepted Ericsson's engines. As Edward Sloan observes, they were sound, but they were not suited for the long narrow clipper ship hull of the *Madawaska*, which could not take their weight and pounding.[25]

The trial of Isherwood's engines in the *Wampanoag* was plagued by construction delays. The trial finally took place in February 1868. Despite heavy seas, the *Wampanoag*, which was identical to the *Madawaska*, having averaged seventeen knots an hour for a twenty-four-hour period, proved the fastest ship in the world. It would be twenty-one years before another American naval vessel would better its speed. Isherwood, who had suffered considerable abuse at the hands of Dickerson and Ericsson, was ecstatic in his moment of triumph. He generously thanked Fox, on 18 February 1868, for "your confidence in me, which . . . never faltered, but with wonderful magnanimity and judgment sustained me throughout." Amazingly, Fox retained the friendship and services of the brilliant inventor Ericsson and the brilliant engineer Isherwood, despite their hostility for each other. Isherwood's triumph was short-lived. Line officers complained that the *Wampanoag* rolled too much and that its engines used too much coal and took up too much space, depriving officers and crew of adequate accommodations. On 5 May 1868, less than three months after it broke all speed records, it was decommissioned. A year later, it was condemned by a naval commission as unacceptable for sea service.[26]

Although he was very interested in the trials of the *Madawaska* and the *Wampanoag*, Fox was no longer in the Navy Department when they were held. His hopes for a diplomatic post had died with Lincoln, but in the spring of 1866 an opportunity to gracefully leave the Navy Department and to represent the nation abroad came his way. An unsuccessful attempt to assassinate Czar Alexander II of Russia prompted Congress in May 1866 to pass a joint resolution congratulating the czar, the Russian nation, and especially the 20 million former serfs whom he had freed earlier, upon his narrow escape. With Fox angling for the honor, Congress asked him to present this resolution to the czar.[27]

Gratified to have been chosen, Fox decided to use the journey to test on the high seas one of the most formidable monitors and to exhibit it abroad. He resolved to cross the Atlantic (which no monitor had attempted) in the twin-screw, two-turreted *Miantonomoh*, designed by Lenthall and Isherwood. Isherwood immodestly but accurately called it "the finest turreted ironclad ever built." Fox confided to Ericsson and John A. Griswold, his associate in building monitors, as well as to Wise, his hope that some European powers—Prussia, Russia, and Sweden, for example—would be interested in buying monitors constructed in private American shipyards. Ericsson did not tell Fox "the unpleasant truth that for want of proper means America cannot at present" compete with Europeans in building monitors "as they ought to be built." Fox would soon be enlightened, because Welles asked him to compare European and American vessels and navy yards. A few days after he resigned as assistant secretary on 22 May 1866, Fox praised Welles for his "judgment, firmness and integrity" and told Welles how proud he was to have been his associate.[28]

For his mission to Russia, Fox received a six-month reappointment as assistant secretary of the navy. In Boston, on 30 May, after putting Virginia on a train for Portsmouth, he departed on the side-wheel gunboat *Ashuelot* for St. John's, Newfoundland. There, on 3 June, he rendezvoused with the *Augusta* and the *Miantonomoh*. The *Augusta* was a side-wheel steamer, which, if necessary, could tow the *Miantonomoh*.[29]

On the evening of 5 June, two bands played "and the harbor was alive with boats to see so strange a vessel depart for a voyage across the Atlantic." The next day, the sea was calm, and Fox strolled around the deck, which was only two feet above the water. On the morrow, a moderate gale brought three to four feet of water over the deck continually. As the *Miantonomoh* lifted, the sea poured off "sounding like the surf breaking upon the beach." Then, for a good part of the voyage, Fox experienced "a pretty rough sea" and was pleased with the performance and accommodations of the *Miantonomoh*. In the roughest weather, it rolled only five and a half degrees, whereas the *Augusta* rolled eighteen and the *Ashuelot* twenty-five. This steadiness in a seaway would enable the *Miantonomoh* to fire its fifteen-inch guns with accuracy. Fox assured Welles that "the monitor type of iron-clads is superior to the broadside" type of vessel as a cruiser on the high seas. His room was excellent, the lighting sufficient "to read the finest print," and the ventilation (a major complaint about the monitors) "perfect." Fox, however, observed that space was wasted on the *Miantonomoh,* and it was underpowered. In fact, he listed twenty-three possible improvements. To conserve its supply of coal, the *Augusta* towed the *Miantonomoh* for most of the eleven-day voyage to Queenstown (Cobh), Ireland. On a personal level, Fox suffered from dyspepsia, brought on, he thought, by too much salmon. In his affliction, he was comforted by the presence of "Monitor," the Newfoundland dog he took to Russia.[30]

Fox went on to Dublin and London, where his little fleet coaled, and then proceeded to the great British naval base at Portsmouth. London disappointed him. Although the navy people there treated him in the "best style," he "never got into tip top society." Sounding as he did when he was a midshipman, he exclaimed, "The real old hidalgos in England won't touch a republican except with tongs, but the middle classes and the Navy people cannot do too much for us." The lords of the Admiralty accompanied him to Portsmouth and boarded the *Miantonomoh* and seemed impressed.[31]

Unlike the aristocracy, royalty did not ignore Fox. Before leaving London, he attended the Queen's ball, "talked with the handsome little Princess of Wales and her lord and his brother the Duke of Edinburgh," and learned the Prince of Wales wished to inspect the *Miantonomoh.* Although Fox adhered to his schedule and left with it on 29 June for Cherbourg, France, he decided the *Miantonomoh* should return to England to go up the Thames, where the prince and "the people can see her and be impressed with our resources." In July the monitor returned to England and anchored at Sheerness, in the Thames, surrounded by British ironclads. The *Miantonomoh*'s unique design, powerful guns, and heavy armor aroused interest and concern that it could sink any of her majesty's vessels in five minutes. "The wolf is in the fold," the *Times* of London observed, "and the whole flock was at its mercy."[32]

In France, the first week in July, Fox moved in the highest circles. He had a frustrating conversation with Emperor Napoleon III. "Every word he said to me about his intentions in Mexico was false," Fox complained, but he "could not with propriety touch upon the truth." Fox perceived that Napoleon was trying "to conceal his real feelings towards us at the act of humiliation he is performing at leaving Mexico." Napoleon probably was preoccupied by news of the Austrian defeat by the Prussians at Sadowa, which he received while talking with Fox. Responding to Napoleon's questions, Fox emphasized American power. He said, "the war had developed our resources," that the North had grown richer, and that the South "acquiesced" in the result of "the contest." Napoleon, who had rejected Ericsson's original plans for the *Monitor,* ordered his marine minister as well as Dupuy de Lome, the designer of French ironclads, to inspect the *Miantonomoh.*[33]

Fox was flattered to learn at a dinner in his honor, given by the French minister of foreign affairs, that the emperor had nominated him an officer of the Legion of Honor. Although a major objective of his trip was to impress the British and French with American power, Fox claimed not to care about their attitude toward the United States. "I think it is a matter of small concern what these Govt's think of us or our people," he wrote Welles. "Our superiority in everything excepting tinsel, epaulettes, and medals can only be felt by coming over here." A five-hour tour of Versailles brought out Fox's distaste for militarism and confirmed his belief in the superiority of American democracy. "Everything is for the *glory* of France," he wrote Virginia. "Battles and warriors fill every room—it is the sword everywhere. Here it is one man, in England it is one class that governs but the result is the same, the people have no voice. . . . It is a blessed country we have and a Gov't that shows its superiority every step I take and every person I visit." A few days later, Fox predicted that the United States might not have the polish of Europe but would have an infinitely greater "effect upon the human race."[34]

Fox had hoped to rendezvous in Paris with Virginia's sisters Nell and Frank and Frank's husband Arch Lowery, but he discovered that they had gone to Geneva. He followed them there and found that, although they had planned to accompany him through northern Europe on his way to Russia, "Frank was entirely used up" and Nell refused to leave her. He was also annoyed that Nell remembered nothing of the "3 or 4 miles of paintings" at the Louvre. Disappointed and not entirely sympathetic with Frank, Fox toured Switzerland and Germany without them. The Strasbourg Cathedral filled him "with admiration and wonder." He found the Rhine River from Bingen to Koblenz— "famous for its beauties, its castles, and its legends"—"inferior" to the Hudson River, and that Köln was so "very dirty" that "all the Eau de Cologne would hardly purify it." But he predicted that its cathedral, once again under construction, "if ever finished . . . will excite the admiration of the world."[35]

With cholera outbreaks at various points in Germany, Fox hastened to Denmark. He arrived in Copenhagen, "the healthiest place in Europe," on 24 July, where the *Miantonomoh* and *Augusta* awaited him. Finding the climate, scenery, and cleanliness of Copenhagen like Portsmouth, he visited museums, Tivoli Garden, and the docks and was presented to King Christian, whom he invited to visit the *Miantonomoh*. Accompanying the king, Princess Dagmar insisted that she and her mother "thoroughly explore" the engine room, from which they emerged with their "handsome dresses covered with oil." The king had Fox and the officers of his vessels to dinner, where the wines were "excellent," but the food "rather poor."[36]

On 31 July Fox and the *Miantonomoh* left Copenhagen, stopped at Helsinki (where he attended a ball and heard the violinist Ole Bull play Russian airs and American tunes), and on 6 August arrived at Kronstadt. From there, he went to St. Petersburg, where on 8 August, accompanied by his fleet's officers and the American minister, Cassius M. Clay, he presented the congressional resolution to Alexander II. On the following day, Alexander, with Fox at his side, visited the *Miantonomoh* and the *Augusta*. Fox spent several days sight-seeing. He visited the Hermitage and inspected ships, forts, and troops with the czar. On 22 August Fox and his entourage dined with Alexander and the czarina and 100 other guests at Peterhof Palace. There the czar toasted his visitors, the prosperity of the United States, and "the continuance of friendly relations." At a charity ball that evening, Fox danced a quadrille with the daughter of a grand duchess, and the emperor waltzed several times. Fox proudly reported that the czar was "very well pleased with me personally and with all I have done." He gave Fox "a gold snuff box, with his portrait surrounded by 26 diamonds and outside of these 6 large ones."[37]

Fox traveled beyond St. Petersburg and was overwhelmed by his reception, which exceeded either diplomatic courtesy or official orchestration. "I would have given any thing in the world," he wrote Virginia, "had you or any of our family witnessed our reception here." In part, it was a tribute to Fox for having the guts to cross the Atlantic in a monitor, and also it is clear that, in its rivalry with Britain, the Russian government wanted the United States for a friend. The immense enthusiastic crowds that greeted the Fox delegation as it traveled circuitously from St. Petersburg to Moscow, to Gorky on the Volga River, to Kalinin 529 miles upstream, and back to St. Petersburg reflected a broad admiration for and identification with America by the Russian people. To be sure, Fox saw the nobility on his travels, but peasants, recently emancipated from serfdom, repeatedly presented him with their traditional welcome of bread and salt. Officials elected under the zemstvo system of local self-government, instituted two years earlier (a major step in the direction of democracy), continually met with him. He felt that he had seen the people, that "they are a great people," and that they "are our friends from the highest to the lowest."[38]

Considering his republican bias, Fox was impressed by Czar Alexander's leadership and ruminated upon the future impact of Russia and the United States. "I cannot help feeling," he wrote Charles Sumner, chair of the Senate Foreign Relations Committee, "that God has permitted two great experiments to be tried in our day. That in His presence shall be established for human

progress an autocracy in the East and a republic in the West and to these powers He commits His people and will surely judge that nation which fails in the
trust reposed by Him." On 15 September, after forty strenuous yet rewarding
days among the Russians, Fox left Kronstadt on the *Augusta.* He was satisfied
that he had "made a favorable impression." The official reception was most
cordial, "but the striking feature of our visit," Fox told Welles, "was the spon-
taneous reception everywhere accorded to us by the people themselves." As he
looked back, the welcoming, cheering, even adoring crowds, seemed "like a
dream."[39]

He arrived in Stockholm, which also reminded him of Portsmouth, on 18
September and remained in Sweden for ten days. He met, chatted, and dined
with Charles XV, who "pumped" him for his impressions of Russia, and who,
with members of his family, inspected the *Miantonomoh.* At Skokloster, Fox
viewed "the original painting" of Gustavus Vasa, for whom he was named. He
appreciated the thin Swedish rye bread and was bored at the opera. He was
most pleased to associate once again with Commodore Axel Adlersparre, assistant minister of the navy, who was a midshipman with Fox, Wise, and Worden
in the *Cyane,* and who now had the "sagacity" to construct monitors for the
Swedish navy. Impressed by the Scandinavian peoples, he declared they had
no equal anywhere for "Christian hospitality, refined civilization, industry,
frugality, courtesy, honesty, freedom from violence, crime and rudeness." After
visiting naval vessels and facilities in both Russia and Sweden, Fox gave up his
idea of selling American-built monitors abroad. As Ericsson predicted, Fox
discovered that "as to monitors both the Russian and Swedish ones are superior to ours and cost just one third less to build."[40]

Fox and the *Augusta* and *Miantonomoh* arrived at Kiel, Prussia, on 29 September. A few days later, he left the ships and embarked on a tour. In Berlin,
he regretted that Bismarck ("the most prominent statesman living") was sick,
but he had twenty minutes with King William I. The broad expanse of Unter
den Linden and the profusion and size of outdoor beer gardens impressed Fox,
while the realistic naked statues about Berlin and the sensuous paintings of
"the passions of love" in its museum raised his New England eyebrows. By the
time Fox got to Prague on 10 October, he preferred to ride about town. The
palaces and paintings had "become as confused in" his mind as an "old paint
shop." In Vienna, he fell in with John Lothrop Motley, the distinguished historian, who was American minister to the Austrian Empire. He saw Emperor
Franz Joseph, whom he found touched with sadness, resulting from Austria's
recent defeat at the hands of Prussia. His trip by rail over the mountains, from

Vienna to Trieste to Venice on the Adriatic Sea, was exciting for Fox, who admired the engineering skill that produced "splendid viaduct bridges and a multitude of tunnels."[41]

Venice was even more fascinating than the railroad. "I have seen no place," Fox told Virginia, "that excites in the mind livelier interest." The treasures from centuries of mercantile supremacy, the crumbling palaces and churches, and the Italian politics of the moment were overwhelming. He arrived on 19 October, the day the Austrians evacuated and Italian troops entered Venice, and "the sight was one of exceeding beauty." The city was covered with the Italian tricolor of green, white, and red; the people were excited "almost beyond control"; and from a gondola that night the "illuminations were superb, and with the moonlight gave the city a fairy like appearance."[42]

At Lake Como on 24 October, Fox again rendezvoused with Nell, Frank, Arch, and their children Wood and Ginny. He was happy to see Virginia's namesake—now a tall, pretty, vivacious teenager—who had "not forgot how to kiss and hug." She, as always, had fun with Fox, but thought he overdid his tendency to "pinch, poke, and bite" and perceived that he missed his physical contact with Virginia. Her parents, to Fox's delight, were ready to travel. The next afternoon, 25 October, they all left for Milan, where they arrived that evening. "We started off sight seeing together," Fox wrote Virginia, "but a journey on top of the Cathedral, half as high again as Bunker Hill Monument Knocked them all up. Ginny wanted you to know that she plaited my beard on top of the Cathedral." Fox loved being with the children but realized that the entourage hampered his travels. While he pushed on to Florence, he advised the others to be present in Venice for the triumphal entry of King Victor Emanuel, on 7 November, celebrating a major step in the unification of Italy. In Florence, Fox viewed paintings and sculptures, churches, and chapels. He took a day trip to Spezia, where he inspected "the immense works under construction for a naval station." While at Florence, thanks to the good offices of his friend Joseph Bertinatti (the Italian minister to the United States), Fox was asked, along with the diplomatic corps, to accompany the king as he entered Venice. He accepted, and his renewed enjoyment of Venice was enhanced by being with his relatives. The pageantry was wonderful, and when, on Sunday evening at ten, they "went out on the Piazza of St. Mark and saw it illuminated in the most superb style," Fox declared it "the best sight we have seen in Venice."[43]

Fox next moved on to Rome, where he divided his time between the Vatican and "numerous antiquities." While there, he received anxiety-ridden letters from Virginia that gave him "such a fit of blues" that he "left without seeing the Pope or Victor Emanuel." Arriving in Paris on 22 November, Fox received Virginia's letter written on 29 October, their eleventh anniversary, "a day," Fox told her, "from which dates all my happiness on Earth." It reinforced his blues, and he lingered there only five days. In Paris, J. F. Loubat, his grateful secretary on the trip to Russia, gave Fox a "Milo Venus bronze," which pleased Virginia. Fox satisfied his curiosity with a visit to "the Paris sewers with the superintending engineer." He spent a few days in London, inspected more vessels, "did a little shopping," and went to Liverpool, where, on 1 December, he sailed for New York on the British & North American Royal Mail Steam Ship *Cuba.* He arrived in New York on 13 December 1866, caught the Old Colony boat for Boston, and the next day boarded a train for Portsmouth. At three that afternoon, he was with Virginia.[44]

Virginia had missed Fox's comforting presence. In addition to her chronic health problems, she was worried about where he would work and where they would live. She was unnerved by attacks in the *New York Herald* on Fox and his mission. She was troubled by the rift between President Johnson (who wished to reconstruct the Union with virtually no changes in the South beyond the destruction of slavery) and the Republican Congress (which was determined to protect the civil and political rights of blacks in the South). Specifically, Virginia was not in step with the pro-Johnson sentiments of her family. When, on 18 August, Montgomery Blair and her brother Charles Levi Woodbury returned in an ecstatic mood from the anti-Radical-Republican "Arm-in-Arm" convention, she wrote: "I'm sick of politics & politicians too much for *success* & too little for principle—self deceived—or—worse!" She yearned for a private existence.[45]

"I shall be perfectly content," Fox had assured her, "to *retire from public life* forever." From Paris, he had reassured her, "I have no desire for worldly honors." As a public man, Fox was identified with the Blair family. Although he was fond of Montgomery Blair, he did not share Blair's hostility to Negro suffrage and was willing to drop out of public life. He predicted correctly that Blair, who after the Arm-in-Arm convention was nominated for Congress in Maryland, "will be beaten out of sight in the coming elections." When the October election went "all for the Republicans," Virginia exclaimed, "What now Mr. Johnson & Co.! Are the Yankees to allow the conquered Rebs to rule them again? Is treason a recommendation to office?" Even when separated by an ocean, she and her husband were on the same wavelength. Along with the Republican radicals, Fox believed, "Our country will never be tranquil until the law recognizes, as God recognizes, no difference for race or color."[46]

CHAPTER NINETEEN

Postwar Career

> We can foot it together and try and find our happiness in our
> mutual affection, that is our property, our bank, our capital; it
> will not give out.   *Fox to Virginia, 24 April 1878*

The trip to Russia was marvelous, but, as Fox told Ericsson, it was taken at
"great pecuniary loss." Before going, Fox had to "decline several civil positions," and, before finding a job on his return, he had to write the official
report of his trip. He especially wanted to make a case for a stronger United
States Navy by comparing its offensive punch with that of foreign navies. In
addition, Welles continued to rely on Fox's expertise, and naval officers still
called upon him to influence Welles. "My interest in naval affairs will not
cease until you retire," he assured Welles. In fact, Fox's commitment to the
navy never ended.[1]

■ ■ ■

Having completed a draft of his report on his Russian mission, Fox was in
Washington by the middle of February 1867 to utilize the editorial skills of
Welles. He also wanted to influence Congress to pass a bill enabling him to
keep gifts received from European royalty, especially the diamond-studded
snuffbox given to him by the czar. The rancorous political climate at the capital disturbed him. He had already written Welles, "The threats of impeachment and uncertainties at Washington are having a disastrous effect upon the
country." Impeachment, he added, "will do more to weaken our people in
their form of Govt. than even the whole rebellion which has rather had an
opposite effect."[2]

Fox had his usual good time in Washington and told Virginia the news and
the gossip. He was delighted by legislation creating a navy yard on League
Island and gratified that congressmen frequently quoted his pamphlet in the
debate. In a lighter vein, he described the refurbished exterior and additional

story on Minna and Montgomery Blair's house. He reported he had dined with his old cronies Wise and Hay (who was back from Paris), attended Welles and Sumner receptions, and had dinner with Seward. He told Virginia that Mary Jane Welles "looks quite fat," that Charlotte Wise "goes out a good deal . . . to show Wise that she is popular," and that Alice Hooper, Charles Sumner's "pretty and agreeable" bride refused to leave parties when he wanted to go home. Although Fox realized Seward was given to exaggeration, he was pleased when he "said at the table that" Fox "had prevented a war with France by impressing upon him . . . our want of preparation for a foreign war and the necessity of keeping peace at least with that power. That this led him to resist the pressure from all sides to push the French to extremities in Mexico." Fox told Virginia that his loss of weight in Europe and additional "little whiskers" had so changed his appearance that for several minutes John Lenthall did not recognize him, but he was quite certain that Lizzie Lee did recognize him after church and deliberately cut him. Her irascible husband, S. P. Lee, believed erroneously that Fox hampered his career and told the world. Fox perceptively noted to Welles that Lee "is one of those men who . . . must always have a grievance to nourish and finally it becomes all their capital to get future favors."[3]

Fox also "came very near being appointed superintendent of the Coast Survey." Its head, Alexander Dallas Bache, died on 17 February. The proposal to place Fox at the head of the survey came from the distinguished mathematician Benjamin Peirce and the equally distinguished geologist Louis Agassiz. Fox did not "fancy the idea" and disappointed them both as well as Admiral Charles Henry Davis, who thought him ideal for the job. Knowing that Virginia had had enough of Washington and with friends divided over Reconstruction issues, he was ambivalent about living in the capital. The only appointment he wanted was minister to Switzerland (to restore Virginia's health), but thinking "Seward would not let me go there," he did not angle for the position.[4]

Naval affairs continued to involve Fox. There were loose ends that Welles wished nailed down. Did Fox authorize the plans by George C. Mason of Newport, Rhode Island, for remodeling the Naval Academy at Annapolis? Fox did not and stated that Mason should not be compensated. When, in March 1867, the idea that a board of admirals should run the navy surfaced again, Fox suggested that his wartime functions be continued not by an inefficient board but by the head of a revamped Bureau of Navigation. To fill that position, the secretary of the Navy should appoint a highly respected naval officer, like William Radford or Melancton Smith, who could combine expertise and efficiency.

A strong head of the Navy Department, like James W. Grimes, would maintain civil control over the navy. Neither the board of admirals nor Fox's idea was adopted.[5]

An expansionist, Fox was interested in the acquisition of Alaska as well as the Danish West Indies. The initiative from the czar to sell Alaska (which threatened to become a fiscal and strategic burden for him) came on the heels of Fox's return from Russia. The time Fox spent with Seward and especially with Sumner, the chair of the Senate Foreign Relations Committee, was devoted to promoting Alaska's purchase. The support of Sumner, who was neither an imperialist nor a friend of the Johnson administration, was crucial. He supported the purchase in a well-informed, two-and-three-quarter-hour speech and gave that vast territory the Aleut name "Alaska." It had previously been known as "Russian America." The speedy, 9 April 1867 ratification of the purchase treaty overjoyed Fox, who from Portsmouth boasted to Wise, "I worked here and in Boston for the treaty. Telegraphed to Sumner and got parties to write to Senators," and sent a communication to the *Boston Advertiser.* "Perhaps [John] Bull will sell out his N.W. Columbia territory. This cession of territory from Russia will help us to the whole Continent."[6]

From 20 May to 5 June, Fox served at Annapolis on the Naval Academy Board of Visitors. He had a busy and occasionally "tedious" time attending examinations and seamanship exercises. The board was pleased that extensive repairs to the physical plant necessitated by four years of neglect were finally being done. Porter especially wanted Fox to see "the steam department. The navy," he told him, "is indebted to you for it." Porter apparently was doing well as superintendent, and it was good to see Welles and Farragut, when they visited for a day. "Our meals are elaborate, and drinks plenty," Fox reported to Virginia. "I rather like you," a member of the board told him, "you eat so much, drink so much, exercise so much and seem to have yourself in perfect control—how do you do it?" Although most of the board went to Governor Thomas Swann's reception given to what Fox dismissed as "the Copperhead convention sitting here," he did not go. Unlike Swann and Montgomery Blair, Fox was not ready to rejoin the Democratic Party.[7]

On weekends, Fox went to Washington and stayed with Minna and Montgomery Blair. "Our brother-in-law," Admiral Lee, he told Virginia, was quarreling with Fox's equally disputatious friend, Dr. Horwitz, over fences, and Fox regaled her with juicy capital gossip about Charles Sumner's marital problems. Fox also examined boxes of minerals, books, and photographs given to him in Russia that were housed at the Smithsonian Institution. He planned to add the minerals to his personal collection and to keep a few of the choice books and photographs, but to give the remainder to the Library of Congress and the Smithsonian. Joseph Henry, secretary of the Smithsonian, displayed some of the items at his house "for the inspection of the Scientific club." Fox talked about Russia for an hour to that group, which included Chief Justice Chase, Secretary of the Treasury Hugh McCulloch, Benjamin Peirce, and about twenty others. He was disappointed that Blair had earlier committed himself to attend the opera.[8]

While serving on the board of visitors, Fox learned that the distinguished lawyer and railroad entrepreneur Frederick Billings and his associates wanted "the best man in the U.S. for the Presidency" of the South West Pacific Railroad of Missouri and its extension, the Atlantic and Pacific Railroad with its huge federal land grant of 55 million acres. The shipping magnate William H. Aspinwall had recommended Fox, and Billings had sounded him out. Fox was interested, if he would have *"full control of affairs."* He consulted his friend James B. Eads, who was involved in western railroads and was a Missourian.[9]

Although Eads would have liked to involve Fox in an enterprise of his own, he was encouraging about the railroad presidency. Eads proposed that Fox help sell to the Navy and War departments his "steam or compressed air gun carriage" for mounting heavy cannon, which increased the rapidity of their fire. With his prestige, Eads reasoned, Fox could "easily have an order issued" to install his invention on every monitor and influence its use by the army in coastal defense, and together "we can build up two colossal fortunes in a few years." Commenting, "Don't want to touch anything before the Dep'ts," Fox realized lobbying would compromise his ethical standards. Eads counseled Fox to secure the presidencies of both the South West Pacific and the Atlantic and Pacific railroads, if he got involved in the project. Eads predicted that, if completed, it would be "the most important of all railroad companies on this, or any other continent." Fox dreamed that, once he got things organized in Missouri, he could move his office to New York, where he and Virginia could live in style.[10]

Although the South West Pacific Railroad had great potential, it was deeply troubled in June 1867. It had been mismanaged by its president, General John Charles Frémont, who early in the Civil War had gone from a political ally of the Blairs to their enemy. After a year of Frémont's control, the eighty-nine-mile road owed the state $1 million (the balance of its purchase price) and its bondholders $1,437,000 and had $435,000 in unsecured debt. It owed its construction laborers two months' back pay for the 11 miles of track laid on its proposed 280-mile route. Because the road had failed to pay the $250,000 installment of its debt to the state, Governor Thomas C. Fletcher had taken possession of it that month and placed it in the charge of General Clinton B. Fisk. The people of southwest Missouri had lost patience with Frémont, as had some of his associates. The *Missouri Democrat* insinuated that he never "honestly meant to build the road," but rather to profit from the sale of its bonds and its 1 million acres of land. Fox reported to Virginia that Frémont's associates say "he has neither character of any kind nor decency in business, or morality nor common honesty."[11]

The dubious condition of the South West Pacific was matched by doubts about who should manage it. Prior to the state takeover, Billings found to his chagrin that he could not manage Fox's appointment as president. He assumed that the state takeover was temporary and that by restructuring the bonded indebtedness, reconstituting the board of directors, and securing Fox as president to attract investors, the road "would go through," with "no humbug, & no stealing." But Frémont and bondholders in New York and Boston, with whom Billings and Fox met, were reluctant to fall in with Billings's plan to give up $800,000 to $1 million in bonds to the company treasury. Billing's proposal, that these bonds "be reissued at eighty with a quantity of stock to go with them as a gift," would realize $800,000 capital. When coupled with the strong investors Fox would attract, Billings thought "the road would go on again."[12]

Although Billings characterized Frémont and his associates as corrupt, he believed it necessary to include them in reorganizing the South West Pacific Railroad, because they controlled its proposed extension, the Atlantic & Pacific. Fox soon questioned that idea. Apart from alleged corruption, the coolness of bondholders to the Billings proposal to turn in bonds to raise capital did not endear them to Fox, and the failure of the Frémont party to lay track and to pay the state had turned southwest Missourians and the governor against them. After consulting with John Murray Forbes, who was heavily involved in the Chicago, Burlington, & Quincy Railroad, and Thomas Scott of the Pennsylvania Railroad, as well as Eads, Fox determined that a new organization was necessary.[13]

Aided by his brother-in-law Charles Levi Woodbury, Fox devised a plan. The Fox party would subscribe enough capital (approximately $1.5 million) to build the road and get the legislature to grant it to the South West Pacific Railroad, with its land grant of 1 million acres. From a position of strength, Fox could negotiate an arrangement with the Atlantic & Pacific Railroad, which existed only on paper, despite its enormous grant of 55 million acres. Governor Fletcher and a delegation of southwest Missourians, who came to New York, liked Fox's plan, but Billings thought it "entirely impractical" to exclude the Frémont party. On 9 October Fox and Billings "parted company." Fox, however, did not ignore the South West Pacific bondholders and secured some support from them.[14]

Throughout the fall of 1867, Fox worked in New York and Boston to obtain twelve $100,000 subscriptions for first mortgage bonds and for three similar pledges in Missouri. "Political excitement" over Reconstruction, he noted, "is considerable" and the price of gold is up. Capitalists, he added, "upon the gloomy appearance of the business future hesitate to embark in so great a scheme." Nathaniel Thayer, a Boston financier, was not alone when he wrote in December, "I find business matters here in a very bad state, and great distrust as to the future and in the present condition of affairs I should decline joining *anything* new." Even Aspinwall hesitated, until John Murray Forbes at Fox's request journeyed to New York "to strengthen" him about the enterprise. Engineering problems and financial misfortunes had given the South West Pacific a bad name with capitalists. Of the remaining 191 miles to be constructed, 20 promised to be difficult. By 21 December Fox had seven subscribers, and felt certain of three more names in New York, one in Rochester, two in Cleveland, and at least three in Missouri.[15]

While trying to raise money, Fox also had to contend with rival parties, hoping to acquire the South West Pacific. Although General Fisk denied it, there were rumors of a "*Missouri* all owned" organization with Fisk as president. There was also the Frémont interest of unorganized South West stockholders. Fox had most to fear from the Boston-based South West Pacific bondholders. They wanted to protect their investment and some of them wished to protect their interest in the Missouri, Kansas, & Texas Railroad, which the extended South West Pacific would intersect and siphon off east-bound traffic. By mid-December, these bondholders had organized a committee to regain control of the South West Pacific. Among their leading spirits were Benjamin E. Bates, president of the Boston Bank of Commerce, his lawyer, Francis B. Hayes, and Andrew Peirce Jr. After they consulted with Forbes and Woodbury, Forbes advised Fox to make an arrangement with them. Although reluctant, he agreed to allow them fifty cents on a dollar in exchanging old for new bonds. Fox did not want the road to "be put up at auction to the highest bidder," and he realized Bates and Peirce could "block the wheels and mar the prospects" of his party.[16]

Between 23 and 28 December, Fox nailed down subscribers and talked to bondholders in New York. He was too busy to escort Virginia, her mother, and her sister Nell to church on Christmas Day. Although Bates said, "The true plan is to unite with the Fox party" and claimed to be "working in that direction," efforts to "concoct some scheme that would enable" his associates to unite the "interests" of all parties failed. Despite differences, an ally confidently wrote Fox, "All these men perfectly understand you are to be President."[17]

Having secured enough subscribers, Fox left for the West on 5 January 1868 and began the crucial political phase of his activities. He had to lobby a bill through the Missouri legislature, granting his party the South West Pacific Railroad. At St. Louis, he stayed with Eads and saw Montgomery Blair's brother Frank to explore what help he and his cousin Benjamin Gratz Brown could be in passing the bill. Frank saw some of his conservative friends, but thought he should keep a low profile and not prejudice Radical Republicans against Fox's bill. Fox arrived in Jefferson City, the capital, on 10 January and began drumming up support for his project. "I am logrolling in the heart of Mo.," he wrote Wise. Meeting with legislators from southwest Missouri, Fox solidified their support, spent an evening with state supreme court judges, and played chess regularly with Governor Fletcher. On 20 January Fox's bill was introduced in the Senate. But Frank Blair was right. Within a few days, William M. Grosvenor, of the Radical *Missouri Democrat*, attacked the Fox bill as a Blair-Fox scheme to enrich the Blair family. It was also "a deep laid plan to control the next election" and propel Frank Blair into the U.S. Senate. Grosvenor was answered effectively and accurately by James Baker from southwest Missouri, who pointed out that Frank Blair's politics were not Fox's politics and that at least ten of the fifteen subscribers Fox had recruited were Radicals.[18]

The effort to portray Fox as an agent of the Blairs had limited success. Political differences were subordinated to geographic and economic considerations. The support Frank Blair gave Fox was tardy, halfhearted, and ineffectual. Southwest Missourians, whatever their political persuasion, were virtually unanimous in favor of the Fox bill. But Fox realized there were opposing forces: rival railroad interests worried about losing traffic to a completed South West road; Governor Fletcher and "a large clique" wanted the South West's "valuable lands sold so they can speculate in them"; Radicals, influenced by Grosvenor, wanted "all roads subordinate" to the upcoming political campaign; and the "Fremont interest [stockholders] are trying to defeat us and the bondholders also. All these we can defeat," Fox predicted, "unless the bondholders choose to make a better offer than ourselves. They are in St. Louis and will soon appear here. In their game I am no match for these sharp lawyers, but the committal of the S.W. to my scheme gives advantage."[19]

Fox was right. He was no match. His bill passed the Missouri Senate on 13 February, but four days later Hayes and Peirce, representing both New York and Boston bondholders and those who controlled the Atlantic & Pacific franchise, arrived in Jefferson City. Fox neither liked nor trusted them. They insisted that no matter how the road was organized they would fight for their claims against the South West Pacific. Rather than have the enterprise bog down in litigation, Fox yielded to pressure to include the bondholders among the new grantees of the road as long as Hayes and Peirce agreed to unite the South West and Atlantic & Pacific franchises. His "distrust of them" grew when Hayes promised to pay "for his services to his entire satisfaction," should he not get the presidency of the united companies.[20]

Getting the altered Fox bill through the Missouri General Assembly, which was deluged by railroad bills, was difficult. To Fox's chagrin, conservative associates of Frank Blair fought his bill and persisted even after Blair telegraphed them to get out of the opposition. Eads urged Fox to work with this financially strong and politically conservative St. Louis group, but their motives were questionable. Despite a severe case of diarrhea, which left him weak and ten pounds lighter, Fox spoke individually with members of the assembly's Committee on Internal Improvements to gain their approval. He was partially successful. His bill and an Iron Mountain Railroad bill passed on 13 March, thanks to considerable logrolling and "much liquor." But Frank Blair's conservative St. Louis friends tacked some "very objectionable amendments" to Fox's bill. Eight St. Louis capitalists were added to Fox's subscription list, and the bill stated that bondholders would forfeit $1 million if certain requirements were not met. The Senate accepted the amended bill, and, to Fox's surprise, Fletcher signed it into law on 17 March 1868.[21]

Organizing the grantees named in the act into a company would be a daunting task. "I think," he wrote Charles Woodbury, "you better try and arrange to meet with us not only as one of our lawyers but to protect and assist me in getting the presidency." Because some, if not all, of his original subscribers were unhappy with the amendments, Fox visited them to shore up their support. The grantees met in New York from 8 to 17 April and elected a nine-member board of directors including Fox, who ominously was not on the slate proposed by the Committee on Organization. Fifteen parties subscribed $100,000 contingent upon a clear title and a satisfactory organization. One of them, Ben Holladay, the stagecoach king who was moving into railroads, telegraphed his attorney from San Francisco, "Vote for Fox for president and tell him he is on the reliable track to the Pacific." And Senator Samuel W. Headlee, who sponsored Fox's bill, told him how pleased southwest Missourians were at "the prospect of an early organization of the Fox Company." James F. Joy, Forbes's associate in the Chicago, Burlington & Quincy who had helped Fox lobby for his bill, knew that his "untiring . . . efforts and reputation" revived the project and emphasized that Fox "ought to be the president."[22]

Fox was cautiously optimistic. The grantees met in St. Louis, and on 8 May adopted a plan of organization to which there were nineteen subscribers. After causing so much trouble, none of the St. Louis conservatives subscribed. Amid "ostensible harmony," the meeting adjourned to reconvene in New York to complete the organization and select a president. "Unless some of my friends fail," Fox assumed he had a majority for the presidency and would prevail over the Boston bondholders, "but . . . I may be cheated out of it."[23]

Some of Fox's friends did falter. They did not like the forfeiture amendment nor the insistence of the Boston people that the new company be organized as a merger with the Atlantic & Pacific and assume its debts. Fox's people wanted to organize first and then negotiate a merger. In addition, some of Fox's strongest supporters were in Europe or in California and were not available for the New York meeting. With his "strong monied friends absent and lukewarm," Fox came to the "mortifying" conclusion that he could not win the presidency. On 19 May he met with Hayes and Peirce, who agreed to compensate him "for past services and for putting road into their possession." At the directors' meeting on 20 May 1868, he "withdrew his name for any position whatever" in the South West Pacific Railroad, after the unanimous passage of a resolution that his claims be referred to mutually chosen arbitrators and, if they should disagree, be sent to an umpire for a final decision. "I doubt its resulting in anything," Virginia exclaimed. "Thus ends fortune!" Hayes was elected president. Within a few days, Fox resigned his directorship, and, within a few weeks, only three members of his original party remained active in the new company. Although Ben Holladay told Hayes that Fox should get $100,000 for lobbying in Missouri and organizing in New York and Boston, the "slippery" Hayes offered $5,000 for his year of hard work and stalled a settlement. After five years, in May 1873, the arbitration umpire awarded Fox $16,624, and after more spiteful delays he received payment in twenty-five Atlantic & Pacific second-mortgage land grant bonds in February 1874.[24]

Fox tried to take his disappointment in stride. He and Virginia left New York, on 25 May 1868, for Boston. There, two days later, in both the morning and evening, they heard Wendell Phillips. Crusading for African American political equality, he addressed the remnant of the American Anti-Slavery Society, of which he was president. That same day, Fox saw John Murray Forbes and "told him briefly about 'Railroad termination.'" A few days later, he was Forbes's dinner guest at the Parker House for a meeting of the intellectually stimulating Saturday Club. From the Saturday Club, Fox joined a small gathering at Samuel Gridley Howe's Perkins Institution for the Blind. He had tea with John Rodgers, the commandant of the Boston Navy Yard, and attended the 10 June meeting at Faneuil Hall, ratifying the Republican Party's nomination of Ulysses S. Grant for president. Having been purged of his desire to be the captain of a railroad, Fox was tempted by the suggestion of his old friends in the textile business, Oliver H. Perry and Joseph S. Fay, that he manage their Middlesex Mill at Lowell, and asked for $8,000 and a rent-free house.[25]

During the summer and fall of 1868, Fox relaxed. He even relaxed his scruples a bit, while on a visit to Washington, to persuade Isherwood to call for standard-sized, rough and finished nuts and bolts and obtain them from his brother, George Fox. He perceived he had a chance for the St. Petersburg mission, but did not try for it when Virginia said she had "neither the strength, taste, nor money for it." In the summer, he boated on Chesapeake Bay and up the Maine coast to Mt. Desert Island. In the fall, he and Virginia went to the White Mountains, where, from Mount Washington, they saw vessels at sea, sixty-seven miles away. Next they visited Montreal, Canada, and turned south and west to Ausable Chasm and Watkins Glen in New York State. A lover of flowers, trees, and natural wonders, Virginia reveled in the beauty of chasm and glen. Intrigued by science and technology, Fox was delighted to discover in Albany, New York, a museum of natural history. Upon his return to Portsmouth, he accepted the agency of the Middlesex Mills at $7,500 plus $1,500 for housing, beginning in January 1869. Considering their recent aspirations, Virginia was depressed at the thought of "mill life for Gus" and life in Lowell for her, but Fox maintained good spirits about his prospects in the textile industry.[26]

Although he was beginning to lean toward the Democrats, Fox was ambivalent about the 1868 presidential election. The impeachment of Andrew Johnson, the praise of the British system of responsible government by Wendell Phillips, and calls for "strong government" by George Jones of the *New York Times* (whom Fox met in the White Mountains) confirmed Fox's fear that Radical Republicans, like his friend Ben Butler, "meditated" a change in our form of government. But, in March, he told Virginia that the recent Republican victory in New Hampshire "did not disappoint me. The North will not consent to put the Gov't into the hands of those who sympathized with the South during the war. Grant will surely be President unless Ben Butler's candidate Farragut is nominated. He will beat Grant." Fox was pleased that the Democrats nominated Frank Blair for vice president, but found their presidential nominee, Horatio Seymour, too difficult to stomach. As governor of New

York, Seymour gave the Union cause only tepid support and blamed the New York City draft riots on the excesses of the Lincoln administration. Fox did not vote in 1868. Farragut did not wish to be president, and, as Fox predicted, Grant triumphed. Shortly after Grant's victory, Fox called on him, hoping to enlist his support for the annexation of the Virgin Islands. Probably realizing that the Senate would not ratify the purchase treaty, Fox did not lobby for the treaty's passage, as his friend Waldemar Raasloff, the Danish minister, urged him to do.[27]

Fox soon had more reasons to be disappointed with Grant and his administration. Like Welles, he was disturbed when Grant appointed, in quick succession, a nonentity and then a corruptionist as secretary of the navy and made Porter the de facto head of the department. If anything, the mutual respect Fox and Welles had for each other grew as they reviewed their years in the Navy Department. Welles was stung by allegations that he had been incompetent, annoyed by Porter's heavy-handed changes in the department, and outraged by the corrupt acts of his successor, George M. Robeson. Beginning in 1870, Welles published a series of articles defending his administration. He consulted with Fox, tried to resolve differences in their recollections, and briefly aroused in Fox a concern that Welles might slight his contributions. Fox supplied Welles with information, including confidential correspondence from line officers. Because Porter (after the death of his foster brother Farragut) claimed credit for capturing New Orleans, Fox appreciated Welles's assertion that Farragut, not Porter, was responsible for the victory. If anything, Fox was more annoyed than Welles over Porter's "reforms" in the department. They included getting rid of Benjamin F. Isherwood and John Lenthall and rerigging steamers for sail, while the British were improving their steam vessels. Porter also brought in new uniforms and designed the *Alarm*, an iron torpedo boat, which proved a failure. In protest, but not certain it would stop "the plundering now going on," Fox in 1870 voted for the Democrats. Still, he had hopes that "the better class of republicans," the "revenue civil service reformers," would restore the balance of powers among the three branches of government.[28]

By 1871 Porter's old habit of disparaging others, which now included Fox and Welles, angered Fox. He exploded to James B. Eads:

> Poor fellow. I stood by him because he fought well. I knew he could not tell the truth, but in the dire necessities of our late war and the poor material to select from *fighting* was the only consideration. Neither Mr. Welles nor Mr. Lincoln ever liked him. I took him as a Lt. and when I let go of him he was a Vice Admi-

ral. I saved his drunken lying relations from disgrace and my influence gave him a fortune in money also. When he took my place at the Dept. we separated as brothers. I asked but one favor the appt of a nephew, a poor boy to West Point. Porter was all powerful with Grant and promised to attend to it. He *forgot it;* he trampled upon the memory and reputation of those who had befriended and gave him priceless opportunities—he belittled our acts, he lied about our services and without provocation disparaged us in every way in his power. I have not lifted a pen in reply. Without reward, or thanks or even acknowledgment of my own services I have kept silent with this traducer filling my place, satisfied that he would at length perish by his own hand and few to regret it.

In time, Fox's rage subsided, and he again saw and corresponded with Porter. Indeed, by 1877 Porter disparaged Robeson, wrote Fox lively, friendly, illustrated letters, and seemed unaware that he had ever irked him. Obviously, it was better for Fox to get along with Porter. He had great influence over the development of the navy, which, along with Virginia, was Fox's true love.[29]

On 4 January 1869 Fox began his new job in the textile industry. On that day, he started working as the agent (manager) of the Middlesex Mills in Lowell and continued in that position until March 1874. From December 1871 to January 1873, Fox also served on the Massachusetts Board of Health and, among other things, decided on an abattoir at Brighton, where the slaughtering of animals in the Boston area would be concentrated. On 2 April 1872 he became president for a short period of the projected Lowell & Andover Railroad. A link between existing lines, it was in operation by December 1874. Earlier that year, on 1 May, he became a partner for 20 percent of the profits plus $6,000 annually in E. R. Mudge, Sawyer & Company, which owned the Washington Mills in Lawrence. He remained in that position for four years. No longer responsible for day-to-day operations, he served in an overall supervisory capacity (occasionally lobbying for a 40 percent ad valorem tariff on woolens in place of 70 cents per pound) and had more time for leisure.[30]

While at the Middlesex Mills in Lowell, Fox had a full social life, but Virginia felt lonely and unhappy. He was in touch with relatives and old friends and colleagues, and he and Virginia vacationed and traveled. His brother-in-law Charles Woodbury and his nephews Woodbury Blair and Woodbury Lowery (who were both attending Harvard) visited in Lowell nearly every Sunday. Wood Lowery was an excellent student and became a distinguished historian, but Wood Blair was so indifferent a scholar that his father gave up on him. Thanks primarily to Fox's constant encouragement and help, Wood Blair made it through Harvard and became a successful lawyer.[31]

For Fox and Virginia, the social event that eclipsed all others while they were in Lowell was the luncheon they gave in their home on 10 December 1871 for Czar Alexander's third son, Grand Duke Alexis. Fox had the house painted a lighter color for the occasion, hired a Boston caterer, and reported that all went as planned.[32]

The Foxes attended weddings and numerous funerals. The death on 2 April 1869 in Naples, Italy, of Fox's best friend, Henry A. Wise, was a severe blow. In July 1870 Fox shuttled between Lowell and Newport, Rhode Island, where Virginia was vacationing. He attended the wedding of Benjamin F. Butler's daughter Blanche to Adelbert Ames, the carpetbag senator from Mississippi, and, a few days later, visited Admiral Farragut on his deathbed in Portsmouth. Fox was with his parents when they died, his father Jesse, on 12 October 1870, and his mother Olivia, on 9 April 1874. A few weeks earlier, in March 1874, he attended the funeral of Charles Sumner in Boston.[33]

In Washington in May 1872, the Foxes socialized with the Porters, and, in front of the War Department, Fox chatted with Grant about the Liberal Republican nomination of Horace Greeley. (Grant correctly thought the Rebels would vote for Greeley). Two days later in New York, John Hay, who was temporarily editing Greeley's *Tribune*, told Fox that Greeley's election depended on the Democrats. Apart from reporting these comments, Fox took little interest in the 1872 campaign. He liked neither Greeley (because of his attacks on the Navy department during the war) nor Grant (because of the state of naval affairs during Grant's first term), but he did like the Liberal Republicans and probably voted for Greeley. Almost a year later, feeling that the financial Panic of 1873 vindicated the revolt against Grant, Fox commented to Welles, "How sad that Greeley was not now alive," referring to Greeley's death shortly after the election. By 1874 Fox was once again a Democrat, but he feared that party would neither "retrench" nor be an improvement.[34]

The Washington Mills position enabled Fox and Virginia to move to the Parker House in Boston. There, their social, intellectual, and cultural opportunities were broader. They attended the opera and the theater regularly and museums occasionally. On 26 December 1874 Fox dined with the Saturday Club, along with Charles Francis Adams, Ralph Waldo Emerson, Oliver Wendell Holmes, John Murray Forbes, William Dean Howells, and others. A couple of months later, he dined with the Friday Club, whose members boasted the proper Bostonian names of Gardner, Adams, Lawrence, Coolidge, Quincy, Amory, and Grey. Virginia's health remained a problem. "Such a winter as the last," Fox exclaimed on 8 September 1875, "she ought not to experience." He thought seriously about retiring early. To improve her health and morale, they got out of Boston on frequent trips and extensive vacations. In New York, Fox called on Ericsson, who expounded on his design for a torpedo and was "furious" about corruption, "cursing" Robeson, Grant, and the "whole Country." In Washington, Fox dropped in at the Coast Survey Office and on relatives, and he and Virginia visited the 1876 Philadelphia Centennial Exhibition. On longer vacations, he was characteristically restless. In August 1875 a "very weak" Virginia spent a few weeks at Lake George with her sister Frank and her family. On the three weekends he spent there, Fox rowed Virginia about the lake. In between, he checked in at the mill, visited Welles at Newport, and stopped at Nahant, a resort town on Massachusetts Bay.[35]

His loose schedule at the Washington Mills enabled Fox to research geographical questions that intrigued him. The *Kearsarge*, which under the command of John A. Winslow sank the *Alabama*, had been named by Virginia after a New Hampshire mountain in Carroll County. There was, however, another mountain named Kearsarge in Merrimack County, New Hampshire, and nearby residents claimed it as the source of the *Kearsarge*'s name. Worse, C. H. Hitchcock, a distinguished New Hampshire geologist, had suggested in a report and on a map that the Carroll County mountain be called Piqwacket or Pequawket. Opposed to this name change, Fox thoroughly researched the earliest histories and accounts of New Hampshire and showed that white settlers in Carroll County had never used any name but Kearsarge for their mountain and that the Indian word pequawket described a level place, not a mountain. Despite his research, he had limited success. The Carroll County mountain is called Pequawket or Kearsarge or North Kearsage (with no second "r"), while the Merrimack Kearsarge is in the middle of Winslow State Park.[36]

On 7 November 1876, at the end of Grant's disastrous second term (marred by cronyism and corruption), Fox voted for the Democratic nominee Samuel J. Tilden for president. With Republicans and Democrats both claiming to have carried South Carolina, Louisiana, and Florida, no clear winner emerged. On the basis of votes actually cast, Tilden would have won, but murder and intimidation had kept many African American Republicans from voting for the Republican nominee Rutherford B. Hayes in many southern states. Where intimidation occurred, the entire vote of an election district could be disqualified by state returning boards, which were empowered to determine the official vote.[37]

Dominated by Republicans, the returning boards in the disputed states could decide the outcome of the election. In an effort to influence those boards, prominent members of both parties descended on the disputed states. Fox had seemed more interested in Kearsarge Mountain than in the campaign, but

Montgomery Blair was a conspicuous supporter of Tilden. Also, Abram S. Hewitt, the steel manufacturer who during the war had apprised Fox on the casting of guns abroad, was both a congressman and the chair of the Democratic National Committee. On Friday, 10 November, Hewitt asked Fox, as well as other "fair men," to go to New Orleans. Fox left at 9:30 that evening with $200 in his pocket.[38]

Consultations with Democrats in Washington changed Fox's destination to Columbia, South Carolina. Thanks to the company of Montgomery Blair and Senator Theodore F. Randolph of New Jersey, the trip was a pleasant one. They arrived in South Carolina on Tuesday. After meeting with Wade Hampton, the Democratic candidate for governor, on Wednesday, the trio, along with Grant's emissary, Chief Judge David K. Cartter, of the Supreme Court of the District of Columbia, called on Daniel H. Chamberlain, the Republican governor of the state. Cartter delivered to Chamberlain a note from Grant calling for "a fair count of the votes cast." It soon became clear that Hayes had carried South Carolina, but the governorship, legislature, and state offices were in doubt. In the two days Fox was in Columbia, he called on Thomas C. Dunn, a Republican member of the returning board and a former U.S. naval officer, who had distinguished himself on blockade duty and at Fort Fisher. Dunn agreed when Fox urged him and his colleagues to act as impartial judges in open sessions before "witnesses on both sides" and to "throw out illegal votes no matter who they affected."[39]

Fox optimistically reassured his partner Mudge back in Boston that South Carolinians had experienced a change of heart.

> No danger of outbreak here. A complete revolution has taken place in the temper of this people in 16 years. I witnessed the beginning of the Civil War by their firing on Fort Sumter. Today I was present when the people then so intemperately passionate, calmly asserted their political rights before a court constituted entirely of Republicans and mostly Negroes where opposing counsel were Negroes and the attendants were chiefly Negroes. So effectively have the disasters of the Civil War taught themselves restraint and the necessity of asserting their rights according to forms of law.

Given his ongoing commitment to political rights for blacks and his current support of Tilden, Fox emphasized the postelection good behavior of Democrats, and, although he wanted illegal votes thrown out, he did not stress the intimidation of black voters prior to the election.[40]

By Saturday, 18 November, Fox was back in Washington, calling on Grant at the White House. Being overcommitted, Grant could not give a second lieutenant's commission in the army to Fox's nephew George William May (Willie) Guild, but Grant wanted Fox to stay and talk about the disputed election. Fox reminded him that his note delivered to Chamberlain by Judge Cartter and his order to General William T. Sherman called for a fair count of the "votes actually cast." Grant countered that the order "should have been legally cast. You might as well count mechanically a bundle of bank bills without scrutinizing and throwing out the counterfeit." In Louisiana, Grant told Fox, only three votes were cast for Hayes in heretofore Republican parishes, a "marshall was killed and ballot boxes seized." Fox asked, "If all illegal votes are thrown out by the Louisiana returning board, who will be in majority there?" Grant replied, "Hayes." To Fox's query, "Is there any appeal from the decision of this board?" Grant replied that he thought not. To Fox's regret, their conversation was interrupted and ended when two cabinet members entered the room. Two days later in New York, Fox spent two hours with Tilden reporting on South Carolina and his interview with Grant. Tilden accurately predicted that the Louisiana, Florida, and South Carolina returning boards would return Hayes electors and that Congress would settle the question.[41]

Congress did decide the election. The Electoral Commission Act, which Fox favored, created a body that decided who carried the disputed states. Congress accepted the rulings of the commission, and to Fox's dismay Hayes was elected "contrary to the votes of the people." Perhaps because his great friend and kinsman Montgomery Blair was so devastated by Tilden's loss, Fox felt it keenly. Four years later, in 1880, Fox referred to Tilden as "the President of the U.S.," when he visited him at Greystone, his Yonkers home, overlooking the Hudson. Tilden's mind was "clear and he talked well and joked," but he spoke only in a whisper and both hands shook continually. Fox realized Tilden's asset was his mind, not his constitution, and again lamented the lost election. "One cannot look at Mr. Tilden without feeling a deep sense of humiliation at the unparalleled crime committed in his person, and almost despair that it has not aroused more intense feeling. He will not live to see another presidential election," Fox inaccurately predicted, "but the crime committed in his person will be the blackest page of our history." Fox, however, did not shun Hayes. When he visited Boston in June 1877, Fox was among the dignitaries who dined with him and members of his cabinet. As a Civil War warrior and an advocate of black voting rights, Fox was not really at ease in the Democratic Party. Although he liked its 1880 nominee, General Winfield Scott Hancock, he thought Hancock would not be elected, because "the solid South is the potent and ugly factor in the case," and it would cost the Democrats northerners' votes.[42]

Fox retired from the Washington Mills in 1878. He calculated that he and Virginia had "enough" to give them an income of $10,000 a year. Because he was only fifty-six, he wished to remain active. He felt he was "fitted for public life" and longed to serve the navy in some civilian capacity. He also had "a strong desire to compile a Naval history of the War," but his "first care" was to improve Virginia's "physical and mental condition. . . . If she is happy," he wrote Montgomery Blair, "I feel like a soldier with a secure base." Because Virginia's three sisters lived in Washington, Fox and Virginia decided to make it their home again. He spent May and June 1878 selling and storing furniture, donating art to the Museum of Fine Arts (including Clark Mills's copy of Milo's *Venus*), and packing large trunks.[43]

In the next few years, they would live as well-to-do vagabonds. Their baggage on one trip weighed 725 pounds. Virginia's medicine trunk weighed 190 pounds, her other one 150, and her maid's trunk 100, while Fox's large trunk was 160 pounds and his small one 125.[44]

After seeing friends, like John Murray Forbes, and paying bills, Fox and Virginia, on 28 June 1878, left Boston for the White Mountains. They remained there for eighty-one days. After a month in New York, followed by a month in Washington, they meandered in December to Florida, where they attended services at the African-Methodist Episcopal and "Baptist colored" churches. They also attended exercises at the Stanton School for black children, where Fox "made some remarks to the pupils." On 18 January 1879 they left Jacksonville, Florida, for three months in Nassau in the Bahamas. Returning in April, they toured the South for nearly a year and a half, taking a long sojourn in Atlanta. Hoping that hot baths would be beneficial for Virginia, they spent the summer of 1879 at Warm Springs, North Carolina, and the next summer at Jordan Alum Springs, Virginia. They returned to Washington for the winter of 1880 to 1881.[45]

Fox's travels were not aimless. They were influenced by Edward Atkinson, an economist who also had been the agent of a textile mill. Fox read Atkinson's publications "with deep interest," while investigating the feasibility of manufacturing cotton textiles in the South. "I have visited," he wrote Atkinson, "the cotton mills at Vaucluse, Augusta, Atlanta, Greenville, &c. and travelled along the Piedmont Region lying between the mts and the coast, low, malarial lands. I am more than ever impressed with the idea that here is the true region for the most economical development of, at least cotton, manufactures, but the managers and the capital must be foreign to the region." Emulating Atkinson, Fox collected statistics on population and schools in the towns he visited, in an effort to project the existence of an educated labor force.[46]

With laborers on his mind, Fox spoke to former slaves. He heard from them that all-white juries would never convict a white for a crime against a black. They also complained that after a year's work a sharecropper had nothing. "Will you just tell me," a former slave asked Fox with great feeling, "how 'tis that the nigger is always underneath?" Fox found the answer in "a thousand years" of history, but suggested that education, energy, and thrift would improve the condition of blacks. He also felt that white oppression of African Americans encouraged the much talked about "exodus," which he feared would ruin the South and not help blacks. Their place, Fox felt certain, would not be taken by European immigrants. He continued to believe in black suffrage and opposed literacy tests for voters. They were, he thought, counterproductive for Democrats, because blacks were learning to read and write at a faster rate than poor whites. He found a "large number of persons" who believed that "political equality for the Negro is inevitable and their best course is to educate him and attach him to their side by kindness and giving him offices to which he may become fit." On the whole, Fox found white southerners "very selfish." They wished "first to be saved from the Negro vote, then appropriations, and office." Worse, he found that the return of the Democrats to power in Tennessee, and he believed elsewhere, led to "the ostracism of every person who contributed to the preservation of the Union."[47]

For Fox, the trip to the Bahamas also served a purpose. There, in early 1879, he took up the question of which island Columbus first landed on in the New World. To delve more deeply into the subject, he waited until returning to Washington, where he "had access to great sources of information." With his Coast Survey experience, sailing know-how, and indefatigable energy, he investigated this unsolvable problem. Previous writers suggested that Columbus landed either on Grand Turk Island, Cat Island, Mayaguana Island, or Watlings Island. After poring over charts, inquiring about currents, and studying the topography of these and other islands, Fox concluded that Columbus landed on Samana Cay.[48]

At work or play, traveling or studying, Fox remained a navy man. He kept in contact with Welles and Welles's son Edgar, and he also saw old navy comrades. Fox zealously guarded the honor, fame, and reputation of the navy and its men. He was most anxious that Farragut be remembered and was gratified by the Augustus Saint-Gaudens statue of him in Madison Square, New York City, and Vinnie Ream's huge statue of him in Farragut Square, Washington. To celebrate the unveiling of the Ream statue on 25 April 1881, Fox spent $407.85 on a dinner for thirty-six dignitaries, including cabinet members, senators, and admirals Porter, Worden, and John Rodgers.[49]

Fox and Porter continued their renewed association. On a professional level, Porter apprised Fox on developments in the navy and, on a personal level, he inquired after Virginia's health and comfort and saw the Foxes whenever possible. He also pitched in to try and get that elusive second lieutenancy for Willie Guild. In doing so, Porter once again evaluated Fox's contribution during the war:

> To his professional knowledge and untiring energy, the country is largely indebted for the rapidity with which we built up a powerful navy. To his advocacy of the building of suitable vessels for the destruction of an enemy's commerce and improvement of Ericsson's system of monitors was the country in a great measure indebted for an avoidance of war with England and France which would have been fatal to the Union cause. . . . I assent from an intimate acquaintance with the facts, that but for Mr. Fox's energy in promptly supplying the requisitions of naval commanders, which at times seemed extravagant important movements would have been unsuccessful.[50]

Fox neither established a textile mill in the South nor wrote a history of the Union navy in the Civil War. It is regrettable that all Fox wrote on the war was a balanced encyclopedia article on the *Monitor*,[51] because he grasped that "the truth of history can hurt nobody and should not be concealed. So far as my administration is concerned," he wrote, "I should wish no credit at the expense of truth from whatsoever source it emanates." Fox recognized that "exaggeration may be a necessary device of war, but not of history."[52]

The summer of 1883 was stressful for Fox. Montgomery Blair died on 27 July. "Next to myself," Virginia wrote Minna, "Gus loved him better than anyone on earth." In addition, Fox experienced a series of sudden, brief, painful "attacks" in the chest accompanied by motor disturbances, a pale pinched look, cold extremities, and sweating. Half the physicians Fox consulted blamed his attacks on "surf bathing." The other "half acknowledged," Virginia noted, "with a truthfulness and modesty rare in the profession, that they did not know what caused them." By 19 October Fox and Virginia were at the Everett House on New York's Union Square for Fox to visit Dr. William A. Hammond, a pioneer neurologist, about his "nervous affection." Between his episodes and medical appointments, Fox remained active, walking about town and viewing, for example, an exhibit of etchings "from nature" by James Abbott McNeill Whistler, whose father came from Lowell.[53]

At the Everett House on the evening of 28 October, while Virginia, as usual, occupied the sofa, Fox had what was undoubtedly a heart attack. He felt chilly and had no appetite. He took "some light wine," rather than call a doctor, as

Virginia suggested. Lest he worry her, Fox did not go to bed, but attempted to make himself comfortable on two chairs he pushed together. At nine, he did go to bed, but the night proved difficult. At four, Virginia sent for a doctor, who found Fox's lungs severely congested. Knowing the end was near, the doctor asked "if he had anything to say." Fox replied, "No." Thirty minutes later, he lost consciousness, and, at about five in the morning of 29 October 1883, Fox died. He was only sixty-two years of age. Virginia outlived him by twenty-five years, dying in 1908 at the age of eighty-three.[54]

Epilogue

Though he never fought in a battle, no one had a greater impact on the Union navy than Gustavus Vasa Fox, and no one made a greater contribution to the navy's success. He was integrally involved in acquiring its ships, determining their armament, choosing their commanders, organizing them into squadrons, and developing the strategy they followed. The tactics he advocated were daring, as was the monitor program he embraced. Admirals and generals have a tendency to fight the current war with the weapons and ships developed in the previous war, until they prove obsolete. That the Union navy did not fall into this trap was largely due to Fox's eagerness to adopt the new. The Civil War is renowned as the first railroad war. It also was the first steamboat war, and no one appreciated that fact more than Fox. Steamboats, many of them armored, enforced the blockade and facilitated drives on the Mississippi and its tributaries that carved up the Confederacy. The earliest significant Union successes were naval victories that bought the army enough time to overcome its early failures. These victories kept the public behind Lincoln long enough for the North to prevail.

Fox was the troubleshooter whom squadron commanders called to clear up snafus and to get quick results. As a former naval officer, related by marriage to a family consumed by politics, Fox was aware of political demands as well as naval needs and capabilities. Welles relied on him to engineer bills through Congress. Fox was able to explain to politicians that the navy required ships and bases and that there were limits to what it could accomplish immediately. To naval officers, he was able to explain that, in a democracy, the support of politicians, beholden to the people, depended on action and victories.

Fox was a loyal subordinate to Welles, who appreciated Fox's nautical expertise and approved his ideas. Welles and Fox were a remarkably balanced team. Welles was knowledgeable and shrewd. Fox was impulsive, energetic, enthusiastic, and gregarious. His ability to get along with people was an invaluable asset. His friendliness and his appreciation for engineering talent enabled Fox to get an incredible amount of work out of Ericsson, Isherwood, and Stimers. Even though they despised each other, they worked together to produce engines and ships that enabled the Union to win the war. Although some ideas for the ships and their armaments originated with Fox, his genius was finding immediate and practical applications for the ideas of Ericsson, Eads, and other inventors and for identifying and making use of aggressive leaders, like Farragut and Porter.

Fox worked morning, noon, and night at the Navy Department. Initially, his major task was coordinating the acquisition of fast, light-draft steamers for the blockade. In securing these vessels, he infused the department with unprecedented energy. Blockading 3,550 miles of coast was a massive organizational task that required strategically located bases for coal and supplies. Fox was the principal organizer of the expedition to capture Port Royal, South Carolina (with its presumably formidable defenses), as a base for the South Atlantic Blockading Squadron. He suggested Du Pont to head the expedition, prevailed at a confused meeting with Lincoln, Seward, and McClellan that nearly canceled it, and persuaded Du Pont to make Port Royal the expedition's objective, rather than the less desirable harbors of Bulls Bay, South Carolina, or Fernandina, Florida.

Du Pont's spectacular success inspired Fox and others to mount a bigger expedition against New Orleans (which was crucial to the Union's ultimate success). Fox was the prime mover of that expedition, and, together with Welles, he selected Farragut to be its commander. Fox was responsible for Farragut's orders to run past Fort Jackson and Fort St. Philip, proceed to New Orleans, and demand its surrender. His plan worked. New Orleans surrendered, and the forts, cut off by the navy and besieged by the army, soon followed. Fox then urged Farragut to move up the Mississippi to meet the Mississippi Flotilla moving downstream and cut the Confederacy in two.

The organization of the Mississippi Flotilla illustrates Fox's role as a troubleshooter. That flotilla was controlled by the army but organized and officered by the navy, with Foote in command. Fox solved problems for all squadron commanders, but the problems he solved for Foote were the greatest of all. After the army ignored requests from Foote for men, matériel, and money, he asked Fox to help him with the War Department. Fox saw that Foote's needs were met, and successful joint operations with generals Grant and Pope followed.

By fortuitous accident, Fox witnessed the battle between the *Virginia* and the *Monitor*. As a result, he enthusiastically promoted the monitor design for the Union navy. It was, in fact, the only ironclad design available that could operate in the shallow waters of the war zone and be rapidly and cheaply produced in private northern shipyards. Noting, during the battle, that the *Monitor* lacked the offensive punch to send the *Virginia* to the bottom, Fox found the solution on shore, where he spotted a fifteen-inch Rodman coastal defense gun. After consulting army ordnance people on the spot, he asked Dahlgren, in whom he had great confidence, to design a fifteen-inch naval gun that would fit in a monitor turret. Dahlgren reluctantly followed orders, and Fox made certain the new coastal monitors had fifteen-inch guns. Those vessels proved more than a match for Confederate ironclads.

Monitors were neither invincible nor invulnerable. They could break down the walls of forts but were not effective against rubble, dirt, and sand artillery emplacements. Du Pont's attack on Charleston's defenses was not successful, nor were subsequent attacks by Dahlgren.

A fixation on destroying Charleston may have clouded Fox's judgment, but it was an important military objective. Until late 1863, it exported more cotton and imported more war matériel through the blockade than any other southern port. But, in addition, Fox hated Charleston for starting the "wicked rebellion." For him and many Union partisans, the desire for revenge exaggerated its undoubted importance. After 1863, however, Dahlgren's increasingly effective blockade made Charleston militarily irrelevant, and Fox, albeit reluctantly, gave up wreaking havoc on it.

Apart from his temporary obsession with the Charleston expedition (which may have succeeded with a commander like Farragut), Fox was the facilitator of Union naval victory. Whether they liked him or not, naval officers regarded Fox as the guiding hand in the Navy Department, but *a* guiding hand would be a fairer assessment. Welles was closely involved in choosing squadron commanders and, like Fox, was willing to ignore the stifling seniority system. Nevertheless, decisions affecting naval operations were usually made by Fox and ratified by Welles. As Porter told Fox at the end of the war, "We are indebted to you more than any other man for our Naval Success."

Abbreviations

ALCW   Abraham Lincoln. *The Collected Works of Abraham Lincoln.*
            Edited by Roy P. Basler. 9 vols. New Brunswick, N.J.: Rutgers Uni-
            versity Press, 1953–55.
ANB   *American National Biography.* 24 vols. New York: Oxford Univer-
            sity Press, 1999.
BFP   Blair Family Papers.
CWNC   *Civil War Naval Chronology, 1861–1865.* 5 parts. Washington, D.C.:
            Naval History Division, Office of the Chief of Naval Operations,
            Navy Department, 1961.
DAB   *Dictionary of American Biography.* 20 vols. New York: Charles
            Scribner's Sons, 1928–36.
DANFS   *Dictionary of American Naval Fighting Ships.* 8 vols. Washington,
            D.C.: Naval History Division, Office of the Chief of Naval Opera-
            tions, Navy Department, 1959–81.
GVFCC   Gustavus Vasa Fox. *Confidential Correspondence of Gustavus Vasa
            Fox: Assistant Secretary of the Navy, 1861–1865.* Edited by Robert
            Means Thompson and Richard Wainwright. 2 vols. New York:
            Naval History Society, 1918–19.
GVFP   Gustavus Vasa Fox Papers.
LC   Library of Congress, Washington, D.C.
NA   National Archives, Washington, D.C.
NHSC   Naval History Society Collection.
NYHS   New-York Historical Society, New York.
NYPL   New York Public Library, New York.
OLNR   Officers Letters, Naval Records.
OR   *War of the Rebellion:… Official Records of the Union and Confed-
            erate Armies.* 128 vols. Washington, D.C.: Government Printing
            Office, 1880–1901.
ORN   *Official Records of the Union and Confederate Navies in the War of
            the Rebellion.* 31 vols. Washington, D.C.: Government Printing
            Office, 1894–1927.

VLW   Virginia Lafayette Woodbury.
VLWF   Virginia Lafayette Woodbury Fox.
WFP   Woodbury Family Papers.

Chapter 1. Midshipman Fox

1. VLWF, Diary, 27 Nov. 1862, WFP, LC.

2. "Remarks of Bishop Clark of Rhode Island," Scrapbook, GVFP, NHSC, NYHS; VLWF, Diary, 29 Nov. 1862, WFP; Fox to VLW, No. 34, 8 July 1849, No. 57, 25 (29) July 1850, Albert C. Perkins to Fox, 1, 17, 28 June 1871, J. A. Hood to Fox, 30 June 1871, Fox to VLWF, 15 June 1864, GVFP. Fox wrote VLW numbered journal letters, which are herein identified by the first day followed in parenthesis by the day cited. Fox was so close to Barnes that he became his guardian when Barnes was on his deathbed, even though his nephew by marriage, Charles Levi Woodbury, was close at hand. Woodbury to Fox, 31 Dec. 1864, GVFP.

3. Edward F. Sherman to Fox, 14 June 1864, Fox, "Address at Phillips Academy, Andover," [1877 or 1878], GVFP. Gus took "a fine sled with his name on it in full" to Andover and, when he left, gave it to the daughter of the woman with whom he boarded. In 1866 it was still in use. VLWF, Diary, 30 July 1866, WFP; John Percival to James K. Paulding, 25 July 1839, Percival to Jesse Fox, 1 Aug. 1839, GVFP; Jesse Fox to Caleb Cushing, 5 Dec. 1837, Caleb Cushing Papers, LC.

4. Jesse Fox to Cushing, 5 Dec. 1837, 10 Jan. 1838, Elisha Bartlett to Caleb Cushing, 4 Dec. 1837, Cushing Papers; Webster et al. to Mahlon Dickerson, [Dec. 1837?], "Capt. Gustavus V. Fox," *Vox Populi* (Lowell), 31 Oct. 1883, Scrapbook, GVFP.

5. J. L. Sibley to Levi Woodbury, 30 Dec. 1834, WFP. When in late 1836 and early 1837 there was "a great press" on Boston banks, Barnes and Henshaw begged for a further infusion of federal funds to aid the Commonwealth Bank "upon which," Barnes reminded Woodbury, "hang all our hopes." If Woodbury helped, his efforts did not save either the Lafayette or the Commonwealth Bank in the Panic of 1837. Henshaw to Woodbury, 26 Nov. 1836, John K. Simpson to Woodbury, 26 Nov. 1836, Barnes to Woodbury, [Apr. 1837], WFP. On David Henshaw and the Commonwealth Bank, see Bray Hammond, *Banks and Politics in America: From the Revolution to the Civil War* (Princeton: Princeton University Press, 1957), especially p. 419, and *DAB*, s.v. "Henshaw, David."

6. Mahlon Dickerson to Fox, 12 Jan. 1838, GVFP; Barnes to Woodbury, 13 Jan., 10, 12 Feb. 1838, WFP.

7. Dickerson to Fox, Navy Department, 23 Apr. 1838, GVFP.

8. *DAB*, s.v. "Percival, John"; *Autobiography of Rear Admiral Charles Wilkes, U.S. Navy, 1798–1877*, ed. William James Morgan et al. (Washington, D.C.: Department of the Navy, 1978), pp. 361–63.

9. Wilkes, *Autobiography*, pp. 44–45, 109, 111, 124–25.

10. Wilkes, *Autobiography*, pp. 362–63; Percival to Jesse Fox, 23 Nov. 1838, GVFP.

11. Fox to Barnes, 7 Jan. 1843 [1844], Wise to Fox, 25 May 1866, GVFP. Wise referred to Adlersparre in 1866 as "our old shipmate . . . who sailed with us in the 'Cyane.'"

12. Fox to Barnes, 22 Nov. 1838, GVFP.

13. Fox, Charles W. Place, and Archibald MacRae to Percival, 1 June 1839, GVFP.

14. Fox to Percival, 21 June 1839, GVFP.

15. Percival to Fox, 21 June 1839, Percival to Jesse Fox, 1 Aug. 1839, Henry A. Wise, Journal, 21 June 1839, Scrapbook, GVFP; James T. Woodbury to Levi Woodbury, 19 Nov. 1839, WFP.

16. Percival to James K. Paulding, 25 July 1839, GVFP; Percival to Paulding, 30 Sept. 1839, OLNR, NA.

17. Fox to Percival, 29 Sept. 1839, Fox to Latimer, 3 Feb. 1840, GVFP.

18. Fox to Barnes, 13 Apr. 1840, Henry S. Allmond to Fox, 3 June and 24 July 1841, W. Branford Shubrick to Fox, 22 June 1841, Latimer to Fox, 22 July 1841, GVFP.

19. Fox to George E. Badger, 5 Sept. 1841, OLNR; J. D. Simms to Fox, 16 Sept. 1841, Fox to Hannah Barnes, 4 Oct. 1846, GVFP. For descriptions of Virginia, see Levi Woodbury to James T. Woodbury, 30 Mar. 1839, WFP; Anne Newport Royall, "Ladies," *The Huntress* (Washington), 26 Mar. 1842. The Woodbury and Fox Papers groan with references to Virginia's health. Her parents, siblings, and Fox took her complaints seriously, but her nieces and nephews doubted the extent of her maladies.

20. Fox to Abel P. Upshur, 24 Oct., 3 Nov. 1841, OLNR; *DANFS*, s.vv. "*Columbus*," "*Ohio*."

21. Minna Woodbury to Elizabeth W. C. Woodbury, 21 July 1842, VLWF, Diary, 13 Aug. 1865, WFP; Fox to VLW, No. 6, 15 May (22 May) 1848, Pearson to Fox, 15 Dec. 1842, GVFP. Iceland moss is an edible lichen found in mountainous and arctic regions.

22. Howard I. Chapelle, *The History of the American Sailing Navy: The Ships and Their Development* (New York: Bonanza Books, 1949), p. 427; *DANFS*, s.v. "*Saratoga*"; Fox to Abel P. Upshur, 15 Nov. 1842, OLNR; Upshur to Fox, 7 Dec. 1842, Joseph Smith to Fox, 16 Dec. 1842, Fox to Israel C. Wait, 23 Dec. 1842, Fox to Barnes, 15 Mar. 1843, GVFP.

23. Fox to Barnes, 21 Mar. 1843, GVFP; Louis M. Goldsborough to Elizabeth W. Goldsborough, 24 Mar. 1843, Goldsborough Papers, LC.

24. Tattnall to Fox, 2 June 1843, Fox to Barnes, 21 Mar. 1843, GVFP.

25. Fox to Barnes, 15 Mar., 4 Mar. [Apr.], 5 July 1843, GVFP.

26. Although it was the navy's first commissioned ship of the line, the *Independence* carried its original seventy-four guns too low in the water and had been razeed into a large, powerful, fast frigate of fifty-six guns by eliminating one of its covered fighting decks. *DANFS*, s.v. "*Independence*." Wilkes, *Autobiography*, pp. 115, 412; Fox to Hannah W. Barnes, 5 July 1843, A. V. Dayton, 21 June 1843, GVFP.

27. Henshaw to Fox, 28 Sept. 1843, Isaac McKeever to Fox, 23 Oct. 1843, GVFP.

28. Fox to Hannah W. Barnes, 5 July 1843, GVFP; McKean to Henshaw, 21 Nov. 1843, Henshaw to McKean, 2 Dec. 1843, OLNR.

29. Fox to Barnes, 7 Jan. 1843 [1844], 31 Mar. 1844, GVFP.

30. Fox to Barnes, 7 Jan. 1843 [1844] GVFP; H. K. Davenport, G. V. Fox, and S. Marcy to John Y. Mason, 28 Mar. 1844, OLNR. Worden left the *Cyane* in 1839, attended the naval school, became a passed midshipman, and had just returned from three years in the Pacific.

31. Fox to Barnes, 7 Jan. 1843 [1844], 31 Mar. 1844, GVFP.

32. Fox to Barnes, 7 Jan. 1843 [1844], GVFP.

33. James Biddle to Fox, 3 May 1844, GVFP; Fox to John Y. Mason, 9, 20 May, 1 June, 10 Aug. 1844, OLNR.

Chapter 2. Master Fox

1. *DANFS*, s.v. *"Preble"*; Fox to Hannah Barnes, 16, 23 Oct. 1844, GVFP, NHSC, NYHS.

2. Fox to Hannah Barnes, 16, 23 Oct. 1844, GVFP; Samuel Eliot Morison, *"Old Bruin": Commodore Matthew C. Perry, 1794–1858*... (Boston: Little, Brown, 1967), pp. 166–68. Perry's precautions kept to a minimum his squadron's contact with mosquitoes, the carriers of both malaria and yellow fever.

3. Fox to Barnes, 23 Dec. 1844, GVFP.

4. Fox to Barnes, 23 Dec. 1844, GVFP.

5. Fox to Barnes, 23 Dec. 1844, 28 Feb. 1845, Fox et al. to Freelon 14, 18 Nov. 1844, Freelon to Fox et al., 15 Nov. 1844, GVFP.

6. Fox to Barnes, 23 Dec. 1844, 28 Feb. 1845, GVFP.

7. Fox to Barnes, 23 Dec. 1844, 28 Feb. 1845, GVFP.

8. Fox to Barnes, 28 Feb. 1845, Fox to VLW, No. 4, 1 (3) May 1848, Matthew C. Perry to Fox, 23 Dec. 1844, GVFP; Morison, *"Old Bruin,"* p. 176. Morison mistakenly has the *Preble* aiding the British colonial settlement of Bathurst on the Gambia River. Fox wrote VLW numbered journal letters, which are herein identified by the first day followed in parenthesis by the day cited.

9. Fox to Barnes, 24 Apr. 1845, Freelon to Fox, 18 May 1845, GVFP.

10. Freelon to Fox, 18 May 1845, GVFP.

11. Fox to Barnes, 26 Sept. 1845, GVFP; Fox to Bancroft, 27 Dec. 1845, OLNR, NA.

12. Fox to Barnes, 8 Feb. 1846, GVFP; Elizabeth W. C. Woodbury to Mary Elizabeth (Minna) Woodbury, 25 Mar. [1846], BFP, LC. Minna, who would in a year marry Montgomery Blair, was visiting his family at Silver Spring, Maryland.

13. Lee to [Bancroft], 9 Apr. 1846, Fox to Bancroft, 20 Apr. 1846, OLNR.

14. Fox to Hannah Barnes, 4 Oct. 1846, Benjamin F. Sands to Fox, 1 Sept. 1865, GVFP; Lee to John Y. Mason, 16 Nov., 4 Dec. 1846, OLNR.

15. Lee to Mason, 5, 9, 18 Dec. 1846, OLNR; Howard I. Chappelle, *The History of the American Sailing Navy: The Ships and Their Development* (New York: Bonanza Books, 1949), p. 378.

16. Fox to Barnes, 10 Jan. 1847, Fox to VLW, No. 18, 25 Dec. 1848, No. 62, 25 Dec. 1850 (1 Jan. 1851), GVFP.

17. Lee to Mason, 18 Dec. 1846, OLNR; Fox to Barnes, 10 Jan. 1847, GVFP.

18. Lee to Mason, 5 Mar., 10 Sept. 1847, OLNR. As an enthusiastic supporter of the war, Fox did not acknowledge (what he must have known) that tardy volunteering for the army in his home state resulted from an antiwar attitude engendered by antislavery feelings. Fox insisted that critics "forget, or don't know, that in Mass'ts everybody has business. There are no loafers." Fox to Barnes, 10 Jan. 1847, GVFP.

19. Lee to Fox, 22 Mar. 1847, Fox to VLW, 3 (4) May 1847, 15 May 1848, GVFP; Elizabeth W. C. Woodbury to Mr. and Mrs. Asa Clapp, 27 Feb. [1847], WFP, LC.

20. Lee to Mason, U.S. Brig *Washington,* Philadelphia Navy Yard, 1 Apr. 1847, OLNR; Fox to Barnes, 4 Apr. 1847, Fox to VLW, 13 (14) June 1847, GVFP.

21. Fox to Barnes, 23 Apr. 1847, Fox to VLW, 3 (4) May 1847, GVFP.

22. Fox to Barnes, 18 May 1847, GVFP; Morison, *"Old Bruin,"* pp. 202–3, 229. Fox participated in the bloodless occupation of Laguna.

23. Fox to Barnes, 18 May 1847, GVFP; Morison, *"Old Bruin,"* pp. 193–98, 230.

24. Fox to VLW, 13 (14, 24) June 1847, GVFP.

25. Fox to VLW, 13 (24) June 1847, GVFP.

26. Fox to VLW, 13 (24) June 1847, GVFP.

27. Fox to VLW, 13 (24) June 1847, GVFP; *Inside Lincoln's White House: The Complete Civil War Diary of John Hay,* ed. Michael Burlingame and John R. Turner Ettlinger (Carbondale: Southern Illinois University Press, 1997), 10 Sept. 1863, p. 84.

28. Fox to VLW, 13 (24, 25, 26) June 1847, GVFP; Hay, *Civil War Diary,* 10 Sept. 1863, p. 84. For an overview of the Tabasco expedition, see Morison, *"Old Bruin,"* pp. 230–38.

29. Fox to Barnes, 31 July (1 Aug.) 1847, GVFP.

30. Fox to Barnes, 31 July (1 Aug.) 1847, GVFP.

31. Lee to Fox, 28 Sept. 1847, GVFP.

32. Fox to Hannah Barnes, 6 Jan. 1848, Fox to VLW, No. 62, 25 Dec. 1850 (1 Jan. 1851), GVFP.

33. Fox to Hannah Barnes, 6 Jan. 1848, GVFP.

Chapter 3. Lieutenant Fox: China

1. Howard I. Chappelle, *The History of the American Sailing Navy: The Ships and Their Development* (New York: Bonanza Books, 1949), pp. 440–42.

2. Fox to Barnes, 18 Feb. 1848, GVFP, NHSC, NYHS.

3. John D. Sloat to Fox, 24 Feb. 1848, Fox to Barnes, 2 Mar. 1848, Fox to VLW, No. 6, 15 (22) May 1848, No. 49, 13 (15) Feb. 1850, GVFP. Fox wrote VLW numbered journal letters, which are herein identified by the first day followed in parenthesis by the day of entry. Levi Woodbury in 1848 had some support for the Democratic presidential nomination.

4. Fox to Hannah Barnes, 6 Aug. 1848, Fox to VLW, No. 4, 1 May 1848, No. 6, 15 (18) May 1848, GVFP. On Hannah Barnes's difficulties with alcohol, see J. T. Woodbury to Levi Woodbury, 29 June 1841, WFP, LC.

5. Fox to VLW, No. 3, 21 (30) Mar. 1848, GVFP.

6. Fox to Barnes, 6 May 1848, Fox to VLW, No. 6, 15 May 1848, GVFP.

7. Fox to VLW, No. 6, 15 May, No. 4, 1 (3, 5) May 1848, GVFP. Fox, at this point, regarded Africans as subhuman, "little removed from . . . apes." Fox to VLW, No. 8, 13 (30) June 1848, GVFP.

8. Fox to Barnes, 6 May 1848, Fox to VLW, No. 6, 15 (21, 22) May 1848, No. 7, 23 (26, 27) May 1848, GVFP.

9. Fox to VLW, No. 8, 13 June (30 June, 4 July) 1848, Fox to Hannah Barnes, 6 Aug. 1848, GVFP.

10. Fox to VLW, No. 9, 2 Aug. 1848, No. 10, 21 Aug. 1848, Fox to Hannah Barnes, 6 Aug. 1848, GVFP.

11. Fox to VLW, No. 10, 21 (26) Aug. 1848, GVFP.

12. Fox to VLW, No. 11, 21 (23) Sept. 1848, GVFP.

13. *DAB*, s.v. "Janvier, Catherine Ann"; Fox to VLW, No. 11, 21 (23) Sept., No. 12, 26 Oct. 1848, D. Geisinger to Fox, 9 Oct 1848, GVFP.

14. Fox to VLW, No. 13, 4 Nov. 1848, GVFP.

15. Fox to VLW, No. 14, 16 (25) Nov. 1848, No. 16, 20 Dec. 1848, GVFP.

16. Fox to VLW, No. 15, 6 Dec. 1848, GVFP.

17. Fox to VLW, No. 16, 20 Dec., No. 17, 23 Dec., No. 18, 25 (26, 27) Dec. 1848, GVFP.

18. Fox to VLW, No. 19, 1 (5) Jan., No. 35, 14 July 1849; Fox to Barnes, 25 Mar. 1849, Fox to My Dear Sir, 30 Apr. 1849, in *The Cabinet* (Amherst), 30 Aug. 1849, in Scrapbook, GVFP. Fox was annoyed by publication of his letters. Fox to VLW, No. 42, 16 Nov. 1849, GVFP.

19. Fox to VLW, No. 41, 5 Nov. 1849, No. 45, 1 Jan. 1850, Fox to Barnes, 12 (19) June 1849, GVFP.

20. Fox to Barnes, 12 (19) June 1849, Fox to VLW, No. 39, 7 Oct. 1849, GVFP.

21. Fox to VLW, No. 43, 1 (4) Dec. 1849, No. 41, 5 (13) Nov. 1849, GVFP.

22. Fox to VLW, No. 43, 1 (5) Dec. 1849, GVFP.

23. Fox to VLW, No. 37, 10 (27) Aug., No. 38, 23 (28) Sept. 1849, Fox to Barnes, 18 (20, 28) Sept. 1849, GVFP.

24. Fox to VLW, No. 38, 23 (28) Sept., No. 40, 17 (21) Oct. 1849, Fox to Barnes, 18 (28) Sept. 1849, GVFP. Emilie Rawles's father was probably the one honest merchant, because he remained relatively poor.

25. Fox to VFW, No. 42, 16 (21) Nov. 1849, Fox to Hannah Barnes, 21 (27) Nov. 1849, GVFP.

26. Fox to VLW, No. 47, 16 (18, misdated 28) Jan., No. 49, 13 (17) Feb. 1850, Fox to Barnes, 22 Jan. 1850, Geisinger to Fox, 30 Jan. 1850, GVFP.

27. Fox to Barnes, 22 Jan. 1850, GVFP.

Chapter 4. Lieutenant Fox: Diplomacy and Home

1. Fox to VLW, No. 51, 24 (25, 26, 27) Feb. 1850, GVFP. Fox wrote VLW numbered journal letters, which are herein identified by the first day followed in parenthesis by the day cited.

2. Fox to VLW, No. 51, 24 Feb. (12 Mar.) 1850, Fox to Barnes, 25 Mar. 1850, GVFP.

3. Fox to VLW, No. 51, 24 Feb. (12, 16 Mar.) 1850, No. 52, 27 (31) Mar. 1850, Fox to Barnes, 25 Mar. 1850, GVFP, NHSC, NYHS. The emperor at Hue in Annam controlled both Tongkin to the north and Cochin China to the south. Fox and his contemporaries tended to refer to the entire present-day Vietnamese coast as Cochin China.

4. Fox to VLW, No. 51, 24 Feb. (16, 21, 25 Mar.) 1850, GVFP; *DAB*, s.v. "Roberts, Edmund."

5. Fox to VLW, No. 53, 16 (17, 19) Apr. 1850, GVFP.

6. Fox to VLW, No. 53, 16 Apr. (24, 30 Apr., 5 May) 1850, GVFP.

7. Fox to VLW, No. 53, 16 Apr. (14 May) 1850, GVFP. Fox and his colleagues did not hear Balestier's side of the story, because his orders, which he evidently wrote himself, were to keep his negotiations secret. Fox admitted that his account was "entirely one sided" and that he was "strongly prejudiced" against Balestier's conduct on ship and shore.

8. Fox to VLW, No. 53, 16 Apr. (5, 9, 14, 23 May), No. 54, 24 (28) May, No. 55, 31 May (3 June) 1850, GVFP.

9. Fox to VLW, No. 55, 31 May (3, 4 June) 1850, GVFP.

10. Fox to VLW, No. 55, 31 May (5 June) 1850, GVFP.

11. Fox to VLW, No. 55, 31 May (7, 10 June), No. 56, 13 (18, 19) June 1850, GVFP.

12. Fox to VLW, No. 56, 13 June (28 June, 7 July) 1850, GVFP.

13. Fox to VLW, No. 56, 13 (21, 23, 24, 28) June, No. 57, 1 (4) July 1850, GVFP.

14. Fox to VLW, No. 57, 1 (5, 6) July 1850, GVFP.

15. *DANFS*, s.v. "*Dolphin*"; Fox to VLW, No. 56, 13 June (9, 21, 22 July) 1850, GVFP.

16. Voorhees to Fox, 13 July 1850, Fox to VLW, No. 56, 13 June (21, 22 July) 1850, No. 57, 1 (26, 29) July 1850, GVFP. Fox added to No. 56 in July after he had begun No. 57 on 1 July 1850.

17. Fox to VLW, No. 57, 1 (25, 27, 30 July, 2, 3, 4, 7 Aug.) July 1850, GVFP.

18. Fox to VLW, No. 58, 15 (16, 27 Sept., 7 Oct.) Sept. 1850, No. 62, 25 (14 Jan. 1851) Dec. 1850, GVFP. Although the population of the Bonin Islands was 5,000 in the 1920s, they have been uninhabited since World War II.

19. Fox to VLW, No. 58, 15 (26 Sept., 16, 20, 22 Oct.) Sept. 1850, GVFP.

20. Fox to VLW, No. 59, 7 (8–10, 13–16, 22) Nov. 1850, GVFP. When copying these letters years later, Virginia Fox misnumbered 11 to 22 November as number 60. That letter began on 6 Dec. 1850. *DAB*, s.vv. "Allen, Elisha Hunt," "Judd, Gerrit Parmele."

21. Fox to VLW, No. 59, 7 (16) Nov. 1850, GVFP.

22. Fox to VLW, No. 59, 7 (17, 22) Nov. 1850, GVFP.

23. Fox to VLW, No. 59, 7 (23, 26, 29) Nov. 1850, GVFP.

24. Fox to VLW, No. 59, 7 (29) Nov. 1850, No. 62, 25 Dec. 1850 (14, 29 Jan., 3 Feb. 1851), GVFP.

25. Fox to VLW, No. 59, 7 (29) Nov. 1850, No. 62, 25 Dec. 1850 (29 Jan. 1851), GVFP.

26. Fox to VLW, No. 62, 25 Dec. 1850 (29 Jan. 1851), GVFP.

27. Fox to VLW, No. 62, 25 Dec. 1850 (30 Jan. 1851), No. 60, 6 (8) Dec. 1850, GVFP.

28. Fox to VLW, No. 62, 25 Dec. 1850 (31 Jan. 1851), GVFP.

29. Fox to VLW, No. 61, 17 (18, 19, 20) Dec. 1850, No. 62, 25 Dec. 1850 (31 Jan. 1851), GVFP.

30. Fox to VLW, No. 62, 25 Dec. 1850 (14, 21, 22 Jan. 1851), GVFP.

31. Fox to VLW, No. 62, 25 Dec. 1850 (6, 15 Feb. 1851), GVFP.

32. Fox to VLW, No. 62, 25 Dec. 1850 (18, 19, 22 Feb. 1851), GVFP.

33. Fox to VLW, No. 63, 17 Feb. (8, 23 Mar.) 1851, No. 64, 7 (28) Apr. 1851, GVFP.

34. Fox to VLW, No. 64, 7 Apr. (5, 6 May) 1851, GVFP.

35. Fox to VLW, No. 64, 7 (12) Apr. 1851, GVFP.

36. Fox to VLW, No. 64, 7 (21, 22) Apr. 1851, GVFP.

37. Fox to VLW, No. 64, 7 (24) Apr. (1, 7 May) 1851, GVFP.

Chapter 5. Captain Fox/Agent Fox

1. Fox to William A. Graham, 8 July 1851, OLNR, NA; Thomas Hart Benton to Montgomery Blair, 29 Aug. 1851, BFP, LC.

2. Rantoul to Wetmore, 30 Sept. 1851, Peaslee to Wetmore, 1 Oct. 1851, Geisinger to Fox, 12 Oct. 1851, Smith to Wetmore, 14 Nov. 1851, GVFP, NHSC, NYHS; Samuel Eliot Morison, *"Old Bruin": Commodore Matthew C. Perry, 1794–1858*... (Boston: Little, Brown, 1967), pp. 256–57.

3. Fox to William A. Graham, 14 Nov. 1851, OLNR; Morison, *"Old Bruin,"* pp. 257–60.

4. Joseph J. Comstock to the president and directors of the N.Y. & Bremen Steam Ship Co., 28 Oct. 1852, Wetmore to Fox, 15 Feb. 1852, GVFP.

5. Clipping, 6 Mar. 1852, from a New York newspaper, Scrapbook, GVFP. George Steers, architect of the yacht *America*, designed the *Baltic* as well as its sister ships *Atlantic, Pacific,* and *Arctic*. The *Arctic* sank in 1854 with most of its passengers and crew, the *Pacific* disappeared with all on board in 1856, and those disasters coupled with a reduction in the congressional subsidy so weakened the Collins Line it could not survive the panic of 1857. Morison, *"Old Bruin,"* pp. 258–59.

6. Wetmore to C. H. Land, 2 Sept. 1852, Comstock to the president and directors of the New York & Bremen Steamship Company, 28 Oct. 1852, Edward K. Collins to C. H. Land, 28 Oct. 1852, James Brown to C. H. Land, 28 Oct. 1852, Jefferson Davis [Acting Secretary of the Navy] to Fox, 9 June 1853, Charles Boarman to Fox, 23 June 1853, GVFP; Fox to James C. Dobbin, 18 Apr., 5, [24] June 1854, Fox to Dobbin, 2 July 1853, Fox to Jefferson Davis, 8 June 1853, OLNR.

7. Thomas A. Bailey, *A Diplomatic History of the American People,* 3rd ed. (New York: Appleton-Century-Crofts, 1946), pp. 158, 295.

8. Fox to Barnes, 29 Aug. 1853, GVFP.

9. Fox to Barnes, 29 Aug. 1853, GVFP. Fox's observations about British unwillingness to fight a war over the fisheries were accurate. The Reciprocity Treaty of 1854 virtually removed restrictions on American fishing in the British Maritime provinces. Bailey, *Diplomatic History,* p. 297.

10. Marshall O. Roberts to Fox, 5 Oct. 1853, 5 Jan. 1854, GVFP.

11. Marshall O. Roberts to Fox, 5 Oct. 1853, GVFP; Logbook, Mail Steamer *Ohio*, 7, 12, 14, 15, 17 Oct. 1853 and 5, 13, 15, 19 Jan. 1854, U.S. Mail Steamship Company Papers, NYHS.

12. Fox, "Journal, June 1851–December 1855," BFP; George Law to Fox, 13 Feb. 1854, Roberts to Fox, 14 Feb., 20 Apr., 20 May, 20 June, 5 Aug., 5 Sept., 5 Oct., 6 Nov., 5 Dec. 1854, 5 Mar., 5 Apr., 5 May, GVFP; Provision List, *George Law,* 5 Aug. 1855, U.S. Mail Steamship Company Papers, NYHS.

13. Roberts to Fox, 3 Aug. 1855, GVFP; Blair to Mary Elizabeth (Minna) Woodbury Blair, 13 June, 30 July 1854, BFP.

14. Blair to Minna Blair, 1, 13 June, 1, 31 July 1854, BFP; VLWF, Diary, 11 Dec. 1862, WFP, LC.

15. VLW to Elizabeth W. C. Woodbury, San Francisco, 25 Dec. 1862 [actually, Washington, 25 Dec. 1849], WFP.

16. List of VLW's property, 1852, WFP. See also Financial Records, GVFP.

17. Fox to VLWF, 11 Sept. 1862, GVFP; Marriage Contract, Gustavus Vasa Fox with Virginia Lafayette Woodbury, 20 Oct. 1855, WFP; "Marriage in High Life," 30 Oct. 1855, [unidentified Boston newspaper], Scrapbook, GVFP. See also Financial Records, GVFP. Perry, whom Fox succeeded, was the son of the hero of Lake Erie.

18. Unidentified newspaper clipping, Scrapbook and Financial Records, GVFP; Ellen De Q. Woodbury to Elizabeth W. C. Woodbury, Friday [probably late 1856], Elizabeth W. C. Woodbury to VLWF, 12 Jan. 1857, Elizabeth W. C. Woodbury to Frances W. Lowery and VLWF, 8 Mar. [late 1850s], WFP; Fox to James C. Dobbin, 5 July 1856, GVFP.

19. *Boston Journal*, 5 Feb. 1858, *Lawrence Sentinel*, 30 Oct. 1858, and unidentified newspaper clipping probably from the *Lawrence Sentinel*, 6 Feb. 1858, Scrapbook, GVFP; Barnes Memorandum, 28 May 1864, Financial Records, GVFP; Helena Wright, Librarian, Merrimack Valley Textile Museum, North Andover, Mass., to Ari Hoogenboom, 7 Dec. 1979.

20. "Democratic Nominations," *Lawrence Sentinel*, 30 Oct. 1858, undated clippings from the *Lawrence Sentinel*, and "The Great Calamity at Lawrence," *Boston Journal*, 12 Jan. 1860, Scrapbook, GVFP.

21. Wife of a Worker [VLWF] to Editor, Lawrence, 27 Jan. 1860, in *Lawrence Sentinel*, 4 Feb. 1860, and "Pemberton Mill Disaster . . . Verdict of the Inquest," newspaper clipping probably the *Lawrence Sentinel*, 4 Feb. 1860, Scrapbook, GVFP.

22. Fox to Blair, 19 June 1860, BFP; Fox to VLWF, 21 June 1860, GVFP; O. H. Perry to Fox, 20 Nov. 1861, *GVFCC*, 1:403. For the hostility of some of the stockholders, see Albert G. Browne to Gideon Welles, 2 Apr. 1862, Welles Papers, LC.

23. Fox to VLWF, 21 June 1860, GVFP.

24. VLWF, Diary, 5, 10, 14–24 July 1860, WFP.

25. VLWF, Diary, 24–25 July 1860, WFP.

26. VLWF, Diary, 26–31 July 1860, WFP.

27. Aspinwall to Fox, 19 Sept. 1860, Charles W. Copeland to Fox, 19, 25 July 1864, GVFP.

28. VLWF, Diary, 29 Aug., 10, 17 Sept. 1860, WFP; Fox to VLWF, Monday, [17 Sept. 1860], mailed 21 Sept. 1860, 21, 24, 27 Sept. 1860, GVFP.

29. Fox to VLWF, 27, 28 Sept., 1 Oct. 1860, GVFP.

30. Fox to VLWF, 2, 5, 6, 12, 13, 15 Oct. 1860, GVFP; Fox to VLWF, 6 Feb. 1861, *GVFCC*, 1:6; VLWF, Diary, 28 Oct. 1860, WFP. Fox's March 1861 letter to the agent accepting his proposal was not answered. In 1864 Charles W. Copeland worked to regain for investors their share in the property. Copeland to Fox, 25 July 1864, GVFP.

Chapter 6. Fort Sumter

1. VLWF, Diary, 17, 21 Nov., 25 Dec. 1860, 8 Jan. 1861, WFP, LC; *DAB*, s.v. "Roberts, Marshall Owen." The inside story of Fort Sumter is best told by Anderson's surgeon, Samuel Wylie Crawford, in his *The Genesis of the Civil War: The Story of Sumter, 1860–1861* (New York: Charles L. Webster, 1887). Fox's own account, a memorandum for Welles in response to a Senate Resolution, is Fox to Welles, 24 Feb. 1865, GVFP, NHSC, NYHS. Virtually the entire report is reprinted in *ORN*, 4:245–51.

2. Philip Shriver Klein, *President James Buchanan: A Biography* (University Park: Pennsylvania State University Press, 1962), pp. 353–402, presents the Sumter crisis from Buchanan's perspective.

3. VLWF, Diary, 12, 14, 24, 29 Jan. 1861, WFP; Blunt to Editor, *New York Tribune*, 27 Sept. 1866, Scrapbook, GVFP; *DAB*, s.vv. "Gibbs, Oliver Wolcott," "Sims, James Marion." Although a medical doctor, Gibbs is renowned chiefly as a chemist. Sims developed the vesicovaginal fistula operation.

4. VLWF, Diary, 29 Jan., 4, 5 Feb. 1861, WFP; Winfield Scott to Fox, 30 Jan. 1861, Montgomery Blair to Fox, 31 Jan. 1861, *GVFCC*, 1:3; Blunt to Editor, *New York Tribune*, 27 Sept. 1866, Scrapbook, GVFP.

5. VLWF, Diary, 31 Jan., 9, 17 Feb. 1861, WFP; Fox to VLWF, 7 Feb. 1861, Fox to Winfield Scott, 8 Feb. 1861, *GVFCC*, 1:6–9.

6. Fox to VLWF, 7 Feb. 1861, Fox to Winfield Scott, 8 Feb. 1861, *GVFCC*, 1:6–9.

7. VLWF, Diary, 8, 9, 17 Feb. 1861, WFP; Fox to VLWF, 7 Feb. 1861, *GVFCC*, 1:6–7. In February 1861 Forbes presented Scott with a relief plan for Sumter utilizing eight light-draft-propeller-driven vessels. Forbes to Montgomery Blair, Boston, 13 Mar. 1861, BFP, LC. For yet another plan, see Elias Hasket Derby to Isaac Toucey, 16 Jan. 1861, *ORN*, 4:221–23.

8. VLWF, Diary, 12 Mar. 1861, WFP; *ALCW*, 4:284–85, n. 1, 288–90; Fox to VLWF, Washington, 19 Mar. 1861, *GVFCC*, 1:9–10; Crawford, *Genesis*, pp. 347–68. Richard N. Current makes the plausible suggestion that Fox spoke of evacuation as a security measure and that this reference should not be taken seriously. Current, *Lincoln and the First Shot* (Philadelphia: J. B. Lippincott, 1963), p. 71. But Fox was not deceptive— especially with his wife—and the emphasis in the Lincoln administration from 15–18 March 1861 was on evacuation. Four years later, Fox said he suggested going to Sumter to strengthen his "arguments in favor of the practicality of sending in supplies." Fox to Welles, 24 Feb. 1865, *ORN* 4:247.

9. F. W. Pickens to Robert Anderson, 21 Mar. 1861, Winfield Scott to Joseph Holt, 26 Feb. 1861, Simon Cameron to Winfield Scott, 19 Mar. 1861, Norman J. Hall to Robert Anderson, 21 Mar. 1861, Robert Anderson Papers, LC; Samuel W. Crawford, "Fort Sumter Diary," 21 Mar. 1861, Samuel W. Crawford to A. S. Crawford, 23 Mar. 1861, Samuel W. Crawford Papers, LC; Fox to VLWF, [25 Mar. 1861], GVFP. After the attack on Sumter, Pickens accused Fox of treachery, but, twenty-one years later, Fox insisted that Hartstene guaranteed him to Pickens without asking "anything about my object being peaceful." Crawford to Fox, 9, 11 May 1882, GVFP. In addition, at the time of

Fox's visit, evacuation was a real possibility, and Fox had earlier thought that a relief expedition would stave off, not precipitate, war.

10. Kenneth P. Williams, *Lincoln Finds a General: A Military Study of the Civil War*, 5 vols. (New York: Macmillan, 1950–59), 1:39; *OR*, 1:208–9, 211, 230, 235, 294; *ORN*, 4:247; Fox to VLWF, [25 Mar. 1861], Crawford to Fox, 8, 9, 11 May 1882, GVFP; Crawford, *Genesis*, p. 371.

11. Anderson to L. Thomas, 22 Mar., 1, 8 Apr. 1861, Anderson Papers, LC.

12. Fox to VLWF, 26 Mar. 1861, GVFP; Fox to VLWF, 27 Mar. 1861, *GVFCC*, 1:11. Abner Doubleday, one of Anderson's officers, apparently thought well of Fox's plan. He wrote his wife that it would be difficult for the Confederate batteries to hit a small boat by day and impossible to do so at night. Current, *First Shot*, p. 62.

13. Current, *First Shot*, pp. 73–76; David Herbert Donald, *Lincoln* (New York: Simon & Schuster, 1995), p. 288.

14. Fox to Lincoln, 28 Mar. 1861, (endorsed by Lincoln and Blair), GVFP; Donald, *Lincoln*, pp. 288–89; Williams, *Lincoln Finds a General*, 1:41–42; Lincoln to Welles and Cameron, 29 Mar. 1861, *ALCW*, 4:301–2. Montgomery Blair exaggerated in 1882 when he recalled that, by accusing Scott of giving political rather than military advice on Pickens, he clarified Lincoln's thinking to the point that he "immediately ordered the reinforcement of Fort Sumter." Crawford, *Genesis*, pp. 365–66. Most authorities, including Current and Donald, believe that Lincoln was unaware of Scott's memorandum until 28 March and that it precipitated the decision by Lincoln and a majority of the cabinet to hold on to Sumter. Scott's memorandum, however, is undated and Williams, *Lincoln Finds a General*, 1:387–88, thinks it was a response to Lincoln's request on 15 March for advice on the wisdom of provisioning Sumter and was in his hands prior to 28 March. Whatever the date of Scott's memo, I believe the key to Lincoln's decision was not the suggestion of appeasement by Scott, but Hurlbut's convincing report that appeasement such as Scott proposed would not preserve the Union. In any event, Lincoln's request that Fox provide him with the specifics of his plan came after getting Hurlbut's report and before the informal cabinet meeting on the evening of 28 March and the formal meeting the following day. Lincoln apparently had at least tentatively decided on holding Sumter.

15. Fox to Blair, 31 Mar. 1861, *GVFCC*, 1:12–13; *DAB*, s.v. "Marshall, Charles Henry." Aspinwall repeated his arguments to Lincoln on Sunday. Aspinwall to Lincoln, 31 Mar. 1861, Lincoln Papers, LC.

16. Fox to Blair, Sunday, p.m., 31 Mar. 1861, *GVFCC*, 1:13–14. Four years later, Marshall remembered being more cooperative. Marshall to Fox, 18 Sept. 1865, GVFP.

17. Blair to Fox, 1 Apr. 1861, Fox to Lowery, 3 Apr. 1861, *GVFCC*, 1:16, 17–18, 19; VLWF, Diary, 2 Apr. 1861, WFP.

18. Donald, *Lincoln*, pp. 290, 292; Richard N. Current, *The Lincoln Nobody Knows* (New York: McGraw-Hill, 1958), pp. 120–23; Current, *First Shot*, pp. 94–102; Cameron to Fox, 4 Apr. 1861, *GVFCC*, 1:20–21; Cameron to Anderson, 4 Apr. 1861, *ALCW*, 4:321–22.

19. Donald, *Lincoln*, p. 291; Scott to H. L. Scott, 4 Apr. 1861, *GVFCC*, 1:21–22; Cameron to Chew, 6 Apr. 1861, Chew to Lincoln, 8 Apr. 1861, *ALCW*, 4:323–24.

20. Current, *First Shot*, pp. 82–86. See Lincoln's orders, dated 1 Apr. 1861, to Foote,

Porter, and Samuel Mercer, *ALCW*, 4:313–14. Robert V. Bruce has called to my attention the existence of a second *Powhatan*—a wooden side-wheel steamer—operating out of Georgetown on the Potomac River, which might explain Lincoln's "accident" in diverting the navy's *Powhatan* from the Sumter expedition, while agreeing it should be a part of that expedition. *DANFS*, s.v. "*Powhatan*." John Niven, *Gideon Welles: Lincoln's Secretary of the Navy* (New York: Oxford University Press, 1973), pp. 332, 613, believes that Lincoln both understood and approved Seward's plan, but I think it more likely that Lincoln was confused by naval vessels with Indian names beginning with the letter P.

21. Niven, *Welles*, pp. 332–33; Welles to Foote, 1 Apr. 1861, *ORN*, 4:229; Lincoln to Foote, 1 Apr. 1861, *ALCW*, 4:313–14 (two communications).

22. Foote to Welles, 4, 5 Apr. 1861, Welles to Mercer, 5 Apr. 1861, *GVFCC*, 1:19, 22–25; Meigs to Seward, 6, 10 Apr. 1861, *OR*, 1:368–70; *ORN*, 4:111–12, 237.

23. *Diary of Gideon Welles: Secretary of the Navy under Lincoln and Johnson*, 3 vols., ed. Howard K. Beale (New York: W. W. Norton, 1960), 1:23–25 (writing in retrospect, Welles misdated the episode with Seward and Lincoln as 6 April); Welles to Mercer, 5 Apr. 1861, Foote to Welles, 6 Apr. 1861 (3 communications), F. A. Roe to Foote, 6 Apr. 1861, *GVFCC*, 1:25, 27–31. Fort Pickens was reinforced when the troops on the *Brooklyn* were landed on the evening of 12 April. More troops from the *Atlantic*—part of the Seward-Meigs-Porter expedition—landed on 16 April and the *Powhatan* arrived on 17 April. H. A. Adams to Welles, 14, 16 Apr. 1861, Porter to Seward, 21 Apr. 1861, *ORN*, 4:115, 118–19, 122–23.

24. L. Thomas to D. D. Tompkins, 4 Apr. 1861, *GVFCC*, 1:20; VLWF, Diary, 6–9 Apr. 1861, WFP. The recruits, whom Fox said were "totally unfit to be thrown into a fort likely to be attacked by the rebels," were supplied by Lieutenant Colonel Henry L. Scott (an aid to Winfield Scott), who "ridiculed" the idea of relieving Sumter. Fox to Welles, 24 Feb. 1865, *ORN*, 4:248.

25. Fox to Blair, 8 Apr. 1861, Lincoln Papers, LC; Fox to VLWF, 8 Apr. 1861, *GVFCC*, 1:26–27 (erroneously dated as Steam Ship Bath, Ap. 6th '61). Sturgis, father of the architect of the same name, was a merchant and the commissioner of pilots in New York City.

26. Fox to Blair, 17 Apr. 1861, *GVFCC*, 1:31–36.

27. Fox to Blair, 17 Apr. 1861, *GVFCC*, 1:32–33; Fox to Welles, 24 Feb. 1865, *ORN*, 4:249.

28. Fox to Blair, 17 Apr. 1861, *GVFCC*, 1:33. Years later, Rowan recalled that the note of 7 April from Mercer (handed him by Captain Faunce of the *Harriet Lane*), only said that Mercer, but not the *Powhatan*, was "detached from duty off Charleston." Rowan's behavior confirms his memory. Although he should have informed Fox immediately of Mercer's removal, it is inconceivable that Rowan would have allowed Fox and the *Baltic* to look for the *Powhatan* on the night of 12 April if he knew that vessel was elsewhere. When Fox learned of Mercer's note, he realized immediately that the ship as well as Mercer was detached. Apart from his lack of clarity, Mercer's chief mistake was his failure to send Rowan his orders from Welles.

29. Fox to Pickens, [12 Apr. 1861], Fox to Blair, 17 Apr. 1861, *GVFCC*, 1:18, 34–36; *OR*, 1:11.

30. Lincoln, "First Inaugural Address," 4 Mar. 1861, *ALCW*, 4:261; Fox to Blair, 17 Apr. 1861, *GVFCC*, 1:36; Anderson to Simon Cameron, 17 Apr. 1861, *OR*, 1:12.

31. Fox to Blair, 17 Apr. 1861, *GVFCC*, 1:33–34.

32. Fox to Blair, 17 Apr. 1861, Fox, "Result of G. V. Fox's Plan for Reinforcing Fort Sumpter," *GVFCC*, 1:34, 40. Foster did not think Sumter was as heavily damaged as Fox believed. Fox was probably influenced by Anderson. See *OR*, 1:24–25; Williams, *Lincoln Finds a General*, 1:58.

33. Fox to Blair, 17 Apr. 1861, Fox, "Result of G. V. Fox's Plan for Reinforcing Fort Sumpter," Fox to VLWF, 2 May 1861, *GVFCC*, 1:35, 40–43; VLWF, Diary, 18 Apr. 1861, WFP.

34. Lincoln to Fox, 1 May 1861, *GVFCC*, 1:43–44.

Chapter 7. Ships for the Blockade

1. *ALCW*, 4:331–33, 338–39, 346–47.

2. VLWF, Diary, 16, 18–20, 24 Apr. 1861, WFP, LC.

3. VLWF, Diary, 22, 24–26 Apr. 1861, WFP; Breese to Fox, 25 Apr. 1861, *GVFCC*, 1:36; Fox to Welles, 24 Feb. 1865, *ORN*, 4:250; Aspinwall to Fox, 29 Sept. 1865, GVFP, NHSC, NYHS.

4. Fox to VLWF, 29 Apr., 2 May 1861, *GVFCC*, 1:41–43; Ellen De Quincy Woodbury, to Elizabeth Clapp Woodbury, [29 Apr. 1861], WFP. Nell and her siblings sympathized with Virginia's physical ailments and usually with her anxieties. Late on the evening of 30 April, John Hay saw Blair, Fox, and Carl Schurz emerge from "the audience chamber," where "the great Map of Virginia" was "newly hung." *Inside Lincoln's White House: The Complete Civil War Diary of John Hay*, ed. Michael Burlingame and John R. Turner Ettlinger (Carbondale: Southern Illinois University Press, 1997), 30 Apr. 1861, p. 15.

5. Fox to VLWF, 4 May 1861, Welles to Fox, 8, 9 May 1861, *GVFCC*, 1:44–46; Lincoln to Welles, 8 May 1861, *ALCW*, 4:363; Fox to Welles, [9 May 1861], GVFP; VLWF, Diary, 11 May 1861, WFP; John Niven, *Gideon Welles: Lincoln's Secretary of the Navy* (New York: Oxford University Press, 1973), pp. 351–54. Faxon felt that Welles had sacrificed him and resented Fox. Faxon to Mark Howard, 10 May 1861, Howard Papers, Connecticut Historical Society, Hartford (courtesy of John D. Hayes).

6. Samuel Francis Du Pont to Matthew Maury, 30 Aug. 1861, in *Samuel Francis Du Pont: A Selection from His Civil War Letters*, 3 vols., ed. John D. Hayes (Ithaca: Cornell University Press, 1969), 1:138; Niven, *Welles*, pp. 351, 615, n. 12; Fox to VLWF, 28 May 1861, Welles to Fox, 30 May 1861, *GVFCC*, 1:46, 358–59; Charles Henry Davis to Harriette M. Davis, 28 May, 7 Aug., 10 Sept. 1861, in Charles Henry Davis, *Life of Charles Henry Davis: Rear Admiral, 1807–1877* (Boston: Houghton, Mifflin, 1899), pp. 128, 133, 146.

7. Niven, *Welles*, p. 353.

8. Niven, *Welles*, pp. 324–25, 349–53; Leonard D. White, *The Jacksonians: A Study in Administrative History, 1829–1861* (New York: Macmillan, 1954), pp. 218–19; Davis to Harriette M. Davis, 11 Sept. 1861, in Davis, *Charles Henry Davis*, p. 133.

9. On the destruction of the Norfolk Navy Yard, see Niven, *Welles*, pp. 339–45.

Although he had no influence on the decision, Fox, in New York, thought that the navy yard should be destroyed. VLWF, Diary, 22 Apr. 1861, WFP. For Welles's actions prior to Fox's arrival in the Navy Department, see under the appropriate dates *CWNC* and E. B. Long and Barbara Long, *The Civil War Day by Day: An Almanac, 1861–1865* (New York: Doubleday, 1971). These two works are indispensable for day-to-day events as well as for apt quotations.

10. For Scott's Anaconda Plan, see Allan Nevins, *The War for the Union: The Improvised War, 1861–1862* (New York: Charles Scribner's Sons, 1959), pp. 151–54.

11. "Introduction," and Fox to Du Pont, 22 May 1861, Du Pont to Bache, 30 May 1861, Du Pont to Henry Winter Davis, 1 June 1861, *Du Pont Letters*, 1:lxviii–lxix, 71, 73–76; Welles to Joseph Smith, 29 May 1861, Joseph Smith to Welles, 1 June 1861, GVFP.

12. Edward William Sloan III, *Benjamin Franklin Isherwood, Naval Engineer: The Years as Engineer in Chief, 1861–1869* (Annapolis: United States Naval Institute, 1965), pp. 30–31; Fox to Du Pont, 24 May 1861, Henry Francis du Pont Winterthur Collection of Manuscripts, Hagley Museum and Library, Wilmington, Del.; Fox to VLWF, 28 May, 10 June 1861, Welles to John Lenthall, 3 June 1861, GVFP; Du Pont to Matthew Maury, 30 Aug. 1861, Du Pont to Fox, 27 Sept. 1861, *Du Pont Letters*, 1:137–38, 157. Fox, who wished to save "from oblivion the beautiful Indian names of our country," got Julia Kean (Mrs. Hamilton) Fish to name the *Unadilla*, enlisted the aid of Joseph Henry of the Smithsonian Institution, the historian Benson J. Lossing, and tried to convince G. and C. Merriam to include a dictionary of Indian place-names in their *Webster Dictionary*. Fox to G. and C. Merriam, 29 Nov., 16 Dec. 1864, G. and C. Merriam to Fox, 1 Dec. 1864, GVFP.

13. Fox to General [Joseph K. F. Mansfield or Charles W. Sandford], 24 May 1861, Chicago Historical Society; Lincoln to Winfield Scott, 24 May 1861, *ALCW*, 4:385; Dahlgren to Welles, 24 May 1861, *ORN*, 4:477. The original Zouaves were French colonial troops serving in Algiers.

14. VLWF, Diary, 16 May, 13 June 1861, WFP; Fox to VLWF, 28 May, 3 June 1861, GVFP. Virginia apparently was illness-prone; it would be difficult to fake the coughing fits, nausea, diarrhea, and other ailments with which she was troubled. Yet her constitution was strong enough to recover from cures like blistering and croton oil, which she afflicted herself with, and to live to a ripe old age. Her parents and siblings took her chronic ill health seriously, but her niece, young Minna Blair, thought she exaggerated her medical problems.

15. Charles H. Marshall to Fox, 24 May 1861, and Alfred Crea to Fox, 29 May 1861, *GVFCC*, 1:357–60.

16. *CWNC*, 30 Apr. to 23 June 1861.

17. Cornelius Vanderbilt to Welles, 16 Apr. 1861, J. D. Jones to Welles, 18 Apr. 1861, Wm. Seligman & Co. to Salmon P. Chase, 17 Apr. 1861, *ORN*, 1:8–9.

18. "Confederate Forces Afloat: *Jefferson Davis*, Privateer," *DANFS*, 2:539, 584–85; *CWNC*, 28 June to 18 Aug. 1861; Fox to S. L. Breese, 14 July 1861, *ORN*, 1:43; Du Pont to Sophie Du Pont, 15 July 1861, *Du Pont Letters*, 1:103.

19. *CWNC*, 16 July 1861; "Confederate Forces Afloat: *Jefferson Davis*," *DANFS*, 2:539.

20. "Confederate Forces Afloat: *Sumter*," *DANFS*, 2:569–70; Semmes to Mallory, 14 June 1861, Semmes to José De La Pozuela, 6 July 1861, *ORN*, 1:615, 619–20.

21. Mahan to Fox, 9 Sept. 1861, Semmes to Mallory, 13 Apr. 1862, Semmes, Journal, 24 May 1861 to 11 Apr. 1862, *ORN*, 1:87–88, 683–84, 691–745; "Confederate Forces Afloat: *Sumter*," *DANFS*, 2:569–70.

22. On the *Jeff Davis*, see the various reports received and orders given by the Navy Department from 12 July 1861 to 24 July 1861, *ORN*, 1:37–46, 49–50. On the *Sumter*, see Fox to Welles, 7 Sept. 1861, Welles Papers, LC; Semmes, Journal, 3 Dec. 1861, *ORN*, 1:727. On the *Nashville*, see Du Pont to Welles, 16 Oct. 1861, Samuel L. Breese to M. Woodhull, 16 Oct. 1861, R. B. Pegram to S. R. Mallory, 10 Mar. 1862, *ORN* 1:115–16, 745–49; "Confederate Forces Afloat: *Nashville*," *DANFS*, 2:551–52.

23. Fox to Delano, 21 Feb. 1862, Fox to Webb, 26 July 1862, *GVFCC*, 1:426–27, 2:333–34.

24. Fox to Paul S. Forbes, 28 Feb., 16 Mar., 15 Sept. 1863, Fox to Delano, 12 Mar. 1863, GVFP; "Statistical Data of U.S. Ships," *ORN*, Series II, 1:85, 107; *DANFS*, s.vv. "*Idaho*," "*Wampanoag*"; *ANB*, s.v. "Isherwood, Benjamin Franklin." Forbes unfortunately decided to use Dickerson-designed engines in his vessel the *Idaho*.

25. Fox to Du Pont, 24 May 1861, Welles to Du Pont, 28 May 1861, du Pont Winterthur Manuscripts; *DANFS*, s.v. "*Keystone State*." Du Pont negotiated the purchase of the *Keystone State*. The exorbitant asking price is unknown.

26. Fox to Du Pont, 31 May 1861, Welles to Du Pont, 28 May 1861, du Pont Winterthur Manuscripts.

27. Fox to VLWF, 10 June 1861, Seward to Fox, 27 Feb. 1862, GVFP.

28. Fox to Du Pont, 17 June 1861, du Pont Winterthur Manuscripts.

29. Forbes to Fox, 20 June 1861, GVFP; Niven, *Welles*, pp. 362–64.

30. Niven, *Welles*, pp. 361–62. Both Draper (1864) and Grinnell (1869) ultimately secured the most coveted patronage plum in the nation—the collectorship of the Port of New York.

31. Stellwagon to Fox, 27 June 1861, GVFP. The navy acquired all three vessels, and Stellwagon's diligence was rewarded with the command of the *Mercedita*, but not before the Navy Department had difficulties forcing its owners, J. C. Jewett & Co., to make agreed upon alterations before it could be commissioned on 3 December 1861. Fox to Morgan, 11 Nov. 1861; *DANFS*, s.v. "*Mercedita*"; Niven, *Welles*, pp. 362–64.

32. Morgan to Fox, 20 June 1861, GVFP; Niven, *Welles*, p. 363.

33. Du Pont to Fox, 21 Aug. 1862, *ORN*, 13:268–70; Morgan to Fox, 20, 28 June 1861, Russell Sturgis to Morgan, 20 June 1861, Marshall? to Morgan, 21 June 1861, endorsed by Morgan, 26 June 1861, Joseph J. Comstock to Fox, 23 June 1861, GVFP. Comstock told Fox that the *Adriatic* could be had for $500,000 and the *Baltic* and *Atlantic* for $250,000 each. When the Collins line went bankrupt following the Panic of 1857, the three vessels were sold at auction in 1858 for a mere $50,000. Ironically, they were supposedly built for easy conversion into warships. See my discussion in chapter 5. *DAB*, s.v. "Collins, Edward Knight." *DANFS*, s.vv. "*Connecticut*," "*Rhode Island*," and "*Charles Phelps*."

34. Morgan to Fox, 21 June, 29, 30 July 1861, GVFP.

35. Forbes to Fox, 22 June 1861, Morgan to Fox, 25 June, 4, 5 July 1861, GVFP.

36. Morgan to Fox, 26 June, 4 July 1861, Forbes to Fox, 26 July 1861, GVFP.

37. Morgan to Fox, 1, 22, 23 (2 letters), 29 July 1861, GVFP.

38. Forbes to Welles, 26 July 1861, Forbes to Fox, 27 July 1861, Fox to Forbes, 30, 31 July 1861, GVFP; *DAB*, s.v. "Creesy, Josiah Perkins." Great seafarers did not always make competent naval officers.

39. Forbes to Fox, 27, 30 July 1861, Fox to Forbes, 30, 31 July 1861, GVFP; Niven, *Welles*, pp. 363–64; *Diary of Gideon Welles: Secretary of the Navy under Lincoln and Johnson*, 3 vols., ed. Howard K. Beale (New York: W. W. Norton, 1960), 1:486–88 (15 Dec. 1863); Welles to Morgan, 25 Dec. 1861, Morgan to Welles, 23, 26, 27, 28 Dec. 1861, Welles Papers, Huntington Library, San Marino, Calif.

40. Du Pont to Sophie Du Pont, 30 June 1862, *Du Pont Letters*, 2:139.

Chapter 8. Implementing the Blockade

1. John Niven, *Gideon Welles: Lincoln's Secretary of the Navy* (New York: Oxford University Press, 1973), p. 358; Kevin J. Weddle, *Lincoln's Tragic Admiral: The Life of Samuel Francis Du Pont* (Charlottesville: University of Virginia Press, 2005), pp. 110–13; "Introduction," and Fox to Du Pont, 22 May 1861, Du Pont to Bache, 30 May 1861, Du Pont to Henry Winter Davis, 1 June 1861, in *Samuel Francis Du Pont: A Selection from His Civil War Letters*, 3 vols., ed. John D. Hayes (Ithaca: Cornell University Press, 1969), 1:lxviii–lxix, 71, 73–76; Fox to Du Pont, 31 May 1861, Henry Francis du Pont Winterthur Collection of Manuscripts, Hagley Museum and Library, Wilmington, Del.; *DAB*, s.vv. "Barnard, John Gross," "Davis, Charles Henry (1807–1877)." Treasury Secretary Salmon P. Chase, in whose department the Coast Survey was lodged, might have originated the idea of the Blockade Strategy Board. Rowena Reed, *Combined Operations in the Civil War* (Annapolis: Naval Institute Press, 1978), p. 7.

2. Fox to Du Pont, 22 May 1861, Du Pont to Henry Winter Davis, 1 June 1861, Du Pont to Sophie Du Pont, 28 June 1861, *Du Pont Letters*, 1:71, 75, 85–86.

3. Du Pont to William Whetten, 26 June 1861, *Du Pont Letters*, 1:82. For summaries of the first three Blockade Board reports, see Reed, *Combined Operations*, pp. 8–9; *Du Pont Letters*, 1:92, n. 1, 103–4, nn. 9, 12. On Fox and the stone fleets, see Fox to Du Pont, 17 June 1861, du Pont Winterthur Manuscripts; John E. Woodman, "The Stone Fleet," *American Neptune* 21 (Oct. 1961): 233–57; Arthur Gordon, "Union Stone Fleets of the Civil War," *DANFS*, 5:424–41, but especially 440, n. 2. Even before the board submitted its third report, Fox was in such a hurry to obstruct the North Carolina inlets that he wanted Du Pont "*to go and do it,*" but Du Pont refused, because the duty belonged to officers already on that coast. He remarked to his wife that he was asked just because he was "*present* and people" were "reminded" of him. Du Pont to Sophie Du Pont, 15 July 1861, *Du Pont Letters*, 1:103.

4. For the fifth memoir, see *Du Pont Letters*, 1:124, n. 4.

5. Du Pont to Sophie Du Pont, 26 July 1861, Du Pont to Matthew Maury, 30 Aug. 1861, *Du Pont Letters*, 1:113, 138.

6. Du Pont to Sophie Du Pont, 15 Sept. 1861, Davis to Du Pont, 25 Sept. 1861, *Du Pont Letters*, 1:147; Davis to Harriette M. Davis, 10 Sept. 1861, in Charles Henry Davis,

Life of Charles Henry Davis: Rear Admiral, 1807–1877 (Boston: Houghton, Mifflin, 1899), pp. 132–33.

7. Porter to Fox, 5 July 1861, *GVFCC*, 2:73–79. Later, after rifled guns tended to burst, Porter replaced them with smoothbore ordnance. See my comments in chapter 17. Du Pont called Mervine (whom Welles appointed to his command a few days before Fox entered the department) "the thickest-headed fellow we have—who will blunder day in and day out." Du Pont to Henry Winter Davis, 9 June 1861, *DuPont Letters*, 1:75, no. 3.

8. Fox to Du Pont, 5 July 1861, Du Pont to Sophie Du Pont, 12 July 1861, *Du Pont Letters*, 1:93, n. 2, 100–101.

9. VLWF to Fox, 1 July 1861, GVFP, NHSC, NYHS; Fox to VLWF, 25 July 1861, *GVFCC*, 1:363–65. Virginia was probably referring to Fox's boon companion, Henry A. Wise, who was in Washington in July.

10. Fox to VLWF, 23, 24 July 1861, GVFP; Du Pont to Sophie Du Pont, 24 July 1861, *Du Pont Letters*, 1:108–9. By 27 July 1861, after appropriate communications between the Navy and War departments, a naval battery was established at Fort Ellsworth. John A. Dahlgren to Welles, 27 July 1861, *ORN*, 4:589.

11. Fox to VLWF, 25 July 1861, *GVFCC*, 1:363; Fox to VLWF, 24 July 1861, VLWF to Fox, 23, 26 July 1861, GVFP. "I knew," Virginia added, "the South held the life & quivering flesh of black men as of little importance, but that they could show such barbarity to whites only proves their long experience of torturing slaves has turned them into fiends."

12. Du Pont to Sophie Du Pont, 25, 26 July 1861, *Du Pont Letters*, 1:111–14.

13. Du Pont to Sophie Du Pont, 1 Aug. 1861, *Du Pont Letters*, 1:117. A minié ball was a cone-shaped bullet with a hollow base that expanded when fired.

14. Du Pont to Sophie Du Pont, 3 Aug. 1861, Du Pont to Henry Winter Davis, 5 Aug. 1861, *Du Pont Letters*, 1:118–19, 125–26; Du Pont to Fox, 9 Aug. 1861, *GVFCC*, 1:49–50.

15. Du Pont to Sophie Du Pont, 3, 4 Aug. 1861, Gideon Welles to Du Pont, 5 Aug. 1861, *Du Pont Letters*, 1:118–24, 126–27.

16. Morgan to Fox, 2 Aug. 1861, Morgan to Welles, 2, 14 Aug. 1861, GVFP. The *Bienville* and *DeSoto* were acquired within a few weeks for a combined $322,500 and were highly successful blockaders. *DANFS*, s.vv. *"Bienville," "DeSoto."*

17. Fox to Du Pont, 17 Aug. 1861, *Du Pont Letters*, 1:131; Welles to H. S. Stellwagon, 3 Aug. 1861, Welles to Stringham, 3, 9, 15 Aug. 1861, *ORN*, 6:50–51, 69–70, 84; Reigart B. Lowry to Fox, 17 Aug. 1861, *GVFCC*, 1:366–68.

18. Stringham to Fox, 16 Aug. 1861, *GVFCC*, 1:365–66; Fox to Du Pont, 17 Aug. 1861, *Du Pont Letters*, 1:132; Elizabeth Blair Lee to Samuel Phillips Lee, 5 July 1861 (journal letter of 3 July 1861), in Virginia Jeans Laas, ed., *Wartime Washington: The Civil War Letters of Elizabeth Blair Lee* (Urbana: University of Illinois Press, 1991), p. 56.

19. Stringham to Welles, 2 Sept. 1861, *ORN*, 6:120–23; Du Pont to Henry Winter Davis, 4 Sept. 1861, *Du Pont Letters*, 1:141–42; Reed, *Combined Operations*, pp. 11–15; Bern Anderson, *By Sea and River: The Naval History of the Civil War* (New York: Alfred A. Knopf, 1962), pp. 48–52. In 1861, when Seward, Meigs, and Porter concocted

their Pensacola expedition, one of the orders they induced Lincoln to sign placed Barron in charge of the Bureau of Detail in the Navy Department, but Welles countermanded the order.

20. Fox to VLWF, 8 Sept. 1861, GVFP; Reed, *Combined Operations,* pp. 12, 15.

21. Fox to Stringham, 1 Sept. 1861, Welles to Stringham, 2, 3 Sept. 1861, Stringham to Welles, 3 Sept. 1861, *ORN,* 6:131–32, 162–63; Joseph S. Fay to Fox, 4 Sept. 1861, GVFP; Welles to Fox, 5 Sept. 1861, J. P. Bankhead to Fox, 29 Sept. 1861, *GVFCC,* 1:373–74, 383–85; Du Pont to Henry Winter Davis, 4 Sept. 1861, *Du Pont Letters,* 1:141–42; Gordon, "Union Stone Fleets," *DANFS,* 5:426.

22. Reed, *Combined Operations,* pp. 16–19; W. N. W. Hewett to Stringham, 7 Sept. 1861, *ORN,* 6:184–85; Du Pont to Sophie Du Pont, 15 Sept. 1861, *Du Pont Letters,* 1:147–48; Lance E. Davis and Stanley L. Engerman, *Naval Blockades in Peace and War: An Economic History* (New York: Cambridge University Press, 2006), pp. 116–19.

23. Welles to Stringham, 3 Sept. 1861, Fox to Stringham, 9, 14 Sept. 1861, Stringham to Welles, 16 Sept. 1861, *ORN,* 6:162–63, 188, 210–11, 216–17; Du Pont to Sophie Du Pont, 17 Sept. 1861, *Du Pont Letters,* 1:149. For examples of reports of consular agents to the State Department forwarded to the Navy Department and then to a squadron commander, see Fox to Stringham, 12 Sept. 1861 (with enclosures), and Welles to Stringham, 18 Sept. 1861 (with enclosures), *ORN,* 6:201–3, 227–31.

24. Welles to Goldsborough, 18 Sept. 1861, *ORN,* 6:233–34; Welles to Du Pont, 18 Sept. 1861, *Du Pont Letters,* 1:152; Louis M. Goldsborough to Elizabeth W. Goldsborough, 23 Aug. 1861, Elizabeth Goldsborough to Goldsborough, 26 Aug. 1861, Louis M. Goldsborough Papers, LC. Elizabeth Goldsborough was the daughter of William Wirt, the attorney general during the administrations of James Monroe and John Quincy Adams. For detailed histories of these blockading squadrons, see Robert M. Browning Jr., *From Cape Charles to Cape Fear: The North Atlantic Blockading Squadron during the Civil War* (Tuscaloosa: University of Alabama Press, 1993) and his *Success Is All That Was Expected: The South Atlantic Blockading Squadron during the Civil War* (Washington, D.C.: Brassey's, 2002).

25. *ANB,* s.vv. "Buchanan, Franklin," "Drayton, Percival," "Du Pont, Samuel Francis," "Farragut, David Glasgow"; *DAB,* s.v. "Page, Thomas Jefferson."

26. Goldsborough to Elizabeth W. Goldsborough, 28 Jan., 2 Apr. 1861, Goldsborough to ?, no day, 1861, Elizabeth W. Goldsborough to Goldsborough, 27 Mar. 1861, Goldsborough Papers.

27. Fox to Forbes, 26 Aug. 1861, Goldsborough Papers. On prize money, see *Du Pont Letters,* 2:380, n. 3.

28. Du Pont to Sophie Du Pont, 17, 18 Sept. 1861, Samuel Mercer to Du Pont, 11 Oct. 1861, *Du Pont Letters,* 1:149–52, 156, no. 9; VLWF, Diary, 4 Mar. 1862, WFP, LC. Porter had recently disparaged Mervine in a letter to Fox. Levy, who died just eighteen days later, also told Virginia that Andrew Jackson "commanded" him to buy Thomas Jefferson's Monticello (the act for which he is renowned) and that "he had lost 60 or 70,000 by it."

29. Reed, *Combined Operations,* pp. 21–23; Gordon, "Union Stone Fleets," *DANFS,* 5:426–27; Morgan to Fox, 14 Aug. 1861, GVFP. Stellwagon warned Fox that blocking

the inlets "can not be done but at great risk." Stellwagon to Fox, 29 Sept. 1861, *ORN*, 6:268.

30. Morgan to Welles, 14 Aug. 1861, Morgan to Fox, 14, 15, 16, 17, 22, 31 Aug., 5, 7 Sept. 1861, GVFP.

31. Du Pont to Sophie Du Pont, 8 Sept. 1861, Du Pont to Fox, 27 Sept. 1861, *Du Pont Letters*, 1:146, 158–59, n. 6; Morgan to Fox, 7, 16 Oct. 1861, Fox to Pook, no date, copy on verso of Morgan to Fox, 16 Oct. 1861, GVFP.

32. Du Pont to Sophie Du Pont, 15, 17 Sept. 1861, Du Pont to Henry Winter Davis, 29 Sept. 1861, *Du Pont Letters*, 1:147, 149, 160.

33. Du Pont to Henry Winter Davis, 8 Oct. 1861, *Du Pont Letters*, 1:162–64.

34. Du Pont to Sophie Du Pont, 8, 15 Sept. 1861, *Du Pont Letters*, 1:146–47.

35. Du Pont to Fox, 11 Oct. 1861, Welles to Du Pont, 12 Oct. 1861, *ORN*, 12:213–15; Du Pont to Sophie Du Pont, 17 Oct. 1861, *Du Pont Letters*, 1:170–71; Davis to Harriette M. Davis, 20 Oct. 1861, Davis Papers, Wayne State University, Detroit (courtesy of Prof. C. Norman Guice).

36. Fox to Welles, 22 Oct. 1861, Welles Papers, LC; Du Pont to Fox, 24 Oct. 1861, *GVFCC*, 1:58. In deciding to attack Port Royal, Du Pont said he was "aided by the professional knowledge and great intelligence of . . . Fox." Du Pont to Welles, 6 Nov. 1861, *ORN*, 12:259–61.

37. Du Pont to Fox, 29 Oct. 1861, *GVFCC*, 1:64.

38. Fox to Lincoln, 5 Nov. 1861, John G. Nicolay Papers, LC; Reed, *Combined Operations*, pp. 23–32.

39. Reed, *Combined Operations*, pp. 30–32.

40. Du Pont to Fox, 9, 11 Nov. 1861, Davis to Fox, 8 Nov. 1861, *GVFCC*, 1:65–66, 69, 396–97. Subordinate officers also congratulated Fox by noting "much of the glory of this victory was due to your personal exertions in organizing the force." Clark H. Wells to Fox, 13 Nov. 1861, GVFP.

Chapter 9. The Monitor *and the Peninsula*

Epigraph: Doris Kearns Goodwin, *Team of Rivals: The Political Genius of Abraham Lincoln* (New York: Simon & Schuster, 2005), p. 437.

1. Du Pont to Fox, 12 Nov. 1861, in *Samuel Francis Du Pont: A Selection from His Civil War Letters*, 3 vols., ed. John D. Hayes (Ithaca: Cornell University Press, 1969), 1:235; *CWNC*, 9, 24 Nov., 5 Dec. 1861.

2. Bache to Du Pont, 4 Sept. 1861, *ORN* 12:207; Du Pont to Sophie Du Pont, 5 Dec. 1861, *Du Pont Letters*, 1:272–73. The stone fleet outraged the British as well as southerners, because they thought southern ports might be permanently closed. Du Pont and Davis may have disliked sinking obstructions because they thought it too extreme a war measure or because they thought new channels would form, bypassing the obstructions. Arthur Gordon, "Union Stone Fleets of the Civil War," *DANFS*, 5:424–41; John E. Woodman Jr., "The Stone Fleet," *American Neptune* 21 (Oct. 1961): 233–59. One of the stone whalers, the 340-ton bark *Edward*, was spared to become that floating machine shop (the navy's first) Du Pont requested.

3. Wilkes to Welles, 8 Nov. 1861, Welles to H. Paulding, 16 Nov. 1861, Welles to

Wilkes, 30 Nov. 1861, *ORN,* 1:129–31, 145, 148; Fox to Du Pont, 19 Nov. 1861, Henry Francis du Pont Winterthur Collection of Manuscripts, Hagley Museum and Library, Wilmington, Del.; David Herbert Donald, *Lincoln* (New York: Simon & Schuster, 1995), p. 322. In 1861 cotton exports from the South were not significantly reduced by the ineffective Union blockade but by a highly effective self-imposed embargo by Confederate state governments and citizens (not the Confederate government) in a failed effort to provoke British intervention. Lance E. Davis and Stanley Engerman, *Naval Blockades in Peace and War: An Economic History since 1750* (New York: Cambridge University Press, 2006), p. 124.

4. VLWF, Diary, 16 Nov., 25 Dec. 1861, WFP, LC; Goldsborough to Fox, 29 Dec. 1861, *GVFCC,* 1:227.

5. VLWF, Diary, 12 Nov., 25, 28 Dec. 1861, WFP; Lord Lyons to Earl Russell, 31 Dec. 1865, *ORN,* 1:194; William Joseph Sullivan, "Gustavus Vasa Fox and Naval Administration, 1861–1866" (Ph.D. diss., Catholic University of America, 1977), pp. 274–75; Donald, *Lincoln,* pp. 322–23. At Christmas dinner, Lincoln promised Virginia his photograph.

6. VLWF, Diary, 5 Nov. 1861, WFP; "Proposition of John Laird & Son . . .," 10 May 1861, GVFP, NHSC, NYHS. This proposal was relayed to the Navy Department in July by their New York agent John T. Howard. See also, Fox to Welles, 15 Aug. 1863, Welles Papers, LC, in Sullivan, "Fox," p. 162; John David Smith, "Yankee Ironclads at Birkenhead? A Note on Gideon Welles, John Laird and Gustavus V. Fox," *Mariner's Mirror* 67 (1981): 77–82.

7. Forbes to Fox, 18, 20 June, 26 July 1861, GVFP; James Phinney Baxter, *The Introduction of the Ironclad Warship* (Cambridge: Harvard University Press, 1933), p. 242. A year later, Lenthall decided that warships should be of iron, despite his personal interest in wooden vessels, and he predicted that wooden vessels covered with iron (ironclads) will rot. Lenthall to Du Pont, 11 May 1862, *ORN,* 12:814.

8. John Niven, *Gideon Welles: Lincoln's Secretary of the Navy* (New York: Oxford University Press, 1973), pp. 364–66; *CWNC,* 18 July, 3 Aug. 1861. Bushnell's recollections of the origin of the *Monitor* (with corrections by Welles) are vivid. Bushnell to Welles, 9 Mar. 1877, Welles Papers, Huntington Library, San Marino, Calif.

9. Niven, *Welles,* pp. 365–66; Baxter, *Ironclad Warship,* pp. 253–54, 273; Howard to Fox, 25 Aug. 1863 (including copies of Fox to Howard, 13 Aug., 29 Oct., 1 Nov. 1861), GVFP.

10. Niven, *Welles,* pp. 366–67; Baxter, *Ironclad Warship,* pp. 181–90, 254–55, 261; John H. Morrison, *History of American Steam Navigation* (New York: Stephen Daye Press, 1958, reprint of 1903 edition), pp. 427–29. Ericsson had misgivings about the design of the Peacemaker by Robert Stockton, which, while based on Ericsson's twelve-inch gun "Oregon," made changes that weakened the Peacemaker. Ruth White, *Yankee from Sweden: The Dream and the Reality in the Days of John Ericsson* (New York: Henry Holt, 1960), pp. 93–94.

11. Niven, *Welles,* pp. 367–69; Baxter, *Ironclad Warship,* pp. 248, 255–62. Fox, in Fox to Ericsson, 18 Mar. 1862, recalled that he asked Ericsson to design a "match" for the *Warrior* "last summer" to be armed with "one 20 inch gun." He did ask Ericsson, in September 1861, to design such a vessel, but probably not with a twenty-inch gun,

because Fox embraced the idea of fifteen- and twenty-inch guns only after 9 March 1862. Ericsson to Fox, 13 Mar. 1862, GVFP.

12. Baxter, *Ironclad Warship*, pp. 273–81, 350–57. Hale apparently delayed the appropriation because he was incensed by the $70,000 commission earned in five months by Welles's brother-in-law George D. Morgan for purchasing ships for the navy. It is possible that Ericsson's partners had a hand in the delay, because the Lenthall-Isherwood design remained on the drawing boards while the *Monitor* was rushed to completion. Edward William Sloan III, *Benjamin Franklin Isherwood, Naval Engineer: The Years as Engineer in Chief, 1861–1869* (Annapolis: United States Naval Institute, 1965), pp. 50–51. For Fox's idea that Du Pont's success lulled Congress, see Elizabeth Blair Lee to Samuel Phillips Lee, 31 Mar. 1862, in Virginia Jeans Laas, ed., *Wartime Washington: The Civil War Letters of Elizabeth Blair Lee* (Urbana: University of Illinois Press, 1991), p. 114.

13. Baxter, *Ironclad Warship*, pp. 283–84.

14. Fox to Ericsson, 30 Jan. 1862, *ORN*, 6:538; Ericsson to Fox, 24 Feb. 1862, GVFP; William N. Still, *Monitor Builders: A Historical Study of the Principal Firms and Individuals Involved in the Construction of the Monitor* (Washington, D.C.: National Park Service, 1988), pp. 7, 24–26; Baxter, *Ironclad Warship*, pp. 260–66. The construction of the *Monitor* graphically illustrates the thesis of Raimondo Luraghi, *A History of the Confederate Navy* (Annapolis: Naval Institute Press, 1996), that the South lost the naval war in the workshops of the North. The tugboat *Seth Low* was named for the grandfather of the identically named mayor of Brooklyn and New York and the president of Columbia University.

15. Goldsborough to Fox, 9–10, 20 Feb., 1 Mar. 1862, *GVFCC*, 1:236–42, 245–48.

16. VLWF, Diary, 6 Jan. 1862, WFP; Barnard to Fox, 12 Feb. 1862, *GVFCC*, 1:419–23; Fox to Barnard, 30 Apr. 1864, GVFP.

17. VLWF, Diary, 5, 7 Mar. 1862, WFP.

18. VLWF, Diary, 7 Mar. 1862, WFP. Fanny Kemble and her daughter, Sarah Butler Wister (mother of the novelist Owen Wister), and her husband Owen J. Wister were friends of the Foxes. Kemble to Fox, no day, 1862, and Sarah B. Wister to Fox, 7–8 July, no year, GVFP. By the end of March, Fox rejoiced that McClellan had "sat them out," after his move to the Peninsula had forced the abandonment of the batteries without sacrificing any lives. Elizabeth Blair Lee to Samuel Phillips Lee, 31 Mar. 1862, in Laas, *Wartime Washington*, p. 117.

19. VLWF, Diary, 8 Mar. 1862, WFP.

20. Fox to Welles, 30 June 1874, Welles Papers, Huntington Library. John L. Worden to Welles, 5 Jan. 1868, copy in GVFP, vividly describes the trip to Hampton Roads. Fox sailed with Worden and called him "my most intimate friend." Fox to Welles, 19 Aug. 1865, Welles Papers, LC. See also, Craig L. Symonds, "Building the Ironclads," in Harold Holzer and Tim Mulligan, eds., *The Battle of Hampton Roads: New Perspectives on the U.S.S. Monitor and C.S.S. Virginia* (New York: Fordham University Press, 2006), pp. 33–34.

21. Fox to Ericsson, 18 Mar. 1862, GVFP; VLWF, Diary, 9, 10 Mar. 1862, WFP; Benjamin P. Thomas and Harold M. Hyman, *Stanton: The Life and Times of Lincoln's Secretary of War* (New York: Alfred A. Knopf, 1962), pp. 179–80; Donald, *Lincoln,*

p. 340. A razee is a vessel with its upper deck cut away, which explains why the *Cumberland* is frequently described as a sloop of war. Reflecting and magnifying her husband's views, Virginia Fox reportedly even "rejoiced" with Elizabeth Blair Lee (Montgomery's sister and the wife of naval officer Samuel Phillips Lee) "over the destruction of the Congress & Cumberland," because "on their ashes or ruin we will build an Iron Navy." Elizabeth Blair Lee to Samuel Phillips Lee, 20 Mar. 1862, in Laas, *Wartime Washington*, p. 114.

22. Fox to Marston, 8 [should be 9] Mar. 1862, *GVFCC*, 1:432–34; Fox to Ericsson, 12 Jan. 1863, GVFP. While in the navy, Fox had also befriended Jones. The latter had been a house guest of the Foxes, when they lived in Lawrence. VLWF, Diary, 12 Mar. 1862, WFP.

23. Samuel Dana Greene to Welles, 12 Mar. 1862, *ORN*, 7:25; John L. Worden to Welles, 5 Jan. 1868, copy in GVFP; Fox, "Monitor," *Johnson's New Universal Cyclopaedia*, 4 vols. (New York: A. J. Johnson, 1875–77), 3:582–84; Alban C. Stimers to Fox, 20 Oct. 1875, Isaac Newton to Fox, 22 Oct. 1875, Greene to Fox, 15 Nov. 1875, Catesby ap R. Jones to Fox, 20 June 1876, GVFP. Jones called Fox's encyclopedia article "the fairest northern account of the fight that I have seen," but corrected some "errors." See also Mabry Tyson, "Believe Only Half of What You Read about the Battle of Hampton Roads," in Holzer and Mulligan, *Battle of Hampton Roads*, p. 99.

24. Robert J. Schneller Jr., *A Quest for Glory: A Biography of Rear Admiral John A. Dahlgren* (Annapolis: Naval Institute Press, 1996), pp. 201–2; Fox to Welles, 9 Mar. 1862, Fox to Ericsson, 9 Mar. 1862, *ORN*, 7:7–8; Fox, "Monitor," *Johnson's New Universal Cyclopaedia*, 3:582–84. Although his doctors leeched Worden, he soon recovered. Wise to Fox, 12 Mar. 1862, *ORN*, 7:97. Worden, Wise, and Fox were all midshipmen together on the *Cyane*.

25. Fox to McClellan, 9 Mar. 1862, *GVFCC*, 1:435; Lincoln to Welles, 10 Mar. 1862, Welles to Fox, 10 Mar. 1862, and Fox to Blair, 11 Mar. 1862, *ALCW*, 5:154.

26. VLWF, Diary, 10–12 Mar. 1862, WFP; Fox to Lenthall, 10 Mar. 1862, Fox to Welles, 10 Mar. 1862, *ORN*, 7:85–86.

27. Fox to Wise, 11 Mar. 1862, T. G. Baylor to J. W. Ripley, 11 Mar. 1862, *ORN*, 7:92–94; Fox, "Monitor," *Johnson's New Universal Cyclopaedia*, 3:582–84; Eugene B. Canfield, "Civil War Naval Ordnance," *DANFS*, 3:805.

28. Fox to Dahlgren, 11 Mar. 1862, Dahlgren to Fox, 11 Mar. 1862, Fox to Grimes, 12 Mar. 1862, *ORN*, 7:93, 98; Schneller, *Dahlgren*, pp. 201–2.

29. McClellan to Fox, 12 Mar. 1862, Fox to McClellan, 13 Mar. 1862, McDowell to McClellan, 13 Mar. 1862, *ORN*, 7:99–100, 102; VLWF, Diary, 13 Mar. 1862, WFP.

30. VLWF, Diary, 14 Mar. 1862, WFP; Fox to Welles, 30 June 1874, Welles Papers, Huntington Library; John A. Griswold to Ericsson, 14 Mar. 1862, Ericsson Papers, NYHS; Ericsson to Fox, 13, 14, 15 Mar. 1862, GVFP.

31. Ericsson to Fox, 15 Mar. 1862, GVFP. Joseph Smith specified desired improvements for Ericsson on 17 March. Baxter, *Ironclad Warship*, pp. 306–7, 309.

32. Schneller, *Dahlgren*, pp. 203–8.

33. Schneller, *Dahlgren*, pp. 206, 208; Ericsson to Fox, 2 Jan. 1865, GVFP. Fox insisted "to Rodman belongs the honor of the name." Fox to Ericsson, 8 Jan. 1865, Charles Thomas Harbeck Collection, Huntington Library.

34. Charles Henry Davis to Harriette M. Davis, 26 June 1863, in Charles Henry Davis, *Life of Charles Henry Davis: Rear Admiral, 1807–1877* (Boston: Houghton, Mifflin, 1899), p. 296; Schneller, *Dahlgren*, pp. 211–12. On the Dahlgren-Fox relationship, see Dahlgren to Fox, 7, 18 Oct. 1863, 22 Jan. 1864, *ORN*, 15:13–15, 51, 251–52. Dahlgren was "grateful" to Fox for his "kind attention" to his son Ulrich, following the amputation of his right leg. Dahlgren to Wise, 29 July 1863, Wise Papers, NYHS. See also, the cordial letter from Dahlgren to Wise, Sept. [no day], 1864, Wise Papers, LC.

35. Fox to Ericsson, 18 Mar. 1862, Ericsson to Fox, 19 Mar. 1862, GVFP; Baxter, *Ironclad Warship*, pp. 306, 309. Fox later opposed putting rams on naval vessels.

36. Fox to Ericsson, 20 Mar. 1862, Ericsson to Fox, 23 Mar. 1862, GVFP.

37. Fox to Ericsson, 22, 24, 28 Mar. 1862, Ericsson to Fox, 25, 26, 29 Mar., 28 Apr. 1862, GVFP; Fox to Ericsson, 25 Apr. 1862, Ericsson Papers, NYHS. On sharing monitor technology, see Fox to Edward de Stoekl, 29 Apr. 1862 (Russia) and Waldemar R. de Raasloff to Fox 16 May, 15 Aug. 1862 (Denmark), GVFP.

38. Richard H. Webber, "Monitors of the United States Navy, 1861–1937," *DANFS*, 3:758–61; VLWF, Diary, 2 Apr. 1862, WFP.

39. Sloan, *Isherwood*, 66–67; Ericsson to Fox, 28 Apr. 1862, GVFP.

40. Fox to Ericsson, 5 June, 1862, Ericsson to Fox, 6 July 1862, Ericsson Papers, LC; *DANFS*, s.v. "*Passaic*."

41. Rodgers to Ericsson, 15 Nov. 1864, Ericsson Papers, LC; Fox to Ericsson, 7 Jan. 1865, Ericsson to Fox, 14 Oct. 1865, GVFP; Webber, "Monitors," *DANFS*, 3:762–66.

42. McClellan to Fox, 14 Mar. 1862, *GVFCC*, 1:438–39; Thomas and Hyman, *Stanton*, p. 181.

43. Thomas and Hyman, *Stanton*, pp. 181–82; Kenneth P. Williams, *Lincoln Finds a General: A Military Study of the Civil War*, 5 vols. (New York: Macmillan, 1950–59), 3:339–40.

44. VLWF, Diary, 17–18, 22 Mar. 1862, WFP; Fox to Goldsborough, 24 Mar. 1862, *GVFCC*, 1:251; Elizabeth Blair Lee to Samuel Phillips Lee, 31 Mar. 1862, in Laas, *Wartime Washington*, p. 118.

45. VLWF, Diary, 6, 7, 9, 11 Apr. 1862, WFP.

46. VLWF, Diary, 18 Apr. 1862, WFP; McClellan to Fox, 14 Mar. 1862, Fox to Goldsborough, 17, 24 Mar. 1862, *GVFCC*, 1:438–39, 250–52; Welles to Goldsborough, 17 Mar. 1862, Goldsborough to D. B. Barton, 20 Mar. 1862, Barton to Goldsborough, 20 Mar. 1862, Goldsborough to Welles, 23 Mar. 1862, Marshall O. Roberts to Welles, 6 June 1862, *ORN*, 7:135, 144–45, 161–64, 165–66; Robert V. Bruce, *Lincoln and the Tools of War* (Urbana: University of Illinois Press, 1989), pp. 174–75.

47. Fox to Goldsborough, 19, 23 Apr. 1862, Goldsborough to Fox, 21, 24 Apr. 1862, *GVFCC*, 1:256–57, 259–63. The commander of the *Wachusett* believed that the *Galena*, with its two- or two-and-one-half-inch armor, would be destroyed if it attempted to run past the Confederate batteries, which Fox assured McClellan it could do "with impunity." J. S. Missroon to Goldsborough, 22 Apr. 1862, *ORN*, 7:256–57.

48. VLWF, Diary, 5, 6 May 1862, WFP; *Inside Lincoln's White House: The Complete Civil War Diary of John Hay*, ed. Michael Burlingame and John R. Turner Ettlinger

(Carbondale: Southern Illinois University Press), 9 Sept. 1863, p. 80. Referring to his trophies, Fox wrote, "I keep my Naval record hieroglyphically." Fox to Porter, 13 May 1862, *GVFCC*, 2:101.

49. Goldsborough to Fox, 21 Apr. 1862, Fox to Goldsborough, 7 May 1862, *GVFCC*, 1:261, 266.

50. Fox to Goldsborough, 27 Mar. 1862, Goldsborough to Fox, 21 Apr. 1862, *GVFCC*, 1:255, 259–60. For a description of the escape of the *Nashville*, which illustrates the futility of using sailing vessels for blockading, see Edward Cavendy (commander of the bark *Gemsbok*) to Fox, 21 Mar. 1862, *GVFCC*, 2:283–85. Goldsborough was relieved to hear that the *Nashville* became the British blockade runner *Thomas L. Wragg*. Goldsborough to Fox, 20 Apr. 1862, *GVFCC*, 1:257–58. In November 1862, it was commissioned as the Confederate privateer *Rattlesnake* and was destroyed in February 1863. "Confederate Forces Afloat: *Nashville*," *DANFS*, 2:551–52.

51. VLWF, Diary, 8 May 1862, WFP. Isherwood and Lenthall calculated that the *Virginia* "must draw 22 to 24 feet of water." It apparently drew twenty-two feet. Fox to Goldsborough, 7 May 1862, *GVFCC*, 1:266.

52. Rodgers to Goldsborough, 16 May 1862, *ORN*, 7:357; Elizabeth Blair Lee to Samuel Phillips Lee, 29 Apr. 1862 (30 Apr.), in Laas, *Wartime Washington*, p. 137. As a midshipman, Fox served under Tattnall in the *Saratoga* when it was dismasted in a gale.

53. VLWF, Diary, 18 May 1862, WFP; Fox to Goldsborough, 17 May 1862, Goldsborough to Fox, 21 May 1862, *GVFCC*, 1:269–72; Buchanan to Jones, 19 June 1862, *ORN*, 7:788–89.

54. Fox to Goldsborough, 3, 5, 14 June 1862, Goldsborough to Fox, 16 June 1862, *GVFCC*, 1:281–82, 285–89; VLWF, Diary, 17, 21 June 1862, WFP.

55. VLWF, Diary, 28, 29 June 1862, WFP.

56. VLWF, Diary, 28, 29 June 1862, WFP; Fox to VLWF, 2, 7 July 1862, GVFP.

57. Welles to Wilkes, 6 July 1862, Goldsborough to Welles, 15 July 1862, Welles to Goldsborough, 21 July 1862, *ORN*, 7:548, 573–74; Welles to Mary Jane Welles, 20 July 1862, Welles Papers, LC.

58. Fox to Barnard, 23 July 1862, *GVFCC*, 2:328–30; Fox to VLWF, 14 July 1862, GVFP. Barnard blamed McClellan's failure on his being "deprived of more than ⅓ of the force he counted on," but he also believed that if McClellan had used his force "more boldly . . . we might have got to Richmond." Barnard to Fox, 19 July 1862, *GVFCC*, 2:325. Fox's letter of 14 July 1862 might be the only example of his being exasperated by Virginia's complaints.

59. Fox to VLWF, 24, 26 July 1862, GVFP; VLWF, Diary, 28 July 1862, WFP.

60. Fox to Grimes, 5 Aug. 1862, *GVFCC*, 2:348–49; Rowena Reed, *Combined Operations in the Civil War* (Annapolis: Naval Institute Press, 1978), pp. 183–87.

Chapter 10. The Mississippi

1. Eads to Welles, 29 Apr. 1861, Welles to Simon Cameron, 14 May 1861, Cameron to McClellan, 14 May 1861, Welles to Eads, 14 May 1861, *ORN*, 22:277–80; James Phinney Baxter, *Introduction of the Ironclad Warship* (Cambridge: Harvard University

Press, 1933), pp. 242–43. The gunboats could implement Scott's Anaconda Plan. Eads was one of the most brilliant engineers of the nineteenth century. He subsequently built the Eads bridge over the Mississippi at St. Louis, solved the problem of silting at the mouth of the Mississippi, and advocated an ingenious ship railway over Mexico's Tehuantepec Isthmus. Melvin Kranzberg, *ANB*, s.v. "Eads, James Buchanan."

2. Baxter, *Ironclad Warship*, pp. 243–45; Fox to Foote, 8 Mar. 1862, *GVFCC*, 2:42–43; *DANFS*, s.vv. "*Cairo*," "*Benton*," "*Essex*."

3. Frémont to Montgomery Blair, no date, GVFP, NHSC, NYHS; Welles to Foote, 30 Aug. 1861, *ORN*, 22:307. Probably because Foote and Welles were schoolmates, Foote to Fox, 2 Nov. 1861, *GVFCC*, 2:9, makes it clear that Fox made this personnel decision.

4. Foote to Dahlgren, 5 Sept. 1861, Dahlgren Papers, LC; Foote to Fox, 8 Sept. 1861, *ORN*, 22:320–22; Ulysses S. Grant, *Personal Memoirs of U. S. Grant*, 2 vols. (New York: Charles L. Webster, 1885), 1:264–67.

5. Foote to Fox, 27 Sept. 1861, 11 Jan. 1862, *GVFCC*, 2:5–7, 30.

6. Fox to Foote, 28 Oct. 1861, GVFP; Foote to Fox, 2 Nov. 1861, *GVFCC*, 2:8–10.

7. Foote to Fox, 2, 4 Nov. 1861, *GVFCC*, 2:10–13. Foote actually suffered from "frequent and severe" headaches.

8. Fox to Foote, 19 Nov. 1861, GVFP; Foote to Fox, 22 Nov. 1861, *GVFCC*, 2:13–16.

9. Fox to Foote, 22 Nov., 28, 30, 31 Dec. 1861, 4, 11, 13, 27 Jan. 1862, *GVFCC*, 2:13–36.

10. Lincoln to Foote, 23 Jan. 1862, Lincoln to Edwin M. Stanton, 24 Jan. 1862, *ALCW*, 5:108, 110; Fox to Foote, 27 Jan. 1861, *GVFCC*, 2:36–37.

11. Fox to Foote, 19, 26, 28, 30 Dec. 1862, Foote to Fox, 19, 30 Dec. 1862, Foote to Halleck, 28 Jan. 1863, *ORN*, 22:467–68, 471–72, 475–78, 524; Fox to Foote, 27 Jan. 1862, Foote to Fox, 31 Jan. 1862, *GVFCC*, 2:36–39.

12. Foote to Welles, 7 Feb. 1862, Fox to Foote, 8 Feb. 1862, *ORN*, 22:537–39, 546; Kenneth P. Williams, *Lincoln Finds a General: A Military Study of the Civil War*, 5 vols. (New York: Macmillan, 1950–59), 3:199–228; Grant, *Personal Memoirs*, 1:288–93. The *Eastport* was converted into a Union ironclad ram at Cairo. *DANFS*, s.v. "*Eastport*."

13. Halleck to Foote, 11 Feb. 1862, Foote to Fox, 11 Feb. 1862, Fox to Stanton, 12 Feb. 1862, Foote to Welles, 15 Feb. 1862, *ORN*, 22:579, 582, 584–85; Williams, *Lincoln Finds a General*, 3:229–39; Grant, *Personal Memoirs*, 1:294–304.

14. Williams, *Lincoln Finds a General*, 3:243–59; Grant, *Personal Memoirs*, 1:304–15.

15. Williams, *Lincoln Finds a General*, 3:238, 244–47.

16. Fox to Foote, 8 Mar. 1862 (actually 5 Mar. 1862), *GVFCC*, 2:42–43. Despite his complaint to Foote, Fox was an admirer and lifelong friend of John G. Barnard, chief engineer of the Army of the Potomac and a builder of fortifications.

17. Eads to Ericsson, 20 June, 23 July, 2 Aug. 1862, Ericsson Papers, LC; Richard H. Webber, "Monitors of the United States Navy, 1861–1937," *DANFS*, 3:781–86.

18. Fox to David Dixon Porter, 3 Nov. 1863, *GVFCC*, 2:195–96; Webber, "Monitors," *DANFS*, 3:781–86.

19. Foote to Halleck, 13 Mar. 1862, Foote to Welles, 17 Mar. 1862, Foote to A. M. Pen-

nock in Pennock to Chief, Bureau of Ordnance, 19 Mar. 1862, *ORN*, 22:688–89, 693–95; Williams, *Lincoln Finds a General*, 3:396–400. Fox relayed the "highly successful results" of the mortars to Lincoln. Fox to Lincoln, 4 Apr. 1862, Lincoln Papers, LC.

20. Scott to Stanton, 19 Apr. 1862, Stanton Papers, LC; William D. Porter to Foote, 12 May 1862, *ORN*, 22:730–31; Williams, *Lincoln Finds a General*, 3:396–400.

21. Davis to Harriette M. Davis, 31 May 1862, Davis Papers, Wayne State University, Detroit (courtesy of Prof. C. Norman Guice); Elizabeth Blair Lee to Samuel Phillips Lee, 18 May 1862, in Virginia Jeans Laas, ed., *Wartime Washington: The Civil War Letters of Elizabeth Blair Lee* (Urbana: University of Illinois Press, 1991), pp. 148–49.

22. Chester G. Hearn, *Ellet's Brigade: The Strangest Outfit of Them All* (Baton Rouge: Louisiana State University Press, 2000), pp. 27–40; Gene D. Lewis, *Charles Ellet, Jr.: The Engineer as Individualist* (Urbana: University of Illinois Press, 1968), pp. 189–208; Warren Daniel Crandall and Isaac D. Newell, *History of the Ram Fleet and the Mississippi Marine Brigade...* (St. Louis: Buschart Bros., 1907), pp. 51–61.

23. Davis to Harriette M. Davis, 10, 11 June 1862, Davis Papers, Wayne State University (courtesy of Prof. C. Norman Guice); *CWNC*, 17 June, 1 Oct., 2 Nov. 1862; Lincoln to Alfred W. Ellet, 7 Nov. 1862, *ALCW*, 5:490.

24. *Diary of Gideon Welles: Secretary of the Navy under Lincoln and Johnson*, 3 vols., ed. Howard K. Beale (New York: W. W. Norton, 1960), (2 Sept. 1864), 2:134–35.

25. Fox to Welles, 19 June, 12 Aug. 1871, Welles to Fox, 8 July 1871, Welles Papers, Huntington Library, San Marino, Calif.; Rowena Reed, *Combined Operations in the Civil War* (Annapolis: Naval Institute Press, 1978), pp. 5–7, 58–61; Chester G. Hearn, *The Capture of New Orleans, 1862* (Baton Rouge: Louisiana State University Press, 1995), pp. 97–100.

26. VLWF, Diary, 14 Nov. 1861, WFP, LC; Welles to W. W. McKean, 2 Nov. 1861, *ORN*, 16:753; Fox to Butler, 19 May 1862, *GVFCC*, 2:301. Fox secured from Bache of the Coast Survey minute descriptions of offshore islands stretching from Mobile Bay to Lake Borgne, adjacent to New Orleans. Bache to Fox, 23 Nov. 1861, GVFP. South of North Carolina the Navy Department almost always received its earliest news of its operations from Richmond, Virginia, newspapers obtained through the army at the front.

27. Hearn, *Capture of New Orleans*, pp. 100–5; VLWF, Diary, 21 Dec. 1861, 11 Jan. 1862, WFP; Fox to Gideon Welles, 24 Jan. 1871, Welles Papers, LC. Because Farragut's mother died when he was seven and he never saw his father after he was nine, David and Evelina Porter, the parents of David Dixon Porter, adopted Farragut. The mortar schooners were far more seaworthy crafts than the leaky log rafts on the upper Mississippi.

28. Welles to Farragut, 20 Jan. 1862, *ORN*, 18:7–8; Farragut to Fox, 30 Jan., 12, 17 Feb. 1862, *GVFCC*, 1:299–303. In naval engagements, many men bled to death from want of early attention.

29. Grimes to Fox, 3 Feb. 1862, *GVFCC*, 1:414–15.

30. Fox to Porter, 24 Feb. 1862, Porter Papers, LC; Farragut to Fox, 12 Feb. 1862, *GVFCC*, 1:300–2; Farragut to Welles, 12 Feb. 1862, *ORN*, 18:28.

31. Farragut to Fox, 12 Feb. 1862, Porter Papers, LC; Porter to Fox, 28 Mar., 8 Apr. 1862, *GVFCC*, 1:301–2, 2:89, 98; Hearn, *Capture of New Orleans*, pp. 154–55. With his mind on

the Mississippi, Farragut did not pay close attention to his blockaders. Commander R. B. Hitchcock, who was blockading Mobile with the *Susquehanna,* complained to Fox that his last orders had come from Fox and that, by the end of July 1862, he had not heard a word from Farragut. Hitchcock to Fox, 31 July 1862, *ORN,* 19:102–3.

32. Farragut to Fox, 12, 17 Feb. 1862, Fox to Farragut, 7 Mar. 1862, *GVFCC,* 1:300–3, 306–7.

33. Farragut to Fox, 21 Mar., 8 Apr. 1862, *GVFCC,* 1:307–8, 310–11.

34. Farragut to Fox, 5 Mar. 1862, Farragut to Fox (note added by Lenthall), 7 Apr. 1862, Porter to Fox, 8 Apr. 1862, *GVFCC,* 1:306, 308–9, 2:99.

35. Barnard to Fox, 28 Jan. 1862, Porter to Farragut, 27 Feb. 1862, Porter Papers, LC.

36. Farragut to Welles, 21 Apr., 6 May 1862, Farragut to Fox, 25 Apr. 1862, Farragut to Porter, 24 Apr. 1862, *ORN,* 18:134–35, 142, 153–59; Butler to Blair, 8 May 1862, BFP, LC. Butler also assured Blair that if left alone, "I will make this a Union City within sixty days." Ibid. Hearn, *Capture of New Orleans,* pp. 196–236, describes in vivid detail the battle for New Orleans. Porter was annoyed at Butler for disparaging his mortar fleet. Chester G. Hearn, *Admiral David Dixon Porter: The Civil War Years* (Annapolis: Naval Institute Press, 1996), pp. 116–17.

37. Wells to Farragut, 20 Jan. 1862, *ORN,* 18:7–8; Hearn, *Capture of New Orleans,* pp. 237–48; Reed, *Combined Operations,* pp. 193–95.

38. Hearn, *Capture of New Orleans,* pp. 248–55; Reed, *Combined Operations,* 193–95. Reed argues persuasively that the capture of New Orleans was a joint army-navy operation that would not have succeeded without Butler's troops. She argues, less persuasively, Butler's point that Farragut should have awaited the fall of the forts before proceeding up river with Butler's army to demand the surrender of New Orleans. To Montgomery Blair, Butler simply said: "Farragut is a splendid fellow and deserves every credit." Butler to Blair, 8 May 1862, BFP.

39. Fox to Farragut, 12 May 1862, Fox to Porter, 13 May 1862, *GVFCC,* 1:313–14, 2:101. Fox obliged Porter by cutting some remarks disparaging Farragut out of Porter's official report. Porter to Fox, 10 May 1862, *GVFCC,* 2:100.

40. Welles to Farragut, 20 Jan. 1862, Farragut to Welles, 29 Apr. 1862, *ORN,* 18:7–8, 148; Fox to Farragut, 12 May 1862, Fox to Porter, 13 May 1862, *GVFCC,* 1:313, 2:101.

41. VLWF, Diary, 9 May 1862, WFP, LC; Fox to Farragut, 17 May 1862, Fox to Porter, 17 May 1862, *GVFCC,* 1:314–15, 2:101–2.

42. VLWF, Diary, 27 Apr. 1862, WFP; Fox to Porter, 17 May 1862, *GVFCC,* 2:101–2.

43. Farragut to Fox, 7 May 1862, *GVFCC,* 1:311–12; Farragut to Fox, 30 May 1862, *ORN,* 18:521–22.

44. Farragut to Fox, 7 May, 12 June 1862, Porter to Fox, 7, 12 June 1862, *GVFCC,* 1:311–12, 315–16, 2:117–18, 121–22; Fox to Farragut, 17 May 1862, *ORN,* 18:499; "Contrabands," in Mark Mayo Boatner III, *The Civil War Dictionary* (New York: David McKay, 1959), p. 172. Authoritative and concise, Boatner's volume is most useful. Lee was Fox's old shipmate on the Coast Survey brig *Washington* and Montgomery Blair's brother-in-law.

45. Porter to Fox, 30 June 1862, *GVFCC,* 2:122–24; Williams, *Lincoln Finds a Gen-*

eral, 3:429–31. More than three-quarters of the men digging the canal either died or suffered from fever before the attempt was abandoned. General Halleck also shared in the wishful thinking that the navy, with little support from the army, could take Vicksburg.

46. Elizabeth Blair Lee to Samuel Phillips Lee, 22 July 1862 (23 July), in Laas, *Wartime Washington,* p. 168; Hearn, *Ellet's Brigade,* pp. 50–59; Crandall and Newell, *Ram Fleet,* pp. 103–5.

47. Fox to Welles, 16, 20 Aug. 1862, Welles Papers, LC.

48. Fox to Welles, 20 Aug. 1862, Welles Papers, LC.

49. Fox to Welles, 20 Aug. 1862, Welles Papers, LC. On the dislike of Indian names, see Edward William Sloan III, *Benjamin Franklin Isherwood, Naval Engineer: The Years as Engineer in Chief, 1861–1869* (Annapolis: United States Naval Institute, 1965), p. 256, n. 5.

50. Fox to VLWF, 27 Aug. 1862, GVFP.

Chapter 11. More Ironclads

1. Fox to Du Pont, 3 June 1862, Fox to Grimes, 5 Aug., 6 Sept. 1862, *GVFCC,* 1:126, 2:348, 369.

2. *DANFS,* s.vv. *"New Ironsides," "Passaic";* Fox to VLWF, 2 Sept. 1862, GVFP, NHSC, NYHS. Fox's contempt for Pope (an "imbecile") was, no doubt, heightened by his earlier criticism of Foote at Island No. 10.

3. Fox to VLWF, 31 Aug., 2, 3 Sept. 1862, GVFP. Charlie still wanted to play a more active role in the war, so Fox arranged at the beginning of 1863 for him to be Porter's secretary in the Mississippi Squadron.

4. Fox to VLWF, 3, 6, 8 Sept. 1862, GVFP.

5. Fox to VLWF, 3, 6 Sept. 1862, GVFP; Fox to A. C. Rhind, 6 Sept. 1862, Fox to Grimes, 6 Sept. 1862, Anthony to Fox, 27 Oct. 1862, *GVFCC,* 2:368–69, 415.

6. Fox to VLWF, 19 Sept. 1862, GVFP; VLWF, Diary, 14 Nov. 1862, WFP, LC. On or about 1 November 1862, Fox and Virginia rented four furnished rooms with meals for four dollars a day with one dollar per day deducted in the summer when Virginia was absent, and Fox ate out. Fox, "Memo," GVFP.

7. Percival Drayton to Du Pont, 11 May 1862, *ORN,* 13:3–4; Fox to Grimes, 28 May 1862, *GVFCC,* 2:304; Fox to Spring, 26 June 1862, Luce to Fox, 27 Jan. 1864, GVFP; Harold D. Langley, *Social Reform in the United States Navy, 1798–1862* (Urbana: University of Illinois Press, 1967), pp. 263–66. As Fox suggested, sailors were compensated for the loss of grog by a pay increase of five cents daily. John P. Hale, whom Fox came to despise as an enemy of Welles and himself, was largely responsible for abolishing the barbaric punishment of flogging seamen with the cat-o-nine-tails. Langley, *Social Reform,* pp. 170–206.

8. On Carr, see Fox to William Wilkins, 3 Apr. 1862, GVFP; *Autobiography of Rear Admiral Charles Wilkes, U.S. Navy, 1798–1877,* ed. William James Morgan et al. (Washington, D.C.: Department of the Navy, Naval History Division, 1978), pp. 418–19; Lincoln to Welles, 14 Dec. 1861, *ALCW,* 5:70. On Gansevoort, see Fox to Du Pont, 6 Sept. 1862, *GVFCC,* 1:154; Du Pont to Sophie Du Pont, 24 (28) Aug. 1862, *Samuel Francis*

Du Pont: A Selection from His Civil War Letters, 3 vols., ed. John D. Hayes (Ithaca: Cornell University Press, 1969), 2:205. For more evidence of the widespread problem of drunkenness among naval officers while on sea duty, see Cornelius K. Stribling to Fox, 13, 16 June 1863, GVFP.

9. For the continuation of the problem, see Godon to Fox, 22 Apr. 1865, GVFP.

10. Du Pont to Fox, 14 Aug. 1862, *ORN*, 13:255; Fox to Grimes, 5 Aug. 1862, *GVFCC*, 2:348. Fox also asked John P. Hale to secure the same pay for "temporary, acting volunteer" officers as received by regular navy officers. Fox to Hale, 8 July 1862, GVFP.

11. Du Pont to Sophie Du Pont, 16 Jan. 1863, *Du Pont Letters*, 2:364. Although John P. Hale, of New Hampshire, was chair of the Senate Committee on Naval Affairs, he was so hostile to Welles and Fox that they usually worked through Grimes, who became Fox's close friend.

12. Fox to Du Pont, 23 Jan. 1863, *GVFCC*, 1:177.

13. Fox to Hale, 7 May 1862, GVFP.

14. A. D. Bache to Fox, 1 July 1862, Fox to Anthony, 5 Aug. 1862, *GVFCC*, 2:322, 347.

15. Fox to Blake, 22 May, 30 Sept. 1862, Blake to Fox, 28 May, 17 June, 2 Oct. 1862, *GVFCC*, 2:302–3, 305–6, 314–16, 389–96; Blake to Fox, 1, 5 Dec. 1864, GVFP. The provision exempting some midshipmen from attending religious services was designed for Catholics but was unused as of October 1862.

16. George S. Blake to Fox, 29 Nov. 1862, 14 Oct., 24 Nov., 1 Dec. 1864, Fox to Blake, 9 Dec. 1862, GVFP. For an egregious example of how far a scheming woman of social standing, with political clout, and a friend of Fox would go to get and keep her boy Edward Linzer Amory in the Naval Academy and subsequently to secure "the very best berth" for him, by stooping to lies, referring to her "weak" feminine nature, and recruiting her congressman to plead her son's cause, see M. B. Amory to Fox, [July], 17 Aug., 5 Dec. 1862, 26 Nov. 1864, GVFP. Fox was annoyed when Lincoln appointed some older students to the academy.

17. Engle to Fox, 21 Feb. 1863, Fox to Everett, 2 Jan. 1862, GVFP. After several months, Everett apparently responded. Everett to Fox, 8 Oct. 1862, 2 Feb. 1863, GVFP. Everett was Henry A. Wise's father-in-law.

18. Richard H. Webber, "Monitors of the United States Navy, 1861–1937," *DANFS*, 3:758–61, 766–67.

19. Webber, "Monitors," *DANFS*, 3:767–68. On Lenthall and Isherwood, see Edward William Sloan III, *Benjamin Franklin Isherwood, Naval Engineer: The Years as Engineer in Chief, 1861–1869* (Annapolis: United States Naval Institute, 1965), pp. 50–52. Neither Lenthall nor Isherwood was enamored with monitors, but the monitors they designed functioned on the high seas. One crossed the Atlantic with Fox as a passenger and another sailed around South America to San Francisco.

20. Webber, "Monitors," *DANFS*, 3:768–71.

21. Stimers to Fox, 10 May 1862, GVFP.

22. Fox to Alexander D. Bache, 28 Sept. 1862, GVFP.

23. Ericsson to Fox, 23 Apr. 1862, enclosing Ericsson to Seward, 23 Apr. 1862, GVFP.

24. Ericsson to Fox, 23, 28 Apr. 1862, Fox to Stimers, 23 Apr. 1862, Stimers to Fox, 24 Apr. 21 Dec. 1862, GVFP.

25. Fox to Ericsson, 4, 5, 8 Aug. 1862, Ericsson to Fox, 9 Aug. 1862, Stimers to Fox, 17 Sept. 1862, GVFP.

26. Fox to Ericsson, 27 Sept. 1862, GVFP. Ericsson possibly had in mind basket-woven iron cable as armor for his "shore-monitor." He told Fox that, if he should "stumble upon a good basket maker and an honest horse dealer," he would send Fox a "sample of what shore-Monitors look like." Ericsson to Fox, 29 Sept. 1862, GVFP. The War Department apparently was not interested, so Ericsson did not send a sample of "the field Monitor Scheme" to Washington. Ericsson to Fox, 16 Oct. 1862, GVFP.

27. Ericsson to Fox, 5, 16 Oct. 1862, Stimers to Fox, 6 Oct. 1862, GVFP.

28. Ericsson to Fox, 24 Oct., 10 Dec. 1862, Fox to Ericsson, 28 Oct. 1862, GVFP.

29. Drayton to Fox, 16 Nov. 1862, *GVFCC*, 2:439–41; Drayton to Du Pont, 24 Nov. 1862, *Du Pont Letters*, 2:292–93; Fox to Ericsson, 29 Nov. 1862, GVFP.

30. Drayton to Fox, 16 Nov. 1862, *GVFCC*, 2:439–41; Drayton to Du Pont, 20 Dec. 1862, *Du Pont Letters*, 2:305–7; Ericsson to Fox, 14 Dec. 1862, GVFP.

31. Ericsson to Fox, 17, 26, 30 Dec. 1862, GVFP. Sheer is the curve of the deck fore and aft.

32. Fox to Gregory, 4 Dec. 1862, *GVFCC*, 2:458. Stimers claimed the stays gave way because of undue steam pressure, Stimers to Fox, 30 Nov. 1862, GVFP.

33. Fox to Ericsson, 16 Dec. 1862, Ericsson to Fox, 17 Dec. 1862, GVFP.

34. Fox to Stimers, 17 Dec. 1862, Stimers to Fox, 21 Dec. 1862, GVFP.

35. Ericsson to Fox, 22 Dec. 1862, GVFP.

36. Fox to Ericsson, 30 Dec. 1862, GVFP. On the need for competent engineers, see Tunis Augustus M. Craven to Fox, 2 Apr. 1864, GVFP.

37. VLWF, Diary, 15 Dec. 1862, WFP.

Chapter 12. Charleston

1. Fox to Du Pont, 12 May, 3 June 1862, *GVFCC*, 1:119, 128; Lance E. Davis and Stanley Engerman, *Naval Blockades in Peace and War: An Economic History since 1750* (New York: Cambridge University Press, 2006), p. 138. Seward, among others, equaled Fox in exaggerating Charleston's importance.

2. Du Pont to Fox, 25 May 1862, *GVFCC*, 1:120–21; Du Pont to Sophie Du Pont, 13 June 1862, in *Samuel Francis Du Pont: A Selection from His Civil War Letters*, 3 vols., ed. John D. Hayes (Ithaca: Cornell University Press, 1969), 2:113. Charles O. Boutelle of the Coast Survey and commander of the steamer *Bibb* marked the channel of the entrance of the Stono on 19–20 May. Boutelle to A. D. Bache, 24 May 1862, GVFP, NHSC, NYHS.

3. Drayton to Du Pont, 30 June, 2, 4 July 1862, copies enclosed in Du Pont to Fox, 9 July 1862, J. P. Bankhead to Fox, 29 June 1862, Fox to Du Pont, 31 July 1862, *GVFCC*, 1:133–38, 141–42, 2:317–20; Du Pont to Sophie Du Pont, 19 June, 1862, *Du Pont Letters*, 2:123–24.

4. Fox to Du Pont, 6 Sept. 1862, Du Pont to Fox, 20 Sept. 1862, Fox to Farragut, 9 Sept. 1862, *GVFCC*, 1:154–56, 317; Du Pont to Fox, 12 Sept. 1862, GVFP. To read

faded passages, see Fox to Du Pont, 6 Sept. 1862, Henry Francis du Pont Winterthur Collection of Manuscripts, Hagley Museum and Library, Wilmington, Del. (courtesy of John D. Hayes). Fox never forgave Pope for disparaging Foote's caution at Island No. 10.

5. Fox to VLWF, 2 Oct. 1862, GVFP; Du Pont to Sophie Du Pont, 17, 18, 20, 21 (22) Oct. 1862, *Du Pont Letters*, 2:247–51, 259.

6. Du Pont to Sophie Du Pont, 1 Dec. 1861, 21 (22) Oct. 1862, Du Pont to Davis, 25 Oct. 1862, *Du Pont Letters*, 1:164, 2:259; Kevin J. Weddle, *Lincoln's Tragic Admiral: The Life of Samuel Francis Du Pont* (Charlottesville: University of Virginia Press, 2005), p. 141.

7. Fox to Lee, 2 Oct., 15 Dec. 1862, *GVFCC*, 2:217, 244–45; Braine to C. P. Patterson, 20 Aug. 1862, *ORN*, 7:655; Du Pont to Sophie Du Pont, 25 Jan. 1863, *Du Pont Letters*, 2:378–79. Two widely separated entrances to the Cape Fear River made Wilmington difficult to blockade. Confederate-government-owned blockade runners carried war matériel exclusively and usually ran into Wilmington. Davis and Engerman, *Naval Blockades*, p. 137.

8. Du Pont to Sophie Du Pont, 25 Jan. 1862, *Du Pont Letters*, 2:378–79; Fox to Lee, 9 Dec. 1862, *ORN*, 8:269. Du Pont doubted that the *Nashville* got into Wilmington, but a large side-wheel steamer did and deserters identified it as the *Nashville*. Goldsborough to Welles, 3 June 1862, *ORN*, 7:266–67.

9. Fox to Lee, 23 Dec. 1862, Braine to Lee, 29 Dec. 1862, 1 Jan. 1863, Lee to Welles, 4 Jan., 26 Feb. 1863, *ORN*, 8:312, 334–35, 343–46, 396, 398–99, 573–75; *DANFS*, s.v. "*Passaic.*" Elizabeth Blair Lee reported to Samuel Phillips Lee on 4 Jan. 1863 that Fox was "au des espoir." Virginia Jeans Laas, ed., *Wartime Washington: The Civil War Letters of Elizabeth Blair Lee* (Urbana: University of Illinois Press, 1991), p. 226.

10. Fox to Du Pont, 6 Jan. 1863, *GVFCC*, 1:173; Welles to Du Pont, 6 Jan. 1863, *Du Pont Letters*, 2:352–53.

11. Fox to Charles P. Clark, 17 Nov. 1862, Fox to George D. Morgan, 18 Dec. 1862, Fox to Cyrus W. Field, 18 Dec. 1862, *GVFCC*, 2:443, 471–72.

12. Fox to Du Pont, 23 Jan. 1863, *GVFCC*, 1:175–77; Rodgers to Fox, 22 Jan. 1863, Fox to Rogers, 23 Jan. 1863, GVFP. Rodgers was overly optimistic about the seagoing qualities of the *Weehawken*. On 6 December 1863, having recently taken on and stowed up forward a heavy load of shot, it took on water in a moderate gale and sank bow first. *DANFS*, s.v. "*Weehawken.*"

13. Fox to Du Pont, 12 Feb. 1863, *GVFCC*, 1:178–79.

14. Du Pont to Sophie Du Pont, 1 (2) Feb. 1863, *Du Pont Letters*, 2:408.

15. Fox to Du Pont, 16 Feb. 1863, *Du Pont Letters*, 2:443–45; VLWF, Diary, 19 Feb. 1863, WFP, LC. For naval matters, Lincoln relied on Fox. A constant refrain in Virginia's diary is "The President sent for Gus," and Fox had better access to Lincoln than Postmaster General Montgomery Blair. Francis Preston Blair Sr., for example, prepared a letter for Lincoln, "which," he remarked, "if Fox would deliver, would ensure its being read." F. P. Blair Sr. to Minna Blair, 23 Feb. 1863, BFP, LC.

16. *Diary of Gideon Welles: Secretary of the Navy under Lincoln and Johnson*, 3 vols., ed. Howard K. Beale (New York: W. W. Norton, 1960), 16 Feb. 1863, 1:236–37; VLWF, Diary, 12 Feb. 1863, WFP.

17. Fox to Du Pont, 16 Feb. 1863, *Du Pont Letters,* 2:444; Welles, *Diary,* 16 Feb. 1863, 1:236–37; VLWF, Diary, 12 Feb. 1863, WFP.

18. Ericsson to Fox, 22 Feb. 1863, GVFP; Fox to Farragut, 28 Feb. 1863, *ORN,* 19:639.

19. Fox to Du Pont, 20 Feb. 1863, *Du Pont Letters,* 2:450.

20. Fox to Du Pont, 12 Feb., 2 Apr. 1863, *GVFCC,* 1:178, 197; Fox to Du Pont, 16 Feb. 1863, *Du Pont Letters,* 2:443–45.

21. Du Pont to Welles, 28 Jan. 1863, *ORN,* 13:543; Du Pont to Sophie Du Pont, 24 Feb., 1 (2), 4 (7) Mar. 1863, Du Pont to Fox, 2 Mar. 1863, Du Pont to James Stokes Biddle, 25 Mar. 1863, *Du Pont Letters,* 2:452–53, 461–64, 466–67, 473, 510.

22. Du Pont to Sophie Du Pont, 4 July 1862, Du Pont to Benjamin Gerhard, 19 (24) Feb. 1863, Du Pont to William Whetten, 17 Mar, 1863, Du Pont to James Stokes Biddle, 25 Mar. 1863, *Du Pont Letters,* 2:149–50, 448, 491, 511.

23. Dahlgren to Welles, 1 Oct. 1862, *ORN,* 13:353–54; Du Pont to Fox, 8 Oct. 1862, *Du Pont Letters,* 2:243; Elizabeth Blair Lee to Samuel Phillips Lee, 6 Apr. 1863, in Laas, *Wartime Washington,* p. 256.

24. Rowena Reed, *Combined Operations in the Civil War* (Annapolis: Naval Institute Press, 1978), pp. 289–94; Du Pont to Sophie Du Pont, 8 Apr. 1863, Du Pont to James Stokes Biddle, 4 May 1863, *Du Pont Letters,* 3:3, 86–87; Du Pont to Welles, 3 June 1863, *ORN,* 14:68–73. The *Keokuk* was an experimental vessel armored with horizontal iron bars, alternating with wood. *DANFS,* s.v. "*Keokuk.*" Du Pont could not see because the *New Ironsides* was unmanageable and forced to anchor between 1,000 and 2,000 yards from Sumter (it fired only one broadside and that was at Fort Moultrie). With its small pilothouse located behind its enormous smokestack, Du Pont's view was further obscured. The pilothouse had room only for Du Pont, his fleet captain, and the pilot, but not Thomas Turner, the captain of the *New Ironsides,* who more than anyone else could have moved his vessel closer to Sumter. For two thoughtful arguments that stress Du Pont was forced, for political reasons by Welles and Fox, into an attack that could not succeed given the lack of offensive capacity of monitors, see *Du Pont Letters,* 1:civ–cv, vol. 3, and Weddle, *Du Pont,* pp. 154–217.

25. Fox to Ericsson, 10 Apr. 1863, GVFP; Fox to Daniel Butterfield, 10 Apr. 1863, *ORN* 14:38; VLWF, Diary, 10, 12, 15 Apr. 1863, WFP.

26. VLWF, Diary, 18, 19 Apr. 1863, WFP.

27. Du Pont to Welles, 8, 15 Apr. 1863, Rodgers to Du Pont, 8 Apr. 1863, Worden to Du Pont, 8 Apr. 1863, *ORN,* 14:3–8, 11–14; Reed, *Combined Operations,* pp. 289–94; Weddle, *Du Pont,* pp. 191–97. On the obstructions, see *Du Pont Letters,* 3:13–14, n. 1. The fullest account of the April assault on Charleston and its aftermath is in *Du Pont Letters,* vols. 2–3. The letters are one-sided, but the extensive notes by John D. Hayes are informative and balanced.

28. Stimers to Welles, 14 Apr. 1863, Welles to Fox, 20 Apr. 1863, *ORN,* 14:41–43, 45; Ericsson to Fox, 15 Apr. 1863, Ericsson Papers, LC.

29. Drayton et al. to Welles, 24 Apr. 1863, *ORN,* 14:45–48. Worden visited the Foxes on the evening of 22 April and was "depressed," presumably about the recent defeat, and also "complained of insufficient air in Iron Clads." VLWF, Diary, 22 Apr. 1863, WFP. Rodgers suggested that experiments were needed to perfect the monitors before

sending them into battle and warned that Ericsson "is a man of genius to be used; he is not a sound man to be followed." Rodgers to Welles, 2 May 1863, Welles Papers, Huntington Library. See also, *Du Pont Letters,* 1:lxxxviii–xc.

30. Du Pont to Welles, 22 Apr. 1863, enclosing Fulton's article "A Disgraceful Result," dateline 8 Apr. 1863, published 15 Apr. 1863, *ORN,* 14:51–59. Du Pont's friend Horatio Bridge, who was in the Navy Department, said neither Welles, Fox, nor Charles Henry Davis saw the article before it was published. *Du Pont Letters,* 3:92–93, n. 3. Fox to Welles, 13 May 1863, *ORN,* 14:64; Davis to Du Pont, 5 June 1864, Du Pont to Davis, 11 June 1864, *Du Pont Letters,* 3:353–56.

31. Welles to Du Pont, 3 June 1863, *ORN,* 14:230; Fox to Francis H. Gregory, 8 June 1863, GVFP; Fox to Welles, 15 Aug. 1863, Welles Papers, LC. Fox saw Farragut in New York and reported their conversation to Welles.

32. Rodgers to Du Pont, 17 June 1863, *ORN,* 14:265–66; Charles Henry Davis to Harriette M. Davis, 26 June 1863, in Charles Henry Davis, *Life of Charles Henry Davis: Rear Admiral, 1807–1877* (Boston: Houghton, Mifflin, 1899), p. 296; *DANFS,* s.v. "*Weehawken.*"

33. Dahlgren to Fox, 9 Apr. 1864, GVFP, describes his "hasty departure." Commodore Thomas Turner, who asked to be relieved of his command of the *New Ironsides* (which, despite his earlier criticisms, he pronounced "the finest ship in service"), would have stayed "if Foote had gone down," but was "unwilling to have remained under the Old (Du Pont) or New (Dahlgren) dynasty." Turner to Fox, 13 July 1863, GVFP. Also see Fox to Edward Simpson, 22 June 1863, GVFP; Fox to Lincoln, 4 Aug. 1863, Stanton Papers, LC. Samuel W. Preston, who had been Du Pont's flag lieutenant, went with Fox to see Lincoln and described the interview to C. R. P. Rodgers, who in turn told Du Pont. Du Pont to Henry Winter Davis, 23 Aug. 1863, *Du Pont Letters,* 3:230. Fox had also come to the conclusion that Wilmington would have to be taken by a combined army-navy operation. "If three or four monitors could have effected anything alone," he wrote Foote, "we should have been in long ago. It must be a joint affair, and there is no army now except at Port Royal." Fox to [Foote], 12 June 1863, GVFP.

34. Fox to Lincoln, 4 Aug. 1863, submitted to Stanton for consideration, Stanton Papers, LC; Fox to Dahlgren, early Aug. 1863, GVFP. Welles, *Diary,* 26, 28 July 1863, 1:382–85; Dahlgren, Diary, 5 Sept. 1863, *ORN,* 14:567; Michael Burlingame, ed., *Lincoln Observed: Civil War Dispatches of Noah Brooks* (Baltimore: Johns Hopkins University Press, 1998), pp. 101, 251–52. Brooks has Lincoln in the early summer of 1863, abetted by Fox, urging on a reluctant Halleck the taking of Morris Island and Fort Wagner.

35. VLWF, Diary, 25 Aug. 1863, WFP.

36. Welles, *Diary,* 24 Aug. 1863, 1:415–16; Welles to Dahlgren, 26 Aug. 1863, *ORN,* 14:519; Fox to Dahlgren, 28 Aug. 1863, GVFP.

37. Fox to VLWF, 10 Sept. 1863, GVFP; Du Pont to Halpine, 9 Sept. 1863, *Du Pont Letters,* 3:231–33; *Inside Lincoln's White House: The Complete Civil War Diary of John Hay,* ed. Michael Burlingame and John R. Turner Ettlinger (Carbondale: Southern Illinois University Press, 1997), 20 Oct. 1863, p. 96; Robert J. Schneller Jr., *A Quest for Glory: A Biography of Rear Admiral John A. Dahlgren* (Annapolis: Naval Institute

Press, 1996), pp. 271–72. Two years later, Halpine, who was friendly with John Hay, asked Fox for a pass to see a fellow Irishman imprisoned at Fort Lafayette. Fox complied, Halpine sent him a copy of *Miles: His Book*, but Fox apparently did not give a job at the New York Navy Yard to a friend of Halpine or steer advertisements to Halpine's *New York Citizen*. Halpine to Fox, 19 Jan., 24 Feb., 10 Apr. 1865, GVFP. Fox also cooperated with Gillmore on plans to shut down Wilmington.

38. Schneller, *Dahlgren*, pp. 264–65; Welles, *Diary*, 25 Aug. 1863, 3 Feb. 1864, 1:427, 520. Charleston was not entirely closed to blockade runners, but its significance was greatly reduced. By 1864 Wilmington's cotton exports were triple those of Charleston. Davis and Engerman, *Naval Blockades*, pp. 138–40; Raimondo Luraghi, *A History of the Confederate Navy* (Annapolis: Naval Institute Press, 1996), p. 286.

39. Schneller, *Dahlgren*, p. 273; Fox to Dahlgren, 18 Sept. 1863, GVFP. Secretary of the Treasury Chase, craving a victory to inspire capitalists to invest in the Union cause, "regretted" that Farragut had not been sent to Charleston, but Welles, asking what Farragut could do beyond what Dahlgren had done, was disinclined to relieve him, especially because he was a Lincoln favorite. Welles, *Diary*, 3 Feb. 1864, 1:520. On Fox and the press, see Fox to Dahlgren, 12 Jan. 1864, Fox to William H. Russell (editor of *Army and Navy Gazette* of London), 1 Mar. 1864, GVFP. Ericsson was embarrassed when both the *New York Times* and *Herald* published the same article. The *Herald* had delayed publication so Ericsson gave the article to the *Times*. Ericsson to Fox, 28 Feb. 1864, GVFP.

40. Ericsson to Fox, 22 Feb., 13 Sept. 1863, GVFP.

41. Fox to Ericsson, 15 Sept. 1863, GVFP. The pervasiveness of obstructions at Charleston is questionable. After Charleston fell, Dahlgren investigated and decided they were as formidable as he had suspected, but the Confederate commanders said they did not seriously block the channel and "were by no means so formidable as was supposed." Schneller, *Dahlgren*, p. 314.

42. Dahlgren to Welles, 7 Oct. 1863, Dahlgren to Fox, 7 Oct. 1863, *ORN*, 15:10–11, 13–15. On the test of Ericsson's antiobstruction torpedo, see Dahlgren to Welles, 6 Nov. 1863, *ORN*, 15:102–3. On the *Spuyten Duyvil*, see William W. W. Wood (its designer) to Fox, 13 Nov. 1864, GVFP and *DANFS*, s.v. "*Spuyten Duyvil*."

43. Dahlgren to Maillefert, 16 Feb. 1864, Dahlgren to Welles, 19 Feb, 1864, *ORN*, 15:326, 329–30; Milton F. Perry, *Infernal Machines: The Story of Confederate Submarine and Mine Warfare* (Baton Rouge: Louisiana State University Press, 1965), pp. 166–69.

44. *CWNC*, 26 Oct. 1863.

45. Fox to Dahlgren, 12 Jan. 1864, GVFP; Dahlgren to Fox, 22 Jan. 1864, *ORN*, 15:251–52.

46. Fox to Porter, 25 May 1864, *ORN*, 26:324–25; Dahlgren to Fox, 24 May 1865, GVFP. Many naval officers were hostile to Dahlgren, feeling (with some justification) that he was advanced because of his friendship with Lincoln.

Chapter 13. The Light-Draft Debacle

1. Ericsson to Fox, 23 Apr., 5, 16 Oct. 1862, Stimers to Fox, 7 Nov., 21 Dec. 1862, 4 Feb. 1863, Fox to Ericsson, 21 Feb. 1863, GVFP, NHSC, NYHS.

2. Stimers to Fox, 26, 30 Dec. 1862, Fox to Stimers, 15 Jan. 1863, Ericsson to Fox, 2 Jan. 1863, GVFP.

3. Ericsson also objected to Stimers's novel water compartments idea as useless, because they would "only change the draught six inches," but wondered if Fox liked the idea well enough to go ahead. "If so I say God speed you!" Ericsson to Fox, 24 Feb. 1863, Ericsson to Welles, 24 Feb. 1863, GVFP.

4. Edward William Sloane III, *Benjamin Franklin Isherwood, Naval Engineer: The Years as Engineer in Chief, 1861–1869* (Annapolis: United States Naval Institute, 1965), p. 69.

5. Fox to Stimers, 16 Mar. 1863, Stimers to Fox, 19, 30 Apr. 1863, Stimers to Nelson Curtis (treasurer, Atlantic Works, Boston, builder of the *Casco*), 29 Feb. 1864, GVFP.

6. Ericsson to Fox, 15 Apr. 1863 (including extracts from the *Catskill* engineer), 8, 11 Apr. 1863, GVFP.

7. Fox to Ericsson, 24 Apr., 2 May 1863, Fox to Stimers, 25 Apr. 1863, Stimers to Fox, 30 Apr. 1863, GVFP. Unable to be in two places at the same time, Fox journeyed to New York to confer with Ericsson instead of to Charleston to talk with Du Pont.

8. Stimers to Fox, 30 Apr. 1863, Fox to Ericsson, 25 May 1863, Fox to Dahlgren, c. 15 July 1863, Ericsson to Fox, 13 Sept. 1863, GVFP. To an English engineer, Ericsson said, Fox "is not a man at home in mechanical detail." Ericsson to John Bourne, 27 July 1866, Ericsson Papers, LC.

9. Fox to Hewitt, 5, 10 Mar. 1863, GVFP. Never a fan of the Bessemer converter, Hewitt from 1867 to 1869 introduced the open-hearth method of producing steel to the United States.

10. Hewitt to Fox, 13 Mar., 3 Apr. 1863, GVFP; Ericsson to Fox, [illegible but probably 1864], Ericsson Papers, LC. Dahlgren denied his guns were useless, but "earnestly" recommended that the government erect the steam hammers Hewitt advocated. Dahlgren to Fox, 1 Apr. 1863, GVFP.

11. Hewitt to Fox 2, 5, 20 Apr. 1863, GVFP. Two years later, Ericsson wrote Fox "that both Armstrong and Whitworth guns of the last pattern have split and burst. So it will ever be until the thin hoop system is adopted. Again on this plan the core is so light that the Bessemer steel now being made in this Country may be employed thus ensuring a sound bore." Ericsson to Fox, 1 May 1865, GVFP.

12. Dahlgren to Welles, 28 Jan. 1864, *ORN,* 14:590–601.

13. James W. King to Fox, 4 Feb. 1864, Fox to Stimers, 25 Feb. 1864, GVFP.

14. Ericsson to Fox, 4 Feb. 1864, Ericsson Papers, NYHS; Stimers to Fox, 29 Feb. 1864, Ericsson to Fox, 27 Feb., 1 Apr. 1864, GVFP. At the very time Fox was chewing out Stimers for his administration in New York of the "General Inspectors Office Iron Clad Steamers," Stimers advocated the establishment of a new "Bureau of Iron Clad Steamers" (presumably with himself at its head) in the Navy Department at Wash-

ington. It would, he argued, "tend to remove most of the difficulties" Fox complained about. Stimers to Fox, 18, 29 Feb. 1864, GVFP.

15. King to Fox, 15 Apr. 1864, Fox to Stimers, 23 Apr. 1864, GVFP; *DANFS*, s.v. "*Chenango.*"

16. Stimers to Fox, 16, 31 and another 31 May 1864, GVFP. With its armament and supplies, the *Chimo* should have had fifteen inches of freeboard.

17. Fox to Ericsson, 3 June 1864, GVFP. For data on the light drafts, see Richard H. Webber, "Monitors of the United States Navy, 1861–1937," *DANFS*, 3:771–76.

18. Stimers to Fox, 8, 16 June 1864, Gregory to Fox, 16 June 1864, Ericsson to Fox, 17, 18 June 1864, Fox to Ericsson, 20 June 1864, GVFP; Ericsson to Fox, 25, 26 July 1864, Ericsson Papers, LC; Fox to Welles, 12, 25 Aug. 1864, Welles Papers, LC.

19. Gregory to Fox, 19, 28 July 1864, Fox to Ericsson, 28 July 1864, Stimers to Fox, 12 Sept. 1864, Stribling to Fox, 19, 23 Sept. 1864, Wood to Fox, 13 Nov. 1864, GVFP; Ericsson to Fox, 20 Sept. 1864, Ericsson Papers, LC.

20. Farragut to Welles, 20 Nov. 1863, *ORN*, 20:691; Farragut to Fox, 3 Jan. 1864, *GVFCC*, 1:340–41; Stimers to Fox, 2 Mar. 1864, GVFP.

21. Fox to Ericsson, 28 July 1864, GVFP.

22. Fox to Ericsson, 28 July 1864, Ericsson to Fox, 13 Jan. 1865, GVFP; Fox to Benjamin F. Wade, Chairman, Joint Committee on the Conduct of the War, 15 Dec. 1864, "Light-Draught Monitors," Sen. Report No. 142, Part III, 38th Cong., 2nd sess., 1865, pp. 3–5. Ericsson and Stimers did not remain enemies. After the war, they saw each other and, when Stimers's widow was destitute, Ericsson paid their daughter's school tuition. S. W. Taylor to Julia A. Stimers, 2 Sept. 1881, Ericsson Papers, NYHS.

Chapter 14. Vicksburg

1. Although it did not work out, Fox hoped that he and Virginia could take a house with the Davises when he returned to Washington. With Fox's support, Davis, in February 1863, would be commissioned rear admiral. Fox to VLWF, 1 Oct. 1862, GVFP, NHSC, NYHS; Porter to Fox, 26 July 1862, Davis to Fox, 15 Sept. 1862, Fox to Davis, 22 Sept. 1862, *GVFCC*, 2:64–66, 125; Davis to Harriette M. Davis, 28 Sept. 1862, Davis Papers, Wayne State University, Detroit (courtesy of Prof. C. Norman Guice). Fox persuaded Welles to appoint his friend Porter to the Mississippi Squadron, even though he was annoyed that Porter had recently complained to Lincoln of his treatment by the Navy Department. Chester G. Hearn, *Admiral David Dixon Porter: The Civil War Years* (Annapolis: Naval Institute Press, 1996), pp. 139–42, 151. Porter was appointed the same day the army's Western Flotilla became the navy's Mississippi Squadron.

2. Farragut to Fox, 12 June, 11 Oct. 1862, Fox to Farragut, 7 Nov. 1862, *GVFCC*, 1:316, 318–21.

3. Fox to Farragut, 9 Sept., 7 Nov. 1862, *GVFCC*, 1:317–18, 321; Elizabeth Blair Lee to Samuel Phillips Lee, 10 Aug. 1863, in Virginia Jeans Laas, ed., *Wartime Washington: The Civil War Letters of Elizabeth Blair Lee* (Urbana: University of Illinois Press, 1991), p. 297. Ironically, while Fox was trying to rein in Farragut he was simultaneously trying to fire up Du Pont.

4. Farragut to H. H. Bell, 4 Dec. 1862, *ORN*, 19:390–91; Fox to James W. Grimes, 3 Mar. 1863, GVFP.

5. Farragut to Fox, 11 Oct. 1862, *GVFCC*, 1:319–20.

6. Farragut to Fox, 23 Dec. 1862, *GVFCC*, 1:322–24.

7. Donald S. Frazier, *Cottonclads!: The Battle of Galveston and the Defense of the Texas Coast* (Fort Worth: Ryan Place Publishers, 1996), pp. 61–85; Fox to Farragut, 6 Feb. 1863, Fox to Porter, 6 Feb. 1863, Fox to Du Pont, 12 Feb. 1863, *GVFCC*, 1:178–79, 324–25, 2:156; Fox to Theodorus Bailey, 16 Feb. 1863, *ORN*, 17:367.

8. Frazier, *Cottonclads!* pp. 93–104; Fox to Farragut, 7 Feb. 1863, Fox to Porter, 6 Feb. 1863, *GVFCC*, 1:325–26, 2:156; *CWNC*, 10, 16 Jan. 1863.

9. Porter to Fox, 12, 17, 21, 29, 30 Oct., 10 Nov. 1862, Fox to Porter, 14 Oct. 1862, *GVFCC*, 2:137–45, 149.

10. Fox to Davis, 2 Oct. 1862, Porter to Fox, 2 Nov. 1862, Fox to Porter, 8 Nov. 1862, *GVFCC*, 2:69, 146–48; Warren Daniel Crandall and Isaac D. Newell, *History of the Ram Fleet and the Mississippi Marine Brigade...* (St. Louis: Buschart Bros., 1907), pp. 137–38; Gene D. Lewis, *Charles Ellet, Jr.: The Engineer as Individualist* (Urbana: University of Illinois Press, 1968), pp. 211–13; Chester G. Hearn, *Ellet's Brigade: The Strangest Outfit of Them All* (Baton Rouge: Louisiana State University Press, 2000), pp. 77–78. Alfred Ellet claimed that Stanton and Halleck wanted him to cooperate with Porter, but told him he "was not under his command." Lewis, *Ellet*, p. 212. Fox was aware that the Ellets (the rams were a family affair) had not cooperated with Davis in the past.

11. Hearn, *Ellet's Brigade*, pp. 70–73; Porter to Fox, 12 Nov. 1862, *GVFCC*, 2:150–51.

12. Porter to Fox, 5 Dec. 1862, Fox to Porter, 11 Dec. 1862, *GVFCC*, 2:151–53.

13. VLWF, Diary, 20–21 Dec. 1862, WFP, LC. To Blair's offer to resign during the cabinet crisis, Lincoln exclaimed: "For God's sake, don't. Do not give me more trouble!"

14. VLWF, Diary, 21, 28 Dec. 1862, 4 Feb. 1863, WFP. Lincoln used his war powers to issue the Emancipation Proclamation. It applied only to the war zone and on 1 January 1863 freed no one, but as the armed forces of the Union advanced, it freed most of the human beings held in bondage.

15. Porter to Fox, 5 Dec. 1862, 16 Jan, 1863, *GVFCC*, 2:151, 153–55.

16. Woodworth to Fox, 3 Mar. 1863, *ORN*, 24:454–55.

17. Porter to Fox, 16 Jan. 1863, *GVFCC*, 2:154–56. On 23 November, Porter received a "confidential order" from the Navy Department to cooperate with McClernand in an attack on Vicksburg in three weeks but heard nothing from McClernand until he appeared up the Yazoo on 3 January 1863. Porter to Sherman, 24 Nov. 1862, *ORN*, 23:501; Fox to Porter, 11 Dec. 1862, *GVFCC*, 2:153.

18. Fox to Porter, 6 Feb. 1863, *GVFCC*, 2:156–57.

19. Fox to Porter, 6 Feb. 1863, *GVFCC*, 2:157.

20. Welles to Porter, 19 Jan. 1863, *ORN*, 24:181; Fox to Porter, 6 Feb. 1863, *GVFCC*, 2:157–58. Ulysses S. Grant in *Personal Memoirs of U. S. Grant*, 2 vols. (New York: Charles L. Webster, 1885), 1:456–58, recalled that by 4 February he had suggested the

Young's Point route to Halleck, but obviously Fox and Lincoln had already thought of it, and Porter was apprised of it.

21. Grant, *Personal Memoirs*, 1:445–56.

22. Fox to Farragut, 2 Apr. 1863, Porter to Fox, 3 Mar. 1863, *GVFCC*, 1:331, 2:161. Iowa senator James W. Grimes of the naval committee, with whom Fox carried on an extensive correspondence, was contemptuous of Grant's military ability, prophesying in March 1863, "Mark my words, Grant will never win a victory!!" and elaborating in May, "The truth is Grant is a dull, thick-headed, obtuse, drunkard & cares nothing for human life, has no plan for a battle & lets every division & corps fight on its own hand." After the fall of Vicksburg, Grimes still called Grant "a blockhead." Grimes to Fox, 26 Mar., 1 June (received), 17 July 1863, GVFP.

23. Crandall and Newell, *Ram Fleet*, pp. 153–82; Fox to James W. Grimes, 3 Mar. 1863, GVFP; VLWF, Diary, 3 Mar. 1863, WFP. Fox conferred with Lincoln while "a barber was shampooing his head, preparing him for evening reception."

24. Farragut to Welles, 2, 16 Mar. 1863, *ORN*, 19:644, 665–69; Farragut to Fox, 27 Mar., 22 Apr. 1863, Fox to Farragut, 2 Apr. 1863, *GVFCC*, 1:329–33.

25. Crandall and Newell, *Ram Fleet*, pp. 183–85; Porter to Fox, 3 Mar. 1863, *GVFCC*, 2:158–63; Fox to Henry Wilson, 18 Mar. 1863, GVFP; *DANFS*, s.v. "*Indianola*." As early as January 1862, Fox investigated types and prices of underwater cables, apparently for use in Chesapeake Bay. Cyrus W. Field & Co. to Fox, 31 Jan. 1862, GVFP; Charles W. Fulton to Fox, 25 Feb. 1862, Lincoln Papers, LC.

26. Fox to Porter, 6 Apr. 1863, *GVFCC*, 2:164–65.

27. Fox to Farragut, 6, 7 Feb. 1863, Fox to Porter, 6 Apr. 1863, *GVFCC*, 1:324–26, 2:164–65.

28. Fox to Smith, 2 Apr. 1863, *ORN*, 19:685–86. Fox referred to James Alden of the *Richmond*, James P. McKinstry of the *Monongahela*, and William H. Macomb of the *Genesee*. Melancton Smith's executive officer on the *Mississippi*, whom he commended for his "coolness," was George Dewey, who in 1898 achieved immortal fame at Manila Bay. Smith to Welles 15 Mar. 1863, *ORN*, 19:681.

29. Porter to Fox, 16 Apr. 1863, *GVFCC*, 2:165–69; Crandall and Newell, *Ram Fleet*, pp. 268–92; Hearn, *Ellet's Brigade*, pp. 148–51.

30. Porter to Fox, 17, 25 Apr., 1 May 1863, *GVFCC*, 2:169–82; Grant, *Personal Memoirs*, 1:460–76; Rowena Reed, *Combined Operations in the Civil War* (Annapolis: Naval Institute Press, 1978), pp. 249–55.

31. Porter to Fox, 1 May 1863, *GVFCC*, 2:178–82; Grant, *Personal Memoirs*, 1:477–81; Reed, *Combined Operations*, pp. 239–40, 255. Reed stresses that Grant's "brilliant" campaign simply evolved when all other options failed.

32. Porter to Fox, 14 May 1863, *GVFCC*, 2:182–83.

33. VLWF, Diary, 2–3, 5–6 May 1863, WFP.

34. VLWF, Diary, 7–8, 16 May 1863, WFP.

35. VLWF, Diary, 23–24 May 1863, WFP.

36. *CWNC*, 21 May 1863; Grant, *Personal Memoirs*, 1:485–547, quotation from p. 532.

37. *CWNC*, 20 May 1863.

38. VLWF, Diary, 30 June 1863, WFP; Grant, *Personal Memoirs*, 1:574. On warm feelings among Porter, Grant, and Sherman, see Porter to Fox, 10 July 1863, GVFP.

39. VLWF, Diary, 24, 28 June, 1, 2, 5 July 1863, WFP.

40. Fox to Farragut, 10 July 1863, Fox to Porter, 16 July 1863, *GVFCC*, 1:335, 2:185. Lee lost slightly more than 20,000 at Gettysburg.

41. Fox to Farragut, 10 July 1863, Fox to Porter, 16 July 1863, *GVFCC*, 1:335, 2:185.

42. Fox to Farragut, 10 July 1863, Fox to Porter, 16 July 1863, Porter to Fox, 16 Aug. 1863, *GVFCC*, 1:335–36, 2:185–89.

43. Fox to Farragut, 10 July 1863, Fox to Porter, 16 July 1863, Porter to Fox, 16 Aug. 1863, *GVFCC*, 1:335–36, 2:185–89; George H. Heap to Porter, 21 Oct. 1863, *ORN*, 25:512–13; Grant, *Personal Memoirs*, 1:578.

44. In September 1863, Welles told Lincoln, "In the selection of Farragut and Porter . . . we had been particularly fortunate, and Du Pont had merit also," but Lincoln agreed only in part. "Du Pont he classed, and has often, with McClellan, but Porter he considers a busy schemer, bold but not of high qualities as a chief. For some reason he has not so high an appreciation of Porter as I think he deserves, but no man surpasses Farragut." *Diary of Gideon Welles: Secretary of the Navy under Lincoln and Johnson*, 3 vols., ed. Howard K. Beale (New York: W. W. Norton, 1960), 21 Sept. 1863, 1:440. In time, Welles would realize that Porter was an intriguer. Ibid., 27 Apr. 1868, 22 Sept. 1868, 3:340, 440.

Chapter 15. Washington

1. Lincoln to James C. Conkling, 26 Aug. 1863, *ALCW*, 6:409; *Diary of Gideon Welles: Secretary of the Navy under Lincoln and Johnson*, 3 vols., ed. Howard K. Beale (New York: W. W. Norton, 1960), 31 July 1863, 1:389–90.

2. VLWF, Diary, 13–15 July 1863, WFP, LC.

3. VLWF to Fox, 16, 18, 20 July 1863, Fox to VLWF, 18–19 July 1862, GVFP, NHSC, NYHS; VLWF, Diary, 13–20, 22 July 1863, WFP.

4. VLWF, Diary, 29 July 1863, WFP.

5. VLWF, Diary, 12 Aug. 1863, WFP; *Inside Lincoln's White House: The Complete Civil War Diary of John Hay*, ed. Michael Burlingame and John R. Turner Ettlinger (Carbondale: Southern Illinois University Press, 1997), 2 Aug. 1863, pp. 69–70; Welles, *Diary*, 3, 7 Aug. 1863, 1:393–94; Welles to Mary Jane Welles, 9 Aug. 1863, Welles Papers, LC; Elizabeth Blair Lee to Samuel Phillips Lee, 10 (11) Aug. 1863, in Virginia Jeans Laas, ed., *Wartime Washington: The Civil War Letters of Elizabeth Blair Lee* (Urbana: University of Illinois Press, 1991), p. 298.

6. For a similar evaluation of the Welles-Fox relationship, see John Niven, *Gideon Welles: Lincoln's Secretary of the Navy* (New York: Oxford University Press, 1973), pp. 353–55.

7. Du Pont to Sophie Du Pont, 26 July 1861, Du Pont to Henry Winter Davis, 14 July 1863, Davis to Du Pont, 6 June 1863, in *Samuel Francis Du Pont: A Selection from His Civil War Letters*, 3 vols., ed. John D. Hayes (Ithaca: Cornell University Press, 1969), 1:113, 3:199–200. Even Lincoln, according to Noah Brooks, Washington corre-

spondent of the *Sacramento Daily Union*, referred to Fox as "the Navy Department." Michael Burlingame, ed., *Lincoln Observed: Civil War Dispatches of Noah Brooks* (Baltimore: Johns Hopkins University Press, 1998), p. 251. Brooks recalled Lincoln's request more than thirty years later and may have put words that were bandied about in Lincoln's mouth. The important point is that the words were bandied about.

8. Laird to Howard, 11 Apr. 1863, enclosing extracts from speech of 27 Mar. 1863, John T. Howard to Fox, 29 Apr. 1863, copies in Welles Papers, NYPL; Welles, *Diary*, 2, 19 May, 7, 10, 13 Aug. 1863, 1:291, 306, 394–96, 401; *New York Times*, 6, 10 Aug. 1863; John David Smith, "Yankee Ironclads at Birkenhead? A Note on Gideon Welles, John Laird and Gustavus V. Fox," *Mariner's Mirror* 67 (1981): 77–82.

9. "Proposition of John Laird & Son . . .," 10 May 1861, John T. Howard to Fox, 25 Aug. 1863 (including copies of Fox to Howard, 13 Aug., 29 Oct., 1 Nov. 1861), GVFP; Fox to Welles, 15 Aug. 1863, Welles Papers, LC; William Joseph Sullivan, "Gustavus Vasa Fox and Naval Administration, 1861–1866" (Ph.D. diss., Catholic University of America, 1977), pp. 165–69; Smith, "Yankee Ironclads," pp. 77–82. On the purchase in England of vessels or even of "good propeller machinery" to be fitted into hulls built at U.S. Navy yards, see John Murray Forbes to Welles, 27 Mar. 1863, Welles Papers, LC. See, also, Forbes to Fox, 3, 10 Dec. 1862, GVFP, suggesting the purchase of Confederate ironclads under construction in England. Fox, in June 1863, was sufficiently concerned about the need for steam engines that he wrote, "I do not know what we can do except go abroad for engines." By November 1863 Fox said he was no longer concerned about the shortage of suitable engines, but he later changed his mind. Fox to George B. Upton, 12 June 1863, Fox to Freeman H. Morse, 10 June, 28 Nov. 1863, Alban C. Stimers to Fox, 28 Apr. 1865, GVFP.

10. Welles, *Diary*, 13 Aug. 1863, 1:401.

11. Fox to George W. Blunt, 19 Apr. 1863, Fox to William H. Aspinwall, 27 Aug. 1863, Fox to Howard, 6 Sept. 1863, GVFP; Fox to Welles, 15 Aug. 1863, Welles Papers, LC; Fox to Welles, 20 Aug. 1863, Welles Papers, NYPL; VLWF, Diary, 13–20, 1863, WFP.

12. Fox to Welles, 7 Sept. 1863, Welles Papers, LC; *DANFS*, s.v. "*Wyoming*." The Sabine Pass expedition aimed in part to counteract French designs on Texas, and neither Halleck nor Stanton informed Welles or Fox of its existence. Welles, *Diary*, 22 Sept. 1863, 1:441–42. On the Japanese "War Steamers," see Joseph J. Comstock to Fox, 10 Mar. 1863, Fox to B. F. Delano, 19 Mar. 1863, GVFP.

13. Welles, *Diary*, 11 Aug., 29 Dec. 1863, 1:396–97, 498–99; Alden to Fox, 24 Feb. 1864, Lee to Fox, 22 Apr. 1864, GVFP.

14. Fox to S. B. Luce, 1 Mar. 1864, GVFP; Welles, *Diary*, 25–26, 28 Mar. 1864, 1:546–48. *CWNC*, 25 Mar. 1864, states that the transfer of 12,000 sailors from the army to the navy "was later effected as a result of a bill sponsored by Senator Grimes of Iowa."

15. Lowry to Fox, 13 Apr., 11, 13 May, 3, 9 June, 25 Oct., 21 Nov., 1 Dec. 1864, GVFP; *DANFS*, s.v. "*Sabine*"; Luce to Fox, 27 Jan., 15 Mar., 1 Apr. 1864, Fox to Luce, 1 Mar. 1864, GVFP; *ANB*, s.v. "Luce, Stephen Bleeker."

Luce elaborated on his ideas for a training ship. He wanted strong boys fourteen to sixteen, of good character, nonsmokers, whom he would work hard, discipline strictly, but be liberal with leaves. Luce, who would command the U. S. Naval Training Squadron and would be the principal founder of the Naval War College, was already on his way to becoming the navy's preeminent educator of seamen and officers. "I trust you will see," Luce wrote Fox, "that the question of the bringing up of our Young officers is a subject of very deep & vital interest to us all." Like Fox, Luce also wanted to keep the Naval Academy at Newport, where the midshipmen "can learn to be seamen."

Dennis Hart Mahan, professor of military engineering at West Point and father of Alfred T. Mahan, also gave Fox suggestions about the overly elaborate initiating examinations at the Naval Academy. He advised that all students, no matter what their standing, should start in the lowest class. He regretted that his son, who had spent two years at Columbia College, was admitted in an advanced class and was unhappy at Annapolis. D. H. Mahan to Fox, 4, 12 Aug. 1864, GVFP.

16. Fox to VLWF, 10, 29, 30 Sept. 1863, Leutze to Fox, 7 Apr. 1864, E. D. Townsend to Fox, 18 Nov. 1865, GVFP; Hay, *Civil War Diary*, 19 Aug. 1863, 10 Sept., 26 Oct. 1863, pp. 75, 81–85, 101, 308, 322. The correspondent of the *Cincinnati Commercial* described the Canterbury. Ibid., p. 312. Virginia feared that Wise was not as straitlaced as she would wish her husband's best friend to be.

17. Hay, *Civil War Diary*, 10 Sept. 1863, pp. 82–84. When Fox mentioned to John Murray Forbes how a war with England would *cement* Americans together against a foreign foe, Forbes urged caution. Louis Napoleon "was against us from the start," he pointed out, and the vast majority of Englishmen who could not vote "have been to a man for us." A war with "England would be to fight chiefly with our friends—for on the *poor* comes the great calamity of war." Forbes to Fox, 13 Oct. 1864, GVFP.

18. Fox to VLWF, 16 Sept., 6 Oct. 1863, GVFP.

19. *DAB*, s.v. "Emmet, Thomas Addis"; VLWF, Diary, 8–10, 13 Nov., 1 Dec. 1863, WFP. According to her sister Frank, with whom Virginia was staying, "It is a most difficult thing to argue with V. because she does not argue from *facts*, but from supposition, and no reason can move her. . . . She makes herself so nervous & anxious by imagining things that have no existence, or if they have she could have no power over them, that I give up in despair trying to sooth her." Virginia wrote a "very cross" letter to Fox because "three years ago" he had urged her to see Sims, but Frank reminded her that "F. has been very delicate now" and convinced Virginia to "modify" the letter. Frances Woodbury Lowery to Minna Blair, 4 Nov. 1863, BFP, LC.

20. VLWF, Diary, 11, 13–14 Nov., 5–6, 25–28 Dec. 1863, WFP; Fox to VLWF, 14, 18 Nov., 2 Dec. 1863, Fox to B. F. Butler, 12 Apr. 1864, Butler to Fox, 14 Apr. 1864, GVFP. Butler stipulated that the brother would be released if he would take the oath of allegiance to the United States.

21. VLWF to Fox, 31 Dec. 1863, Fox to VLWF, 2 Jan. 1864, GVFP; VLWF, Diary, 16, 19–20, 24 Jan. 1864, WFP. Wormley opened his famous hotel in 1871. *ANB*, s.v. "Wormley, James."

22. VLWF, Diary, 23 Feb., 2, 12, 14, 16, 24 Mar., 1, 11–13, 15–16, 21–23 Apr. 1864, 18 Jan. 1865, WFP. Virginia enjoyed the Bertinatti dinner all the more because dinners were often in those days all-male affairs.

23. Fox to Ericsson, 17 Feb. 1864, GVFP; Welles, *Diary*, 26 Feb. 1864, 1:531; VLWF, Diary, 18 Feb. 1864, WFP. Davis referred to Fox's brief career in textiles. Hale's ani-

mosity possibly dates back to the 1840s when he was an antislavery Democrat and Levi Woodbury, although opposed to slavery, upheld the constitutionality of the Fugitive Slave Laws, accepted the Compromise of 1850, and, had he lived beyond 1851, would have been called a "Doughface." Fox's salary had been the sea pay of a U.S. navy captain.

24. Detectives were "regarded with more or less obloquy by the general public." Olcott to Welles, 29 Jan., 1 Feb. 1865, Welles Papers, LC.

25. For attitudes of New York newspapers, see George D. Morgan to Fox, 26 Feb. 1864, GVFP. Fox's friend George W. Blunt visited the offices of both the *Post* and the *Tribune* on behalf of the Navy Department and thought he did some good. Greeley thought Fox and his buddy Wise "had made a great deal of money," until he was disillusioned by Blunt. Blunt to Fox, 23 Feb. 1864, 10 Feb. 1865, GVFP. On the attitude of the *Post*, see Bryant to Lincoln, 30 Aug. 1864, Lincoln Papers, LC; Lincoln to Bryant, 27 June 1864, *ALCW*, 7:409–10. On naval officers as navy agents, see Fox to Porter, 25 May 1864, *ORN*, 26:324–25. For a critique of the bill designed to replace civilian navy agents with naval officers, see John Murray Forbes to James W. Grimes, 19 Mar. 1864, GVFP. Senator Grimes urged that Fox "finally and forever dispose of all the Navy Agents." Grimes to Fox, 24 July 1865, GVFP.

26. VLWF, Diary, 12 Feb. 1864, WFP; William Whiting to Fox, 18 Apr. 1864, Grimes to Fox, 29 July, 6 Sept. 1864, 1 June 1865, William E. Chandler to Fox, 19 Feb. 1865, Fox to Welles, 24 Feb. 1865, GVFP; Welles, *Diary*, 18 Dec. 1863, 1, 12 Feb., 7, 8 Mar., 20 June 1864, 1:489, 518–19, 522, 536–38, 2:54. On the court-martial, see William K. Latimer (President of the Court) to Fox, 5, 19, 21 June, 4 Aug., 6, 17 Sept., 27 Oct., 28 Nov. 1864, GVFP.

27. Forney to Fox, 17 Oct. 1864, Stribling to Fox, 9 Feb. 1864, GVFP.

28. Blunt to Fox, 26 Feb., 5 Mar., 25 July 1864, John Murray Forbes to James W. Grimes, 19 Mar. 1864, GVFP. See, also, Fox's explanation to Robert B. Forbes, on 18 Mar. 1864, GVFP, of why he was not paid promptly for the sale of the *Cherokee* to the navy and how delays in paying bills prevented "honest dealers . . . from selling their goods to the Navy Department." The government paid bills "according to the condition of the Treasury."

29. Welles, *Diary*, 13, 15 Oct. 1864, 2:175, 177; Charles Jones to Raymond, 2 Aug. 1864, Raymond to Seward, 5 Aug. 1864, Welles Papers, NYPL; Hay, *Civil War Diary*, 12 Oct. 1864, p. 241; Ericsson to Fox, 9 Nov. 1864, GVFP; David Donald, *Lincoln Reconsidered: Essays on the Civil War Era* (New York: Alfred A. Knopf, 1956), pp. 78–79. In Boston, two congressmen, one of whom was A. H. Rice of the House Naval Committee, having been reelected with the support of the navy yard, asked that its employees be given a pay increase. S. Hooper to Welles, 10 Nov. 1864, Welles Papers, NYPL.

30. Wiegel to Fox, 5, 11 Nov. 1864, GVFP. Fox noted on the 5 November letter "Done Nov. 6th. and $75—check sent him for the cause."

31. Welles, *Diary*, 16, 17 Dec. 1864, 2:199–201. For details of frauds perpetrated by thirty scoundrels (of whom Scofield was the most corrupt) at the Philadelphia Navy Yard, see William E. Chandler to Welles, 31 Dec. 1864, Welles Papers, NYPL. Apparently, the conviction of the Smith brothers was set aside. John Niven, *Gideon Welles: Lincoln's Secretary of the Navy* (New York: Oxford University Press, 1973), p. 465.

32. Fox to Lee, 7 Dec. 1863, *ORN*, 9:340–41; Fox to Morse, 28 Nov. 1863, GVFP.

33. Lee to Fox, 20 Feb. 1864, *ORN*, 9:495–97; Dahlgren to Fox, 22 Jan. 1864, *ORN*, 15:251; Farragut to Fox, 13 Feb. 1864, *GVFCC*, 1:344. For an example of extracts from consular dispatches, see Fox to Du Pont, 14 Mar. 1863, *ORN*, 13:753–55.

34. Lance E. Davis and Stanley L. Engerman, *Naval Blockades in Peace and War: An Economic History since 1750* (New York: Cambridge University Press, 2006), p. 113; David G. Surdam, *Northern Naval Superiority and the Economics of the American Civil War* (Columbia: University of South Carolina Press, 2001), pp. 6, 8, 53, 72–85, 209.

35. J. M. Forbes to Fox, 26, 27 July, 2 Aug. 1864, Fox to Comstock, 28 July 1864, Fox to J. M. Forbes, 30 July 1864, R. B. Forbes to Fox, 31 July 1864, Fox to R. B. Forbes, 3 Aug. 1864, GVFP.

36. Sherman to Porter, 21 Dec. 1863, Frank M. Ramsay to Porter, 8 Jan. 1864, *ORN*, 25:645, 679–80; Ulysses S. Grant, *Personal Memoirs of U. S. Grant,* 2 vols. (New York: Charles L. Webster, 1885), 1:578. Porter noted the presidential aspirations of Banks, but observed that "Grant could not be kicked into the Presidency, he would not have it at $40,000 per year; he dont like anything but fighting and smoking, and hates politics as the devil hates holy water." Porter to Fox, 13 Jan. 1864, GVFP. I have relied on Ludwell H. Johnson's excellent *Red River Campaign: Politics and Cotton in the Civil War* (Kent, Ohio: Kent State University Press, 1993).

37. Sherman to Porter, 30 Jan. 1864, Porter to James A. Greer, 13 Feb. 1864, *ORN*, 25:723–24, 747–48; Porter to Fox, 13 Jan. 1864, GVFP.

38. Porter to Welles, 15, 24 Mar. 1864, *ORN*, 26:24–26, 35; Guild to Fox, 21 Mar. 1864, Porter to Fox, 25 Mar. 1864, GVFP; Johnson, *Red River Campaign,* pp. 101–4.

39. Porter to Fox, 25 Mar. 1864, GVFP; Porter to Sherman, 14 Apr. 1864, *ORN*, 26:56; Johnson, *Red River Campaign,* pp. 106–45, 210–14, 236–41; VLWF, Diary, 9 May 1864, WFP.

40. *Minnesota,* Log, 9 Apr. 1864, Butler to Fox, 21, 22 Apr. 1864, Fox to Ericsson, 21, 22 Apr. 1864, *ORN*, 9:603, 649–51, 667, 683; Ericsson to Fox, 22 Apr. 1864, Ericsson Papers, NYHS; Farragut to Welles, 16 May 1864, Welles to Farragut, 8 June 1864, *ORN*, 21:225–26, 232. The *Albemarle* killed Lieutenant Commander Charles W. Flusser, the gallant, promising skipper, of the *Miami.*

41. Porter to Welles, 28 Apr. 1864, *ORN*, 26:92–95; Porter to Fox, 4 May 1864, GVFP.

42. Johnson, *Red River Campaign,* pp. 248–50.

43. Johnson, *Red River Campaign,* pp. 260–66; Porter to Welles, 16 May 1864, *ORN*, 26:130–35; Porter to Fox, 27 May 1864, GVFP.

44. Charles Henry Davis to Harriette M. Davis, 7, 8 May 1864, in Charles Henry Davis, *Life of Charles Henry Davis: Rear Admiral, 1807–1877* (Boston: Houghton, Mifflin, 1899), pp. 303–4. Davis was in Fox's office when Lincoln dropped in.

45. Welles to Porter, 26 Apr., 31 May 1864, Fox to Porter, 25 May 1864, *ORN* 26:92, 160–61, 324–25. Captain Thornton A. Jenkins of the *Richmond* was concerned about Porter's "tight place." If anyone can, he told Fox, Porter "will relieve himself from it at the least expense to the country." Jenkins to Fox, 16 May 1864, GVFP.

46. Fox to Porter, 25 May 1864, *ORN* 26:324–25.

47. Porter to Welles, 11 May 1864, *ORN*, 26:292–93; Hay, *Civil War Diary*, 16 Nov. 1864, p. 250; Johnson, *Red River Campaign*, pp. 285–88.

Chapter 16. Commerce Raiders and Ironclad Rams

1. See Chester G. Hearn, *Gray Raiders of the Sea: How Eight Confederate Warships Destroyed the Union's High Seas Commerce* (Baton Rouge: Louisiana State University Press, 1996), for the history of these commerce destroyers. Although it is clear that the decline of the American merchant marine began during the Civil War with the depredations of the Confederate raiders, it is not certain that the raiders were responsible for its continued decline. In the past, other devastated merchant marines have quickly recovered. Probably, the failure to adopt steam engines and steel hulls, on one hand, and the lure of domestic industry rather than foreign trade, for capital investment, accounts for the long-term decline of American shipping.

2. On the *Florida* (also known as the *Oreto* and as the *Manassas*), see James D. Bulloch to J. N. Maffitt, 21 Mar. 1862, Welles to Francis Winslow, 1 July 1862, and Maffitt, Journal, 4 May to 31 Dec. 1862, *ORN*, 1:397–98, 755–56, 763–69.

3. Welles to Wilkes, 15 Dec. 1862, Semmes to Mallory, 4 Jan. 1863, Semmes, Journal, 20 Aug. 1862 to 4 Jan. 1863, *ORN*, 1:587–88, 778–80, 783–817; Charles H. Baldwin to Fox, 2 Feb. 1864, GVFP, NHSC, NYHS. Semmes described his crew on 29 Dec. 1862. Journal, *ORN*, 1:816. The *Peterhof* was initially condemned as a prize, but that decision was reversed four years later. Its seizure also led to a further dispute over prize money, between the squadron commander, Wilkes, and Charles H. Baldwin, commander of the *Vanderbilt*, which made the actual capture.

4. Welles to S. P. Lee, 19, 24 Oct., 3 Nov. 1862, Welles to Wilkes, 19 Oct. 1862, Welles to J. P. McKinstry, 24 Oct. 1862, Semmes, Journal, 20 Aug. 1862 to 29 Oct. 1862, *ORN*, 1:508–11, 518–19, 529, 783–802.

5. E. D. Morgan to Welles, 8 Nov. 1862, Edward S. Torrey to Welles, 12 Nov. 1862, William Ronckendorff to Welles, 19 Nov. 1862, Semmes, Journal, 30 Oct. 1862 to 4 Jan. 1863, *ORN*, 1:539, 542–44, 549–50, 802–17.

6. Semmes, Journal, 5–11 Jan. 1863, John N. Maffitt, Journal, 13–16 Jan. 1863, *ORN*, 2:720–22, 667–68.

7. Abstract Log of CSS *Georgia*, 9 Apr. 1863 to 18 Jan. 1864, Semmes, Journal, 12 Jan. 1863 to 31 Mar. 1864, 1 Apr. to 16 June 1864, *ORN*, 2:811–18, 722–807, 3:669–77; P. S. Forbes to Fox, 8 June 1864, GVFP.

8. Maffitt, Journal, 19 Jan. to 30 Apr. 1863, C. Manigault Morris, Cruise of the CSS *Florida*, 29 Feb. to 26 Apr. 1864, Abstract Log, 1 Apr. to 19 Aug. 1864, *ORN*, 2:668–73, 3:609, 643–46; Fox to S. P. Lee, 12 July 1864, *ORN*, 10:261.

9. Winslow to Welles, 19 June, 30 July 1864, Welles to Winslow, 12 July 1864, *ORN*, 3:59, 74–75, 79–81. Winslow's father, who resided in Charleston, suffered at the hands of South Carolinians for his son's victory over the *Alabama*. "As for the old man," Winslow wrote Fox, "they beat him hit with a stone which laid it [him] up, then set fire to his bed while he was asleep. Robbed him of clothes & everything valuable. And his cares ceased only with his death." Winslow also had his property confiscated and sold, in December 1864. Winslow to Fox, 21 June 1865, GVFP.

10. Edge to Fox, 21 July 1864, GVFP. Edge had been the U.S. correspondent for the *London Star* and had been allowed by Fox to accompany Du Pont's Port Royal expedition. He published a pamphlet on the battle of the *Kearsarge* and *Alabama* in 1864. *Samuel Francis Du Pont: A Selection from His Civil War Letters,* 3 vols., ed. John D. Hayes (Ithaca: Cornell University Press, 1969), 1:180–81, n. 3. For depictions of the battle by Manet and others, see Juliet Wilson-Bareau and David C. Degener, *Manet and the American Civil War: The Battle of U.S.S. Kearsarge and C.S.S. Alabama* (New York: Metropolitan Museum of Art, 2003). After viewing the French ironclad fleet in 1865, an American naval officer concluded that a monitor could sink any of them in fifteen minutes. R. H. Wyman to Fox, 14 Nov. 1865, GVFP.

11. Edge to Fox, 21 July 1864, Fox to Edward de Stoeckl, 29 Apr. 1862, Fox to Baron von Gerolt, 10 July 1863, Waldemar R. de Raasloff to Fox, 16 May, 15 Aug. 1862, Ericsson to Fox, 11 Jan. 1864, GVFP. Fox believed that harboring military secrets did not pay. When urged to deny the French information about the monitors, Fox said, if it was "denied we would get the credit of fear & discourtesy & they would buy all the information." Elizabeth Blair Lee to Samuel Phillips Lee, 12 Aug. 1863, in Virginia Jeans Laas, ed., *Wartime Washington: The Civil War Letters of Elizabeth Blair Lee* (Urbana: University of Illinois Press, 1991), p. 299.

12. On taking the *Florida,* see Collins to Welles, 31 Oct., 11 Nov., 1864, Collins to Charles Wilkes, 1 Dec. 1864, *ORN,* 3:255–57, 264. On Fox's hearing the news of the *Florida*'s capture, see VLWF, Diary, 8 Nov. 1864, WFP, LC.

13. On the sinking of the *Florida,* see K. R. Breese to David D. Porter, 22 Nov. 1864, Jonathan Baker, 28 Nov. 1864, Finding of the Court of Inquiry, *ORN,* 3:274, 277, 280; Moses H. Grinnell to Fox, 28 Nov. 1864, GVFP. On freeing the *Florida*'s crew, see Welles to H. A. Allen, 1 Feb. 1865, *ORN,* 3:288. On Collins's court-martial, see *ORN,* 3:268–69.

14. Osbon to Fox, 12 Aug. 1864, *ORN,* 3:137–38. When Confederate raiders stopped a U.S. merchant vessel with a neutral cargo, they released the vessel under a ransom bond covering the value of the vessel but not the cargo. To collect the ransom, however, the Confederacy had to win its independence to gain standing in appropriate courts.

15. Wood to S. R. Mallory, 31 Aug. 1864, Welles to John D. Jones, 13 Aug. 1864, Welles to H. Paulding, 14, 19 Aug. 1864, M. M. Jackson to Welles, 18 Aug. A.M., 18 Aug. P.M. 1864, Welles to Paulding, 19 Aug. 1864, Welles to S. H. Stringham, Paulding, and C. K. Stribling, 25 Aug. 1864, S. P. Lee to Welles, 26 Aug. 1864, *ORN,* 3:141, 144, 151, 152, 157, 168, 170–71, 701–4.

16. Cruise of the CSS *Chicamauga,* 28 Oct. to 19 Nov. 1864, Cruise of the CSS *Olustee,* 29 Oct to 7 Nov. 1864, Search for the CSS *Chicamauga* and *Olustee* (*Tallahassee*), *ORN,* 3:308–40, 712–14, 836.

17. James D. Bulloch to Waddell, 5 Oct. 1864, Abstract Log of the CSS *Shenandoah,* *ORN,* 3:749–50, 785–92; Moses H. Grinnell to Fox, 28 Nov. 1864, GVFP.

18. Welles to Seward, 11 Dec. 1865, *ORN,* 3:602.

19. Buchanan to Jones, 14 Apr. 1864, *ORN,* 21:892; Virginia L. Farragut to Fox, 2 Sept. 1864, GVFP. Richard "Ram Rod" Page, a former naval officer, was "an old friend and neighbor" of the Farraguts.

20. Farragut to Welles, 22 Jan. 1864, *ORN*, 21:52–53; Farragut to Fox, 13 Apr. 1864, GVFP.

21. Farragut to Fox, 14 June 1864, *ORN*, 21:335–36. In this letter, Farragut calls the carpenters German, but in another letter of the same date he calls them Danes. Farragut to Alexander Asboth, 14 June 1864, *ORN*, 21:336. The *Nashville* never was completed. "Confederate Forces Afloat: *Nashville*," *DANFS*, 2:552. For Fox's prophetic warning about torpedoes, see Fox to Farragut, 27 June 1864, GVFP.

22. Welles to Farragut, 25 June 1864, Farragut to Welles, 12 Aug. 1864, *ORN*, 21:344, 415–17; Fox to "Admiral" Henry A. Wise, 13 Aug. 1864, Wise Papers, NHSC, NYHS. Wise at times addressed Fox as "Gunboat." Farragut told his wife that "he was glad to find himself so securely fastened in an elevated position as he felt then if 'I am wounded fatally I may with my dying breath give an order that may lead to victory.'" Virginia L. Farragut to Fox, 23 Apr. [1873], GVFP.

23. Farragut to Welles, 12 Aug. 1864, *ORN*, 21:417–23; Farragut to Fox, no date, but approximately 10 Aug. 1864, GVFP; *CWNC*, 5, 7, 23 Aug. 1864. Despite a tragic accident at its launching in St. Louis, the *Chickasaw* proved to be a lucky ship. When launched, its anchor line swept women of the christening party into the Mississippi, and the wife of the chief clerk of the works drowned. *St. Louis Union*, 10 Feb. 1864.

24. Fox to Butler, 6 Aug. 1864, Butler to Fox, 8 Aug. 1864, *ORN*, 21:439–40.

25. Welles to Farragut, 5 Sept. 1864, *ORN*, 21:545; Nicholson to Fox, 8 Aug., 2 Nov. 1864, Nicholson to George Bankhead, 27 Aug. 1864, GVFP; Fox to Welles, 4 Aug. 1864, Welles Papers, Huntington Library, San Marino, Calif. Actually, Fox flirted briefly with rams for monitors. Fox to Ericsson, 18 Mar. 1862, GVFP. Eads and Ericsson each had a malfunctioning turret on the *Winnebago*. Simon Schultice to Thomas H. Stevens, 6 Aug. 1864, *ORN*, 21:497.

26. Farragut to Welles, 4 Sept., 8 Nov. 1864, *ORN*, 21:544–45, 721. See also Farragut's informal undated letter to Fox, of August 1864, in the Fox Papers, written a few days after the battle. GVFP. The Union navy did not build rams apart from those on the *New Ironsides* and the *Dictator*, and their rams were never used.

27. Fox to VLWF, 19, 25 June 1864, GVFP; VLWF, Diary, 21, 24 June 1864, WFP; Lee to Grant, 23 June 1864, Lee to Fox, 24 June 1864, *ORN*, 10:184, 207–8.

28. Fox to VLWF, 3 July 1864, GVFP; VLWF, Diary, 5 July 1864, WFP.

29. VLWF to Fox, 16 July 1864, GVFP; Fox to Lincoln, 12 July 1864, Lincoln Papers, LC.

30. Catherine Drinker Bowen, *Yankee from Olympus: Justice Holmes and His Family* (Boston: Little, Brown, 1943), p. 194; Fox to VLWF, 14, 18 July 1864, GVFP.

31. Welles to Lee, 10, 14 July 1864, Fox to Lee, 12 July 1864, Lee to Welles, 13 July 1864, *ORN*, 10:252, 261, 265, 272; Elizabeth Blair Lee to Samuel Phillips Lee, 10 Aug. 1861, 26 July 1864, in Laas, *Wartime Washington*, pp. 59, 410. For Lee's defense of his act, see Lee to Welles, 14 July 1864, *ORN*, 10:272–73. Up to this point, there is no evidence that Fox hampered Lee's career. Fox, however, was the very good friend of Montgomery Blair, who hated his brother-in-law Lee. Lee was a difficult man, and Fox, having served with him, evidently did not care for him personally. See Edward Donaldson to Fox, 5 Feb. 1864, GVFP.

32. Fox to VLWF, 28 July 1864, GVFP.

33. Fox to VLWF, 2 Aug. 1864, GVFP.

34. Fox to VLWF, 28 July 1864, GVFP; VLWF, Diary, 11 Aug. 1864, WFP; Fox to "Admiral" Wise, 13 Aug. 1864, Wise Letterbooks, NHSC, NYHS. For Porter's gift of horses to Fox, see Porter to Fox, 15 Oct. 1864, GVFP; Elizabeth Blair Lee to Samuel Phillips Lee, 17 Sept. 1864, in Laas, *Wartime Washington*, p. 430. Porter boasted that he had a "good time" down the Mississippi and came East on leave with six horses, cows, and various luxuries and that the mare he gave Fox was "Jeffs." Ibid.

35. Fay to Fox, 11 Aug. 1864, Grimes to Fox, 6 Sept. 1864, GVFP; VLWF, Diary, 13, 23–24 Aug., 12 Sept. 1864, WFP.

36. Fox to VLWF, 29 Aug. 1864, Fay to Fox, 22 Sept. 1864, MacDonough to Fox, 23 Sept. 1864, GVFP; VLWF, Diary, 27 Sept. 1864, WFP.

37. L. S. Baker to John N. Maffitt, 6 July 1864, S. M. Mallory to James A. Seddon, 30 July 1864, *ORN*, 10:718, 720.

38. Cushing to Lee, 9 May, 9 July 1864, Lee to Cushing, 14 May, 9 July 1864, Welles to Lee, 6 June 1864, Lee to W. H. Macomb, 30 June 1864, *ORN*, 10:39–40, 57, 127–28, 220, 247–48.

39. Lee to J. W. Livingston, 26 July 1864, Lee to Cushing 26 July 1864, Welles to Cushing, 28 July 1864, Cushing to Fox, 9 Sept. 1864, Fox to Cushing, 11 Sept. 1864, *ORN*, 10:308–9, 315, 448–49, 459.

40. Cushing to David Dixon Porter, 30 Oct. 1864; Porter, General Orders No. 47, 15 Nov. 1864, *ORN*, 10:611–13, 11:26–27.

41. Welles to Cushing, 10 Sept., 9 Nov. 1864, *ORN*, 10:451–53, 619.

42. For Ammen's comments, see Elizabeth Blair Lee to Samuel Phillips Lee, 9 Nov. 1864, in Laas, *Wartime Washington*, p. 439.

Chapter 17. End of the War

1. *Inside Lincoln's White House: The Complete Civil War Diary of John Hay*, ed. Michael Burlingame and John R. Turner Ettlinger (Carbondale: Southern Illinois University Press, 1997), 25 Sept. 1864, p. 233; Lee to Welles, 20 May 1863, Welles to Stanton, 2 Jan. 1864, *ORN*, 9:33–34, 384.

2. Fox to VLWF, 29, 31 Aug., 4 Sept. 1864, Fox to Gillmore, 28 Aug. 1863, Grant to Fox, 19 Sept. 1864, GVFP, NHSC, NYHS; Welles to Farragut, 5 Sept. 1864, Grant to Fox, 10 Sept. 1864, *ORN*, 10:430–31, 450; Rowena Reed, *Combined Operations in the Civil War* (Annapolis: Naval Institute Press, 1978), pp. 329–31.

3. Elizabeth Blair Lee to Samuel Phillips Lee, 5 Oct. 1864, in Virginia Jeans Laas, ed., *Wartime Washington: The Civil War Letters of Elizabeth Blair Lee* (Urbana: University of Illinois Press, 1991), p. 437; Welles to Farragut, 22 Sept. 1864, Welles to Porter, 22 Sept. 1864, Welles to Lincoln, 28 Oct. 1864, *ORN*, 10:473–74, 11:3; Reed, *Combined Operations*, pp. 331–33. Lee and Porter exchanged commands. Together, Fox and Stanton had selected Gillmore for the Fisher operation a year earlier, before relations between him and Dahlgren deteriorated.

4. Porter to Fox, 15, 19 Oct. 1864, GVFP.

5. Virginia declared that October was a "glorious" month for Union arms, "which the 8th [election day] will show." VLWF, Diary, 1 Nov. 1864, WFP, LC.

6. Fox to VLWF, 23 Sept. 1864, GVFP; VLWF, Diary, 26, 27 Sept. 1864, WFP.

7. Hay, *Civil War Diary*, 8 Nov. 1864, pp. 244–46; *Diary of Gideon Welles: Secretary of the Navy under Lincoln and Johnson*, 3 vols., ed. Howard K. Beale (New York: W. W. Norton, 1960), 25 Nov. 1864, 2:178–79; VLWF, Diary, 9 Nov. 1864, WFP. The Foxes stayed with Minna and Montgomery Blair, until they could find suitable rooms. Rents were high, and Virginia refused to rent one place, complaining "it would take all our salary for housekeeping. . . . A stingy reward for the services of a man who could be receiving $10,000 a year." VLWF, Diary, 14 Nov. 1864, WFP. A few days later, Virginia rented their old conveniently located rooms (184 F Street) at $120 per month, plus $17 for fires, which were "the cheapest we have found." Ibid., 17 Nov. 1864. After they moved in, on 8 December, Virginia reported, "Gus feels at home & so do I." Ibid., 8 Dec. 1864.

8. Fox to Butler, 17 Nov. 1864, GVFP; VLWF, Diary, 10 Dec. 1864, WFP. Fox probably referred to securing for Butler his command at New Orleans.

9. Porter to Fox, 8 Nov. 1864, GVFP. Butler informed Fox by messenger about the powder-ship idea. Butler to Fox, 1 Nov. 1864, GVFP.

10. Mary R. Simpson to Fox, 15 Oct. 1864, GVFP; Grant to Fox, 11 Nov. 1864, *ORN*, 11:60; VLWF, Diary, 12, 15–16 Nov. 1864, WFP.

11. On the City Point explosion, see Richard Delafield to Charles A. Dana, 18 Nov. 1864, *ORN*, 11:211.

12. Fox to Porter, 16 Nov. 1864, Porter to Fox, 20 Nov. 1864, Porter to W. H. Macomb, 20 Nov. 1864, *ORN*, 11:68, 78–79.

13. Delafield to Charles A. Dana, 18 Nov. 1864, Benton to Henry A. Wise, 18 Nov. 1864, Jeffers to Wise, 23 Nov. 1864, *ORN*, 11:207–15; VLWF, Diary, 19, 20 Nov. 1864, WFP. Reed, *Combined Operations*, p. 338, characterizes the Benton and Jeffers reports as "more favorable," but less negative seems a better characterization to me.

14. Memorandum, 23 Nov. 1864, *ORN* 11:215–16.

15. Fox to Lincoln, 21 Nov. 1864, Lincoln Papers, LC.

16. VLWF, Diary, 24 Nov. 1864, WFP; Fox to Butler, 25 Nov. 1864, Fox to Wood, 29 Nov. 1864, *ORN*, 11:95, 105–6. Lenthall and Isherwood were responsible for the design of the *Monadnock*, which was built at the Boston Navy Yard.

17. Porter to Grant, 30 Nov. 1864, Porter to Fox, 2 Dec. 1864, Fox to Porter, 4 Dec. 1864, *ORN*, 11:110, 119, 134.

18. Reed, *Combined Operations*, pp. 339–41; Grant to Butler, 6 Dec. 1864, *ORN*, 11:149–50; Porter to Fox, 10 Dec. 1864, GVFP. Porter said, Weitzel's troops were "all negroes and I dont expect much of them." Porter's disparagement of black troops is inconsistent with his appreciation of black crewmen on the Mississippi. A master at creating alibis and shifting blame to others for his own failings or miscalculations, Porter, in finding fault with everyone connected with the expedition, was laying the groundwork for his excuses if the powder ship, which was supposed to devastate everything for miles around, turned out to be an expensive firecracker.

Wise, who usually functioned effectively in the Bureau of Ordnance, was in poor health. Prior to the war, he suffered a serious injury in an accident and, to relieve his pain, had become addicted to morphine. Under its influence, he was often "drowsy." Perhaps too much morphine caused the mistakes with the powder ship. Treatment after the war in Carlsbad, Germany, did not restore his health. He died in 1869, shortly before his fiftieth birthday. Porter to Fox, 13 Jan., 8 Nov. 1864, Wise to "Gun Boat" [Fox], 4 July 1865, GVFP; *ANB*, s.v. "Wise, Henry Augustus."

19. Porter to Fox, 22 Dec. 1864, GVFP. Calling Butler "a perfect marplot," Porter said, "I dont expect anything from the army, they will only land in case *we take the forts*, and if we do, I shall land first, and turn them over to him." Ibid.

20. On the preparation of the powder ship, see Jeffers to Wise, 16 Jan. 1865, and Rodman to Wise, 27 Jan. 1865, *ORN*, 11:233–37; Reed, *Combined Operations*, pp. 341–42. Had the powder ship been run aground, had the preparations of Jeffers and Rodman succeeded in producing a simultaneous blast of all the powder, and had that blast been coordinated with an assault by the army, the powder ship might have been a success.

21. Reed, *Combined Operations*, pp. 342–54.

22. Lincoln to Grant, 28 Dec. 1864, Grant to Lincoln, 28 Dec. 1864, *ALCW*, 8:187.

23. Porter to Fox, 28 Dec. 1864, Fox to Porter, 3 Jan. 1865, GVFP; Porter to Welles, 26–29 Dec. 1864, *ORN*, 11:253–65, quotations from 262, 264. In his original official report of 27 December, Porter said, "I sincerely trust this will be the last time I shall have anything to do with the army &c." He asked Fox to omit his hostile words, because it was "unjust to the army generally." Porter to Fox, 28 Dec. 1864, GVFP. Fox "expunged that sentence." Fox to Porter, 3 Jan. 1865, GVFP.

24. VLWF, Diary, 30 Dec. 1864, 6 Jan. 1865, WFP. Preston, accompanied by Porter's wife, called on the Foxes at home to denigrate Butler and protect Porter. Naval officers' wives and other members of their families—especially if they had political clout—often lobbied officials in the Navy Department. Louis M. Goldsborough's wife, who was the daughter of William Wirt, looked after his interests, and Samuel P. Lee had an advocate in his father-in-law Francis Preston Blair (but not in his brother-in-law Montgomery, who detested him).

25. Grant to Stanton, 1 Jan. 1865, Stanton Papers, LC; Fox to Porter, 3 Jan. 1865, GVFP. In 1870 Comstock would become Montgomery Blair's son-in-law.

26. Fox to Gillmore, 3 Jan. 1865, GVFP.

27. Welles to Grant, 29 Dec. 1864, Fox to Grant, 29 Dec. 1864, *ORN*, 11:388, 391–92.

28. Grant to Welles, 30 Dec. 1864, Grant to Porter, 30 Dec. 1864, 3 Jan. 1865, Welles to Porter, 31 Dec. 1864, Porter to Grant, 1 Jan. 1865, *ORN*, 11:392, 394, 396, 401–2, 405; Dahlgren to Fox, Christmas, 1864, GVFP. In a postscript to Fox, Dahlgren added, "You would be delighted with Sherman." Ibid.

29. Grant to Terry, 3 Jan. 1865, *ORN*, 11:404.

30. Porter to Fox, 7 Jan. 1865, GVFP. Porter elaborated: "I don't believe in Grant's troops coming—he says to me—'hold on Dear Admiral, I will be back with more troops soon, and with another commander'—that says a good deal but no troops are yet in sight. We want white men here—not niggers—I don't believe in them." Ibid.

31. VLWF, Diary, 2 Jan. 1865, WFP.

32. Fox to John Rodgers, 25 Dec. 1864, Fox to Fulton, 3 Jan. 1865, Fox to Grant, 4 Jan. 1865, *ORN*, 11:205, 403, 409. Osbon was tried by court-martial and ultimately found not guilty. See J. Cutler Andrews, *The North Reports the Civil War* (Pittsburgh:

University of Pittsburgh Press, 1955), pp. 614–15, 618–19. In 1864 Osbon sent Fox useful information about the Confederate commerce destroyer *Tallahassee*. See chapter 16.

33. VLWF, Diary, 6 Feb. 1865, WFP. For examples of contact with the press, see Fox to Young, 5 Jan. 1864, Fox to White, 12, 22 Dec. 1864, White to Fox, 1 Mar. 1865, Fox to Russell, 1 Mar. 1864, GVFP.

34. Fox to Grant, 2, 4, 5 Jan. 1865, *ORN*, 11:403, 409, 411.

35. Fox to Grant, 29 Dec. 1864, 2 Jan. 1865, Grant to Fox, 29 Dec. 1864, *ORN*, 11:388, 409; VLWF, Diary, 30 Dec. 1864, 2 Jan. 1865, WFP; E. B. Long and Barbara Long, *Civil War Day by Day: An Almanac, 1861–1865* (New York: Doubleday, 1971), 30 Dec. 1864.

36. Fox to Grant, 17, 19 Jan. 1865, *ORN*, 11:605, 614; VLWF, Diary, 18 Jan. 1865, WFP; Long and Long, *Civil War Day by Day*, 12, 16, 18 Jan. 1865; Varina Davis to Minna Blair, [12 Jan. 1865], BFP, LC. In a severe storm, Barnes was buried at Mt. Auburn Cemetery, next to his wife, Hannah Woodbury.

37. The second attack on Fort Fisher is described in Reed, *Combined Operations*, pp. 359–79; Long and Long, *Civil War Day by Day*, 13–15 Jan. 1865; Porter to Welles, 17 Jan. 1865, *ORN*, 11:436–44. Wise was, and Porter had been, an advocate of Parrott guns, but in the first attack on Fisher, the fleet's casualties came from their bursting.

38. Porter to Fox, 7, 21 Jan. 1865, GVFP. Preston was outstanding. "Such men," Du Pont earlier remarked to Fox, "are born about once in a quarter of a century." Du Pont to Fox, 14 Aug. 1862, *ORN*, 13:255.

39. Gregory to Fox, 19 Jan. 1865, GVFP.

40. Porter to Fox, 20 Jan. 1865, GVFP; Reed, *Combined Operations*, pp. 379–83.

41. *CWNC*, 23–24 Jan. 1865; Parker to Porter, 23 Jan. 1865, Grant to Fox, 24 Jan. 1865, Grant to Welles, 24 Jan. 1865, *ORN*, 11:632–33, 635–36.

42. Fox to Grant, 24, 24 Jan. 1865, *ORN*, 11:637, 641. Grant and Fox exchanged several telegrams on that day. VLWF, Diary, 24 Jan. 1865, WFP; Radford to Fox, 7, 14, 23 Feb. 1865, GVFP.

43. Fox to Grant, 24 Jan. 1865, Grant to Fox, 24, 25 Jan. 1865, Farragut to Welles, 26 Jan. 1865, Log of the *Onondaga*, 24 Jan. 1865, John K. Mitchell to S. R. Mallory, 3 Feb. 1865, Joseph Lanman to Welles, 27 Jan. 1865, *ORN*, 11:641, 646, 656, 669–73, 695, 703; VLWF, Diary, 25 Jan. 1865, WFP.

44. On Blair's mission and the Hampton Roads conference, see Abraham Lincoln to the House of Representatives, 10 Feb. 1865, *ALCW*, 8:274–85; James M. McPherson, "No Peace without Victory, 1861–1865," *American Historical Review*, 109 (Feb. 2004): 14–17.

45. Fox to Grant, 24 Jan. 1865, Grant to Fox, 24 Jan. 1865, *ORN*, 11:641, 694–95; Porter to Fox, 19 Feb. 1865, GVFP.

46. Log of the *Rhode Island*, 27 Jan. 1865, *ORN*, 27:710; Fox to John W. Hogg, 21 Mar. 1877, GVFP.

47. Fox to Barnard, 10 Feb. 1865, GVFP. Barnard's better known brother, Frederick A. P. Barnard, became president of Columbia College in New York.

48. Gregory to Fox, no day, Jan. 1865, GVFP. Because Welles and Fox were usually

together and Welles signed virtually everything, examples of Fox's role in naval operations are found when they were apart. While at Fortress Monroe in April 1864, Fox was apprised of a contemplated joint offensive up the James River by Butler and S. P. Lee. Fox immediately asked Welles to order "all Farragut's tugs, which were ordered to the Gulf last Sunday, from New York, be sent here as early as practicable; also the *Canonicus*, at New York, and *Saugus*, at Philadelphia, and *Eutaw*, at Washington? All the double-enders and tugs at New York should be hurried to this point." Fox to Welles, 26 Apr. 1864, *ORN*, 9:698.

49. Porter to Fox, 26 Dec. 1865, GVFP.

50. Fox to A. H. Rice, 15 Feb. 1865, Fox to Grimes, 1 June 1865, GVFP. Fox told Rice not to oppose Hale's clever maneuver, because "the other assistants should have their pay increased." Fox to Rice, 15 Feb. 1865, GVFP. Fox wrote a fifty-page "response to the allegations of the Hon. John P. Hale," which included the charge that Fox ordered an investigation into the "conduct & business transactions" of members of Congress, for Welles to use. Fox to Welles, 24 Feb. 1865, GVFP. Fox called Hale's speech on the Sumter expedition "a tissue of lies." VLWF, Diary, 2 Feb. 1865, WFP. Virginia Fox also pointed out that Hale was a lame duck, with "only one month more & he's extinguished." Ibid.

51. Du Pont to Davis, 4, 9 Feb. 1865, William Whetten to Du Pont, 16 Feb. 1865, in *Samuel Francis Du Pont: A Selection from His Civil War Letters*, 3 vols., ed. John D. Hayes (Ithaca: Cornell University Press, 1969), 3:430–37, 442–44; Welles, *Diary*, 4, 6, 21 Feb. 1865, 2:236–37, 240–42; VLWF, Diary, 8 Feb. 1865, WFP. John P. Hale, as perhaps his last act as a senator, attacked Fox once again. Ibid, 3 Mar. 1865.

52. Welles, *Diary*, 30 Jan. 1865, 2:233; Jenkins to Fox, 20 Mar. 1864, Jouett to Fox, 25 Mar. 1863, GVFP.

53. Welles, *Diary*, 30 Jan., 21 Feb. 1865, 2:232–33, 241–42; Faxon to Mark Howard, 15 Feb. 1865, Howard Papers, Connecticut Historical Society, Hartford (courtesy John D. Hayes); Sedgewick to Wise, 22 Nov. 1864, Wise Letterbooks, NYHS.

54. Welles, *Diary*, 30 Jan. 1865, 2:233; Fox to Welles, 5 Aug. 1865, Welles Papers, LC. Farragut tattled to Welles about telegrams at Grant's headquarters bearing Fox's signature, and Welles assumed Fox had "substituted his own name for mine." In fairness to Fox, Grant had been bombarding him with telegrams on 24 Jan. 1865, and the telegrams Fox sent were in response to those he received. Farragut also told Welles that Fox substituted his name on telegrams to Parker at the same time, but those in the *ORN* have Welles's signature. This entry in Welles's diary reveals more of his and Farragut's pettiness than of Fox's "intrusive or obtrusive" nature. The Fox correspondence is full of examples of his good relations with naval officers. See, for example, the response of Commander J. R. Madison Mullany, an old friend and shipmate who lost an arm at Mobile Bay, to Fox's letter of "sympathy and good will." Mullany to Fox, 3 Oct. 1864, and see also Jenkins to Fox, 20 Mar. 1864, GVFP. For good measure, see Virginia L. Farragut to Fox, 2 Sept. 1864, GVFP, thanking him "for your consideration in telegraphing me so promptly the good news from Fort Gaines." Fox did assume and presume, but more often than not the results were beneficial. Farragut's annoyance with Fox was short-lived. Within a year, Farragut proposed that the Foxes live near him and his wife.

55. Welles, *Diary*, 30 Jan. 1865, 2:233.

56. Fox to Porter, 3 Jan. 1865, William T. Sherman to Fox, 9 July 1865, GVFP.

57. Fox to Welles, 5 Apr. 1865, Welles Papers, LC; VLWF, Diary, 28–31 Mar., 1 Apr. 1865, WFP. On the rough trip to Charleston, Fox got "sea sick for the first time in my life."

58. VLWF, Diary, 1–4 Apr. 1865, WFP.

59. VLWF, Diary, 5–7 Apr. 1865, WFP. Columbus was buried in Spain in the convent of Santa Maria de las Cuevas. Virginia and Ellen were shopping with John Murray Forbes, when he "wanted to know if the President smoked to take some cigars to him." Virginia "couldn't inform him." Fox, who smoked many cigars when with Lincoln, could have told Forbes that Lincoln did not smoke.

60. VLWF, Diary, 7–8 Apr. 1865, WFP. The German naturalist Alexander von Humboldt called the valley of the Gumiere the "most beautiful in the world," but Virginia thought its equals could be found in New England. Virginia misspells Jenckes as Jackes. Despite his cousin's embrace of slavery, Congressman Jenckes, a Republican, supported Lincoln and would back Radical Reconstruction measures, extending civil and political rights to former slaves. He is remembered as the father of civil service reform.

61. VLWF, Diary, 8 Apr. 1865, WFP.

62. VLWF, Diary, 9 Apr. 1865, WFP. Bellamer Cave was discovered in 1861.

63. VLWF, Diary, 9, 11–13 Apr. 1865, WFP.

64. Tilton to Fox, 6 May 1865, GVFP.

65. VLWF, Diary, 14, 17 Apr. 1865, WFP; "Programme of the Order of Exercises at the Re-Raising of the United States Flag, on Fort Sumter, Charleston, S.C., April 14th, 1865," GVFP; Ari Hoogenboom, "Gustavus Fox and the Relief of Fort Sumter," *Civil War History* 9 (Dec. 1963): 398. Fox participated in some of the festivities, but Virginia, "oppressed" by a headache and aware that it was Good Friday, only briefly went into the ward room, where there was "singing & eating cake & wine." VLWF, Diary, 14 Apr. 1865, WFP. Dahlgren thought Beecher's oration "not too long, and moderate, seemingly acceptable." Dahlgren, Diary, 14 Apr. 1865, *ORN*, 16:373.

Chapter 18. From War to Peace

1. VLWF, Diary, 17 Apr. 1865, WFP, LC.

2. VLWF, Diary, 19 Apr. 1865, WFP. Recognizing how close Fox was to Lincoln, Robert Lincoln gave Fox a lock of Lincoln's hair. Ibid., 13 May 1865.

3. Farragut to Fox, 18 May 1865, Robert Townsend to Fox, 11 Apr. 1865, GVFP, NHSC, NYHS.

4. Ericsson to Fox, 1 May 1865, GVFP. Rodgers assured Fox that "properly built monitors can go anywhere that other vessels can go," but Ericsson bristled when Rodgers was critical about the *Dictator*'s coal-carrying capacity and its steering in shallow water. Rodgers to Fox, 20 July 1865, Ericsson to Fox, 14 Sept. 1865, GVFP.

5. Fox to Augur, 21 May 1865, GVFP; VLWF, Diary, 24 May 1865, WFP.

6. VLWF, Diary, 13 Feb., 21 Mar. 1865, WFP. Fox was invited to a reception for the First Regiment, District of Columbia Volunteers (Colored). James Wormley et al. to

Fox, 9 Oct. 1865, GVFP. For an example of a black perceiving Fox as a trustworthy friend, see VLWF, Diary, 1 Mar. 1865, WFP. In the same entry, Virginia did not accept an invitation "to the colored church" for the presentation of a "beautifully painted" banner by a black artist to the Washington "colored odd fellows." Virginia also "shuddered" when an eloquent black steward on board the *Santiago* spoke to fellow crewmen about achieving equality by moving to the West, establishing black communities, and electing black members of Congress. VLWF, Diary, 2 Apr. 1865, WFP. In short, Fox and Virginia were moving toward racial equality but were not fully committed to it.

7. Fox to Grimes, 1 June 1865, GVFP; VLWF, Diary, 7 Dec. 1865, WFP. Had Welles been in town and attended that cabinet meeting, he probably would have supported the president. In September, he wrote Fox that "extremists," whom he thought would be unsuccessful, were trying "to get up a counter policy to that of the Administration on the subject of re-establishing the Union, and especially to enforce Negro suffrage in the rebel states." Welles to Fox, 9 Sept. 1865, GVFP. At this point Fox apparently shared the views of John Murray Forbes, who wished that Fox could make Johnson "see the impolicy of this extreme haste for reconstruction in the South." Forbes to Fox, 5 July 1865, GVFP.

8. Lenthall to Fox, 20 Aug. 1865, GVFP. For evidence of Fox writing orders, see Goldsborough to Fox, 21 June 1865, GVFP. For an example of Welles relying on Fox in a personnel question involving the captain of the *Powhattan,* see Porter to Fox, 16 Aug. 1865, GVFP.

9. *CWNC*; Forbes to Fox, 14, 18 July 1865, GVFP. Forbes told Fox, "You need a Jay Cook to do justice to your sales." The banker Jay Cooke was the highly successful salesman of government bonds and has been renowned as the financier of the Civil War. On naval trash, see Goldsborough to Elizabeth W. Goldsborough, 3, 17 June 1869, Goldsborough Papers, LC, and for Fox's prediction of trash, see Fox to Alexander D. Bache, 28 Sept. 1862, GVFP.

10. Fox to Welles, 26 Aug. 1865, Welles Papers, LC; *CWNC*, 4 Dec. 1865; Raasloff to Fox, 20 June 1865, Fox, Diary, 13 July, 11 Dec. 1868, GVFP; Erik O. Pedersen, "The Attempted Sale of the Danish West Indies to the United States of America, 1865–1870" (Ph.D. dissertation, City University of New York, 1992). VLWF, Diary, 21 Apr. 1865 gives an example of Fox's association with Raasloff.

11. Fox to William G. Morehead, 18 Dec. 1865, Fox to William Hunter Jr., 27 Dec. 1865, Fox to Grimes, 1 June 1865, William H. Aspinwall to Fox, 8 Nov., 13 Dec. 1865, Richard I. Fay to Fox, 27 Dec. 1865, GVFP. John Murray Forbes was glad Fox did not get involved with the Cooke associates, whom he suspected were speculating in extravagantly priced coal lands and wanted to use Fox's "name and reputation" to sell their stock to independent investors, who in a year would be very unhappy and angry with Fox. Forbes to Fox, 27 Dec. 1865, GVFP.

12. VLWF, Diary, 27 Feb., 16 Mar., 3 May, 28 Mar. 1866, WFP. See also 11, 15, 16, 27 Jan., 13, 28 Feb., 4, 13 Apr., 1 May 1866, WFP. A Mr. Knapp of Pittsburgh wanted Fox to take charge of ironworks there. Ibid. 12 May 1866.

13. Fox to Grimes, 1 June 1865, Fox to Alexander Dallas Bache, 9 June 1862, Ericsson to Fox, 22 Mar. 1866, GVFP. One of Fox's friends assumed he was on Fox's wave-

length when he suggested that Marine Corps officers be eliminated and naval officers take over their duties. R. H. Wyman to Fox, 14 Nov. 1865, GVFP. For a description of the "miserable food" midshipmen were served on the *Macedonian* (standard fare for sailors), see Emanuel Leutze to Fox, 17 Aug. 1865, GVFP. Leutze, the painter, was a sometime dinner companion of Fox, and his son, who was on the *Macedonian,* became an admiral.

14. On League Island, see Fox to G. H. Tatham, 21 Dec. 1865, GVFP and Fox's own seventy-four-page pamphlet, *Advantages of League Island for a Naval Station . . . by a New England Man* (Philadelphia: Board of Trade of Philadelphia, 1866). John Lenthall credited Fox with securing League Island for a navy yard and thought it should be renamed Fox Island. Lenthall to Fox, 10 Aug. 1868, GVFP. Grimes, in particular, questioned placing so much emphasis on steam engineering and of recruiting midshipmen from an apprentice system. As a senator Grimes could appoint students to the service academies and was satisfied with that arrangement. Grimes to Fox, 9 July 1865, GVFP. For information on the steam engineering program at the academy, see D. M. Greene to Fox, 24 May 1865, GVFP. Fox had already pushed the Academy to adopt a steam engineering program. See chapter 11.

15. John Huntington Crane Coffin to Fox, 12, 26 July 1865, GVFP. Wishing to remain at the academy, Coffin had a stake in his opposition to rotation. He had heard that he might be transferred to the Nautical Almanac Office in Cambridge, Massachusetts. Within a short time, he was appointed superintendent of that office and became the editor of the *American Ephemeris and Nautical Almanac.* He had been promoted as well as rotated.

16. Fox to Welles, 26 Aug. 1865, GVFP; Porter to Fox, 28 Mar 1862, *GVFCC,* 2:95; Porter to Fox, 10 Dec. 1865, GVFP; VLWF, Diary, 4, 11, 12 May 1865, WFP. Virginia complained that Fox should ride horses less and drive them more, with her accompanying him in the carriage. While Fox was horseback riding with Porter's twelve-year-old daughter, they were caught in the rain and were soaked. Ibid., 8 May 1865. Grimes warned Fox that Porter was "no scholar." Grimes to Fox, 2 Aug. 1865, GVFP.

17. R. B. Lowry, "Circular," 1 July 1865, Drayton to Fox, 1 June 1865, GVFP. The autobiography of James Holley Garrison, *Behold Me Once More: The Confessions of . . ., Brother of William Lloyd Garrison,* ed. Walter McIntosh Merrill (Boston: Houghton Mifflin, 1954), is by a derelict who ended up in the navy.

18. Shirley to Fox, 8 Apr. 1865, Sands to Fox, 28 Oct. 1865, GVFP. On political pressure, see the entries in the index of *Diary of Gideon Welles: Secretary of the Navy under Lincoln and Johnson,* 3 vols., Howard K. Beale (New York: W. W. Norton, 1960), under Isaac Henderson, Pasco of the Philadelphia Navy Yard, and the Smith Brothers.

19. Ruschenberger to Fox, 25 Jan., 7 Feb., 2, 12 June 1865, Fox to VLWF, 23 July 1865, GVFP.

20. On questions of steam engineering, I have leaned heavily on Edward William Sloan III, *Benjamin Franklin Isherwood, Naval Engineer: The Years as Engineer in Chief, 1861–1869* (Annapolis: United States Naval Institute, 1965), in general and for this paragraph on p. 145. The supercruisers were conceived as the American counter to the *Alabama* and *Florida,* which in case of war with Britain would prey on its commerce and engage in hit-and-run attacks on its ports. *DANFS,* s.v. "*Wampanoag.*"

21. Sloan, *Isherwood*, pp. 107–19.

22. Sloan, *Isherwood*, pp. 114–16, 118. Dickerson's attacks on Fox dismayed Paul Forbes, who did not wish to alienate the Navy Department. Fox remained close enough to Forbes to invite him to the flag raising at Fort Sumter, but a mix-up prevented his going. Paul S. Forbes to Fox, 2 May 1865, GVFP. Welles summarized his and Fox's attitude when he wrote, "I . . . want the best engine that is made regardless who is the inventor, or what the principle." Welles, *Diary,* 29 July 1865, 2:346.

23. Sloan, *Isherwood*, pp. 123–31; Fox to Welles, 19, 26 Aug. 1865, Welles Papers, LC; Isherwood to Fox, 13, 16, 21 Sept. 1865, GVFP. Beginning on 8 September 1865, Admiral Francis H. Gregory kept Fox fully posted on the tests of the *Algonquin* and *Winooski*. GVFP. In the summer of 1865, Fox felt Paul S. Forbes "disgraced himself" by signing one of Dickerson's attacks, but he remained friendly enough to dine with Forbes on 17 January 1866. VLWF, Diary, 17 Jan. 1866, WFP.

24. Ericsson to Fox, 30 Sept. 1865, Ericsson Papers, NYHS; Isherwood to Fox, 6 Oct. 1865, Ericsson to Fox, 8 Oct. 1865, GVFP; Sloan, *Isherwood*, pp. 126–27.

25. Sloan, *Isherwood*, pp. 155–56.

26. Sloan, *Isherwood*, pp. 176–80; Isherwood to Fox, 18 Feb. 1868, GVFP; *DANFS*, s.v. "*Wampanoag.*" Isherwood continued to regard Fox "with the warmest esteem." Isherwood to Fox, 7 Nov. 1873, GVFP.

27. *Narrative of the Mission to Russia, in 1866, of the Hon. Gustavus Vasa Fox, Assistant-Secretary of the Navy. From the Journal and Notes of J. F. Loubat,* ed. John D. Champlin Jr. (New York: D. Appleton, 1873), pp. 11–16. Having experienced the horror of an assassination, Congress was especially sympathetic with Alexander II, who had introduced reforms, including the abolition of serfdom. Relations with Russia were good. The United States would soon purchase Alaska from the czar's government. Ironically, the 1866 attempt on Alexander's life by a mentally disturbed student marked the end of reforms. Reaction brought further attempts on his life, until one succeeded in 1881. Fox's daily movements can be traced in Fox, Diary of trip to Russia, 23 May to 14 Dec. 1866, GVFP, and in Loubat, *Narrative*.

28. Isherwood to Fox, 21 Sept. 1865, GVFP; Ericsson to John Bourne, 27 July 1866, Ericsson Papers, LC; Fox to Welles, 30 May 1866, Welles Papers, LC. Loubat, *Narrative*, pp. 16–19. On the scheme of selling monitors abroad, see Griswold to Ericsson, 23 May 1866, Ericsson Papers, NYHS; Fox to Wise, 30 Sept. 1866, Wise Letterbooks, NYHS. The *Miantonomoh* was equipped with Isherwood's engines, which he carefully examined in April 1866. Isherwood to Fox, 22, 24 Apr. 1866, GVFP. The *Monadnock*, sister ship of the *Miantonomoh*, had already passed through the Straits of Magellan and would anchor in San Francisco on 21 June 1866, but it had not crossed an ocean.

29. VLWF, Diary, 30 May 1866, WFP; Fox to VLWF, 3 June 1866, GVFP; Fox to Wise, 5 June 1866, Wise Letterbooks, NYHS. Fox's reappointment, from 31 May to 26 November 1866, passed the House only "by the most active efforts of all his friends." John A. Griswold to Ericsson, 23 May 1866, Ericsson Papers, NYHS.

30. Fox to VLWF, 10–16 June 1866, GVFP; Fox to Welles, 16 June 1866, in Loubat, *Narrative*, pp. 31–34; Fox, List of suggested improvements to the *Miantonomoh*, c. 16 June 1866, GVFP; Fox to Wise, 15 June 1866, Wise Letterbooks, NYHS. Fox was accompanied across the Atlantic by Captain John Bythesea, the naval attaché of the

British embassy in Washington, as well as by the dog Monitor, who died at Elm Place on 6 September 1877. Fox, Diary, 12 Sept. 1877, GVFP.

31. Fox to Henry A. Wise, 1 May 1867, Wise Letterbooks, NYHS. Letters of introduction from Sir Frederick Bruce, the British minister at Washington, "were of no account" and were ignored by Lord John Russell. Ibid. Loubat, *Narrative*, pp. 39–43.

32. Fox to VLWF, 29 June 1866, GVFP; Fox to Welles, 5 July 1866, Welles Papers, LC; Loubat, *Narrative,* pp. 47–53. The Prince of Wales gave the commander of the *Miantonomoh,* John Colt Beaumont (Old Beau), an autographed picture of himself. Fox, who had numerous friends in the diplomatic corps, was especially close to Bruce. VLWF, Diary, 21 Apr. 1865, WFP. Fox, however, mentioned some of his invitations to Virginia and uncharacteristically complained he was tired of dinners. Ibid., 16 July 1866.

33. Fox to Welles, 5, 11 July 1866, Welles Papers, LC; Loubat, *Narrative*, pp. 43–47.

34. Fox to Welles, 5, 11 July 1866, Welles Papers, LC; Fox to VLWF, 5, 14 July 1866, GVFP.

35. Fox to VLWF, 5 Sept., 11, 20, 24 July 1866, GVFP; Fox, Diary, 9–23 July 1866, GVFP; VLWF, Diary, 25 July 1866, WFP.

36. Fox to VLWF, 24 (29) July, GVFP; VLWF, Diary, 18 Sept. 1866, WFP; Fox to Welles, 30 July 1866, Welles Papers, LC. In jest, Fox's friend Raasloff (the Danish minister to the United States), seconded by Sir Frederick Bruce (the British minister), urged Fox to regale the queen with his story about the late Arctic explorer Elisha Kent, "Kane's remains," which probably was not fit for mixed company. Raasloff to Fox, 2 June 1866, GVFP. John Hay thought "Kent's Remains" was "a most wonderful story." *Inside Lincoln's White House: The Complete Civil War Diary of John Hay,* ed. Michael Burlingame and John R. Turner Ettlinger (Carbondale: Southern Illinois University Press, 1997), 10 Sept. 1863, p. 83.

37. Fox, Diary, 31 July-22 Aug. 1866; Fox to VLWF, 23 Aug., 12 Sept. 1866, GVFP; Loubat, *Narrative,* pp. 69–97, 201–7, 359–61.

38. Fox to VLWF, 5, 28 Sept. 1866, GVFP; Fox, Diary, 23 Aug.–5 Sept. 1866, GVFP; Loubat, *Narrative,* pp. 208–331.

39. Fox to Sumner, 4 Jan. 1867, Sumner Papers, Harvard University, Cambridge, Mass.; Fox to VLWF, 16, 28 Sept. 1866, GVFP.

40. Fox to Welles, 17 Jan. 1867, Fox, Diary, 18–27 Sept. 1866, Fox to Adlersparre, 12 Sept. 1865, GVFP; Fox to Wise, 30 Sept. 1866, Wise Letterbooks, NYHS; Loubat, *Narrative,* pp. 384–409.

41. Fox to VLWF, 14, 31 Oct. 1866, GVFP; Loubat, *Narrative,* pp. 409–12.

42. Fox, Diary, 19 Oct. 1866, Fox to VLWF, 31 Oct. 1866, GVFP.

43. Fox to VLWF, 31 Oct. 1866, GVFP; Virginia Lowery to Minna Blair, 12 Nov. 1866, BFP, LC; Fox, Diary, 28 Oct.–2 Nov., 6–11 Nov. 1866, GVFP.

44. Fox to VLWF, 4, 31 Oct., 22 Nov. 1866, Fox, Diary, 15–17, 22–30 Nov., 13–14 Dec. 1866, GVFP.

45. VLWF, Diary, 18 Aug., 8 Sept., 13 Oct., 14 Dec. 1866, WFP. With the onset of cold weather, Virginia was troubled by a continuously sore throat, chest pains, colds, and worry about their economic future. VLWF, Diary, Oct., Nov., and Dec. 1866.

46. Fox to VLWF, 4, 31 Oct., 22 Nov. 1866, GVFP; VLWF, Diary, 8 Sept., 13 Oct. 1866, WFP.

Chapter 19. Postwar Career

1. Fox to Ericsson, 21 May 1866, Ericsson Papers, NYHS; Fox to Welles, 24 Dec. 1866, 7 Jan. 1867, Welles Papers, LC; Charles Henry Davis to Fox, 15 Mar. 1867, GVFP, NHSC, NYHS. Welles continued to consult with Fox about appointments and departmental matters. See Welles to Fox, 19 June, 5, 31 Aug. 1868, GVFP. To support Virginia in what they regarded as a proper style, Fox needed a well-paying job. VLWF, Diary, 30 June 1867, WFP, LC.

2. Fox to Welles, 5 Feb. 1867, Welles Papers, LC.

3. Fox to VLWF, 19, 28, 16, 24 Feb., 30 May 1867; Fox to Welles, 7 Jan. 1867, Welles Papers, LC.

4. Fox to VLWF, 28 Feb. 1867, GVFP; Fox to Welles, 2 Nov. 1868, Welles Papers; Davis to Fox, 20 Mar. 1867, GVFP. Fox assured Virginia that he would never go to Washington, and he would never leave her again. VLWF, Diary, 11 Feb. 1867, WFP. Peirce was named as head of the Coast Survey.

5. Fox to Welles, 12 Mar. 1867, GVFP; Fox to Welles, 25 Mar. 1867, Welles Papers, LC. Two years later, a variant of Fox's idea occurred when Porter ran the navy, but Porter was uncontrolled by the inept Secretary of the Navy Adolph Borie. His spoils-minded successor, George M. Robeson, reined in Porter a bit.

6. Fox to Wise, 16 Apr. 1867, Wise Letterbooks, NHSC, NYHS; David Donald, *Charles Sumner and the Rights of Man* (New York: Alfred A. Knopf, 1970), pp. 303–10. Sumner, like Fox, preferred "indigenous, aboriginal" names. Ibid., 310. VLWF, Diary, 7, 12 Apr. 1867, WFP. When Congress delayed paying for Alaska, Edouard de Stoeckl, the Russian minister, told Fox that "his orders are to present it to the U.S. as they have taken possession." Ibid. 29 Mar. 1868. Fox to Frederick W. Seward, 8 Apr. 1867, F. W. Seward to Fox, 12 Apr. 1867, William Henry Seward Collection, University of Rochester, Rochester, N.Y.; Fox to Sumner, 2 Apr. 1867, Sumner Papers, Harvard University, Cambridge, Mass.

7. Porter to Fox, [May 1867?], Fox to VLWF, 25 May 1867, GVFP; Fox, Diary, 20, 27 May, 3–5 June, 1867, GVFP.

8. Fox to VLWF, 27 May, 2 June 1867, GVFP.

9. Billings to Fox, 11 June, 9 July 1867, Fox to VLWF, 30 May 1867, 11 May 1868, Carlisle P. Patterson to Fox, 2 June 1867, GVFP. On Billings's distinguished career, see Robin Winks, *Frederick Billings: A Life* (Berkeley: University of California Press, 1998; originally published by Oxford University Press, 1991), and, for his relationship with Fox, see pp. 183–84.

10. Eads to Fox, 8, 30 June, 19 July 1867, Fox to VLWF, 30 May 1867, GVFP; Fox to Wise, 13 July 1867, Wise Letterbooks, NYHS. For more on Fox's reaction to the Eads proposal that Fox promote his machinery for big guns, see VLWF, Diary, 22 July 1867, WFP. "Gus dont like the thing." Ibid. Virginia was not anxious to move away from family to New York, a city where there was no social visiting morning or evening by

men or women, and she emphatically did not wish to live in St. Louis. Ibid., 31 May 1867, 25 Apr. 1868.

11. *Daily Missouri Democrat* (St. Louis), 9 July 1867; Fox to VLWF, 30 May 1867, GVFP. The Frémont party was to have spent $1 million on construction in one year and was required to pay off its indebtedness to the state in four equal payments. Despite his connection with the Blairs, Fox did not participate in their feuds and maintained cordial relations with Frémont. In July 1867, while together on the boat from New York to Boston, Frémont asked Fox to procure for him Admiral Charles H. Davis's "last report upon Isthmus Routes." Fox to Edgar Welles, 20 July 1867, Gideon Welles Papers, Connecticut Historical Society, Hartford. Frémont's request gives credence to the charge by Billings that he "sold & got three times the money he put in" the South West to invest in other roads, including a "Costa Rica R.R." Billings to Fox, 2 Aug. 1867, GVFP. Interest in a Central American road does not prove malfeasance. Among the feelers Fox received was the presidency of a proposed Tehuantepec Isthmus railroad. Fox to VLWF, 22 Feb. 1867, GVFP. Earlier, while attached to the Freedmen's Bureau, Fisk had established the school that became Fisk University.

12. Billings to Fox, 28 July, 2, 5 Aug., 11 June 1867, GVFP.

13. Billings to Fox, 2, 5, 30 Aug., 5 Sept. 1867, Eads to Fox, 27 July, 5 Aug. 1867, Fox Diary, 16–19, 22, 25 July, 17, 23–26 Aug. 1867, GVFP. Fox had forged friendships with Forbes, Eads, and Scott during the Civil War. Eads and Scott were especially negative about dealing with the Frémont associates. Billings to Fox 30 Aug. 1867, GVFP. Eads also distrusted Billings because of his past close association with Frémont, but Fox, while disagreeing with Billings, trusted him.

14. Billings to Fox, 28 Sept. 1867, Fox, Diary, 9 Oct. 1867, 14–15, 26–28 Sept., 4, 9 Oct. 1867, GVFP. Despite their differences, Fox admired the ability of Billings, who later became president of the Northern Pacific Railroad from 1879 to 1881.

15. Fox to VLWF, 13, 20, 22 Sept. 1867, Thayer to Fox, 1 Dec. 1867, C. B. Fisk to Fox, 21 Nov. 1867, Thomas C. Bates to Fox, 21 Dec. 1867, GVFP; "The Southwest Railroad," *Missouri Democrat* (St. Louis), 19 Nov. 1867.

16. Thomas C. Bates to Fox, 19, 26 Nov. 1867, Fox to Woodbury, 24, 28 Dec. 1867, Woodbury to Fox, 26 Dec. 1867, E. G. Paris to Fox, 4 Dec. 1867, Fisk to Fox 5, 6 Dec. 1867, William Auferman to Fox, 14 Dec. 1867, GVFP.

17. Benjamin E. Bates to William Auferman, 30 Dec. 1867, Fox to Woodbury, 27 Dec. 1867, Thomas C. Bates to Fox, 23 Dec. 1867, Fox, Diary, 23–28 Dec. 1867, GVFP.

18. Fox to Wise, 21 Jan. 1868, Wise Letterbooks, NYHS; Vindex [Grosvenor], "The Southwest Pacific R.R.," *Missouri Democrat* (St. Louis), 22 Jan. 1868; James Baker, "The Southwest Pacific Railroad," *Missouri State Times* (Jefferson City), 24 Jan. 1868. For these letters to newspapers, see Scrapbook, pp. 122–23, GVFP. Fox, Diary, 5 Jan. 1868, Fox to VLWF, 10, 12, 15 Jan. 1868, Fox to Woodbury, 19 Jan. 1868, GVFP.

19. Fox to VLWF, 29 Jan., 7 Feb. 1868, GVFP.

20. Fox to Woodbury, 20 Feb. 1868, "Arbitration Papers," Fisk to Fox, 13 Feb. 1868, Fox to VLWF, 16 Feb. 1868, GVFP. On the New York bondholders, see Ward & Company to William Auferman, 11 Feb. 1868, GVFP. Fox said Auferman represented the "old gang of shysters," and Billings earlier told Fox that Hayes was "smart but rather

unscrupulous" and "a man not of the right stripe." Fox to VLWF, 21 Jan., 2 Feb. 1868, Billings to Fox, 30 July, 5 Aug. 1867, GVFP.

21. Fox, Diary, 13 Mar. 1868, Fox to VLWF, 14 Mar. 1868, 13 Feb., 11, 18 Mar. 1868, Eads to Fox, 27 Feb. 1868, Fisk to Fox, 28 Feb. 1868, Fox, Diary, 1, 3–5, 9, 14, 16, 17 Mar. 1868, GVFP.

22. Fox to Woodbury, 22 Mar. 1868, Holladay to W. L. Halsey, 15 Apr. 1868, Headlee to Fox, 27 Apr. 1868, James F. Joy to Fox, 24 Apr. 1868, Freeman Clarke to Fox, 20 Mar. 1868, GVFP.

23. Fox, Diary, 8 May 1868, Fox to VLWF, 7, 11 May 1868, Ward Clarke to Fox, 11 May 1868, GVFP; VLWF, Diary, 11, 18 Apr., 8 May 1868, WFP.

24. Fox to Woodbury, 20 May 1868, GVFP; VLWF, Diary, 13, 20 May 1868, WFP; Fox, Diary, 19, 20, 23 May, 22 June, 22, 24, 27–29 Oct. 1868, 29 May 1869, 16, 17 May 1873, 20 Feb. 1874, William Norris, Attorney for Ben Holladay, to F. B. Hayes, 13 Apr. 1869, GVFP. After speaking with Hayes, John Murray Forbes wrote Fox, "I did not like his manner or looks—think he means to screw you." Forbes to Fox, 26 Aug. 1868, GVFP. The South West Pacific ultimately became a part of the St. Louis–San Francisco Railroad (The Frisco Line). H. Craig Minor, *The St. Louis–San Francisco Transcontinental Railroad: The Thirty-fifth Parallel Project, 1853–1890* (Lawrence: University Press of Kansas, 1972).

25. Fox, Diary, 25, 27, 30 May, 7, 10, 17, 19 June 1868, GVFP. Ben Holladay gave Fox's ego a boost when on 17 June 1868 he telegraphed him to come out to California "now." VLWF, Diary, WFP. Given Virginia's state of health and strong preference to be near her family, Fox could not consider Holladay's offer.

26. VLWF, Diary, 22 July, 7 Nov., 27 June, 18 July, 2, 8, 26 Sept., 3, 9 Oct., 4 Nov., 22 Dec. 1868, WFP; Fox, Diary, 29 June, 2, 4, 5, 7, 17 July, 16 Aug., 8 Sept. 1868; Fox to Fay, 3 Dec. 1868, GVFP.

27. Fox to Gideon Welles, 2 Nov. 1868, Welles Papers, LC; Fox to VLWF, 18 Mar. 1868, Fox, Diary, 6, 7 Nov., 3, 11, 26 Dec. 1868, Welles to Fox, 29 Oct. 1868, GVFP; VLWF, Diary, 3 Nov., 22 Dec. 1868, WFP. Virginia, who was on the same political wavelength as Fox, found in March 1868 "so much I object to in both parties," even while living with Montgomery and Minna Blair, who by then were ardent Democrats. VLWF, Diary, 11 Mar. 1868, WFP. Fox, however, used what little influence he had to advocate Frank Blair's nomination. Ibid., 11 July 1868. For Fox's support of the annexation of the Virgin Islands, see Porter to Fox, 15 Dec. 1868, Fox to Sumner, 27 Feb. 1869, GVFP.

28. Fox to Welles, 1 Dec. 1870, Welles Papers, LC. Also, see Fox to Welles, 26 May, 10 July, 17 Aug., 22 Sept., 26 Oct., 16 Nov., 29 Dec. 1869, 14 Jan., 1, 6 Dec. 1870, Welles Papers, LC; Fox to Welles, 28 Jan., 15 June, 3 Dec. 1870, Welles Papers, LC, cited by John Niven, *Gideon Welles: Lincoln's Secretary of the Navy* (New York: Oxford University Press, 1973), p. 637. See Niven's excellent summary of Welles's essays, pp. 570–75. Welles's growing disgust with Porter may be seen in Welles to Fox, 14 June, 14 July, 20 Aug., 27 Sept., 23 Oct., 8, 24, 29 Nov. 1869, GVFP. On reconciling their recollections about the New Orleans expedition, see Welles to Fox, 25 July 1871, Welles Papers, NYPL. On Fox's concern that his own role might be shortchanged, see Montgomery Blair to Fox, 26 July 1871, GVFP. Porter invited Fox to see the *Alarm* when launched

(Porter to Fox, 6 Mar. 1876, GVFP), but he did not see it for over a year. Fox, Diary, 16 Sept. 1877, GVFP. For Porter's hostility to Lenthall and Isherwood, see chapter 8.

29. Fox to Eads, 3 Jan. 1871, Eads Collection, Missouri Historical Society, St. Louis. I am indebted to John Kouenhoven for this and other Eads citations. Fox wrote Welles that Porter "has cunning, audacity and perseverance and is totally unrestrained by any principle of honor or truth." Fox to Welles, 22 Sept. 1869, Welles Papers, LC. Porter did not see Grant about Fox's nephew until 1 July and by then "it was too late." Porter to Fox, 1 July 1869, GVFP. For evidence that Fox and Porter subsequently got on better, see Porter to Fox, 7 Nov. 1877, 7, 9 Sept. 1883, GVFP.

30. Fox, Diary, 1 Jan. 1869, 16, 23, 25 Dec. 1871, 2 Apr. 1872, 24 Jan. 1873, 14, 31 Mar., 1 May, 2 Dec. 1874, 26, 29 Feb., 6 Mar. 1876, 20 Apr., 1 May 1878, GVFP. Although Fox remained on the board of directors and the executive committee of the Lowell & Andover Railroad, he was no longer president on 11 Feb. 1874. Fox, Diary, GVFP.

31. Elizabeth W. C. Woodbury to VLWF, 29 Jan. 1873, WFP. Woodbury Lowery wrote *Spanish Settlements within Present Limits of the United States, 1513–1561* (1901) and *Spanish Settlements in Florida, 1562–74* (1905). *DAB*, s.v. "Lowery, Woodbury."

32. Fox, Diary, 4, 5, 10 Dec. 1871, GVFP; *Narrative of the Mission to Russia, in 1866, of the Hon. Gustavus Vasa Fox, Assistant-Secretary of the Navy. From the Journal and Notes of J. F. Loubat,* ed. John D. Champlin Jr. (New York: D. Appleton, 1873), pp. 440–44.

33. Fox, Diary, 1–5, 15–18, 21, 24, 31 July, 12 Oct. 1870, 16 Mar., 9 Apr. 1874, GVFP.

34. Fox to Welles, 7 Oct. 1873, Welles Papers, LC; Fox to Welles, 26 Feb. 1875, Welles Papers, Huntington Library, San Marino, Calif.; Fox, Diary, 3, 5, 28–29 May 1872, GVFP.

35. Fox to Montgomery Blair, 18 Aug., 8 Sept. 1875, BFP, LC; Fox to VLWF, 8 Feb. 1876, GVFP; Fox, Diary, 17 Sept., 26 Dec. 1874, 29–30 July, 1–23 Aug. 1875, 15, 17 Apr. 1876, GVFP.

36. Fox, *Facts about the Carroll County Kearsarge Mountain, of New Hampshire. Read before the Appalachian Mountain Club* (c. 1876); Fox to Nathan Clifford (Justice of the U.S. Supreme Court), 31 Mar. 1876, GVFP; Fox to Charles Deane, 1, 6, 14 June, 3 Oct. 1876, Massachusetts Historical Society Collections, Boston. On principle, Fox was opposed to changing names "established by long usage." Fox to Deane, 17 Dec. 1877, ibid.

37. Fox, Diary, 7 Nov. 1876, GVFP.

38. Fox, Diary, 10 Nov. 1876, GVFP. Montgomery Blair was confident that Tilden would "send Fox out as a Diplomat."

39. Fox, Diary, 18, 16 Nov. 1876, GVFP. Also see Fox, Diary, 11, 13–15, Fox to Hewitt, 11 Nov. 1876, GVFP.

40. Fox to E. R. Mudge, c. 15 Nov. 1876, GVFP. Ironically, four months later, Tilden's opponent, Rutherford B. Hayes, prior to removing the federal troops propping up Chamberlain's government, shared Fox's optimism that South Carolinians would assert "their rights according to the forms of law." Ari Hoogenboom, *Rutherford B. Hayes: Warrior and President* (Lawrence: University Press of Kansas, 1995), pp. 304–10.

41. Fox, Diary, 18, 20 Nov. 1876, GVFP. Fox's quest for Willie Guild was unsuccessful. Fox to Grant, 18 Nov. 1876, E. D. Townsend to Fox, 12 Mar. 1877, GVFP.

42. Fox, Diary, 2 Mar., 27 June 1877, 16 Oct. 1880, Fox to VLWF, 16, 18 Oct. 1880, GVFP.

43. Montgomery Blair to Minna Blair, 14 Oct. 1877, Fox to Montgomery Blair, 10 May 1878, BFP; Fox to VLWF, 24 Apr. 1878, Fox, Diary, 30 May, 10, 27, 28 June 1878, GVFP.

44. Fox, Diary, 29 Aug. 1882, GVFP.

45. Fox, Diary, 24 Dec. 1878, 19, 28 June, 17 Sept., 17 Oct., 13 Nov., 3, 24 Dec. 1878, 12, 18 Jan., 16 Apr., 4 July 1879, 9 June, 15 Sept., 3 Nov 1880, GVFP.

46. Fox to Edward Atkinson, 13, 27 July 1880, Atkinson Papers, Massachusetts Historical Society; Fox, Diary, 1880, GVFP. Charles A. Dana hoped Fox would write four or five reports for the *New York Sun* on recent developments of manufacturing in the South. Dana to Fox 2 Jan. 1882, GVFP.

47. Fox to Arch Lowery, 29 May 1879, Fox to Montgomery Blair, 28 Dec. 1879, BFP.

48. Fox to Samuel Abbott Green, 17 May 1881, Green Papers, Massachusetts Historical Society; Fox, *An Attempt to Solve the Problem of the First Landing Place of Columbus in the New World* (Washington, D.C.: Government Printing Office, 1882). Sixty years after Fox wrestled with the problem, Samuel Eliot Morison in an equally exhaustive study concluded that Columbus landed on Watlings or San Salvador Island. Morison, *Admiral of the Ocean Sea: A Life of Christopher Columbus* (Boston: Little, Brown, 1942), pp. 227–28. Both Fox and Morison were expert seamen, and both were certain that their intelligent guesses were right.

49. Fox, Diary, 11, 15, 18 Jan. 1875, 25 Apr. 1881, GVFP.

50. Porter to Richard W. Thompson, 10 Nov. 1879, Porter to Fox, 13 July 1880, 21 Apr. 1883, GVFP.

51. Fox, "Monitor," *Johnson's New Universal Cyclopaedia*, 4 vols. (New York: A. J. Johnson, 1875–77), 3:582–84.

52. Fox to Catesby ap Jones, 13 Aug., 2 Dec. 1874, Museum of the Confederacy, Richmond, cited in Mabry Tyson, "Believe Only Half of What You Read about the Battle of Hampton Roads," in Harold Holzer and Tim Mulligan, eds. *The Battle of Hampton Roads: New Perspectives on the U.S.S. Monitor and C.S.S. Virginia* (New York: Fordham University Press, 2006), p. 106.

53. VLWF to Minna Blair, 2 Aug. 1883, VLWF, to Gist Blair, 19 Oct. 1883, BFP; J. C. Wilson to P. J. Horwitz, 30 Aug. 1883, Horwitz to Fox, 15 Oct. 1883, GVFP.

54. Mary G. Ray to Minna Blair, 29 Oct. 1883, BFP Two days before Fox died, he walked three or four miles and felt fine. Minna Blair to Gist Blair, 1, 4 Nov. 1883, BFP. Earlier the same month Fox died, he and Virginia were at Spring Lake, New Jersey, "for the benefit of Mrs. Fox's health." Fox to Simon Cameron, 6 Oct. 1883, Cameron Papers, LC. For Fox's obituary, see the *New York Times*, 30 Oct. 1883. The clipping of an obituary from an unidentified source is in the Blair Family Papers. Fox and Virginia are buried in Rock Creek Cemetery, Washington, D.C. Although she still complained of ill health, Virginia grew stronger.

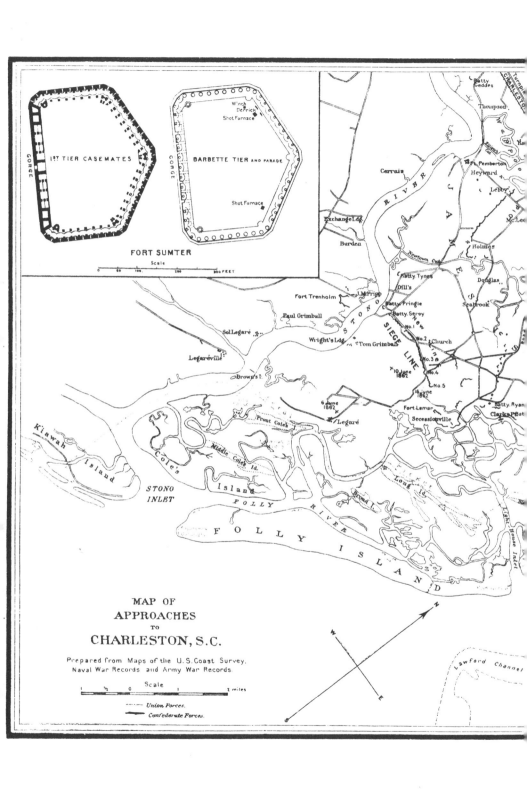

1ST TIER CASEMATES

GORGE

BARBETTE TIER AND PARADE

GORGE

Winch
Derrick

Shot Furnace

Shot Furnace

FORT SUMTER

Scale

0   50   100   200   300 FEET

Batty Geddes

CHARLESTON

Thompson

RIVER

Pemberton

Cerrais

Heyward

Lebby

Exchange Ldg.

McLee

Burden

Holmes

Newtown Cut

Batty Tynes

Douglas

Dill's

Fort Trenholm

J. McTripp

Batty Pringle

Seabrook

Paul Grimball

Batty Seroy

STONO

No.1

SIEGE LINE

No.2

Sol Legaré

Wright's Ldg.

Tom Grimball

Church

No.3

Legaréville

No.4

10 June
1862

Brown's I.

No.5

16 June
1862

6 June
1862

Batty Ryan

Front Coles

Legaré

Fort Lamar

Clarks P. Bat

Kiawah

Secessionville

Island

Coles

Middle Coles Id.

STONO
INLET

Island

Long Id.

FOLLY

Bread I.

Lighthouse Inlet

F O L L Y   I S L A N D

RIVER

MAP OF
APPROACHES
TO
CHARLESTON, S.C.

Crawford Channel

Prepared from Maps of the U.S. Coast Survey,
Naval War Records and Army War Records.

Scale

1   ½   0   1   2 miles

N

W

E

S

-------- Union Forces.
————— Confederate Forces.